Music!
Its Role and Importance in Our Lives

Teacher's Annotated Edition

Glencoe
McGraw-Hill

New York, New York   Columbus, Ohio   Woodland Hills, California   Peoria, Illinois

Table of Contents

Glencoe/McGraw-Hill
A Division of The McGraw·Hill Companies

Copyright © 2000 by The Charles Fowler Estate and the University of Maryland; copyright © 2000 by Glencoe/McGraw-Hill; copyright © 1994 by Charles Fowler. All rights reserved. Except as permitted under the United States Copyright Act, no part of this publication may be reproduced or distributed in any form or by any means, or stored in a database or retrieval system, without prior written permission of the publisher.

Send all inquiries to:
Glencoe/McGraw-Hill
21600 Oxnard Street, Suite 500
Woodland Hills, CA 91367

ISBN 0-02-655692-8 (Student Text)
ISBN 0-02-655693-6 (Teacher's Annotated Edition)
ISBN 0-02-655694-4 (Instructor's Guide)

Printed in the United States of America
1 2 3 4 5 6 7 8 9   027/043   05 04 03 02 01 00 99

Glencoe/McGraw-Hill announces the most comprehensive music program available today.

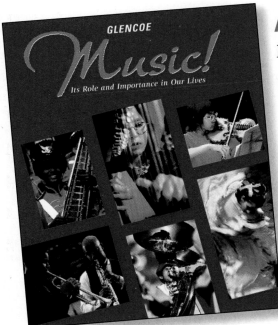

Music! surveys music and its role in our lives. It is an active study of how music says who we are as human beings and how we express ourselves through music.

Music! engages students in listening and in learning interpretive skills. Nine units cover the range of human experience and expression in music.

Music! is correlated to the National Standards for Arts Education.

Music! provides 20 fully integrated **Compact Discs**, a music-in-life and performance **Video**, a correlated **Teacher's Annotated Edition**, a completely keyed and easy-to-use **Instructor's Guide**, an engaging **MIDI Activities** binder, a **Performing Arts Package**, and hundreds of supportive and pre-selected activities in the **Teacher's Resource Binder**.

▶ **The Student Text** is designed to actively engage your students in the learning process.

Throughout the text, bright, bold illustrations and activities reinforce the information. Special features will stimulate thinking and encourage students to learn by doing.

■ **Action Learning:** Activities designed to involve students to learn by doing.

■ **Perceptive Listening:** Students are invited to listen at various levels of musical experience. Both the external and internal aspects of music are explored.

■ **Cooperative Learning:** Some activities present questions or mini-projects where students make observations, record information, survey selections, and make decisions while they apply important interpersonal skills.

 Unit **Encore!** features offer high-interest topics related to unit themes. The features are activity-based and introduce new music selections to expand students' listening experience.

NEW A new **Music Theory Handbook** addresses five major theory studies: Beat and Meter, Notation and Rhythm, Pitch, Key Signatures and Tonality, Harmony.

NEW **Technology/MIDI Options** allow students to play, improvise, create, and analyze music with a MIDI sequencer.

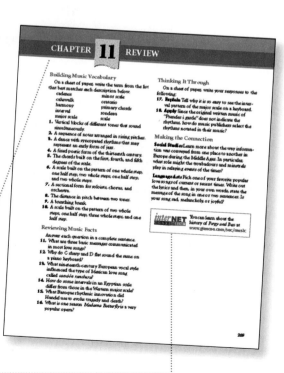

NEW **Photo Connections** to history, art, and culture enhance the caption program.

NEW **Chapter Reviews** assess student learning in vocabulary, factual recall, and critical thinking. Making the Connections activities connect chapter concepts to other curriculum areas.

NEW **Internet Connections** encourage further exploration using computer resources.

THE TEACHER'S ANNOTATED EDITION

NEW ▶ The **Teacher's Annotated Edition** brings together point-of-use cross-references for the multiple components of the program.

Cross-references to the Music Theory Handbook

Video Segments

Answers to Chapter Review Questions

THE TEACHER'S ANNOTATED EDITION

TRB Blackline Masters

Additional Chapter Activities

CD Tracks used with Chapter Activities

MIDI Activities Binder

Artsource® Performing Arts Package

Caption Answers

ACTIVITY ▶ Compare Musical Styles

How would you describe two compositions in different styles and from different historical periods?

Listen:

- Allegro movement from Concerto in D Major for Trumpet and Orchestra by Michael Haydn (performed by Wynton Marsalis).
- "You'd Be So Nice To Come Home To" by Cole Porter (performed by Ella Fitzgerald).

Write down the musical similarities and differences you hear. What can you tell about these pieces just by the verbal clues—the names of the composers, the performers, and the titles of the musical selections? Use your notes to discuss these comparisons in class.

PROFILE

Wynton Marsalis

Although he was born in New Orleans, a city known for jazz, Wynton Marsalis stood out as a classical musician. Guided by his musician father, Marsalis picked up the trumpet when he was twelve, and within two years he had joined the New Orleans Symphony Orchestra. He later attended the Juilliard School of Music in New York.

It was in New York that Marsalis first became interested in jazz. He began going to libraries, museums, and clubs to read about, listen to, and meet jazz musicians. Marsalis's background in classical music and his love of jazz proved to be a winning combination. He became a recognized recording artist by the age of 20.

Marsalis now focuses most of his energies on jazz. He spends much of his time visiting schools to encourage an interest in this style of music among American youth. Wynton Marsalis has become a major force in American music, winning Grammy awards in both jazz and classical categories in 1984. He became Artistic Director of the jazz program at New York City's Lincoln Center in 1991 and won a Pulitzer Prize in music in 1997.

Wynton Marsalis
American Trumpeter
1961–

What We Like and Why We Like It

The old Latin expression *De gustibus non est disputandum* ("There is no disputing taste") seems to suggest that differences in taste cannot be substantiated. For some people, "I like it" or "I don't like it" are sufficient explanations. However, understanding why you like or dislike something is important, if only to validate your perceptions to yourself. Then, too, you may want to be able to persuade others.

Before you can fully and fairly judge whether you like a new piece of music, you have to be certain you hear what the sounds are doing. You have to know what you are hearing and become familiar with the characteristics of the music. This implies a willingness to listen, even if the sounds do not readily appeal to you. You have to give unfamiliar music a chance, which may mean giving it your attention more than once in order to feel comfortable with it.

This text invites you to explore many different forms of music. It does not present one type of musical style as best or ask you to like a particular kind of music. The goal of this text is to expand your horizons. The skill you acquire in analyzing music and learning to listen to it perceptively will enable you to make musical choices and to know why you made them.

ACTIVITY ▶ Develop Perceptive Listening

Can you identify more distinguishing characteristics about music by listening with greater focus?

Listen again to the compositions by Michael Haydn and Cole Porter, first heard on page 12. Use the following criteria to deepen your understanding of the music characteristics:

1. Determine the musical means (the source of sound and the size of the groups for each piece).
2. Describe the musical expression (the rhythm, melody, and mood).
3. Determine each piece's order or organization (the amount of repetition and contrast that is used).
4. Determine the possible origin (the where, when, and by whom the music was created).
5. Characterize the type of music (its function or purpose and its intended audience).

TECHNOLOGY OPTION

- **Music with MIDI** Use a MIDI program to experiment and compose with various instrumentations, musical expression, and organization. You might also create a composition combining musical ideas from different musical styles.

Religious Music

Throughout the ages and in every part of the world, people have sought help from a divine being. For many, religion becomes a central guiding hand that permeates all that they do and everything they are.

All major religions or belief systems use sound as an expression of faith and spirituality which are difficult to understand through words alone. Like the great cathedrals, temples, holy shrines, and other religious works of art, music evokes the spiritual and helps people stay in touch with it. It expresses the mysteries of life and the search for meaning. In this sense, music joins religion to give life direction, wholeness, and purpose.

Hinduism

Hinduism is one of the oldest religions still practiced in the world. Aside from the island of Bali and the mountain kingdom of Nepal, India is the only Hindu country in the world. However, Hindu people live in nearly all countries, particularly on the Asian continent.

Hindus worship many gods and goddesses, each with his or her own name, shape, and character. One of the most important of the many gods is Vishnu, who is thought of as the creator of life and substance. The god Shiva is the lord of the dance. Saraswati is the goddess of music and learning. Although there are many different gods and goddesses, some Hindus believe that these deities are all aspects of a single divine power.

Hindus believe that all creatures are in a process of spiritual evolution; that their souls strive through successive rebirths to achieve union with Brahma, the Supreme Being and source of universal life; and that people must live righteously according to their caste, or station in life.

ART SOURCE

Use Artsource® VHS segment 7 in the Performing Arts Package to show a performance by the Rangasharata Cultural Arts Troupe.

Dance and music are deeply rooted in Hindu life. Here, a dancer from the Rangasharata Manipuri Cultural Arts Troupe performs "Rasa Lila," a classical dance believed to have been created by the Hindu god Krishna. It was communicated to King Jai Singh in 1780 through a vision and was re-created to exact specifications, including both style and costumes.

Music & Art

Saraswati is the Hindu goddess of music and wisdom. The arts are such an integral part of Hinduism that it is difficult to separate the two. Religion, art, music, and drama merge in Hindu life. Can you name other cultures where the same occurs?

Saraswati, Goddess of Learning, c. 1960. Victoria and Albert Museum, London, Great Britain.

Music & Art
Responses might include Native American cultures, among others.

The Music of Hinduism

Natural connections are made between faith and the arts, which are inseparable in Hinduism. These connections are so pervasive that it is difficult to think of one without the other. *Keltis* (KRI-tees) are Hindu religious songs that are sung in praise of a particular god or gods. Many kritis including "Bruhi Mukundeti," were composed in southern India during the eighteenth and nineteenth centuries by deeply religious individuals, many of whom are considered today to be Hindu saints. Kritis are usually sung by a solo artist in a concert setting.

Much of Indian music uses the principle of theme and variations. Sometimes the variations are improvised, sometimes composed. In kritis, the variations are often both composed and improvised. The example you will hear includes only composed variations. In "Bruhi Mukundeti," the poet asks his tongue to keep repeating the different sacred names of God (Keshala, Madhava, Govinda, Krishna, Sadanand, Radha, Ram). The repetitions of God's names is, in itself, often seen as a religious act.

▶ **The Instructor's Guide** ties the entire program together for you. It furnishes you with a plan showing you the variety of ways you can achieve success in the music classroom.

It includes:

- Detailed step-by-step lesson plans
- Brief chapter introductions
- Scope and Sequence chart
- Detailed teaching suggestions and background information for each activity
- Answers to Chapter Reviews
- Comprehensive Index to the CD Program

A flexible curriculum design provides the direction you need to teach this course in a 9-, 18-, or 36-week format. A new theory course outline suggests a 9- or 18-week course based on the Music Theory Handbook.

Scope and Sequence Chart

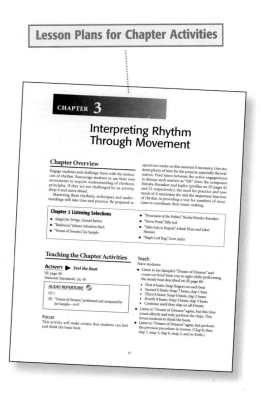

Lesson Plans for Chapter Activities

THE INSTRUCTOR'S GUIDE

Answers to Chapter Review Questions

Lesson Plans for Unit Evaluation Projects

Lesson Plans for Unit Encores!

Music Theory Handbook

Comprehensive CD Index

Lesson Plans for Music Theory Handbook

▶ The extensive repertoire of music selections on 20 compact discs immerses your students in the world of music.

Pre-Selected and Fully Integrated: All music and related activities are pre-selected for quick and easy preparation.

Over 450 selections: This large selection includes:

- Pop
- Jazz
- Art
- Ethnic
- Rock
- Film
- Classical

- Theatre
- Gospel
- Rap
- Renaissance
- Folk
- Big Band
- Contemporary

Music Theory CD: CD 20 includes listening selections and ear training segments that are correlated to, and reinforce, the Music Theory Handbook in the Student Text. Corresponding blackline masters in the Teacher's Resource Binder are designed to work with the ear training segments.

MIDI TECHNOLOGY

▶ A new **MIDI Activities** binder provides exciting new approaches to experimenting with, practicing, understanding, and recording music.

One activity in each chapter of the Student Edition is further developed in a Project in the *MIDI Activities* binder, and each Project contains these three levels:

- Basic
- Intermediate
- Advanced

These levels are often cumulative while others are designed to allow students the flexibility to begin at a level appropriate to their skill with the MIDI program.

Project topics include:

- Combining Different Musical Styles
- Creating with West African Rhythms
- Create a Fugue
- Explore Unusual Keyboard Sounds
- Score an Action Scene
- Compose Balinese Music

▶ A separate **Teacher's Resource Binder** provides you with a correlated supplemental resource for *Music! Its Role and Importance in Our Lives*. It contains a wealth of additional handouts, teaching strategies, and resource materials designed for more effective teaching. You can choose the materials that complement the skill level, time framework, and interest level of your class. The Teacher's Resource Binder provides:

■ Perceptive Listening Grids

■ Music Scores

■ Activity Blackline Masters

■ Composer Profiles

■ Music Theory Blackline Masters

■ Unit Tests

■ Fine Art Transparencies

Teacher's Resource Binder

GLENCOE

Music!

INCLUDES:
• Unit and Chapter Blackline Masters
• Music Theory Masters
• Unit Tests and Answer Key
• Fine Art Transparencies
• Fine Art Transparency Instructor's Guide

▶ A music-in-life and performance **Video** expands the cultural impact of music by presenting a wide variety of musical situations and expressions. Selections include excerpts from

Campanas de America

Lakota Eagle Dance

We Shall Overcome

New Orleans Funeral Parade

Balinese Gamelan

Music of the Movies

Jazz Is My Native Language

▶ In collaboration with the Music Center of Los Angeles County, Glencoe/McGraw-Hill has revised *Music! Its Role and Importance In Our Lives* to reflect an emphasis on the performing arts.

This exceptional resource helps teachers integrate the visual and performing arts, creates a strong multicultural performing arts perspective, and links music to other curriculum areas.

Each unit opens with a photo of performing artists or groups with a caption that links the group and their performance to the unit theme.

The features are extended with a separate multimedia *Artsource® Performing Arts Package* (one VHS tape, one audiocassette, and an Instructor's Guide). These motivational, multicultural examples will help address the *National Standards for Arts Education*, which call for more integration among the arts—visual art, music, dance, and theatre.

National Standards · High School · Grades 9-12
MUSIC

▶ The study of music contributes in important ways to the quality of every student's life. Every musical work is a product of its time and place, although some works transcend their original settings and continue to appeal to humans through their timeless and universal attraction. Through singing, playing instruments, and composing, students can express themselves creatively, while a knowledge of notation and performance traditions enables them to learn new music independently throughout their lives. Skills in analysis, evaluation, and synthesis are important because they enable students to recognize and pursue excellence in their musical experiences and to understand and enrich their environment. Because music is an integral part of human history, the ability to listen with understanding is essential if students are to gain a broad cultural and historical perspective. The adult life of every student is enriched by the skills, knowledge, and habits acquired in the study of music.

Every course in music, including performance courses, should provide instruction in creating, performing, listening to, and analyzing music, in addition to focusing on its specific subject matter.

1 Content Standard: Singing, alone and with others, a varied repertoire of music

Achievement Standard, Proficient:
Students
a. sing with *expression and *technical accuracy a large and varied repertoire of vocal literature with a *level of difficulty of 4, on a scale of 1 to 6, including some songs performed from memory
b. sing music written in four parts, with and without accompaniment
c. demonstrate well-developed ensemble skills

Achievement Standard, Advanced:
Students
d. sing with expression and technical accuracy a large and varied repertoire of vocal literature with a level of difficulty of 5, on a scale of 1 to 6
e. sing music written in more than four parts
f. sing in small ensembles with one student on a part

2 Content Standard: Performing on instruments, alone and with others, a varied repertoire of music

Achievement Standard, Proficient:
Students
a. perform with expression and technical accuracy a large and varied repertoire of instrumental literature with a level of difficulty of 4, on a scale of 1 to 6
b. perform an appropriate part in an ensemble, demonstrating well-developed ensemble skills
c. perform in small ensembles with one student on a part

Achievement Standard, Advanced:
Students
d. perform with expression and technical accuracy a large and varied repertoire of instrumental literature with a level of difficulty of 5, on a scale of 1 to 6

3 Content Standard: Improvising melodies, variations, and accompaniments

Achievement Standard, Proficient:
Students
a. improvise stylistically appropriate harmonizing parts
b. improvise rhythmic and melodic variations on given pentatonic melodies and melodies in major and minor keys
c. improvise original melodies over given chord progressions, each in a consistent *style, *meter, and *tonality

Achievement Standard, Advanced:
Students
d. improvise stylistically appropriate harmonizing parts in a variety of styles
e. improvise original melodies in a variety of styles, over given chord progressions, each in a consistent style, meter, and tonality

4 Content Standard: Composing and arranging music within specified guidelines

Achievement Standard, Proficient:
Students
a. compose music in several distinct styles, demonstrating creativity in using the *elements of music for expressive effect
b. arrange pieces for voices or instruments other than those for which the pieces were written in ways that preserve or enhance the expressive effect of the music
c. compose and arrange music for voices and various acoustic and electronic instruments, demonstrating knowledge of the ranges and traditional usages of the sound sources

Achievement Standard, Advanced:
Students
d. compose music, demonstrating imagination and technical skill in applying the principles of composition

⑤ Content Standard: Reading and notating music

Achievement Standard, Proficient:

Students

a. demonstrate the ability to read an instrumental or vocal score of up to four *staves by describing how the elements of music are used

Students who participate in a choral or instrumental ensemble or class

b. sightread, accurately and expressively, music with a level of difficulty of 3, on a scale of 1 to 6

Achievement Standard, Advanced:

Students

c. demonstrate the ability to read a full instrumental or vocal score by describing how the elements of music are used and explaining all transpositions and clefs

d. interpret nonstandard notation symbols used by some 20th-century composers

Students who participate in a choral or instrumental ensemble or class

e. sightread, accurately and expressively, music with a level of difficulty of 4, on a scale of 1 to 6

⑥ Content Standard: Listening to, analyzing, and describing music

Achievement Standard, Proficient:

Students

a. analyze aural examples of a varied repertoire of music, representing diverse *genres and cultures, by describing the uses of elements of music and expressive devices

b. demonstrate extensive knowledge of the technical vocabulary of music

c. identify and explain compositional devices and techniques used to provide unity and variety and tension and release in a musical work and give examples of other works that make similar uses of these devices and techniques

Achievement Standard, Advanced:

Students

d. demonstrate the ability to perceive and remember music events by describing in detail significant events3 occurring in a given aural example

e. compare ways in which musical materials are used in a given example relative to "rays in which they are used in other works of the same genre or style

f. analyze and describe uses of the elements of music in a given work that make it unique, interesting, and expressive

⑦ Content Standard: Evaluating music and music performances

Achievement Standard, Proficient:

Students

a. evolve specific criteria for making informed, critical evaluations of the quality and effectiveness of performances, compositions, arrangements, and improvisations and apply the criteria in their personal participation in music

b. evaluate a performance, composition, arrangement, or improvisation by comparing it to similar or exemplary models

Achievement Standard, Advanced:

Students

c. evaluate a given musical work in terms of its aesthetic qualities and explain the musical means it uses to evoke feelings and emotions

⑧ Content Standard: Understanding relationships between music, the other arts, and disciplines outside the arts.

Achievement Standard, Proficient:

Students

a. explain how elements, artistic processes (such as imagination or craftsmanship), and organizational principles (such as unity and variety or repetition and contrast) are used in similar and distinctive ways in the various arts and cite examples

b. compare characteristics of two or more arts within a particular historical period or style and cite examples from various cultures

c. explain ways in which the principles and subject matter of various disciplines outside the arts are interrelated with those of music

Achievement Standard, Advanced:

Students

d. compare the uses of characteristic elements, artistic processes, and organizational principles among the arts in different historical periods and different cultures

e. explain how the roles of creators, performers, and others involved in the production and presentation of the arts are similar to and different from one another in the various arts

⑨ Content Standard: Understanding music in relation to history and culture

Achievement Standard, Proficient:

Students

a. classify by genre or style and by historical period or culture unfamiliar but representative aural examples of music and explain the reasoning behind their classifications

b. identify sources of American music genres,6 trace the evolution of those genres, and cite well-known musicians associated with them

c. identify various roles that musicians perform, cite representative individuals who have functioned in each role, and describe their activities and achievements

Achievement Standard, Advanced:

Students

d. identify and explain the stylistic features of a given musical work that serve to define its aesthetic tradition and its historical or cultural context

e. identify and describe music genres or styles that show the influence of two or more cultural traditions, identify the cultural source of each influence, and trace the historical conditions that produced the synthesis of influences

3. E.g., fugal entrances, chromatic modulations, developmental devices

4. E.g., language arts: compare the ability of music and literature to convey images, feelings, and meanings; physics: describe the physical basis of tone production in string, wind, percussion, and electronic instruments and the human voice and of the transmission and perception of sound

5. E.g., creators: painters, composers, choreographers, playwrights; performers: instrumentalists, singers, dancers, actors; others: conductors, costumers, directors, lighting designers

6. E.g., swing, Broadway musical, blues

7. E.g., entertainer, teacher, transmitter of cultural tradition

The National Standards for Music Education were developed by the Music Educators National Conference. Reprinted by permission.

A Unique, Interactive Approach to Music Studies

Music! Its Role and Importance in Our Lives

Student Text   0-02-655692-8
Teacher's Annotated Edition   0-02-655693-6
Instructor's Guide   0-02-655694-4
Teacher Resource Binder   0-02-655696-0
MIDI Activities   0-02-655697-9
Compact Disc Program   0-02-655699-5
Music! **Video**   0-02-655695-2
Artsource® Performing Arts Package   0-07-820374-0

Music!

Its Role and Importance in Our Lives

Charles Fowler

Timothy Gerber   Vincent Lawrence

Glencoe McGraw-Hill

New York, New York   Columbus, Ohio   Woodland Hills, California   Peoria, Illinois

AUTHORS

Dr. Charles Fowler was a lifetime educator, author, and spokesperson, championing the right of students to acquire an understanding of their musical heritage. For this text he created a broad and engaging structure and assembled an impressive team in order to produce a set of educational materials that will open the study of music to many more students.

Dr. Timothy Gerber teaches in the School of Music at The Ohio State University. He is a frequently published authority on adolescent musical development and has served for 14 years as the principal author of educational materials published by the Columbus Symphony Orchestra. He has been honored with the Distinguished Teaching Award in the OSU School of Music, and was selected as the Roy Acuff Chair of Excellence in the Creative Arts at Austin Peay State University (1995).

Dr. Vincent Lawrence is widely recognized as an expert in secondary general music education. For 21 years he was Professor of Music at Towson State University in Maryland, where he was the chairperson of Music Education and directed the University Chorale. During that time he was actively involved in teaching general music in the middle school. Vincent is an author of *Music and You* and a coordinating author of *Share the Music* (Grades K-8), both published by the McGraw-Hill School Division.

Glencoe/McGraw-Hill

A Division of The **McGraw·Hill** *Companies*

Send all inquiries to:
Glencoe/McGraw-Hill
21600 Oxnard Street, Suite 500
Woodland Hills, CA 91367

ISBN 0-02-655692-8 (Student Text)
ISBN 0-02-655693-6 (Teacher's Annotated Edition)

CONTRIBUTORS

EDITORIAL CONSULTANT

Dr. William Anderson
Professor of Music Education
Kent State University
Kent, OH

WRITERS/REVIEWERS

Dr. Stuart Goosman
Asst. Professor
The University of Texas at
    Austin
Austin, TX

Dr. Katherine Hickey
Asst. Professor of Music
    Education
So. Illinois University at
    Carbondale
Carbondale, IL

Dr. Mark Lochstampfor
Asst. Professor of Music
Capital University
Columbus, OH

ARTSOURCE® CONTRIBUTORS

Joan Boyett
Executive Director
Music Center Education
    Division
The Music Center of Los
    Angeles County

Melinda Williams
Concept Originator and
    Project Director

Susan Cambique-Tracey
Project Coordinator

REVIEWERS

Dr. Bobby Adams
Assoc. Professor of Music
    Education
Director of Bands
Stetson University
DeLand, FL

Dwight E. Dodd
Music Educator
South Fulton HS
South Fulton, TN

Christopher Heidenreich
Director of Bands
Lancaster HS
Lancaster, OH

Gary Hodges
Director of Bands
Dublin Scioto HS
Dublin, OH

Charlotte Brooks Polk
Director of Choirs
South Side HS
Memphis, TN

Dr. Dennis Waring
Ethnomusicologist
Westlyn University
Middleton, CT

CONTRIBUTING SPECIALISTS

Dr. Barbara Baker
    Gospel Music
Katherine Bond
    Laotian and Tibetan Music
Dr. Greg Booth
    Indian and Pakistanian Music
Robert T. Bryan
    Swing Music
Dr. Virginia Danielson
    Arabian Music
Mr. George DeGraffenreid
    Music Education
Dr. John Doyle
    Music of Gottschalk
Robb Goldstein
    American Folk Music
Dr. Harold Kacanek
    Indonesian Music
Benedict Lim
    Indonesian Music
Dr. Terry Liu
    Chinese Music
Dr. Barbara Lundquist
    Sub-Saharan African Music
Dr. Salomáo Manhica
    Sub-Saharan African Music
Dr. James E. Mumford
    African-American Music
Dr. Daniel Sheehy
    Hispanic Music
Dr. Robert Myers
    Jazz, Pop, and Rock
Dr. James Reid
    Japanese Music
Edwin Schupman
    Native American Music
Dr. Anne Dhu Shapiro
    American and Western Music
Dr. Christopher Waterman
    African Music and Its
    Influence

TABLE OF CONTENTS

UNIT SIX

From the time of the Olmec Indians
(c.1200 B.C.), more than thirty distinct
cultures have flourished in the region we now know as
Mexico. Ballet Folklorico de Mexico researches these
cultures and performs dance and music that express the
soul of the Mexican people. In "Los Concheros," brightly
costumed dancers use strong, unison movement to
connect the group spiritually to nature. Look at the photo
for clues about the traditions and theme of the dance.
What ideas come to mind?

Ballet Folklorico de Mexico. "Los Concheros." Amalia Hernández, artistic director.
Photo courtesy of Ballet Folklorico de Mexico.

Music!...
To Tell Us Who We Are

You may wish to use Fine Art Transparency 1, *Broadway Boogie Woogie,* in the TRB to introduce Unit One.

Chapter 1
Music in
Our Culture

Chapter 2
Music in
Other Cultures

Use Artsource® VHS Segment 1 in the Performing Arts Package to show "Los Concheros" by Ballet Folklorico de Mexico.

4

Music in Our Culture

Music is one of the great pleasures of life. It has the power to command our attention and inspire us. It speaks to our spirit and to our inner feelings. It provokes thoughts about the mysteries of life, such as why we exist, the vastness of the universe, and our purpose on earth. Music reaches deep into our nature to console us, to reassure us, and to help us express who and what we are as human beings.

*There are as many different kinds of music in the United States as there are different peoples. The variety of musical styles tells us who we are as a nation. **What does your favorite music say about you?***

Caption answer
Encourage students to identify a variety of music styles and discuss how that variety adds interest to the musical choices we have in our culture.

Objectives

By completing the chapter, you will:
- Understand how the variety of music performed in America reflects the diverse people.
- Become familiar with many different styles of music.
- Begin to identify a wider range of musical styles.
- Learn how to describe and compare contrasting musical compositions.

Vocabulary

classical music
concerto
culture
homophony
jazz
musical style
perceptive listening

Musicians to Meet

Wynton Marsalis
Cole Porter

Who We Are

As Americans, we are part of a culturally diverse group of people. Immigrants came to America from every part of the globe. Your classmates, neighbors, and community members probably represent a mixture of racial or ethnic backgrounds. How do you feel about people whose backgrounds are different from yours? Perhaps you interact little with these people. Then again, perhaps you go to school together, understand each other, and get along well.

One way to relate with others is by sharing your culture. **Culture** is *the customs, ideas, tastes, and beliefs acquired from a person's background.* It is the sum total of one's lifestyle. Your culture may be your most personal and important possession. Sharing your culture is the greatest gift you can give others.

One of the most revealing ways that people share their culture is through the arts. The arts radiate the lifestyle of the people who created them. This helps define people's culture. Music, perhaps more than any other art form, reflects the diverse cultures of the American population. Music is as varied as the cultures that create it. All these different musics define who we are as a nation.

You may wish to use "Compare Listening Habits" or "Research Listening Time" at this time. Lesson plans for the activities are found on page 37 in the Instructor's Guide.

Our Affinity for Music

All people, from the earliest recorded history, have created music. Like birds and whales, humans have a natural tendency for making sounds and responding to them. When music is pleasurable, it says something to you. It communicates a feeling or conveys a message. It speaks to your inner being.

Obviously, the amount of time you devote to listening to music will vary according to your interests and schedule, but the amount of time you actually spend is a clear indication of how much you enjoy music. If you are like most teenagers, you probably enjoy listening to music because you are getting something in return. It is saying something that you want to hear.

Preference of Musical Styles

The kind of music you prefer tells something about who you are and what you know. Your likes and dislikes—your musical preferences—express your personal taste. They reveal something about you. Music helps define who you are. This may be one of the reasons it is valued so highly. As a human being, you have the ability to narrowly or broadly define your musical preferences. Your musical preference often reflects your lifestyle.

Variety of Styles

As humans, we can be more than one-dimensional. We can stretch our likes and understandings beyond the narrow range of one type of music. In so doing, we define ourselves more broadly and probably more completely. People need not be limited in their musical likings, any more than they need to limit the hairstyles they admire or the kinds of food they enjoy. We are as narrow and limited, or as broad and all encompassing, as we choose to be.

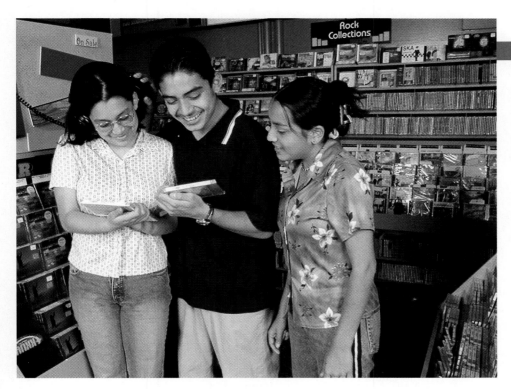

Music & CULTURE

Contemporary music stores usually organize music into categories such as pop, classical, jazz, and world music. **What sections would attract you?**

Music & Culture
Students' responses will vary. Encourage them to recognize the variety of styles available.

Like all forms of communication—speech and written language, scientific symbols, graphics, visual arts, and gestures—music must be learned. If you want to fully understand and respond to its power, you have to study it. By paying careful attention to music, you can come to know it better, and you can broaden and deepen your range of understanding and your ability to respond to it.

ACTIVITY ▶ *Radio Scan*

What kind of music do you like?

When you scan radio stations to find the music you like, you hear many different musical styles. If you are like most people, you quickly skip over several stations until you find your musical preference.

Listen to the musical selections in the Radio Scan. Pretend that each comes from a different radio station. Indicate your reactions to each example by writing down how long you would listen to each station.

Expanding Your Musical Tastes

Different music serves different purposes, different moods, and different human needs. You may find that you are less tolerant of a new type of music. Unfamiliar music may make you suspicious, just as you are cautious when meeting a stranger. This course and this text will help you open your ears to new kinds of music so that you can broaden your musical tastes. By studying music, you will be able to stretch your likes and deepen your understanding.

Different types of music have different characteristics—different styles. **Musical style** refers to *the distinct manner or character of musical expression.* This is best understood when qualities between one piece of music are compared to those of another piece of music. For example, just as you learn to recognize different models of cars, you can learn to distinguish between different styles of music and develop a vocabulary (descriptors) to define them.

The musical world contains an enormous variety of musical styles. This variety helps to characterize and document what we are like and who we are as a society. Some of these styles are broad categories that cover a wide range of music. For example, the term "popular music" refers to commercial music that the general public uses for dancing and entertainment. Subcategories under pop might include rock, heavy metal, Top 40, rap, and reggae, to name a few.

Activity *Radio Scan*
Instructor's Guide, pages 33–34
TRB 1-1, *Radio Scan*
CD 1 [1] Symphony No. 3 in F Major, Op. 90, first movement (0:40)
CD 1 [2] "I Fall to Pieces" (0:44)
CD 1 [3] "Kogetsu Cho" (0:42)
CD 1 [4] "Your Smiling Face" (0:46)
CD 1 [5] "Menuetto/Vivace" (0:45)
CD 1 [6] "Changing Opinion" (0:43)
CD 1 [7] "Kyrie eleison" (0:40)
CD 1 [8] "Pick Up the Pace" (0:49)
CD 1 [9] "Dovúnque al mundo loYankee" (0:44)
CD 1 [10] "A Foggy Day" (0:45)

You may wish to use "Identify Musical Styles" or "Classify Musical Styles" at this time. Lesson plans for the activities are found on pages 38 and 39 in the Instructor's Guide.

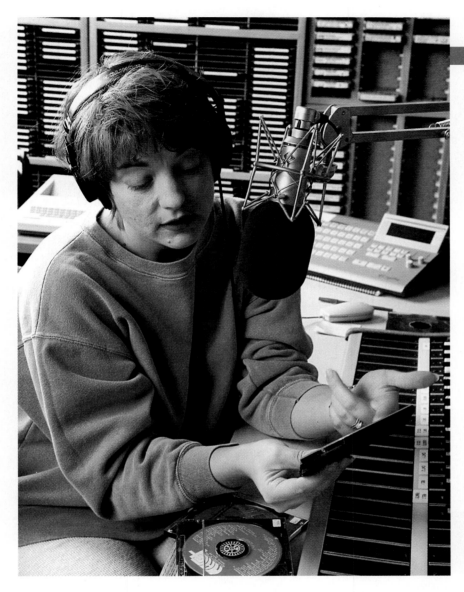

Music & CULTURE

Radio stations are usually noted for playing one particular style or category of music. **List the types of radio stations in your listening area and their formats.**

Music & Culture
Responses will vary.

Activity   *Musical Style Check*
Instructor's Guide, pages 34–35
TRB 1-2, *Musical Style Check*
CD 1 ⑪ "How I Got Over" (0:32)
CD 1 ⑫ "A Mighty Fortress" (0:35)
CD 1 ⑬ Symphony No. 9 in D Minor (0:30)
CD 1 ⑭ "Sweet Home Chicago" (0:39)
CD 1 ⑮ Concerto No. 21 in C Major, second movement (0:35)
CD 1 ⑯ "The Entertainer" (0:34)
CD 1 ⑰ "Ice Nine" (0:30)
CD 1 ⑱ "Northern Plains" (0:34)
CD 1 ⑲ "Islands" (0:34)
CD 1 ⑳ "La Negra" (0:30)
CD 1 ㉑ "Know How" (0:34)
CD 1 ㉒ "As Vesta Was Descending" (0:30)
CD 1 ㉓ "Which Side Are You On?"(0:37)
CD 1 ㉔ "Stone Coal" (0:38)
CD 1 ㉕ Toccata and Fugue in D Minor (0:34)
CD 1 ㉖ "When the Saints Go Marchin' In" (0:38)
CD 1 ㉗ "Mr. Snow" (0:37)
CD 1 ㉘ "Cherokee" (0:37)
CD 1 ㉙ "The Washington Post March" (0:30)
CD 1 ㉚ "Since I Found You" (0:40)

ACTIVITY ▶ *Musical Style Check*

How broad is your aural knowledge of musical styles?

As you listen to the short musical examples in the Musical Style Check, try to identify and match the styles. Discuss:
(1) What percent of this music are you familiar with?
(2) How does this music define America?

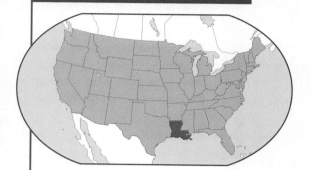

LOUISIANA is located at the mouth of the Mississippi River, where it meets the Gulf of Mexico. It was in the city of New Orleans, Louisiana, that African, Creole, French, Spanish, and other European cultures mixed. The New Orleans style of jazz was one result of this unique blend. *In what other American cities did jazz music develop?*

Music in the World
New York, Chicago, Kansas City, and parts of East Texas.

Jazz and Classical Music

One of the ways to distinguish the many styles of music is by comparison. Jazz and classical music, for example, are easy to distinguish because they have very different characteristics. **Jazz** is *a popular style of music that developed in America during the late 1800s and early 1900s.* It was instrumental music of exuberant spirit, often improvised (invented) on the spot. It most likely emerged from the rhythmic music played during lively street parades and funeral processions in New Orleans. However, jazz music was developing in New York, Chicago, Kansas City, and East Texas at the same time.

Among those who cultivated jazz were Joseph "King" Oliver and Louis Armstrong. Intended for small audiences and for participation, jazz was the kind of music that set feet tapping. Jazz was dance music.

In music, the term classical has two meanings: **classical music,** in its broadest sense, refers to *a style of "art" music as distinguished from folk, jazz, or popular music.* More specifically, **classical music** refers to *European music of the Classical period;* that is, music composed from about 1725 to 1810 by composers such as Franz Joseph Haydn and Wolfgang Amadeus Mozart.

The Classical period was a time when musicians and other artists looked back to the simple, stately, uncluttered, classical architecture of ancient Greece. It was a time in which revolutions overthrew the old social order in France, and when American independence and democratic rule began. People were searching for a sense of order. The result was a

Music & HISTORY

Louis Armstrong is an American jazz legend. In Chicago, he joined the Creole Jazz Band to make the first recording of authentic jazz. **When did this style of American music first develop?**

Music & History
During the late 1800s and early 1900s.

trimmer, clearer music. Instead of many melodies occurring simultaneously, as in the preceding period, Classical composers opted for a more transparent style in which one melody sang out, while the other parts provided a simple accompaniment. This form of music is known as **homophony**, *a single melody with chordal accompaniment.* This new homophonic style projected a sense of aristocratic elegance. The music was known for its symmetrical, balanced phrases. Moods changed freely, and composers used dramatic changes of soft and loud, fast and slow, and high and low to make the music expressive and full of surprises.

Classical composers explored new instrumental combinations. The **concerto** (con-CHAYR-toh), *a composition usually written in three lengthy sections or movements featuring the interplay between one or more soloists and an orchestra,* became a popular vehicle for showing off the

Students can learn more about harmony in section E. of the *Music Theory Handbook.*

Music & Art

Wearing the formal dress of the Classical period (c.1725–1810), Mozart, his father, and his sister are shown here making music. **Describe ways in which modern families share and encourage music making.**

Louis Carmontelle. *Leopold Mozart Making Music with Wolfgang and Nannerl.* c. 1763. Museé Conde, Chantilly, Paris, France.

Music & Art
Encourage a variety of responses.

skill of an instrumental soloist accompanied by the newly formed symphony orchestra. Strings, woodwinds, and brass instruments were combined and contrasted to create a whole new world of musical expression.

Activity *Compare Musical Styles*
Instructor's Guide, pages 35–36
TRB Profile—*Ella Fitzgerald*
CD 1 ⟨31⟩ "Allegro" (2:54)
CD 1 ⟨32⟩ "You'd Be So Nice To
Come Home To" (2:48)

ACTIVITY ▶ *Compare Musical Styles*

How would you describe two compositions in different styles and from different historical periods?

Listen to:

■ Allegro movement from Concerto in D Major for Trumpet and Orchestra by Michael Haydn (performed by Wynton Marsalis).

■ "You'd Be So Nice To Come Home To" by Cole Porter (performed by Ella Fitzgerald).

Write down the musical similarities and differences you hear. What can you tell about these pieces just by the verbal clues—the names of the composers, the performers, and the titles of the musical selections? Use your notes to discuss these comparisons in class.

PROFILE

Wynton Marsalis
American Trumpeter
1961–

Wynton Marsalis

Although he was born in New Orleans, a city known for jazz, Wynton Marsalis started out as a classical musician. Guided by his musician father, Marsalis picked up the trumpet when he was twelve, and within two years he had joined the New Orleans Symphony Orchestra. He later attended the Juilliard School of Music in New York.

It was in New York that Marsalis first became interested in jazz. He began going to libraries, museums, and clubs to read about, listen to, and meet jazz musicians. Marsalis's background in classical music and his love of jazz proved to be a winning combination. He became a recognized recording artist by the age of 20.

Marsalis now focuses most of his energies on jazz. He spends much of his time visiting schools to encourage an interest in this style of music among American youth. Wynton Marsalis has become a major force in American music, winning Grammy awards in both jazz and classical categories in 1984. He became Artistic Director of the jazz program at New York City's Lincoln Center in 1991 and won a Pulitzer Prize in music in 1997.

What We Like and Why We Like It

The old Latin expression *De gustibus non est disputandum* ("There is no disputing taste") seems to suggest that differences in taste cannot be substantiated. For some people, "I like it" or "I don't like it" are sufficient explanations. However, understanding why you like or dislike something is important, if only to validate your perceptions to yourself. Then, too, you may want to be able to persuade others.

Before you can fully and fairly judge whether you like a new piece of music, you have to be certain you hear what the sounds are doing. You have to know what you are hearing and become familiar with the characteristics of the music. This implies a willingness to listen, even if the sounds do not readily appeal to you. You have to give unfamiliar music a chance, which may mean giving it your attention more than once in order to feel comfortable with it.

This text invites you to explore many different forms of music. It does not present one type of musical style as best or ask you to like a particular kind of music. The goal of this text is to expand your horizons. The skill you acquire in analyzing music and learning to listen to it perceptively will enable you to make musical choices and to know why you made them.

ACTIVITY ▶ *Develop Perceptive Listening*

Can you identify more distinguishing characteristics about music by listening with greater focus?

Listen again to the compositions by Michael Haydn and Cole Porter, first heard on page 12. Use the following criteria to deepen your understanding of the music characteristics:

1. Determine the musical means (the source of sound and the size of the groups for each piece).
2. Describe the musical expression (the rhythm, melody, and mood).
3. Determine each piece's order or organization (the amount of repetition and contrast that is used).
4. Determine the possible origin (the where, when, and by whom the music was created).
5. Characterize the use of the music (its function or purpose and its intended audience).

MIDI TECHNOLOGY OPTION

- **Music with MIDI** Use a MIDI program to experiment and compose with various instrumentations, musical expression, and organization. You might also create a composition combining musical ideas from different musical styles.

You may wish to use "Analyze Musical Preferences" at this time. Lesson plans for the activity are found on page 38 in the Instructor's Guide.

Activity *Develop Perceptive Listening*
Instructor's Guide, pages 36–37
TRB 1-4, *Perceptive Listening*
CD 1 ³¹ "Allegro" (2:54)
CD 1 ³² "You'd Be So Nice To Come Home To" (2:48)

Students can learn more about rhythm and harmony in sections B. and E. of the *Music Theory Handbook.*

Technology Option
Use Project 1 in the *MIDI Activities* binder.

PROFILE

Cole Porter

Cole Porter was a songwriter famous for his witty lyrics and memorable melodies. Born into a wealthy family, Porter managed to publish his first song when he was only 11 years old. Later, against his grandfather's wishes, he dropped his law school studies in order to pursue music.

After some initial failures, Porter began to write many hits. His grandfather's will soon made him a millionaire, and he married a woman who was even richer! The two of them lived lavishly in Europe and traveled the world. If you had that much money would you work? Porter did. In fact, few people have ever worked harder. He composed Broadway shows, sometimes two a year.

In 1937, both of Porter's legs were crushed in a horse-riding accident. Although he could not walk again, Porter continued to write. His many fine songs include: "Love for Sale," "I Get a Kick Out of You," and "I've Got You Under My Skin."

Cole Porter
American Composer
1892–1964

Perceptive listening is *the ability to discern musical characteristics and describe them.* These characteristics are both internal (dealing with sound) and external (dealing with the social aspects). In its sound, every piece of music uses a distinctive *means* (the source of sound), *expression* (feeling), and *order* (organization). In its social aspects, every musical piece has a distinctive *origin* (the where, when, and by whom the music was created) and *use* (function or purpose). To develop the capacity to listen perceptively, you must analyze what you hear. You need to perceive the internal and external characteristics of the work and develop the ability to describe them. For this purpose you may have to acquire some new vocabulary, or "descriptors." This new vocabulary will permit you to communicate your likes and dislikes persuasively.

SUMMARY

Music is one of the ways in which we define who we are, as individuals and as a society. Through music and the other arts, we express our cultural lifestyles as Americans. Music gives us a rich and unique heritage. All we have to do is open our ears and our minds. We can learn to appreciate the great variety that surrounds us by becoming perceptive listeners.

Building Music Vocabulary

On a sheet of paper, write the term from the list that best matches each description below.

(4) classical music   (7) jazz
(2) concerto   (3) musical style
(5) culture   (6) perceptive listening
(1) homophony

1. A single melody with chordal accompaniment.
2. A composition usually written in three lengthy sections or movements featuring interplay between one or more soloists and an orchestra.
3. The distinct manner or character of musical expression.
4. A style of "art" music, as distinguished from popular music.
5. Customs, ideas, tastes, and beliefs acquired from a person's background.
6. The ability to discern musical characteristics and describe them.
7. A popular style of music that developed in America during the late 1800s and early 1900s.

Reviewing Music Facts

Answer each question in a complete sentence.

8. Haydn and Mozart are associated with what musical period?
9. When and where did the musical style we call "jazz" first develop?
10. What are some of the characteristics of jazz?
11. Identify three internal characteristics of music.
12. Identify two external characteristics of music.
13. What earlier culture did Classical musicians and artists look back to for inspiration?
14. Why is it possible to distinguish between classical music and jazz simply by listening to it?

Answers to Chapter 1 Review
8. The Classical period.
9. During the late 1800s and early 1900s in New Orleans.
10. Answers may include: an exuberant spirit, improvisation; simple, heartfelt, dancelike, rhythmic.
11. Means, expression, and order.
12. Origin and use (or function).

Complete answers to the Chapter 1 Review are found in the Instructor's Guide, pages 39–40.

Thinking It Through

On a sheet of paper, answer each of the following questions.

15. **Explain** In your own words, explain how a person might develop perceptive listening.
16. **Analyze** How do you believe your personal musical taste developed?
17. **Apply** What are some of the ways you might expand your musical taste to include different kinds of music?

Making the Connection

Social Studies Find out more about the social conditions of African Americans in the 1800s and early 1900s. Use what you have learned to connect these conditions to the development of musical styles during that same time.

Art Create original drawings or find examples of period art that "illustrate" the styles of the classical concerto and the popular song heard in this lesson. Drawings should reflect the various elements that shape the two contrasting styles.

 Learn more about music styles, resources, composers, and popular musicians at **www.glencoe.com/sec/music**

13. Ancient Greece.
14. We can hear differences in musical "style."
15. Answers may include: by listening to many styles of music; by contrasting and comparing styles; by learning about the origin of various selections; by developing a music vocabulary.
16. Individual answers will vary.
17. Answers may include: by listening to different kinds of music and by developing knowledge and vocabulary to understand and explain different musical styles.

CHAPTER 2

Music in Other Cultures

Do you realize that much of the music you hear in the United States comes from other countries? Most people who immigrate to America gradually adapt to and acquire much of the lifestyle of their new homeland. However, they do not generally give up their music. Their musical tastes may be influenced and adjusted, but they will continue to like, and perhaps even favor, the music of their original homeland. Eventually, people hear new sounds that attract their attention. However, rather than give up the music of their heritage, their tastes stretch to accommodate new types of music.

We become knowledgeable about music in other cultures by discovering and experiencing it. Then, since musical expression comes from the depth of who we are, we come to know something important about others at the same time. **What can the instrument shown here tell you about the person's culture?**

Caption answer
Students will probably speculate that he lives near a large body of water where the shell was found.

Objectives

By completing the chapter, you will:
- Assess your familiarity with music of other cultures.
- Understand how music can allow a person to develop empathy for people of different cultures.
- Begin to associate musical styles with their place of origin in the world.
- Be able to recognize and discuss music from cultures represented by Americans of African, Mexican, and Chinese descent.
- Understand and describe how different cultures use music for a variety of purposes.

Vocabulary

anthropologist
empathy
ethnomusicologists
heterophony
Lali
mariachi
mestizo
Peking opera
timbre

Discovering New Soundscapes

As Americans, we collectively embrace the larger world of sound represented by our multicultural society. We all have some affinity for rhythm and blues, gospel, jazz, or other musical traditions given to us by African Americans. We can hear Chinese music when we visit Chinatown or attend a Chinese New Year's celebration. When we eat in ethnic restaurants, we are apt to hear music from countries such as Germany, Italy, Japan, or Mexico. You are probably familiar with a wider variety of the world's music than you think!

Although different kinds of music come from different countries, people have not always had the opportunity to enjoy music from other lands. Prior to Thomas Edison's invention of the phonograph in 1877, the only way to hear music was to experience it live. If you wanted to hear music of other lands, you had to travel to the place where it was performed. The phonograph changed this. It made music from around the world easily accessible to everyone. Perhaps without even being aware of it, you have learned to associate certain sounds with certain cultures.

Regardless of the musical style or the origin, almost all music shares several common elements: melody, rhythm, and **timbre** (TAM-bur), *the quality of sound*. When you listen to music from various countries, consider the type of melody, the type of rhythm, and the type of timbre. Think of descriptive words such as "lively" or "dancelike" to associate with the various musical styles.

ACTIVITY ▶ *Discover Music from Other Countries*

How familiar are you with the music of different countries and cultures?

Listen to musical examples that represent the musical traditions of people from Africa, Asia, Europe, Central America, and North America. Rate your familiarity using a scale of 0–3 (0 = no familiarity; 1 = little familiarity; 2 = some familiarity; 3 = great familiarity). Can you identify the example recorded in Africa? In the United States? What musical characteristics guided you in your decision?

Who They Are

Throughout history, people have always engaged in the creation of art. Magnificent cave paintings and carvings from the late Ice Age reveal that early people did not simply make tools; they decorated them. They had a

---

Activity *Discover Music from Other Cultures*
Instructor's Guide, pages 41–42
TRB 2-1, *Musical Familiarity Worksheet*
CD 1 33 "Raga Kaushi Kanada" (0:35)
CD 1 34 "Scarce O' Tatties" (0:37)
CD 1 35 "Drumming Song in Praise of Blacksmiths" (0:35)
CD 1 36 "Juan Colorado" (0:34)
CD 1 37 "Vienna Remains Vienna" (0:30)
CD 1 38 "Ake—the Break of Day" (0:34)
CD 1 39 "Hawaiian Wedding Song" (0:34)
CD 1 40 "Toasting Song" (0:37)
CD 1 41 "Horos Toa Sakena" (0:37)
CD 1 42 "Semarandana" (0:36)

sense of craftsmanship and design. Their artifacts give us an indication of how these people lived, thought, and conducted their lives.

In Mesopotamia, around the ruins of Babylon, archaeologists uncovered rattles, flutes, and harplike instruments dating back to almost 2000 B.C. The purported splendor of King Nebuchadnezzar's hanging gardens leads us to envision magnificent entertainments as well. Ancient people were fascinated with music.

Your musical preferences help define who you are. The music of other people and cultures helps define who they are. The use of musical instruments by ancient people tells us that they were not that different from us. They, too, had dreams and found ways of coping with the human struggle. They, too, were sensitive and considered the arts important in their lives.

Try to imagine the music of these people. What did they sing when they were victorious in battle? What were their love songs like? How did they dance? If we knew, we would understand much more about them. But their music was not written down; in fact, a system for writing music was not developed in Western Europe until about the ninth century A.D., and the recording of music has only been possible for a little more than 100 years. From the standpoint of being able to hear the music of other peoples, we have accessible to us only about 1,000 years of written music. We can become acquainted with some of the unwritten cultural traditions through examples of music that were recorded "in the field" by **anthropologists**, *scientists who study the physical and cultural characteristics and social customs of a group of people,* and **ethnomusicologists**, *professionals who study the music of different cultural groups.*

You may wish to use "Music in Your Community" at this time. Lesson plans for the activity are found on page 45 in the Instructor's Guide.

Music & Art

This marble sculpture is more than 4,000 years old. **How does it show you that music was important to the people of that civilization?**

Cycladic Art. *Seated Harp Player.* c. 3000-2500 B.C. Marble. The Metropolitan Museum of Art, New York, New York. Rogers Fund, 1947. (47.100.1)

Music & Art
Music was important because the artist took the time to preserve the image of a man with a harp.

You may wish to use "Investigate Musical Origins" at this time. Lesson plans for the activity are found on page 46 in the Instructor's Guide.

Developing Empathy

Through familiarity with and understanding of the music of other cultures comes **empathy**, *the ability to look at the world from another person's perspective*. Empathy gives us an understanding of someone else's viewpoint. Music gives us an indication of how other people express themselves and communicate their feelings. It invites us to know other people and to be empathetic toward them.

What makes music universal is its capacity to speak to our inner being. It touches our feelings and expresses the rituals of our lives. Music is a richness of knowing people and of exploring the world of humanity, past and present.

Crossing the Cultural Chasm

Having easy access to the wonder of sound created by all the peoples of this world does not mean that you are going to readily like or understand all of it. There are vast differences in the ways various cultures express themselves musically. These chasms may be difficult to cross, because our ears tend to get stuck in our own culture or because music of other people may not readily communicate its message to those outside the culture. In spite of the difficulties you may have in breaking out of your musical comfort zone, exploring music that is unfamiliar can be highly rewarding. It's like making new friends.

To grow in your tolerance of music from other cultures, all you have to do is be willing to explore what is unfamiliar. The more you are will-

Use Artsource® VHS Segment 2 in the Performing Arts Package to show a performance by Korean Classical Music and Dance Company.

The Korean Classical Music and Dance Company, under the artistic direction of Don Kim, performs classical and folk dances that are an integral part of Korean culture. The dances and music are presented with the grace and elegance that characterize these ancient traditional dance forms.

Korean Classical Music and Dance Company. Don Kim, artistic director. Photo by Craig Schwartz.

ing to listen, the more rapidly you can accustom yourself. It is like sampling food from foreign countries. At first you may not like it, but then you begin to savor it because it is different. If you can find out what music is trying to communicate and how it is intended to be used, you will have some basis for understanding it.

Finding Similarities

People from all cultures value music. Even though "musical language," or the way people use sounds, may be vastly different, music serves many of the same purposes—ceremonial, religious, and social—in different cultures. Similarities in the use of music throughout the world indicate that human beings are far more alike than different. You may discover that music that sounded very strange at first has familiar aspects. To begin your exploration of music of other cultures, you will be introduced to music from three cultural traditions that are well represented in the American population: African (Cameroon), Hispanic (Mexico), and Asian (China). For each culture, you will be provided with background about the country, the people, and the musical traditions. Then, in that context, you will be asked to listen to typical examples of the music.

Music in the World
Tribal unity and pride.

Cameroon (Africa)

Cameroon is a republic in western central Africa. Two official languages, English and French, help people from more than 150 ethnic groups, with many different languages and dialects, communicate with each other. In 1472, Portuguese sailors visited the coast of what is now called Cameroon and enjoyed eating the prawns they caught in the Wouri River. They called this river Rio dos Cameroes, or "River of Prawns," and the name "Cameroon" soon identified the entire country.

Cameroon lies on a volcanic belt that separates western and central Africa. This double chain of volcanic peaks rises to an elevation of 13,350 feet (4,069 meters) at Mt. Cameroon, the highest point in West Africa. The terrain in Cameroon is diverse. The hot, humid coastal plain that extends inland from the Atlantic Ocean to the slopes of these mountains is among the wettest places on earth. The central Adamawa Plateau has a relatively cool, pleasant climate with little variation in annual temperature. This plateau is the home of the Bamileke (bah-mee-LAY-KAY) people, who live in neighborhoods of family homesteads. The Bamileke people are divided into chiefdoms, subgroups that have some distinct traits within the overall common culture.

MUSIC in the WORLD

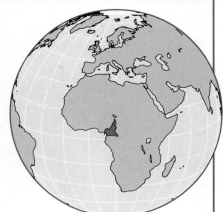

CAMEROON's location in western central Africa made it vulnerable to European colonialism. Warrior dances such as "Lali" were viewed with suspicion by colonial rulers. *What do they symbolize today?*

The Music of Cameroon

The Bamileke people perform **Lali** (LAH-LEE), *a warrior dance.* The example you will hear was performed by the Menne (me-NAY), a sub-group of the Bamileke people. Lali is a music of great rhythmic energy and subtlety. Centuries ago in the sub-Sahara, warrior dances served preparatory and celebratory purposes. These male dances expressed bravery, virility, and brotherhood. They celebrated prowess (ability and skill) in battle, self-confidence, and manliness. But they served other, perhaps even more important, purposes.

From the fifteenth through the early twentieth century, colonialism—the imposed rule of a European power—stripped many African peoples of their independence. Warrior dances were viewed by colonial rulers as a symbol of self-assertion. They became a metaphor for local pride and revolution. In her studies of these dances, Judith Hanna observes that "throughout Africa, warrior dances were usually crushed, as were other dances that might loosen the colonial grip through their expression of

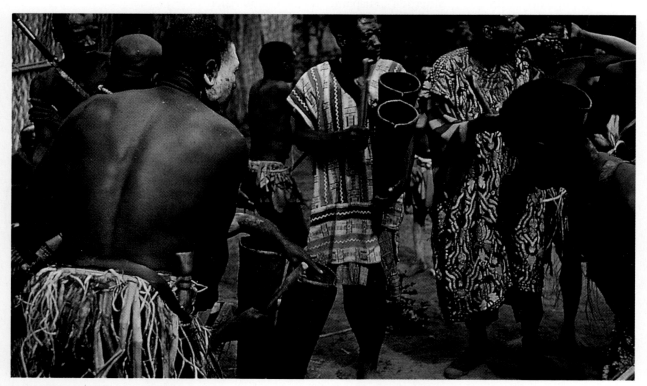

Music & CULTURE

The Bamileke people, like their Cameroon neighbors the Kwifon, shown here, perform dances that express bravery, virility, and brotherhood.

Members of the *Kwifon* society. The Metropolitan Museum of Art, New York, New York. The Robert Goldwater Library, Paul Gebauer Collection. Photograph by Paul Gebauer at Nkwen.

communal life." Such expressions were widely prohibited. Missionaries often feared them because of the sense of solidarity they proclaimed.

Today, these dances still symbolize tribal unity and pride. The Bamileke present these dances now as musical performances expressing these sentiments, rather than as expressions of war. Lali was originally danced by members of a secret society. In all probability, the performers wore ceremonial masks that are typical of this region. The iron bells heard in this music are now used in other music of Cameroon.

ACTIVITY ▶ *Discover Pattern Changes*

Activity *Discover Pattern Changes*
Instructor's Guide, pages 42–43
CD 1 43 "Lali" (2:32)

Can you detect when the two-tone woodblock changes its initial pattern?

Listen to "Lali" performed by the Bamileke-Bamoungoun percussion ensemble from Cameroon and "air perform" with your index fingers the following pattern of eight pulses, high-low, high-low:

Determine when it changes. Do you hear other changes in the woodblock?

How many of the following instruments can you hear?

- Four two-tone bells of different sizes. (How many pitches can you distinguish? Can you hear more than six?)
- N'to (n-TOH), a medium-sized tubular drum that is open on one end.
- N'ket (n-KET), a large closed drum with a carved-out base on which it stands. (Can you hear its low tones?)
- Three rattles that seem to be playing the following pattern:

Students can learn more about rhythm and notes and their values in section B. of the *Music Theory Handbook.*

Can you tap the rattles' pattern along with the recording? Can you detect how the other instruments also repeat their rhythms and vary them subtly? Is there an underlying sense of shared rhythm throughout? When are the parts occasionally silent?

MIDI TECHNOLOGY OPTION

Technology Option
Use Project 2 in the *MIDI Activities* binder.

- **Music with MIDI** Use a MIDI program to explore and create rhythmic and compositional ideas of Cameroon and West Africa. These techniques can be used to compose a piece featuring evolving musical patterns.

Mexico

Mexico is a large country with many regions. As in the United States, these regions differ in dialect, foods, clothing, and music. Although the country is largely mountainous, more than half of the work force engages in agriculture. Industry and commerce are growing. The official language is Spanish, but sizable minorities speak Native-American tongues.

For many centuries music has had a special place in the lives of the Mexican people. Before Hernán Cortés and his Spanish conquistadors arrived in what is now Mexico in 1519, both religious and social music were important to the Indian civilizations. The Spaniards introduced a rich musical heritage, including a wide variety of music and instruments. African slaves and Caribbean immigrants also influenced Mexican music. The cross-fertilization and blending of the Spanish, Indian, and African cultures produced a rich **mestizo** (mes-TEE-soh), *mixed culture*, and a musical life that has been envied and enjoyed by people worldwide.

The Music of Mexico

In today's Mexican music, the legacy of the past has been reworked through centuries of creativity into strikingly different, yet in some ways similar, regional forms of music. These separate traditions have original musical forms and compositions, but they also share Spanish-derived instruments such as the folk harp, violin, and guitar-type instruments, as well as a special musical feeling that is unique to Mexico.

Visit any Mexican town and you will hear music. Mexicans use music to celebrate events such as baptisms, birthdays, weddings, anniversaries, funerals, civic ceremonies, and religious holidays. The people like music, and they show it. They sing along with the musicians and burst out with enthusiastic yells, laughter, clapping, and dancing.

Music & CULTURE

The instruments used in the Veracruzan-style jarocho ensemble include: six-string guitar, harp, requinto jarocho, *and* jarana. **How are they similar to instruments that you have seen or played?**

Music & Culture
Answers will vary.

Two types of regional music popular throughout Mexico are from the states of Veracruz (in the east) and Jalisco (in the west). Typically, Veracruzan music is performed on four instruments: a 35-string harp called *arpa* that plays both melody and bass; a four-string guitar called *requinto jarocho* (reh-KEEN-toh hah-ROH-choh) that provides melody; a thin guitar called *jarana* (hah-RAH-nah); and a six-string guitar that, along with the jarana, provides rhythmic and harmonic accompaniment. Traditional songs are called *sones* (SOH-nehs) *jarochos*. One of the most famous *sones jarochos* is "La Bamba."

ACTIVITY ▶ *Identify Repeated Patterns*

Can you hear the repeated rhythmic and chordal patterns in "La Bamba"?

Hear the 4 beats: 1   2   3   4
Chordal pattern: I   IV   V   V

Rhythmic flow:

Clap bass rhythm:

Can anyone in the class play the chordal pattern of the bass rhythm on a guitar, piano, or another instrument (Key of C)?

Listen to the four different instruments and add a fifth. Can you distinguish the four stringed instruments? Often a fifth instrument is added—the feet of a dancer stamping on the floor while dancing. Can you stamp the following rhythmic pattern along with the repeated cycle above?

Rhythm of feet:

Foot pattern: l   r - l   r   l - r
(l=left, r=right)

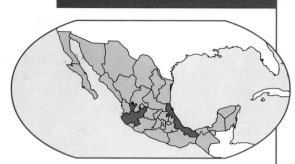

MUSIC in the WORLD

VERACRUZ is a long and narrow state on the Gulf of Mexico. **JALISCO** is in west central Mexico. Both states have dense forested regions. *How might this natural resource influence the types of instruments common to the music of Mexico?*

Music in the World
Forests provided the raw materials to make guitars.

Activity *Identify Repeated Patterns*
Instructor's Guide, page 43
CD 1 44 "La Bamba" (2:49)

Students can learn more about rhythm and notes and their values in section B. of the *Music Theory Handbook*.

Mariachi Tradition

Music from Jalisco is usually played by the **mariachi** (mah-ree-AH-chee), *a musical group with several violins, two trumpets, a bass guitar called "guitarrón" (qhee-tah-ROHN), a short five-string rhythm guitar called "vihuela" (vee-WAY-lah), and a six-string guitar.* The mariachi plays many types of music. Two are the *son jalisciense* (hah-lee-see-EN-seh),

You may wish to use "Listen for the Meaning" at this time. Lesson plans for the activity are found on page 47 in the Instructor's Guide.

a type of *son* from Jalisco, and the *canción* (cahn-see-OHN) *ranchera,* a country song. "La Negra" ("The Dark Woman") is the most well known of the *sones jaliscienses.*

Activity *Experience the Difference*
Instructor's Guide, page 44
CD 1 45 "La Negra" (2:53)

ACTIVITY ▶ *Experience the Difference*

Can you perform the rhythmic shifting from a feeling of three to a feeling of two in the son jalisciense "La Negra"?

	Feeling of three:	Feeling of two:
Count:	1 & 2 & 3 &	1 2 3 4 5 6
Tap:	● • ● • ● •	● • • ● • •

Try tapping four verses in the pattern of three, then four verses in the pattern of six. Can half the class tap in three and half the class tap in six while counting together?

Now follow the guitarrón (bass) line and hear it when it plays in three:

1 & 2 & 3 &   or   1 & 2 & 3 &
● _ ● _ ● _   (rest) ● _ ●

It also plays the following tricky pattern in six:

1 & 2 & 3 &
_ ● _ ● _

To get the feeling of the constant flow of six beats and how the guitarrón line fits in, pair up so that one person claps a repeated cycle of 12 while the other claps on 2, 5, 9, and 11:

1 2 3 4 5 6 7 8 9 10 11 12
_ ● _ _ ● _ _ _ ● _ ● _

Start slowly, then speed up until you are going as fast as the music.

Students can learn more about rhythm and notes and their values in section B. of the *Music Theory Handbook.*

Music & CULTURE

Many of the performers in Campanas de America learned to play in high school mariachi ensembles. Here they perform with the traditional mariachi instruments: trumpets, violins, guitarróns (large bass guitars), and vihuelas (small guitars).
The mariachi style of music is from what part of Mexico?

Music & Culture Jalisco.

ACTIVITY ▶ *Recognize Mariachi Characteristics*

Can you identify the musical and cultural characteristics of mariachi?

Watch the video of "Campanas de America" and answer the following questions:

1. Identify the instruments used in a mariachi.
2. What does each instrument contribute to the mariachi ensemble?
3. On what occasions do mariachis typically play?
4. Describe traditional mariachi costumes.

Activity *Recognize Mariachi Characteristics*
Instructor's Guide, pages 44–45
Music! VHS Segment 1, "Las Mañanitas," performed by Campanas de America

China

China, one of the world's largest countries, has a mainly temperate climate. Even though it is one of the world's largest mineral producers, its economy is primarily agricultural. Many great rivers, among them the Yangtze and the Yellow, still serve as important arteries of transportation. China's ruling dynasties extended from about 2,000 B.C. to the early twentieth century. Today, the People's Republic of China is ruled by a communist government that was established in 1949.

The long history of the Chinese people is rich in literature and the arts. Chinese arts, often expressions of religious belief, are among the oldest in the world. In religion, the Chinese practice a mixture of Confucianism, Buddhism, and Taoism. Early writings include the works of Confucius, a philosopher and teacher of court officials. Confucius believed that only by learning justice, self-sacrifice for the good of all, and correct behavior could one achieve peace. Appreciation of the best music was part of one's development.

MUSIC in the WORLD

BEIJING (once called Peking) is the capital of China. It was in this city that the many styles of Chinese opera were combined and known as Peking opera. *What might you see in a typical Peking opera performance?*

Music in the World
An orchestra with singing, acrobatic martial arts, and pantomime.

The Music of China

During the sixth century A.D., a new, wealthy middle class developed a combination of music and theatre called Chinese opera. Soon there were public performances of opera throughout China. Hundreds of different styles developed. In the nineteenth century, a number of these styles were combined in the capital city of Peking (now Beijing). This style of opera became known as **Peking opera**, *an art form that combines an orchestra with speaking, singing, acrobatic martial arts, and pantomime.* The vocal

You may wish to use "Compare Peking Opera with Western Opera" at this time. Lesson plans for the activity are found on page 47 in the Instructor's Guide.

range of singing is generally higher than in Western opera. Whereas European and American opera singers resonate sound in their chests, Chinese opera singers make the sound vibrate in their head cavities, producing a shrill tonal quality.

The accompanying instrumental ensemble sits to the right of the stage in full view of the audience. Loud cymbals, gongs, a bright sounding drum, and a wood clapper (the latter played by the ensemble leader) accompany the actors' movements. Singing is accompanied by stringed instruments. The *jinghu* (jing-who), a small two-stringed bowed lute, accompanies male roles; a larger one, called *jing erhu* (jing AR-who), accompanies female roles. A round plucked lute, called *yuegin* (you-ay-chin), accompanies both. The musical texture is heterophonic. **Heterophony** is *musical texture that occurs when performers sing or play the same melody, but each in its own appropriate way, according to voice or instrument.* Melodies and rhythms serve the mood of the drama. Generally, the stories are taken from Chinese history or folklore.

Even though Chinese opera developed as a form of entertainment, the Confucian values of patriotism, loyalty, fidelity, and respect for elders and those in authority remain embedded in it. The cast of a Chinese opera is made up of a number of characters: ancient bearded men, flirtatious girls, aspiring students, women warriors, and others symbolizing various aspects of society. Generals and kings with distinctive costumes are presented in a larger-than-life manner. Clowns portray common people. In symbolic plots, these characters entertain and educate their audiences.

Music & HISTORY

Peking opera originated in the nineteenth century, when public performances of various styles throughout China were brought together in the city of Peking. It combines exciting drama, beautiful dance, stylized movement, and expressive movement with song. **How is Peking opera similar to theatre productions you have seen?**

Music & History
Responses will vary.

The Story of White Snake

One well-known Peking opera, *The Story of White Snake,* tells the story of two goddesses, White Snake and Green Snake, who decide to visit the mortal world. They each assume a woman's form. Soon White Snake meets, falls in love with, and marries a mortal man, Xu Xian (sue see-EN). The antagonist, or opponent, Fa Hai (fah high), religious leader of the town, knows the true identity of White Snake. He convinces Xu Xian to make White Snake drink wine, revealing her as a snake. Xu Xian shrieks and falls dead with fright.

White Snake dashes back to heaven, fighting her way through the heavenly guards to obtain an herb that will save her husband's life. She returns and saves him, and she eventually bears his child. Still, Fa Hai makes Xu Xian frightened of her, and Xu Xian leaves for a monastery. In a final meeting on a bridge, White Snake, whose love is as real as it is immortal, forgives Xu Xian. Her friend Green Snake is ready to skewer the cowardly man. As White Snake lets down her guard, a monk uses his power to imprison her and Green Snake in a pagoda for 10,000 years.

This story contains everything that Chinese audiences love: beautiful ladies, wonderful costumes, a wide range of emotions, acrobatic martial arts, and animal gods and goddesses. The Chinese audiences know that there are lessons to be learned here. Marriage is an important institution in Chinese society. Most Chinese believe that marriage and a stable family are the basis for social order. Love is a powerful emotion that all people feel, but like many tragic lovers, White Snake and her husband sacrifice their love because of rigid social conventions. The established ways of religion, represented by Fa Hai, do not permit true love in unusual circumstances. So, the kindhearted White Snake loses everything in the end. Chinese audiences leave the world of the theatre with much to talk about, as they return to the real world where the strict ways of society prevail.

Caption answer
Responses will vary.

In Peking opera you will see larger-than-life portrayals of generals and kings played by men with masklike painted faces, who wear elevated shoes and move like giants. **How would you describe the action in this scene from The Story of White Snake?**

Activity *Experience Peking Opera*
Instructor's Guide, page 45
CD 1 46   "Baishe Zhuan" (3:36)

ACTIVITY ▶ *Experience Peking Opera*

Can you determine how this excerpt from the Peking opera expresses heartbreak and forgiveness?

In the scene, White Snake is heartbroken to learn that Xu Xian, her husband, is leaving her to enter a monastery. However, she understands his fear and forgives him because her love for him is so strong. Try to perceive the themes of heartbreak and forgiveness and how the Chinese depict emotions in this musical example. Listen carefully and think about this particular moment in the story. Then listen again to the excerpt and answer the following questions:

1. How many different sources of sound can you distinguish? Do they blend or contrast?
2. Do the two instruments (yuegin and jing erhu) that accompany White Snake play totally independent parts and melodies that contrast with her melody, or do their parts relate to hers?
3. Do we have any forms of expression in the United States that ask us to "suspend reality" and accept the unreal in order to understand the meaning?

SUMMARY

Musical traditions must be viewed in the context of the culture from which they come. When you hear music with some understanding of how and why it was developed, and you know something about its use and meaning, then you can begin to relate to it. You have to hear it enough to become accustomed to its musical conventions before it can speak to you emotionally. Then you can feel empathy for the people who created and shared the expression. People become knowledgeable in the ways of this world by discovering and experiencing a larger universe. One way is through music. Musical expression comes from the depths of who and what we are as humans. It is a way that we share our inner being with others. To know the music of other people is to know something very important about them—their spirit and their feeling.

Building Music Vocabulary

On a sheet of paper, write the term from the list that best matches each description below.

- (2) anthropologist
- (8) empathy
- (6) ethnomusicologists
- (7) heterophony
- (3) Lali
- (4) mariachi
- (9) mestizo
- (5) Peking opera
- (1) timbre

1. The quality of sound.
2. Scientists who study characteristics and customs of a group of people.
3. A warrior dance.
4. A Mexican instrumental ensemble consisting of violins, trumpets, and guitars.
5. A Chinese musical art form that combines instruments, speaking, singing, acrobatics, martial arts, and pantomime.
6. Professionals who study the music of different cultural groups.
7. A musical style where all performers sing or play the same melody, but in a manner appropriate to each voice or instrument.
8. The ability to look at the world from another person's perspective.
9. A Spanish term for "mixed culture."

Reviewing Music Facts

Answer each question in a complete sentence.

10. What invention made music from around the world accessible to everyone?
11. Why are we unable to know very much about the music of very early cultures?
12. What are some of the ways we can know a little about the music of early peoples?
13. What instruments are typical to the music of Veracruz and to the music of Jalisco?
14. What is one of the most obvious differences between the singing style in Western opera and Peking opera?

Complete answers for the Chapter 2 Review are found in the Instructor's Guide, pages 48–49.

Thinking It Through

On a sheet of paper, answer each of the following questions.

15. **Compare** Identify similarities between the African Lali music and the Mexican musical examples.
16. **Explain** In your own words, explain the "rhythmic shifting" in the Mexican *son jalisciense* "La Negra."
17. **Analyze** What are two characteristics common to the African, Mexican, and Chinese musical examples in this chapter?

Making the Connection

Language Arts Find and share traditional stories or poems that illustrate cultural traditions.

Social Studies Choose an instrument from the chapter that is associated with the music of Cameroon, Mexico, or China. Discover how the materials, design, and construction reflect natural resources common to its place of origin.

 Discover more about music traditions from Africa, Mexico, and China at **www.glencoe.com/sec/music**

Answers to Chapter 2 Review
10. The invention of the phonograph.
11. They had no system for writing music down and no recordings.
12. Instruments and drawings of musicians and instruments; field recordings which may be an unwritten, oral record of earlier music are clues to early music.
13. Veracruz: Harp (arpa), guitars (requinto jarocho, jarana), six-string guitar. Jalisco: violins, trumpets, guitars (including guitarrón, vihuela, and six-string guitar.)
14. Western opera singers resonate their voices in the chest; Peking opera singers resonate in the head; the latter has a more shrill tonal quality.
15. Both are strongly rhythmic, with repeating patterns.
16. The pattern shifts from a feeling of two to a feeling of three.
17. All illustrate a traditional style and traditional material.

Chapter 1 Project

You may also wish to use Assessment Master 1, Unit One Test, in the TRB.

Chapter 1 Project
Instructor's Guide, page 50

▶ *Match Music with Environment*

How well can you associate different environments with different types of music?

Look at the photographs on this page. For each photo, answer the following questions:

- What is the environment or place?
- What style of music is being performed?
- What is the source of sound? (Describe the means.)
- What is the function of the music? (Describe the use.)
- Who is the intended audience?

When you have finished, discuss your answers. Are there times when other music might be heard in the same environments?

1.

2.

3.

4.

5.

Chapter 2 Project

▶ *Connect Music with Culture*

On the basis of (1) what you have learned about African, Mexican, and Chinese music, and (2) clues that you identify in the music, determine which broad culture the music represents.

Listen to the musical examples and make notes on as many of the musical characteristics as you can. On the basis of your analysis of each of the three pieces and what you know about music of other cultures, place each work in its proper cultural context. Be prepared to discuss the reasons for your choices.

Chapter 2 Project
Instructor's Guide, page 51
TRB Unit One Evaluation: Chapter 2,
Perceptive Listening
CD 1 ⁴⁸ "Zhonghua Liuban" (4:10)
CD 1 ⁴⁹ "Bako" (3:13)
CD 1 ⁵⁰ "El Gustito" (2:40)

A Transatlantic Experience

If you grew up in an American city like New York or a small town in the Midwest, you might remember songs that were part of the games you played with your friends. These kinds of songs and chants are called "game songs," and they are found in many cultures. "Kye Kye Kule" is a popular game song of children in the African county of Ghana. They learn this song from their parents. It is part of their early musical training, and it remains important to their musical heritage.

"Kye Kye Kule"
Instructor's Guide, page 53
CD 18 [1] "Kye Kye Kule" (0:46)

Analyze Call and Response
Instructor's Guide, page 53
CD 18 [1] "Kye Kye Kule" (0:46)

See Chapter 8, page 129, for more about call-and-response form.

▶ *"Kye Kye Kule"*

As you listen to "Kye Kye Kule," follow the music below and imagine children singing this game song while they are at play. It is the sound of the words, not their meaning, that is significant.

▶ *Analyze Call and Response*

"Kye Kye Kule" is performed in call-and-response form, where a group of singers responds to a leader. It's like a musical question and answer. Follow the notation as you listen again and answer these questions:

1. What is the relationship between the leader and group?
2. Why do you think this song has no accompaniment?
3. How are the repetitions the same? How are they different?
4. What musical characteristics make this song easy to learn?

Kye Kye Kule

An Akan Call-and-Response Exercise Song
From the Repertoire of Abraham Kobena Adzenyah*

Kye   kye ku - le.   Kye kye ku - le.   Kye kye ko - fi nsa.   Kye kye ko - fi nsa.
(Chay chay koo - lay)   (Chay chay ko - feen - sah)

Ko - fi nsa lan - ga.   Ko - fi nsa lan - ga.   Ka - ka shi lan - ga.   Ka - ka shi lan - ga.
(Ko - fee sah - lahn - gah)   (Kah - kah shee lahn - gah)

Kum   a - den - de.   Kum   a - den - de.   Kum   a - den - de.   Hey!
(Koom   ah - den - day)

*As sung in *Let Your Voice Be Heard: Songs from Ghana and Zimbabwe*

Name the Instruments
Instructor's Guide, page 54
CD 18 [2] "tché-tché" (4:31)

▶ *Name the Instruments*

In Ghana, contemporary adult musicians might honor the game songs of their childhood by incorporating them in their compositions. However, the song might sound different because it is accompanied by instruments usually associated with Western popular music.

Listen to Angelique Kidjo perform "tché-tché," a contemporary song that uses the music of "Kye Kye Kule." Identify the instruments used by the performers that you might also hear in a popular Western rock band, such as a trap set and electric bass guitar.

▶ *Identify Cross-Atlantic Influences*

Listen again to both performances and discuss the following:

1. Describe how Angelique Kidjo used "Kye Kye Kule" in her song.

2. During what part of the entire song do you recognize "Kye Kye Kule"?

3. Why do you think an Afro-Pop musician like Kidjo might include a game song as musical material in her arrangement?

4. Can you think of any contemporary Western popular music groups that include game songs as part of their music repertoire

Identify Cross-Atlantic Influences
Instructor's Guide, page 54
CD 18 [1] "Kye Kye Kule" (0:46)
CD 18 [2] "tché-tché" (4:31)

MUSIC in the WORLD

GHANA, Africa, became an independent nation in 1957. The music of Ghana often shows the influence of British and native Ghanaian styles.

Angelique Kidjo is an energetic Afro-Pop musician. Much of her music reflects the values and traditions of Ghana, her native country.

Lily Cai, a Chinese-American,
preserves her traditional Chinese
culture by performing ancient classical court dances.
This stunning dance from the T'ang Dynasty
(619–907 A.D.), represents the spirit of a goddess,
celebrated by the flying and floating of the brilliant
red ribbons. All classical Chinese dances base
movements, gestures, and floor patterns on the
concept of the circle. As the dancer moves, she
strives to achieve variety in the flowing movements
of circular forms. Imagine the type of designs the
movement of the ribbons might make. Can you
demonstrate these movements to the class?

Lily Cai. "The Flying Goddess." Photo: Lee Hanson.

Music!...
To Invite Us To Move

You may wish to use Fine Art Transparency 2, *Jitterbugs IV*, in the TRB to introduce Unit Two.

Chapter 3
Interpreting Rhythm Through Movement

Chapter 4
Rhythms that Dance

Use Artsource® VHS Segment 3 in the Performing Arts Package to show a performance of "The Flying Goddess."

Interpreting Rhythm Through Movement

Music progresses through time. Like a film, a play, or a speech, a musical work has a beginning, middle, and an end. If it is well conceived, it provokes our interest. It teases us and catapults us along from its start into its interior and on to its finish. To hold our attention, it presents us with a series of events—surprises or revelations, frustrations and satisfactions—that stir our excitement and draw us into deeper involvement. It promises a conclusion or resolution—and delivers it.

Rhythm is the unmistakable aspect of making music that tells us it moves through time. It is what the human body feels first in music and responds to so eagerly. In this photo, Cuban rumba dancers respond to the syncopated rhythms of the rumba. **Can you describe rhythms that move you to do the following: sway, march, stomp your feet, or clap your hands?**

Caption answer Encourage students to think of the rhythms of a lullaby, a school pep song, a fast rock song, or a folk song.

Objectives

By completing this chapter, you will:
- Use body movements to understand rhythm in music.
- Differentiate between "felt" time and "real" time in music.
- Become familiar with tempo designations, pulse, meter, and accent.
- Learn to improvise rhythms.
- Recognize some rhythmic aspects in the music of India.
- Understand and create syncopation.

Vocabulary

accelerando
accent
a tempo
"felt" time
improvisation
meter
rhythm
rhythm cycle
ritardando
syncopation
tempo

Musicians to Meet

Scott Joplin
Nicolai Rimsky-Korsakov

The Beat of Music

The beat, or pulse, gives music much of its energy, excitement, and drive. More than any other factor, it is the beat that conveys **"felt" time**, *the space that music appears to carve out for itself.*

Activity *Feel the Beat*
Instructor's Guide, page 57
CD 1 [59] "Dream of Dreams"
(4:47)

Students can review the concept of beat in section A.1 of the *Music Theory Handbook.*

ACTIVITY ▶ *Feel the Beat*

Can you internalize a steady beat?

While you listen to "Dream of Dreams" by Joe Sample, count out loud from one to eight and perform the following:

First 8 beats: Snap fingers on each beat

Second 8 beats: Snap 7 beats, clap 1 beat

Third 8 beats: Snap 6 beats, clap 2 beats

Fourth 8 beats: Snap 5 beats, clap 3 beats

Continue until you clap on all 8 beats.

Now repeat the sequence but count silently and perform only the claps! Now you are thinking the beats. Can you do this in reverse? (Clap 8; then clap 7, snap 1; clap 6, snap 2; and so forth.)

Music & Art
Students may wish to improvise and perform music to accompany the dance or identify familiar songs that might be appropriate.

Music & ART

In the early 1800s, plantation slaves in the South created the cakewalk, a dance of exaggerated walk, promenade, or high step. The dancers often competed for the prize of a cake. By the 1900s, it became a social dance associated with ragtime. **How would you describe the music that might accompany the dance shown here?**

George Luks. *Cake Walk.* 1907. Delaware Art Museum, Delaware. Gift of Helen Farr Sloan.

The Momentum of Music

If the music is effective, it will provoke expectations. It commands our attention by making new sounds occur in a momentum that is so inviting it pulls us along with it. We begin to anticipate what is coming but delight in the surprising turns along the way. When we are excited and engaged in a film, play, speech, or piece of music, we feel that time flies by; when we are bored, time seems to drag. This sense of time has little to do with real, or clock time. It is "felt" time. Music seems to stretch and expand time, condense it, or make us forget it altogether. The quality of the "felt" time that the artist creates depends on many factors, not just activity but the tension that is created and then resolved.

ACTIVITY *Discover "Felt" Time*

Without looking at your watch, determine which of these two contrasting musical pieces seems longer.

You will hear (1) the *Adagio for Strings* by Samuel Barber and (2) the "Badinerie" from the *Orchestral Suite No. 2* by Johann Sebastian Bach. As you listen, decide which of the following words describe the character of each selection.

slow	hurried	strong pulse
calm	detached	tension
spirited	short sounds	repose
fast	weak pulse	smooth sounds

1. Which of these words describe both selections?
2. Which piece seems longer? Why?

Activity *Discover "Felt" Time*
Instructor's Guide, page 58
CD 1 [51] *Adagio for Strings* (1:15)
CD 1 [52] "Bandinerie" (1:15)

You may wish to use any of the following additional activities. Lesson plans are found in the Instructor's Guide.
"Designate Tempo Markings" (page 62)
"Create a Story Line" (page 63)
"Create a Film Soundtrack" (page 63)

Accent

The pulse moves by steady beats, some of which are accented to create strong and weak beats. An **accent** (represented by the symbol >) is *the emphasis placed on a beat.* These stressed and unstressed pulses usually fall into groups of twos or threes. Being aware of rhythmic organization helps us to be more conscious of how the music is moving forward. We have to be aware of the beat when we are marching or dancing. In march or dance music, some beats are deliberately accented so that people can easily move "in time," that is, in coordination with the rhythm. The beat is exaggerated, but it is important to be able to feel the pulse of the music even when it is not overstated.

Activity *Accent the Beat*
Instructor's Guide, page 58
CD 1 [59] "Dream of Dreams"
          (4:47)

Students can review beat in section A.1 of the *Music Theory Handbook*.

ACTIVITY *Accent the Beat*

Can you accent some of the beats as you listen to "Dream of Dreams" by Joe Sample?

While listening to "Dream of Dreams," perform the following patterns of accented (●) and nonaccented beats (•) by clapping on the accented beats and snapping on the others.

```
        1   2   3   4   5   6   7   8
a.    [ ●   •   •   •   ●   •   •   • ]
b.    [ •   ●   •   •   •   ●   •   • ]
c.    [ •   •   •   ●   •   •   •   ● ]
d.    [ •   •   ●   •   •   •   ●   • ]
```

Challenge Tap the steady beat with your left foot and perform each of the patterns by clapping only the accented beats while the other beats remain silent.

PROFILE

Nicolai Rimsky-Korsakov

Nicolai Rimsky-Korsakov showed his musical talent at a very young age. Although he followed his parents' wishes and joined the Russian navy, he eventually left to devote himself to music, his real love. He did not have a great deal of formal training in music, but he became a brilliant writer for orchestra and a famous teacher of composition. In composing for orchestra, Rimsky-Korsakov paid special attention to combinations of instrumental sounds. He was one of the great orchestrators of the nineteenth century. His textbook on orchestration remains an important source of study for serious composers in the twenty-first century.

Nicolai Rimsky-Korsakov
Russian Composer
1844-1908

Meter

These repeating patterns of beats create what is called **meter,** *the aural aspect of music in which a certain number of beats are grouped together.* These *groups or sets of beats* are called **measures**. Usually, the first beat in each measure is accented. Hearing that accent helps us establish the meter. To determine the meter, feel where the accented beat is and call it "one." Then count the beats in between until you hear another strong beat, which is "one" again.

Students can review meter in section A.2 of the *Music Theory Handbook*.

ACTIVITY ▶ *Practice and Determine Meter*

Activity *Practice and Determine Meter*
Instructor's Guide, page 59
CD 1 |60| "Procession of the Nobles" (3:00)

Perform duple and triple meter to determine the meters in "Procession of the Nobles" by Nicolai Rimsky-Korsakov.

As you listen to the music, perform these duple-and triple-meter patterns by clapping on the accented beat (●) and snapping on the others (●). Note that the vertical bars mark the measure.

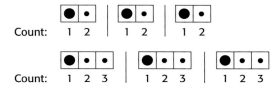

Show that you can hear the changes in meter by performing the duple and triple meters in clapping "Procession of the Nobles."

Challenge Listen again to determine the order of meters in this music. Which of the combinations below correctly reflects the order?

    A. duple/triple/duple

    B. triple/duple/triple

    C. triple/triple/duple

Rhythm

Rhythm is *the way music paces itself and moves through time.* Like a stream, music can flow gently or forcefully, smoothly or roughly. It might move in a trickle or broadly and majestically. The movement can be rapid or slow, deliberate or tentative, powerful or timid, depending upon what the composer wants to express.

Tempo is *the pace with which the music moves.* The pace of music is one of its most expressive elements. There are many gradations of tempo. In classical music, these are often expressed in Italian terms:

Largo	*Adagio*	*Andante*	*Allegretto*	*Allegro*	*Presto*
very slow	slow slow	moderately fast (walking)	moderately	fast	very fast

- **Accelerando** (aht-cheh-leh-RAHN-doh): *gradually growing faster.*

- **Ritardando** (ree-tar-DAHN-do): *gradually growing slower.*

- **A tempo** (ah TEM-poh): *in normal time, or a return to the preceding rate of speed.*

Music can change pace. In this way our interest is sustained. Changing the pace means varying the tempo (and usually the mood, since the two are practically inseparable). Change can be abrupt or gradual. Abrupt change might be from *adagio* to *presto* or vice versa. Gradual change might move from slow to fast *(accelerando)* or from fast to slow *(ritardando).*

Music & ART

Fernando Botero uses line, color, shape, form, emphasis, proportion, and balance to create movement and rhythm in his painting Dancing in Colombia. ***How does music convey its own sense of movement and rhythm?***

Fernando Botero. *Dancing in Colombia.* 1980. Anon. Gift, 1983. © Fernando Botero, The Collection of The Metropolitan Museum of Art. Courtesy, Marlborough Gallery, New York.

Music & Art
The music's tempo conveys a sense of movement.

ACTIVITY *Determine the Tempo*

Listen to these musical selections and write down what you think would be an accurate tempo marking for each one. Use appropriate Italian terms.

As you listen a second time, match the titles of the compositions with the selections. Consider (1) the title (verbal clue), (2) tempo, (3) style of the music, and (4) possible uses of the music. Be careful—the titles are listed in random order:

- "Trio" from *Pomp and Circumstance, March No. 1* by Sir Edward Elgar

- "Little Train of the Caipira" from *Bachianas Brasileiras No. 2* by Heitor Villa-Lobos

- "Cripple Creek" (American Folk Dance)

- "Flight of the Bumblebee" from the opera *Tsar Saltan* by Nicolai Rimsky-Korsakov

- "Ase's Death" from *Peer Gynt Suite No. 1* by Edvard Grieg

- "The Strings of God's Lute Are in My Body" (Islamic music from Pakistan)

Activity *Determine the Tempo*
Instructor's Guide, page 59
CD 1 53 "Flight of the Bumblebee" (1:00)
CD 1 54 "Cripple Creek" (1:00)
CD 1 55 "Ase's Death" (1:00)
CD 1 56 "The Strings of God's Lute Are in My Body" (1:00)
CD 1 57 "Little Train of the Caipira" (1:00)
CD 1 58 "Trio" (1:00)

Coordination

Musicians learn how to keep more than one rhythm going at one time. While they keep a steady beat, they may perform one or more complex rhythms with it. For example, a pianist might play one rhythmic pattern in the right hand, and another in the left. An organist might add yet another rhythmic pattern with both feet on the pedal board. At some time you probably have demonstrated your coordination by rubbing your stomach with one hand while patting your head with the other. This type of psychomotor challenge is similar to what all trap-set (drum) players do. Their hands, arms, and feet have to work independently.

ACTIVITY *Count and Coordinate Rhythmic Patterns*

Can you get your right hand, left hand, and left foot to perform different rhythms simultaneously while listening to Eddie Grant's "Electric Avenue"?

Imitate the skills of a fine trap-set drummer. Follow these steps:

Activity *Count and Coordinate Rhythmic Patterns*
Instructor's Guide, page 60
CD 1 61 "Electric Avenue" (0:30)

1. Listen to the recording and establish the accent on beat 1. Tap this accent with your right foot every time you hear it.
2. While your right foot continues to tap on 1, use your left hand to tap regular pulses of four. Tap these four even beats on your desk. Make sure you accentuate the first beat.
3. While you continue to tap your foot on 1 and use your left hand to tap regular pulses of four, use your right hand to double the speed of your left hand so you are playing eight even beats. Use your pencil as a drumstick, holding it lightly as you tap these eight beats on your desk. In your head, think the eight beats by counting to eight silently as you play. Do not speed up!

Play all three rhythms with the recording.
In a musical score, what you are doing looks like this:

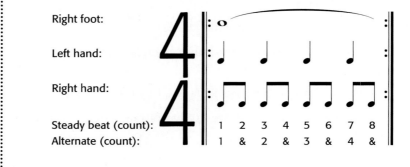

Right foot:

Left hand:

Right hand:

Steady beat (count):   1 2 3 4 5 6 7 8
Alternate (count):   1 & 2 & 3 & 4 &

Use section B.1 in the *Music Theory Handbook* to review notes and their values.

Improvisation

Music is not something fully created that has to be passed on and learned as is. When we learn music, we bring to it something of our own talent, feeling, and personality. But music also invites us to invent. We may find ourselves humming or whistling our own tune or tapping a rhythm that we make up. This kind of *spontaneous musical invention* is called **improvisation**. The improviser is a composer and a performer simultaneously. For example, members of the performing group STOMP improvise many of their rhythms.

Do improvisers do anything they want? Not usually. Most musical improvisation is done within certain boundaries that help to reduce the number of choices, making it easier. The improviser might elaborate upon—or embellish—a familiar melody, adding tones and altering rhythms to enhance a particular feeling. A jazz clarinetist or trumpeter might "take" a solo—that is, improvise—while the other musicians in the band provide the accompaniment. Rendered on the spot, these improvisations add an element of expectation and surprise for the audience. In live performance, improvised music is never the same old thing, and it is *never* read from music notation.

Improvisation is an art with a technique. It is a way of making music a form of direct self-expression. However, improvisation is risky. It requires musicians to take chances. They have to think ahead to where the music is going and how they want it to sound, then be able to perform what they want to hear. Some authorities believe that music improvisation is among the highest forms of human thinking.

In an African musical ensemble, a master drummer often sets a "time line" that serves as the basic rhythmic foundation throughout a performance. Other performers improvise over this steady beat of the master drummer.

ACTIVITY ▶ *Improvise Rhythmic Patterns*

Try your hand and mind at improvising different rhythms and creating a rhythmic ostinato with your own rhythm instruments.

A master drummer is frequently used to keep an African musical ensemble together. Working in a group of four, have one person assume the role of the master drummer while the others improvise individual rhythmic patterns on other percussion instruments. The objective is to create a group composition that is musically interesting.

The master drummer should set a steady tempo and play all eight beats in the 8-beat pattern. The first improviser should think a pattern of sound, selecting a combination of those beats, for instance, 1, 3, 6, and 7. Try to hear the pattern (in your mind) before you play it. Repeat the pattern four times (for four counts of 8); then if you are satisfied that this is what you want, write the numbers down so you do not forget them. Improvisers two and three then take their turns, creating their own individual patterns and writing down the numbers. Now put the whole composition together with each person entering after a repetition of two 8-beat counts. Once everyone is playing, keep this rhythmic ostinato going for eight counts of 8. After this is going smoothly, switch roles and start again inventing new patterns.

When writing down the patterns you have invented, use a dot (●) on beats to be played and a blank for silence, as in this example:

Activity *Improvise Rhythmic Patterns*
Instructor's Guide, page 60

Ostinato—a rhythmic or melodic passage that is repeated continuously.

Counting Pattern:	1	2	3	4	5	6	7	8
Master Drummer:	●	●	●	●	●	●	●	●
First Improviser:		●		●		●	●	

Rhythm and Improvisation in the Music of India

With a population of over 800 million people (three times the population of the United States!), India is the world's largest democracy. In all aspects of life, contrast and variety prevail. There are huge cities and over half a million tiny villages, sophisticated factories and small family farms, automobiles and elephants, richness and poverty. The people speak 14 languages and many more dialects. Although the majority of Indians are Hindus, five other religions, including Christianity, are common.

Indian music is as varied as this land of snake charmers and filmmakers. Take a walk down any street in India and you will probably hear Western pop music played on trumpet, saxophone, guitars, and drums, but you will also encounter quite different music. From a Hindu temple you might hear people singing with a pump organ, string instruments, Indian drums, and cymbals.

MUSIC in the WORLD

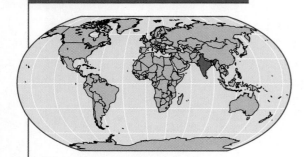

INDIA is one-third the size of the United States, yet it has three times the number of people. It's music is as varied as its people. The music you would hear in an Indian city might reflect Western influences. *Can you describe any music from India that you have heard?*

Music in the World
Encourage a variety of responses.

Indian Instruments

Indian instruments include a number of strings or "chordophones," such as the *sitar, sarangi, vina,* and the *tambura*. The tambura supplies the drone. Just as important is the pair of small drums called *tabla*. The larger (lower pitched) drum is made of metal and shaped like a small kettledrum, while the smaller (higher pitched) drum is made of wood and is more cylindrical in shape. The tabla are played with the hands and fingers.

Tabla

Sitar

This simple looking instrument can produce an astonishing variety of sounds or timbres. Tabla players develop the skill of moving their hands and fingers very rapidly.

Indian music is performed to a basic beat, but the beats are not grouped into regularly recurring patterns of two, three, and four as in much of Western music. The tabla player, for example, performs in a rhythm cycle that may be anywhere from seven to 104 beats in length! A **rhythm cycle** is *a fixed number of beats in a series that repeats itself over and over.* When audiences in India listen to music that includes tabla, they sometimes use a series of hand motions to keep track of their place in the rhythm cycle. One of the most popular rhythm cycles—tintal (TEEN-tal)—is 16 beats long. In Hindi, *tin* means "three" and *tal* means "clap"—a reference to the three claps used in following this cycle.

For a review of beat and meter, see sections A.1 and A.2 in the *Music Theory Handbook.*

Music & CULTURE

The music of India is as varied as the country itself. During a typical Indian performance, you might hear arrangements ranging from Western pop or brass marching bands to traditional Indian music. **What musical instrument do you recognize in this photo?**

Music & Culture
The tabla on the far right.

You may wish to use "Compose a Rhythm Score" at this time. Lesson plans for the activity are found on page 63 in the Instructor's Guide.

ACTIVITY ▶ *Understand the Tintal Cycle*

Use your hands and fingers to keep your place in the tintal cycle, while you listen to the narrated examples of Indian music.

As you count beats 1 through 16 of the tintal cycle, mark groups of four beats with the following movements of your hands and fingers:

1. Clap beat 1 bringing your right hand down onto your upturned left palm.
2. Mark beats 2, 3, and 4 by bringing the fifth, fourth, and third fingers of your right hand, one after the other, onto your left palm.
3. Repeat step 2 for beats 5 through 8.
4. Use a small hand wave rather than a clap on beat 9 and continue with fingers on beats 10, 11, and 12.
5. Repeat clap and fingers on beats 13, 14, 15, and 16.
6. Begin the pattern all over again.

Keeping track of 16 beats in a tintal cycle

Beats	1	2	3	4	5	6	7	8	9	10	11	12	13	14	15	16
Hands:	clap				clap				wave				clap			
Fingers:		❺	❹	❸		❺	❹	❸		❺	❹	❸		❺	❹	❸

When you have learned to keep your place in the tintal cycle, use the hand and finger movements while listening to the tabla play the cycle six times. Can you find a musical reason for the wave segment that begins on beat 9?

Challenge See if you can clap tintal, just as a knowledgeable Indian might, while you listen to a sitarist and tabla player improvise. Can you hear the bass drum pattern? The sitarist's melodies are also connected to the pattern.

When students learn the tabla, they learn a special drum language, which is sung much like a melody. All drums can make at least two sounds. One sound is a deep booming sound that is made by playing close to the center of the head and letting the sound ring. The second is a dry sharp sound made by playing close to, or on the edge of, the head or rim and "damping" the sound by leaving one's fingers on the head. The word *dum* (doom) refers to the center stroke; the word *te* (tay) refers to the rim stroke. These are two words from the Indian drum language.

ACTIVITY ▶ *Perform an Indian Rhythm Cycle*

Activity *Perform an Indian Rhytm Cycle*
Instructor's Guide, page 61
CD 2 ⑤ "Adi Tal" (1:06)
CD 2 ⑥ Variations on the rhythm cycle (1:02)

Practice the 8-beat hand and finger pattern called "Adi Tal," as the recording guides you through the music.

Beats:	1	2	3	4	5	6	7	8
Fingers:		❺	❹	❸				
Hands:	clap				clap	wave	clap	wave

When you can clap the pattern easily, recite the drum pattern with it using the two words *dum* and *te*.

Beats:	1		2		3		4		5	6		7		8		
Words:	*dum*		-	*dum*	-	-	*te*	*te*	*te*	*te*	*te*	*te*	*dum*	-	-	-

When you are comfortable with this pattern, transfer it to a drum or tambourine. Remember to play the "dum" in the middle of the instrument; play the "te" on the rim.

You may wish to use "Improvise" at this time. Lesson plans for the activity are found on page 64 in the Instructor's Guide.

Challenge Working in pairs, have one person recite the rhythm cycle with fingers and hands while the other practices making variations in Indian drum language. Try some of the following variations.

Cycle :	1		2		3		4		5	6		7		8		
Variations:	*dum*	*te*	*dum*	*te*	*dum*	-	*te*	*te*	*te*	*te*	*te*	*te*	*dum*	-	-	-

Cycle:	1		2		3		4		5	6		7		8		
Variations:	*dum*	*dum*	*te*	*dum*	-	*dum*	*te*	*dum*	*te*	*te*	*te*	*te*	*dum*	-	-	-

Cycle:	1		2		3		4		5	6		7		8		
Variations:	*dum*	*te*	*dum*	-	-	*dum*	*te*	*dum*	-	-	*te*	*te*	*dum*	-	-	-

Cycle:	1		2		3		4		5	6		7		8		
Variations:	*te*	*te*	*dum*	*te*	*dum*	-	-	*te*	*dum*	-	*te*	*te*	*dum*	-	-	-

Change places with your partner. Transfer these to a drum and try to improvise your own patterns.

PROFILE

Scott Joplin
American Composer
1868–1917

Scott Joplin

Called a forgotten genius when his *Collected Piano Works* were finally published in 1971, Scott Joplin has enjoyed a long-overdue revival. During the early part of the twentieth century, Joplin was in the forefront of American popular music, composing "rags" that established one of the influential dance styles of the period—ragtime. The terms "rag" and "ragtime" were not meant to be complimentary. Joplin considered them to be grossly abusive. However, his music was original and immediately likeable.

With Joplin's death on the eve of World War I, ragtime fell out of favor and was completely overshadowed by American jazz. It was not until the film *The Sting* (1973) and its theme song, Joplin's rag "The Entertainer," that Americans were reawakened to his music. Since then, Joplin's music has reemerged triumphantly after more than half a century of neglect. His works—including more than 40 rags, waltzes, marches for piano, and his opera, Tremonisha—are now regarded as American classics.

Syncopation

If music were simply a progression of steady beats with regularly recurring accents, it would hardly be as exciting as it is. Once the ongoing, steady pulse is established, accents can be shifted from the strong to the weak beats and even between the main beats. This is called **syncopation**, *deliberate shifts of the accent so that it conflicts with the steady beat and tries to upset the steady pulse.* Syncopation emphasizes the weak beats and denies the strong beats their usual stress. This creates a feeling of imbalance, a kind of teasing and thwarting of the steady recurrence of beats and accents. Syncopation is something unexpected, and that is a good part of its pleasure.

Ragtime

Ragtime, an American music full of syncopation, was a dance form that appeared in the nineteenth century and became popular during the first decades of the twentieth century. While jazz, at first, was primarily improvised, ragtime was usually written down. This may account, in part, for its popularity. Amateurs could buy piano "rags" in sheet music and play them, note for note, like the great rag pianists and composers—Scott Joplin, Jelly Roll Morton, and Eubie Blake. When Scott Joplin's "Maple Leaf Rag" was published in 1899, it quickly sold a million copies.

These rags were popular because they had a catchy, syncopated melody set against a moving bass that emphasized a steady beat in duple meter. From that collision of accents came a new musical feeling—exuberant and infectious. Soon people could play the syncopated strains of ragtime on piano rolls in penny arcades and hear rags performed on the pianos that accompanied the silent films in nickelodeons. American popular music and show music would never get over the feeling.

*Music & **HISTORY***

When "Maple Leaf Rag" was published in 1899, almost every home had a piano. People could buy the sheet music for ragtime and play it themselves, which may account for its popularity. **How did ragtime differ from jazz?**

Ragtime was written down; jazz was improvised.

ACTIVITY ▶ *Create Syncopation*

Can you feel and create syncopated rhythms?

To feel syncopation, you have to know where the steady beat is, because two rhythms are juxtaposed. To understand this, divide the class in half and try tapping the following rhythms together, beginning with the steady beat (1) and adding the syncopation (2):

Accent:	●	·	●	·		●	·	●	·	
(1) Steady beat:	1 2 3 4 5 6 7 8					1 2 3 4 5 6 7 8			repeat
(2) Syncopation:	·	·	·	· ●	·		·	·	· ●	

Now listen to the opening (or "A") section of Scott Joplin's "Maple Leaf Rag"; with a partner, see if you can clap the steady beat in the left hand (lower part) while your partner claps the syncopation in the right hand (upper part or melody). The main syncopated notes have been colored blue to correspond with the above example.

Activity Create Syncopation Instructor's Guide, page 62
CD 2 [7] "Maple Leaf Rag" (3:02)

Use sections A.1 and A.2 in the *Music Theory Handbook* to review beat and meter.

You may wish to use "Take Rhythmic Dictation" at this time. Lesson plans for the activity are found on page 64 in the Instructor's Guide.

Challenge Can you tap out the rhythms for both the left- and right-hand parts simultaneously?

Now listen to the entire rag to enjoy the syncopated rhythms.

MIDI TECHNOLOGY OPTION

Technology Option
Use Project 1 in the *MIDI Activities* binder.

■ **Music With MIDI** Use a MIDI program to explore how syncopation can create interest and tension, and to compose with syncopation in both traditional and modern styles.

SUMMARY

Rhythm is much of the excitement and fun of music.

It conveys a good deal of the spirit we feel. The variety of moods it can establish is infinite—from slow and sedate to rapid and robust. However, it has other important functions. It is rhythm that gives music its sense of movement, its energy, its drive, and life. Rhythm provides music with its sense of continuity—the feeling that it is cut from one piece of cloth. However, its most important function may be the underlying structure it provides so musicians can perform together even when each is doing something different. It is rhythm that pulls us along through the music, that gives us a sense of time and space, and that carries us out of the real world and into a world of imagination and mystery.

Building Music Vocabulary

On a sheet of paper, write the term from the list that best matches each description below.

(7) accelerando   (11) accent
(2) a tempo   (4) "felt" time
(8) improvisation   (6) meter
(1) rhythm   (9) rhythm cycle
(5) ritardando   (10) syncopation
(3) tempo

1. The way music paces itself and moves through time.
2. In normal time, or a return to the preceding tempo.
3. The pace with which the music moves.
4. The space that music appears to carve out for itself.
5. Gradually growing slower.
6. A rhythmic measure of a certain number of beats.
7. Gradually growing faster.
8. Spontaneous musical invention.
9. A fixed number of beats in a series that repeats itself over and over.
10. Deliberate shifts of the accent so that it conflicts with the steady pulse and tries to upset the steady pulse.
11. The emphasis placed on a beat.

Reviewing Music Facts

Answer each question in a complete sentence.
12. Scott Joplin is best known as a composer of what kind of music?
13. Why is improvisation considered risky?
14. How is the music of India grouped?
15. How many beats are in the Indian tintal?

Complete answers to the Chapter 3 Review are found in the Instructor's Guide, page 65.

Thinking It Through

On a sheet of paper, answer each of the following questions.
16. **Analyze** How do you know when a musician is improvising?
17. **Explain** In your own words, explain how musical beats are commonly arranged.
18. **Apply** Why does dance and march music often have an accented beat?

Making the Connection

Social Studies At the turn of the century, in what kinds of places and in what ways might teenagers have heard ragtime music? How would a student in a remote part of the country have been able to know about the music of Scott Joplin?

Math Using various combinations of notes, create ten "musical math" problems using notes in 4/4 meter.

 You will learn more about such composers as Bach, Joplin, and Jelly Roll Morton at **www.glencoe.com/sec/music**

Answers to Chapter 3 Review
12. Ragtime.
13. It requires musicians to think ahead, to take chances.
14. Into rhythm cycles.
15. Sixteen.
16. The performance will always vary, may never sound the same twice.
17. They are grouped into measures with a certain number of beats, with measures distinguished by stressed or accented beats.
18. So people can easily move in time, in coordination with the music.

Rhythms That Dance

Dance has been part of the life of every tribe, society, and culture. It is one way of expressing our essence: who we are and what life is about. In ancient societies, people danced to celebrate a marriage, a birth, a successful hunt, a good crop, or a victory. They danced to ward off evil spirits, to prevent sickness and danger, to bring good fortune, to ask for rain, and to cope with the other mysteries of life. Dance was, and is, a communal form of solidarity.

Dance is a hugely popular form of human expression both on stage and in social settings. Here, ballet dancers perform a dance from The Nutcracker *by Peter Ilyich Tchaikovsky.* **What types of music might accompany this dance?**

Caption answer
Most students will describe music with a slow and graceful tempo.

Objectives

By completing the chapter, you will:
- Understand how different rhythms create different dances.
- Learn the rhythms of a variety of dances and acquire vocabulary for explaining and discussing them.
- Become acquainted with Tex-Mex and Native American dance and learn about their origins and purpose.
- Learn some of the basic differences in music for popular, folk, theatrical, ballet, and modern dance.
- Become familiar with the instrumental suite.
- Differentiate between the minuet as a dance and the minuet as a movement of a symphony.
- Recognize how composers have incorporated dance rhythms in their instrumental works.
- Become acquainted with the work of American composers Louis Gottschalk and William Grant Still.

Vocabulary

ballet	samba
conjunto	suite
minuet	tango
reggae	waltz

Musicians to Meet

Leonard Bernstein
William Grant Still
Igor Stravinsky

Dance in American Heritage

Dance is more than mere physical movement. It is expression. It uses the human body as a musical instrument. Music generally serves as the springboard to dance, giving it much of its expressive power. Because it can be sensuous, dance has been forbidden by some religious sects. Today, dance is accepted as a popular social diversion, as well as an expressive art form.

Music and dance burst with energy. Rhythm is the heart of this energy and the means for regulating it. Humans have a built-in rhythmic impulse that is transformed through dance. By giving "voice" and order to the energy within us, dance uplifts the human spirit.

Music & Culture
Students will likely name a program such as *Soultrain* or cable stations such as TNN, MTV, and Univision.

Activity *Dance Music*
Instructor's Guide, page 66
TRB 4-1, *Perceptive Listening*

Social Dance

Dances are popular because of their distinctive rhythms. In fact, American dances often have such distinct personalities that they characterize their social period. The Charleston, for example, evokes the 1920s just as disco characterizes the 1970s. The macarena was a dance craze of the 1990s. Since the days of *American Bandstand*, hosted by Dick Clark, the highly visual nature of social dance has made it a lucrative target of television programming. Today thousands of music videos feed our appetites for dance. Cable television networks such as BET and TNN devote prime viewing time to music for dancing.

ACTIVITY ▶ *Dance Music*

Analyze dance music using a perceptive listening grid.

Analyze your favorite piece of dance music (whether you have danced to it or not). Identify the title and the performer of the work and briefly describe its overall style and character. As you listen to it, list as many characteristics of this music as you can.

The Latin Influence

The dance music of Latin America and Cuba became popular in urban centers of the United States during the 1930s and 1940s. The conga, an African-Cuban dance, gained popularity because of its catchy rhythm and because it was easy and fun. Later, the cha-cha, rumba, mambo, calypso, samba, and tango were among the new Latin-American dances that captivated American dancers.

The roots of many of the exciting dance rhythms in Latin-American and Caribbean music can be traced to Africa. The music and dance of these cultures are generally inseparable. Throughout the Americas, dance music shares some basic features: highly syncopated rhythms, improvised drumming, and a variety of percussion instruments.

The delightful mixture of African and Latin-American rhythms has become the primary international influence on social dancing in the world today, and it continues prominently in the world of jazz.

ACTIVITY ▶ *Perform Dance Rhythms*

Listen and then learn to perform the rhythms of an Argentine tango, Brazilian samba, and Jamaican reggae.

Work in small performing ensembles of four people. Follow these instructions for each of the three dances you hear:

1. As you listen to the rhythm, tap even eighth notes, eight beats to the measure. (This means that the meter signature is 8/8.)

2. Assign the various rhythmic parts in each dance to members of your group. First count and then tap each of the rhythms. After you have mastered them, transfer your tapping to instruments.

3. Play your rhythm section along with each recording. Your group may want to perform for the class or join with other groups in playing these characteristic dance patterns.

Challenge Add an improvised, syncopated rhythm that fits each dance pattern.

MIDI TECHNOLOGY OPTION

- **Music with MIDI** Use a MIDI program to compose with different Afro-Cuban rhythm styles and to examine some of the many variations within these styles.

Activity *Perform Dance Rhythms*
Instructor's Guide, page 67
CD 2 [8] "Tango Apasionado" (1:46)
CD 2 [9] "So Danco Samba" (2:04)
CD 2 [10] "One Love" (2:02)

Refer to section B.1 and B.3 in the *Music Theory Handbook* to review notes and their values.

Technology Option
Use Project 4 in the *MIDI Activities* binder.

The Tango

The **tango** is *a Latin-American dance performed at a moderately slow, walklike tempo in 4/4 meter.* The primary accents on beats 1 and 3 mean this dance has no backbeat (accents on 2 and 4). Each pattern below is one measure long and should be repeated throughout. Every second measure, try an improvisation based on the first measure.

Counting Guide (Steady Eighth Notes)	1	2	3	4	5	6	7	8

BASS

CLAVES

ACCORDION

GUIRO (optional)

The Samba

The **samba** is *an Afro-Brazilian dance that is faster and jazzier than the tango.* Although you may count the samba in a fast 4/4 meter, you should feel it in strong two-beat groupings. Like the tango, the samba uses no backbeat, but it is more syncopated. The rhythmic pattern is two measures long. Bring out the guitar line because it distinguishes the typical samba rhythm. Add improvisation where you think it will fit.

Reggae

Reggae is *a popular musical style mixing African and Caribbean rhythms created by Jamaican musicians.* Reggae's sound comes from the combination of backbeat (accents on beats 2 and 4) with syncopated "afterbeats" often played on rhythm guitar. The other significant feature is a syncopated and quickly moving melodic bass line. Can you hear the frequent improvisation in this bass melody?

The samba developed from regional urban dances in Brazil. As with other Latin dances, mostly from Argentina, Brazil, Cuba, and Mexico, the samba has been widely accepted by American culture.

Tex-Mex Music

Although dance is almost universally practiced among all peoples, it is not performed in the same way. One of the traditions of the Southwest is **conjunto,** *a dance music created by Texas-Mexicans.* It is often called "Tex-Mex" music, since it is derived from the unique Texas-Mexican cultural mix.

Three influences shaped conjunto music: (1) several kinds of dance music, especially the polka and the waltz, were brought to Mexico

from European countries in the nineteenth century; (2) Germans, Czechs, and Poles, for whom these dances had special importance, immigrated to southern Texas and continued to play and dance them; and (3) around 1900, these immigrants brought to Texas and popularized the button accordion. Influenced by their new European neighbors, *tejano* (teh-HAH-noh), or Texas-Mexican, musicians created a body of music in which the polka is still the most important dance, and in which songs in polka rhythm are by far the most popular.

Conjunto music, one of the most notable forms of traditional music created in the United States, is dance music in a one-two, one-two (duple) polka rhythm. The primary musical instrument of the conjunto is the button accordion.

button accordion

Music & CULTURE

Before 1836, most of what is now Texas was part of Mexico. This Mexican heritage lives on in Texas, but the cultural mix has evolved into the unique musical style of Texas Mexicans. **What European dance rhythm is central to Tex-Mex music?**

Music & Culture
The polka.

It is accompanied by a 12-string Mexican guitar, called *bajo sexto* (BAH-hoh SEX-toh), which plays fast bass runs and a chordal accompaniment; an electric bass guitar; and a drum set. The Spanish lyrics are often sung in the typically Mexican style of close harmony in parallel thirds.

ACTIVITY ▶ *Sing a Spanish Refrain*

Can you sing the refrain in Spanish while accompanied by the four instruments of the conjunto tejano?

■ Listen to "Ay te dejo en San Antonio" and try to sing in Spanish the refrain that follows each strophe, or stanza, of the song. The text of the refrain is "Te gusta mucho el baile, y bailas al compas, te vas hasta Laredo, y quires mas y mas." (Translation: "You like dancing a lot, and you dance with the beat, you go over to Laredo, and you want more and more.")

■ Can you identify the four instruments: the button accordion (main melody), electric bass, *bajo sexto* (playing bass runs and chordal offbeats), and drum set?

Activity *Sing a Spanish Refrain* Instructor's Guide, page 68 CD 2 ⏹11 "Ay te dejo en San Antonio" (2:48)

Refrain: a chorus (melody and text) that is repeated at intervals in a song, especially following each verse.

Native American Dance

There are more than 300 different Indian tribes in North America, each with its own culture. Every tribe has its own music and dance, its own purposes for performing, and its own musical styles. Within this diversity are some general musical characteristics that are shared by many of these tribes. To the Native American, music and dance have always been essential parts of life, expressing the mystical elements of religion, love, birth, death, hunting, war, and celebration. Tribal dance is functional, ceremonial, and participatory. It is never used as merely passive entertainment.

Native American music is primarily sung. Drums and rattles are the main types of musical instruments, and they come in many different sizes, shapes, and natural materials. Rattles, for example, are made out of gourds, turtle shells, carved wood, leather, baskets, coconuts, cocoons, cow horns, rattlesnake rattles, bird beaks, animal bones, and seashells.

Some tribes used various types of flutes and string instruments. The making of musical instruments is often a highly regarded vocation in the Native American world because of the social responsibilities and artistic talents it requires. Some of the instruments are beautifully crafted works of art.

Most American tribal languages do not contain a word for music. If they did, its meaning would be quite different than an European or Western definition of music. The notion of a composer attempting to create a work of art does not exist. For the Native American, one of the most traditional and valued means of acquiring new songs is through dreams or visions. Spiritual guidance often indicates how the music is to be used. Music is a gift from the Creator or other spiritual sources. It is sacred.

Unlike such Western art music as symphonies, operas, and concertos, Native American music is not performed to provide an aesthetic experience for the listeners. Instead, music is generally one component of an event that fulfills a function within the society—a religious ceremony, a healing ritual, the honoring of an individual, or ensuring a successful hunt or crop.

Like traditional music in other parts of the world, Native American music is not written down. It is committed to memory and passed on orally (or aurally) from generation to generation—creating an unbroken strand of performance practice that originated in the distant past. This achievement is often impressive, given the extreme complexity of certain ceremonies that last several days and include hundreds of songs. Any individual who becomes a carrier of a musical tradition accepts a huge responsibility within the community.

Native Americans dance and sing to show their pride in who they are; to honor their families, their ancestors, and their tribes; to assure the continuance of traditions; and to bring good fortune to their people. On less sacred occasions, social songs and dances are performed.

Music & ART

This mask is from the Kwakiutl tribe of the Northwest Coast. The Kwakiutl incorporate these powerful masks into their dance ceremonies. During a dance, the beaks move as if the figures were alive. **How would that movement add to the drama of a ceremonial dance?**

George Walhous. *Secret Society Mask.* 1938. Denver Art Museum, Denver, Colorado.

Music & Art
It would give a sense of life to the figures in the mask.

Lakota Eagle Dance

The Lakota are one of many Native American tribes that people commonly refer to as the "Sioux." The traditional culture of these horsemen and buffalo hunters of the Great Plains has for a long time been popularized in literature and film. Unfortunately, much of what has been depicted of Lakota culture in the past has been incorrect, oversimplified, or stereotypical. The Lakota people still enjoy a rich heritage of traditional music and dance. The singers and dancers you will hear and see come from the Rosebud Reservation in southwestern South Dakota.

ACTIVITY *Understand the Lakota Eagle Dance*

Use your powers of observation to find out more about Native American music and dance.

In the video segment, you will see and hear the Lakota Indians tell of some of the significance and meaning that their tribal music and dance holds for them. Then you will see the Eagle Dance. Based on your observations, see if you can answer the following questions:

1. What are the functions of Lakota music and dance?
2. Why is the Eagle Dance performed?
3. What does the whistle imitate?
4. What does the eagle symbolize?

Activity *Understand the Lakota Eagle Dance*
Instructor's Guide, page 68
Music! VHS Segment 2, Lakota Eagle Dance

Music & CULTURE

In this modern example of the Eagle Dance, a Lakota dancer gracefully and respectfully honors an animal that holds a great deal of importance to his people. The eagle symbolizes the Great Spirit known as Wakan Tanko. **Why is music considered sacred to Native Americans?**

Music & Culture
It is a gift from the Creator.

Theatrical Dance

America loves theatrical dance. In nineteenth-century minstrel shows, dances were commonplace. Operettas in the late 1800s and early 1900s contained ample dancing, as did the vaudeville shows that flourished in the early decades of the twentieth century.

Tap dancing is distinctly American. It has its roots in the African-American community. Tap seems to have originated in the rhythmic dances of African slaves that merged with the fancy footwork of Irish clogging. It made its Broadway debut in the early 1920s in black musicals. The tap craze was sparked by Bill "Bojangles" Robinson, grandson of a slave, who was born in 1878 in Richmond, Virginia. As a young man, Robinson first saw the shuffling dances of the black performers in traveling minstrel shows in Washington, D.C. He used the basics of clogging to develop his own more intricate, energetic, and syncopated style. He soon became a headliner on the vaudeville circuit and was called "The King of Tap Dancers." Nicknamed "Bojangles," Robinson won America's heart and established a new art form in the process.

In tap dancing, the feet are used as percussive instruments. The shoes, with their bright-sounding metal taps at the toe and heel, become a way of tapping out complex rhythms. Tap dancers improvise elaborate rhythms, shifting their weight nimbly from foot to foot, using their arms for balance, and turning in space. The rhythms are as complex as those of the jazz drummer and include much syncopation. Today, tap artists such as Gregory Hines and Savion Glover are admired as much for their musicianship as for their remarkable dancing.

Use Artsource® VHS Segment 4 in the Performing Arts Package to show a performance by tap dancer Eddie Brown.

Tap dancing legend Eddie Brown (1918–1995) began his career at New York's Apollo Theatre during the 1930s. He appeared with great musicians such as Billie Holiday, Joe Turner, Dizzy Gillespie, Count Basie, and Duke Ellington. His style of dancing was called "scientific rhythm," so named because the rhythm could be heard but the movement that created it was difficult to see.

Eddie Brown, Linda Sohl-Donnell, and musicians. "At the Savoy."

Dance is an integral part of American musical theatre. It is a standard part of any Broadway musical. Jerome Robbins's dances from *West Side Story*, performed to music composed by Leonard Bernstein, are particularly memorable examples, perhaps because they are so integral to the story. This show opened on Broadway in 1957 and is a modern-day fictional version of William Shakespeare's *Romeo and Juliet* transplanted to New York City's West Side. It revolves around the conflict between two street gangs: the Jets, who are white, and the Sharks, who are Puerto Rican. Tony, a former member of the Jets, meets and falls in love with Maria, a Puerto Rican girl, whose brother is a member of the Sharks. Tony and Maria meet in secret, but their relationship is doomed because of the conflict between these rival gangs.

American composer Leonard Bernstein combined Latin dance rhythms, big-band jazz, and expressive love songs in his Broadway musical West Side Story, *based loosely on Shakespeare's play* Romeo and Juliet. *In 1968 the musical was adapted for film, shown here.*

Bernstein incorporates jazz style to convey youthful vigor and violence, and he uses Latin-American dance rhythms to characterize the Sharks. The dances portray the tension between the gangs. They help to tell the story, so much so that the dances alone embody the plot. Realizing this, Bernstein made an arrangement of the dances in a separate work for orchestra entitled *Symphonic Dances from "West Side Story."*

Activity *Listen to the Music of West Side Story*
Instructor's Guide, page 68
TRB 4-2, *Symphonic Dances*
CD 2 [12] "Prologue" (4:07)
CD 2 [13] "Somewhere" (3:52)
CD 2 [14] "Scherzo" (1:17)
CD 2 [15] "Mambo" (1:25)
CD 2 [16] "Cha-cha" (0:49)
CD 2 [17] "Meeting Scene" (1:41)
CD 2 [18] "Cool" (3:03)
CD 2 [19] "Rumble" (1:52)
CD 2 [20] "Finale" (2:47)

ACTIVITY ▶ *Listen to the Music of* West Side Story

Can you match the dance titles with the music from *West Side Story?*

Listen to *Symphonic Dances from "West Side Story"* by Leonard Bernstein and determine the order of the story line. Write down the titles of the sections of the composition in the proper order on the Symphonic Dances Worksheet. Use the musical descriptions to help you make your decisions.

Leonard Bernstein
American Composer
1918–1990

PROFILE

Leonard Bernstein

As a composer, conductor, and spokesperson, Leonard Bernstein did much to advance music in the United States and throughout the world. He began studying the piano at the age of 10, but by the early 1940s Bernstein started to focus his musical energies on conducting. In 1944, while serving as assistant conductor of the New York Philharmonic Orchestra, he was called upon to conduct a concert when the principal conductor was ill. Bernstein's brilliant performance launched his career in the United States and around the world. He went on to become the chief conductor of the Orchestra from 1958 to 1969, during which time the orchestra gained international fame. Bernstein also introduced and conducted televised concerts for young people. He had a remarkable ability to discuss music in a way that was clear to people with little musical knowledge.

As his conducting career flourished, Bernstein also performed as a piano soloist and developed his skills as a composer. He wrote a variety of works but is most famous for his musical theatre compositions such as *West Side Story* and the ballet *Fancy Free*. His music combined jazz, dance, and popular rhythms and styles with classical elements.

Ballet

The art of telling a story through music and movement originated in **ballet**, *a style of classical dance that emerged in France during the sixteenth century*. Because ballet is physically strenuous, dance solos or duets (pas de deux) normally last from two to four minutes. Dancers need constant breaks to catch their breath, so dance stories must be told in many scenes. Consequently, music that is suitable for ballet should be rhythmic and colorful, and full of short, changing, and clearly delineated moods.

In 1910, Igor Stravinsky, an unknown young Russian composer, created his first ballet score, *L'Oiseau de feu (The Firebird)*. When the ballet premiered at the Paris Opera with dance steps by choreographer Michel Fokine, it caused a sensation and launched Stravinsky's career. The work continues to be performed by ballet companies throughout the world. The music from *The Firebird* is frequently performed in concert halls in a seven-movement suite that Stravinsky arranged for a very large orchestra.

The story of *The Firebird* is adapted from several Russian fairy tales. In *The Firebird*, the curtain rises on the enchanted garden of the wicked wizard, Kashchei. Soon the firebird appears and performs a glorious dance. She is pursued and captured by Prince Ivan Tsarevitch. She pleads for her release, plucking out one of her bright red feathers to give to him. Then 13 enchanted princesses enter and play with golden apples. Suddenly Ivan appears, and they dance to a theme Stravinsky borrowed from a Russian folk song. When daybreak comes, the princesses disappear. Kashchei's guards rush out of their subterranean home and capture

This is a scene from the American Ballet Theatre's production of The Firebird *with music by Igor Stravinsky. Prima Ballerina Natalia Makarova (center stage) dances the role of the firebird.*

Ivan. Kashchei confronts Ivan, but the princesses intercede on Ivan's behalf. Again the firebird appears, casting a spell on Kashchei's subjects and making them dance fiendishly.

Kashchei and his court are put to sleep so that Ivan can seize the egg that contains the secret power of Kashchei. By breaking it, Ivan brings about Kashchei's death. Stravinsky lets us hear the egg break. The prince and princess then marry. The music of the finale is composed in the style of a Russian chorale. Stravinsky alters its accents by changing it from six beats to seven, giving the ballet a triumphal, majestic close.

Activity *Visualize the Musical Drama*

Instructor's Guide, page 69
CD 2 21 Finale, *The Firebird* (3:06)

ACTIVITY ▶ *Visualize the Musical Drama*

How does the music support the dramatic action?

You will hear the conclusion of *The Firebird* by Igor Stravinsky. All the tensions in the plot are resolved after Ivan breaks the magic egg, putting an end to the evil Kashchei. How does Stravinsky's music convey the drama? If you were to choreograph this ballet, how would you describe the movements to your dancers?

PROFILE

Igor Stravinsky
Russian Composer
1882–1971

Igor Stravinsky

Born in Russia, Stravinsky spent much of his life in the United States, settling in Hollywood in 1939 and becoming an American citizen in 1945. Before leaving Russia he studied with Nicolai Rimsky-Korsakov, the great Russian composer and orchestrator.

When Stravinsky was a young man, he teamed up with the famous ballet manager Serge Diaghilev to write three ballet master-pieces. The first two were *The Firebird* and *Petrouchka*, followed by the primitive and revolutionary modern work *Rite of Spring*. The innovative orchestrations, violent rhythms, and unusual harmonies of this work actually caused a riot at its first performance!

From 1919 to 1951 most of Stravinsky's compositions were modeled on the styles and harmonies of Baroque and Classical composers. These works include the *Octet for Winds* and Symphony in C. In his final works, Stravinsky turned to the 12-tone system invented by Arnold Schoenberg. Even when he chose to use the styles and techniques of other composers, he always wrote in an inventive and distinctive way. Stravinsky is considered by many to be the greatest composer of the twentieth century.

Modern Dance

Musical rhythm and movement alone can arouse and convey a wide range and variety of moods. Modern dance, developed by American dancers as an alternative to ballet, is made up of a variety of dance styles unimpeded by the strict traditions of classical ballet. This free expression of a free people was pioneered by Isadora Duncan, Ruth St. Denis, Ted Shawn, and Martha Graham during the first half of the twentieth century and continues to be explored today.

Among those who have contributed to the development of modern dance are African Americans. One outstanding example is Alvin Ailey, who founded the Alvin Ailey American Dance Theatre. Ailey translated African American folk music and jazz into dance forms that capture the soul of his people.

ACTIVITY *Find the Theme in* **Revelations**

What music does Alvin Ailey use to express a biblical theme in this excerpt from his dance choreographed as *Revelations*?

Look at the movements and listen to the music to determine Ailey's theological interpretation of *Revelations*. What is he trying to say to us through this dance and this music? What African-American music spirituals do you hear?

Activity *Find the Theme in Revelations*
Instructor's Guide, page 69
Music! VHS Segment 3, "Rock-a-my Soul in the Bosom of Abraham"

Music & **CULTURE**

From the beginning, Alvin Ailey (1931–1989) had a vision of creating a company dedicated to the preservation and enrichment of the American modern dance heritage and the uniqueness of African-American cultural expression. Revelations *was originally choreographed in 1960.* **What two music styles did Ailey use in his choreographies?**

Music & Culture
Folk music and jazz.

The Undanced Dance

Dance rhythms carved out a place and a purpose for instrumental music. Vocal music had its message in the texts. In contrast, instruments could deliver a snappy rhythm and make us celebrate with our feet. The sheer delight of dance rhythms inspired the development of instrumental music, and this delight followed the instruments right into the concert hall. Today, modern dance companies started by Twyla Tharp, Bill Robinson, and Alwin Nikolais have developed great popularity.

The Suite

During the first half of the eighteenth century, Johann Sebastian Bach and George Frideric Handel arranged the popular dances of their day— the allemande, courante, sarabande, gigue, and so forth—into suites. A **suite** is a *set of instrumental pieces each in the character of a dance.* Suites were composed for a keyboard instrument or a small orchestra. Although much of the music of this period—Baroque—incorporated dancelike rhythms, these rhythms were meant more to be played and heard than to be danced to.

Activity *Distinguish the Source*
Instructor's Guide, page 70
CD 2 |22| "Minuet" (1:48)
CD 2 |23| "Bourée" (1:23)
CD 2 |24| "Sarabande" (1:59)

Sarabande: a dance in triple meter with an accent on beat two.
Bourée: a French dance usually in quick duple meter with a single upbeat.

ACTIVITY ▶ *Distinguish the Source*

Listen to three movements from George Frideric Handel's *Water Music Suite* and decide which of the three dances he used as inspiration.

Tap the following rhythmic patterns of three eighteenth-century dances observing tempo, meter, and accent:

- Which dance rhythm inspired each movement in Handel's suite?
- After you have decided the order of the dance patterns, clap the appropriate pattern as you listen to the music. Describe the differences between the three dance styles. Which are similar? How are they different?
- Why is Handel's work a stylized use of these dance rhythms and not the actual dances?

Through the suite, composers learned how to make instrumental music expressive. The various types of dances found in the suite permitted composers to change tempos, shift accents, and alter dynamics. They found that instruments could portray affections (feelings) just as effectively as vocal music.

The Minuet

Another dance form that has entered the musical mainstream is the minuet. The **minuet**, *a rather slow and charming old French dance in triple meter*, probably originated as a country dance. It was danced at the court of Louis XIV during the seventeenth century. In the hands of Franz Joseph Haydn (1732–1809) and Wolfgang Amadeus Mozart (1756–1791), the minuet was turned into an art form that epitomized the graceful dignity and elegance of the Classical period. Composers began to include a minuet as a contrasting movement in their sonatas, quartets, and symphonies. As the third (occasionally second) movement in these three or four-movement works, the minuet often provided a lighthearted contrast to the more serious musical statements that preceded and followed. Even though the minuet became a piece to listen to, it retains its triple rhythm and its catchy charm.

You may wish to use "Compare Minuets" at this time. Lesson plans for the activity are found on page 73 in the Instructor's Guide.

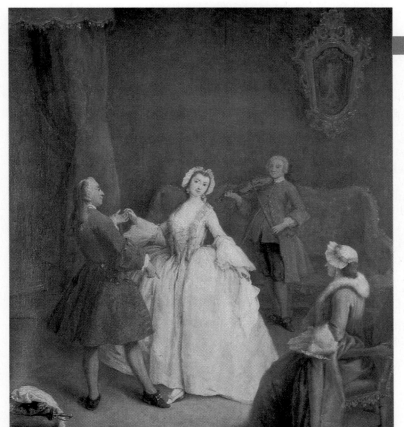

Music & HISTORY

Aristocrats at the court of Louis XIV danced the minuet, a stately old French dance in triple meter. Later, Classical composers such as Haydn and Mozart incorporated the minuet in their multimovement musical forms, such as the sonata, the string quartet, and the symphony. ***Within a larger work, what was the purpose of the minuet?***

Pietro Longhi (1702–1788). *The Dancing Lesson.* 1884. Galleria dell' Accademia, Venice, Italy.

Music & History
It provided lighthearted contrast to more serious movements.

The Waltz

Like the minuet, the **waltz** is *a dance in triple meter.* Both the minuet and the waltz started out as social dances that eventually graduated to the concert hall. Compared to the stately minuet, the waltz was unsophisticated and unrestrained. Unlike the minuet, the waltz has enjoyed great popularity for nearly 200 years. In the early nineteenth century, it prevailed as the most fashionable and favorite of all dances. At that time, one of the dance halls in Vienna, the Apollo, could accommodate 6,000 dancers.

Activity *Recognize the Waltz*
Instructor's Guide, page 70
CD 2 28 *The Blue Danube* (2:02)

ACTIVITY ▶ *Recognize the Waltz*

How can you identify the vintage Viennese waltz?

Listen to *The Blue Danube* by Johann Strauss, Jr., and answer the following questions:
1. Using the second hand of your watch or the classroom clock, determine the length of the introduction. That is, precisely how many seconds go by before Strauss begins the main theme? How do you know where the first theme begins?
2. Try to tap three even quarter notes in each measure during the main theme of the waltz. Is the tempo the same throughout the dance? Which of the three beats is sometimes delayed or lengthened? Is Strauss's music actually danceable, or would it be more successful in a concert hall?

Summarize Based on your listening to *The Blue Danube*, list 3 characteristics of the Viennese waltz.

Activity *Compose a Dance Melody*
Instructor's Guide, page 71
TRB 4-3, *Waltz Worksheet*
CD 2 28 *The Blue Danube* (2:00)

ACTIVITY ▶ *Compose a Dance Melody*

In the style of the Viennese waltz, compose a 16-measure dance melody.

Work with a partner to create two 4-measure answers to the waltz phrases written on the waltz worksheet. Keep your melody in C major (use the white keys on a keyboard) and the rhythm in 3/4 meter. Experiment on any melody instrument (keyboard, mallet percussion, recorder, etc.) while you compose.

By the mid-nineteenth century, Vienna had become the center of waltz music. Vienna's most beloved citizen, composer Johann Strauss, Jr. (1825–1899), also known as the "Waltz King," composed almost 400 waltzes. *The Blue Danube* reigns as one of his most famous. It remains a classic example of the vintage Viennese waltz.

The waltz usually begins with an introduction that includes a short announcement of the waltz rhythm before the dance actually begins. Often, the waltz itself is in two parts (16 measures each), and several waltzes (usually five) follow one another in a row with a concluding finale. The waltz is lighthearted, optimistic music, conveying happiness and good feelings.

The waltz was elevated to concert music during the nineteenth century when Frédéric Chopin (1810–1849) and other composers wrote instrumental waltzes that were not meant for dancing. Maurice Ravel (1875–1937), was inspired to write his choreographic poem for orchestra, entitled *La Valse*, in 1920. He imagined this waltz as a fantastic and fatal sort of dervish's dance. A brilliant orchestrator, Ravel created *La Valse* as a glorified tribute to the symphonic waltz style. He considered his exalted orchestral waltz more as a ballet to be choreographed than as a ballroom dance for couples.

ACTIVITY ▶ *Identify Characteristics of the Waltz*

Is this piece really a waltz?

Listen to the beginning of *La Valse* to answer question 1 below. Then listen to its surprising and fantastic ending to answer question 2.
1. At what point can you confirm with confidence that this piece is written in the Viennese waltz style? (Use the second hand of a watch to get an idea of where an identifiable waltz theme begins.) How is the beginning of *La Valse* different from the beginning of *The Blue Danube*?
2. What has Ravel done to the waltz style at the end of *La Valse*? What similarities does the ending share with *The Blue Danube*?

Activity *Identify Characteristics of the Waltz*
Instructor's Guide, page 71
CD 2 [28] *The Blue Danube* (2:02)
CD 2 [29] *La Valse* (3:00)

Latin Dance Rhythms in Classical Works

The highly celebrated American pianist and composer Louis Moreau Gottschalk (1829–1869) was among the first to incorporate creole and African-American folk idioms into his compositions. He had heard these rhythms and tunes growing up in New Orleans and

Inspired by Cuban, Puerto Rican, and Latin-American rhythms, American pianist and composer Louis Moreau Gottschalk (1829–1869) was one of the first composers to incorporate native folk materials into his classical compositions.

Caricature of Louis Gottschalk. Corbis.

MUSIC in the WORLD

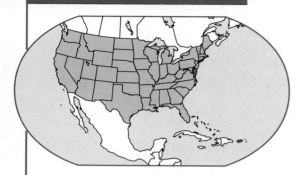

Composer and pianist Louis Moreau Gottschalk was strongly influenced by the rhythms of music in PUERTO RICO. Consider how the closeness of Puerto Rico to the United States would increase the likelihood that music styles would be mutually influenced.

Music in the World
Frequent travel back and forth would contribute to an exchange of styles.

Activity *Perform Puerto Rican Rhythms*
Instructor's Guide, page 72
CD 2 30 *Souvenir de Porto Rico*
      (6:00)

thought it natural to include them in his works. As a virtuoso pianist, he performed throughout the world, traveling to Europe, South and Central America, and the islands of the Caribbean. He was fascinated by the local music, particularly the Latin-American rhythms, and he boldly incorporated them in his music. While visiting Puerto Rico in 1857, Gottschalk heard strolling musicians perform traditional Christmas carols. He freely adapted one of these in composing *Souvenir de Porto Rico*, which he subtitled *Marcha y danza de gibaros* ("March and Dance of the Peasants").

ACTIVITY ▶ *Perform Puerto Rican Rhythms*

Learn to perform the syncopated Puerto Rican rhythms Gottschalk used in his *Souvenir de Porto Rico*.

First practice tapping each of the following measures slowly and separately (one and three are alike), counting the pattern of eight. Gradually increase the tempo. Put all four measures together and repeat them until you can tap them easily. Then try tapping the rhythms while you count in two.

Now listen to Gottschalk's piano work and see if you can hear when this four-measure rhythmic pattern comes in. (Hint: It does not occur until after the three-minute mark).

African dance rhythms have been incorporated in the work of a host of African-American classical composers, led by William Grant Still (1895–1978) and Ulysses Kay (1917–1994). In the mid-1940s, a friend brought Still a set of Panamanian dance tunes and asked him to use the new melodies as a basis for composing a string quartet. Still did just that, and the result was his *Danzas de Panamá* composed in 1948. The fourth movement of this quartet, written for the customary two violins, a viola, and a cello, bursts with Latin-American dance rhythms.

ACTIVITY ▶ *Match the Rhythms*

Activity *Match the Rhythms*
Instructor's Guide, page 72
CD 2 31 "Cumbia y Congo" (3:04)

Match the rhythms of William Grant Still's themes to the correct sections of his "Cumbia y Congo," the fourth movement of his string quartet *Danzas de Panamá*.

This movement contains several distinct themes and tempo changes. All four string instruments use a technique called pizzicato (plucking the strings with the fingers). The musicians also tap the wood of their instruments to imitate the sound of native Panamanian drums.

Each of the four sections of this movement—Introduction, Section A, Section B, and the Coda (the last four bars)—uses a different melodic rhythm. Can you match each of these sections with its proper rhythm as notated below?

(1)

(2)

(3)

(4)

PROFILE

William Grant Still

One of the most famous African-American composers of classical music, William Grant Still wrote operas, ballets, choral works, and symphonies that have been performed around the world. Determined to develop a style of classical music that reflected and expressed African-American tradition, Still incorporated African-American folk song melodies in his musical works. His *Afro-American Symphony*, composed in 1931, was the first symphony by an African-American composer to be played by a major orchestra.

Still grew up in Little Rock, Arkansas. His musician father died when Still was a baby. However, his stepfather encouraged his interest in music. In college, he majored in science but changed to music. After graduating, he wrote jazz arrangements and then went on to study composition. Still also became an accomplished oboist. He eventually settled in Los Angeles, where he lived and continued to compose until his death in 1978.

William Grant Still
American Composer
1895–1978

SUMMARY

Music invites us to move. It calls our rhythmic impulse into action, translating it into the expressive movements we call dance. Rhythm is the underlying organizational pattern that gives music and dance its distinct and expressive order.

Like music, dance is a cultural expression. It springs from the soul of a people. Its rhythms convey the special way people view themselves in relation to the world around them. The music of the dance radiates life. It emits the glow of the human spirit and the vitality of being alive. This rhythmic energy is the basis for much of the expressive quality of music.

Originally, it was dance that gave instrumental music its reason for being. Eventually, instrumental music incorporated dance rhythms into purely musical statements, raising them to a level of art so that they served the mind, not just the feet. The spirited rhythms of real-life dance still fascinate composers and inspire them to incorporate the feeling into their musical expressions. The dance element in music is one of its most attractive and compelling characteristics.

CHAPTER 4 REVIEW

Complete answers to the Chapter 4 Review are found in the Instructor's Guide, page 74.

Building Music Vocabulary

On a sheet of paper, write the term from the list that best matches each description below.

(7) ballet   (8) conjunto   (3) minuet
(6) reggae   (4) samba   (1) suite
(2) tango   (5) waltz

1. A set of instrumental pieces, each in the character of a dance.
2. A Latin-American dance performed at a moderately slow, walk-like tempo.
3. An old French dance, rather slow and stately, in triple meter.
4. An Afro-Brazilian dance that is quite fast and jazzy.
5. A dance in triple meter, made famous in Vienna in the late 1800s.
6. Jamaican dance music, mixing African and Caribbean rhythms.
7. A physically strenuous style of classical dance that originated in France in the sixteenth century.
8. A dance music created by Texas-Americans.

Reviewing Music Facts

Answer each question in a complete sentence.

9. The samba and tango originated in what part of the world?
10. What instrument is most important in the conjunto music of the Tejano people in Texas?
11. How have the Lakota people preserved their traditional music?
12. Why are ballets usually broken up into a series of "scenes"?
13. What style of dance is usually associated with the African-American choreographer Alvin Ailey?
14. What were some of the musical styles borrowed by the composer Louis Moreau Gottschalk for his concert pieces?

Thinking It Through

On a sheet of paper, answer each of the following questions.

15. **Identify** What are some of the elements that give reggae music its distinctive style?
16. **Compare and Contrast** What are some of the similarities and differences between the waltz and the minuet?
17. **Apply** Why were the "dances" in the Baroque suites popular with composers of the period?

Making the Connection

Social Studies Choose one of the dance styles described in Chapter 4 and trace its roots. Using a world map or globe, explain how one style influenced another and how this influence spread from country to country and culture to culture.

Language Arts Choose one of the dance pieces heard in this chapter and create a poem or paragraph about that dance style.

 More information on the tango, the Eagle Dance, and American musical theatre is available at **www.glencoe.com/sec/music**

Answers to Chapter 4 Review
9. Latin America.
10. The button accordion.
11. It is passed orally (or aurally) from generation to generation.
12. So dancers could rest between scenes.
13. Modern dance.
14. Creole and African-American folk idioms; music of Latin America and the Caribbean.
15. A combination of backbeat and syncopated "afterbeats"; a syncopated, quickly moving melodic bass line; improvisation.
16. *Similarities:* Both are in triple meter; both are dance forms; both began as dance music and were later used as concert forms. *Differences:* The minuet is quite slow, stately, reserved, formal. The waltz is fast, unrestrained, with pulsating rhythms.
17. They could write pieces that were expressive and could utilize shifts in tempo, dynamics, and accents.

Unit Two Evaluation

You may also wish to use Assessment
Master 2, Unit Two Test, in the TRB

Chapter 3 Project

▶ *Create a Rhythm Soundtrack*

Chapter 3 Project
Instructor's Guide, page 75

**Using your knowledge of rhythm, create a rhythm soundtrack
and record it.**

Put what you have learned about rhythm to the test. Working in a
small group of five to seven of your classmates, organize, compose,
perform, and record a 32-measure soundtrack for percussion.

Follow these musical requirements:

1. Select percussion instruments whose sounds you like.

2. Use the 8-beat set (measure) as the organizing metric device
(1 measure = 8 beats) for the soundtrack.

3. Prepare the composition in four sections of eight measures
each. The four sections should have an organizational plan
of A A' B A: that is, the A sections should be alike, the B
section different. The A' (A-prime) section should be
somewhat different from A. (You can
introduce some slight variations here.)

4. Develop section B in a different tempo.
This section should be improvised.

5. Include regular and syncopated
rhythmic patterns in both sections.

Create a score for your work using the count of
eight and X's to mark where each instrument
should play. Here is the plan for your soundtrack:

Organizational Plan

Section	A	A'	B	A
Length	8 measures	8 measures	8 measures	8 measures
Rhythms	8-beat sets with syncopation	Sets that are similar to A, but varied	Sets in a different tempo and improvised	Exactly the same as the first A section
Instruments	You decide!			
Tempo	You decide!			
Other expressive ideas	You decide!			

Remember this is one continuous piece; the sections have to connect.
Record your soundtrack. Compare your percussion piece with others
in the class.

Chapter 4 Project

▶ *Connect Rhythms to Dance*

Summarize what you have learned about rhythm in danced and undanced music.

Check your listening knowledge of types and origins of dance music and their basic metric organization. Respond to the musical examples and identify the type of dance (i.e., waltz). Determine the meter of the dance (i.e. duple or triple). Finally, indicate whether the musical example is best suited for the dance hall or the concert hall.

Pick the correct dance or dance rhythm from the following list:

Minuet	Tap	Charleston
Cha-cha	Ballet	Waltz
Native American Dance	Square Dance	Theatrical Dance
Disco	Tex-Mex Polka	Sarabande
Modern Dance	Tango	Social Slow Dance
Twist	Samba	Hip Hop

Chapter 4 Project
Instructor's Guide, page 76
TRB, *Identify and Define*
CD 3 [1] "Sarabande" (1:59)
CD 3 [2] "So Danco Samba" (2:04)
CD 3 [3] "Ay te dejo en San Antonio" (2:01)
CD 3 [4] *Symphonic Dances from "West Side Story"* (2:01)
CD 3 [5] "Tango Apasionado" (1:46)
CD 3 [6] *The Blue Danube* (2:02)
CD 3 [7] "War Dance Song" (2:01)
CD 3 [8] "The Twist" (2:03)
CD 3 [9] Symphony No. 40, third movement (2:01)
CD 3 [10] *The Firebird* (2:05)

Hip Hop

Native American

Ballet

The Twist

81

Unit Two *Encore!*

Rhythms in Everyday Life

Did you know that rhythms can be made out of anything? You can use your mouth, hands, fingers or feet, your pencil, keys, backpack, or desk to create interesting rhythms. Founder and dancer Luke Cresswell states that the goal of STOMP is to invite people to "listen to the world in a different way and hear music where maybe they didn't think there was music before." STOMP uses ordinary objects to play their rhythms—pots, pans, trash cans, brake drums, and street signs. Can you identify these objects when you hear them?

Identify Rhythm Instruments
Instructor's Guide, page 79
Music! VHS Segment 4-A, STOMP Out Loud (1:04)
CD 17 ③ STOMP Out Loud
(sound excerpt) (2:00)

Improvise "Off-Beat Arias"
Instructor's Guide, page 79

▶ *Identify Rhythm Instruments*

Use your ears to tell you what ordinary objects are used as rhythm instruments. Listen to the segment and write down the sounds you can identify.

Now watch the video as the members of STOMP dangle from rock-climbing harnesses attached to a billboard on the Manhattan skyline. How many of the terms below can you apply to their rhythm and dance? Use the Glossary to understand any terms that are unfamiliar to you.

call and response	diminuendo	improvisation	solo
accelerando	ritardando	ostinato	tutti
unison	pianissimo	fortissimo	pause
polyrhythm	duple meter	syncopation	accent

Does the music of STOMP invite you to listen to the world in a different way? Why or why not? Would you classify this performance as dance? How is it theatre?

▶ *Improvise "Off-Beat Arias"*

STOMP members perform some of their dances using brooms and other non-traditional percussion instruments. Can you do the same to improvise your own "off-beat aria"?

1. Using ordinary objects like trash cans, tin cups, rubber storage tubs, brooms, and small pieces of lumber, create a 32-bar improvised rhythm piece that includes movement. Try using foot stomps as well.

2. Turn this activity into an "additive improvisation." In groups of eight, have two people begin by setting a tempo and playing for 8 measures. At the second set of 8 bars, add the next pair of players while the first pair continues; then add the third pair at measure 17 and the final pair in your group at measure 25. How will you select which instruments each pair will play? Will each pair have different movements or will everyone do the same thing? Compare the "off-beat arias" of different groups in your class. For an added challenge, combine two groups of eight students. Record your improvisations on video.

3. Determine how you would polish your work for a performance before the entire school.

An ordinary, everyday object such as a basketball becomes a rhythm instrument in the hands of musicians. Here, members of the performing group STOMP coordinate their movements to create rhythms that dance.

▶ *Bounce, Slap, Dribble, Move!*

Watch STOMP members perform their basketball street scene aria. Then try the following.

1. As you watch the video, identify the meter of the piece performed by STOMP. How many different ways do they get sounds with their basketballs? Use their performance as a basis for creating your own basketball rhythms that dance.

2. Work in groups of four, practice your coordination and counting ability. Make sure each of the four dancer/musicians has a basketball. Assign each a number between 1 and 4. In number order, begin on their number and play each of the parts below in sequence as you keep the tempo steady.

Bounce, Slap, Dribble, Move!
Instructor's Guide, page 79
Music! VHS Segment 4-B, STOMP
Out Loud (0:51)
CD 17 ② "Odun de! Odun de!" by
Babatunde Olatunji
(4:36)
CD 17 ③ "Mona Lisa" by Wyclef
Jean and the Refugee
Allstars (4:30)
CD 17 ④ "Rockin' After Midnight"
(instrumental) by
Marvin Gaye (7:00)
CD 17 ⑤ "One Love" by Bob
Marley (3:20)

The California E.A.R. Unit performs a new style of music with energy, humor, and wit. Their ability to communicate musical artistry with a sense of fun entices the audience to enjoy their nontraditional performance style. This inventive group combines classical instruments like the flute and violin with everyday objects such as blow dryers, table tennis paddles, and hoses. What elements do you think make a good performance? What type of musical performances do you enjoy? Why?

California E.A.R. Unit. Dorothy Stone (keyboard), Amy Knoles (percussion), Robin Lorentz (far right). Photo: Richard Hines.

Music!...
To
Let Us
Perform

You may wish to use Fine Art Transparency 3, *Jane Avril*, in the TRB to introduce Unit 3.

. . . .

Chapter 5
From the Performer's Perspective

Chapter 6
From the Audience's Perspective

Chapter 7
Virtuoso Performers

Chapter 8
Alone and Together

Use Artsource® VHS Segment 5 in the Performing Arts Package to show a performance by the California E.A.R. Unit.

From the Performer's Perspective

To live is to be active, to do, to perform. One way we perform or feel alive is to make music. We make music because the capacity to think sound is built into the human mind. We call this capacity **audiation**, *the ability to imagine or hear in our heads the sound of a melody, a rhythm, various musical timbres, or a performance*. Most people possess this talent, not just a fortunate few, as is sometimes believed.

Objectives

By completing the chapter, you will:
- Find out that you can "think" music.
- Learn about how to use your voice to express yourself musically.
- Understand musical communication as a performer.
- Learn how voices are classified musically.
- Try your skill at the art of interpretation.
- Learn to sing in a style appropriate to the music.

Vocabulary

alto	countertenor
audiation	crescendo
baritone	decrescendo
bass	mezzo soprano
basso	phrase
profundo	soprano
bel canto	tenor
coloratura	vocal range
contralto	vocal register

Musicians to Meet

John Cage
Marian Anderson

The fun of performing begins with individuals who use music to expressive themselves in unique ways. Here, two members of the Broadway show Bring in da Noise, Bring in da Funk *improvise rhythms on common objects attached to their clothing.* **What reaction from the audience members do you think these performers would like to have?**

Caption answer Students most likely would imagine that these performers would enjoy seeing their audiences respond with cheers, laughter, and excitement.

The Art of Performance

You may wish to use "Interview a Musical Performer" at this time. Lesson plans are found on page 90 in the Instructor's Guide.

Performers use the capacity to think sound (to audiate) in order to hear the music before they actually play it. They can "hear it with their eyes." Composers do this too; they think the sounds first, then write them down. Some people assume that composers have to work at a piano. This is not true. Although some do, others prefer to sit at a desk away from any musical instrument. They can create musical sounds and alter them—all in their mind. You, too, have the capacity to think sound, even when the sounds are not physically audible.

Music is a basic and unique part of us. Through music we can express ourselves and communicate with one another. In fact, some of humanity's most profound thoughts have been expressed through music. By making music—being a performer—music becomes self-expression. Delivering a musical performance can be both exhilarating and demanding. Musicians must work to develop control and confidence. They have to be certain they can produce a high level of musical quality. This takes a great deal of practice, such as going over a musical passage again and again until it is mastered.

Music & CULTURE

Young people throughout the world perform music, expressing their society's character and the values in which they believe. **How can musical performances—instrumental as well as vocal—convey a community spirit and pride in who we are?**

Music & Culture
Because a voice is unique to each person, it is a powerful means to express beliefs and values.

ACTIVITY ▶ *Think the Musical Sound*

Can you "think" music without actually hearing the sound waves?

Refining your audiation skills can make you a better performer. See how well you can audiate the following:

1. *Audiate a major scale.* Think the syllables DO RE MI FA SOL LA TI DO as you silently sing the pitches of a major scale, beginning with DO on C. As a class, sing the high DO out loud together to see if you have all arrived on the same pitch.

2. *Audiate instrumental timbres.* Can you hear in your mind's ear the sound of an electric guitar and the sound of a tuba playing "The Star-Spangled Banner"? How are they different?

3. *Audiate a melody.* Think of the melody for the first line of "America": "My country 'tis of thee, sweet land of liberty, of thee I sing." When you come to the word "sing" (on DO), sing it out loud to see if everyone in the class arrived on the same pitch at precisely the same time.

Musical Communication

Music is an art of communication. Musical communication, like all communication, is a two-way street. We send, and we receive. Most often, music is more than self-expression. It makes connections between people.

Performers bring us music by repeating from memory traditional musical expressions learned "by ear" from others, by inventing sounds from the mind's imagination (audiating and improvising), or by reading and interpreting the notations on a musical score. Can music be made any other way?

American composer John Cage (1912–1992) tried to bring greater freedom to musical expression. For Cage, music was not limited to sounds we select and organize for communicative purposes. He believed that any kind of sound can be heard as music. According to Cage, if we attend to the sounds around us, we could interpret them as musical expression. To illustrate his point, Cage produced a "piece" entitled *4'33"* (1952) in which no sounds are intentionally performed. Instead, the "performer" sits at the piano for four minutes and thirty-three seconds and does not play a note. The audience listens as usual. The ambient sounds that occur in the room become the musical expression.

PROFILE

John Cage

*John Cage
American Composer
1912–1992*

With his innovative use of chance and nontraditional sounds, John Cage helped to direct the course of music and art in the modern era. His compositions focused on timbre, loudness, and duration of sound rather than pitch or harmony. They are often made up of many unrelated layers of sound. *Imaginary Landscape No. 4* (1951) involves twelve radios, each with two performers—one to manipulate volume, the other the stations. Such chance effects reflect his belief that humans should not try to mold nature to their will but should discover music in everyday life. His composition *4'33"* exemplifies these beliefs.

Cage was born in Los Angeles in 1912. He was an excellent student and went on to develop interests in many areas, including architecture, writing, painting, and modern dance. Cage eventually returned to his childhood love of music and studied composition with Arnold Schoenberg. He later collaborated with other artists such as the painter Robert Rauschenberg and the choreographer Merce Cunningham on performance art events called "happenings." Scorned by some, revered by many, Cage was one of the most influential American composers of the twentieth century.

Activity *Make Your Own Music*
Instructor's Guide, page 84

ACTIVITY ▶ *Make Your Own Music*

Set up and attend a performance of John Cage's *4'33"*, then discuss the questions listed below.

Choose a performer who will designate the beginning of the composition by opening the keyboard cover of the piano. The conclusion of the composition will be designated by the closing of the keyboard

As you listen to the live performance of *4'33"*, make a list of the sounds you hear.

Arrange a second performance. Compare the list of sounds you heard during the second performance with the list you compiled during the first. Working in small groups, discuss the following:

1. Which of the sounds you heard, if any, are considered to be music?

2. Does the term "music" refer to the entire spectrum of sounds in the world?

3. Does the organization of music just happen randomly?

4. Is there such a phenomenon as silence?

Using Your Voice to Express Yourself

Your voice is one of your most distinguishing characteristics. It is part of your personality, part of what makes you unique. Your voice is like your fingerprint—different from anyone else's. It is the most important means by which you express yourself and convey your moods and beliefs. Your voice gives you enormous power—the power to communicate in both speech and song.

Singing is sustained speech. When we sing, we aim for the vowels. They support the tone. With the possible exception of *N* and *M*, we cannot sustain or sing consonants. Singers try to develop pure vowel sounds for tonal clarity and beauty. They also strive for an evenness in sound throughout their low, middle, and upper registers, working to eliminate any "breaks" so there is smoothness throughout their entire vocal range.

ACTIVITY ▶ *Determine Your Vocal Range*

Find and notate the pitches that represent the highest and lowest points of your voice range.

Your **vocal range** is *the highest and lowest pitches you can sing.* Use these steps to find your range:

1. As a class, review music notation on a grand staff. Practice singing the syllable pattern DO RE MI RE DO TI DO on each of several pitches beginning on middle C.

2. Working in small groups of the same gender, gather around a piano, portable keyboard, or mallet percussion instrument to find the pitches you produce vocally.

3. To find your lower range, sing the pattern DO RE MI RE DO TI DO together beginning on middle C; move downward one half step at a time. Find the lowest pitch you can sing comfortably at medium volume. Notate this pitch on your staff paper.

4. To find your upper range, go back to middle C and sing the same pattern, this time ascending in pitch one half step at a time. Keep your voice light and sing as high as you can comfortably without straining. When you have found the highest pitch you can sing easily, notate this pitch on the staff paper.

5. Your high and low pitches represent your vocal range. How wide is it? Compare your range to that of others in your group.

Activity *Determine Your Vocal Range*
Instructor's Guide, page 85

You might wish to use Music Theory Transparency 4, The Grand Staff, in the Teacher's Resource Binder.

Learning the Art of Interpretation

For music to communicate, it must be expressive. When composers do not designate exactly how a work is to be performed, performers must decide how to sing or play it. They ask:

- What is the most appropriate tempo for the piece?
- What is the most fitting tone quality, or timbre?
- Should the notes be smooth and connected, or short and choppy?
- Where should special emphasis be given?
- What dynamics should be used?

Musical expression is directly tied to interpretation. Figuring out how to interpret a piece of music requires some ingenuity. The performer has to try to understand what the composer is trying to communicate, then tailor the performance to realize that intent. There is no single "correct" way to perform a piece of music. There are many interpretations.

Interpretation requires an attention to detail. Performing music is not just a matter of getting the notes right, it is making every note *mean* something. The performer has to "phrase," that is, convey the logic of the melodic flow. A **phrase** is *a musical thought—a series of pitches that makes sense*. Composers sometimes mark the phrase by a curved line over a series of notes, indicating that they are connected to form a statement. All music breathes. There have to be resting points or places that mark the end of the phrase.

Musicians are challenged to interpret music and make decisions about how to sing or play it. They consider appropriate tempo, tone quality or timbre, how notes are connected to each other, emphasis, dynamics, and phrasing. **Can you explain why one of your favorite songs is a successful interpretation?**

Caption answer
Responses will vary.

ACTIVITY ▶ *Learn to Interpret*

Activity *Learn to Interpret*
Instructor's Guide, pages 85–86
TRB 5-2, *Read the Rhythms*
TRB 5-3, *Artist's Life*
CD 3 ⊡11⊡ "Dona Nobis Pacem"
    (2:56)

Interpret this Latin prayer for peace, paying particular attention to the dynamics and phrase markings.

Practice your interpretation so that the entire class is able to sing this piece expressively. Find and observe the dynamic levels of: *pianissimo (pp)* very soft, *piano (p)* soft, *mezzo forte (mf)* moderately loud, and *forte (f)* loud.

Dona Nobis Pacem

Composer Unknown

Practice the **crescendo** (⟨), *a gradual increase in the loudness of the sound;* **decrescendo** (⟩), *a gradual decrease in the loudness of a sound,* and ritardando (*rit*), a gradual slowing down at the end. Practice singing each phrase in one breath or by "staggering" your breathing (sneaking a breath in so it cannot be detected). Sing to express a prayer for peace. Make your performance musical; that is, find the meaning in these notes.

Vocal Timbres

When we identify someone by his or her speaking voice, we base our recognition on the tone color or timbre of the voice and on the **vocal register**, *how low or high someone speaks.* Once we are familiar with television personalities, for example, we do not need to see them to identify them. We associate the sound of their voice with who they are. Without being aware of it, we recognize familiar singers the same way— by the distinctive timbre and register of their voices.

Activity *Characterize the Voices*
Instructor's Guide, page 86
CD 3 12 "Oh, Pretty Woman" (0:47)
CD 3 13 "Mame" (0:47)
CD 3 14 "Rhythm Is Gonna Get Ya" (0:46)
CD 3 15 "Magic of Love" (0:47)

ACTIVITY ▶ *Characterize the Voices*

Try to recognize these vintage pop artists by the tone quality (timbre) of their voices.

As you listen to these distinctive twentieth-century pop music voices, develop a list of words that describe the tone color and register of each voice. Some terms that describe tone color are: bright, dark, harsh, heavy, hoarse, husky, light, mellow, and warm. Registers are usually high, low, or medium in pitch. On the basis of their timbre and register, can you determine the identities of the voices? Compare and discuss your list with those of your classmates.

Roy Orbison

Each of these twentieth-century musicians—Roy Orbison, Louis Armstrong, Gloria Estefan, and Janis Joplin— has a unique tone quality. **Name three other singers whose voices could be described as husky, dark, or mellow.**

Janis Joplin

Caption answer
Responces will vary.

Louis Armstrong

Gloria Estefan

The human voice is imperfect. It can sing out of tune and have a breathy or nasal quality. It can lack adequate strength or sustaining power. It can also be highly expressive. The voice naturally projects a humanness because it comes from within. It therefore speaks directly to other people's feelings. What is considered a beautiful tone in some cultures might be less appealing in others. For example, the chesty and nasal timbres of some Eastern European countries are criticized as crude vocal sounds in other European countries.

ACTIVITY ▶ *Compare Timbres*

Activity *Compare Timbres*
Instructor's Guide, pages 86–87
CD 3 16 "Homage a Baba Cissoko" (1:46)
CD 3 17 "Mamo Marie Mamo" (2:20)

Listen to two popular singers from Bulgaria and Mali. Describe the differences in their vocal coloration.

Make a list of adjectives that describe the vocal qualities of each singer, then answer the following questions:

1. How do these singers differ from one another, particularly in timbre?
2. Which singer comes from West Africa (Mali)? (Hint: Pay attention to the accompaniment.)
3. Do you think these voices have carrying power? Why might this be necessary?
4. What makes these voices expressive?

As an instrument, the human voice has a wide range and a variety of timbres. Female voices are usually higher than those of males.

FEMALE VOICES

Soprano (so-PRAH-noh)—*the high female register.*

Coloratura (col-or-ah-TOO-rah)—*the soprano voice that is light and flexible enough to perform rapid scales and trills.*

Mezzo soprano (or mezzo)—*the intermediate female voice.*

Alto—*the low female register.*

Contralto (con-TRAL-toh)—*a low female register with a full, rich, dark, and powerful quality.*

MALE VOICES

Countertenor (coun-ter-TEN-or)—*the highest male voices with a falsetto range and quality and a register in the female alto range.*

Tenor—*the high male range with a powerful, ringing quality.*

Baritone—*the intermediate male voice.*

Bass—*a lower male register with a rich, robust, resonant, and full quality.*

Basso profundo (BAS-soh pro-FUN-doh)—*the lowest of the adult male voices with a dark, rich, powerful quality.*

ACTIVITY ▶ *Designate Voice Categories*

What are the qualities that determine voice categories?

Match the picture of the artist and the description of his or her voice category with the voice you hear. How would you describe the differences and the similarities between the voices? Which type of voice is the most unusual? Why?

Activity Designate Voice Categories
Instructor's Guide, pages 87–88
CD 3 ⟦18⟧ "Nessun dorma," *Turandot* (2:53)
CD 3 ⟦19⟧ "Queen of the night," *The Magic Flute* (2:23)
CD 3 ⟦20⟧ "Flowers of the purple dye," *A Midsummer Night's Dream* (2:03)
CD 3 ⟦21⟧ "Old Man River," *Show Boat* (3:00)
CD 3 ⟦22⟧ "Non più andrai," *The Marriage of Figaro* (2:03)
CD 3 ⟦23⟧ "Queen of the abyss, make haste," *The Masked Ball* (2:05)
CD 3 ⟦24⟧ "Farewell aria," *Boris Godunov* (2:48)

Edita Gruberova—Coloratura soprano
Character: Queen of the Night
Aria: "Queen of the night"
Opera: The Magic Flute (1791) by Wolfgang Amadeus Mozart (1756–1791)

Marian Anderson—Contralto
Character: Ulrica
Aria: "Queen of the abyss, make haste"
Opera: The Masked Ball (1859) by Giuseppe Verdi (1813–1901)

Alfred Deller—Countertenor
Character: Oberon
Aria: "Flowers of the purple dye"
Opera: A Midsummer Night's Dream (1960) by Benjamin Britten (1913–1976)

Luciano Pavarotti—Tenor
Character: Calaf
Aria: "Nessun dorma" ("No one will sleep")
Opera: Turandot (1926) by Giacomo Puccini (1858–1924)

José van Dam—Baritone
Character: Figaro
Aria: "Non più andrai" ("Life
   in the Army")
Opera: The Marriage of Figaro
   (1786) by Wolfgang
   Amadeus Mozart
   (1756–1791)

William Warfield—Bass
Character: Joe
Aria: "Old Man River"
Opera: Show Boat (1927) by
   Jerome Kern
   (1885–1945)

Nicolai Ghiaurov—Basso
   profundo
Character: Boris
Aria: "Farewell aria"
Opera: Boris Godunov (1874)
   by Modest Mussorgsky
   (1839–1881)

Marian Anderson
American Singer
1902–1993

PROFILE

Marian Anderson

The great American singer Marian Anderson broke through racial barriers firmly but gently. She grew up in Philadelphia and developed her voice by singing in church choirs. In the late 1920s she went to Europe to study and tour. There, the renowned conductor Arturo Toscanini called Anderson's voice a "voice heard once in a century."

However, when she returned to the United States, she found many doors closed to her because she was African American. In 1939 she was refused access to the most prestigious concert hall in Washington, D.C. First Lady Eleanor Roosevelt helped remedy this injustice. Instead of singing at Constitution Hall, her concert was moved to the steps of the Lincoln Memorial. An audience of 75,000 people assembled to hear her. Anderson walked onto the steps, paused to look at Lincoln's statue, then, choked with emotion, sang "My country 'tis of thee, sweet land of liberty, of thee I sing . . ." She later said, "I had no bitterness then. I have no bitterness now." Today, the recording of her 1939 concert at the Lincoln Memorial is one of the most requested records at the Library of Congress.

Activity *Recognize Parts of a*
        Chorus
Instructor's Guide, page 89
TRB 5-1, *Listening/Performance*
CD 3 25 "Kyrie," (first 14 bars)
        Mass in B Minor (1:33)
CD 3 26 "Kyrie," *Mass in B Minor*
        (4:46)

ACTIVITY ▶ *Recognize Parts of a Chorus*

Can you identify the four parts of a chorus when you hear them?

Listen to the first 14 measures of the "Kyrie" from Johann Sebastian Bach's *Mass in B Minor* and see if you can tell when the principal theme is sung and which section of the chorus (soprano, alto, tenor, or bass) is singing it. Try to sing or play the theme:

Ky - ri - e   e - lei - son, e - lei - son.

Note that the theme is in 4/4 meter and uses several chromatic or half-step intervals. All the voices sing the same text. *Kyrie eleison* is Greek for "Lord have mercy."

Count measures and listen for the four vocal entrances of the theme. The first entrance occurs in the first measure on beat 1. Locate the remaining three entrances of the theme.

Listen a second time to check your answers. Then, as you listen a third time, circle the number of the beat in the measures where each new voice begins singing the "Kyrie" theme. Do all the voices enter on the same beat?

Listen again and label which voice section of the chorus (soprano, alto, tenor, or bass) actually sings each entrance of the theme. Is there a pattern to the way Bach introduced each entrance?

MIDI TECHNOLOGY OPTION

Technology Option
Use Project 5 in the *MIDI Activities*
binder.

■ **Music with MIDI** Use a MIDI program to create a four-part composition (soprano, alto, tenor, bass) featuring a theme that is heard at different times in all four voices.

Matching Timbre with Style

If all the sounds in the world can be used for expressive purposes, then which sounds do we select for what purposes? Are some sounds more suitable for expressing certain emotions than others? To express a variety of emotions in music and to attain maximum impact, we must choose the most suitable timbre.

The voice can be adapted to sing many different types of music, and each type has its own appropriate style. The style of the music dictates the

An artist's use of color is similar to a musician's use of timbre (tone colors). **How has the artist Miriam Schapiro used color to make these figures come alive as dancers?**

Miriam Schapiro. *Pas de Deux*, 1986. © Miriam Schapiro. Private collection. Courtesy Steinbaum Krauss Gallery, New York, New York.

Music & Art
She uses bright colors suggesting a festive, spirited mood.

style of the singing. You have some idea of the differences in sound that exist between a pop and an operatic singer. A natural, unaffected, easygoing sound best conveys the intimate thoughts and feelings expressed in pop and folk music. In contrast, the more formal, lofty expression of opera suits a tradition of vocal production called **bel canto** (literally, "beautiful singing"), *a style characterized by lyrical and flowing phrases, beauty of vocal color, and brilliant technique.* Just as we probably would not like to hear a country-and-western singer attempt opera, we most likely would not want to hear an opera singer attempt to sing pop music in a bel canto style.

ACTIVITY ▶ *Identify Differences in Musical Styles*

What musical style matches the notation below?

Listen to the arrangements of "Amazing Grace" played in four different musical styles: jazz, gospel, classical, and pop. Which of these four styles is noted on the following page?

Sing along with the arranged accompaniment of "Amazing Grace." Can you match your vocal timbre with the style? How well can you and your friends harmonize this melody? (See page 100.)

Activity *Identify Differences in Musical Styles*
Instructor's Guide, page 90
TRB 5-4, "*Amazing Grace*"
CD 3 [27] "Amazing Grace" (jazz) (1:04)
CD 3 [28] "Amazing Grace" (gospel) (1:12)
CD 3 [29] "Amazing Grace" (classical) (1:09)
CD 3 [30] "Amazing Grace" (pop) (0:55)

Amazing Grace

Composed by John Newton
Arranged by Rob Landes

A - maz - ing ___ grace! How ___ sweet ___ the ___

sound that ___ saved a ___ soul like ___ me! ___ I

once ___ was ___ lost, but ___ now ___ am ___ found; was ___ blind ___ but ___

now I see. ___

SUMMARY

People express themselves musically in many different ways and with an array of sounds—instrumental, vocal, and electronic. The variety of timbres increases the range of musical expression.

Performing music together requires a considerable degree of cooperation and coordination—a sense of togetherness or ensemble. Musical communication requires technique (performing the right sounds, in time and in tune) and expression (effectively conveying the mood of the music). Musicians perform a piece of music in order to realize its expressive power. They communicate the meaning of a musical work by paying careful attention to such matters as appropriate tempo, dynamics, timbre (tone color), blend, balance, and phrasing.

CHAPTER 5 REVIEW

Building Music Vocabulary

On a sheet of paper, write the term from the list that best matches each description below.

(6) alto
(4) audiation
(3) baritone
(17) bass
(9) basso profundo
(16) bel canto
(15) coloratura
(10) contralto
(13) countertenor
(11) crescendo
(8) decrescendo
(1) mezzo soprano
(5) phrase
(12) soprano
(14) tenor
(2) vocal range
(7) vocal register

1. The intermediate female voice.
2. The span from the highest to the lowest pitch you can sing.
3. The intermediate male voice.
4. The ability to hear, think, or imagine music in your head.
5. A musical thought—a series of pitches that makes sense.
6. The low female register.
7. How high or low someone speaks.
8. A gradual decrease in the loudness of a sound.
9. The lowest male voice, with a dark, rich, and powerful quality.
10. A low female voice with a full, dark, rich, and powerful quality.
11. A gradual increase in the loudness of a sound.
12. A high female register.
13. The highest adult male voice, with a register in the female alto range.
14. A high male voice, with a powerful, ringing quality.
15. The highest female voice that is light and flexible enough to perform scales and trills.
16. A style of singing characterized by flowing phrases and beauty of vocal color.
17. A lower male voice, with a rich, robust, resonant, full quality.

Answers to Chapter 5 Review
18. Vowels support the tone and can be sustained; most consonants cannot.

Complete answers for the Chapter 5 Review are found in the Instructor's Guide, pages 90–91.

Reviewing Music Facts

Answer each question in a complete sentence.
18. Why do singers aim for vowels as they sing?
19. How does a singer use phrasing to create interpretation?
20. What is the voice quality we hear when we recognize a familiar voice?

Thinking It Through

On a sheet of paper, write the answers to the following questions:
21. **Analyze** How might a singer use phrasing to interpret a folk song about being lonely?
22. **Contrast** How would you describe the difference between the singing styles of a folksinger and an operatic singer?
23. **Apply** How would you determine your own vocal register and vocal range?

Making the Connection

Science Learn more about how a voice type is determined by a person's physiology. Discover which parts of the body affect the vocal range.

Language Arts Find song lyrics you like and read them aloud as a poem or a story. Does speaking the words give you ideas about the phrasing of the music when those same words are sung?

 Marian Anderson and Luciano Pavarotti are featured at **www.glencoe.com/sec/music**

19. To convey the logic of the melodic flow.
20. The timbre or tone quality.
21. By using crescendos, decrescendos, and ritardandos to shape the musical ideas, to help interpret feelings about loneliness.
22. Folk style: more natural, easygoing, unaffected. Operatic style: more formal, lofty, using more brilliant technique.
23. By finding the highest and lowest pitches you can sing.

CHAPTER 6

From the Audience's Perspective

By completing the chapter, you will:
- Explore the various levels of experiencing music as a listener.
- Learn about the sources of instrumental sounds.
- Be able to recognize and categorize instrumental timbres.
- Become familiar with how dynamics serve as a powerful expressive aspect of music and how loudness can be harmful.
- Understand the role of the music critic.
- Begin to develop your own ability to critique music.

Vocabulary

aerophones
authenticity
chordophones
electrophones
idiophones
membranophones
music critic

We can engage ourselves with music as a creator (composer), re-creator (performer), or receiver (listener). As a listener, we respond to music with different levels of receptivity. We may be very casual about the way we hear music, paying almost no attention to it. Elevator music, for example, is not meant to be listened to intently. We have all used music as background sound, a pleasant atmosphere for our own thoughts and tasks. An "easy listening" station can create a dreamlike haze, and we may deliberately tune out the music. We are oblivious to the sounds.

*As a member of an audience, you participate in music making by involving yourself with the sounds of the music as they unfold. Each experience has a different purpose; therefore, you respond differently each time. **Can you describe a situation when you are actively involved with listening to music and one when you are not?***

Caption answer
Responses will vary, but students will likely say that they pay more attention to music that engages their senses and suits their tastes, and less attention to music that is unfamiliar and/or belonging to other generations.

Perceptive Listening

There are different ways to experience music. Some people let sounds wash over them like a sonic bath, an emotional flood. This is the *sensuous* level. Other listeners delineate the sounds and savor various aspects of the music as they unfold. This is the *perceptive* level. They listen for musical events and how they accumulate to form an expressive composition. The sensuous level of attending to music is purely emotive. The perceptive level raises our awareness because it is more analytical. Ideally, we listen more perceptively in order to increase the emotional impact.

The ultimate experience is being so caught up in the music that we lose ourselves in it. This is often called the "aesthetic experience." It involves focus, intellect, affect (emotion), and our cultural conditioning. The following diagram illustrates the various levels of experiencing music:

LEVELS OF EXPERIENCING MUSIC

Experience Level	Oblivious	Sensuous	Perceptive	Peak
Psychological Level	Subconscious	Conscious	Analytical	Revelatory

Each level of experiencing music is valuable for a different reason. The analytical approach, however, has to be learned. It requires some knowledge of musical events, the elements of music, and what makes music expressive. As an intermediary stage of bringing music to life, the analytical stage can complement the purely emotional response and boost it. This is the approach used in this text. It is the process of paying attention to the details and trying to hear everything that is happening.

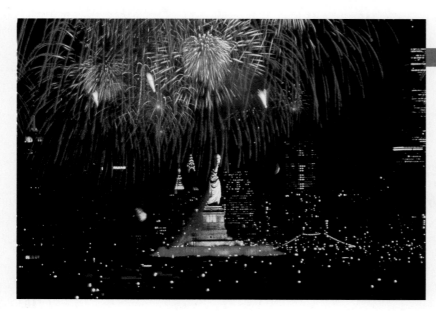

Music & HISTORY

In 1986, America celebrated the one hundredth anniversary of the Statue of Liberty. American composer John Williams wrote and conducted "Liberty Fanfare" to honor the occasion. **What emotions would you anticipate experiencing during a performance of "Liberty Fanfare"?**

Music & History Possibilities include patriotism and pride, excitement, and respect for the historical importance of the event.

ACTIVITY ▶ *Listen Perceptively*

How does the "Liberty Fanfare" call attention to itself?

Listen to a work that John Williams was commissioned to write for the one hundredth birthday of the Statue of Liberty.

How does the composer command our attention? Write your thoughts on a piece of paper and be prepared to discuss them.

Now listen again and complete the Perceptive Listening Grid.

Does an awareness of what is going on in the music help you to get more out of it or increase your enjoyment? Does knowing the purpose for which the piece was created, the function of the music, and the intended audience/occasion increase your response?

Activity *Listen Perceptively*
Instructor's Guide, pages 92–93
TRB 6-1, *Perceptive Listening*
CD 3 |31| "Liberty Fanfare" (4:12)

ACTIVITY ▶ *Use Your Imagination!*

What variables affect the way we experience music?

With your classmates, simulate the three circumstances described below. Then determine the level at which you are interacting with John Philip Sousa's "The Washington Post March" in each situation. Choose one of these levels: (A) Oblivious (B) Sensuous (C) Perceptive (D) Peak.

1. You are attending a parade celebrating the Fourth of July. You can faintly hear in the distance the band playing Sousa's march.
2. The band arrives. They turn, face you, and play the march. You can feel the beat of the drums, and the brilliance of the woodwinds and high brass slice the air.
3. While in class, you are analyzing and focusing on the various internal aspects of the march as well as the social function of the music.

Activity *Use Your Imagination!*
Instructor's Guide, pages 93–94
TRB 6-1, *Perceptive Listening*
CD 3 |32| "The Washington Post
     March" (2:21)

Being an Audience Member

We often listen to music in the company of other people. How you react to music depends on the type of music, how it is being used, and where you are listening to it. At a basketball game, you probably would not analyze the music being played by the band. At a dance, music appeals to your sense of movement and you react in a sensuous way. In church, you may sing or even clap along with the choir. Attending a concert, you may try to hear all the details in the music being performed and applaud the performers for their effort and achievement. In a sense, then, the context in which the music is performed dictates what is expected of the listener.

Identifying Instrumental Timbres

As listeners of music, our perception is sharpened when we can delineate the variety of the sounds we are hearing. While the human voice is the most primary and natural source of music, every culture in the world has created musical instruments by using the natural materials of their region—fiber, metal, reed, gut, skin, and even stone—to fashion ways to produce sound. Ethnomusicologists have classified all musical instruments in five fundamental categories, based on how the sound is produced:

Aerophone: bagpipes

■ **Aerophones**, *instruments that produce sound by a vibrating column of air.* Usually these consist of a pipe made out of wood, metal, or plastic, sometimes with a reed attached. Examples of aerophones include flute, tuba, and harmonica.

■ **Idiophones**, *simple, solid instruments that produce sound by being struck, scraped, or shaken.* This includes gongs, cymbals, rattles, and xylophones.

All instruments belong to the five fundamental categories: aerophones, idiophones, membranophones, chordophones, electrophones. **Can you identify another instrument for each category?**

■ **Membranophones**, *instruments that produce sound by striking or rubbing a skin or membrane stretched across a resonating air chamber.* This category includes conga drums, tabla, and timpani.

Idiophone: Vietnamese dan t'rung

■ **Chordophones**, *instruments that create sound by striking, rubbing, or plucking a taut string (or chord).* These include guitar, harp, violin, and string bass. The strings on many of these instruments are attached to a resonating box.

Membranophone: Gamelan drum

■ **Electrophones**, *instruments that generate sound from electricity.* Electronic organs and synthesizers are in this category.

All instruments of the modern symphony orchestra and of the Indonesian gamelan orchestra can be classified in one of the five categories: aerophones, idiophones, membranophones, chordophones, or electrophones. Each of these sources of sound produces a particular tone color, or timbre, that is distinct and clearly identifiable by the ear. As a listener, you can learn to identify the timbre with the instrument that produces its sound.

Chordophone: *sitar*

Electrophone: *keyboard*

APPROXIMATE RANGES OF ORCHESTRA INSTRUMENTS

Piccolo
Flute
Oboe
Clarinet
Bassoon
French horn
Trumpet
Trombone
Tuba
Timpani
Harp
Violin
Viola
Cello
Double bass

A B C D E F G A B C D E F G A B C D E F G A B C D E F G A B C D E F G A B C D E F G A B C D E F G A B C

Middle C

Chart from Music: A Listener's Introduction *by Kenneth Levy. ©1983 by Kenneth Levy. Reprinted by permission of HarperCollins Publishers.*

Another way to identify instruments is by their range of audible pitch from very low to very high. While some instruments do not have discernible pitches (a cymbal or rattle, for example), others produce tones that are in the high, low, or mid-range. Except in the case of some electrophones, pitch is affected by the size of the instrument. The larger the instrument, the lower the pitch. The smaller the instrument, the higher the pitch. Similarly, the longer the string or pipe, the lower the pitch. Stretching a membrane raises the pitch, while loosening a membrane lowers it. In these ways people have been able to create musical instruments that span the full range of audible pitch.

ACTIVITY ▶ *Name the Source*

Discriminate among instrumental timbres that you hear.

Listen to these seven musical excerpts. Identify all the timbres and the instruments producing the sound you hear. Then, classify the instruments according to their appropriate category. Hint: All five classification categories are represented.

TECHNOLOGY OPTION

■ **Music with MIDI** Use a MIDI program to experiment with tone colors and evaluate the success of your keyboard or sound module at emulating other instruments.

Listening to Music Alone

We frequently listen to music in private. Often, recorded music is played for an audience of one. Sometimes we listen to music on the radio by ourselves. In these private situations, we can choose our own level of experience: oblivious, sensuous, or perceptive. If we are fortunate, we may even achieve a peak experience.

Many people enjoy listening to music using headphones. With headphones we can create our own sound space, an environment that shuts out the discordant elements of modern life.

One important expressive aspect of music is its volume. The capacity to hear music depends on how well our ears function. The human hearing mechanism is sensitive and can be damaged easily and permanently. The tendency of people to listen to music at high volumes has alarmed physicians, audiologists, and even social psychologists. Do we really need to listen to music that is so loud?

ACTIVITY *Investigate Volume Levels*

Why do people listen to music at very loud volumes?

Investigate and discuss these questions:

Science and Health Issues

1. Amplitude, dynamics, loudness, and intensity are related but distinct terms. How are they different?
2. How are sound intensity levels (SIL) measured? When are sound levels dangerous and damaging?

Social Issues

3. Why do people like loud music?
4. What are the pros and cons of using personal headphones?

Deciding What You Like

There are many ways to coax the beauty out of music. Some people champion **authenticity**, *performing music as closely as possible to the way it was performed at the time it was created.* Others apply modern standards and contemporary tastes to reinterpret a work for today's world. The way a work is performed can alter its meaning. When you purchase recordings, you often have different interpretations from which to choose. It is up to you to select the performance that pleases you.

Making a decision depends on comparing the various aspects of one performance with those same aspects in another. But when we are unable to hear the music ourselves, we have to depend on published reviews. Published reviews are written by the **music critic**, *a person who judges the quality of a performance and the music.*

Stereo headphones allow listeners to enclose themselves in their own musical world. However, they pose a serious health risk to our hearing if the music is played at high volumes. **How would you convince a friend to recognize this risk?**

Caption answer
Responses will vary.

Activity *Investigate Volume Levels*
Instructor's Guide, page 96
TRB 6-3, *How's Your Hearing?*

The Role of the Music Critic

When the British team of Sir William Gilbert and Sir Arthur Sullivan premiered their comic operetta *H.M.S. Pinafore* in London in 1878, they quivered at the thought of how Queen Victoria would react to this burlesque of the revered Royal Navy and the stiff social class system. She had one curt remark: "We are not amused." Nonetheless, the operetta was a smash success and played 700 performances. (Queen Victoria was not a professional critic.)

Activity *Compare Performances*
Instructor's Guide, pages 96–97
TRB 6-4, *Compare Performances*
CD 4 ⑧ Toccata and Fugue in D
       Minor (2:22)
CD 4 ⑨ Toccata and Fugue in D
       Minor (3:26)

ACTICITY ▶ *Compare Performances*

Which version of Johann Sebastian Bach's Toccata and Fugue in D Minor do you like better and why?

Compare the original organ version of this work with Leopold Stokowski's transcription for symphony orchestra. Try to substantiate why you think one version is better than the other. Listen again to Stokowski's version of Bach's Toccata and Fugue in D Minor and answer the following questions:

1. Bach might have performed his toccata on the organ of the Church of St. Thomas in Leipzig. This long, narrow, and high building had a reverberation (echo) of 3.5 seconds. How does Stokowski take that phenomenon into account in his orchestral transcription?
2. Bach probably created this brilliant toccata "on the spot" as a prelude or recessional to the religious service. How does Stokowski's transcription, which was intended for the concert hall, take away from, or add to, the sacred and mystical character of the composition?

A music critic may comment on the performer, the composer, the conductor, the acoustics, the size of the audience and its reaction, or on anything else that relates to the performance. Music critics can influence public opinion. Because of this, they shoulder considerable responsibility. Depending on how fairly they treat the musical performer, for example, they can make or break a career. For this reason, their views can be controversial. Of course, when you read a review, your most important task is to distinguish between fact and opinion.

ACTIVITY *Investigate Music Reviews*

Can you distinguish between fact and opinion in newspaper columns about music?

Read both newspaper columns about Midori, the Japanese-born violinist who was 16 years old at the time they were published. Then answer these questions:

1. Which one is a music review and which one is a news article?
2. Which does the music review contain? What is the focus of each article?
3. Now watch a video performance of Midori. Write your own review of her performance.

At age 11, violinist Midori made her first appearance with the New York Philharmonic. Now she travels worldwide giving concerts and making recordings.

Activity *Investigate Music Reviews*
Music! VHS Segment 5, Midori Performance
Instructor's Guide, pages 97–98
TRB 6-5, *Newspaper Column 1*
TRB 6-6, *Newspaper Column 2*
TRB 6-7, *Music Criticism Work-*
      sheet

Developing Critical Skills

Critics can be wrong, especially when they offer their personal opinions. When George Gershwin's opera *Porgy and Bess* was first performed in 1935, some critics liked it; others did not. Virgil Thomson, writing in *Modern Music*, stated, "I do resent Gershwin's shortcomings. I don't mind his being a light composer, and I don't mind his trying to be a serious one. . . . [Porgy and Bess] is crooked folk-lore and half-way opera, a strong but crippled work." After a revival of the opera in 1941, Thomson expressed a change of heart and wrote: "After six years George Gershwin's *Porgy and Bess* is still a beautiful piece of music. . . . Its inspiration is authentic, its expressive quotient high. . . . One is inclined to be more than proud of our little Georgie."

All of us are forced to make choices every day. We have to distinguish between good and bad, right and wrong, and we must make a host of other decisions. When it comes to music, we have a right to exercise our own judgment. We are apt to run into problems when all we have to say is our opinion, with nothing to support it. As audience members, we can act as music critics for ourselves, making decisions about our likes, dislikes, and preferences. By using perceptive listening skills to improve our understanding of the music, we can develop a descriptive language that permits us to express our judgments and share them.

You may wish to use "Analyze Music Reviews" at this time. Lesson plans are found on page 98 in the Instructor's Guide.

In making judgments about music, the professional critic can provide a model for us. Critics' comments range from scorn to praise. They use colorful language—descriptive nouns, adjectives, and adverbs—to communicate their reactions and judgments. These words help them explain or clarify their points of view, substantiate their claims, and present a fair assessment.

When Porgy and Bess was first presented in 1935, the reviews were mixed. The opera tells the story of a disabled man's love for a woman who eventually deserts him. The opera is now hailed worldwide as an American musical masterpiece.

SUMMARY

We experience music live, on recordings, on the radio, in films, and on television. As listeners we can decide how much attention we give to the music around us. We can ignore it, enjoy the sonic blur, or listen to it intensely. When we give music our fullest attention, we listen perceptively. This combined emotional and intellectual involvement with music may move us profoundly.

As listeners, we are all critics. We make judgments and determine our preferences. To share our likes and dislikes with others, we have to acquire insight into the music and vocabulary with which to describe it. We learn to substantiate our judgment based upon what we hear. We can also learn something from professional critics or reviewers by observing how they support their opinions. Like professional music critics and reviewers, we can become more discerning and descriptive. By developing the ability to critique what we hear, we become active participants in the listening process. By awakening our mental antennae, we can experience music more fully.

Building Music Vocabulary

On a sheet of paper, write the term from the list that best matches each description below.

(4) aerophones   (6) idiophones
(7) authenticity   (2) music critic
(1) chordophones   (5) membranophones
(3) electrophones

1. Instruments that produce sound when a string or chord is struck, rubbed, or plucked.
2. A person who judges the quality of a musical performance.
3. Instruments that generate sound from electricity.
4. Instruments that produce sound by a vibrating column of air.
5. Instruments that produce sound when a membrane or skin is struck or rubbed.
6. Simple, solid instruments that produce sound by being struck, scraped, or shaken.
7. Performing music as closely as possible to the way it was performed at the time it was created.

Reviewing Music Facts

Answer each question in a complete sentence.
8. Violins and guitars can be classified as what kind of instruments?
9. Name three aerophones.
10. Gongs, cymbals, and xylophones are in what instrumental category?
11. Identify two membranophones.
12. Why and how can headphones be harmful?
13. How can you tell which instruments will sound higher and which will sound lower?
14. What elements of a music performance might be part of a critical review?

Answers to Chapter 6 Review
8. Chordophones.
9. Flute, tuba, and harmonica.
10. Idiophones.
11. Conga drums, tabla, or timpani.
12. When used at high volumes they can damage hearing.
13. Larger instruments generally sound lower; smaller instruments sound higher.

Complete answers for the Chapter 6 Review are found in the Instructor's Guide, page 99.

Thinking It Through

On a sheet of paper, write the answers to the following questions:
15. **Explain** In your own words, describe four levels of experiencing music.
16. **Identify** Name the one category of instruments that would not be found in ancient cultures and explain why not.
17. **Apply** In your own words, describe the reasons you might, or might not, prefer an "authentic" performance of a piece from the 1700s.
18. **Apply** How might you go about improving your own critical skills?

Making the Connection

Science Create a "pop bottle" xylophone. Fill pop bottles with varying amounts of water. Strike the bottles with a spoon. Decide whether the sound is higher or lower with more water in the bottle. Now blow across the open top of the bottle to create a sound. Is the sound higher or lower with more water? Explain your finding.

Social Studies Choose an instrument that is familiar to you, then find at least three examples of a similar instrument from another culture.

 You can access an instrument encyclopedia at **www.glencoe.com/sec/music**

14. The performer, the composer, the conductor, the acoustics, or the size and reaction of the audience.
15. Explanations should cover listening subconsciously, then consciously, then analytically, resulting in a heightened response or peak experience.
16. Electrophones, which require modern technology.
17. Responses should show students' awareness that an authentic performance re-creates a composer's original intent, reflecting musical styles, forms, and instruments of the era.
18. By developing perceptive listening, reading, comparing critics' reviews, and acquiring descriptive language.

CHAPTER 7

Virtuoso Performers

What makes a performer or a performance great? Great performers breathe excitement into music. They captivate the public by making themselves and their art one. Some are superstars who have extraordinary technical ability, beauty of sound, and personal charisma. Their performances have conviction, and they persuade us that this is the way the music should sound. They make us feel their passion for the music.

Objectives

By completing the chapter, you will:
- Become acquainted with some of the great musical performers of the past and present.
- Learn to recognize and describe characteristics of a virtuoso performer.
- Discover what makes music difficult to master.
- Develop criteria for judging musical performances.

Vocabulary

child prodigy
double bass
musical expression
technique
virtuoso

Musician to Meet

Louis Armstrong

Virtuosos are musicians who seem to do what no one else can do. They amaze us with their extraordinary talent. Shown here is violinist Sarah Chang making her 1993 debut performance at Lincoln Center in New York City at the age of 12. **What commitments to music do you think Sarah had to make to reach this point at such a young age?**

Caption answer
Most students will recognize the hours of practice required to reach this level of skill. Some might also identify the maturity needed to perform in front of large audiences.

The Virtuoso Performer

What is musical virtuosity? The **virtuoso** is *a person with a flawless and brilliant technique, who can seemingly do what no one else can.* Like Olympic gold-medal athletes, virtuosos redefine human ability. They break through established limits and set new standards. They achieve the impossible.

ACTIVITY ▶ *Discover Musical Virtuosity*

What makes these performers great?

Listen to an excerpt from a performance by each of the following artists. Make a list of the qualities that make them unique.

1. **Louis Armstrong** jazz trumpeter and singer
   "West End Blues"
2. **Andrés Segovia** classical guitarist
   "Gavotte en Rondeau" from Partita No. 3 in E Major (J. S. Bach)
3. **Maria Callas** opera singer
   "Gualtier Maldè!...Caro nome" from *Rigoletto* (Guiseppe Verdi)
4. **Jim Walker** jazz/classical flutist
   "Caprice" (Niccolò Paganini)
5. **Cho-Liang Lin** classical violinist
   Violin Concerto in E Minor (Felix Mendelssohn)
6. **Ustad Alla Rakha**
   Indian tabla player
   Pancham Sawari
7. **Umm Kulthum**
   Egyptian singer
   "Ana fi intizarak"

Activity *Discover Musical Virtuosity*
Instructor's Guide, pages 100–103
CD 4 ⏹10 "West End Blues" (3:13)
CD 4 ⏹11 "Gavotte en Rondeau" (2:00)
CD 4 ⏹12 "Gualtier Maldè!...Caro nome," (5:00)
CD 4 ⏹13 "Caprice" (2:50)
CD 4 ⏹14 Violin Concerto in E Minor (3:00)
CD 4 ⏹15 *Pancham Sawari* (1:43)
CD 4 ⏹16 "Ana fi intizarak" (2:18)

Maria Callas (1923–1977), a brilliant operatic soprano, enhanced her vocal virtuosity with her musically intelligent interpretations, her superb sense of drama, and the intensity and authority she brought to every aspect of the roles she performed.

PROFILE

Louis Armstrong

Louis Armstrong
American Jazz Trumpeter and
Entertainer
1901–1971

Born in New Orleans, virtuoso Louis Armstrong was introduced to the bugle and cornet at the age of 14. His extraordinary talent became his ticket from poverty to riches.

After performing in bands in New Orleans and Chicago, Armstrong moved to New York City to join the Fletcher Henderson Band, the best African-American orchestra of the time. Armstrong then returned to Chicago to lead his own bands, the Hot Five and later the Hot Seven. During this period he switched from cornet to trumpet and was largely responsible for shifting jazz from a group art form toward a more individual form. Armstrong's sensational solos extended the high range of his instrument and set a new jazz performance standard. After recording such classics as "Potato Head Blues" and "Hotter Than That" in the 1920s, he went on to lead big bands in the 1930s and 1940s.

Aside from his trumpet innovations, he also invented scat, or meaningless, improvised singing. Armstrong's raspy but tender voice can be heard on many recordings, including "Heebie Jeebies" and "Hello, Dolly!" Audiences loved his sense of humor and his gentleness. He was the first to learn to swing, and the world followed in his footsteps.

Although there have been musical virtuosos throughout history, the nineteenth century spawned a spectacular number, and they are inevitably interesting people. The violin virtuoso Niccolò Paganini (1782–1840), for example, was so gaunt and frightening in appearance that it was rumored that he had made a pact with the devil. How else could he play so brilliantly? And he played the viola just as well as the violin! Paganini wrote showpieces for the violin, some of them only to demonstrate that he could play anything, even just on the G string.

Franz Liszt (1811–1886) was a Hungarian pianist and composer. Like Mozart, he was a **child prodigy**, *someone who excels at a very early age*, who composed and concertized at a surprisingly young age. By the time he was 12 he was dazzling audiences in Continental

After one of Niccolò Paganini's performances in Italy in 1810, an awestruck critic wrote: "It fairly took one's breath away. In a sense, he is without question the foremost and greatest violinist in the world." Rumors at that time held that Paganini learned all his technical feats while he was in prison. Such fabrications sold many tickets.

Europe and in England. At 16, upon the death of his father, he had to fend for himself in Paris. Fortunately, he was able to make a livelihood teaching piano and concertizing. Just as Paganini had composed virtuoso works for the violin, Liszt wrote fiendishly difficult works for the piano—works that no one else at that time could play. He even transcribed some of Paganini's difficult works so that he could show off his own technical fireworks.

The Challenge of Music

Music can be difficult to perform. It can require an extraordinary technical facility on the part of the performer, as well as sheer physical stamina. Rock musicians who perform an entire two-hour concert expend enormous physical and mental energy. Musicians have to be alert and totally immersed in their performance. This takes a high degree of concentration. All of their resources of technical ability and expressiveness—their musicianship—must come into play.

Music & ART

Nineteenth-century musicians often performed for one another in salons. Here Franz Liszt plays the piano as his friends listen. From left to right are Alexandre Dumas, Victor Hugo, George Sand, Niccolò Paganini, Giocchino Rossini, and Mademoiselle d'Agoult. In the background are a bust of Beethoven and a portrait of Lord Byron.

Joseph Danhauser. *Franz Liszt and His Friends.* 1840. Historisches Museum der Stadt Wien. Vienna, Austria.

Technique is *the ability to perform the music with the correct notes, played (or sung) in tune and in proper rhythm.* This can pose considerable difficulties to the performer. Occasionally a composer will indicate that a piece of music must be played at a tempo so rapid that average performers cannot play the notes that quickly without mistakes. Sometimes, for example, Liszt's works call for the pianist to make difficult leaps at high speed, a feat that involves considerable risk of striking the wrong key.

ACTIVITY ▶ *Figure Out*

What makes this music by Franz Liszt difficult?

Challenge yourself to play (or find someone in your class who can play) the relatively simple melody that is the basis for this work:

Then listen to and discuss Jorge Bolet's performance of Franz Liszt's piano transcription of Paganini's variations on *La Campanella*:

1. **Count:** How many times is the melody repeated?
2. **Describe:** What does Liszt do to this melody each time it returns?
3. **Conclude:** Why might this piece be a challenge to performers?

MIDI TECHNOLOGY OPTION

■ **Music with MIDI** Use a MIDI program to compose and sequence a theme and variations for the piano. As a challenge, you can make each variation increasingly difficult until it sounds "impossible" for a live performer to play.

Activity *Figure Out*
Instructor's Guide, pages 103–104
TRB 7-1, *La Campanella*
TRB 7-2, Profile—Franz Liszt
CD 4 ⟨17⟩ *La Campanella* (5:04)

Technology Option
Use Project 7 in the *MIDI Activities* binder.

Mastering technique means that performers conquer the problems of their particular instrument or voice. A piano poses one set of difficulties, a trumpet another, an electronic instrument yet another. A melody of wide leaps, for example, can be difficult to sing but relatively easy to play on a piano or mallet percussion. Fast runs may be fairly simple to play on a violin or flute but extremely difficult on a double bass. A **double bass** is *the largest instrument in the bowed, stringed family.* Moving from pitch to pitch on the long strings of the bass requires a fairly wide and awkward reach between the fingers of the left hand.

Activity Listen
Instructor's Guide, page 104
CD 4 [18] "Caprice" (1:06)

ACTIVITY ▶ *Recognize Virtuosity*

Try to recognize virtuosity when you hear it.

Gary Karr, the well-known American double-bass virtuoso, has transformed the technique on this instrument, managing to play this instrument as no one has before.

Listen to his performance of Edouard Nanny's "Caprice." Working in small groups, discuss the following questions:

1. Is this the timbre you expected from a double bass?
2. Is the double bass capable of musical expression?
3. Can the double bass be played as a solo instrument?

For the musician, playing all the notes correctly and in the proper tempo is just the beginning. Technique itself can be cold and expressionless. The performer must capture the spirit of the work and communicate it.

Musical expression is *the feeling the performer brings to the sound.* It is what lies beyond the notes on the page. It is the tasteful combination of tempo, dynamics, tonal shading, phrasing, and musical sense and style that the performer uses to transform notes into sounds that command and stir us. Without musical expression, music would lack the warmth of human emotion. This incredibly important dimension is the performer's creative contribution.

Activity *Experience an Expressive Melody*
Instructor's Guide, pages 104–105
CD 4 [19] "Deep River" (1:46)

ACTIVITY ▶ *Experience an Expressive Melody*

Listen to Gary Karr perform the spiritual "Deep River" on the double bass. Discuss how he conveys its expressiveness.

1. How does he make his instrument expressive?
2. Does Karr do more than simply play the right notes and rhythms?

Virtuoso musician Gary Karr (b. 1941) was born into a family of double bassists who for many generations have chosen this instrument. In high school he played in professional community orchestras, sometimes seven different ones each week. Now he performs in symphony orchestras worldwide.

Quality Performance

While outside factors can affect your judgment, a musical performance must be judged on its own merits. Being able to judge musical performance depends on a number of factors:

Criteria for Judging Musical Quality

Timbre. The tone quality or timbre, range, variety, appropriateness, and appeal.

Expressiveness. The interpretation, style, and phrasing.

Technique. The performer's skills in bringing the notes to life.

Presentation. The choice and appropriateness of the music, and whether the performance meets your expectations.

Impact. The artist's charisma, the familiarity or newness of what you hear, and, perhaps, how the performance compares with similar performances you have heard.

ACTIVITY ▶ *Critique a Performance*

What qualities make a performance really fine?

You will hear three guitarists who are considered to be virtuosos. (Their names will be revealed later.) Their performances illustrate three types of guitars, as well as the wide spectrum of musical styles the guitar is uniquely able to express:

1. Classical (6-string Spanish guitar).
2. Folk/Jazz Crossover (12-string acoustic guitar).
3. Heavy Metal Rock (6-string electric guitar).

While you are listening to these performances, analyze their quality using the Judging Quality Grid provided by your teacher. Determine why these guitarists are regarded as virtuosos.

Being outstanding in any human endeavor is a rare achievement that happens in all races and in all countries. Recognizing musical greatness when you hear it requires musical knowledge and the ability to discern quality.

Activity *Critique a Performance*
Instructor's Guide, page 105
TRB 7-3, *Judging Quality*
CD 4 [20] "Danza Española No. 5 in E Minor" (4:08)
CD 4 [21] "Agile N" (1:48)
CD 4 [22] "Ice Nine" (3:29)

You may wish to use "Comparing Critiques" at this time. Lesson plans are found on page 106 in the Instructor's Guide.

Some performers simply play better than others. No matter what type of music people play, doing it well requires extraordinary effort and ability. Rock performers work very hard at what they do. Eddie Van Halen is an example of a rock musician who has strived for greatness.

Music & ART

Like musicians, artists exhibit virtuosity. A Woman Dancer, *a woodblock print, demonstrates the use of clear and precise lines to capture the grace of the dancer. This technical brilliance is comparable to a musician who can improvise with a seemingly flawless flow of expression.* **In both cases, how are these artists masters of their field?**

Torii Kiyonobu. *A Woman Dancer*. c. 1708. The Metropolitan Museum of Art. Harris Brisbane Dick Fund, 1949. (JP 3098)

Music & Art
They combine talent, technique, and interpretation to create masterpieces of music and art.

SUMMARY

What makes a musical performance great? The more we know about music, the better we will be able to answer this question. We know that a quality performance depends on a performer's timbre, technique, and expressiveness. Does the performer make sense out of the music? Does the performance command our interest and move us? Behind every great musical performance there is the force of a human personality and charisma. Ultimately, it is the humanity that is expressed that reaches out to captivate, enchant, and spellbind us. The performer's personality is one of the intangibles that makes music so fascinating, so surprising, so intriguing, so mystifying. A great performance can be analyzed and explained up to a point; then there is that extra something that can touch us, but we know not why.

Complete answers for the Chapter 7 Review are found in the Instructor's Guide, pages 106–107.

Building Music Vocabulary

On a sheet of paper, write the term from the list that best matches each description below.

(5) child prodigy   (4) technique
(3) double bass   (2) virtuoso
(1) musical expression

1. The feeling a performer brings to music.
2. A performer with brilliant, flawless technique.
3. The largest instrument in the bowed, stringed family.
4. The ability to perform an instrument or sing music in tune and in proper rhythm.
5. Someone who excels at a very early age.

Reviewing Music Facts

Answer each question in a complete sentence.

6. On which instrument was Paganini a virtuoso?
7. What were some of Liszt's musical accomplishments?
8. What aspect of their childhoods did Liszt and Mozart have in common?
9. What musical accomplishments did Liszt and Paganini have in common?
10. What are some characteristics of the double bass that make it difficult to play?
11. What is another term for "tone quality"?
12. Name five factors that help a listener judge a performance.

Thinking It Through

On a sheet of paper, write your responses to the following:

13. **Compare** In what sense are the mental and physical tasks required of a sports star and a virtuoso musician similar?
14. **Explain** How do we know, without recordings to listen to, that Paganini was a great virtuoso artist?
15. **Explain** Describe some of the nonmusical aspects that can influence a listener's judgment of a performance.
16. **Apply** Choose a recording you like and describe how the expressive quality affects your response to the performance.

Making the Connection

Language Arts Imagine that you have attended a concert by Paganini or Liszt. Write a review of the "concert," describing the performance, including your own and the audience's response.

Physical Education Find out more about how a star athlete prepares for a big game and how a virtuoso musician prepares for a concert. Use what you have learned to draw parallels between them.

 Find out more about classical virtuosos such as Liszt and Paganini as well as rock and roll musicians in the Hall of Fame at **www.glencoe.com/sec/music**

Answers to Chapter 7 Review

6. The violin (also the viola).
7. Lizst was a child prodigy; he could read any music on sight; he could memorize immediately; he composed, transcribed, and played very difficult music.
8. Both were child prodigies.
9. Both were virtuoso performers and accomplished composers.
10. It requires wide, awkward reaches and rapid physical movement to play the long strings.
11. Timbre.
12. Timbre, expressiveness, technique, presentation, and impact.

13. Both require innate talent, long hours of practice, and physical stamina in performance.
14. He wrote extremely difficult music for his instrument, and he was able to perform it successfully. Written accounts from his time describe his skill.
15. The setting, companions, and feelings for the performer.
16. Students should choose recordings that "move" and affect them and describe their responses in terms of such qualities as interpretation, style, and phrasing.

CHAPTER 8

Alone and Together

Music can be a solitary act—a person playing a guitar or shakuhachi or singing alone unaccompanied. You have probably whistled, hummed, sung, or even played an instrument by yourself, when you had the privacy to express yourself musically without feeling the pressure to perform or having the fear of being criticized. During these private moments, music becomes a means of personal expression. We speak through it, and it speaks back to us in a very intimate way. We can lose ourselves in its magic.

Objectives

By completing the chapter, you will:
- Find out how people make music alone and together.
- Discover Native American flute music.
- Learn to recognize and describe basic textures of music.
- Be able to describe the characteristics of the concerto.
- Understand the problem of coordination and describe how it is solved.
- Learn how to conduct in meters of 2, 3, and 4.

Vocabulary

call and response
canon
conductor
counterpoint
homophonic texture
imitation
monophony
neumes
polychoral music
polyphony
solmization
texture

Musician to Meet

Giovanni Gabrieli

Performing music is an expressive act. Sometimes we might perform music alone as a way to get in touch with our feelings. At other times, we perform with others to achieve a social expression. **Do you favor performing music alone or together?**

Caption answer
Although responses will vary, encourage students to understand that each situation has personal and social value.

Music as Solo Expression

Throughout the ages and in all cultures, people have been compelled to make music by themselves. We have a need to express ourselves, to get in touch with our inner feelings and spirit. In this sense, making music is similar to writing a poem, making a sketch, or dancing alone.

People enjoy expressing themselves in solo musical performance. The sound of a single voice or instrument can be haunting in its beauty. There is an intensity about focusing on one timbre and one pitch at a time.

Activity *Music as Solo Expression*
Instructor's Guide, page 108
TRB 8-1, *"Oh, Danny Boy"*
CD 4 [25] "Oh, Danny Boy" (3:08)
CD 4 [26] "Londonderry Air" (4:20)

ACTIVITY ▶ *Identify Expressive Qualities*

How do performers make a folk song expressive?

Listen to two versions of "Oh, Danny Boy." The first version is sung by a professional tenor from England. A choir sings the second version. Which version do you think is more expressive? Why?

Our emotional reaction to music is largely based on the expressive qualities of a performance, whether it be solo or ensemble, vocal or instrumental. Members of this bell choir work together to convey the spirit of the music they perform. **Can you identify a choral performance that has moved you?**

Caption answer
Responses will vary.

Activity *Describe the Sounds*
Instructor's Guide, page 109
CD 4 ⟦27⟧ "Hifumi hachigaeshi"
         (2:24)
CD 4 ⟦28⟧ "Maeng poo dawn dawk"
         (1:11)

Music & **CULTURE**

Both solo and group performances are common in most cultures. Here a musician plays a Laotian kaen. Instruments of this kind were first described in China about 3,000 years ago. **What instrument does it resemble?**

Music & Culture
Most students will identify the harmonica or mouth organ.

ACTIVITY ▶ *Describe the Sounds*

Listen to the following solo instrumental performances.

1. The first is a performance of the Japanese *shakuhachi* (sha-ku-HAH-chee), a vertical bamboo flute with five holes.
2. The second is a performance of the *kaen* (can), an instrument used in Thailand and Laos that is a cousin of the harmonica. Constructed of wood and bamboo, it has as many as 16 bamboo tubes, each with a small brass reed enabling more than one tone to be sounded at the same time.

Now try the following:

■ Categorize each instrument (i.e., idiophone, aerophone, etc.)
■ What words describe the sound or timbre of each instrument?

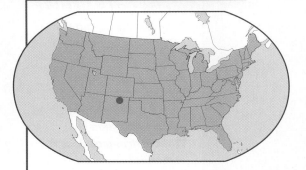

TAOS, NEW MEXICO, is in an area of the southwestern United States that is home to the Pueblo Indians. Much of Pueblo life, including many songs and dances, centers on agriculture. The flute is a common solo instrument and is made of various woods, cane, and animal bones.

Native American Flute Music

The flute is the one melodic instrument widely used by Native Americans, and it is always played as a solo instrument. Native Americans use a large variety of flutes of different sizes, shapes, and materials. Most are end-blown with three to six finger holes to vary the pitch. The flutes are made of various woods, cane, and animal bones.

According to Native American legends, the flute was given to the Indian people by the Creator for enjoyment, easing loneliness, and other important purposes. Some tribes used the flute as a courting instrument. Other tribes used the flute for quiet, introspective moments.

During the late nineteenth and early twentieth centuries, Native American flute playing nearly became extinct, along with other rich cultural expressions—language, music, dance, art, and knowledge of herbal medicine. Fortunately, many tribes were able to cling to their culture. Today, there is a resurgence of interest among young Native Americans in preserving tribal traditions.

Music & CULTURE

Flutist John Rainer, Jr., is a member of the Taos Pueblo in New Mexico. His playing, like that of many contemporary Native American flutists, has a lyrical and expressive quality. He enriches the melody with ornaments that suggest bird calls and echoes in deep canyons.

ACTIVITY ▶ *Visualize the Melody*

Activity *Visualize the Melody*
Instructor's Guide, pages 109–110
CD 5 ☐1 "Northern Plains" (3:35)

Listen to John Rainer, Jr., play the traditional Native American song "Northern Plains." Visualize the contour of the melody.

This traditional song is normally sung by Native American performing groups at pow wows. It is an exciting and energetic song and dance, which is adapted for the flute in this recording.

The melody consists of four phrases—A, B, and C—that correspond to the breaths the performer takes (C takes two breaths). Listen to each phrase and try to visualize its contour based on the highness or lowness of the pitches in the melody. Pick out the appropriate general contour for each phrase: (1) descending (moving downward), (2) ascending (moving upward), or (3) level. (Hint: Two answers are correct for phrase C.)

On a sheet of paper, draw a line graph to represent the contour of each phrase. Note that the starting pitch of each successive phrase is lower than the previous one.

TECHNOLOGY OPTION

Technology Option
Use Project 8 in the *MIDI Activities* binder.

■ **Music with MIDI** Use a MIDI program to explore the visual and aural contours of melodies, and to "see" how different phrases of a melody can be related in contour.

Music as Social Expression

Another important function of music is its use as a form of group expression and social communication. Performing music with other people has its own special satisfactions and rewards. People generally enjoy working together toward a goal that cannot be achieved alone. If the goal is to enrich the texture of the music, other people are usually needed.

Organizing people to function together in a cooperative and orderly manner is not always easy. Perhaps the most obvious solution is to have everyone sing the same melody together monophonically, that is, in unison with everyone sounding the same note or octave at the same time.

Another way people make music together is by combining solo and choral response. **Call and response** is *a question-and-answer pattern in which a group responds to a leader.* It is part of the oral tradition—the way music was passed along from person to person and from one generation to the next. Crews on board old sailing ships had leaders who called out the verses while the others sang the repeated response.

The leader must know the changing lyrics and be able to sing the more complex melody that sometimes goes with them. The group usually has a simple response that is repeated each time. This way, the group has the part that can be learned rapidly and is easy to remember, enabling them to join in quickly and participate with confidence. The call-and-response form of coordination is found frequently in spirituals and gospel music and is audible in music from Africa and from other cultures. Its influence today can be heard in jazz, blues, rock, rap, folk songs, and backup vocal responses.

Activity *Call and Response*
Instructor's Guide, page 111
CD 5 [2] "Oh Happy Day" (5:07)

ACTIVITY ▶ *Call and Response*

Can you identify patterns in a call-and-response song?

Listen to "Oh Happy Day," a call-and-response gospel song that was made famous in the early 1970s by the Edwin Hawkins Singers. As you listen to the song, learn the lyrics and try to anticipate the responses in answer to Hawkins's call. Then answer these questions:

1. How many responses did you hear in the first chorus?
2. Are all the responses exact repetitions of the call? If not, where did the divergence occur?
3. Does the verse use call and response?

Homophonic Texture

Musical **texture** refers to *how sounds are woven together*. Like fabric, music can be almost transparent, or relatively dense. Generally, the more parts in the music, the more complex and dense the texture.

We can think of music horizontally with different melodies sounding together at the same time, or we can think of music vertically with clumps of notes (chords) accompanying one melody. **Homophonic texture** is *a musical texture in which a single melodic line is supported by a chordal accompaniment* (*homophonic* means "same" or "similar" sounding). "Oh Happy Day" is homophonic in texture; one melody predominates, and the voices join together to give that melody a chordal accompaniment.

During the seventeenth century, composers studied the vertical aspects of music closely and discovered certain combinations of notes on each tone of the scale that sounded well together. They called them triads. By using these triads, or chords, to accompany a melody, composers further developed homophonic texture.

Triads in the scale of C major:

This triadic chordal system gave composers a whole new range of harmonic expression that is still being explored today.

Homophonic or chordal music can be performed on keyboard instruments by solo performers. Usually, a pianist or an organist plays the melody with the right hand and the chordal accompaniment with the left hand, or a guitarist will play the chords by picking and strumming while singing the melody.

The Concerto

Another way to contrast solo and group performance is in a musical form known as the concerto. In a concerto, a soloist, or a solo group of instrumentalists, is set off against the larger orchestra. Sometimes the orchestra accompanies the soloist; sometimes the soloist plays along with the orchestra; sometimes they play individually. Sometimes they are friends, sometimes rivals, which sets up a tension that can be exciting to see resolved. There are usually three movements in a concerto, so there is ample time to explore the various contrasting textures and timbres.

Activity *Map the Forces*
Instructor's Guide, pages 111–112
TRB 8-2, *Listening Map*
CD 5 ③ Horn Concerto No. 3
       (6:56)

Caption answer
Students will likely identify the musical energy that is generated between the soloist and orchestra.

The concerto provides the opportunity for both solo and group performances. Sometimes the soloist accompanies the orchestra, and sometimes the orchestra accompanies the soloist. At other times they will play individually. **How does this interplay create interest in a performance?**

ACTIVITY ▶ *Map the Forces*

Can you identify the different musical forces as they perform Mozart's Horn Concerto No. 3?

As you listen, complete the music map showing the relationship between the horn soloist and the orchestra. Sometimes each plays alone; sometimes they play together. Categorize the relationship using the following codes:

A = orchestra alone
B = French horn solo with orchestral accompaniment
C = cadenza, a French horn solo without accompaniment

After you have completed your map, answer these questions:

1. Are all of the sections of equal length?
2. Can you detect any repetition?
3. Which sections (by number) seem to create the most intensity and drive?
4. Which section was the most unique?
5. What is the basic pattern of the first movement of this concerto?

The Problem of Coordination

People were not always able to combine different timbres to make music as interesting or as expressive as it is today. During the early Middle Ages, people had not yet developed a way to coordinate different instruments and melodies. Their music was monophonic (*mono* means "one," *phonic* means "sounds"). Strictly speaking, **monophony** consisted of *a single melodic line without accompaniment.* The underlying rhythmic meter in Western music had not been defined. Without it, performers found it difficult to stay together, even when everyone was singing or playing one melody!

Nonetheless, medieval composers were determined to find a way to combine different sounds to broaden the range of musical expression. Since singing and playing together required a way to coordinate the performers, the simplest kind of organization—everyone singing the same tune—was tried first. You can still hear this effect in Gregorian chants. Then composers became more adventurous. They tried having one part of the group sing the same melody at the interval of a 4th above. This early attempt at creating harmony was known as parallel organum.

To help his choristers learn to sing more easily, Guido of Arezzo (c. 991–1033), an Italian Benedictine monk and music theorist, devised a system of **solmization**, *a method of sight-singing by syllables.* This method forms the basis of the Western DO-RE-MI system of solfège or sight-singing. In order to help his choristers remember the various tones of the scale when singing plainsong, Guido used the well-known "Hymn to St. John the Baptist" as a memory aid. Since the melody of each phrase of the hymn begins one tone higher than the previous phrase, the corresponding six tones (represented by the syllables UT, RE, ME, FA, SOL, LA) could be extracted from the hymn and applied to the tones of the scale:

UT   RE   MI   FA   SOL   LA

Music & HISTORY

During the Middle Ages, Western music was mono-phonic, consisting of a single line of melody. The notes on this decorative page of music show a melody line combined with the text below it. **What style of music is most often associated with monophony?**

Music & History
Gregorian chant.

Guido of Arezzo found that by associating these syllables with the scale degrees, people were able to read music. Eventually UT was changed to DO and a seventh tone (SI or RI) was added to create our seven-tone major or diatonic scale. This method of sight-singing, solmization, was used in monasteries throughout the Middle Ages. It continues to be one of the basic skills taught to musicians.

Activity *Go Back in Time*
Instructor's Guide, page 112
CD 5 [4] "Hymn to St. John the Baptist" (0:36)

You may wish to use "Perform a Gregorian Chant" at this time. Lesson plans are found on page 115 in the Instructor's Guide.

ACTIVITY ▶ *Go Back in Time*

Given the absence of a formal rhythmic structure, how did medieval choirs solve the problem of coordination?

Learn to perform the Gregorian chant (or plainsong) "Hymn to St. John the Baptist."

1. Say the words of the Latin text until the stresses fall naturally.
2. Play the pitches of the lower line of the hymn while saying the words. Note that the syllable UT begins on C; RE of "Resonare" begins on D, and so on, forming the basis of Guido's solmization. Let the flow of notes follow the flow of the text. Gradually start to sing the words, but resist feeling any steady pulse.
3. Perform together as a class, remembering to stress the first syllable of each line of text as you feel it and sense it together.

Hymn to St. John the Baptist

c. 1000
in parallel organum

The chants used in the church services during the early Middle Ages had to be learned by rote. Committing them to memory was a long and arduous process. Sometime during the sixth to the eighth centuries a method of notation was invented that placed **neumes** (*neume* is the Greek word for "sign"), or *marks over the words*. These markings showed the direction of the melodic line.

The neumes were eventually placed above and below a line that signified a definite pitch. This line provided singers with a general idea of how the pitches related to one another. From this one-line beginning, a four-line staff was developed and, finally, the five-line staff that is still used today. By assigning individual lines and spaces to specific pitches, singers were able to sing unfamiliar melodies from a musical score.

Polyphonic Texture

The capacity to notate music and give it a rhythmic structure led to the development of polyphony in the twelfth century. **Polyphony** is *the simultaneous combination of different melodies and rhythms.* Literally, it means "many sounds." Now voices sang more than one melody at the same time and even entered at different times.

By the fourteenth century, European composers began to relate the various vocal parts by having them exchange melodies or parts of

Music & Art
The choir is on the left in white robes; the instrumentalists are in the center in red robes.

Music & Art

The Italian painter Gentile Bellini (1429–1507) painted contemporary life in Venice during the Renaissance. In his Procession in St. Mark's Square, *the Basilica of St. Mark dominates the background.* **Can you locate a choir and a band of instrumentalists in the painting?**

Gentile Bellini. *Procession in St. Mark's Square.* 1496. Academy, Venice, Italy.

melodies. The use of **imitation**, *exact repetition or resemblance between the parts*, helped to organize the piece by giving it a sense of consistency and order. One of the most remarkable and ingenious examples of this device of having the different parts share the same melody can be heard in a round or **canon**, *a musical form that uses exact imitation.* You may have sung the rounds "Three Blind Mice" or "Row, Row, Row Your Boat."

By the sixteenth century, composers were creating polyphonic music by using **counterpoint**, *a system of countering one note or point against another.* Different melodies were cleverly interwoven to create a uniform texture. Imitation and counterpoint today appear in various guises in all kinds of music. Arrangements of pop music, for example, often incorporate imitation; a melody played by one instrument is taken up later by another.

In the sixteenth and seventeenth centuries, composers throughout Europe and England were writing polyphonic music that was highly expressive and complex. One result of being able to coordinate multiple parts is the elaborate textures that became possible when more than one choir or instrumental group performed together. For example, at the Byzantine Basilica of St. Mark in Venice, Giovanni Gabrieli composed **polychoral music**, *music for several choirs singing in answer to each other.* Substituting instruments for voices, Gabrieli composed music for alternating choirs of brass instruments.

Giovanni Gabrieli
Italian Composer
c.1553–1612

PROFILE

Giovanni Gabrieli

Giovanni Gabrieli (c. 1553–1612) was an influential figure in the transition of European music from the Renaissance style to the Baroque style in the late sixteenth and early seventeenth centuries. He was among the first to create vocal works with instrumental accompaniment and to specify dynamics, or loud and soft markings in his scores. He became known for his imaginative polychoral style in which two or more groups of soloists, choirs, or instrumental ensembles performed in alternating (and often overlapping) dialogue. Many of his large-scale works are published in the multiple volumes of his *Sacrae symphoniae.*

ACTIVITY *Visit Venice Around 1600!*

Listen to *Canzon in Double Echo* by the Italian Renaissance composer Giovanni Gabrieli as it might have sounded in 1600.

This work is performed by three brass quintets—15 instruments in all. Each choir consists of two trumpets, a French horn, a trombone, and a tuba. Try to hear how the second and third choirs echo the first.

1. How does Gabrieli's interweaving of many parts create an expressive musical texture?
2. How does Gabrieli achieve contrast?
3. Why is a steady pulse so important in this music?

Activity *Visit Venice Around 1600!*
Instructor's Guide, pages 112–113
TRB 8-3, *Canzon in Double Echo*
CD 5 ⑤ *Canzon in Double Echo*
(3:33)

While European composers during the Renaissance created much new and beautiful music, people in other parts of the world were also busy making music. The basic idea of polyphony, that blending of musical lines moving together with rhythmic independence, is characteristic of some African music. Polyphony therefore could have been practiced in Africa as early as it was in Europe, or even earlier. Obviously, people wanted to combine sounds to form more interesting and more expressive textures, and they found their own ways of doing so.

Activity *Discover Polyphonic Texture*
Instructor's Guide, page 113
CD 5 ⑥ "Music for Entertainment"
(1:57)

ACTIVITY ▶ *Discover Polyphonic Texture*

Can you identify the sources of sound in this African polyphony?

The Ba-Benzele people of the Central African Republic (see map) in the equatorial region of West Africa sing this music to accompany a dance in which both men and women participate. Try to hear the principal melody that uses only three pitches, and listen for a variety of other melodies that are sung at the same time. Try to hear the different rhythms of the melodies. As you listen, answer the following questions:

1. How many different sound sources are there? What are they?
2. Approximately how many singers are performing?
3. How do you suppose the singers learned this music? When they perform this piece, do you think it always sounds exactly the same?
4. What makes this music polyphonic?

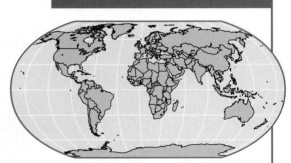

MUSIC in the WORLD

CENTRAL AFRICAN REPUBLIC is home to the Ba-Benzele people, who live in the densely forested areas. Because they historically are a nomadic people, they carried few instruments and developed a mainly vocal music. Like the forests of their home, their music is densely textured.

Conducting

Around the time of Ludwig van Beethoven (1710–1827), when orchestras began to grow in size, it became essential to have someone in front of the musicians to keep them together. This person became known as the **conductor**, *the director of an orchestra, choir, or other performing group.* Conductors do more than just beat time. In addition to maintaining the beat with a baton, conductors interpret the music as it unfolds. They make important musical decisions regarding such expressive matters as tempo, dynamics, spirit, and phrasing. Conductors give visual clues to the performers to help them play as one force and make a unified statement. These gestures often help the audience understand and feel the music as well.

Conductors are the musical leaders of their group. Their instrument is a chorus or an orchestra. They determine the programming, select the music, and rehearse the performers in the repertoire so that there is agreement about how the various works are to be performed. Conductors inspire the group to perform at their highest level and with appropriate feeling. They must exercise sufficient authority and leadership ability to pull all the musicians together and make them perform as one. This means conductors have to know the music very well. The conductor is the key to effective musical communication.

Asian-born Apo Hsu, conductor of the Women's Philharmonic of San Francisco, picked up her first conducting baton in the ninth grade. Now, she brings variety and balance to the symphony's performances with a mix of classical pieces and rediscovered ones. **How do conductors help the audience understand and feel music?**

Caption answer
Through their gestures.

Conducting requires technique and a superb sense of rhythm. Conductors indicate the meter of the music by beating a pattern that shows the number of beats in a measure and the tempo or speed of those beats. The first beat of each measure (on the count of one) is always straight down—the strongest motion the arm can make. Conductors follow this downbeat with patterns for the other beats (2, 3, 4 or more) ending with an upbeat that prepares them again for the downbeat of one. The patterns are not difficult to learn. The real skill is to beat these patterns and interpret the music at the same time!

ACTIVITY ▶ *Learn to Conduct*

Activity Learn to Conduct
Instructor's Guide, pages 114–115
CD 5 [8] *William Tell* Overture (1:00)
CD 5 [9] *Emperor Waltz* (1:18)
CD 5 [10] "March Past of the Kitchen Utensils," (1:00)
CD 5 [11] "Power in the Blood (1:02)
CD 5 [12] Symphony No. 7, Op. 92 second movement (1:02)
CD 5 [13] Symphony No. 1 in D, second movement (1:01)
CD 5 [14] Symphony No. 88, third movement (1:02)
CD 5 [15] Prelude, *Carmen*, Act 1 (1:01)

Can you conduct the music of great composers?

Follow the diagrams and practice beating these patterns:

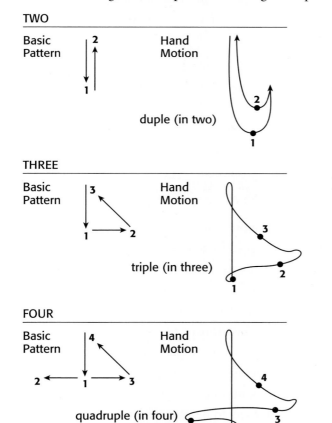

These musical works are in duple, triple, and quadruple meter. Listen to each example, identify the meter, then conduct it.

PROFILE

Arturo Toscanini

Arturo Toscanini began his formal musical studies at the age of nine when he enrolled in the Royal Conservatory of Music in his hometown of Parma, Italy. When he left the conservatory at 18, he joined a traveling opera company. One evening while on tour in Rio de Janeiro, he left the cello section to conduct from memory Verdi's opera *Aïda,* a feat that caused a sensation and launched his conducting career.

Toscanini challenged the popular Romantic conducting style of the era by performing works as literally as possible. Instead of expressing his own ideas and emotions through a work, Toscanini attempted to convey the spirit of the composer. He remained true to his idealistic vision of music throughout his 70-year career. Toscanini also conducted and directed at the Metropolitan Opera and conducted the New York Philharmonic and the NBC (National Broadcasting Company) Symphony.

Toscanini's success greatly influenced the direction of European music in the 1900s. No longer were conductors expected to create flamboyant arrangements. When Toscanini conducted the music of Debussy or Wagner, it was straightforward and structurally precise.

Arturo Toscanini
Italian-American Conductor
1867–1957

SUMMARY

People perform music alone and in groups. A single voice or instrument can be highly expressive and moving. Sometimes a soloist will perform with a group, creating contrast and tension that is dramatic and exciting. The call-and-response form of singing is common in Africa and in the gospel music of African Americans. The concerto usually features the interplay between a solo instrument and a group of instruments. Combining a variety of sounds adds impact to our musical expression.

Learning how to coordinate a musical group took a considerable amount of ingenuity. It took hundreds of years and the inventiveness of many musicians and composers to develop a system of musical notation, the concept of an underlying meter, and a means of sight-singing. Homophonic and polyphonic textures represent two expressive ways we have learned to put sounds together. Today, the conductor plays a major role in this coordination process, helping people perform together with ease and inspiration.

Building Music Vocabulary

On a sheet of paper, write the term from the list that best matches each description below.

(4) call and response
(12) canon
(1) conductor
(7) counterpoint
(11) homophonic texture
(10) imitation
(2) monophony
(6) neumes
(5) polychoral music
(8) polyphony
(9) solmization
(3) texture

1. The director of an orchestra, choir, or other performing group.
2. A single melodic line with no accompaniment.
3. The way sounds are woven together.
4. A question-and-answer pattern in which a group responds to a leader.
5. Music for several groups performing in answer to each other.
6. Marks written over the words of a song.
7. Music that counters one note against another.
8. Simultaneous combination of different melodies and rhythms.
9. A method of sight-singing by syllables.
10. Exact repetition or resemblance between parts.
11. Musical texture in which a single melodic line is supported by chordal accompaniment.
12. A musical form using exact imitation.

Reviewing Music Facts

Answer each question in a complete sentence.

13. How did some Native Americans use the flute for courting?
14. What popular music styles use call-and-response form?
15. What is a musical triad?
16. What is the origin of the DO-RE-MI syllables?
17. What kind of music was Giovanni Gabrieli famous for?

Answers to Chapter 8 Review
13. A man might play the flute outside the home of a woman he was courting.
14. Spirituals, gospel, jazz, blues, rock, rap, and folk songs.

Complete answers for the Chapter 8 Review are found in the Instructor's Guide, pages 115–116.

Thinking It Through

On a sheet of paper, write your responses to the following:

18. **Contrast** Describe how a performer might feel when performing alone as compared to performing in a group situation.
19. **Analyze** How does a concerto reflect human interactions?
20. **Explain** In your own words, explain how a conductor coordinates the performance of a group of musicians.

Making the Connection

Social Studies Find more examples of how Native Americans use music in their lives. Compare what you learn with the way you use music in your life.

Theatre Find out how the director of a play works with actors to create a performance. Using what you have learned, compare that process with the work of an orchestra conductor, describing similarities and differences.

 There is more to learn about the Native American flute and Gregorian chant at **www.glencoe.com/sec/music**

15. Chords or groups of notes sounding together.
16. The opening phrases of a hymn ("Hymn to St. John the Baptist").
17. Polychoral music, music for alternating choirs or brasses.
18. A solo performance provides the chance to express personal feelings and musical interpretation. Group performance requires cooperation and coordination, but it provides social communication and the excitement of being part of a group effort.
19. The dynamics between the solo performer and the group might be tense, friendly, or competitive.
20. By conducting patterns that are understood by everyone in the group; by giving visual clues and gestures that help unify the group.

You might also wish to use
Assessment Master 3,
Unit Three Test, in the TRB.

Chapter 5 Project

Chapter 5 Project
Instructor's Guide, page 117
CD 3 27 "Amazing Grace" (jazz)
(1:04)
CD 3 28 "Amazing Grace"
(gospel) (1:12)
CD 3 29 "Amazing Grace"
(classical) (1:09)
CD 3 30 "Amazing Grace" (pop)
(0:55)

 ### *Perform in an Appropriate Style*

Try to make your vocal style appropriate to the musical style.

Use the recordings played by your teacher as accompaniment while you sing the melody and words to "Amazing Grace" in the classical, jazz, gospel, and pop versions (see page 100 for one version). Use appropriate vocal style and inflection (changes in tone, dynamics, and modulation of the voice). Decide how the various versions should be interpreted to be consistent with their styles. Note the differences in the melody line and rhythm.

Extra credit: Set up a mini-recording lab with a tape recorder and microphone and record your voice singing in the style of one of the accompaniment versions of "Amazing Grace."

Listen to the tape recordings of members of the class. Using the musical descriptors you developed for each of the styles, decide which of the performances is most suitable and appropriate.

Chapter 6 Project
Instructor's Guide, pages 117–118

Chapter 6 Project

Write a Music Review

How clearly can you express your opinion about a recorded performance?

Here are some basic guidelines for writing your first music review:

1. Select a recording that you believe is particularly good or notably bad. Review the entire recording, describing the variety of music it contains. Highlight the compositions you feel are well performed.
2. Take a stance—either positive or negative. Make it clear to the reader where you stand and why.
3. Include some informed opinion and authority in your review.
4. Write a minimum of three paragraphs, but no more than two pages.

Chapter 7 Project

 Identify a Quality Performance

Can you distinguish a difference in quality when comparing performances?

In both pairs of performances you will hear, one of the performers is acclaimed to be a virtuoso; the other is not. Your job is to pick the virtuoso, regardless of whether you like the music or not. You probably will not know the names of the artists or the pieces they are performing. Judge both pairs of performances on the merits of their performance alone.

Comparison 1

Performer A: Recorded in a studio with synthesized sounds

Performer B: Recorded live with a jazz quartet

Comparison 2

Performer C: Lied (song) by Franz Schubert, recorded in German

Performer D: Lied (song) by Franz Schubert, recorded in German

Chapter 7 Project
Instructor's Guide, page 118
CD 5 16 "You Say" (2:12)
CD 5 17 "Scrapple from the Apple" (2:46)
CD 5 18 *The Erkling* (3:40)
CD 5 19 "Aufenhalt" (2:17)

Chapter 8 Project

Identify Music Textures

Listen to the musical excerpts and name the textures of these solo and group performances.

The musical examples you will hear are woven together in a number of basic ways:

A. monophonic
B. call and response
C. unison chant
D. homophonic
E. polyphonic
F. parallel organum
G. canonic
H. heterophonic

Identify the terms that best describe the music in each example.

Chapter 8 Project
Instructor's Guide, pages 119–120
TRB Unit 3 Evaluation, *Identify the Musical Textures*
CD 5 20 "Density 21.5" (0:51)
CD 5 21 "Alleluia, *Vidimus stellam*" (0:52)
CD 5 22 "African Singing Game" (0:48)
CD 5 23 "Little Fugue in G Minor" (0:53)
CD 5 24 "Parallel Organum" (0:34)
CD 5 25 "The Gambler" (0:57)
CD 5 26 "Fantasia à deux" (0:46)
CD 5 27 *Songs of a Wayfarer, No. 2* (0:51)
CD 5 28 *Ricercar on the 12th Tone* (0:49)
CD 5 29 Aria from Peking Opera (0:50)

Heterophonic texture occurs when performers sing or play the same melody simultaneously, but in different ways. (See Chapter 15, page 298.)

Musical Artistry in High Schools

Many high schools in America have a band and a choir. Some also have a jazz band, an orchestra, a glee club, or other types of small ensembles. Have you attended a performance by one of these groups? Are you or any of your friends involved in one as performers? Here is an opportunity to become familiar with the musical talents of your peers. You will also discover how the teenage years are a time when performing musicians develop from beginning skill levels to sophisticated heights.

Junior High or High School?
Instructor's Guide, pages 121–122
CD 18 8 "Hodie Christus Natus Est" arranged by Healey Willan (1:54)
CD 18 9 "Hodie Christus Natus Est" arranged by Healey Willan (1:29)
CD 18 10 "Colonel Bogey March" by K.J. Alford (1:53)
CD 18 11 "Colonel Bogey March" by K.J. Alford (2:22)

High School or Professional?
Instructor's Guide, page 122
TRB, *Judging Quality*
CD 18 12 "Allegro non troppo," fourth movement, Symphony No. 5 in D Minor, Opus 47 by Dmitri Shostakovich (3:46)

▶ *Junior High or High School?*

What would happen if a junior high school basketball team played the senior high school varsity? Would one team have an advantage over the other? Which one and why? There are similar disparities in the field of music. Try to tell the difference between junior high and high school performing groups. As you listen to each pair of examples, list words and phrases from your music vocabulary to help you make clear distinctions.

■ Listen to a junior high and high school choir singing "Hodie Christus Natus Est." Describe the main differences between the performances.

■ Next, compare a junior high and high school band. Both play "Colonel Bogey March" by K. J. Alford. However, the arrangements are different. Which is performed by a high school band? How do you know?

▶ *High School or Professional?*

Listen to this excerpt from the fourth movement of Symphony No. 5 in D Minor by Dmitri Shostakovich. Is it performed by a professional orchestra or by a high school group? Be prepared to explain your choice. Would you call this a virtuoso performance? Why or why not?

Unit Three *Encore!*

▶ *Evaluate Performances*

Listen to two high school band performances of "Dance" from John Barnes Chance's *Incantation and Dance*. Then determine which band performs at a higher level. What reasons would you cite for your decision?

▶ *Which Choir Would You Join?*

Which would you find easier to do—play or sing? The demands on vocalists are quite different than they are on instrumentalists. For example, rather than playing with just one or two performers on each part, choral musicians are often one of many performers who sing the soprano, alto, tenor, or bass parts. Also, some musicians feel that *singing* a solo can make one more nervous than *playing* an instrumental solo. Some people claim it's easy to sing in a choir. You be the judge.

- Analyze the quality of the performances of these two choirs and write a critique comparing the two groups.

- In which choir would you be most proud to be a member? Why?

▶ *Choose an Arrangement*

Many great pieces originally written for a large orchestra have been transcribed for the smaller concert band. Can you guess why? The difference is subtle, yet obvious.

Listen to these two high school performances of Leonard Bernstein's Overture to *Candide* played by an orchestra and a band.

- Which do you like best? Finish this sentence by writing your reasons: "I prefer the (band/orchestral) arrangement because. . ."

- Which sounds more professional? Explain your response.

▶ *What's Your Taste?*

Jazz, as you will learn in Chapter 24, has many forms. Both instruments and voices can perform as soloists, combos, or with big bands. If you like jazz, do you favor vocal or instrumental jazz? Listen to two recordings by high school jazz groups. Then discuss the following:

- If you had the choice, which of the recordings would you buy? Why?

Evaluate Performances
Instructor's Guide, page 123
CD 18 13 "Dance" from *Incantation and Dance* by John Barnes Chance (3:00)
CD 18 14 "Dance" from *Incantation and Dance* by John Barnes Chance (3:02)

Which Choir Would You Join?
Instructor's Guide, pages 123–124
CD 18 15 "Sound the Trumpet" by Henry Purcell (1:55)
CD 18 16 "Kyrie" by Wolfgang Amadeus Mozart (1:41)

Choose an Arrangement
Instructor's Guide, page 124
CD 18 17 Overture to *Candide* by Leonard Bernstein (4:24)
CD 18 18 Overture to *Candide* by Leonard Bernstein (4:14)

What's Your Taste?
Instructor's Guide, pages 124–125
CD 18 19 "Just the Way You Are" arranged by Kirby Shaw (2:29)
CD 18 20 "Cherokee" arranged by Frank Mantooth (3:52)

Music and dance enhance story-telling, as in *The Nutcracker,* a ballet based on E. T. A. Hoffman's delightful story, *The Nutcracker and the King of the Mice* (1851). Inspired by Tchaikovsky's musical score for the ballet, the Joffrey Ballet's production is an American expression of the Russian story, made more dramatic by elaborate costumes, sets, and props. Have you seen a performance of *The Nutcracker*? If so, what impressed you the most? Describe the mood captured here in the photo and compare it to your experience.

The Joffrey Ballet. *The Nutcracker,* "Waltz of the Flowers." Gerald Arpino, artistic director. Photo by Herbert Migdoll.

Music!...
To
Enhance
Expression

You may wish to use Fine Art Transparency 4, *Boy Playing the Flute,* in the TRB to introduce Unit Four.

. . . .

Chapter 9
The Power of Emotion

Chapter 10
The Beauty of Order

ART
SO U
RC
ARTSOURCE

Use Artsource® audio segment 1 in the Performing Arts Package to hear a retelling of *The Nutcracker* with musical excerpts.

The Power of Emotion

Music and the other arts play a special role in every society. They provide us contact with the intuitive, mysterious, and emotional realms of life that logic is hard-pressed to explain. In this way, music balances the part of us that is logical, rational, and factual with the part of us that is imaginative, sensitive, and spiritual.

Objectives

By completing the chapter, you will:
- Find out how music stirs our emotions.
- Discover that music, like language and mathematics, is a symbolic system of communication.
- Learn that you can respond to a wide range of music.
- Become familiar with the Balinese gamelan orchestra and the music of the *Barong Dance*.
- Become acquainted with German Romanticism and learn about the music of the Romantic period.

Vocabulary

a cappella
gamelan
libretto
music drama
Requiem Mass
Romantic period
symphony

Musicians to Meet

Ludwig van Beethoven
Wolfgang Amadeus Mozart

*The emotional impact of music lies in its performance, which results from the sounds created by humans. What we react to is as much from what musicians put into the music as from the music itself. This emotional power of music is a window into the world of human emotions. **Can you describe an experience when music affected you emotionally?***

Caption answer
Encourage students to share all types experiences, happy and sad. Remind them that music can provide a way to examine the entire range of emotions that they encounter.

What Music Expresses

Music is the way we give concrete representation to such inner mental states as love, grief, faith, hope, and a host of other feelings. Music is the way we get our feelings and intuitions outside ourselves in a form in which they can be expressed and communicated. Music permits us to capture, share, and even store perceptions about our feelings or emotions that might otherwise escape us. No art has more emotional impact than music, and none is harder to describe in words. What music conveys to us is largely indescribable. Like words, music is a symbolic system of communication completely different from any other. What words can do in music is help us share our insights about it.

Activity *Understand Musical Characteristics*
Instructor's Guide, pages 129–130
TRB 9-1, *Perceptive Listening*

ACTIVITY ▶ *Understand Musical Characteristics*

Determine why your favorite piece of music moves you.

List the internal and external qualities that move you in your favorite piece of music. Use the following questions to qualify your list:
1. What musical characteristics affect you?
2. What other factors influence you?
3. What aspects of the performance and the performers make you react to this music?

Music & ART

In most cultures, love is a common subject in both music and art. French painter Jean Watteau (1684–1721) painted the theatrical character Mezzetin, the lover who sang and played the guitar but was usually rejected. **How does Watteau capture the feeling of melancholy in this painting?**

Jean Antoine Watteau. *Mezzetin.* c.1718. The Metropolitan Museum of Art. New York, New York. Munsey Fund, 1934. 34.138.

Music & Art
Responses will probably focus on Mezzetin's solitude in the garden and his sad expression.

How Music Expresses Emotions

A symbol is something that stands for or represents another thing. We can describe an Egyptian pyramid in geometric terms and by giving its mathematical measurements. A photograph or painting of a pyramid might be equally revealing. Each of these forms of representation—mathematical and graphic—are symbolic. They are not the pyramid itself, but rather representations of it in another form that helps us grasp what it is.

Music is a symbolic system, too. Like numbers, scientific formulas, and words, music represents something else. Science can explain a sunrise; music expresses its emotive meaning. The earth turning on its axis every 24 hours is one part of the truth about a sunrise; the exhilaration we feel at the birth of a new day is another part of the meaning or truth of a sunrise. The arts and the sciences often describe different aspects of the same fact or event. That is why, together, they give a more complete picture than either one alone. We need all these ways to express our understanding of the world because no one way can say it all.

ACTIVITY ▶ *Experience a Musical Sunrise*

> **Listen to three different composers' musical representation of a sunrise.**
>
> 1. "Daybreak" from *Daphnis and Chloé* by Maurice Ravel.
> 2. "Sunrise" from *Also sprach Zarathustra* by Richard Strauss.
> 3. "Sunrise" from *The Grand Canyon Suite* by Ferde Grofé.
>   Which setting is the most subtle? Which is the most literal? Why?

Activity *Experience a Musical Sunrise*
Instructor's Guide, pages 130–131
CD 5 30 "Daybreak," Daphnis and Chloé, No. 2 (2:01)
CD 5 31 "Sunrise," Also sprach Zarathustra (2:01)
CD 5 32 "Sunrise," The Grand Canyon Suite (2:15)

A familiar saying is "A picture is worth a thousand words." A sunrise can be described; it can also be captured and interpreted by a photographer. Music too can convey a sunrise, evoking its emotional aspects— the hope and wonder of a new day.

PROFILE

Wolfgang Amadeus Mozart
Austrian Composer
1756–1791

Wolfgang Amadeus Mozart

Wolfgang Amadeus Mozart (MOAT-zart) is among the world's greatest geniuses. As a child prodigy at eight, he astounded Europe's royalty with his skill at improvisation on the harpsichord. He composed his first symphony when he was ten years old and his first opera at age 11. During a visit to Rome when he was 14 years old, he heard a performance of Gregorio Allegri's *Miserere* in the Sistine Chapel and wrote out all nine parts of the work from memory after a single hearing!

Mozart wrote sacred works, piano music, orchestral works, vocal music, chamber music, concertos, and operas—literally hundreds of works. His operas include *The Marriage of Figaro, Don Giovanni,* and *The Magic Flute*—works still widely performed. His music reflects his abundant wit and wisdom and expresses a wide range of moods. Always there is a formal perfection, rich harmony, ingenious coloration, and melodic beauty. Yet even though he was highly regarded in his day, his income was modest and he died in poverty at the age of 35. Music lovers will probably always wonder what he might have accomplished had he lived a longer life.

Stirring Our Emotions

Music makes connections between our head and our heart—between our cognitive, or intellectual, being and our affective, or emotional, state. These two domains work together. Often, they can influence our psycho-motor, or physical, state, such as when music makes our heartbeat accelerate, gives us goose bumps, or makes us teary-eyed. How does this happen?

The emotions expressed through music encompass a range that extends well beyond what most of us experience in a normal day, perhaps even in our lifetime. Music confronts us with feelings that are similar to those we have experienced and those that are unlike any we have ever known. Through music we can experience certain kinds of feelings for the first time.

Activity *Identify Emotional Qualities*
Instructor's Guide, pages 131–132
TRB 9-2, *Cause and Affect*
CD 5 33 "Oh, Danny Boy" (3:08)
CD 5 34 Piano Concerto No. 21, second movement (4:11)
CD 5 35 "The People United Will Never Be Defeated!" (3:28)

ACTIVITY ▶ *Identify Emotional Qualities*

Determine what musical characteristics stir your emotions as you listen to the following three pieces:

1. "Oh, Danny Boy," a traditional Irish favorite song sung **a cappella**, *without musical accompaniment.*

2. Second movement of the Piano Concerto No. 21 by Mozart.
3. "The People United Will Never Be Defeated!" a Chilean song of solidarity. (See the Spanish text and English translation below.)

For each piece, write down a word or two in a column marked "affective" that describes the emotions this music brings out in you. Then, in the column marked "cognitive," note what you heard in the music that made you react this way.

¡El Pueblo Unido Jamás Será Vencido!

The People United Will Never Be Defeated!

by Sergio Ortega

De pie, cantar
que vamos a triunfar.
Avanzan ya
banderas de unidad
y tú vendrás
marchando junto a mí.
Y así verás
tu canto y tu bandera
florecer. La luz
de un rojo amanecer
anuncia ya
la vida que vendrá.

Stand up, sing
We are going to triumph.
Flags of unity
are advancing now
and you will come
marching together with me.
In this way you'll see
your singing and your flag
blossom. The light
of a red dawn
already announces
the life that will come.

La patria está
forjando la unidad.
De norte a sur
se movilizará
desde el salar
ardiente y mineral
al bosque austral
unidos en la lucha
y el trabajo irán,
la patria cubrirán
su paso ya
anuncia el porvenir.

The homeland
forging unity
from north to south
will be mobilized.
From the fiery
salt mine
to the southern forests
united in struggle
and work they will go.
They will cover the country,
their step already
announces the future.

De pie, luchar
el pueblo va a triunfar.
Será mejor
la vida que vendrá
a conquistar
nuestra felicidad.
Y en un clamor
mil voces de combate
se alzarán, dirán,
canción de libertad
con decisión
la patria vencerá.

Stand up, struggle,
the people will triumph.
It will be better
The life that will come
To win
our happiness.
And there will be a clamor of
a thousand embattled voices:
They will speak
a song of freedom.
With determination
the homeland will win.

De pie cantar
el pueblo va a triunfar.
Millones ya
imponen la verdad.
De acero son
ardiente batallon.
Sus manos van
llevando la justicia
y la razón. Mujer
con fuego y con valor
ya estás aquí
junto al trabajador.

Stand up, sing
people will triumph.
Millions now
impose the truth.
The fiery army
is as steel.
Its hands
carry justice and reason.
Women with fire
and with courage
already you are here
close to the worker.

Y ahora, el pueblo
que se alza en la lucha
con voz de gigante
gritando: ¡adelante!

And now the people
rising up in the struggle
with a great voice
shout "forward!"

Y ahora, el pueblo
que se alza en la lucha
con voz de gigante
gritando: ¡adelante!

And now the people
rising up in the struggle
with a great voice
shout "forward!"

Emotion in the Music of Bali

Even when the music of another culture is different from our own, it may communicate its emotional content to us more readily than we might guess. Maybe this is so because, as human beings, we are far more alike than we are different.

The Culture of Bali

Bali is a province of the Republic of Indonesia. Located directly north of Australia, Indonesia stretches east to west for more than 3,000 miles, like a necklace hung from the equator. Bali is approximately 90 miles (145 kilometers) long and 60 miles (97 kilometers) wide.

The Balinese people are known for their physical beauty and their uniquely ritualistic forms of music, drama, and dance. Although Islam is the predominant religion in Indonesia, most Balinese people are Hindu, and it is their form of Hinduism that inspires all their arts, including music. Males and females of all ages participate in the island's dance traditions. All children learn to dance and sing both in and out of school.

MUSIC in the WORLD

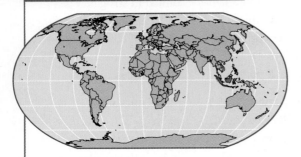

THE REPUBLIC OF INDONESIA consists of a chain of over 13,000 islands between Australia and the mainland of southeast Asia. Bali is a province of this republic, with a culture rich in art, dance, music, and sculpture. *What type of ensemble is the center of Balinese music?*

Music in the World
The gamelan.

The Music of Bali

Everyone in Bali is an artist—a sculptor, painter, dancer, or musician. After a busy day in the rice fields, the men gather in the late afternoon to practice gamelan music. The **gamelan** is *a Balinese ensemble.* The term is generic. There are many different types of gamelan ensembles on the island. Some gamelans have as many as 25 performers or more who play on metallophones and gongs of several sizes, cymbals, drums, a flute, and sometimes a simple string instrument. It is the center of Balinese music.

Boys take up the instruments of the gamelan when they are young and learn "by ear" from the older men. Girls often take up weaving and dancing. Both young men and women dance with the gamelan when they have mastered the difficult movements that relate to stories often taken from their religion.

In Bali, there is no dance or drama without music. In the *Barong Dance,* for example, the orchestra accompanies the male and female dancers who portray various animals, humans, and gods.

This story, like so many others in the Hindu faith, represents the eternal fight between good and evil. Barong, a mythological tiger played by two men, represents a good spirit, while Rangda, a mythological monkey,

The gamelan ensemble is the center of Balinese music. It usually consists of 25 or more performers who play on metallophones of several sizes and pitches, gongs of different sizes, cymbals, drums, a flute, and simple string instruments.

represents an evil spirit. For the Balinese, good and evil exist in equal measure in the world. In their drama, good never triumphs over evil. The two are locked in an eternal struggle. The story of Barong, enacted in elaborate costumes, is told in several acts with many characters.

ACTIVITY ▶ *Sense the Emotions*

Use your musical knowledge to identify two basic emotions expressed in this music.

Listen to this overture to the *Barong Dance* performed by a gamelan orchestra in a small village in Bali.

- Can you detect two very distinct moods? Can you describe them?
- Is there any repetition?
- Does the tempo stay the same or change often?
- What instrument leads the group?

TECHNOLOGY OPTION

- **Music with MIDI** Use a MIDI program to compose a Balinese gamelan-style composition that follows some of the compositional "rules" associated with Balinese music.

Activity *Sense the Emotions*
Instructor's Guide, page 132
Music! VHS Segment 6, Gamelan
Ensemble
CD 5 36 Overture to the *Barong Dance* (3:49)

Technology Option
Use Project 9 in the *MIDI Activities* binder.

The External Aspects

The external or social aspects of music often help us understand its meaning. Knowing that John Williams's *Liberty Fanfare* was commissioned for the unveiling of the newly refurbished Statue of Liberty on July 4, 1986 (its one hundredth birthday) helps to put us in the right frame of mind to accept this music on its own terms. Knowing something about the nonmusical aspects of the music—the background of the work, the occasion of the performance, the composer, the performer, and so forth—can establish a rapport between the listener and the musical work. In this way, historical knowledge enhances our musical understanding.

One of the most electrifying events of the 1980s was the tearing down of the Berlin Wall in November, 1989. As the most visible symbol of the Cold War between the Communist East and the democratic West, the Wall had been an obstruction to freedom for almost three decades. East German authorities erected the 29-mile wall around West Berlin in August, 1961, to halt the exodus of their citizens to the West. Tearing down the wall was a cause for worldwide celebration: the triumph of freedom over totalitarianism.

To celebrate the overwhelming joy of this event, musicians from the East and the West assembled in Berlin for a festival of jubilation on New Year's Eve, December 31, 1989. American conductor and composer Leonard Bernstein was invited to lead these artists in a performance of Ludwig van Beethoven's *Ninth Symphony* on both sides of the Berlin Wall. The nationalities of the performers reflected the victors and the vanquished in the Second World War (1939–1945), people now united in music to proclaim the harmony of the world.

No other musical work would have celebrated human freedom as well that day. A **symphony** is *an extended work in several movements for orchestra*, but Beethoven added voices. He incorporated Friedrich von Schiller's "Ode to Joy" as the chorale finale of this work. To give special meaning to the occasion, Bernstein had the singers substitute the word *Freiheit* ("freedom") for the term *Freude* ("joy") in Schiller's poem.

The first performance of the *Ninth Symphony* took place 165 years earlier in Vienna, in 1824. The four-movement work moves through darkness to light, encompassing the grim and the magnificent, despair and joy. Beethoven, totally deaf when he composed the work, was no stranger to suffering. The fourth movement sings of the triumph of the human spirit over adversity. Beethoven had struggled for months to find the right melody for Schiller's ode. His solution is simple and unforgettable.

MUSIC in the WORLD

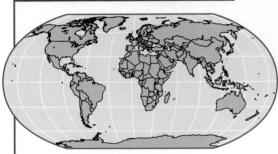

GERMANY is one of the largest countries in Europe. German composers such as Beethoven, Wagner, and Bach made important contributions to Western music, especially to the symphonic form. *Who conducted the performance of Beethoven's* Ninth Symphony *to celebrate the tearing down of the Berlin Wall in 1989?*

Music in the World
Leonard Bernstein.

Music & HISTORY

On November 22, 1989, the Bradenburg Gate, which marked the division between Communist East Berlin and democratic West Berlin, was opened once more. Musicians from both East and West gathered together and performed Beethoven's Ninth Symphony to celebrate the historical event. **How long had the wall separated the city of Berlin?**

Music & History
28 years (1961–1989).

ACTIVITY ▶ *Perform the "Joy" Theme*

Using the following notation, read and perform Beethoven's theme from his *Ninth Symphony.*

Activity *Perform the "Joy" Theme*
Instructor's Guide, page 133
TRB 9-3, *"Ode to Joy" Notes*
TRB 9-4, Beethoven's *Ninth Symphony*

The "Joy" Theme

Ludwig van Beethoven

■ Which phrases sound the same?
■ Which are different?

PROFILE

*Ludwig van Beethoven
German Composer
1770–1827*

Ludwig van Beethoven

Ludwig van Beethoven, one of the world's greatest composers, was born in Bonn, Germany. Despite the family's poverty, his father began teaching him the piano and violin at age four. After studying with Joseph Haydn, Beethoven became the world's first freelance composer, though his income barely paid the rent.

Beethoven's compositions are generally divided into three distinct style periods: the early Vienna years (1792–1802), the middle period (1802–1815), and the final years (1815–1827). In the early years, Beethoven composed in the Classical style. These were also the years that he first noticed his loss of hearing. During the middle period he began to show his true genius, writing some of his most important works, including the *Fifth Symphony* and many great sonatas, concertos, string quartets, and other works.

It was during the final years that Beethoven became totally deaf. At this time he wrote the magnificent *Missa Solemnis* and the *Ninth Symphony*. When he finished conducting his triumphant *Ninth Symphony*, a singer had to tug at Beethoven's sleeve and direct his attention to the audience before he bowed to an ovation he did not hear.

The fourth movement opens with discord. The orchestra appears to be at war with itself, some instruments interjecting with calls for peace. Violence tries to prevail; a strain of the "Joy" theme gently coaxes but is dismissed. It tries to sound again and is rejected. Finally, the whole orchestra states the theme. Then the solo baritone calls for people to join in rejoicing. The basses of the chorus, the solo quartet, and the full orchestra take up the cause. The mood becomes more and more jubilant, rising to shouts of ecstasy—Beethoven's dream of a liberated humanity.

Activity *Feel the Emotion*
Instructor's Guide, page 133
CD 6 1 *Ninth Symphony*, fourth
  movement (15:10)

ACTIVITY ▶ *Feel the Emotion*

Use your imagination as you listen to the fourth movement of Beethoven's *Ninth Symphony*. Imagine that you were present as it was being performed at the Berlin Wall in 1989.

Use these questions to guide your analysis:

1. What is there about this music and this theme that is uplifting?
2. Imagine that the singers are people who are celebrating their own newly won freedom. Can you detect their own joy and conviction in their performance?

3. Try to follow the text during the performance. Does it help to know the meaning of the words?
4. Listen to the entire fourth movement. Can you sense the tension in the orchestra as it builds to the statement of the "Joy" theme? Does Beethoven alter the "Joy" theme?

Music permits us to speak with a depth and an emotional power that would not be possible in any other artistic medium. Knowing the external aspects—the historical context of this particular performance and the background of this work and its composer—are the keys that help us unlock the layers of meaning in a musical score. That is why the study of music is so important. Without it, these meanings could not be known or shared.

As exemplified in Beethoven's *Ninth Symphony,* text can add to the emotional impact of music. Words present specific meanings and emotions that are then reinforced by the music. The two, words and music, have to work together if the total expression is to be effective. This is just as true in a simple song as it is in Beethoven's complex symphony. There is an art to the successful marriage of words and music.

Communicating Emotion

All truly effective songs speak from the heart. The words and music meld together to make one unified statement. The performance can make or break this expressive sense of rightness and oneness. A performance should capture this marriage of words and music and make it seem natural and right.

Blind Willie Johnson was born in Texas around 1900. When he was seven years old, he was blinded by his stepmother who, in a fit of rage, threw a pan of lye in his face. Later, as a young man, he survived on the streets of Dallas with his musical talent. However, life was never easy. He had a strong voice, and he learned to accompany himself on guitar by sliding a pocketknife along the strings to create chords. He sang his own blues on the street corners and became a master of slide-guitar technique, a way of playing that cut through the clatter on the street. In 1927, Johnson recorded "Dark was the Night, Cold was the Ground." This was at a time in his life when, on a good day, he might earn enough to afford shelter for the night. Otherwise, he slept in the street.

Blind Willie Johnson wrote and performed music that told of the hardship he knew in his own life. He sang a form of the blues that mixed sacred and secular music. The result was an intense emotional impact on listeners, allowing them to feel his sorrow.

Activity *Recognize Emotional Qualities*
Instructor's Guide, page 134
CD 6 [2] "Dark was the Night, Cold was the Ground" (3:18)

ACTIVITY ▶ *Recognize Emotional Qualities*

Use the following criteria to grasp the emotional impact of "Dark was the Night, Cold was the Ground," an early blues song composed and sung by Blind Willie Johnson.

■ Is the spiritual moaning just as effective as words, or more so?

■ Does Johnson create empathy for the homeless?

■ What does Johnson's slide-guitar accompaniment add?

■ Does knowing something about Johnson help you to feel the emotion of his music?

The Internal Aspects

When composers want to express themselves, they must choose the particular combination of sounds that will convey their sentiments. These choices include a multitude of musical options—all kinds of melodies, rhythms, and harmonies, plus the voices and instruments to perform them!

The "Dies irae" (DEE-ace ee-RAY) is a Latin medieval poem written sometime during the thirteenth century. The text describes the day of judgment—the terrifying time when life on earth, according to Christian theology, will end and all people will be judged by God for their actions. On this day, humans face either eternal salvation or damnation. This powerful text has served as part of the **Requiem Mass**, or *Mass for the Dead, in the Catholic liturgy.* French composer Hector Berlioz (1803–1869) and Polish composer Krzysztof Penderecki (b. 1933) were both inspired to create works on this theme using large instrumental and vocal forces. The Berlioz work uses the text to paint a sonic picture of the end of the world, while Penderecki creates a memory of the millions of Jews slaughtered by the Nazis during the Second World War at the concentration camp in Auschwitz, Poland.

Activity *Compare Treatments of a Theme*
Instructor's Guide, pages 134–135
TRB 9-2, *Cause and Effect*
CD 6 [3] "Dies irae," *Requiem* (7:01)
CD 6 [4] "Dies irae," *Auschwitz Oratorio* (4:46)

ACTIVITY ▶ *Compare Treatments of a Theme*

Determine how two composers expressed the Judgment Day theme.

As you listen to the "Dies irae" from Hector Berlioz's *Requiem* (1837) and the "Dies irae" from Krzysztof Penderecki's *Auschwitz Oratorio* (1967) answer these questions:

1. In what ways are these works similar musically? In what ways are they different?

2. Do they generate different emotions in the listener?
3. In what ways have both composers made their music reflect the message of a terrifying, final day of judgment?

Romanticism

Music is the language of human feeling. It is always emotive, but during the Romantic period it was especially dramatic and emotional. The **Romantic period** was *a period during the nineteenth century and early twentieth century when composers created music that often exploded with emotion.* Composers of this period created supercharged expressions. Romantic music invited the heart to reign.

The Romantic spirit expressed the rise of the middle class, the triumph of the individual. The American Revolution (1776) and the establishment of the new social order in France (1789) affected the entire world. The American Constitution with its appended Bill of Rights and the new French Constitution with its famous preamble, the Declaration of the Rights of Man and Citizen, broke the rule of the old aristocracy. The restraints characterized by the music of Haydn, Mozart, and early Beethoven were cast aside. The feelings, beliefs, and aspirations of the common man would now be heard.

Earlier in the eighteenth century, during the Age of Enlightenment, the intellect dominated thinking. We see this in the geometric patterns of the gardens of the Schönbrun Palace in Vienna. Here geometry, not nature, rules. The pattern of every garden and size and color of every tree

The well-ordered symmetrical gardens of Vienna's Schönbrun Palace, created in the eighteenth century (left), contrast with the freer and more natural treatment of nature in New York's Central Park, created in the nineteenth century (right). They illustrate the difference between the rational thinking of the Classical period and the emotional spirit of the Romantic period.

and plant were planned on paper, then planted. The plants were trained to conform to the perfect order—symmetry and elegance.

While the gardens at Schönbrun Palace are impressive, one can become tired of such rigidity. When rules are strong, humans tend to rebel. The roots of Romanticism lie in just such a revolt against sheer formalism. People sought a more natural order. The nineteenth-century design of Central Park in New York City illustrates the vast difference in feeling between the Classical and Romantic spirit. There, nature is permitted to assert itself. Romanticism did not impose laws over nature. It set emotions free.

The problem in the nineteenth century was how far to go with this new freedom. The opposite of complete intellectual rule is complete emotional rule. Both extremes present disadvantages and difficulties.

Robert Schumann (1810–1856) was among the first of the new breed of German Romantic composers. In many of his works he created short mood pictures. These highly personal pieces were almost always written for the piano, which he considered the most expressive instrument of the period. His *Carnaval* (*Carnival*, 1834–1835) presents scenes of clowns and dancers interspersed with various masquerading personalities— some imaginary, some real. This work, a suite of character pieces strongly influenced by dance, includes two waltzes, a promenade, and a march. This *Carnaval*, like many real ones, is full of oddities that are not explained, but the imagery can still be felt.

Activity *Describe the Character*
Instructor's Guide, page 136
CD 6 ⑤ "Chopin," *Carnaval* (1:05)
CD 6 ⑥ "Harlequin and
        Columbine," *Carnaval*
        (0:59)

ACTIVITY ▶ *Describe the Character*

Can you identify the character Robert Schumann is describing in two contrasting movements of *Carnaval*?

Use these questions to give focus to your analysis:

1. Describe the mood of "Chopin." It may help to know that Schumann greatly admired the piano compositions of Frédéric Chopin. In this piece, he even imitates Chopin's style.
2. Describe the mood of the characters Harlequin and Colombine. Can you differentiate between the two characters? Can you tell from the music which is the male and which is the female?

Richard Wagner (VAHG-ner) (1813–1883) was one of the greatest composers of the Romantic period. Success did not come easily for him, and few men have been as vicious to those who offered them help. His was a stormy, egotistical personality, perhaps the epitome of the worst quality of Romanticism—unconstrained emotion. Wagner spent his lifetime borrowing money and eluding his creditors. Despite all his faults, he produced works of notable power and expressiveness. Wagner's term for his *operas of the Romantic period* was **music dramas.**

One of Wagner's greatest achievements is *The Ring of the Nibelung*, which is based on Nordic legends. This vast work, comprising four full operas, explores just about every human emotion from hate and greed to love and sacrifice—a perfect Romantic tale. Wagner wrote the **libretto**, *the text of an opera*, as a set of sequels—but backwards! He first wrote the *Death of Siegfried*, the young hero, which he later renamed *Die Götterdämmerung (The Twilight of the Gods)*. Then he developed the story that led up to Siegfried's death, which was turned into three other operas: *The Rhine Gold, The Valkyrie,* and *Siegfried.* Wagner created a world where gods and goddesses have all the flaws and feelings that we do—from stealing to falling in love! But these gods have powers and curses and magic that make them superhuman. It took Wagner 28 years—from 1848 to 1876—to complete the libretto and the music and to produce the Ring cycle.

One of the most dramatic moments in the whole opera is the death of Siegfried. This fearless young man has rescued Brünnhilde from her long sleep by penetrating the ring of magic fire that surrounds her. Later, after drinking a magic potion, he is deceived and falls in love with another woman while pledging Brünnhilde (whom he no longer remembers) to his best friend. By the time his memory is restored, it is too late. Hagen, the evil perpetrator of the scheme, plunges a spear deep into Siegfried's back. Now Brünnhilde understands why her hero betrayed her. As night falls, the servants place Siegfried's body on his shield and carry him in a solemn procession. Wagner's funeral music produces a mighty lament.

Richard Wagner (1813–1883) was one of the nineteenth-century Romantic composers who used new harmonies, soaring melodies, and vivid orchestral colors to express the mystical world of the supernatural. He created dramas that brought German Romantic opera to its heights.

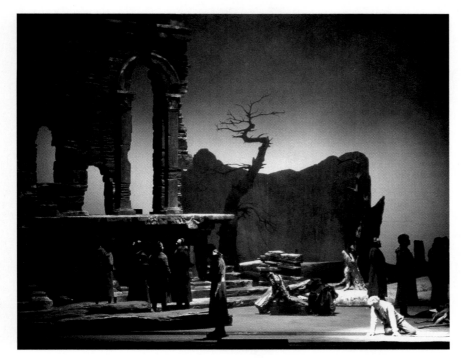

In Wagner's music drama Siegfried, *the third of the four operas in* The Ring of the Nibelung, *the young hero slays the dragon and gains possession of the magic ring. The struggle for his ring, which the gods need in order to survive, leads to Siegfried's death in the final opera,* The Twilight of the Gods.

The moon breaks through the clouds, and mist rises from the Rhine River. Toward the end, the bass trumpet and horns sound the stately hero's theme. Gradually the mist engulfs the scene.

Wagner thoroughly explored the expressive qualities of the various instruments of the orchestra. He learned how to wring every drop of expressiveness out of an orchestra, and he used the same sense of adventure and determination that the pioneers in this country used as they were exploring the new continent. He was able to portray emotion effectively because he used the orchestra to comment on the action on stage.

Activity *Recognize Timbres of the Orchestra*
Instructor's Guide, pages 136–137
CD 6 ⬜7 "Siegfried's Funeral March," *Die Götterdämmerung* (8:30)

ACTIVITY ▶ *Recognize Timbres of the Orchestra*

How does Wagner use the orchestra to express the death of a hero?

Listen to "Siegfried's Funeral Music" from Wagner's music drama *The Twilight of the Gods.* Use these questions to arrive at your answers:
1. How does Wagner use instruments to convey Siegfried's good deeds, his heroism, and his tragic end?
2. Is this a real funeral march? Why or why not?

Prior to the First World War (1914–1918), the world turned against the sometimes exaggerated, emotional outpourings of nineteenth-century Romanticism. Reason began to reassert itself. We hear the last expressions of the Romantic spirit in the early decades of the twentieth century in the works of Richard Strauss (1864–1949) and Sergei Rachmaninoff (1873–1943).

SUMMARY

Music expresses our emotions in clear and convincing ways. It is not unreasonable to ask whether we could feel the meaning of patriotism, love, peace, freedom, fear, faith, loss, suffering, and other emotional states as well if we did not have music to express them. In expressing these emotions, music reinforces them, helping us experience them in a more objective way. Music helps to bring our feelings into focus, to intensify them, and to sustain them so that we can grasp their impact fully. The emotional power of music is a window into the very real emotional world of other human beings, past and present.

CHAPTER 9 REVIEW

Complete answers for the Chapter 9 Review are found in the Instructor's Guide, page 137.

Building Music Vocabulary

On a sheet of paper, write the term from the list that best matches each description below.

(4) a cappella (1) Requiem Mass
(6) gamelan (3) Romantic period
(2) libretto (5) symphony
(7) music dramas

1. Part of the Catholic ritual for the dead.
2. The text of an opera.
3. A period during the nineteenth and early twentieth century marked by music that emphasized emotion.
4. Without musical accompaniment.
5. An extended work for orchestra, with several movements.
6. A Balinese instrumental ensemble.
7. Wagner's term for his operas of the Romantic period.

Reviewing Music Facts

Answer each question in a complete sentence.
8. What is the usual instrumental makeup of a Balinese gamelan orchestra?
9. Why did conductor Leonard Bernstein substitute the word *Freiheit* ("freedom") for *Freude* ("joy") in the 1989 Berlin performance of Beethoven's *Ninth Symphony*?
10. How did Blind Willie Johnson play "slide guitar"?
11. Identify some of the social changes that occurred during the Romantic period.
12. Robert Schumann was best known for what kind of compositions?
13. How did Richard Wagner use the orchestra in his music dramas?

8. Metallophones, gongs, cymbals, drums, flute, and sometimes a string instrument.
9. The concert marked the tearing down of the Berlin Wall, which had been a barrier to freedom.
10. He slid his pocketknife across the strings.
11. Answers may include the triumph of the individual, the breaking down of aristocracy, and the rise of the "common man."

Thinking It Through

On a sheet of paper, write your responses to the following:
14. **Compare and Contrast** How is Penderecki's "Dies irae" similar to and different from the "Dies irae" of Berlioz?
15. **Analyze** How did Blind Willie Johnson's life affect his music?
16. **Apply** How can knowing the nonmusical aspects of a piece of music enhance the way you understand and enjoy it?

Making the Connection

Science Use classroom or homemade instruments to demonstrate how tuning two instruments slightly apart can create a "wavering" sound like that of the gamelan orchestra. Find the scientific explanation for this effect and include it in your demonstration.

Social Studies Find out more about the construction and history of the Berlin Wall. Using what you have learned, discuss how citizens of Berlin might have felt during the New Year's Eve 1989 performance of Beethoven's *Ninth Symphony*.

 Hear audio examples of gamelan music and discover more about classical form at **www.glencoe.com/sec/music**

12. Small piano pieces.
13. To create emotion and to comment on the action on stage.
14. Both pieces use the "judgment day" text; both depict terror; both use large chorus and orchestra. The Berlioz is a Romantic-period piece that depicts the end of the world; the Penderecki is a twentieth-century work in memory of the Jews who were slaughtered in World War II.
15. He was poor, blind, and homeless; his music is sad, dark, and weary-sounding.
16. It provides more understanding of the underlying emotional message of the music.

CHAPTER 10

The Beauty of Order

Inside each of us, there is a constant struggle between our emotions and our intellect. We may have an urge to do something, but our judgment may put a damper on it. Our intuition tells us one thing; reason tells us another. The reconciliation of these two extremes takes many forms. Sometimes our emotions rule, sometimes our intellect rules.

The order in music provides its continuity. Through it, we sense the way the music is put together, from the smallest motive to its complete work. To this order the performer applies emotions, resulting in a performance that touches us deeply. **Can you identify any songs that have a distinct order?**

Caption answer
Have students first think of a round such as "Row, Row, Row Your Boat." Then have them recognize popular songs that repeat a chorus or refrain.

Objectives

By completing the chapter, you will:
- Learn about some of the ways music is organized.
- Understand how composers use repetition and contrast to create cohesive musical expressions.
- Find out what gives order to popular songs, the Afro-Cuban rumba, the march, and ragtime.
- Understand and be able to describe the forms of the rondo and the sonata.
- Become familiar with the fugue and chance music.

Vocabulary

aleatory music
fugue
hook
motive
ostinato
rondo
sonata

Musicians to Meet

Johann Sebastian Bach
John Philip Sousa

Order in Music

Music is more than emotion. It is a representation of thought and intelligence as well. One of the ways humans bring intelligence into play is by ordering the sound. Just as there is emotion in all music, so, too, is there order. In general, music stands in opposition to chaos and stands on the side of order, although it represents order of many different kinds and degrees.

Without some sense of order and agreement, society cannot function as a community. It would not hold together. Music expresses this social order. It is logically constructed. It has consistency because its parts relate. Quite simply, it makes sense.

Orders Based on Repetition

Just as there is a certain ugliness in anarchy and disorder, there is a certain beauty in order and coherence. Even when music expresses disorder, it uses an underlying structure to do so. How does music express order? In music, order is expressed through the relationship of the parts. One musical part relates to another because of its similarities. Musical structure, or form, is a plan of organization for all the musical events that take place within the composition. One way that musical forms achieve a sense of order is through the use of repetition. In music, repetition is a device that uses familiarity to create a sense of order.

Music & CULTURE

Music is the model of an ordered world. Likewise, dance offers a visual depiction of order, as seen in this photo from the stage production of Riverdance. **In how many ways do you see order and repetition in this photo?**

Music & Culture
Answers may include the position and stance of the dancers as well as their dress and general body shapes.

Order in American Popular Songs

American popular songs achieve a sense of cohesiveness because of their melodic repetition. Many songs use a standard 32-bar song form consisting of four sections of eight bars each, in an A A B A pattern.

Composers often use a musical **motive**, *a short, distinctive musical pattern or figure*, as a building block. In popular music, the essence of the song is expressed in the **hook** (sometimes called the "grabber"), *the musical motive that generally accompanies the words to the title of the song*. The title is usually sung to a short melodic or rhythmic motive or pattern that is repeated, copied at a higher or lower pitch, or played in some altered form (and sometimes imitated). It is the repetition and imitation of this musical motive, or hook, that holds the song together and makes it memorable.

ACTIVITY ▶ *Find the Order*

Activity *Find the Order*
Instructor's Guide, pages 138–139
CD 6 [8] "My Funny Valentine"
    (3:07)

Determine the melodic organization of the classic 1937 song "My Funny Valentine."

Use the following questions as a basis for your analysis:

1. Which of these letters could best be used to designate the melodic form of the song?
   1. A A A A   2. A B B B   3. A B B A   4. A A B A
2. Are the repetitions of the A section exactly the same? How does the B section contrast with A?
3. Identify the hooks or musical motives in measures 1–2 and 3–4.
4. Compare the hooks used in measures 5–6 with those in measures 13–14.

My Funny Valentine

Words by Lorenz Hart

Music by Richard Rodgers

fav - 'rite work of art. _____ Is your fig - ure less than Greek; Is your

mouth a lit - tle weak, when you o - pen it to speak, Are you

smart?_____ But don't change a hair for me, Not if you

care for me, Stay lit - tle Val - en - tine, stay! _____

Tag

Each day is Val - en - tine's day. _____ day. _____

"My Funny Valentine," by Lorenz Hart, Richard Rogers. Copyright © 1941. Robbins Music Corporation. International Copyright Secured.

Music & Art

As in music, art can portray interest within order. Artist Robert Silvers used multiple images of flowers to create a larger, unified image. **How does a composer provide the same sense of order and interest in a composition?**

Robert Silvers. Based on Diego Rivera's *The Flower Carrier*. 1935, in the Collection of the San Francisco Museum of Modern Art. Photomosaic™. 1997.

Music & Art
By composing repetition and imitation of a motive.

Architecture, like all the arts, is ordered. In the general A B A structure of the U.S. Capitol building, there is a repetition of forms that gives stability, at the same time that the central, or B, section gives added interest and climax. The A B A form is common to Western art forms, including music, because it balances unity and variety.

Song form is generally organized into three sections, that is, in A B A, or ternary, form—even though the first A section is often repeated to form an A A B A structure. There is a comfortable and satisfying symmetry about this arrangement. In the A B A form, the A sections function like bookends, enclosing the form and supporting it structurally. Many forms in nature, including the human torso, have this kind of structure, which gives a balance between unity and variety. The music of the repeated sections is set in contrast to the middle section. This repetition is a return to the familiar. The repetition can be exact, or it can have some degree of variation or modification.

The interplay of contrast and repetition is a basic device used in the creation of much of the world's music. Subconsciously, we expect to hear repetition. Most of the musical examples we have heard during our lifetime have led us to expect it. Contrasting material takes us momentarily away from the main theme that has been introduced, and this sets up tension. Returning to the main theme is like greeting a familiar friend. We experience a sense of comfort, repose, and security.

You may wish to use "Analyze the Organizational Devices" at this time. Lesson plans for the activity are found on page 145 in the Instructor's Guide.

Order in the Cuban Rumba

A large portion of Cuba's population is of African descent. Although Cubans speak Spanish and share many traditions with other Latin Americans, Afro-Cubans maintain a culture with a strong African character. Many retain African tribal identities, practice African religions, speak adapted versions of African languages in addition to Spanish, and preserve forms of music that closely resemble African models. Out of this African heritage, Afro-Cubans have gradually developed new musical forms well suited to modern Cuban tastes. One of these is the rumba.

Music & CULTURE

The Cuban rumba form known as guaguancoi *uses claves as a time line and a two-part formal structure. As a dance and drum performance, it has influenced Latin American popular music, notably salsa. Shown here is a 1998 performance of Los Muñequitos de Matanzas.*

Rumba is performed with percussion instruments, singing, and dancing. It should not be confused with the ballroom rumba, which is a pale, foreign imitation. The most popular of the several types of rumba is *guaguanco* (wah-WAHN-coh), a form that has influenced today's popular Latin-American dance music called salsa.

Guaguanco is an original, distinctly Afro-Cuban musical form that is ordered in two important ways. Both ways are common to many types of African music. First, there is a short, repeated rhythm that is played by *claves* (CLAH-vehs), short, round, resonating wood bars. This time line serves as a reference point for the rest of the musicians and lends an orderly forward motion to the music. Linked to the time line is a repeated rhythmic pattern of the same length that is played by two *tumbadoras* (toom-bah-DOR-ahs), which are similar to conga drums. Along with this, another drum called *quinto* (KEEN-toh), a higher pitched master drum, improvises, often playing rhythms that mimic or direct the movements of the dancers. Second, there is a two-part, formal structure that is marked by two singing styles. The initial section has a fixed melody and text and is often sung in two-part harmony. This is followed by a *montuno* (mohn-TOO-no), a second section that alternates soloist and chorus (refrain). In the montuno, a short, repeated refrain alternates with solo singing of changing, often improvised, verses of text. In this section, the quinto plays more actively. Each of the two main sections is preceded by a *diana* (dee-AH-nah), a shorter section of solo singing.

Activity *Test Your Skill*
Instructor's Guide, pages 139–140
CD 6 10 "Negra Sandunguera"
        (4:16)

ACTIVITY ▶ *Test Your Skill*

Can you perform rhythmic patterns to show the form of "Negra Sandunguera"?

Read and perform the following repeated rhythm or time line pattern of guaguanco played by the claves. In a repeated cycle of 16 sixteenth notes, the claves accent the following pulses.

Claves:																
Count:	1	2	3	4	5	6	7	8	1	2	3	4	5	6	7	8
Basic Beat:	>		&		>		&		>		&		>		&	

Start by tapping the sixteenth notes, accenting the clave rhythm as indicated. Increase the tempo until you can clap only the accented notes. Try to feel the rhythm. Now work in pairs with one person clapping the basic beats (four to a measure), while both of you audiate the sixteenth notes. The other person claps the clave rhythm.

Note that accents 1 and 5 come on the beat, the second and third accents come just ahead of the basic beat, and the fourth accent comes on "&." Try counting and clapping with a beat of four until you can perform this quite rapidly:

Claves:												
Count:	1		&	a	2		&	a	3		&		4		&
Basic Beat:	1				2				3				4		

Once you have mastered this rhythm, try tapping along with the claves in "Negra Sandunguera." Can you hear the pattern of the two tumbadoras?

Perhaps the easiest part of the tumbadora pattern to single out is the following:

Claves:												
Count:	1		&	a	2		&	a	3		&		4		&

Tumbadoras
Higher pitch:
Lower pitch:

Can you tell when the montuno begins?

The two-part form illustrated in the guaguanco represents another basic way to organize music. Examples of A B, or binary, form are common. Nonetheless, three-part (A B A), or ternary, form is more common and perhaps more satisfying because of the sense of return.

The Ostinato

As you have heard in the guaguanco, order in music can be established by means of a short musical pattern that is repeated persistently. This pattern might be rhythmic, or rhythmic and melodic. Superimposed upon this recurring pattern is a variety of other rhythms and melodies. The time line rhythmic pattern in the guaguanco is an **ostinato**, *a repeated musical figure*. It gives stability and uniformity to the composition. The ostinato gives an underlying unity while still permitting variety in the other parts. It is like wearing the same uniform every day with different accessories.

You have seen how melodic repetition can give order to popular songs and how an ostinato, a constantly repeated musical pattern, gives order to the Afro-Cuban rumba and to some classical symphonic music. This type of repetition almost always occurs at the same pitch in the same part (or instrument).

Activity *Judge the Ostinato Patterns*
Instructor's Guide, page 140
CD 6 [11] "Carillon," *L'Arlesienne Suite No. 1* (4:39)

ACTIVITY ▶ *Judge the Ostinato Patterns*

Determine how the ostinato patterns that Georges Bizet (1838–1875) uses in his *L'Arlésienne Suite No. 1* give unity to the work.

Play this ostinato melody during the A section of "Carillon":

 (repeat 56 times)

Perform this ostinato rhythm during the B section:

 (repeat 89 times)

Play this ostinato melody again during the return of A:

 (repeat 39 times)

1. Describe the experience of performing these ostinatos.
2. What is the structural function of these ostinatos? Do they function expressively as well?

Imitation

Using a short musical motive as a building block is another way composers give order to their music. One outstanding example that you have probably heard is the "dot-dot-dot-dash" motive in Ludwig van Beethoven's *Fifth Symphony*. During the Second World War, this ♪♪♪♩...—pattern, which represents the letter V in Morse code, became the Allies' symbol of victory.

Beethoven used a simple pattern to create a movement that expresses conflict with incredible force and emotion. Sometimes, he repeats the pattern exactly. Sometimes, the pattern is imitated—repeated higher or lower, or with some other modification. Imitation is the successive statement of identical or nearly identical material in two or more parts.

You may wish to use "Find the Imitation" at this time. Lesson plans for the activity are found on page 146 in the Instructor's Guide.

The Fugue

Organization in contrapuntal music posed a different challenge. How do you establish a relationship between two or more melodic parts, or voices, when they are sounding together? One technique that composers used was to place the same melody in each voice but to offset its entrance so that it overlaps and therefore interacts with itself. As you may recall, this is the way the canon is constructed. Another method was to create a **fugue**, *a polyphonic composition consisting of a series of successive melody imitations*. This chasing of the melody from part to part explains why works created in this manner were called fugues. The term means flight.

Music & ART

A fugue is like a musical echo, where a melody is chased from one part to another. Artist Paul Klee (1879–1940) explored this same concept in his painting Fugue in Red. ***Why is the term "fugue" appropriate for this artwork?***

Paul Klee. *Fugue in Red*. 1921. Felix Klee Collection, Bern.

Music & Art
Various shapes seem to chase each other across the canvas in a sequence, varying slightly with each repetition.

Musical works are considered contrapuntal when two or more melodies are sounded together. They are fugal when those melodies exchange the same thematic material. A fugue is an ingenious creation that was brought to its highest perfection by Johann Sebastian Bach in the first half of the eighteenth century. Bach's Fugue No. 16 in G Minor from Book I of *The Well-Tempered Clavier* shows how this exchange of melodic material is accomplished. This fugue has four voices, or parts (melodic lines), though all four are not always in play. For example, the first voice enters with the theme in measure 1; the second voice responds in measure 2; the third voice enters in measure 5; and the fourth voice responds only in measure 12. But when the fourth voice finally enters in measure 12, two other voices are at rest. All four voices sound together for the first time in measure 15. A fugue is not like a canon. While the voices in a fugue share some of the same material, each is quite different, taken as a whole.

The themes that are exchanged among the voices have been color coded so that you can see how they dart from part to part (see page 177). The theme, or subject (in red), is first stated in one voice alone. It is then answered (in imitation) by the second voice at a higher pitch, by a third voice at a lower pitch, and repeated in other sequences throughout.

PROFILE

Johann Sebastian Bach
German Composer
(1685–1750)

Johann Sebastian Bach

Johann Sebastian Bach was born into a family that would produce more than seven generations of important musicians. As a youth he studied harpsichord with his older brother. He went on to play violin in a chamber orchestra before becoming an organist.

Bach spent the rest of his life as either a court or church organist, where his duties included composition. He wrote an astonishing amount of music: instructional pieces for students; virtuoso keyboard works; instrumental sonatas, suites, and concertos; works for harpsichord and organ; and much sacred music of the highest caliber. While director of music for the town of Leipzig and the Church of St. Thomas, Bach composed numerous sacred vocal and instrumental compositions called cantatas for the Sunday services. Often he provided a new cantata each week, composing more than 200 in all.

In his own day Bach was much more famous for his organ and improvisation skills than for his compositions. Yet most of his over 1,000 works have survived to this day. Bach surpassed all other composers in the art of writing contrapuntal music.

When the answer enters at the end of bar 2, the subject continues with a melody in counterpoint with it. This countersubject (blue) is heard throughout the fugue and is also exchanged between the voices. The space between statements of the subject is filled in with freely invented counterpoint, which is often based on melodic motives from the subject and the countersubject. In this way, the entire work is thoroughly integrated in all its parts. Toward the end of some fugues, the subject enters in such rapid succession in various voices that it overlaps itself. This pressing together of the entrances is called "stretto," and it can have the grand effect of a series of reverberating echoes.

Fugues can be played by an orchestra or a small ensemble, sung by a chorus, or performed on a single instrument such as an organ or piano. The challenge in performing a fugue is to give emphasis to the particular voice that has the subject. Sooner or later all the voices have it, so all the melodic lines are of equal importance—a very democratic kind of music.

Activity *Analyze Bach's Fugue*
No. 16
Instructor's Guide, pages 140–141
CD 6 ⑬ Fugue No. 16 in G Minor
(2:10)

ACTIVITY ▶ *Analyze Bach's Fugue No. 16*

Can you determine how every voice in a fugue is treated equally by sharing the subject and the countersubject?

First, learn to play the theme, or subject, of Fugue No. 16 in G Minor from Book I of *The Well-Tempered Clavier* by J. S. Bach. Clap this rhythm as you sing the notes on "ta."

Number the fingers of your right hand by making the thumb 1 and the little finger 5. Practice crossing your second finger over your thumb to play the G–F#–G.

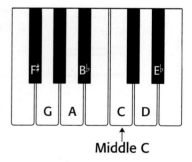

Middle C

Perform this two-measure melody using the rhythmic pattern you clapped and chanted. Now listen to this fugue, and as you follow the score, point to each new entrance of the subject (red). Listen again to the fugue, and as you follow the score, point to each entrance of the countersubject (blue). Listen to the fugue a third time and identify the rhythmic and melodic motives used to fill the space between the statements of the subject and the countersubject. Where does this material come from?

Can you find the stretto, the place where the subject enters in various voices in such quick succession that they overlap?

TECHNOLOGY OPTION

- **Music with MIDI** Use a MIDI program to experiment with imitation and compose a fugue with a subject, countersubject, and stretto section.

Technology Option
Use Project 10 in the *MIDI Activities* binder.

The March and the Rag

Repetition or recurrence is used in other musical designs as well, but not so insistently. For example, the march, familiar to most Americans through bands and parades, uses repetition in a modest and direct way. Although this is not a symmetrical A B A form, it has a definite sense of order and clarity. The march shows us that continuity and unity do not need to depend solely on repetition. Cohesiveness can be achieved with a modest amount of repetition if there is a consistent use of musical materials: rhythm, tone color, and spirit.

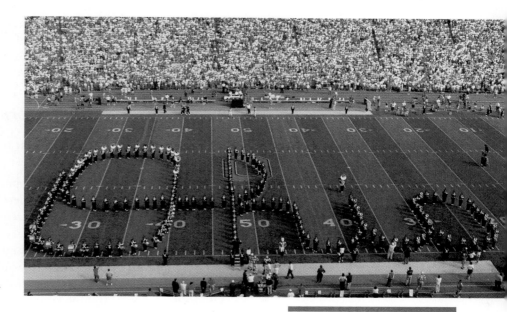

The marching band is one performance style that crisply coordinates music and movement. Each are dependent on the other. Thanks to John Phillip Sousa, American march music is a national institution. Here, the Ohio State University marching band performs during halftime at a football game.

ACTIVITY ▶ *Analyze the Structure of a March*

How does a composer structure the sections of a march?

While you listen to a short section of "The Washington Post March" by John Philip Sousa, count and tap the basic meter (beats per measure). This metric grouping is usually associated with the march:

left, right left, right

After you have listened to this march and heard the various sections, answer the following questions:

1. Which of the following series of letters—a, b, or c—represents the form of this march? ("I" stands for Introduction.)
   (a) I AA BB CC;   (b) I AA BB AA;   (c) I AA BB BB.
2. Are the sections of equal length?
3. How does Sousa create contrast?
4. How does Sousa establish the feeling of unity?

Activity *Analyze the Structure of a March*
Instructor's Guide, pages 141–142
TRB 10-1, *"The Washington Post March"*
CD 3 32 "The Washington Post March" (2:21)

"The Washington Post March," "El Capitan," "The Stars and Stripes Forever," and other military marches by American bandmaster John Philip Sousa were highly popular with the American public. Equally popular was the music of Scott Joplin, the great American composer of rags (1868–1917). A common ground exists between Sousa's marches and Joplin's rags, as Joplin likely was influenced by the tradition of African-American march and dance music popular in the nineteenth century.

Activity *Compare Two Forms*
Instructor's Guide, page 142
TRB 10-2 *"Maple Leaf Rag"*
CD 2 ⑦ "Maple Leaf Rag" (3:02)
CD 3 ㉜ "The Washington Post March" (2:21)

ACTIVITY ▶ *Compare Two Forms*

How is the form of the march similar to the form used by composers of ragtime?

You have already studied the syncopations in Scott Joplin's "Maple Leaf Rag" on page 53. Now identify the distinct sections of the composition. There are four different melodies: A, B, C, and D. Can you distinguish them?

Now listen to this rag again and assign the appropriate letters to each of the nine sections. Unlike the Sousa march, this Joplin rag does not have an introduction. Are all the sections of equal length?

Unlike the Sousa march, the rag uses only one type of tone color, the piano. How does the composer create variety? Unity? Compare and contrast the form and musical characteristics of Sousa's "The Washington Post March" with Joplin's "Maple Leaf Rag."

PROFILE

John Philip Sousa

John Philip Sousa
American Composer and Bandmaster
1854–1932

Did you ever make a connection between the sousaphone and John Philip Sousa? If so, you were right. The biggest instrument in a marching band was made according to Sousa's specifications in the 1890s and named after him.

Known as the March King, Sousa was born in Washington, D.C., where his father was a trombonist with the United States Marine Corps Band. When he was growing up, Sousa learned trumpet, trombone, and other brass instruments, although his main instrument was the violin. At the age of 25 he was asked to become the conductor of the U.S. Marine Corps Band, which he directed for 12 years. During that time Sousa composed some of the greatest of his 136 marches, including "The Washington Post March."

In 1892, he formed the Sousa Band, which toured widely in North America and Europe. His brilliant showmanship kept the band a popular success for four decades. He composed many songs, a dozen operettas, and other music. Yet Sousa is best remembered for his rousing marches like "The Stars and Stripes Forever."

The Rondo Form

Composers sometimes give stability to a musical work by returning to the principal theme again and again, with other themes occurring in between. It is like making a sandwich out of several thin slices of bread with something different between them. A **rondo** is *an instrumental form based on an alternation between a repeated (or recurring) section and contrasting episodes.* The result is repetition in the recurrent sections and contrast in the inner episodes. If you were to repeat one of the episodes (A B A C A B A), you would achieve repetition, contrast, and symmetry all at once!

Composers repeat musical material for effect and to build their musical forms. Repetition unifies and orders the parts. It signifies that the music is planned and not haphazard. But most important, it assures a familiarity that fixes the music in our memory.

ACTIVITY ▶ *Determine the Form*

Can you determine the form of the "Rondo all' Ongarese" from Trio No. 39 by Franz Joseph Haydn?

Listen to the portion of the opening section of "Rondo all' Ongarese" and show the tempo and meter of the music by clapping the accented beats and snapping the unaccented beats.

Listen again to the entire A section of the work and count the number of measures. Your teacher will indicate when the A section is completed. Listen a third time to the entire work and count the number of times you hear the A section performed. How would you label the sections between the repetitions of A?

Which of the following represents the form of the "Rondo all' Ongarese"?

(a) A A A   (b) A B A   (c) A B A C A

Activity *Determine the Form*
Instructor's Guide, pages 142–143
CD 6 16 "Rondo all'Ongarese"
(3:09)

Orders Based on Other Devices

Although most music has order, it is not governed by hard-and-fast rules or formulas. Musical structures are seldom rigid. There are no organizational traditions or systems in music that have not been violated. Music can be molded, but usually it breaks out of the mold. In other words, music is not always as ordered as we might think. Just as parallel lines, circles, and right angles are the exception in the real world, perfect order is the exception in music. Composers sometimes use preexisting forms or designs to order their music, but they reshape them to serve their own expressive and communicative needs. Composers also structure their music in ways that do not involve repetition or depend solely upon it.

From the beginning, the piano sonata has come to be one of the most popular and exciting of all performance compositions. Typically it has three movements that unify the entire composition.

The Sonata

Classical composers often write works that have several sections or movements. One such type of composition is a **sonata** (suh-NAH-tah), *a work in several movements for one or more instruments.* Sonatas for a single instrument usually have three movements. The first and last are usually energetic and fast. The second movement is usually slow. The three-movement form is generally marked *allegro, adagio, allegro.*

In the sonata, the design of each movement is complete within itself. Yet each movement remains incomplete without the other movements. These movements might be compared to chapters in a book, each satisfying in itself but not completing the story. The tragedy that engulfs us in the first movement of Beethoven's Piano Sonata in C Minor needs the calm and solemn second movement to allow us to collect our feelings, before the third movement carries us swiftly to a tragic fate. The movements of this sonata are unified through the serious mood established at the onset of the work. Sonatas have emotional unity—the movements are held together by an expressive order.

Activity *Find the Overall Unity*
Instructor's Guide, pages 143–144
Piano Sonata in C Minor, Op. 13
(*Pathétique*)
CD 6 17 First Movement (2:03)
CD 6 18 Second Movement (1:33)
CD 6 19 Third Movement (1:33)

ACTIVITY ▶ *Find the Overall Unity*

Can you determine how a composer unifies a large work made up of three separate movements?

Listen to excerpts from each of the three movements of Beethoven's Piano Sonata in C Minor (*Pathétique*) and try to determine the central organizing device. To begin, clap the rhythmic pattern from the introduction to the first movement and chant the different durations as indicated:

Now listen to the introduction and determine the number of times this rhythmic pattern is heard. The introduction is marked "grave," meaning slow and serious. What other terms would describe the mood?

As you listen to the excerpts from each of the three movements, select words from the following lists that best describe the expressive qualities of each movement:

- **First Movement:** calm, agitated, delicate, aggressive, anxious, dreamy, turbulent, passionate, graceful, restless, soothing, tense.

- **Second Movement:** happy, longing, cheerful, serious, jolly, sorrowful, impulsive, meditative, pleading, lighthearted, gloomy.

- **Third Movement:** joyous, intense, determined, weak, agitated, hopeful, carefree, resigned, piteous, sunny, bright, hopeless.

Aleatory or Chance Music

When music is performed live, a chance factor is operating. We are never quite certain what may happen! Aleatory music, or chance music, makes the most of this uncertainty. **Aleatory music** is *music in which composers deliberately leave parts of the composition and performance undetermined.* They relinquish some of their control, giving those who perform the work the option to determine how the work will ultimately sound and be performed. They invite the performers to join them in the creative process.

Composers of aleatory music offer performers choices or ask them to make certain creative decisions. For example, a composer might suggest a sliding sound from low to high without specifying exact pitches or timing. Sometimes composers provide a graph of the composition that contains new signs that have to be learned, then interpreted, by the performer. In this way, the performer collaborates with the composer.

ACTIVITY ▶ *Create Order in a Performance*

Activity *Create Order in a Performance* Instructor's Guide, page 144

Can performers have a role in giving order to the events in a musical composition?

Earle Brown's score for *Piece for Any Number of Anythings* on page 186 provides broad descriptions for five musical events that are to be improvised by the performers. The conductor must make the following musical choices:

- What the order of the events will be.

- How long each event will last.

- What the dynamic level of each event will be.

- Whether any of the events will be repeated.
  Perform this composition for your classmates with different conductors.

Piece of Any Number of Anythings   By Earle Brown

1	2	3	4	5
long high notes	quick angular melodic lines	very legato lines	highly fragmented lines	very small noisy sounds <u>on instruments</u>*
slowly changing melodic lines	abrupt dynamic changes (normal sounds but vary timbres*—pizzicato, arco, etc.)	note-to-note intervals <u>no more than a perfect 5th</u>	note-to-note intervals <u>always more than one octave!</u>	
small intervals	vary durations			

* Timbral conditions may be translated into comparable or similar sounds from voices.

Aleatory music, though left to the conductor and performers to complete, does not lack order. The composer may specify an order for the musical events or leave this to the preference of the performers. In any event, there is a plan that may or may not include some repetition.

Activity *Compose Aleatory Music*
Instructor's Guide, pages 144–145

ACTIVITY ▶ *Compose Aleatory Music*

Can you create an aleatory or chance composition?

Select three contrasting colors as inspiration for your composition, then follow these steps:

1. Discuss the emotion that each color suggests.
2. Experiment with ways to express these emotions with sounds at hand.
3. Create a simple three-part descriptive (verbal) score similar to Earle Brown's.
4. Try performing each section with different tempos, dynamics, length, and tone colors to see the range of expressive possibilities.
5. Perform the composition with different conductors, creating the form (order) as you proceed.

SUMMARY

Much of what we call order in music is what we perceive as its continuity. As performers or listeners, we sense the way a musical piece is put together, working from the smallest motive, to the parts that make up the movement, to the movements that make up the complete work. Today, composers are free to use the organizational devices of the past, as well as to invent new ones. What is important to remember is that they strive to bring order to their musical compositions. They apply their intellect, not just their emotions, to their work. Composers create vast and magnificent musical structures out of nothing more than vibrations, creating amazing worlds that can touch our inner beings and stir us to our depths.

Complete answers for the Chapter 10 Review are found in the Instructor's Guide, pages 146–147.

Building Music Vocabulary

On a sheet of paper, write the term from the list that best matches each description below.

- (7) aleatory music
- (4) fugue
- (6) hook
- (2) motive
- (5) ostinato
- (1) rondo
- (3) sonata

1. A composition consisting of a recurring theme alternating with contrasting sections.
2. A short, distinctive musical pattern or figure.
3. A work in several movements for one or more instruments.
4. A polyphonic composition consisting of a series of successive melody imitations.
5. A repeated musical figure.
6. The motive or "grabber" phrase in a song that generally accompanies the words of the song's title.
7. Music with sections that are left undetermined, or left to chance.

Reviewing Music Facts

Answer each question in a complete sentence.

8. What is the usual form for an American popular song?
9. What is binary form?
10. Why was the opening pattern of Beethoven's *Fifth Symphony* used to symbolize victory during the Second World War?
11. How is a fugue different from a canon?
12. What important element holds together the various movements of a sonata or symphony?

Thinking It Through

On a sheet of paper, write your responses to the following:

13. **Analyze** How does imitation give a piece of music a sense of unity?
14. **Apply** What musical element gives both marches and rags a sense of cohesiveness?
15. **Explain** Describe how a composer might create written parts for performers of "chance music" when there are no specific pitches to write down.

Making the Connection

Theatre Find out about the form of a typical three-act play. Compare what you have learned with what you know about the sections of sonata-allegro form. How are they similar?

Visual Art Find examples of modern art that seem to have no recognizable subject (nonobjective). Describe how the elements of art (color, line, shape, form, space, and texture) give the artwork a sense of unity. Compare the artist's technique to what you have learned about aleatory or "chance" music.

 Hear clips from Sousa's marches and sample more musical forms at **www.glencoe.com/sec/music**

Answers to Chapter 10 Review

8. Responses include A A B A, A B A, three-part form.
9. A B, or two-part form.
10. The three short, one long, note of the opening is the same as Morse Code for V (victory).
11. A canon uses exact repetition; a fugue uses imitation, not exact copies of musical material.
12. Emotional unity, an expressive order.
13. Repetition and interrelation between the parts can create unity.
14. A consistent use of rhythm, tone color, and spirit.
15. A composer may create charts and graphs.

Chapter 9 Project

You may also wish to use Assessment Master 4, Unit Four Test, in the TRB.

Chapter 9 Project
Instructor's Guide, page 148
CD 6 [20] Piano Concerto No. 2, first movement (3:05)
CD 6 [21] "All by Myself" (2:28)

▶ *Describe Expressive Qualities*

Listen to an excerpt from the first movement of Rachmaninoff's Piano Concerto No. 2 (1901) and compare it with Eric Carmen's song "All by Myself" (1975) that was inspired by it. Make notes about each piece so you can answer these questions:

1. What gives each of these works its expressive power?

2. Do the song lyrics correspond to the emotions expressed in the concerto?

3. Based on just one hearing, which do you prefer and why?

4. Using these two pieces as examples, how would you describe the ways music can express and touch our feelings?

Chapter 10 Project

Chapter 10 Project
Instructor's Guide, page 149
CD 7 [1] "On the Street Where You Live" (2:55)
CD 7 [2] "Song" from Divertimento for Band (2:03)
CD 7 [3] "The Stars and Stripes Forever" (3:14)
CD 7 [4] *Little Fugue in G Minor"* (4:04)
CD 7 [5] "Troika," *The Lieutenant Kije Suite*, Op. 60 (3:02)
CD 7 [6] "The Entertainer" (4:01)

▶ *Compare Artistic Unity*

From the following list, choose the name of the musical organization that you identify as you listen to each of the six recorded examples:

march	song form (A A B A)	rondo
fugue	ostinato	rag

Artists often use a balance of repetition, imitation, and contrast to give their works a sense of order and interest. Study the painting on the facing page and determine what device the artist, Fred Kabotie, used to give order to this work. Then answer the following questions:

1. What structural element does the artist use for repetition and imitation? How does this repetition and imitation give the work a sense of order? How does the artist achieve contrast?

2. Compare the use of repetition in this work with Beethoven's use of a short motive in the opening of his Fifth Symphony. Explain how they function similarly as structural devices.

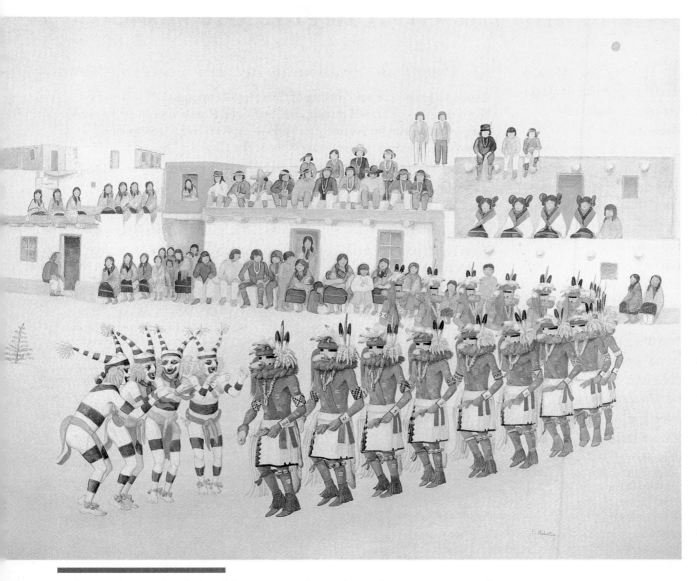

In the painting Hopi Tashaf Kachina Dance, *artist Fred Kapotie creates a sense of order with repeating shapes. He provides interest by showing slight variations both within and among groups of similar shapes. As with music, the art holds our interest when it has a balance between order and contrast.*

Fred Kabotie. *Hopi Tashaf Kachina Dance.* c. 1945. The Philbrook Museum of Art, Tulsa, Oklahoma.

Music and the Civil Rights Movement

During the 1960s, a new form of popular music evolved in America. The "protest" or "message" song was an emotional statement associated with the Civil Rights movement. This movement, led by Martin Luther King, Jr., protested injustice and discrimination against African Americans. Musicians responded by writing songs about the racial struggles. "We Shall Overcome" became the music that set America marching toward racial equality.

Identify the Relationship Between Words and Music

Instructor's Guide, page 150 CD 18 21 "We Shall Overcome" (3:30)

▶ *Identify the Relationship Between Words and Music*

Listen to Joan Baez's recording of "We Shall Overcome." This live performance was recorded during the 1963 Civil Rights march on Washington, D.C. Use the following questions to understand why "We Shall Overcome" became the rallying song of the Civil Rights movement:

1. Does this recording feature only Ms. Baez as soloist?
2. What emotions are expressed by the words and music of the song?
3. To whom is the song addressed?
4. Does this song suggest any solutions to the issues/problems addressed?
5. What, if any, importance does this song have to American society today?

We Shall Overcome

American Freedom Song
Words by Zilphia Horton, Frank Hamilton,
Guy Carawan, and Pete Seeger

1. We shall o-ver-come, _____ We shall o-ver-come, _____
2. We'll walk hand in hand, _____ We'll walk hand in hand, _____
3. Truth shall make us free, _____ Truth shall make us free, _____

We shall o-ver-come some day. _____ Oh, _____
We'll walk hand in hand some day. _____ Oh, _____
Truth shall make us free some day. _____ Oh, _____

deep in my heart I do be-lieve,
deep in my heart I do be-lieve,
deep in my heart I do be-lieve,

We shall o-ver-come some day. _____
We'll walk hand in hand some day. _____
Truth shall make us free some day. _____

TRO © Copyright 1960 (Renewed) Ludlow Music, Inc., New York. International Copyright Secured. Made in U.S.A. All Rights Reserved Including Public Performance for Profit.

Unit Four *Encore!*

American folk singer Joan Baez is shown here in performance in the 1960s. Like many other musicians of her time, Baez used the "protest" or "message" song to further the causes of the Civil Rights movement.

Trace the Source
Instructor's Guide, pages 150–151
Music! VHS Segment 7, "We Shall Overcome"

▶ *Trace the Source*

Watch the video *We Shall Overcome* and answer the following questions:

- Describe the history and sources of the song.
- Describe how the song "We Shall Overcome" functioned both as a tool for social protest and as a historical document.
- Suggest reasons why this song would continue to inspire people to struggle for social justice.

Martin Luther King, Jr., waves to the crowd in Washington, D.C. in 1963. His "I Have a Dream Speech" and the song "We Shall Overcome" are forever linked to the Civil Rights movement and the historic march on the nation's capital.

▶ *Compare Performances*

Listen to two additional arrangements of "We Shall Overcome." The first performance is by the Reunion Concert of Freedom Singers in 1988. The second is by the Howard Gospel Choir in 1998. After listening, discuss them using the following questions:

- What musical elements are similar in each performance? Which are different?
- How do these performances differ from Joan Baez's historic 1963 recording?
- Which version is the most powerful? Why?
- Can a song written in response to a specific historical event transcend time and place and have lasting appeal? Explain your answer.

Compare Performances
Instructor's Guide, page 151
CD 18 [22] "We Shall Overcome" (2:42)
CD 18 [23] "We Shall Overcome" (5:10)

The American Indian Dance Theatre researches and collects traditional dances from many Native American cultural groups. Often, these dances are inspired by animals and their perceived qualities. Although the Eagle Dance (shown here) varies from region to region, it is believed that eagles are messengers between man and the Creator. The Hoop Dance, originally designed to teach and tell stories of creation, symbolically portrays aspects of nature. What do you know about Native American cultures? What animal would you select to inspire a dance? What traits would you stress and why?

American Indian Dance Theatre. "Eagle Dance." Hanay Geiogamah, artistic director. Photo by Don Perdue.

Music!...

To

Understand Life's Meaning

You may wish to use Transparency 5, *Onkto 'Mi Dreaming,* in the TRB to introduce Unit Five.

Chapter 11
Love Songs

Chapter 12
Religious Music

Chapter 13
The Music of Celebration

Chapter 14
Condolences in Death

Use Artsource®
VHS Segment 6 in the Performing Arts Package to show the American Indian Dance Theatre's performance of the "Eagle Dance."

Love Songs

Song as a form of human expression is the largest and oldest category of music. People sing of work and play, of birth and death, of joy and sorrow, of faith and hope, of triumph and despair, and especially of love. Secular songs, songs that contain nonsacred subject matter, can be traced back to ancient Greece, but all we have are some of the texts. After the development of musical notation in the ninth century, it took another 300 years before secular songs were written down. Now they are a large and respected part of what music is all about.

Objectives

By completing the chapter, you will:

- Find out how universal the subject of love is in all kinds of music throughout history and around the world.
- Become familiar with the style of American popular love songs today and in the nineteenth century.
- Be introduced to typical Mexican and Egyptian love songs and see how they are similar to, yet different from, our own.
- Learn more about the elements of musical expression, including major and minor scales, intervals, chords, phrases, and cadences.
- Become familiar with two of the greatest love songs in opera.

Vocabulary

cadence	minor scale
cakewalk	oratorio
harmony	primary chords
interval	rondeau
major scale	scale

Musician to Meet

George Frideric Handel

Popular singer Mariah Carey, shown here, is known for the expressive qualities that she brings to her performances. Her love songs convey common human themes and help us understand our own feelings of love. **Can you identify a current popular love song that touches you deeply?**

Caption answer
Encourage a variety of responses.

You may wish to use "Analyze Love Songs" at this time. Lesson plans for the activity are found on page 164 in the Instructor's Guide.

More about scales and tonal centers is found in section D. 1 of the *Music Theory Handbook.*

Patsy Cline (1932–1963) was a favorite country and pop singer during the 1950s and 1960s. Like most of her love songs, "Why Can't He Be You" conveys a sadness for lost love.

Activity *Compare Love Songs*
Instructor's Guide, pages 155–156
CD 7 ⑦ "You Are the Sunshine of My Life"
CD 7 ⑧ "Why Can't He Be You" (3:25)
CD 7 ⑨ "Stormy Weather" (3:37)

Love Songs of Today

One of the most universal themes in music is love. People of every culture throughout the world sing love songs, and we can assume that, as soon as humans discovered singing, they must have serenaded their loved ones. Love may well have been the reason humans invented singing! The vast majority of love songs communicate just three basic messages: lost love, longing for love, and celebration of love. The first conveys sadness, the second melancholy, the third joy and hope.

The Major Scale

How are the three states of love expressed musically? What gives this music its special character? Usually, songwriters rely on melody to give greater expression to their lyrics of love. By analyzing a melody, we can look at the tonal material itself and how a composer uses it. In music, a **scale** is *a sequence of tones arranged in rising pitches.*

The **major scale** is *a scale built on the pattern of two whole (w) steps, one half (h) step, three whole steps, and one half step.* This sequence is easy to see on the keyboard because the major scale can be played on the white keys, from C to C. This pattern can be transposed to any of the other 11 tones on the piano (each of the black and white keys). There are, therefore, a total of 12 major scales or keys, one on each of the 12 tones that make up the Western tonal system.

ACTIVITY ▶ *Compare Love Songs*

Each of the popular songs you are going to hear contains a different message about love. Can you determine the basic message of each song?

Listen to three love songs in different popular styles. See if you can identify (1) the style of the music and (2) the basic message—whether lost love, longing for love, or a celebration of love. Write down your answers, then compare and discuss them with your classmates.

Intervals

Melodies are created by selecting scale tones and putting them in an order that has an expressive quality. Even with just the seven basic tones of the scale, there is considerable choice. A melody can move up by step or skip, down by step or skip, or remain the same by repeating the tone. An **interval** is *the distance in pitch between two tones.* In determining the difference in pitch between two tones, we count both tones as well as the lines and spaces between them.

| unison | 2nd | 3rd | 4th | 5th | 6th | 7th | octave |
| DO/DO | DO/RE | DO/MI | DO/FA | DO/SOL | DO/LA | DO/TI | DO/DO |

Use section C. 4 in the *Music Theory Handbook* to review intervals.

The smallest interval in the 12-tone Western scale is a half step, or minor (meaning small) 2nd. In the major scale, as we have seen, the minor 2nd occurs between the scale degrees MI (3) and FA (4), and TI (7) and DO (8). The distance between the other adjacent tones of the scale is a major (meaning large) 2nd. A major 2nd (or whole step) is made up of two minor 2nds (or half steps). Melodies generally use whole and half steps (major and minor 2nds) and few large leaps.

Music & Art

Next to the human voice, perhaps the one instrument that Western cultures associate most with love songs is the guitar. Here, painter Edouard Manet (1832–1883) depicts the solitary Latin singer with his guitar. **Judging from his expression, would his love song be of sadness, melancholy, or joy and hope?**

Edouard Manet. *The Spanish Singer.* 1860. The Metropolitan Museum of Art, New York, New York. Gift of William Church Osborn, 1949. (49.58.2)

Music & Art
Students may be able to support any of the three possibilities. Encourage detailed explanations.

Activity *Discover*
Instructor's Guide, pages 156–157
CD 7 [7] "You Are the Sunshine of
My Life" (Phantom Track)
CD 7 [8] "Why Can't He Be You?"
(3:25)
CD 7 [9] "Stormy Weather" (3:37)

ACTIVITY ▶ *Discover*

How do composers use the major scale to create different feelings?

1. Study the following two melodies from the song "You Are the Sunshine of My Life."

   a. In which section (A or B) does the melody move in a smooth, scalelike motion? In which section does the melody move in a series of excited leaps?
   b. What is the largest interval in section A? section B?
   c. What is the range of the melody in section A? section B?

2. Study the melodic "hook" of Hank Cochran's song "Why Can't He Be You?"

   a. How many notes of the G major scale are used in this hook? Can you hear what is basically a descending scale?
   b. How many times do you hear this hook in the song?
   c. Where is the hook somewhat different? Why?

3. Composer Harold Arlen added tones to the G major scale in order to capture a bluesy quality in his song "Stormy Weather."

Slow lament

Don't   know   why ————————   there's   no

sun   up   in   the   sky,   storm- y   weath- er, ——

a. Can you tell which notes he added to the G major scale?
b. What effect do these "blue" notes have?
c. Point out where you hear and see half steps in this melody.

The love songs of Mexican pop singer Selena (1971–1995) expressed the joys and hardships of young love. She was also recognized as a gifted, rising star who updated cultural themes about love. **How might a younger person's song of love differ from that of an older person?**

Mexican Love Songs

All cultures throughout history have connected love with music. In Mexico, it is common for individuals to express their emotions in a love song. Unlike traditional types of Mexican vocal music that create a rhythm for dancing, this style of singing allows the singer the opportunity to express emotion through melody and text. This romantic style was influenced by European styles of singing—especially those of Italian opera—that were popular in Mexico in the nineteenth century. Today the love song thrives in the *canción ranchera* (kahn-see-OHN rahn-CHEH-rah), or "country song," as one of the most popular types of music in the repertoire of the mariachi ensemble. Like love songs in other cultures, the *canción ranchera* speaks of love lost, sought, or found. It can speak of tragedy and betrayal, longing, or joy. In the love song "Se me olvido otra vez" ("I forgot once again"), a lonely woman tells of returning again and again to the place where she fell in love. Sadly, the familiar surroundings make her forget once more that her love was not returned and that the relationship is over.

Most *canciónes rancheras* have a simple A A B structure. Following an instrumental introduction, the vocalist sings one or two strophes (or stanzas) of the text. Then, the singer sings an additional section that has a different character, possibly because it passes to the IV chord of the key or has a different melodic shape. Following a short instrumental interlude, the song may repeat one of the strophes and the final section (A B) and come to an end. The instrumental introduction and interlude are usually derived from the vocal melody, often the B section. The simplicity of form, the repetition of melody and words, and the echoing of the vocal melody in the instrumental introduction, interlude, and *adornos* (countermelodies in the accompaniment) all serve to highlight the message and the singer's interpretation.

Activity *Feel the Drama*
Instructor's Guide, page 157
CD 7 ☐10 "Se me olvido otra vez"
(2:40)

ACTIVITY ▶ *Feel the Drama*

Listen to the *canción ranchera* "Se me olvido otra vez" and determine which emotions the singer communicates.

As you hear the music, follow the text to find out exactly what the singer is feeling. Is this a song of love lost, sought, or found? How do you know? Make a list of the emotions the singer is trying to convey.

Se me olvido otra vez	I forgot once again
Probablemente ya	You have probably
de mi te har olvidado	forgotten me by now.
y mientras tanto yo	And in the meantime
te seguiré esperando	I continue waiting for you.
no me he querido ir	I have not wanted to leave
para ver si algún día	in order that someday
que tú quieras volver	if you were to want to come back
me encuentres todavía	you would find me here still.
Por eso aún estoy	So, I am still here
en el lugar de siempre	in the same place as always,
en la misma ciudad	in the same city,
y con la misma gente	and with the same people,
para que tú al volver	so that on your return
no encuentres nada extraño	you would find nothing different
y seas como ayer	and you would be like yesterday
y nunca más dejarnos	and we would never again part.
Probablemente estoy	Maybe I am asking
pidiendo demariado	too much.
se me olvidaba que	I was forgetting
ya habíamos terminado	that we were finished
que nunca volverás	that you will never return
que nunca me quisiste	that you never loved me.
se me olvidó otra vez	I forgot again
que sólo yo te quise	that only I loved you.

Egyptian Love Songs

To unfamiliar listeners, most Arab music may sound similar, but the various regions of the Arab world have distinct musical styles. Like Western or Chinese music or the music of India, Arab music has a long history. Its theory dates from the writings of the philosopher al-Fārābī in the tenth century. Melodic and rhythmic modes serve as the basis for musical composition. The melodic modes often include notes that lie between the half steps of the Western scale. These may seem to be "out of tune" at first, but in fact, they are carefully tuned.

The song "Ana fi intizarak" (AH-na fee in-ti-ZA-rak) ("I am waiting for you") is about a woman whose man has left her, and she does not know whether he will return. The poem describes the woman's feelings of anger and despair. It is clear that she still loves him. The phonetic spelling of the Arabic text and the English translation are as follows:

> AH-yiz AH-raf lat koon rad-BAHN
> I want to know that you're not angry,
>
> ow SHA-gil el-back in-SAN
> Or whether your heart belongs to someone else.

Although the poem speaks to common, everyday personal emotions, it also expresses the pain of waiting for something good to happen. This theme appeals to many listeners in twentieth-century Egypt and the Arab world who wait for political independence, for wars to end, for families

Music & ART

We know about ancient Egyptian music through pictures, inscriptions, and sculptures such as the one shown here. In addition to flutes, instruments included harps and double clarinets— two cane tubes connected by a single reed and mouthpiece. **Can you imagine how an Egyptian love song played on this flute may have sounded?**

Egypt. Figure of Aulos-Player. c. 650–550 B.C. The Metropolitan Museum of Art, New York, New York. The Cesnola Collection, purchased by subscription, 1874–1876. (74.51.2517)

Music & Art
Responses will vary.

to be reunited, and for economic conditions to improve. Although the song is a love song, it expresses more general emotions. Such duality of meaning is common in songs of many cultures.

The song was recorded by Umm Kulthum (oom kool-THOOM). The composition is in a traditional style. The melody she sings moves stepwise and is based on one of the Arab melodic modes:

(♮ is higher than B♭)

Music in the World
Responses will vary.

MUSIC in the WORLD

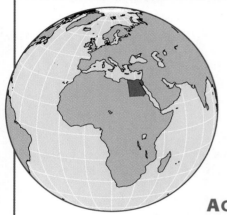

EGYPT is located on the continent of Africa. Its history and culture, however, are more closely tied to the Middle East and Islam, where music making was considered socially acceptable for males, not females. *How, if at all, do the roles of male and female musicians differ in your culture?*

Activity *Follow the Melody*
Instructor's Guide, pages 157–158
CD 7 [11] "Ana fi intizarak" (2:51)

The instrumental accompaniment is deliberately simple so as not to interfere with the singer's line. In the excerpt you will hear, the *ūd* (ood), an Arab lute, is the predominant instrument used, along with a string bass and violins.

Once the listener is completely enveloped by the song, the artist and listener become one with the music. This state of oneness is called *tarab*. This process requires time and attention. The ear and the imagination are captured slowly and gradually. Arab music is primarily melodic. To appreciate it, you need to focus your attention on the vocal line, listening to every note so that you are able to follow the singer's interpretation of the text.

ACTIVITY *Follow the Melody*

Listen to Umm Kulthum's rendition of this excerpt from the Egyptian love song "Ana fi intizarak" and try to feel the meaning of the text.

Review the text above so that you are familiar with its meaning and the pronunciation of the Arabic. Pay particular attention to the key words "angry" (rad-BAHN) and "someone else" (in-SAN).

Listen to the excerpt several times, focusing your attention on Umm Kulthum's voice and the text. Judging by this excerpt, how would you describe her vocal style?

American Love Songs of the Nineteenth Century

The history of American popular music can be told through love songs. Americans have always sung about love. During the nineteenth century, families in the bustling eastern cities gathered around the parlor piano and sang the popular songs of the day. It was customary for young, middle-class girls to take piano lessons and to be able to play for important social occasions. Since there was no radio or television, people had to invent their own entertainment.

Although a bit too formal and sentimental by today's standards, nineteenth-century parlor songs were sincere expressions. Some of these songs came from Europe; some were composed here. New music publishing houses made these songs available in sheet music. Traveling entertainers circulated the latest songs, carrying them from the eastern cities to the frontier towns. Americans everywhere were making music!

These early parlor songs use simple melodies and straightforward accompaniments. They were clearly European in musical origin and character. "Annie Laurie" is a good example. This song, published in 1838, became a national hit, even though it was not an American song. The words and music are by Lady John Douglas Scott of Berwickshire, Scotland. The sentiment, however, is universal. British troops who sang the song in the Crimean War thought of Annie as the girl they left behind.

Music & ART

In this painting, French artist Pierre-Auguste Renoir (1841–1919) depicts two girls practicing the piano. In nineteenth-century Europe, almost all middle-class young ladies were given music lessons. Middle-class America saw a similar development with the rise of affordable pianos and printed music. **How were love songs of this time characterized?**

Pierre Auguste Renoir. *Two Young Girls at the Piano*. 1892. The Metropolitan Museum of Art. Robert Lehman Collection, 1975. (1975.1.201)

Music & Art
They were somewhat formal and sentimental.

Chords

Use section E. in the *Music Theory Handbook* to review harmony.

You have already heard enough **harmony**—*vertical blocks of different tones that sound simultaneously*—to know that it is one of the most expressive elements in music. These tonal blocks, or chords, consist of three or four notes that form a harmonic unit. The accompaniments of parlor songs like "Annie Laurie" rely on just a few basic chords. The combination of melody and harmony is carefully designed to create an appealing tension that teases us and then resolves itself. To understand how this expressive quality is achieved, it is necessary to learn how melody and harmony work together.

In any scale or key, we can build a chord above each tone or "root" by adding notes that are a 3rd and a 5th above that tone. In C major, for example, seven different chords can be formed, one above each note:

Look at the difference between the chord on C and the chord on D. The chord on C (I) is major; the chord on D (ii) is minor. Can you tell what is different about them? Clue: Both chords have an interval of a 3rd between the bottom two tones and an interval of a 3rd between the upper two tones, but the 3rds are not the same. The minor chord uses a small (minor) 3rd above the root. The major chord uses a large (major) 3rd above the root.

Three of these chords—*the chords built on the first (DO), fourth (FA), and fifth (SOL) degrees of the scale*—are **primary chords** or harmonies. The V chord is frequently enhanced by adding a minor 7th above its root, 3rd, and 5th.

Note that collectively these three chords, even without the 7th added to the V chord, incorporate all seven tones of the scale. This means that, no matter which note of the scale appears in the melody, it can be found in one of these three chords. If the tone in the melody is in the I, IV, or V chord, that chord will probably harmonize the tone and sound all right as the accompaniment. It is a matter of compatibility and preference. You will discover that tunes usually begin and end on the I chord (like starting and ending on home base), and that the V7 chord likes to move to the I chord.

In "Annie Laurie," the accompaniment uses the chords V7, I, V, I in bars 16–19 ("Gave me her promise true"). When the phrase is repeated in bars 20–23, different harmonies are used: V, vi, ii, III. The repetition of the melody is given variety, richness, and added expressiveness by these different chords. The new chords are secondary harmonies that are substituted for the primary chords:

secondary chords:

	ii	iii	vi	vii°
Roots:	RE	MI	LA	TI

ACTIVITY ▶ *Discover*

Can you follow the chord changes?

Use the sheet music provided by your teacher to read and audiate "Annie Laurie." Listen for the chord changes that are indicated above the melody. Note that the composer does not change chords on every note of the melody. In this way, the chord changes become important. These harmonic changes have a certain rhythm that helps to carry the melody along.

Read and audiate the song with the accompaniment again and try to find the primary and secondary chords. In which measures do secondary chords occur?

Activity *Discover*
Instructor's Guide, page 158
TRB 11-1, *"Annie Laurie"*
CD 7 13 "Annie Laurie" (0:46)

Stephen Foster (1826–1864) was American's first popular song composer. He used simple, straightforward melodies that a listener could easily remember. His use of musical phrases in "Jeanie with the Light Brown Hair" demonstrates natural cadences.

Phrases and Cadences

A stanza of a song or a poem usually consists of four or more lines with a set meter and rhyme scheme, a pattern that is generally repeated in other stanzas. Each of these lines is usually short enough to be spoken or sung in one breath. As it is, poems and songs have a pause built in after each line to give singers a chance to inhale a new supply of air so they can say or sing the next line. In music, these pauses at the end of a line or phrase are marked by a **cadence**, or *breathing break*. These cadences provide a natural pause in the melodic line.

Sometimes these cadences come at the end of a thought, where we want to convey the feeling of finality, like a period at the end of a sentence. In this case, the resting point is called a perfect or full cadence. The V or V7 chord resolves to the I (tonic) or home chord. This is often how you know the music is over. The tension has been resolved.

At other times the cadences come in the middle of an idea, indicating a temporary pause. This kind of pause corresponds to a comma and is called an imperfect or half cadence. The music comes to rest momentarily on a V or V7 chord, which immediately conveys the feeling that the music has not ended. The half cadence sustains the tension that has been created. The V chord needs to be resolved, so it establishes the feeling that there is more to come.

Activity *Find the Phrases*
Instructor's Guide, page 159
TRB 11-2, *"Jeanie with the Light
       Brown Hair"*
TRB 11-3, *Profile—Stephen Foster*
CD 7 12 "Jeanie with the Light
       Brown Hair" (2:32)

ACTIVITY ▶ *Find the Phrases*

Can you hear the musical phrases in a classic American love song?

The song "Jeanie with the Light Brown Hair," by the American composer Stephen Foster, was published in 1854, after Foster was reconciled with his wife Jane and their three-year-old daughter Marion. No doubt, when he wrote the song, the composer was thinking about Jane and how much he had missed her. Listen to the arrangement of "Jeanie" and identify the musical phrases on the music provided by your teacher.

■ As you listen, write down the words in the text that indicate where there are pauses or breathing breaks. Discuss. Do you agree on where the pauses occur?

■ Listen to the arrangement again and next to each phrase-ending word, label the type of cadence: "full cadence" if there is the sound of the V7–I resolution, "half cadence" if there is a hesitation on the V7 chord that wants to be resolved. (Hint: the first cadence on the word "hair" is a full cadence.)

Incorporating African-American Traditions

While families at home sang parlor songs such as "Annie Laurie" and "Jeanie with the Light Brown Hair," a new form of public entertainment was introduced in 1828 by Thomas "Daddy" Rice who performed in blackface. At New York's Chatham Square Theater in 1843, Dan Emmett, the composer of "Dixie," transformed this form of entertainment into the first minstrel show. His Virginia Minstrels was a theatrical sensation. Soon other groups tried performing in blackface, but it was Ed Christy who gave the minstrel the unique form that made it the most popular type of entertainment in America during the second half of the century. Stephen Foster wrote many of his songs for Christy's minstrels.

As Christy developed it, the minstrel was a variety show consisting of comic songs and sentimental ballads, soft-shoe dancing and clogging, instrumental playing, comedy skits, sight gags, jokes, and amusing patter. Minstrel shows toured widely and many of their songs became popular throughout the country. The minstrel song-and-dance routines incorporated many of the rich musical traditions that were part of the African-American culture at that time. After the Civil War, minstrel shows provided many African-American entertainers with their first opportunities to perform for white audiences.

By the last decade of the nineteenth century and the early years of the twentieth century, American popular music was not only absorbing and reflecting the African-American traditions, but it had also become more vital and unique because of them. One example is the song "Bill Bailey, Won't You Please Come Home?" (1902) by Hughie Cannon (1877–1912), who was one of the best of the minstrel song-and-dance men of that time. The song relates the story of how Bill Bailey's wife threw him out of the house and then begged him to come back with promises ("I'll do the cookin', darlin', I'll pay the rent"). She becomes even more distressed when she discovers he has struck it rich!

Music & HISTORY

White minstrel shows were a tremendously complicated, powerful, and unique American phenomenon that began around 1820. By 1840 minstrel shows had become more numerous and more popular. However, they often stereotyped African-American culture through song and dance. After 1865 African-American performers themselves began to organize minstrel shows. **What American composer wrote songs for early minstrel shows?**

Music & History
Stephen Foster

Bill Bailey, Won't You Please Come Home?

Words and Music by Hughie Cannon

"Won't you come home Bill Bai - ley, Won't you come home?" She moans the whole day long. _____ "I'll do the cook - in', dar - lin', I'll pay the rent; I know I done you wrong. _____ 'Mem - ber that rain - y eve that I drove you out, With noth - ing but a fine tooth comb? _____ I know I'm to blame, well ain't that a shame? Bill Bai - ley, won't you please come home?" _____

Activity *Write a Love Song*
Instructor's Guide, page 160
TRB 11-4, *New Lyrics Worksheet*
CD 7 ⑭ "Bill Bailey, Won't You
    Please Come Home?"
    (3:06)
CD 7 ⑮ "Bill Bailey, Won't You
    Please Come Home?"
    (1:17)

ACTIVITY ▶ *Write a Love Song*

Use the melody from the chorus of "Bill Bailey, Won't You Please Come Home?" as the basis for creating your own love song.

Working in small groups, listen to the melody and analyze it. Then, write new lyrics for this melody and perform it.

1. Learn to sing the chorus. Find the basic pattern of syncopation

that characterizes this piece. How many times is this rhythmic pattern repeated?

2. How many different chords are used to accompany the chorus? If the F chord is the I chord, and the B-flat chord is the IV chord, which chord is the V7? the II7? the VI7?

3. Determine the places where phrases end. Set up the number of accented (●) and unaccented (•) syllables you need in each line. The first line would look like this:

Quarter note count: 1 2 3 4 | 1 2 3 4 | 1 2 3 4 | 1 2 3 4
Word syllables:

4. Select one of the major love-song themes to guide your lyric creativity (lost love, longing for love, or celebrating love). Determine what you want to say in your song. Note the rhyme scheme of the original and develop one of your own.

5. Write your lyrics on a sheet of paper, then hyphenate them and place them under the proper melody notes.

6. Practice performing your new version. You may choose to have someone: (a) play the melody on a keyboard instrument while you sing your lyrics; (b) accompany the song on a guitar or keyboard instrument using the six chords written above the melody; (c) improvise a rhythmic accompaniment while you sing the words; or (d) employ any combination of these performance options. Make sure your tempo and dynamics correspond to the type of love song you have written.

MIDI | TECHNOLOGY OPTION

Technology Option
Use Project 11 in the *MIDI Activities* binder.

■ **Music with MIDI** Use a MIDI program to create an interesting version of "Bill Bailey" to use with your new lyrics. Be prepared to explain how your arrangement complements your lyrics.

The delightful humor of these lyrics was not the only reason the song was an immediate hit and became popular from coast to coast. The song is a **cakewalk,** *an exuberant dance with syncopated rhythms that may represent an early form of jazz.* The infusion of African-American musical style gave American popular music a distinction that makes it familiar anywhere in the world. In style, "Bill Bailey" is a giant leap away from earlier, European-based parlor songs like "Annie Laurie." The stilted language is gone. In its place is a directness and an honesty expressed in the vernacular—the ordinary language of the street. The rhythms, too, are fresh and catchy. The music captures the vigor and confidence of a new society discovering itself and incorporating the best of its diverse creative resources.

Love Songs of Other Times and Places

We know that the art of communicating through original songs flourished in Europe during the twelfth, thirteenth, and fourteenth centuries. Poet-musicians called "troubadours" in southern France, "trouvères" in northern France, and "minnesingers" in Germany composed music and poetry and traveled widely, entertaining in the palaces of the feudal lords. Their songs told the news and other stories. Like today's troubadours— rap singers are one example—their songs were often about love.

As early as the tenth century in Europe, minstrels (troubadours and jongleurs) performed secular poems set to an uncomplicated melody. They also composed and performed simple narratives accompanied by theatrics or dance. **What contemporary musicians are similar to these early minstrels?**

Caption Answer
Folk singers and rap artists are two possibilities.

A Thirteenth-Century Monophonic Song

Like other trouvères of the late thirteenth century, Guillaume d'Amiens, (William of Amiens [France]), sang of love. The text of one of his songs, "Prendes i garde" ("Be on your guard"), tells of the secret meeting between two lovers. It is not known how trouvère melodies were originally performed. Only the melodies (not the rhythms) were notated in the manuscript.

Prendes i garde (Be on your guard)   by Guillaume d'Amiens

Take care, lest anyone see us
If someone sees us, tell me.
It's just there in that wooded grove.
Take care lest anyone see us.
The pleasant lass was looking after the animals,
"Charming brunette, I would like to meet with you"
Take care lest anyone see us,
If someone sees us, tell me.

The Minor Scale

"Prendes i garde" is in the minor mode. The **minor scale** is *a scale built on the pattern of one whole step (w), one half step (h), two whole steps, one half step, and two whole steps.* On the keyboard, the natural minor scale can be played on the white keys from A to A:

Use section C. 3 in the *Music Theory Handbook* to review scales.

The pattern of the natural minor scale is w, h, w, w, h, w, w; or 1, 1/2, 1, 1, 1/2, 1, 1. Because this scale starts on A, it is called the A minor scale. An easier way to remember the minor scales is to relate them to their major counterpart. Play or sing any major scale from LA to LA instead of from DO to DO and you have the "relative" natural minor scale:

Activity *Determine Musical Form*
Instructor's Guide, page 161
TRB 11-5, *"Prendes i garde"*
CD 7 ⌈16⌉ "Prendes i garde (0:40)

ACTIVITY ▶ *Determine Musical Form*

How does Guillaume d'Amiens, the thirteenth-century composer of this French rondeau, organize the music and the poetic form of the text?

Listen to a recording of "Prendes i garde" as you follow the music provided by your teacher and decide which of the following patterns represents the musical form of the eight phrases of the song.

(1) A B A B A C A C
(2) A B A A A B A B
(3) A B A B A B A B
(4) A B C A D E A B

Now determine which of the above patterns represents the poetic form of the text. The poetic form you have just identified is called a **rondeau**, *a fixed poetic form of the thirteenth century*. Which lines repeat the same music with different text?

Learn to play "Prendes i garde" on a keyboard instrument. Which phrases convey a sense of completeness or finality? How do you know?

Challenge You may have noticed the absence of a meter sign in the music. However, when you performed the work, you projected the presence of an underlying metric organization of triple meter. Create a rhythmic accompaniment to be played on percussion instruments while you perform the melody on a keyboard instrument.

An Eighteenth-Century Chorus

Not all expressions of love are composed as solo songs. During the Baroque period, George Frideric Handel composed the **oratorio**, *a sectional form for soloists, chorus, and orchestra*. Like his earlier *Messiah* (1742), *Solomon* (1749) is a sacred work in three parts. In the third part, Handel composed the chorus entitled "Draw the tear from hopeless love," a vivid comparison of the anguish of lost love with death and despair.

Handel's chorus, "Draw the tear from hopeless love," depicts the emotions clearly and dramatically, as Baroque composers always tried to do. The pathos of hopeless love is exaggerated in order to arouse feelings of sympathy and compassion. The moods or affections (as they were called then) are designed to affect the listener. He achieves this intensity of emotion through the basic elements of melody, harmony, and rhythm. The melody, for example, begins with a powerful, descending octave leap immediately followed by an ascending leap of a 7th. The words "tear" and "hopeless" are set with dissonance—notes that clash harmonically:

Then there is the dotted rhythm, one of the great discoveries of the Baroque. The dotted rhythm, occurring in the minor mode at the words "wild despair," evokes tragedy and death. Appropriately, Handel sets "death" with a diminished chord.

PROFILE

George Frideric Handel

George Frideric Handel
German Composer
1685–1759

George Frideric Handel was born in 1685 in Halle, Germany. He showed an early talent for music but was forbidden by his father to study it. To get around this, young George smuggled a clavichord into the attic and practiced on it secretly. Reluctantly, his father finally allowed the boy to study music as well as law.

In 1703, Handel moved to Hamburg, where he performed in opera orchestras. He composed his first opera the following year. Then in 1706, he went to Italy, where he absorbed the free-flowing Italian lyricism, which was to be a hallmark of his later music. There he refined his opera composing and wrote concertos, sonatas, cantatas, and oratorios. Yet it would be in England that Handel would make his mark as one of the greatest composers of the Baroque era. His opera *Rinaldo* was a triumph during his first visit in 1711. He moved to London the next year, remaining there until his death in 1759.

Handel's finest achievement was the invention of the English oratorio, a form of storytelling for soloists, chorus, and orchestra. Oratorios are dramas without scenery. The uniqueness and grandeur of oratorios like the *Messiah* make them still popular today.

Activity *Sing a Chorus from the Baroque Era*
Instructor's Guide, pages 161–162
CD 7 17 "Draw the tear from hopeless love," *Solomon* (3:43)

ACTIVITY ▶ *Sing a Chorus from the Baroque Era*

How does Handel's music express the anguish of lost love?

Sing the opening line of "Draw the tear from hopeless love" on page 213, paying attention to the dissonance on the words "tear" and "hopeless." Sing the line "full of death and wild despair," making the dotted rhythm clipped and dramatic. Now listen to the recording of this work while you follow the text:

> Draw the tear from hopeless love;
> lengthen out the solemn air,
> full of death and wild despair.

1. Which sections of the text did Handel set polyphonically?
2. Which sections of the text are set homophonically?
3. How and where does Handel use silence to good effect?

An Early Twentieth-Century Opera Aria

The three basic emotional states of love—lost, sought, or found—are just as common in classical music as they are in popular music. As in popular music, classical songs expressing the tragedy of lost love and the search for love outnumber songs that celebrate the joys of love. We see this in the opera *Madama Butterfly* (1904) by Giacomo Puccini

The opera Madama Butterfly *by Italian composer Giacomo Puccini is among the great tragic love stories. The story focuses on a young Japanese girl who falls in love with an American naval officer. She marries him against her father's wishes, not knowing the love is one-sided. Puccini's music, performed here by Renata Scotto, is the reason this opera continues to be performed throughout the world.*

(1858–1924). This story-told-in-song is a very popular opera because the action is realistic and the characters are understandably human. Like most operas, this is a love story.

The story of *Madama Butterfly* recounts the tragic relationship between a young Japanese lady and an American naval officer named Pinkerton. At the age of 15, Butterfly marries the visiting lieutenant, who promptly abandons her. Despite Butterfly's responsibility as a single parent for raising their son, Butterfly remains hopeful about their marriage. She fantasizes about her husband's return and their ensuing happiness in the famous aria "Un bel di" ("One fine day"). Unfortunately, when he does arrive, three years after leaving her, it is with Kate, his American wife. Realizing that her love has been a delusion, Butterfly blindfolds her son and then stabs herself to death.

This opera was given its world premiere at La Scala Opera House in Milan, Italy, in 1904, and its American premiere at the Metropolitan Opera in 1907. The opera continues to be one of the most popular in the world, and its essence is summed up in its most famous aria, "Un bel di."

Another successful Puccini opera, La Bohème *(1896), tells the story of a young poet (Rodolfo) and his love (Mimi). Like* Madama Butterfly, *the theme of love appeals to a universal audience.* Rent *is a Broadway musical that retells the story of* La Bohème, *set in New York City in the 1990s.*

Activity *Discover Through Analysis*
Instructor's Guide, page 162
TRB 11-6, *"Un bel di"*
TRB 11-7, *Profile—Giacomo Puccini*
CD 7 [18] "Un bel di," *Madama Butterfly* (4:45)

ACTIVITY ▶ *Discover Through Analysis*

How does Puccini's music reflect the hopes and feelings of Madame Butterfly?

Listen to "Un bel di" as you follow the Italian words and their translation and focus on the ideas that occur. Describe the dramatic action portrayed in each of the events.

1. Listen again and select the letter that matches each of the four dramatic sections with one of the following musical descriptions.
   a. The most intense section, with the loudest dynamic level. A climactic pitch in high register is held for a long duration.
   b. Strong, powerful melody in triple meter that begins in a high register. Singing is legato (smooth and connected), with much rubato (give and take in the tempo), and a wide vocal range.
   c. Vocal phrases are short. At first the vocal range is narrow and speechlike; then it turns impassioned and full voiced, changing from duple to triple meter.
   d. The meter changes to duple. The singing is hushed, calm, and thoughtful, then more excited and expectant.
2. Which words mark the return of the opening melody? What is the text referring to at this point?
3. Which section employs the greatest dynamic contrasts? How do these dynamic contrasts support the text?

An American Opera Duet

Love songs are sometimes presented in the form of a duet. This can serve as the perfect medium for a lovers' quarrel or to show the emotion of two people who are happily in love. One of the most famous love songs of the latter type is the duet "Bess, You Is My Woman Now" from George Gershwin's opera *Porgy and Bess* (1935), which incorporated the local dialect of the Gullah African Americans of Charleston, South Carolina, about 1912, where and when the opera takes place.

In the opera, Porgy and Bess sing their famous love duet. At first, Porgy sings alone to Bess. Then, after an expressive modulation (a change of key), Bess sings her response to Porgy. At the end of Bess's solo, Porgy echoes the "mornin' time an' evenin' time" theme before the two join in singing together. Here, both Porgy and Bess are singing different lyrics and different melodies to each other at the same time. These combined lyrics are as follows:

Bess: Porgy, I's yo' woman now, I is, I is, An' I ain' never goin' nowhere 'less you shares de fun.

Porgy: Bess, you is my woman now an' forever. Dis life is jes' begun, Bess, we two is one now an' forever.

Bess: Dere's no wrinkle on my brow, no-how, but I ain' goin' you hear me sayin'

Porgy: Oh Bess, don' min' dose women. You got yo' Porgy, you loves yo' Porgy. I know you means it.

Bess: If you ain' goin', wid you I'm stayin'. Porgy, I's yo' woman now. I's yours forever.

Porgy: I seen it in yo' eyes, Bess. We'll go swingin' through de years a singin'

Bess: Mornin' time an' evenin' time an' summer time an' winter time.

Porgy: Hmmm—

Bess: Hmmm—

Porgy: Mornin' time an' evenin' time an' summer time an' winter time.

Bess: Oh my Porgy, my man Porgy, from dis' minute I'm tellin' you, I keep dis vow:

Porgy: My Bess, my Bess, from dis' minute I'm tellin' you, I keep dis vow:

Bess: Porgy, I's yo' woman now.

Porgy: Oh, my Bessie, we's happy now—we is one now.

One of the emotional climaxes in any piece of musical theatre is the love duet, which can suspend time, place, and belief. In Porgy and Bess, the two lovers embrace and sing "Bess, You Is My Woman" at a point in the story where love overwhelms their troubles. Clamma Dale and Donnie Ray Albert played the lead roles in this Houston Grand Opera's production of the George Gershwin opera Porgy and Bess.

ACTIVITY ▶ *Expand Your Listening Focus*

What makes a great love song? Listen to the duet "Bess, You Is My Woman Now" from *Porgy and Bess* and describe the musical qualities that make it so expressive.

Listen to this duet three times while you list your comments in each of the blocks of the Perceptive Listening Grid.

■ The first time you listen to the lovers singing together on the third chorus, try to focus your attention exclusively on the melodic line sung by Bess.

■ The second time, focus your attention on Porgy's line.

■ The third time, see if you can follow both of their lines and lyrics simultaneously.

Activity *Expand Your Listening Focus*
Instructor's Guide, pages 162–163
TRB 11-8, *Perceptive Listening*
CD 7 [19] "Bess, You Is My Woman Now" (5:30)

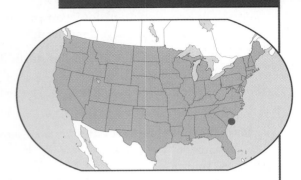

MUSIC in the WORLD

GULLAH culture originated in the Sea Islands off the coast of Georgia and South Carolina. Here the first African families settled and spoke a dialect that maintained words closely related to Bantu, a language group found in parts of Africa. *Porgy and Bess* is set in a fictional Gullah community named Catfish Row.

SUMMARY

The love song is one of the most compelling and frequent forms of musical expression. Love songs turn up in all cultures throughout history. As highly inventive and intensely expressive musical creations, they capture some of the strongest emotions we experience in our lives. Perhaps no other form of artistic expression can surpass music in representing these powerful emotions: the tragedy and anguish of lost love, the disturbingly empty and lonely search to find love, and the joy of love secured. The subject of love can reveal the best of any composer. We know it when all the elements of music come together to express these common human themes in ways that illuminate our own emotional state and let us know that we are not alone in feeling the way we do.

Complete answers for the Chapter 11 Review are found in the Instructor's Guide, pages 164–165.

Building Music Vocabulary

On a sheet of paper, write the term from the list that best matches each description below.

(9) cadence   (6) minor scale
(3) cakewalk   (7) oratorio
(1) harmony   (5) primary chords
(8) interval   (4) rondeau
(10) major scale   (2) scale

1. Vertical blocks of different tones that sound simultaneously.
2. A sequence of notes arranged in rising pitches.
3. A dance with syncopated rhythms that may represent an early form of jazz.
4. A fixed poetic form of the thirteenth century.
5. The chords built on the first, fourth, and fifth degrees of the scale.
6. A scale built on the pattern of one whole step, one half step, two whole steps, one half step, and two whole steps.
7. A sectional form for soloists, chorus, and orchestra.
8. The distance in pitch between two tones.
9. A breathing break.
10. A scale built on the pattern of two whole steps, one half step, three whole steps, and one half step.

Reviewing Music Facts

Answer each question in a complete sentence.

11. What are three basic messages communicated in most love songs?
12. Why do C sharp and D flat sound the same on a piano keyboard?
13. What nineteenth-century European vocal style influenced the type of Mexican love song called *canción ranchera*?
14. How do some intervals in an Egyptian scale differ from those in the Western major scale?
15. What Baroque rhythmic innovation did Handel use to evoke tragedy and death?
16. What is one reason *Madama Butterfly* is a very popular opera?

Thinking It Through

On a sheet of paper, write your responses to the following:

17. **Explain** Tell why it is so easy to see the interval pattern of the major scale on a keyboard.
18. **Apply** Since the original written music of "Prendes i garde" does not indicate the rhythms, how do music publishers select the rhythms notated in their music?

Making the Connection

Social Studies Learn more about the way information was conveyed from one place to another in Europe during the Middle Ages. In particular, what role might the troubadours and minstrels play in relaying events of the times?

Language Arts Pick one of your favorite popular love songs of current or recent times. Write out the lyrics and then, in your own words, state the message of the song in one or two sentences. Is your song sad, melancholy, or joyful?

 You can learn about the history of *Porgy and Bess* at **www.glencoe.com/sec/music**

Answers to Chapter 11 Review
11. Lost love, longing for love, celebration of love.
12. C sharp and D flat are played on the same piano key.
13. European singing styles, especially Italian opera.
14. Some fall between the half steps of the Western scale.
15. Dotted rhythms.
16. The action is realistic and the characters are human.
17. The key of C is all the white notes on the piano keyboard.
18. Possibilities include determining the rhythm of the music by looking at the rhythm of the words.

CHAPTER 12

Religious Music

Music has always had its practical uses. Worldwide, music seems to be directly connected to, and stand at the heart of, every aspect of human life. In addition to practical needs, much of the world's music is made to serve spiritual needs. Music evokes the spirit and mystery of life better than any other form of human expression. By interpreting the meaning of sacred texts, music clarifies and intensifies their implications. Through music, the words are lifted to a higher power. By this means, music transports us into the spiritual world so that we can connect with our own spirituality and our quest for salvation.

Music is a part of most religious services. Furthermore, may of the great musical traditions of the world grew directly from religious traditions. **Can you identify any of these traditions?**

Caption answer
Students might recognize the spiritual, gospel music, Gregorian chant, hymn, cantatas, the Hindu kritis, Mahayana chant, or Islamic qawwali.

Objectives

By completing the chapter, you will:
- Realize how music reflects religious feeling and interprets the meaning of sacred texts.
- Understand the importance of music in the practice of most of the world's religions.
- Become acquainted with music of different religions including Hindu, Buddhist, Jewish, Christian, and Islamic faiths.
- Learn the history and style of gospel music.

Vocabulary

cantata
chorale
chorale preludes
conjunct
disjunct
harmonics
kritis
mass
overtones
qawwali
word painting

Musicians to Meet

Thomas Andrew Dorsey
Felix Mendelssohn

Religious Music

You may wish to use "Investigate Religious Music" at this time. Lesson plans for the activity are found on page 175 in the Instructor's Guide.

Throughout the ages and in every part of the world, people have sought help from a divine being. For many, religion becomes a central guiding hand that permeates all that they do and everything they are.

All major religions or belief systems use sound as an expression of faith and spirituality, which are difficult to understand through words alone. Like the great cathedrals, temples, holy shrines, and other religious works of art, music evokes the spiritual and helps people stay in touch with it. It expresses the mysteries of life and the search for meaning. In this sense, music joins religion to give life direction, wholeness, and purpose.

Hinduism

Hinduism is one of the oldest religions still practiced in the world. Aside from the island of Bali and the mountain kingdom of Nepal, India is the only Hindu country in the world. However, Hindu people live in nearly all countries, particularly on the Asian continent.

Hindus worship many gods and goddesses, each with his or her own name, shape, and character. One of the most important of the many gods is Vishnu, who is thought of as the creator of life and substance. The god Shiva is the lord of the dance. Saraswati is the goddess of music and learning. Although there are many different gods and goddesses, some Hindus believe that these deities are all aspects of a single divine power.

Hindus believe that all creatures are in a process of spiritual evolution; that their souls strive through successive rebirths to achieve union with Brahma, the Supreme Being and source of universal life; and that people must live righteously according to their caste, or station in life.

A R T S O U R C E *ARTSOURCE*

Use Artsource® VHS segment 7 in the Performing Arts Package to show a performance by the Ranganeketan Cultural Arts Troupe.

Dance and music are deeply rooted in Hindu life. Here, a dancer from the Ranganiketan Manipuri Cultural Arts Troupe performs "Rasa Lila," a classical dance believed to have been created by the Hindu god Krishna. It was communicated to King Jai Singh in 1750 through a vision and was re-created to exact specifications, including both style and costumes.

Ranganiketan Manipuri Cultural Arts Troupe. "Vansanta Rasa Lila." Dr. T.D. Singh, founder and director. Photo by Craig Schwartz.

Saraswati is the Hindu goddess of music and wisdom. The arts are such an integral part of Hinduism that it is difficult to separate the two. Religion, art, music, and drama merge in Hindu life. **Can you name other cultures where the same occurs?**

Saraswati, Goddess of Learning. c. 1960. Victoria and Albert Museum, London, Great Britain.

Music & Art
Responses might include Native American cultures, among others.

The Music of Hinduism

Natural connections are made between faith and the arts, which are inseparable in Hinduism. These connections are so pervasive that it is difficult to think of one without the other. **Kritis** (KRI-tees) are *Hindu religious songs that are sung in praise of a particular god or gods.* Many kritis, including "Bruhi Mukundeti," were composed in southern India during the eighteenth and nineteenth centuries by deeply religious individuals, many of whom are considered today to be Hindu saints. Kritis are usually sung by a solo artist in a concert setting.

Much of Indian music uses the principle of theme and variations. Sometimes the variations are improvised, sometimes composed. In kritis, the variations are often both composed and improvised. The example you will hear includes only composed variations. In "Bruhi Mukundeti," the poet asks his tongue to keep repeating the different sacred names of God (Keshala, Madhava, Govinda, Krishna, Sadanand, Radha, Ram). The repetitions of God's names is, in itself, often seen as a religious act.

Bruhi mukundeti rasane
    (BROO-hee mu-KOOND E-tee RA-sa-ney)
Keshava madhava govindeti
    (KE-sha-va MAA-dha-va go-VIND E-tee)
Krishna nanta sadanandeti
    (KRISH-na NAN-ta sa-DAAN-nand E-tee)
Bruhi mukundeti rasane
Radha ramana hare rameti
    (RAA-dha RAAM-a-na HA-re RAAM E-tee)
Raji baksha ghana shyameti
    (RAA-jee BAK-sha GHA-na SHYAAM E-tee)
Bruhi mukundeti rasane

The first line serves as a kind of refrain and is sung six times initially, with an additional half line ("Bruhi mukundeti") repeated as a cadence. It recurs two more times (lines 4 and 7) and is sung two and one-half times at each appearance. This song is sung by M. S. Subbalakshmi (SOOB-ba-LAK-shmee), one of India's most famous vocalists. She sings in an ancient Indian language called Sanskrit and is accompanied by a violin and a barrel-shaped drum called a *mrdangam* (mir-DUN-gum). In the background, you will also hear a drone instrument called a *tambura*. By repeating the tonal center, this four-stringed instrument establishes a firm foundation for the melodic activities occurring above it.

Activity *Explore Repetition and Contrast*
Instructor's Guide, pages 166–167
CD 7 [20] "Bruhi Mukundeti" (3:28)

ACTIVITY ▶ *Explore Repetition and Contrast*

Listen to the kriti "Bruhi Mukundeti" and note the balance between repetition and contrast.

Read the words to this kriti aloud. Line 1 (see above) is sung six and one-half times, and lines 4 and 7 are performed two and one-half times.

Listen to the performance and answer the questions below. After the singer introduces each line, she repeats it a number of times. The composer has added musical variations to these repeated lines:
1. How many times are lines 2, 3, 5, and 6 heard?
2. Why is this repetition important?
3. What musical elements provide contrast in this performance? (Possibilities include altering the melodic contour, melodic rhythm, dynamics, and adding ornamentation.)

Technology Option
Use Project 12 in the *MIDI Activities* binder.

MIDI TECHNOLOGY OPTION

■ **Music with MIDI** Use a MIDI program to create a theme and variations using ideas from classical Indian music.

Buddhism

Through meditations on his thirty-fifth birthday, Siddhartha Gautama (c. 563–483 B.C.) received revelations that made him Buddha (meaning "awakened"), the Enlightened One. He then set a mission for himself to show others how to attain this enlightenment, and the faith known as Buddhism was born. After 2,500 years, this faith still guides more than 200 million people, mostly in southeastern Asian countries such as Myanmar (formerly Burma), Thailand, Cambodia, and Vietnam.

Buddhists believe that in order to attain enlightenment the individual must look inward, not to any gods. They believe that God does not intercede on earth. The ideal is to shed earthly desires to reach the state of nirvana, a peace of mind devoid of any desires or thoughts of pleasure. It is also believed that a life well lived brings rewards in the next life.

The basic teachings of Buddhism are contained in the Four Noble Truths. These describe life as suffering, sorrow as arising from craving, the elimination of suffering, and the path of actions by which one can escape from suffering. After Buddha's death, Buddhism separated into two schools: Therevada (TEH-ra-VAH-da) and Mahayana (MAH-ha-YAH-na). Both schools follow Buddha's basic teachings but differ in interpretation and practice.

Caption answer
Awakened.

Historical images of Buddha vary somewhat between China, India, Japan, and Indonesia. The first image of Buddha as a human appeared around the first century. As with sound and music, symbols, images, and structures are important to Buddhism. **What does the word "Buddha" mean?**

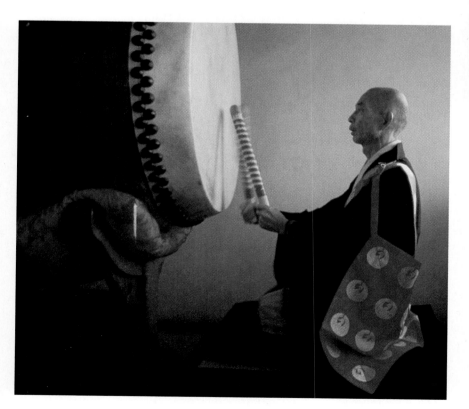

A Buddhist monk plays a temple drum. Music is an important part of Buddhist ceremonies. Buddhism is a major religion or belief system in spite of the fact that Buddha made no claim to divinity, nor did he offer reliance on any gods. He taught that we must look for salvation within ourselves.

Music in Therevada Buddhism

Religious ceremonies in Therevada Buddhism, as practiced in Southeast Asia, include chants, drums, and gongs. Since instrumental and vocal music are viewed as the cause of deviation and distraction from the solemn meditation that leads to enlightenment, this type of music is prohibited as part of religious worship inside the Buddhist temple.

Outside the temple, music is an integral part of Buddhist ceremonies and rituals. It is heard at weddings, funerals, and religious festivals and celebrations, where its function is to establish atmosphere and entertain. The music may invoke spirits and gods that are considered animist or Hindu but still fit within Southeast Asian Buddhist tradition.

"Krida Pinihan" (KREE-dah pin-e-HAN), a piece from Laos, is performed at the beginning of Therevada ceremonies and court recitals. The piece accompanies a dance in which the performers wish the audience prosperity and bless them by sprinkling flower buds on them.

This work is performed by the traditional Laotian *piphat* (bee-PAHD), an ensemble consisting of the *ranat ek* (ran-at EK) and *ranat thoum* (ranat TUM), xylophones of hard wood that provide the melody; *kong wong* (KONG wong), a bronze gong that also sounds the melody; *kong taphone* (gong TAH-pon), a drum that maintains tempo and rhythm; *so u* and *so ee*, stringed instruments made from coconut shells and hard wood that follow the melody; and *sing* and *sap*, small cup-shaped cymbals that establish and maintain the rhythm. The *pi* or oboe, after which the ensemble is named, is more common in Cambodia and Thailand than in Laos.

Activity *Imagine a Buddhist Ceremony*
Instructor's Guide, pages 167–168
CD 7 21 "Krida Pinihan" (3:14)

ACTIVITY ▶ *Imagine a Buddhist Ceremony*

Listen to "Krida Pinihan," a dance performed by an instrumental ensemble at Buddhist ceremonies in Laos.

Envision a religious festival or court ceremony in a palace. This piece is meant to welcome the guests. Working in small groups, discuss the following:

- Why is this music more suitable for ceremony than worship?
- How does the rhythm played by the drums and cymbals change from the beginning to the end?
- Try to identify the following instruments of the piphat and classify them according to the "world music" categories (idiophone, chordophone, membranophone, aerophone).

ranat ek	ranat thoum
kong wong	kong taphone
so u	so ee
sing	sap
pi	

Music in Mahayana Buddhism

In the Tibetan Buddhist tradition, chants and instrumental music are a unique blend of musical styles. These Buddhists view music as a means of preparing the mind for spiritual enlightenment. Choral chants and instrumental hymns are important parts of monastic rituals.

One example of the Mahayana tradition in Tibet is the "Prayer for the welfare of all sentient [conscious] beings and preservation of the Buddha-Dharma [the teachings of the Buddha]." The text may be translated as follows:

> Kye! Source of all glory, mundane
> and transcendent
> Teachings of Shakyamuni, may they
> long endure.
> May the holy beings who uphold
> them
> Live long and be preserved in glory.

The chant is performed primarily by a Tibetan monk, although two other voices interject syllables of the chant. The main voice has the capability of producing choral **overtones**, *the series of faint tones that are generated when any one tone is sounded.* This gives the effect of many voices. These overtones show that the sounds we hear are more complex than just a single tone. A string, for example, vibrates as a whole but also in smaller segments—in halves, thirds, fourths, fifths, and so on. These secondary vibrations produce **harmonics**, *a series of tones generated by the fundamental tone:*

Vibrations per second
55   110   165   220   275   330   385   440   495   550   605   660 *etc.*

Harmonic Series on A

Only two monasteries in Tibet teach monks how to sing in overtones, a technique not taught in the West. Performing the chant this way requires extraordinary skill developed with much discipline and practice. This skill, viewed as an integration of the powers of mind, body, and

Music & CULTURE

Tibetan monks use both vocal and instrumental music as a spiritual means toward enlightenment. Pictured here is a style associated with only two Tibetan monasteries. It is very difficult to master and takes many years of training. Each individual vocalist, singing in a group, is able to produce two pitches that resonate in the throat simultaneously. **What term refers to this technique?**

Music & Culture
Overtones.

speech, represents the existence of a reality beyond our day-to-day perceptions. In this way, the Mahayana Buddhists believe music is connected directly with the deities who guide them to higher states of consciousness.

Activity *Sense the Other-
worldliness*
Instructor's Guide, page 168
CD 7 22 "Offerings for General
Protectors" (3:47)

ACTIVITY ▶ *Sense the Otherworldliness*

Listen to the chanting of the Mahayana Buddhists of Tibet and try to feel how it transports them into a spiritual state.

Sit quietly and concentrate on eliminating every sound, feeling, and thought from your mind as though you were meditating. Listen to the Tibetan chant and answer the following questions:

1. How is the chant different from Western melodies?
2. How does chanting with overtones help express a spiritual state? How many voices do you hear?
3. Is there a steady rhythm (meter)?
4. Try to sing two tones at once. Do you find it difficult? Why or why not?

Judaism

Judaism, one of the oldest faiths, is the spiritual root of both Christianity and Islam. The centerpiece of Jewish law is the Ten Commandments, which God gave to Moses. Jewish holy days remind believers of the struggles and calamities their ancestors experienced throughout the centuries and the lessons they learned from them. In early autumn, the shofar, or ram's horn, sounds the start of the ten-day penitence that begins with Rosh Hashanah, the Jewish New Year, and ends with Yom Kippur, a solemn Day of Atonement for all sins, marked by abstinence from food and drink.

In synagogues on the eve of Yom Kippur, the haunting tones of the chant "Kol Nidrei" (kohl NEE-dray) beckon the faithful to atone for their sins. In medieval times, Jews were often forced to deny their God or else forfeit their life. The plaintive music of "Kol Nidrei" begs for release from such forced vows, as indicated in the text of the prayer:

> All vows and oaths we take, all promises and obligations we make between this Yom Kippur and the next Yom Kippur—may it come to us for good—we hereby publicly retract in the event that we should forget them or could not keep them, and hereby declare our intention to be absolved of them. May these oaths not be considered as oaths, nor these obligations as obligations.

Kol Nidrei

Largo

Kol   nid - rëy____   v' - e - sa - rëy____   va - cha - ra

mey____   v' - k'o - na - mëy ____   v' - chi - nu -

yëh ____   v' - ki - nu - sëy ____   u - sh' - vu - ōt.

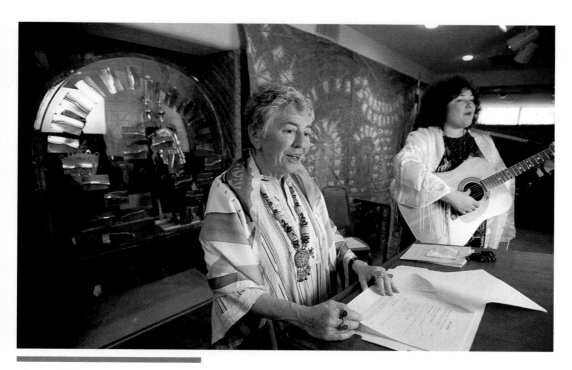

The Jewish cantor is a synagogue official who sings or chants liturgical (worship) music and leads the congregation in prayer. In this photo, a female rabbi leads a prayer while the cantor accompanies on a guitar.

ACTIVITY ▶ *Music and Prayer*

How does music enhance the meaning of this Hebrew prayer?

A. Listen to a cantor sing "Kol Nidrei" as you follow the English translation of the Hebrew text, then do the following:

1. Think of words that describe the mood of the text and the music. Make a list of the musical elements that express this mood.

2. Decide whether this melody is basically **conjunct**, *a melody formed by successive pitches of the scale*, or **disjunct**, *a melody formed by intervals larger than a 2nd*. Is the range of the melody (from lowest to highest pitch) generally small or large? Is the melody based on the major or minor scale?

Challenge Learn to play the refrain of "Kol Nidrei" on mallet percussion or a keyboard instrument.

B. Now listen to a version of "Kol Nidrei" as it was adapted for solo cello and orchestra by the German composer Max Bruch (1838–1920).

1. Why do you think Bruch chose to set this Hebrew folk song for solo cello?

2. How is Bruch's adaptation of "Kol Nidrei" different from the original vocal version?

At the end of this prayerful day, the shofar sounds once more, a signal that the heavenly book of judgment has been closed for the coming year. The sound evokes ancient calls to battle and the heralding of peace.

Christianity

The Christian faith is based on the writings of the New Testament of the Holy Bible. Christians worship the Trinity (Father, Son, and Holy Spirit) and believe that Jesus Christ, as the son of God, was crucified, buried, and rose from the dead. Christians aspire to a sublime life after death with the heavenly father.

As one of the great civilizing forces of the Western world, the Catholic church educated its people through magnificent pageants and passion plays (that told the Christmas and Easter stories), and splendid celebrations on feast days—all with glorious music. For almost 1,500 years, Rome was the center of Christianity. The early history of music, therefore, is largely a history of Catholic church music—from Gregorian chants, motets, cantatas, and organ works to compositions for chorus and orchestra.

The Mass

The *principal form of the Catholic liturgical service* is the **mass**. Through the ages, composers have written music for the sung portions of the mass, and the tradition has continued into our own time. One of the functions of religious music is to interpret the text of the mass and express its ultimate meaning. Music forces us to linger over the words and ponder them.

Ludwig van Beethoven was a master at **word painting**, *the technique of making the music portray the meaning of the words.* This technique was developed by Renaissance composers. Beethoven's *Missa Solemnis* ("Solemn Mass") provides some excellent examples of word painting and the meaning it can impart.

This work is unusually long, and it requires a great number of performers—soloists, chorus, and a large orchestra. It seems more suited to the concert hall than to a liturgical service, and that is generally where it is performed today. (Beethoven originally conceived his *Missa Solemnis* as a liturgical work, although one for an event of exceptional magnificence. His good friend and patron, the Royal Archduke Rudolph, was to be installed as archbishop of Olmutz, and this was to be the music for the grand service. Unfortunately, Beethoven did not complete the work until two years after the occasion had taken place!)

The *Missa Solemnis*, like most other masses, is organized in five poetic sections: Kyrie, Gloria, Credo, Sanctus, and Agnus Dei. An excerpt from the Gloria, the second section of the mass, illustrates how he uses sound to interpret the words. If we were merely to speak these words, we might find it difficult to decide which lines exalt and praise God and which are more prayerlike:

Music & Art

*Inspired by Christianity, the architecture of great cathedrals gave people a glimpse of what heaven might be like. Spanish architect Antonio Gaudi (1825-1926) continued this tradition in his as yet unfinished Church of the Sacred Family (Sagrada Familia) in Barcelona. **What similar technique did Beethoven use to have music portray religious meaning?***

Music & Art
Word painting.

Gloria in excelsis Deo,	Glory to God in the highest,
Et in terra pax hominibus bonae voluntatis.	And on earth peace to men of good will.
Laudamus te,	We praise Thee,
Benedicimus te,	We bless Thee,
Adoramus te,	We adore Thee,
Glorificamus te.	We glorify Thee.

Beethoven's musical setting of the text makes clear his sense of divine glory as well as his humility as man in the face of it.

Activity *Discover Word Painting*
Instructor's Guide, pages 169–170
CD 5 [4] "Hymn to St. John the Baptist" (0:36)
CD 7 [25] "Gloria in excelsis Deo," *Missa Solemnis* (4:55)

ACTIVITY ▶ *Discover Word Painting*

How does Beethoven paint different musical pictures to convey the meanings of the text in the Gloria of his *Missa Solemnis*?

Listen to the opening of the Gloria, and describe how Beethoven's theme paints the meaning of the words "Gloria in excelsis Deo." Show the melodic contour with your hand.

- Describe the tempo and rhythm. Is the setting polyphonic or homophonic?

- Listen again to the opening Gloria, focusing on the second line of text, "Et in terra pax hominibus bonae voluntatis." How does Beethoven paint the meaning of these words?

- How is such a musical contrast between these two lines of text justified?

- Describe Beethoven's musical treatment of the next lines of text. How does he interpret these words (Laudamus te, Benedicimus te, Adoramus te, Glorificamus te)?

- How did Beethoven create a sense of musical unity and variety through word painting in this opening section of the Gloria?

The Hymn

On October 31, 1517, when Martin Luther (1483–1546) posted his "Ninety-five Theses Upon Indulgences" on the door of the Wittenberg Castle Church in Germany, he ended the preeminent role of the Catholic church in Western Europe. At the time, Luther, himself a Catholic priest, took issue with the right of his churchmen to extract monies for certain favors they bestowed. He created an uproar that finally split the church. In 1529, when Luther was prohibited from teaching by the Catholic rulers in Germany, his supporters protested, and the Protestant movement was born. Protestantism extolled the authority of the Bible and each person's direct relationship with God. Since that time, Protestantism has grown in many different forms and has deeply affected Western thought and civilization.

Music **& History**

The invention of the moveable type press in the 1450s enabled Martin Luther to spread his ideas on faith. However, music symbols were too complex to create on a printing press. Early books of printed music finally appeared in Germany in the late 1400s. **How did the printing press enable music to reach a wider audience?**

Music & History
The printing press made mass production of the same music possible for faster and greater distribution.

Luther's idea that people should have a direct relationship with God can be seen in his music. He translated the Bible into German so that people could read it themselves. (At the time, the official language of the Catholic church was Latin.) He composed simple, yet powerful, hymns in the people's own language. "A Mighty Fortress Is Our God" is a good example.

ACTIVITY ▶ *Count the Phrases*

Activity *Count the Phrases*
Instructor's Guide, page 170
CD 8 ☐1 "A Mighty Fortress Is Our
God" (1:41)

How does the melodic contour affect the expressiveness of a melody?

Listen to Martin Luther's hymn "A Mighty Fortress Is Our God" and try to hear the logic and power of the form.
1. Count the total number of phrases you hear.
2. Listen again, and facing a partner, create a mirror image of the phrases by moving your hand in an arc. Which phrases convey a sense of completeness or finality? What is the basis for your determination? Why is this tune so powerful?
(**Hint:** Study the use of DO [tonic] and SOL [dominant], the two most important tones in the scale, throughout the tune.)

Later composers used the **chorale**, or *hymn tune*, as the basis for various kinds of musical works. For example, Felix Mendelssohn used the chorale "A Mighty Fortress Is Our God" as the first theme in the fourth movement of his Symphony No. 5 in D Major (*Reformation*).

Mendelssohn composed the work in celebration of the three-hundredth anniversary of the Augsburg Confession, the document that set forth the principles of Protestantism in 1530. In this orchestral work, he used the chorale theme in a dramatic rather than religious way.

A Mighty Fortress Is Our God

Words and Music by Martin Luther, 1529

A might-y for-tress is — our God, A tow'r of strength n'er fail - ing. A

help - er might-y is — our God. For it's a light pre - vail - ing. He

o - ver com - eth — all. He sav - eth from the fall. His might and pow'r are

great. He all things did cre - ate. And He shall reign for e - ver more.

Activity *Track the Musical Events*
Instructor's Guide, page 171
TRB 12-1, *Symphony No. 5 in D Minor*
CD 8 ② Symphony No. 5 in D Minor, fourth movement (8:080)

ACTIVITY ▶ *Track the Musical Events*

Listen to the fourth movement of Felix Mendelssohn's Symphony No. 5 in D Minor and hear how he builds the movement around the chorale theme.

Try to identify each of the successive musical events shown on the map of this movement provided by your teacher.

All nine phrases of the chorale "A Mighty Fortress Is Our God" (first theme) are presented.

Johann Sebastian Bach also borrowed chorale melodies and used them as the basis for constructing new works. He often improvised on the organ, using a familiar chorale melody as the basis. These became known as **chorale preludes**, *compositions that served as introductions to the singing by the congregation.* Today these works are often used as preludes or postludes to the religious service.

Many of Bach's cantatas rely on hymn tunes as sources of their inspiration. As developed in the seventeenth century, a **cantata** is *an accompanied vocal work in a number of movements with a sacred or a secular text.* Bach incorporated the sacred cantata into the Protestant church service. These works have magnificence because of Bach's skills as a composer in expressing his unflagging faith. Normally, these cantatas end with a simple harmonized chorale or hymn that was sung by the congregation. In this sense, cantatas were participatory. Sometimes the chorale served as the basis for other movements of the cantata. The use of recognizable hymn tunes made these works readily familiar and gave them a kind of popular appeal. Cantatas were the Protestant equivalent of the mass. They became increasingly elaborate, with movements for soloists interspersed with choruses, all accompanied by a small orchestra. The chorale, however, remained the essential ingredient.

Sleepers Awake!

J. S. Bach

Wake, A - wake! E - vents are call - ing. The peal - ing bells_ an -
nounce, en - thrall - ing. A - rise, Je - ru - sa - lem,_ A - rise!
The bride - groom comes in sight. Raise high your torch - es
bright! Al - le - lu - ia! The wed - ding song swells_
loud and strong. Go forth and join the fes - tive throng.

Activity *A Class Performance Project*
Instructor's Guide, pages 171–172
TRB 12-2, *"Sleepers Awake"*
TRB 12-3, *"Sleepers Awake" Bass*
CD 8 3 *"Sleepers Awake"* (3:56)

ACTIVITY ▶ *A Class Performance Project*

Experience how Bach added counterpoint to a chorale to give it new interest. Follow these five steps.

1. Learn to sing or play the chorale tune "Sleepers Awake." Analyze and compare the melody of this chorale to "A Mighty Fortress Is Our God." Is the melodic contour similar or dissimilar?
2. Go to the music supplied by your teacher. Learn to sing the chorale melody or play it on a keyboard instrument or mallet percussion. How did Bach change this tune?
3. Have someone who can read music play the countermelody. Why do the chorale and countermelody contrast so starkly with each other?
4. Now perform the chorale melody with the countermelody. This is a good example of two-part nonimitative counterpoint.
5. Learn to play the bass line on a keyboard instrument or a synthesizer. Perform all three parts together in counterpoint.

Challenge Listen to the recording of this movement from Cantata 140 and make a listening map of the texture by indicating an "R" for the instrumental melody or "ritornello" sections and a "C" for the chorale melody with the countermelody. (A ritornello is a repeated section in a Baroque concerto.)

PROFILE

Felix Mendelssohn

Felix Mendelssohn
German Composer
1809–1847

Felix Mendelssohn was born into a wealthy family in Hamburg, Germany, in 1809. Felix and his sister, Fanny, who was also an accomplished musician, received their early musical education from their mother, Leah. When he was only nine years old, Mendelssohn made his musical debut. At the age of ten, the Berlin *Singakademie* performed his setting of Psalm 19, and when he was 17, he composed his most popular work, the overture to *A Midsummer Night's Dream*.

After attending a university, Mendelssohn made his first of ten visits to Britain, where audiences adored him. Inspired by the scenery, he composed the *Hebrides* Overture and later his Symphony No. 3 (*Scottish*). His works also include music for piano and voice, his famous Violin Concerto in E Minor (1844), and his great oratorio, *Elijah* (1846). Throughout his life, he campaigned for high standards of musical performance and composition. Mendelssohn founded and administrated the Leipzig Conservatory and is credited with popularizing the music of Johann Sebastian Bach after almost a century of neglect.

Gospel Music

After the Civil War in the United States, African-American churches emerged with their own kind of Protestantism. The Negro spiritual, which had its roots in slavery, was the predominant style of African-American sacred music in the latter part of the nineteenth century. Between 1871 and 1879, the Fisk University Jubilee Singers toured America and Europe, popularizing concert versions of the spiritual. These spirituals were sung without instrumental accompaniment, and singers were not permitted to improvise or interject their own personal emotions.

Around 1895 in Lexington, Mississippi, a group of Baptist clergymen led by Charles Henry Mason left the Black Baptist church because of doctrinal and liturgical differences. By 1906 this splinter group had evolved into the fundamentalist Church of God, centered in Memphis, Tennessee. Members believed in the literal meaning of the Bible and sang spirited songs accompanied by tambourines, drums, and piano. Although these were not called by any particular name, they were early gospel songs.

The Fisk Jubilee Singers began as an institution at Fisk University in 1867. Under the director, George L. White, a white teacher at the school, this small group of African-American students began to transform the folk spirituals of their parents and grandparents, turning them into recital pieces. "Jubilees" were fervent religious gatherings that included song and dance.

Later, members established the Church of God in Christ in other major cities across the United States. They spread these musical traditions and influenced the development of African-American gospel music. The gospel song borrowed three basic song types from the spiritual: (1) call-and-response chant, (2) the slow, syncopated, long-phrased melody, and (3) the fast, syncopated motivic melody.

ACTIVITY *Distinguish the Musical Events*

Listen to a typical gospel song, "Perfect Praise," sung by Lecresia Campbell, Walt Whitman, and the Soul Children of Chicago. Can you distinguish what is going on musically?

Using the perception chart of the successive musical events provided by your teacher, try to hear each event described as it occurs. Note: The events are not all of the same length. Answer all twelve questions in the chart.

Activity *Distinguish the Musical Events*
Instructor's Guide, pages 172–173
TRB 12-4, *"Perfect Praise"*
CD 8 ☐4 "Perfect Praise" (6:01)

Other styles of music in the early 1900s also influenced the development of gospel music. While many spirituals tended to be somber, the jubilee was primarily happy and lively. The spirit of the jubilee became the spirit of gospel music. Then, too, the white revival hymns or white gospel songs that were sung at large religious crusades and camp meetings contained lively rhythms as well as call-and-response chants. The antiphonal style was also used, along with the term "gospel."

The Negro spiritual, jubilee, and white gospel song influenced the first major African-American gospel hymn composer, the Rev. Charles Albert Tindley (c. 1851–1933), who was born in Berlin, Maryland. Tindley wrote over 50 hymns for his East Calvary Methodist Church in Philadelphia. Itinerant preachers carried them everywhere.

African-American gospel music gained national recognition during the 1940s and 1950s. Through recordings and tours, Sister Rosetta Tharpe and Mahalia Jackson were among the first gospel singers to achieve a national following. Today, gospel music permeates the fabric of music in America. The fervent religious feeling, the personal expression of the singers, the infectious harmonies and syncopated rhythms, and the strong rhythmic drive of the instrumental accompaniment continue to evolve and change.

PROFILE

Thomas Andrew Dorsey
American Composer, Performer,
and Bandleader
1899–1993

Thomas Andrew Dorsey

Known as the Father of Gospel Music, Thomas Dorsey began his career as a blues pianist, composer, and bandleader for the singer Gertrude (Ma) Rainey. Dorsey then returned to his religious upbringing and began to write and record gospel music. His settings of religious texts used blues notes, lively rhythms, and syncopated piano accompaniments.

In the 1930s, Dorsey had to persevere in order to have his music accepted by many of the large orthodox African-American Baptist churches. They called gospel music "the devil's music" because of its similarity to the popular music of the day. Traveling from church to church, Dorsey sang his music and taught it whenever ministers gave him the chance.

Eventually, the spirit and the sincerity of his music won acceptance, and he published more than 400 gospel songs. Renowned gospel performers like Mahalia Jackson recorded his songs. His most famous song, "Precious Lord," was written after the death of his first wife and son during childbirth. It has been sung in more than 40 languages.

The word "gospel" literally means "good news." It expresses in song the message of Jesus Christ's birth, mission, and gift to mankind. Gospel music can now be heard in religious services of every type, Protestant and Catholic. No other style of sacred music incorporates the free interpretation of the vocal and instrumental parts by the performers, or invites the kind of audience participation, that gospel music does. This is an original American creation that is recognized worldwide.

ACTIVITY ▶ *Sing a Gospel Song*

Sing your own version of the gospel song "Ordinary People" by Danniebelle Hall.

Listen to the recording of this song while you follow the solo line in the music provided by your teacher. Repeat several times until you know the melody and rhythms and can sing along.

Now use the recorded accompaniment to sing your own version of this song, being free with your expression. Try creating a call and response by having a group repeat the phrase "ordinary people" where you feel it is appropriate.

This piece is in slow 4/4 time. Does it lend itself to clapping on the offbeats—2 and 4? Why or why not?

Islam

Islam, the youngest of the great religions, is second only to Christianity in numbers of followers. The term Islam refers to the "peace that comes when one's life is surrendered to God." A follower of Islam is called a Muslim, meaning "one who submits." The Prophet Mohammed (A.D. 570–632), founder of the religion, is considered to be the last of God's prophets, along with Adam, Noah, Abraham, Moses, and Jesus. After Mohammed's death, his followers carried this new religion westward to Spain and West Africa, and eastward as far as Indonesia and China. It is now the dominant religion of North Africa, the Middle East, Pakistan, Malaysia, and Indonesia.

Muslims believe in only one God, Allah. The Koran, the sacred text written in Arabic, is believed to be God's revelations to Mohammed. It provides guidelines to help people cope with human situations.

Activity *Sing a Gospel Song*
Instructor's Guide, page 173
TRB 12-5, *Ordinary People*
CD 8 5 "Ordinary People" (4:32)
CD 8 6 "Ordinary People" (3:43)

The Koran is the sacred text of Muslims that records the revelations Mohammed received from God (Allah). Like the decorative script of this page from the Koran, Islamic music often consists of ornamental melodies.

Leaf from Koran (Qur'an) in Maghribi Script. Islamic. North African. c. 1300. The Metropolitan Museum of Art, New York, New York. Rogers Fund, 1942. (42.63)

The Culture of Pakistan

Pakistan is a small country in comparison with India, its giant neighbor. It encompasses low coastal areas on the Arabian Sea as well as some of the world's most remote regions in the high Karakoram Mountains, an extension of the Himalayas. The separate nations of Pakistan and India were created in 1947 when the British gave up their control over most of these regions. Most of the people in Pakistan are Muslim and speak a language called Urdu. Their lives reflect their geographic location halfway between the Middle East and India.

The Music of Pakistan

Because some orthodox Muslims do not approve of music, a number of fundamentalist Muslim rulers have tried to suppress the practice of music in their countries. Even so, most Muslims and Muslim cultures enjoy a wide variety of musical activities. Some even use music in the practice of their religion. Pakistan is such a country.

One of the most popular forms of religious music in Pakistan (and parts of India) is called **qawwali** (kha-WAA-lee). This rhythmic, fast-paced music is used especially by groups of devout Muslims called Sufis (SOO-fees). During religious celebrations, these men dance to qawwali.

Muslims come to worship at the mosque in Bander Seri Begawan, capital of Brunei, on the northwest coast of Borneo, near Malaysia and Indonesia (southwest of the Philippines). Islam, the religion of these people, spread from the birthplace of Mohammed in Mecca, Saudi Arabia, both westward and eastward.

One group within Islam closer to music than other sects is Sufism, which was founded by the Persian poet Rumi. Sufis believe that music is a means to know God better. It is no surprise, then, that many musicians in Islamic society are Sufis. The dholak drum, shown in this photo, is native to South Asia (India and Pakistan).

Through drumming, hand-clapping, and repetitive religious lyrics, the dancers are induced into a religious trance. The rhythms help create the sense of religious ecstasy the dancers seek. By this means, Sufis believe that they may better experience the blessings of God. During a performance, everyone may clap—the singers in the chorus, the dancers, and the members of the audience.

Another important stylistic feature of qawwali is the use of both solo singers and chorus. The text is sung by soloists and chorus, whose parts alternate and sometimes overlap. In the qawwali excerpt from "The Strings of God's Lute Are in My Body," performed by the Sabri Brothers and their ensemble, the words are as follows:

> Even those who think that they know you
> Have not reached the depth of you;
> Only you know the extent of your divinity.

> Oh, my God, my God, God of all creation
> You can capture a river in a cup.
> I pray to you to grant peace to the whole world.

Activity *Discover Voice Inter-*
        relationships
Instructor's Guide, page 174
TRB 12-6, *Call and Response Chart*
CD 8 8 "Allah hi Allah tan
        meintar" (1:26)

ACTIVITY ▶ *Discover Voice Interrelationships*

Listen to this excerpt from a performance of qawwali. Can you figure out the rhythmic movement and interrelationship between soloists and chorus?

One of the drums is the tabla; the other is a barrel-shaped instrument called a dholak.

Clap along with these qawwali musicians and try to answer the following questions:

1. Is this music moving in groups of threes or groups of fours?
2. Are there sounds that are moving steadily faster than your hand claps? steadily slower?
3. Are there sounds that seem to move consistently in contrast to your hand claps?
4. Are there many places where the singing of these two groups overlaps?
5. Can you decide which is more important, the soloists or the chorus?

SUMMARY

All of the world's great religions are practiced in North America, and all the music of these faiths is also performed here. The United States is as pluralistic in its religions as it is in its cultures and ethnicities. No one religion is dominant. Today, rock, jazz, country and western, and soul music have entered the sanctuary, as churches and synagogues have become involved in the concerns of our contemporary world—discrimination, hunger, injustice, drugs, poverty, illness, and homelessness. These common concerns, like the music that expresses them, blur the distinction between the sacred and secular worlds. Ultimately, we discover that many of the great musical traditions of the world grew directly from religious traditions.

Complete answers for the Chapter 12
Review are found in the Instructor's Guide, pages 175–176.

Building Music Vocabulary

On a sheet of paper, write the term from the list that best matches each description below.

- (5) cantata
- (8) chorale
- (6) chorale preludes
- (7) conjunct
- (3) disjunct
- (1) harmonics
- (4) kritis
- (10) mass
- (9) overtones
- (11) qawwali
- (2) word painting

1. A series of tones generated by the fundamental tone.
2. A technique of making music portray the meaning of the words.
3. A melody formed by intervals larger than a 2nd.
4. Hindu religious songs that are sung in praise of a particular god or gods.
5. An accompanied vocal work in a number of movements with a sacred or secular text.
6. Compositions serving as introductions to congregational singing.
7. A melody formed by successive pitches of the scale.
8. A hymn tune.
9. Faint tones that are generated when any one tone is sounded.
10. The principle form of the Catholic liturgical service.
11. One of the most popular forms of religious music in Pakistan and parts of India.

Reviewing Music Facts

Answer each question in a complete sentence.

12. What two kinds of variations are used in the Hindu kritis?
13. Identify at least four instruments found in the Laotian piphat ensemble.
14. What unique singing technique is used by some Tibetan monks?
15. What chant beckons faithful Jews to atonement on the eve of Yom Kippur?
16. How did composer Felix Mendelssohn use the hymn "A Mighty Fortress Is Our God"?

Thinking It Through

On a sheet of paper, write your responses to the following:

17. **Explain** Why is music prohibited in the Therevada Buddhist temples?
18. **Analyze** Why did composers of chorale preludes and cantatas often make use of recognizable hymn tunes?
19. **Contrast** What is the principal difference in character between a jubilee and a spiritual?

Making the Connection

Science Find out more about overtones and harmonics. Then demonstrate how string players create harmonics on their instruments.

Social Studies Learn about other religions which, like Therevada Buddhism, exclude music in religious services.

Religious music from around the world is explored further at **www.glencoe.com/sec/music**

Answers to Chapter 12 Review
12. Composed and improvised variations.
13. Possibilities are: ranat ek and ranat thoum (wood xylophones), kong wong (bronze gong), kong taphone (drum), and so u and so ee (stringed instruments), sing and sap (cymbals).
14. Choral overtones.
15. The "Kol Nidrei."
16. As a theme in the last movement of his Fifth Symphony.
17. Vocal and instrumental music is thought to be a distraction from the meditation that leads to enlightenment.
18. The familiarity of the hymn tunes gave the cantatas and chorale preludes popular appeal.
19. A spiritual is somber, a jubilee is happy and lively.

CHAPTER 13

The Music of Celebration

All humans celebrate. The expression of joy, pride, solidarity, triumph, and other emotions that make our spirits soar is universal. Music is one of the most important ways humans express these feelings. Usually national celebrations commemorate the life of a great leader or a pivotal event in the nation's history. They might also be solemn and dignified in the case of a hero's death or recognition of those who have died in service to the nation. Invariably these are public events that bring the community together and demonstrate its unity. The music for such events allows the group to share its social values and unite in spirit. In a very real sense, music is often the means by which the feelings of community are coalesced.

The music that accompanies celebrations can draw people together in spirit, thought, and feeling. The music that you hear at a graduation, such as the one shown here, captures the importance of the occasion. ***Name an important celebration in your life and identify music that creates the appropriate mood.***

Caption answer
Encourage a variety of responses.

Objectives

By completing the chapter, you will:
- Find out how all cultures use music as an essential part of celebration.
- Realize how Irving Berlin's music celebrates the human spirit.
- Learn the characteristics of national anthems.
- Investigate the role of the band in celebration.
- Learn about the music of Charles Ives, Sir Edward Elgar, and Peter Ilyich Tchaikovsky.
- Discover how music is used in celebrations in Nicaragua and Japan.

Vocabulary

band
bugaku
concert band
gagaku
marimba
national anthem

Musicians to Meet

Irving Berlin
Peter Ilyich Tchaikovsky

245

Pomp and Circumstance— American Style

In American society, celebration is expressed with such symbols as flags, and through events such as parades, parties, and fireworks exhibitions. Some celebrations, such as the Fourth of July and Thanksgiving, happen on a regular basis. Others such as inaugurations, weddings, anniversaries, homecomings, graduations, and championships occur less regularly and more spontaneously. Almost always there is music involved.

Irving Berlin—Celebrating Life

One American who had a genius for tapping into the American spirit was Irving Berlin. He wrote the melodies and lyrics for songs that celebrate special occasions: "Easter Parade" (1933) and "White Christmas" (1942). He celebrated America through songs such as "God Bless America" (1938) and "Oh, How I Hate to Get Up in the Morning"

Irving Berlin
American Composer
1888–1989

PROFILE

Irving Berlin

Irving Berlin was born Israel ("Izzy") Baline in a Siberian village in 1888. He and his parents fled a pogrom—the organized persecution of a minority group—and immigrated to America. Berlin grew up in the Russian-Jewish ghetto of the Lower East Side of New York City, where he apprenticed as a singing waiter. His gift of playing the piano by ear drew him to Tin Pan Alley, where music publishers had their offices. Here he pounded out the new tunes to sell the popular sheet music of the day.

In 1911, Berlin wrote his first big hit, "Alexander's Ragtime Band." It made him famous. As with most of the thousand or so songs he composed during his lifetime, he wrote both the words and the music. However, he couldn't read music, so a music secretary wrote down his melodies and harmonized them for him.

Berlin was an ardent patriot and had the gift of expressing the universal sentiments of the American people. He wrote the scores for a number of successful musicals starring Fred Astaire. Among his many Broadway musicals are *Annie Get Your Gun* and *Call Me Madam*, two shows that are still widely performed today.

(1942), the latter a spoof on being a private in the army. But many of Berlin's songs simply celebrate the joy of being alive: for example, tunes such as "There's No Business Like Show Business" (1946) and "Top Hat, White Tie, and Tails" (1935). Berlin was a master at grasping and expressing the subtle, internal aspects of human experience.

One of Berlin's most celebratory songs is "Puttin' on the Ritz" (1930). In it he captures the rhythm of ragtime, contrasting a syncopated melody played with the right hand against a steady beat in the left-hand accompaniment. Now, however, the melody was sung rather than just played on the piano. This meant that he had to invent lyrics that ragged—words that have verbal accents and rhymes that deliberately go against the steady beat—no easy feat! The result is vocal ragtime:

DIFF-'rent TYPES
who WEAR a DAY coat
PANTS with STRIPES
and CUT-a-WAY-coat,
PER-fect FITS,
PUT-tin' on the RITZ!

COME let's MIX
where ROCK-e-FELL-ers
WALK with STICKS
or UM-ber-EL-las
IN their MITTS,
PUT-tin' on the RITZ!

Singer/dancer/actor Fred Astaire (1899–1987) performed many of Irving Berlin's compositions in film musicals. He is shown here in the 1935 movie Top Hat, *dancing to the movie's title song.*

TH-48
P-824-56

Activity *Master a Psychomotor Challenge*
Instructor's Guide, pages 177–178
CD 8 [9] "Puttin' on the Ritz"
(2:49)

ACTIVITY ▶ *Master a Psychomotor Challenge*

As you listen to Irving Berlin's song "Puttin' on the Ritz," tap the steady beat and the rhythm of the melody at the same time.

First, listen to "Puttin' on the Ritz" and tap the steady beat. Identify the meter and tempo of the song. What is the song about?

Listen to the song again and concentrate on the rhythm of the melody. The unique character of this rhythm is based on this syncopated pattern:

Tap this rhythm. Recite the words (above) to it.

Now try tapping both the steady beat and the rhythm of the syncopated melody at the same time.

National Anthems

Nearly every country has its own officially designated **national anthem**, *a song of praise or devotion to one's country.* These anthems are the musical equivalent of the country's motto or flag and are meant to stir up pride and evoke patriotism. They are often performed on ceremonial occasions, particularly to honor the head of state. On international occasions, they are useful as a salute to participating nations. At the Olympic Games, for example, winners are honored by the performance of their country's anthem. In the United States and Canada, most athletic events officially begin with the playing and singing of the national anthems.

Most national anthems have a marchlike character. The first such anthem was Spain's "Marcha real" (1770). The model for this type of anthem, however, is the French anthem, "La Marseillaise" (Chant de guerre pour l'armee du Rhin, "the war song for the army of the Rhine") (1792). Many national anthems were written during wartime and reflect martial themes of sovereignty, conquest, freedom, and other national sentiments. Although "The Star-Spangled Banner" celebrates a victory, its 3/4 meter, rather than 4/4 meter, makes it less martial in feeling.

Some anthems are stately hymns. The primary model for this type of anthem is Great Britain's "God Save the King/Queen." Many of the countries that use this type of anthem are former British colonies.

At Olympic games, medalists are honored with a performance of their countries' national anthem. Here, figure skaters Michelle Kwan, Tara Lipinski, and Chen Lu stand at respectful attention during the 1998 medal ceremony in Nagano, Japan. **What events do you attend where the national anthem is performed?**

Caption answer
Responses will vary, but may include sporting events and school assemblies.

Fanfares constitute anthems for some Middle Eastern countries such as Kuwait and the United Arab Emirates. The operatic anthems popular among South American countries were undoubtedly influenced by nineteenth-century Italian opera. In contrast, Asian countries tend not to rely on European models but use their own folk music traditions. Good examples are the national anthems of Japan and Tibet.

ACTIVITY ▶ *Reach an Informed Opinion*

Adopt a Different National Anthem?

Should the United States adopt a different national anthem? Put your research skills to work to answer the question.

The issue: Many people believe that "The Star-Spangled Banner" is too difficult to sing. Others believe that it is too militaristic and does not reflect peaceful democratic ideals. Should Congress maintain the present anthem or adopt a new one?

Read the news articles about the suitability of our national anthem provided by your teacher. Then study the words and melodies of the leading contenders for the new national anthem. Are there other choices that should be considered? Which one do you think best suits this nation, and why? Write your own "letter to the editor" that describes your personal point of view in this debate.

Activity *Reach an Informed Opinion*
Instructor's Guide, page 178
TRB 13-1, *"America"*
TRB 13-2, *"America, the Beautiful"*
TRB 13-3, *"This Land Is Your Land"*
TRB 13-4, *Should We Change Our National Anthem?*
TRB 13-5, *The Anthem Under Fire*
TRB 13-6, *Conduct a Public Opinion Poll*

National anthems function with varying degrees of success. Neither the words nor the music of many of these anthems are the finest examples of the poetry or music of their countries. Still, the words and the melodies are generally stirring and often memorable. The national anthems of the United States and France, both revolutionary and militaristic tunes, are among the most inspiring and memorable.

"The Star-Spangled Banner" was adopted as the official national anthem only in 1931. The melody already existed when Francis Scott Key wrote his verses to it in September, 1814, while being held on board a British ship in Baltimore Harbor. The British had bombarded Fort McHenry during the night, but when morning broke, the American flag was still flying. The melody by the English composer John Stafford Smith was based on "To Anacreon in Heaven," a well-known song of the era.

MUSIC in the WORLD

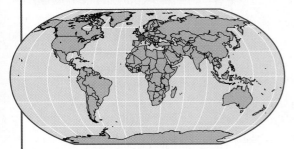

FRANCE is an important cultural and economic European country, whose history reflects a fierce struggle for equality and liberty. The French national anthem, "La Marseillaise," became popular in the nineteenth century as feelings of nationalism swept through Europe and America. *How does your national anthem provoke a feeling of pride in your country?*

Music in the World
Responses will vary.

Activity *Compare National Anthems*
Instructor's Guide, pages 178–179
TRB 13-7, *French Call for Toned-Down Anthem*
CD 8 10 "The Star-Spangled Banner" (2:31)
CD 8 11 "La Marseillaise" (3:58)

ACTIVITY ▶ *Compare National Anthems*

Can you determine what makes the national anthems of the United States and France difficult to sing?

Listen to the national anthems of the United States and France and discover what makes them sound patriotic.

Once you are familiar with the sound of both anthems, look at the notation on pages 251 and 252 and audiate their melodies. Compare the anthems and try to find the elements they have in common. On a sheet of paper, make a column for each anthem and answer these questions:

1. What is the range of each piece?
2. What is the length (total number of measures) of each anthem?
3. What is the meter of each?
4. How would you describe the form?
5. What melodic similarities do you hear?
6. What rhythmic similarities do you hear?
7. What messages do the texts convey?

Many people have complained that both of these anthems are difficult to sing. Based on your analysis, what are the difficulties in each piece?

The Star-Spangled Banner

Lyrics by Francis Scott Key, 1814

Music by John Stafford Smith

1. Oh, — say can you see, by the dawn's ear - ly light, What so
2. Oh, — thus be it ever, when — free men shall stand, Be -

proud - ly we hailed at the twi - light's last gleam - ing, Whose broad
tween their loved home and the war's de - so - la - tion! Blest with

stripes and bright stars, through the per - il - ous fight, O'er the
vict' - ry and peace, may the h'v'n res - cued land, Praise the

ram - parts we watched were so gal - lant - ly stream - ing? And the rock - et's red
pow'r that hath made and pre - served us a na - tion! Then — con - quer we

glare, The bombs burst - ing in air, Gave proof through the night that our
must, when our cause it is just, And this be our motto: "In

flag was still there. Oh, say, does that — Star- Span - gled Ban - ner — yet —
God is our trust." And the Star Span - gled — Ban - ner in tri - umph — shall —

wave — O'er the land — of the free and the home of the brave?
wave — O'er the land — of the free and the home of the brave!

La Marseillaise

Translation by Charles Fowler

Music and Words by
Claude-Joseph Rouget de Lisle, 1792

Music for Special Occasions

Americans celebrate in many different ways, and music is usually there to give the occasion just the right spirit. Even though we are not fond of pomp, we have invented our own kinds of celebrations. About as close as we come to real pomp is in the playing of "Hail to the Chief" whenever the president of the United States appears in person. On the Fourth of July, our most important national holiday, we hang flags, parade down the city's main street, and have a fireworks display. Otherwise, our celebrating is more modest and homespun. We commemorate important stepping-stones in our lives—graduations, weddings, and anniversaries of various kinds—by joining together in a public ceremony with appropriate music.

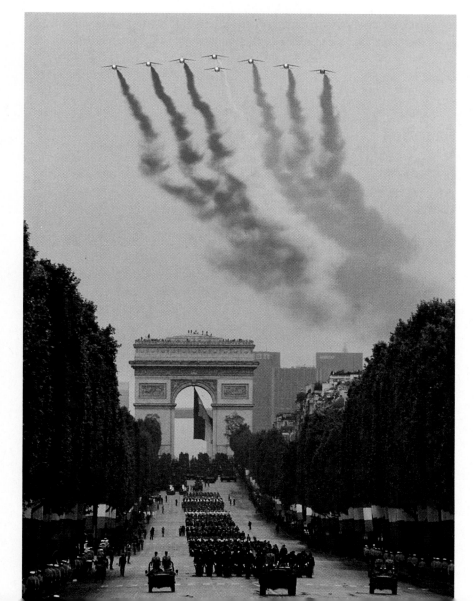

Celebrations are often a combination of music and great displays of pageantry. Here, military planes fly over the Arc de Triomphe in Paris during a Bastille Day parade (July 14). "La Marseillaise" is the French national anthem played during the celebration of independence.

Activity *Identify the Instruments*
Instructor's Guide, pages 179–180
TRB 13-8, *"American Salute" Time
    Line*
CD 8 [12] "The Washington Post
    March" (2:21)
CD 8 [13] "American Salute" (4:26)

ACTIVITY ▶ *Identify the Instruments*

Can you name the instruments you hear in an American concert band?

A. Notice: To test your knowledge of the instrumentation in the concert band, review John Philip Sousa's "The Washington Post March." Working in small groups, write down the names of all the instruments you hear.

B. Apply: Just as Sousa's march conveys a feeling of celebration, so too does "American Salute" by Morton Gould. Gould based his band composition on the short, familiar folk song "When Johnny Comes Marching Home." Gould's band version is written as a type of theme and variations in which different instruments play successive statements, each in a new key.

Listen to a performance of this piece, and using the perception chart, see if you can identify the instruments that are featured in each variation.

Parades

What would a parade be without a band? In many parts of the world, but above all in the United States, the band has a revered place as a celebratory musical ensemble. Almost without exception, high schools, colleges, and universities have bands that perform for sporting events, community celebrations, and patriotic holidays. A **band** is *a large instrumental ensemble consisting primarily or solely of wind and percussion instruments.* There are military bands, marching bands, and symphonic or concert bands. The word "band" has also been applied to jazz and dance ensembles, although the term "combo" is more often used to designate small groups, and "big bands," groups of 15 or more.

Bands have always had, and still have, a role in the military. In the United States, each of the services—army, navy, marines, coast guard, and air force—has its own bands. Military bands rallied the troops during the Revolutionary War, so they predate the founding of the nation. Bands buoyed up the spirits of men enduring hardships, and the familiar tunes provided a link with home.

The **concert band** is basically *an expanded version of the wind and percussion sections of the orchestra.* Unlike orchestral music, however, band music is not written for stringed instruments. Concert bands usually include saxophones (invented by Adolphe Sax of Brussels in 1840), instruments rarely heard in orchestral music. This basic difference in instrumentation tells the listener whether an ensemble is a band or an orchestra. There is a reason why stringed instruments are not included.

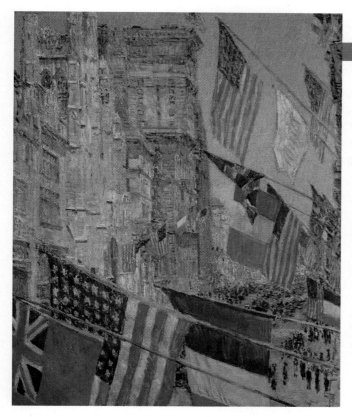

Music & *ART*

When America entered World War I, American painter Childe Hassam (1859–1935), created a series of flag paintings to celebrate Anglo-French-American cooperation and American's patriotism. **How does the painting represent a "coming together of the three peoples in the fight for democracy"?**

Childe Hassam. *Allies Day, 1917.* 1917. National Gallery of Art, Washington, D.C. Gift of Ethelyn McKinney in memory of her brother, Glenn Ford McKinney.

Music & Art
Flags from the three countries are represented.

Bands frequently perform outdoors and while marching. The sound of stringed instruments outdoors does not have much carrying power, nor do cellos and basses lend themselves to being carried down the street! The band, by its very nature, is a noisy ensemble. That is why it can be so exciting to watch.

Holidays

Americans like their national holidays, which are always a cause for celebration. Charles Ives (1874–1954), a remarkable composer from Danbury, Connecticut, wrote *Symphony: Holidays* in four movements: "Washington's Birthday," "Decoration Day," "Fourth of July," and "Thanksgiving and/or Forefathers' Day." He composed these movements between 1904 and 1913. Ives had often heard bands marching down Main Street on the Fourth of July, their sounds overlapping so that the various tunes—always very American—were like counterpoint, one fading into the next. This is the effect he tried to capture. Ives was so inspired by our American tunes and our national holidays that he based this symphony on them.

Activity *Experiment with American Tunes*
Instructor's Guide, page 180
CD 8 14 "Fourth of July,"
        Symphony: Holidays
        (6:02)

ACTIVITY ▶ *Experiment with American Tunes*

What is the musical and expressive effect when several familiar American tunes are performed at the same time?

Learn to perform a phrase from each of the following American songs on keyboard instruments or mallet percussion. Members of your class who play band or orchestral instruments can also perform any of these songs on their chosen instruments.

Columbia, the Gem of the Ocean

The Battle Hymn of the Republic

The Battle Cry of Freedom

Reveille

Perform the four melodies at the same time. Change the tempo, meter, and dynamics. Describe the musical and expressive effect.

Now listen to how Charles Ives used this same musical device in his composition "Fourth of July." Make a list of the tunes you recognize.

After you have listened to "Fourth of July" a second time, discuss how Ives created a sense of celebration in this work. How did he paint a musical picture of this holiday?

Graduations

You may wish to use "Plan the Music for Your Graduation" at this time. Lesson plans for the activity are found on page 183 in the Instructor's Guide.

One of the principal events in the lives of Americans is high school graduation. More than any other event, it marks the division between adolescence and adulthood. This, surely, is a time for rejoicing. There is the ceremony, serious and formal, when diplomas and awards are conferred on the graduates. Later, there is usually a certain amount of celebration. Music plays a role in each part. College graduation is also a time of celebration.

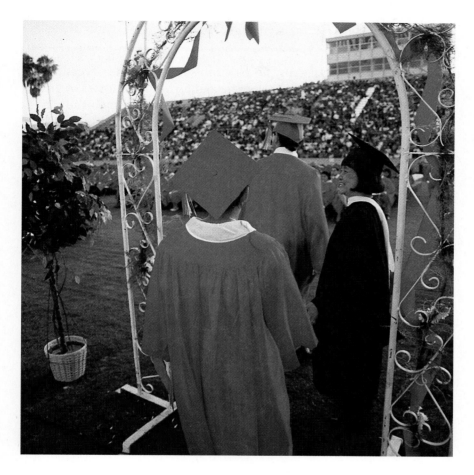

Sir Edward Elgar's March No. 1 from Pomp and Circumstance *is a traditional piece played at high school graduation ceremonies because its musical characteristics add formality and seriousness to this important occasion.* **At what celebrations would you likely hear this piece?**

Caption answer
Most students will identify college graduations.

ACTIVITY ▶ *Associate Music with Events*

What musical characteristics make a composition appropriate for pomp and celebration?

Listen to the musical selection and decide the type of event at which you might hear it. List the musical characteristics you used to make your decision.

Analyze *Pomp and Circumstance*, March No. 1, by Sir Edward Elgar (1857–1934).

- How does the composer capture a sense of celebration and pomp in this composition?

- How is contrast achieved?

- Which musical characteristics have made this famous melody one of the most popular tunes in all of Western music?

Activity *Associate Music with Events*
Instructor's Guide, pages 180–181
TRB 13-9, *Perceptive Listening*
CD 8 ⑮ *Pomp and Circumstance, March No. 1* (5:59)

Celebrations in Other Countries

Celebrations can take many forms, from simple, heartfelt occasions with dancing in the streets, to elaborate and formal ceremonies of great splendor. In other countries, celebrations reveal an amazing breadth of expression. Without exception, music is a central element in these celebrations, evoking both the culture and the particular occasion. Quite often, music is tailor-made for these celebrations. In some cultures, however, there is a whole array of music ready-made for festive occasions, with its own style and even its own particular instrumentation.

Festivals in Central America

Much of the music heard at festival celebrations in Central America is played on the marimba (mah-REEM-bah). Marimbas throughout the region are similar to one another, but their exact shape, sound, and way of being played varies from country to country. The Central American **marimba** is *a wooden xylophone that can be played by as many as eight musicians.* The number of musicians depends on the size of the instrument and local custom. Each player strikes the keys with two to four sticks with rubber knobs at the ends. Some marimbas have wooden keys arranged and tuned to the white keys on a piano (diatonic scale). Others

In Nicaragua and Guatemala, the marimba is played in the streets on festive occasions. Depending on the size of the instrument, several musicians often join together to perform, creating melody and harmony parts by improvising on the low, middle, or high tones.

have keys arranged to correspond to both the white and black keys (chromatic scale). Below each key is a resonator tube with a small membrane stretched across a hole, which makes a buzzing sound when the marimba is played.

The model for these marimbas was probably brought to Central America by African slaves during colonial times (from approximately the sixteenth through eighteenth centuries). Although slaves were not permitted to bring musical instruments with them on slave ships destined for the New World, they could have easily fashioned new instruments from the abundant hardwoods in Central America. While the instrument derives from African prototypes, most of the older music played on the marimba is Hispanic in character. It has a 6/8 meter and generally involves only three chords—I, IV, and V7. Many pieces that accompany dancing consist of only two or three melodic sections that are repeated many times.

The Masaya province of Nicaragua features a type of marimba that is tuned to the diatonic scale. Generally it is accompanied by two guitars. Music performed on the Nicaraguan marimba is public music, especially suited for festive occasions and dancing. Popular occasions for marimba playing are birthdays, festivals for the patron saints of villages, and Sunday afternoons in town plazas. "El Sapo" (ehl SAH-poh, "The Frog") is a well-known folk dance of Masaya.

ACTIVITY ▶ *Perform "El Sapo"*

See if you can capture the lively and spirited rhythm of "El Sapo" in your own performance.

Listen to the recording of "El Sapo" and tap along on the rapid eighth notes while you count the six beats.

Starting with a comfortable tempo, practice tapping and counting the following rhythms, keeping the eighth note steady. Feel the accents switch from two to three in a measure. This is the playful ambiguity that you have heard before in Hispanic music.

Chords:

E   A   B7

I   IV   V7

Guitar strokes: up with thumb (↑) and down with fingers (↓):

Activity Perform "El Sapo"
Instructor's Guide, page 181
TRB 13-10, *"El Sapo"*
CD 8 ⏹16 "El Sapo" (2:29)

Use section B. in the Music Theory Handbook to review notation and rhythm.

Celebrations in the Music of Japan

The music of celebration is not always as relaxed as the folk music of Nicaragua. Some ceremonies are more formal and demand a different kind of music. Japan is a nation steeped in ancient traditions. Celebrations there treat rulers with deference and dignity, and the music reflects this attitude.

Japanese Music

The Japanese place much emphasis on preserving that which is old. Thus, you might hear contemporary music in Japan like that in the United States. At the same time, you will hear music that is hundreds of years old.

Festivals in all parts of Japan provide many opportunities for celebration. Music for these occasions is generally a type of folk music that uses drums and flutes. You will hear one form of traditional Japanese music that expresses celebration: music that is part of the ceremonies of the imperial court, and therefore of an old and stately tradition.

Traditional Japanese music is often constructed from stock melodic and rhythmic patterns. **Gagaku** (gah-gah-kuh) is *Japanese orchestral music (sometimes with singing) that is performed as it has been for centuries at imperial court ceremonies, temples, and shrines.* The term "gagaku" means "elegant music." It is one of the oldest surviving types of music, extending back to the time of early Christian music in Europe. It was performed at the coronation of Emperor Akihito in 1990, continuing a musical tradition that is more than 1,200 years old. Much gagaku was originally imported from the Asian mainland, particularly China. Typically, it was absorbed and heavily adapted to conform to Japanese tastes and needs. It reached its full development in the years A.D. 750 to 950.

The term "gagaku" refers both to purely instrumental music and to music for **bugaku** (buh-gah-kuh), *danced portions of gaguku.* Bugaku consists of a wide variety of costumed dances, many using striking masks. A current example of the influence of bugaku can be seen in the masks used in the Broadway hit *The Lion King.* These bugaku-inspired masks were designed by *The Lion King* director, Julie Taymor, after years of study in Japan.

Another example of bugaku is "Batoo" (ba-toh). The "Batoo" is a dance believed to have originated long ago in Southeast Asia. It is thought to have been brought to Japan around A.D. 740 by a Buddhist

MUSIC in the WORLD

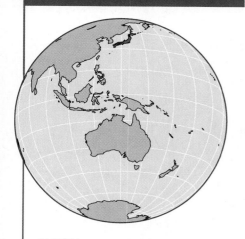

JAPAN is a country rich in music tradition. Its court music is as much a part of modern ceremonies as it was 1,200 years ago. The traditional gagaku and bugaku reflect early influence of music and dance from China, Korea, and areas in Central Asia.

Bugaku Dancers (detail). Handscroll. 1408. Asian Art Museum of San Francisco, California. The Avery Brundage Collection.

Music & CULTURE

One example of bugaku is "Batoo," which is an ancient Japanese dance that is still performed frequently, usually at temples and shrines on ceremonial occasions. The movements are highly stylized, and the music is played on traditional Japanese instruments.

priest. Over the centuries, it has remained a relatively popular, frequently performed composition. The title "Batoo" seems to refer to the downward pull of the hand over the dancer's head. It may also describe the prominent forehead on the mask. The dance has two possible interpretations. The solo dancer may be celebrating the slaying of a tiger that killed his father, or he may be pulling at his hair in sorrow over the slaying of his father.

The danced version of "Batoo" uses the following six instruments—three wind and three percussion:

ryuteki (ree-yoo-teh-kee)—a lacquered bamboo transverse flute;

hichiriki (hee-chee-ree-kee)—a lacquered bamboo double-reed pipe;

sho (show)—a free reed multipipe mouth organ;

san-no-tsuzumi (sahn-noh-tsoo-zoo-mee)—a small double-headed drum played with one stick;

taiko (tie-koh)—a large suspended drum played with knobbed sticks; and

shooko (show-koh)—a small suspended gong played with hard sticks.

The melody of the prelude, played on the ryuteki and hichiriki, is in free rhythm (no definite meter) and is heterophonic, meaning that it is played simultaneously on both instruments but with variants appropriate to the traditional way these instruments are played. Free rhythm is common in Japanese traditional music. Free rhythm does not mean improvisation. On the contrary, each detail of this music, including the relationship between the instruments, is precisely determined and is played the same way each time.

Activity *Write a Haiku*
Instructor's Guide, page 182
TRB 13-11, *Batoo*
CD 8 17 *Bato Netori* (0:47)
CD 8 18 *Uho Bato* (3:02)

ACTIVITY ▶ *Write a Haiku*

As you listen to the Japanese "Batoo" dance music, imagine a beautiful scene in nature that will serve as the topic for a haiku.

Haiku is a traditional Japanese lyric poem made up of only 17 syllables. Read the example below. Listen to the music. Then write your own poem.

> The falling flower
> I saw drift back to the branch
> Was a butterfly.
>
> Matsuo Bashō (1644–1694)

TECHNOLOGY OPTION

- **Music with MIDI** Use a MIDI program to create a composition that serves as a musical backdrop for a haiku.

Technology Option
Use Project 13 in the *MIDI Activities* binder.

Coronations and Other Celebrations

For sheer majesty and stately grandeur, the ceremonies of the courts of Europe and Russia have been difficult to surpass. Coronations, the crowning of a new monarch or sovereign, are lavish events that demand opulence and extravagance. Music for such events is equally as impressive. One of the most famous musical coronations is within Modest Mussorgsky's (1839–1881) opera *Boris Godunov*. This opera tells the story of Godunov, one of the early czars of Russia.

Another well-known piece for celebration is the *1812 Overture* by the Russian composer Peter Ilyich Tchaikovsky (1840–1893). However, the overture does not celebrate the War of 1812, as the title suggests, since Russians had nothing to do with that particular war. Instead, this overture was written to commemorate the Russian defeat of Napoleon when he tried to invade Russia with his French forces in 1812.

The overture is distinguished by its gigantic proportions. The composer used cannons, bells, and an unusual collection of percussion instruments to achieve his bombastic effects. In fact, the cannoneer rests for the first 406 measures of this piece. Then, according to Tchaikovsky's direction, he fires (plays) the cannon for 16 measures at volumes ranging from forte (*f*) to very, very, very loud (*ffff*). The overture contains some recognizable Russian folk tunes, as well as the stirring melodies of "La Marseillaise" and the Russian national anthem.

In many ways, this overture typifies the romantic and expressive ideals of music written during the late nineteenth century. Although it is often played at festive events such as fireworks exhibitions on the Fourth of July, it has also been criticized as being shallow and tasteless. In 1946, music historian Gerald Abraham called the work "one of the most dreary and most repulsive works in the whole of music," labeling it "noisy, vulgar, and empty." Still, this work is played frequently and is a smashing success with the public.

PROFILE

Peter Ilyich Tchaikovsky
Russian Composer
1840–1893

Peter Ilyich Tchaikovsky

Tchaikovsky was the first Russian composer to combine native traditions with a training in Western-style music. His music was successful both in his homeland and in Europe and America.

Tchaikovsky was a melancholy youth. He turned to music for consolation in difficult times such as the death of his mother when he was 14. At age 23 he decided to devote his life to music. After studying at the St. Petersburg Conservatory, he accepted a teaching position in Moscow, where he composed his first symphony, his first opera, and in 1869, his first masterpiece—the orchestral overture fantasy, *Romeo and Juliet*.

Tchaikovsky's tendency toward melancholy was often expressed in his music. He combined passionate melodies and a sense of drama with his formal knowledge of classical traditions to create music that embodied the spirit of Romanticism. Although he wrote great works in several genres, he is best known for ballets such as *The Nutcracker* (1892) and his symphonic works. He died nine days after the premiere of his magnificent Symphony No. 6 in B Minor, the *Pathétique*.

Activity *Examine the* 1812
Overture
Instructor's Guide, pages 182–183
TRB 13-12, *Judging Quality*
CD 8 [19] *1812 Overture* (2:17)

ACTIVITY ▶ *Examine the* 1812 **Overture**

How would you rate the quality of Tchaikovsky's famous work?

Many people consider Tchaikovsky's *1812 Overture* to be one of the best examples of musical celebration ever created. But, is it good music? Opinion is divided on this question. Some critics rate it highly while others condemn it. Where do you stand?

Listen to the overture and rate it according to:

■ Quality of the overture as music for celebration.

■ Quality of the overture as a musical masterpiece.

Write a paragraph that supports your critical judgment. How does your opinion compare with Gerald Abraham's (above)? Who is right?

SUMMARY

Whenever and however people celebrate, music is usually there proclaiming, reinforcing, and dramatizing the occasion. In fact, music is such a natural part of human festivity in all cultures that it is difficult to think of celebrating without it. In the United States, we regularly salute our nation and commemorate our national holidays with music. In other nations, people dance and observe ancient rituals using their own native instruments and forms of music. Ceremonial events such as royal weddings and coronations are cause to call forth the heralding trumpets, massed choirs, bands, and orchestras.

Why music? Why are great orations and fantastic fireworks displays not enough? The answer bores deeply into what music is and what it does for us. Music, perhaps better than any other means, permits us to express the particular spirit of human celebration. It can proclaim dignity and stateliness, solemnity and honor, heartfelt devotion and belief, jubilation and triumph, and the simple, joyous fun of human camaraderie. Periodically, as humans, we have to parade our feelings and know that we all feel the same way. That is how we bond with communities and care about each other. Music allows us to share our humanity in the common experience of elation. Without it, life would be diminished.

Complete answers for the Chapter 13 Review are found in the Instructor's Guide, pages 183–184.

Building Music Vocabulary

On a sheet of paper, write the term from the list that best matches each description below.

(3) band   (2) gagaku
(1) bugaku   (5) marimba
(6) concert band   (4) national anthem

1. Danced portions of Japanese gagaku.
2. Japanese orchestral music (sometimes with singing) used at imperial court, ceremonies, and shrines.
3. A large instrumental ensemble consisting primarily or solely of wind and percussion instruments.
4. A song of praise or devotion to one's country.
5. A wooden xylophone that can be played by as many as eight musicians.
6. An expanded version of the wind and percussion sections of the orchestra.

Reviewing Music Facts

Answer each question in a complete sentence.

7. What is unusual about the lyrics of Irving Berlin's "Puttin' on the Ritz"?
8. What musical element of "The Star-Spangled Banner" is not typical for a national anthem?
9. Identify at least three occasions on which Americans join in public celebration with appropriate music.
10. What band instrument is not usually found in an orchestra?
11. What Central American instrument was derived from an African prototype?
12. Music for traditional Japanese celebrations is usually performed on which two categories of instruments?

Answers to Chapter 13 Review

7. The words have verbal accents that go against the steady beat (the lyrics create a vocal ragtime).
8. Most national anthems are in 4/4 meter; "The Star Spangled Banner" is in 3/4 meter.
9. Graduations, weddings, anniversaries, Fourth of July celebrations, the public appearance of the president.

Thinking It Through

On a sheet of paper, write your responses to the following:

13. **Analyze** Describe some of the reasons why the songs of Irving Berlin became and have remained so popular with Americans.
14. **Analyze** What are some possible reasons why bands do not use stringed instruments?
15. **Explain** Tell how Charles Ives created the feeling of being at a parade in his orchestral work *Symphony: Holidays*.

Making the Connection

Social Studies Learn more about African instruments that resemble marimbas, how they are made, and of what materials. Create diagrams for constructing a marimba-like instrument out of materials that can be found in the area where you live.

Language Arts Create or find a story or description of a celebration to share with the class. It should be different from any in the chapter, but may be from any ethnicity or background. What kind of music is used?

 National anthems and music for celebrations are further explored at **www.glencoe.com/sec/music**

10. The saxophone.
11. The marimba.
12. Flutes and drums.
13. They reflect the American spirit, mark important holidays, celebrate joy, express internal aspects of human experience.
14. Bands often play out of doors, at parades and festivals, where softer-sounding string instruments might not be heard; string instruments are difficult to play while marching.
15. Ives overlapped the sound of one band approaching and another band marching away, as in a real parade.

Condolences in Death

All human beings have a natural instinct to survive, to live, and to create more life. Death is the antithesis of life, yet it is part of life's process. All living things wither and die. For young people, understanding and coping with death is particularly difficult. From the beginning of our lives, we fill our minds and our days with learning how to live. We spend our time finding out what life is and can be. Death seems remote. It appears to be something that only the elderly need to think about. That is why, perhaps, when an accident suddenly claims a young person's life, there is a tragic sense of shock and loss.

*Death is one of our most difficult emotional experiences. In a variety of ways, music helps us comprehend death and express our sorrow. **How would you describe the music that accompanies the funeral march shown here?***

Caption answer Students would most likely describe music that is slow and somber.

Objectives

By completing the chapter, you will:
- Learn how music is used to express emotions connected with death.
- Find out how music is used in the funeral ceremonies in Bali and in West Africa.
- Discover the relationship between New Orleans jazz and West African music.
- Experience how music is used to express death in the opera *Wozzeck*.

Vocabulary

atonal
gambang
lieder
opus
through-composed
tonality

Musicians to Meet

Frédéric Chopin
Eric Clapton
Billie Holiday
Franz Schubert

Expressions of Death

Death—the loss of a loved one, an admired leader, a cherished friend—is a reality in our lives. It is one of our most difficult emotional experiences. Religion is one place we look for help in understanding and coping with death. All religions give hope and consolation despite the inevitability of death. In almost all the rituals humans have developed to memorialize and commemorate a life that has been stilled and to console those who mourn, music plays an essential and compelling role.

"Taps"

One of the most haunting musical expressions of closure, or ending, is the deceptively simple "Taps," a melody attributed to General Butterfield at the Battle of Richmond (1862). This short instrumental piece is usually performed by a single trumpet or bugle to signal the end of the day at military bases. It is also used as a final farewell at most military funerals. The melody is based on the "open" natural tones of the trumpet or bugle—those pitches that result naturally by blowing air through one length of the pipe. To play these different tones, the player has to increase or decrease the air pressure and change the formation of the lips on the trumpet. These tones are played without the use of the valves, which allow the performer to vary the length of the pipe. In contrast to the trumpet, the bugle does not have any valves and is, therefore, more limited in the tones that it can produce.

You may wish to use "Analyze Expression of Death" at this time. Lesson plans for the activity are found on page 193 in the Instructor's Guide.

Activity Demonstrate Musical Characteristics
Instructor's Guide, pages 185–186
CD 8 20 "Taps" (0:51)

ACTIVITY ▶ *Demonstrate Musical Characteristics*

What musical characteristics give "Taps" its farewell quality?

Listen to a performance of "Taps" and make a list of the musical and emotional qualities that create the haunting mood. Try to comment on each of the elements listed. Is the piece in major or minor tonality? Try to sing or play "Taps," attempting to reproduce the same type of mood.

The New Orleans Funeral Parade

People deal with death in many different ways, and music reflects these differences. "Taps" seems to speak of our vulnerability and mortality. It evokes the silence and emptiness that results when someone dies. Other expressions of death celebrate the life of the deceased and the entry of the soul into a better world. Surprisingly, perhaps, these are basically happy expressions. Like "Taps," the New Orleans funeral parade is also a send-off, but its message and feeling are different.

From the earliest times, New Orleans was a mixture of cultures. The population consisted largely of whites from various backgrounds, Africans, and Creoles—people of mixed parentage. By the 1860s, Creoles and African-Americans began to form their own marching bands. These bands, which usually numbered no more than a dozen performers, were connected with lodges and social clubs. The organizations paid their bands to accompany dead members to their graves. Marching to and from the grave site was a practice peculiar to New Orleans, documented as early as 1820. Notices of these parades were published in the newspaper.

Music & CULTURE

*In New Orleans, the funeral procession, led by a jazz band, is a part of the ritual that accompanies death. Here music is used not to mourn, but to celebrate the life of the deceased. **What music would you expect to hear at this parade?***

Music & Culture
Because the band consists of jazz musicians, the music would be lively.

Activity *Experience a New Orleans Funeral Parade*
Instructor's Guide, page 186
Music! VHS Segment 8, New Orleans Funeral Parade

ACTIVITY ▶ *Experience a New Orleans Funeral Parade*

Watch the video of the New Orleans funeral parade, then discuss the following questions:

1. Is there anything about the parade that would tell you it is connected with a funeral?
2. What tells you that this music is jazz?
3. What instruments are used?
4. What justification is there for the "up" mood?
5. How does this music help people to cope with the loss of a loved one?

The African-American bands had a freer and more rhythmic way of playing than the Creole bands, and there was intense competition between them. But by the late 1870s and 1880s, musicians from both backgrounds joined to play jazz. Typically, the bands were composed of trumpets or cornets, trombones, horns, clarinets, and drums, but other instruments such as tubas and flutes were added if they were available. Usually the march to the gravesite was accompanied by a slow hymn or mournful dirge, but the march back had a definite "up" mood. On its return, the band might strike up a lively spiritual such as "When the Saints Go Marchin' In."

Funeral parades, which enable people to join in the happy celebration of the life of the departed, are still part of life in New Orleans.

Non-Western Expressions of Death

Music has been used in all cultures as a way to express grief, to give tribute, and to console the survivors. Death has a haunting mystery that music somehow embodies. But music does something more. It makes our grief universal. It reaches into the soul of humankind to make the lament larger than our own personal sorrow and thereby provides more solace and comfort.

The arts play an important role in marking the rites of passage—from birth and infancy, through childhood, adolescence, and early adulthood, to middle age, old age, and death. The extent to which various cultures celebrate these passages differs widely. Some societies, for example, have elaborate marriage ceremonies and funerary rites but pay little attention to birth. In the United States, graduation exercises are a form of passage from adolescence into early adulthood. Societies often celebrate such passages in elaborate public rituals.

Music & **CULTURE**

People, often unconsciously, try to leave something of themselves behind when they die. The tomb of Tutankhamen, which contained the Egyptian king who died about 1352 B.C., was discovered in 1922 and contained great art treasures befitting his status. **Why might these tombs be decorated with scenes of everyday life?**

Music & Culture
The dead will be assured the comfortable continuance of their previous lives.

Cremation Music of Bali

Some cultures use music as an essential part of the ceremonies connected with death. One of those countries is Bali, a small tropical island (about the size of Delaware) that is known for its artistic traditions. The climate and the landscape are so beautiful, and the people so friendly and peaceful, that Bali has frequently been compared to paradise.

Cremation (*nagaben*) is considered to be one of the most sacred duties of the Balinese. After a period of interment, the bones of the dead are gathered and placed inside elaborate, brightly colored coffins fashioned in the form of bulls, cows, and other animals and decorated with golden streamers. Usually many families join together to cremate their dead at the same time.

An important part of the daylong ritual is the procession, accompanied by bright music played on gongs, drums, and cymbals, that takes the coffins to the cremation site. As the remains are burned, the souls of the dead are liberated. Later, another procession takes the ashes down to the sea in tall white spires decorated with gold foil and thousands of mirrors

Music & **CULTURE**

In the Indonesian province of Bali, people perform the ceremony of cremation according to their Hindu religious beliefs. Music and other arts are an integral part of this festive ritual. **What type of music is often included in American funeral ceremonies?**

Music & Culture
Responses will vary, but may include songs of sadness and loss or celebration of life.

that flash in the sunlight. While they sing, relatives wade out into the water and cast away the ashes, finally releasing the soul. The cremation ceremony in Bali is an occasion for celebration, not for mourning.

On the eve of the cremation day, a great procession is held to take the effigies of the deceased to the house of the high priest for a final blessing. All the relatives of the dead parade in their finest clothes, accompanied by a gamelan orchestra, dancers, banner- and flag-bearers, and files of women bearing offerings. The processional music is an essential part of the ceremony. The gamelan orchestra consists of metal gongs of various sizes and wooden and metal instruments resembling xylophones that are struck. The precisely coordinated five- or seven-tone music combines rapid cross rhythms and intricate syncopated melodies to create an intoxicating music of dramatic and mystical moods.

The gamelan **gambang**, *a Balinese sacred instrumental ensemble*, consists of four *gambangs* (wooden xylophones) and two *gangsas* (metallic xylophones). The 14 keys of the gambang are arranged to permit octaves to be played with special forked hammers. These hammers are used chiefly to play rhythmic figures. The rhythms, played in interlocking style, dovetail in a complicated manner to create a rapid continuity. The melody, which is in a syncopated rhythm, is sounded in octaves on a pair of seven-keyed sarons. The melody is played in what seems to be a casual, almost faltering way, as though deliberately independent of the basic beat. Actually, this music uses a complex form of polyrhythm.

In 1947, Colin McPhee, an American composer then living in Bali, wrote this account of the gamelan gambang music that is played only for the rites of death, prior to the great procession:

> Above the dry, wooden sound of ancient xylophones that rattled a hollow accompaniment there range the hard metallic tones of *gangsas* [metal instruments that play the melody] in a strange, anvil-like chorale, irresolute, uncertain, as though the players could barely recall the melody. On and on the music played, passionless, colorless, filling the air with mournful sound that seemed curiously at variance with all the excitement and confusion. There were many guests, and the rich aroma of festive cooking floated over the walls from the kitchens, the smell of spice and freshly grated coconut, of roasting turtle and pig.

ACTIVITY ▶ *Analyze the Balinese Gambang*

How would you describe Balinese gambang music?

Using the perceptive grid, identify the means, expression, order, origin, and use of this music.

Watch the video of the cremation ceremony and determine the mood or moods the music conveys.

Honoring the Dead in West Africa

Throughout Africa, music functions as an integral part of social life. Ceremonies and rituals that reflect life's passages—birth, adolescence, marriage, and death—typically include music. To most sub-Saharan Africans, death is believed to be a transformation from one state of being to another. The person enters another form of existence, joining the company of others who have died. There is a sense of going home.

Through the many elaborate rituals connected with death, the living maintain contact with those who have died. Great importance is placed on remembering and paying respect to ancestors who have made possible the lives of those who have followed, as well as those who have made important contributions to the well-being of the group. The music performed in funeral processions and at festivals often commemorates ancestral figures.

Activity *Analyze the Balinese Gambang*
Instructor's Guide, pages 186–187
Music! VHS Segment 9, Balinese Cremation Ceremony
TRB 14-1, *Perceptive Listening*
CD 8 21 "Sekar Kesumba" (1:29)

West African Culture

The Hausa (HOW-sah) people use music to honor their dead. This African ethnic group, which numbers about ten million people in northern Nigeria and southern Niger, is almost exclusively Muslim.

Although the Hausa are deeply involved in agriculture, they also have a reputation as merchants, which is understandable in view of their location near the ancient trade routes that cross the Sahara Desert. Theirs is the prevailing trade language along the southern edge of the Sahara, and their adaptation of the Arabic alphabet has long been used in business in the area.

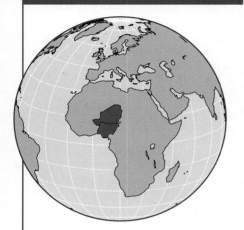

MUSIC in the WORLD

NIGERIA and **NIGER** are home to the largest culture group in this African region, the Hausa. Their music, which always features body movement, is an important and useful part of everyday life. Its texture is a result of complex cross rhythms between instruments.

The Music of West Africa

The Hausa believe in the power of music to make things happen. They value music for its usefulness. They also see a close relationship between music and movement. The two go hand in hand. Body motion is an integral part of their music making. They venerate their ancestors in burial rites that include funeral processions.

The music played during the processions frequently uses repetition. It often includes ostinatos (melodic and rhythmic) as a background for continuous variation. The timbres tend to be complex. For example, percussion sounds are combined with a wide variety of instruments and often with voices. There are complex cross rhythms between the instruments. This combination of sounds gives the music a multilayered texture.

One example of this music is "Sara" (SAH-ra), which is performed in honor of the dead Hausa kings. "Sara" is performed on official occasions, including feast days. It retraces the history of the Hausa kings in the Kantche area of Niger. It might be heard on Islamic holy days when the emirs or rulers ride in procession to and from the mosque.

This excerpt from "Sara" uses seven *ganga* (GAH-ngah) drums, somewhat shorter than conga drums, that are hung by straps from the shoulders of the musicians and played with curved sticks. These ganga drums are double-headed and have attached snares—lengths of spiraled wire or gut strung across the bottom for added vibration.

The ensemble includes a conical double-reed instrument, the *algaita* (al-GAH-ee-tah), and two long trumpets called *kakaki* (kah-kah-kee). The latter add a proud and grandiose sound befitting Hausa dignitaries. These horns have two pitches that are sounded at the interval of a 5th. A bell or *kougue* (koh-oo-goo-eh) completes the ensemble.

ACTIVITY ▶ *Compare Funeral Ceremonies*

Activity   *Compare Funeral
Ceremonies*
Instructor's Guide, pages 187–188
Music! VHS Segment 8, New
Orleans Funeral Parade
CD 8 [22] "Sara" (1:35)

What are the similarities and differences between "Sara," a West African musical salute to the dead Hausa kings, and the processional music of a New Orleans funeral parade?

- Listen to "Sara" and try to identify the drums, double-reed instrument, trumpets (with just two tones), and the bell. Think of the meter as if it were in 12. Can you count it? Is there any repetition? What is the tempo?

- Watch the video of the New Orleans funeral procession you saw earlier. Concentrate on the music that is played on the return from the cemetery. What is the meter? Is there any repetition? What is the tempo?

- Compare the African and American funeral music according to the following:
  (1) the relationship of music and movement
  (2) the spirit of the music (in the context of death)
  (3) the variety of timbres that are used
  (4) the tempo
  (5) the texture—simple or complex
  (6) rhythmic repetition and variety.

- Are there similarities between the two examples, and if so, how do you account for them?

Death Expressed in Classical Music

Throughout the ages, Western classical musicians have dealt with the emotions of death. One of the most moving expressions of death was composed by J. S. Bach during the first half of the eighteenth century. For his *Mass in B Minor*, Bach composed a short chorus on the subject of the crucifixion of Jesus. Actually, he adapted the music from one of his cantatas, taking great care to refine and improve it.

This work may be the most profound statement ever made of human pity, divine suffering, and the mysterious silence of death. It is given added emphasis through the underlying, or ground bass, a four- or eight-measure bass line that repeats constantly under one or more changing upper parts. In this case, it produces an emotional throb. The chromatic descent of this melodic ostinato expresses the grief.

Activity *Explore Expressions of Grief*
Instructor's Guide, page 188
CD 8 23 "Crucifixus," *Mass in B Minor* (6:10)

ACTIVITY ▶ *Explore Expressions of Grief*

How does Bach's melodic ostinato embody the meaning of grief?

Read the English translation of the Latin text for the "Crucifixus" from J. S. Bach's *Mass in B Minor* (below).

Crucifixus etiam pro nobis   And He was crucified also for us
sub Pontio Pilato,   under Pontius Pilate.
passus et sepultus est.   He suffered and was buried.

What is the general mood and focus of the text? What key words help you make your decision?

Learn to play this ostinato (ground bass) melody on a keyboard or bass instrument (below). Try to answer the questions that follow.

1. What is the general direction of the melody?
2. Does the melody move by leaps or by steps?
3. Describe the tempo of the melody.
4. Is the melody based on a major or a minor scale?
5. How does this ground bass convey the meaning of the text?

Challenge Listen again to the "Crucifixus" and determine how many times the ostinato is repeated throughout the composition.

The Funeral March in Classical Music

Use section D. in the *Music Theory Handbook* to review tonality.

Although Ludwig van Beethoven wrote a funeral march as the third movement of his Piano Sonata in A-flat Major, Op. 26, the most famous funeral march is probably Frédéric Chopin's *Marche funèbre*, from his Piano Sonata in B-flat Minor, Op. 35. **Opus** (Op.) refers to *a musical work or set of works*. The term also refers to the order in which the works were composed. It was this music that was used to accompany the horse-drawn caisson holding the coffin of President John F. Kennedy as the funeral procession moved from the United States Capitol down Pennsylvania Avenue on its way to Arlington Cemetery. The president was assassinated on November 22, 1963, in Dallas, and the entire world mourned his death.

Chopin's march is in minor tonality (B-flat minor). He uses a heavy plodding bass with a somber melody in dotted rhythm that evokes tragedy. The slow (*lento*) tempo and dramatic dynamics create a powerful expression of reverence and sorrow.

PROFILE

Frédéric Chopin

Frédéric Chopin was born and raised in Poland, the son of a French father and a Polish mother. He learned to play the piano at an early age and became a brilliant improvisor. His love for the piano became the focus of his creative energies.

Settling in Paris at the age of 21, Chopin established himself as a leading teacher of piano and one of the greatest pianists of his time. Yet he seldom performed in public, savoring his privacy and preferring to devote his time to piano composition.

In 1837 during a period of depression, he composed his well-known *Funeral March*. The next year, he fell in love with George Sand (Aurore Dudevant), a novelist known for her unconventional ideas and well-publicized love affairs. During their ten-year relationship, Chopin wrote some of his most impressive works. Many of these pieces have a Polish flavor, particularly his dances—mazurkas, polonaises, and waltzes. His melodies draw their expressiveness from his harmonically inventive, technically brilliant accompaniments. Chopin died of tuberculosis at the age of 39.

Frédéric Chopin
Polish Composer
1810–1849

ACTIVITY ▶ *Evaluate the Funeral March*

Work cooperatively to examine this music.

Why was Frédéric Chopin's *Funeral March (Marche funèbre)*, an appropriate choice for the funeral procession of President John F. Kennedy on November 25, 1963?

Look at the photo of the funeral procession on page 278 while you listen to the funeral march as originally composed for the piano.

In discussion groups, talk about your answers to these questions:

1. What kind of an arrangement would be appropriate for this outdoor procession?
2. What musical characteristics make this music so gripping in its effect?
3. Would you have chosen any other piece for the occasion of President Kennedy's funeral?

Activity *Evaluate the Funeral March*
Instructor's Guide, page 189
CD 9 ☐1☐ *Funeral March (Marche funèbre)* (4:24)

In November of 1963, the coffin of President John F. Kennedy was carried in a horse-drawn caisson from the U.S. Capitol, down Pennsylvania Avenue, past the White House, and on to its final resting place in Arlington National Cemetery. **What music accompanied the procession?**

Music & History
Frédéric Chopin's *Funeral March.*

Death Expressed in the "Art Song"

The Erlking is a narrative ballad composed in 1815 by Franz Schubert (1797–1828), one of the masterful German composers of the nineteenth century. The poem is by Johann Wolfgang von Goethe (1749–1832), a German poet of Schubert's time. Goethe's poem describes a father carrying his dying son, who is delirious with fever, on horseback through a storm. Four characters tell the story: a narrator, the father, his son, and the Erlking, who symbolizes death. In the central part of the poem, the father and the Erlking, a phantom figure, vie for possession of the child in a dialogue that mounts in tension and anguish. The rapid triplet pattern of repeated notes of the piano accompaniment portrays the galloping horse, the storm, and the father's frantic ride to save his child.

Schubert treated each character differently, and the baritone who sings this song usually varies his voice quality to distinguish between them. Schubert set the father's part in the lowest register and gave his melodies a firmness and strength. In contrast, the Erlking's part lies in the middle-voice register, and Schubert has him speak in hushed tones, as if he is from another world. He beckons his prey with sinister seductiveness, singing in major while the rest of the work is in minor. In further contrast, Schubert set the boy's part in the upper register where each of his abrupt and desperate appeals is sung at a higher pitch and announced with a shrill dissonance.

ACTIVITY ▶ *Play the Piano*

Learn to play the triplet pattern of repeated notes that Schubert uses in the piano accompaniment of *The Erlking* to suggest the fleeting horse:

Using the translation master, read the translation of the poem and bracket the lines and label them according to who speaks them: N for Narrator, F for Father, S for Son, and E for Erlking.

Now listen to the performance in German while you follow the English text provided by your teacher. (In order to follow the text, it will help to know that there are the same number of syllables in both the German and the English. Unlike the English translation, the German text rhymes at the end of each line.) How does the singer help you to know when the speaker changes? How does Schubert use dynamics to help you tell who is speaking?

How many times does Schubert interrupt the repeated triplets in the piano accompaniment? Which one of the people in the story speaks without the triplet figure?

This poem does not have a series of verses and a recurring chorus like many of our folk and popular songs. For this reason the poem is **through-composed,** *a setting of text in which different music is provided for each stanza of the poem,* rather than one in which musical themes repeat in a consistent pattern. In this through-composed form, each part of the text is given a distinctive musical setting befitting the sentiment of the words. Schubert sets each stanza to different music that evokes the emotional meaning of that particular text. Notice how Schubert's triplet rhythm serves as the musical device that holds the music together.

Activity *Play the Piano*
Instructor's Guide, page 189
TRB 14-2, *The Erlking*
CD 9 ☐2 *The Erlking* (4:01)

Activity *Analyze Unity in Music*
Instructor's Guide, page 190
TRB 14-3, *Listening and Perfor-
mance*
CD 9 ☐2 *The Erlking* (4:01)

ACTIVITY ▶ *Analyze Unity in Music*

How does Schubert achieve a sense of unity?

Schubert's accompaniment contains a violent rising and falling figure in the bass that begins with a triplet figure.

Using the *Listening and Performance* grid, count the measures from the beginning of the piece and place an "X" in the first row of boxes in the bars in which you hear this rhythmic figure recur. Is there a consistent pattern? What feeling is conveyed?

Listen again. In the second row of boxes, mark an "X" on the correct beat and in the bars where one narrative voice changes to another.

TECHNOLOGY OPTION

Technology Option
Use Project 14 in the *MIDI
Activities* binder.

- **Music with MIDI** Use a MIDI program to create an art song that utilizes musical motives as well as both modern and traditional song elements.

PROFILE

Franz Schubert

Although he only lived to be 31 years old, Franz Schubert was the supreme creator of the German song. Before him, other composers had put their best efforts into composing long musical forms. Schubert took his genius for melody and applied it to the simple, short popular song, thereby raising it to a highly expressive art form.

Schubert was born in Vienna and spent his entire life there. As a young boy, he studied violin, piano, organ, singing, and theory. At the age of 11, he was admitted to the Vienna court choir. When he was 17 Schubert composed 144 songs including *The Erlking* (The elf king). He waited six years for the first public performance of the song and did not publish it until 1821, as his Opus l.

In his brief life Schubert composed prolifically. He wrote several operas, six masses, nine symphonies, a number of works for piano, and many chamber works. The latter, along with his songs, are among his most performed works today.

*Franz Schubert
Austrian Composer
1797–1824*

Similar to the works of Schubert and Berg, Mexican painter Diego Rivera (1886–1959) painted scenes that evoked strong emotions. In Liberation of the Peon, *he portrays the sadness of comrades over a poor man's death. The grief appears controlled, yet deeply felt.* **How does the artist communicate grief in the painting?**

Diego Rivera. *Liberation of the Peon.* 1931. Philadelphia Museum of Art, Philadelphia, Pennsylvania. Gift of Mr. and Mrs. Herbert Cameron.

Music & Art
Responses might include the kneeling figures, their effort to cover the man, and the bound hands of the victim.

As a composer of more than 600 **lieder** (LEE-der), *German art songs,* Schubert had a profound ability to capture the emotional essence of a poem in his music. The ideal of any song composer is to interrelate the words and music so completely that they become one message. That was Schubert's genius.

The Death Scene from the Opera *Wozzeck*

There are many "death scenes" throughout the world of opera, but one of the most dramatic is in the opera *Wozzeck* (VOT-zehk) by the Austrian composer Alban Berg (1885–1935). This opera, completed in 1922, uses dissonance with powerful effect. The work uses a melodic and harmonic vocabulary that breaks out of the major-minor tonal system. **Tonality** refers to *the major-minor system of pitches.* Berg's opera is **atonal,** *without tonality or a tonal center.* Once you are absorbed in the story, however, you probably will not miss the feeling of the traditional tonality.

Berg's imagination was sparked in 1914 when he saw the play *Wozzeck* by the German dramatist Georg Büchner (1813–1837). Berg adapted the play as an opera. No doubt the traumatic experience of the war helped Berg relate to the tragic figure of Wozzeck, a soldier who is driven to murder and madness by a hostile society.

Through the music, we are drawn into Wozzeck's world to experience his hallucinations and grotesque visions. The music projects his disturbed and abnormal mental state, especially his effort to murder his mistress, Marie.

The music seems as chaotic as the mind it portrays. Surprisingly, it is highly structured even though it may not sound at all ordered. Throughout the murder scene in Act III (Scene 2), a single note B is sounded, as if it were the idea of murder itself rising and submerging and rising again in Wozzeck's thoughts, finally exploding in the horrifying act itself. The music for this scene is an invention on a single pitch!

Activity *Create Mood with a Single Pitch*
Instructor's Guide, pages 191–192
TRB 14-4, *Wozzeck*
CD 9 ③ *Wozzeck*, Act III, Scene 2 (1:38)

ACTIVITY ▶ *Create Mood with a Single Pitch*

Does the repetition of a single pitch function as a structural or an expressive device?

Isolate the single pitch B on any melodic instrument. Using only the pitch B, create a musical idea that expresses these moods:

- calm, delicate, dreamy, and soothing;

- turbulent, agitated, passionate, and tense.

What musical elements did you use to create the two contrasting moods?

In *Wozzeck*, the uncontrolled obsession of Wozzeck to murder Marie is symbolized by the use of the insistent pitch B. This pitch appears throughout the scene in various instruments, registers, rhythm patterns, and dynamic levels.

Follow the German words and their translation on the translation master as you hear them. How do Berg's treatment of the pitch B as well as other musical devices reflect the feelings embodied in the text?

Death Expressed in Spirituals

Because death is something all humans must face, it is a subject that has been explored in all kinds of music—classical, folk, jazz, and popular. We try to give expression to it because we need to understand and cope with it. Many Negro spirituals, for example, speak of the promised land:

> I'll meet you in de mornin',
> When you reach de promised land;
> On de oder side of Jordan,
> For I'm boun' for de promised land.

For many slaves, such songs had powerful double meanings. True, they spoke of the hope of reaching heaven, but heaven also referred to reaching the North and freedom. In the spiritual "Swing Low, Sweet Chariot," the line "I looked over Jordan and what did I see, Coming for to carry me home" might refer to the Ohio River. The "band of angels" could be a group of friends, or abolitionist members of the Underground Railroad. "Home" might refer to the states where slaves had been freed.

ACTIVITY ▶ *Identify Musical Characteristics*

What musical characteristics illuminate the emotions in the words of the spiritual "Hush, Hush, Somebody's Callin' Mah Name"?

Read the text of the spiritual (see page 284). What is the text describing? What specific words tell you this?

Now listen to the recording or sing the spiritual and decide how the music conveys what the text is describing.

Activity *Identify Musical Characteristics*
Instructor's Guide, page 192
CD 9 4 "Hush, Hush, Somebody's Callin' Mah Name" (3:55)

Negro spirituals developed during the time of enslavement. Today, they continue to demonstrate the strong influence of African-American culture in American music. As expressions of death, spirituals convey powerful emotions through text and music.

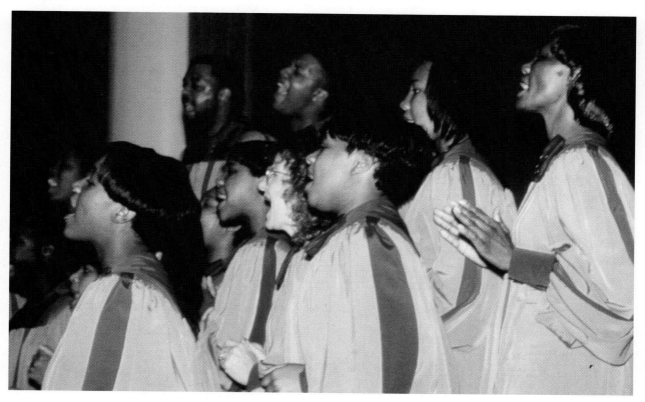

Hush, Hush, Somebody's Callin' Mah Name

Arrangement by J. Jefferson Cleveland
and Verolga Nix

Death Expressed in Jazz and Blues

Even though its tunes are usually thought of as "upbeat," jazz is often tinged with the blues. This blues tint can sometimes assert itself to shade the whole. This is usually the instance on those rare occasions when jazz musicians turn their attention to the subject of death. The New Orleans funeral parade is one way that death is expressed through the jazz medium, but there are others.

Music and Controversy

John Ruskin, a nineteenth-century art critic, wrote that "Great nations write their autobiographies in three manuscripts—the book of their deeds, the book of their words, and the book of their arts. Not one of these books can be understood unless we read the other two, but of the three, the only trustworthy one is the last." In Ruskin's view, the arts present a more honest overall picture because they sometimes probe the meaning of life and events and raise troublesome questions about them. They dig at the truth.

It is this quality of probing for the truth that has sometimes caused the arts to be considered controversial. Some people become irritated when their beliefs and practices are questioned. When the arts express alternative views that challenge the way people think and act, people sometimes react against them. They view them as subversive and dangerous, even immoral. Often such people prefer to impose their own viewpoints on others. Those who would limit viewpoints to their own are not supporters of American freedom and democratic ideals as guaranteed by the First Amendment to the Constitution of the United States.

The arts are often outspoken. They can console us. They can also disturb and rile us up when they present different and unexpected visions of the world. The arts often confront us with more than the comfortable aspects of life. Music expresses love, joy, spirituality, celebration, and hope; but it also explores life's darker aspects: distress, anxiety, loss, sorrow, and death. Like the other arts, music expresses the highest human aspirations. It also awakens us to our failings and to truths about life that may be disturbing. Music helps us better our human ways.

One example of how music can be controversial is the song "Strange Fruit," which Billie Holiday recorded in 1939. The poem and the music, both by Lewis Allen, dared to express in metaphor the subject of lynching in the South. Holiday's performance of the song is pained but never self-pitying. She tells it "like it is." A muted trumpet sets the mood. Then the piano states the melody. The singing is dramatic but controlled in a blues style. The accompaniment has a funereal beat.

Billie Holiday
American Jazz Singer
1915–1959

PROFILE

Billie Holiday

Eleanora ("Billie") Holiday sang the blues with a warm, uniquely expressive voice and was probably the best interpreter of popular songs of her day. She grew up in a Baltimore ghetto and moved to New York in 1929, where she performed in small clubs. Her appearance at New York's Apollo Theater and the invention of the jukebox in 1935 boosted her career.

Yet, like other African-American artists of the jazz era, Holiday was at the mercy of predominantly white club owners and record industry moguls. At clubs she was prevented from mingling with customers and was forced to use service entrances. Often these conditions got the best of her, and she left without pay or prospects of another job.

Although Holiday worked with several big bands in the mid-1930s, she returned to singing at clubs where she did not have to compromise her unique style. In songs such as "T'ain't Nobody's Business," "Don't Explain," and countless others, she sang about real aspects of life, including racism and abusive husbands. Single-handedly, she brought the "real" world to popular singing, an innovation that fundamentally changed popular music. Her addiction to drugs and alcohol led to her death at the age of 44.

Activity *Find the Meaning*
Instructor's Guide, pages 192–193
TRB 14-5, *"Strange Fruit"*
CD 9 ⑤ "Strange Fruit" (3:08)

ACTIVITY ▶ *Find the Meaning*

Why would the song "Strange Fruit" have been controversial in 1939?

- Why might some people not have wanted to hear this song or allow it to be sung?

- Why did it take courage for Billie Holiday to perform this song?

- Why is a blues style appropriate for this song?

Death Expressed in Popular Music

During the latter half of the twentieth century, the popularization of folk music put memorial songs into the Top Forty on a regular basis. For example, the Kingston Trio had a hit with "Tom Dooley" (1958). Peter,

Paul, and Mary's "Where Have All the Flowers Gone" became an antiwar anthem of the 1960s.

The early 1960s saw many pop songs about death. Some described tragic road accidents, such as Mark Dinning's "Teen Angel" (1960), as did Jan and Dean's "Dead Man's Curve" and the Beach Boys' "A Young Man is Gone." Other songs such as "Tell Laura I Love Her" and the Beatles' "Eleanor Rigby" have a sadness to them, with such lines as "Eleanor Rigby, died in the church and was buried along with her name. Nobody came."

The assassinations of famous people have been chronicled in popular music. Dick Holler's "Abraham, Martin, and John" (sung by many artists including Dion and Marvin Gaye) paid tribute to Abraham Lincoln, Martin Luther King, Jr., and President John F. Kennedy. In 1981, George Harrison ("All Those Years Ago") and Elton John ("Empty Garden") composed memorials to John Lennon. Lennon himself wrote the popular "Let It Be" in memory of his mother. More recently, rapper Sean "Puff Daddy" Combs composed an entire CD in tribute to his fallen mentor, Christopher "Notorious B.I.G." Wallace. Near the end of the album, Puff Daddy transitions from Barber's "Adagio for Strings" directly into "I'll be Missing You," a remake of Sting's "Every Breath You Take." In 1997, Naughty By Nature documented the murder of Tupac Shakur with the rap hit "I'll Mourn You Til I Join You."

Historical Events and Popular Music

Some popular tunes about death document historical events. Graham Nash's "Ohio" criticized the needless deaths of four Kent State University students gunned down by the Ohio National Guard during a campus protest of the Viet Nam war. Sting's "They Dance Alone" called attention to the tragic disappearance and murders of Chilean family men at the hands of Augusto Pinochet in the 1970s. The Broadway musical hit *Les Miserables* includes the mournful song "Empty Chairs at Empty Tables." This musical, based on Victor Hugo's novel of the same name, presents a story of love and death during a time of politcal and social revolution in eighteenth-century France. It demonstrates how both literature and history can be kept alive in popular music about death.

Public Expressions of Personal Grief

It is common that well-known personalities respond with public gestures when confronted with private grief. In the case of British rock singer Eric Clapton, the accidental death of his young son resulted in a song, a video, and numerous performances of the song. Many musicians and entertainers, like Clapton, often respond to personal grief by quickly returning to their work and doing what they do best—performing.

PROFILE

Eric Clapton
English Guitarist
1945–

Eric Clapton

Eric Clapton is considered to be one of the world's greatest rock guitarists. His guitar method based on the blues has been emulated by many guitarists and earned him the nickname "Slowhand."

Born in England and raised by his grandparents, Clapton began playing when he was 14 years old by carefully imitating, note-for-note, the great blues guitarists of the time, such as Muddy Waters. He began playing in rock bands in his late teen years and continued to do so until the early 1970s. Many of his bands were highly successful, most notably two very influential groups—the Yardbirds and Cream.

In the early 1970s, after recording the famous song "Layla" with the group Derek and the Dominoes, Clapton began to devote himself to a solo career. It was at this time that he also became addicted to heroin, but after a long struggle, he overcame it. Despite other personal problems and tragedies such as the accidental death of his four-year-old son, he has remained at the forefront of rock performance for much of four decades. Clapton received his eleventh Grammy Award in 1997 for the song "Change the World."

SUMMARY

Humans express death in a variety of ways, in all kinds of music. We honor the deceased by celebrating the life of the individual with a jazz parade or a solemn funeral march. We memorialize people through jazz and classical music, by a lone trumpet, by a voice raised in song, and by instruments that give expression to our sorrow and loss. Through music we can begin to understand the terror and violence that sometimes accompany death, and we can learn to be compassionate.

Death is part of the unfolding drama of life. It is music that so often permits us to express what is otherwise inexpressible—those quiet, unexpected, or powerful events that sweep a human life away. It lets us know that the hurt we feel is shared by others and that it is natural and human. It permits us to pause and remember, to console and to cherish, to weep and to mourn. In other words, music helps us get in direct touch with our deepest feelings, distill them, release them, and put them outside of ourselves where we can understand them better.

CHAPTER 14 REVIEW

Complete answers for the Chapter 14 Review are found in the Instructor's Guide, page 193.

Building Music Vocabulary

On a sheet of paper, write the term from the list that best matches each description below.

(4) atonal   (1) opus
(6) gambang   (3) through-composed
(5) lieder   (2) tonality

1. A musical work or set of works.
2. The major or minor system of pitches.
3. A setting of a text in which different music is provided for each stanza of the poem.
4. Without tonality or a tonal center.
5. German art songs.
6. A Balinese sacred instrumental ensemble.

Reviewing Music Facts

Answer each question in a complete sentence.

7. How does the player change pitches on a bugle?
8. Describe the origin of the tradition of New Orleans funeral parades.
9. What instruments are used in the sacred gambang ensemble?
10. What aspects of Hausa music create its multilayered texture?
11. What famous classical piece accompanied President John F. Kennedy's funeral procession?
12. What unusual musical device did Berg use in the murder scene of *Wozzeck*?

Thinking It Through

On a sheet of paper, write your responses to the following:

13. **Compare** What are some similarities between the New Orleans and Balinese funeral traditions?
14. **Analyze** What musical devices did Schubert use to create different characters and set the scene in his art song *The Erlking*?
15. **Analyze** What musical devices in Billie Holiday's recording of "Strange Fruit" evoke death?

Making the Connection

Social Studies Find out more about spirituals and their possible double meanings (code words).

Theatre The words of *The Erlking* tell a story. Divide into groups of four and assign parts (Narrator, Father, Child, Erlking) and read the English translation as a radio play.

 More information about composers Chopin and Schubert and singer Billie Holiday is available at **www.glencoe.com/sec/music**

Answers to Chapter 14 Review

7. The player changes lip formation and air pressure.
8. Lodges and social clubs paid their bands to play for funeral processions of their members to the gravesite.
9. Gambangs (wooden xylophones) and gangsas (metal xylophones).
10. Continuous variation, complex timbres, a wide variety of instruments and voices, and cross rhythms.
11. Chopin's *Funeral March*.
12. Repetition of a single note (B).

13. Both traditions involve musical processions; both have a high degree of energy and sense of celebration of the life of the departed.
14. Different characters have different vocal styles (low, firm for the father's character, middle register and hushed for the Erlking, high and desperate for the boy); the Erlking is set in major mode to contrast with the minor mode of the father and child; the galloping horse is evoked with the triplet figure in the accompaniment.
15. The sound of the muted trumpet, controlled singing, piano melody, and the funeral beat of the accompaniment.

Unit Five Evaluation

You might also use
Assessment Master 5,
Unit Five Test, in the TRB.

Chapter 11 Project
Instructor's Guide, page 195
CD 9 ⑦ "Stormy Weather" (3:37)
CD 9 ⑧ "Un bel di" (4:45)

Chapter 11 Project

▶ *Compare Love Songs*

What are the differences and similarities between two love songs?

Listen to Harold Arlen's song "Stormy Weather" and Giacomo Puccini's song "Un bel di" ("One fine day") and make a list of the differences and similarities between the two. Comment about as many musical characteristics as you can, including the basic style, message, mood and intended audience, and such musical characteristics as the sources of sound, rhythm, melody, and dynamics.

Chapter 12 Project
Instructor's Guide, page 196
CD 9 ⑨ "African Sanctus" (3:01)

Chapter 12 Project

▶ *Identify Sacred Music*

What characteristics determine whether a musical composition is religious (sacred) or nonreligious (secular)?

Listen to "African Sanctus" by David Fanshawe, then answer these questions:
1. Which aspects of the piece might be considered religious?
2. Which aspects sound secular?
3. Which styles of religious music that you have studied in this unit are represented in this composition?
4. Would you consider this composition a sacred work? Why or why not?

When we come together to celebrate events, whether they are formal or informal, joyful or sad, religious or secular, we add meaning to our lives. Almost always, music is a significant part of those events.

Chapter 13 Project

Chapter 13 Project
Instructor's Guide, page 196
CD 9 [10] *Festive Overture* (6:17)

 Map the Musical Events

What musical characteristics support and embody the sense of celebration in Dmitri Shostakovich's *Festival Overture* (1954)?

As you listen to *Festival Overture,* create a map of the musical events in this composition. Focus your attention on the musical qualities that make this work festive. In creating your map, try to include musical descriptors of the following:

- How the composition begins and ends.
- The ebb and flow, including crescendos and decrescendos.
- Orchestral tone color and the use of the four families of tone color (brass, woodwind, strings, and percussion).
- Tempo designations.
- Texture—the contrast of homophonic and polyphonic sections.
- Melodic rhythm (use of long and short durations).
- The use of dancelike rhythms.
- The expressive use of percussion.
- The extensive use of syncopation.

Use your map of the *Festival Overture* as the basis for a written composition describing how Shostakovich ordered the musical events as a statement of celebration.

Chapter 14 Project

Chapter 14 Project
Instructor's Guide, page 197

Create a Performance

Determine what musical devices make a song express death.

Create a performance of "Johnny Has Gone for a Soldier." Decide if the performance would be more effective as a solo or as an ensemble. What instruments would provide an appropriate accompaniment? Include your suggestions for tempo, dynamics, harmony, and tone color.

Name the pitches that make up the I and V chords in A minor. Harmonize "Johnny" using these two minor chords by following this procedure: Examine each melody tone and find the chord to which it belongs, then place the root of the chord in the bass (left hand), and play the chord with your right hand.

Unit Five *Encore!*

A Musical Memorial

Death remains one of the most sorrowful experiences for all human beings. In response, we rely on family, friends, and religion. Often, we turn to music to help us cope with a devastating loss. It is logical, then, that many musicians and composers have turned to their own musicianship to find and offer comfort.

Use your ears, your voice, and your sense of compassion to examine how music not only provides solace but enables us to celebrate life.

▶ ### Listen to "Tears in Heaven"

In response to the accidental death of his four-year-old son in 1990, Grammy-winning guitar legend Eric Clapton composed the song "Tears in Heaven."

Listen to an instrumental performance of this tune. While you listen, try to identify characteristics of the music that touch you most deeply.

▶ ### Read a Poetic Tribute

For most people, finding the "right thing" to say in response to death will always be difficult. Poetry and song lyrics often provide clues to an appropriate reaction.

Read the first verse of the poem "Do Not Go Gentle into That Good Night" by poet Dylan Thomas. Then read four lines of the chorus from songwriter Vince Gill's "Go Rest High on That Mountain."

- What message does each of the poems convey?
- How are they similar? How are they different?
- In what ways might this poetry provide comfort to those who are grieving? (You may read Thomas' entire poem and Gill's complete lyrics on the page provided by your teacher.)

> Do not go gentle into that good night,
> Old age should burn and rave at the close of the day;
> Rage, rage against the dying of the light.
>> *Dylan Thomas*

> Go rest high on that mountain.
> Son, your work on earth is done.
> Go to heaven a shoutin'
> Love for the Father and the Son.
>> *Vince Gill*

Listen to "Tears in Heaven"
Instructor's Guide, page 198
CD 19 [1] "Tears in Heaven"
    (instrumental) (3:30)

Read a Poetic Tribute
Instructor's Guide, page 199
TRB Unit 5 Encore!, *Poetic Tributes*

▶ Discuss Historical Events

Songwriters throughout history have used music to express their reactions to the monumental losses associated with war and revolution.

- Read the lyrics to "Vacant Chair," a civil war song popular in both the north and south.

- Listen to a recording of "Vacant Chair" and discuss how the music conveys sadness.

- How does a song such as "Vacant Chair" keep history alive?

- Can you cite important examples of literature that are related to these events? How do they, like music, keep history alive?

▶ Compose Lyrics for a Musical Memorial

When Diana, Princess of Wales, was tragically killed in an automobile accident in Paris in 1997, the whole world grieved. The most widely acclaimed tribute to her life was musical. English songwriter Elton John presented "Candle in the Wind, 1997 (In loving memory of Diana, Princess of Wales)."

Originally composed in memory of actress Marilyn Monroe, John changed the words of the verses and modified the chorus of his 1973 tune "Candle in the Wind." The early version began with the words "Good-bye, Norma Jean." The later tribute began with "Good-bye, England's Rose." Within weeks, this recording became the largest-selling single of all time.

Use "Ashokan Farewell," a song from the soundtrack of *The Civil War*, to compose your own musical tribute.

- Look at the music for "Ashokan Farewell" provided by your teacher while you listen to the song.

- Use the music as a basis for creating your own musical memorial. Work with a friend and create lyrics to celebrate someone's life.

- If you wish, use the recording as an accompaniment while you perform your tribute for the class.

Discuss Historical Events
Instructor's Guide, page 199
TRB Unit 5 Encore!, *"Vacant Chair"*
CD 19 [2] "Vacant Chair" (4:06)

Compose Lyrics for a Musical Memorial
Instructor's Guide, page 200
TRB Unit 5 Encore!, *"Ashokan Farewell"*
CD 19 [3] "Ashokan Farewell" (4:08)

English singer/songwriter Elton John is shown here performing a moving tribute at the funeral of Diana, Princess of Wales, in 1997. His recording of "Good-bye, England's Rose" quickly became a best-selling song.

The **Dance Theatre of Harlem** is an African-American ballet company, internationally acclaimed for its skill and artistic vision. Artistic Director, Arthur Mitchell, states, "I am a fighter, and I fight with my art." His life goal is to provide African Americans the opportunity to create and perform ballets. *Firebird,* a traditional Russian ballet, was re-created for his company and recast in a Haitian Jungle, as shown here. This timeless story entails an evil spell, a magical bird, two lovers, fear, conflict, and courage. What do you think is being expressed in this scene?

The Dance Theatre of Harlem. *Firebird*. Arthur Mitchell, founder and artistic director. Photo by Jack Vartoogian; courtesy of the Dance Theatre of Harlem.

Music!...
To
Let Us
Create

You may wish to use Transparency 6, *In Ochre and Yellow with Sheet Music*, in the TRB to introduce Unit Six.

Use Artsource® VHS Segment 8 in the Performing Arts Package to show an interview with Arthur Mitchell and a segment of *Firebird*.

Communicating with Sound

S ound is the basic raw material of all musical communication. It might consist of the distinct pitches of a particular scale, a set of noises of indeterminate pitch, or a combination of both. During the creative process, sound is manipulated in a number of ways to give it character and dimension. Musical creators shape sound by giving it a particular melody, rhythm, dynamics, form, timbre, and texture. These elements are the tools a composer or arranger uses to shape sound into an expressive statement.

Musicians communicate by shaping sound with basic musical elements and their own creative expression. Steel drummers, pictured here, communicate unique sounds that are influenced by each drum's depth, the pattern and shape of its surface, and the size and shape of the drum beaters. **What sounds would you expect to hear at a performance by these steel drummers?**

Caption answer Students will likely identify the unique sound of metal drums and the quick rhythms that are common to music played by steel-drum bands.

Objectives

By completing the chapter, you will:
■ Understand how musical communication depends on the combination of musical elements.
■ Learn the important role of texture in musical expression.
■ Discover the uniqueness of Balkan vocal textures.
■ Learn about and be able to discuss expressive tools such as harmonizing, modulation, and arranging.
■ Understand the important role of the music arranger.
■ Be able to distinguish an arrangement from a transcription.

Vocabulary

arranger
harmonizing
idée fixe
modulation
obbligato
program symphony
transcriptions

Musicians to Meet

Hector Berlioz
Gioacchino Rossini

297

The Integration of Musical Elements

We have already investigated many of the musical elements the composer uses. Up to this point, we have looked at and listened to these various elements as separate and distinct entities. Now we will begin to see and hear them in a more comprehensive way.

There is no melody without rhythm. Most often, rhythm is expressed in combination with the melodic movement of tones. Dynamics are not heard in isolation, but as they affect the melody and rhythm in all parts. Form, timbre, and texture are applied across the board, affecting the other elements and emerging from them. Music is a cohesive consolidation of related events.

Texture

Musical texture is introduced on page 123.

One of the most expressive aspects of music is its texture, the arrangement of the horizontal and vertical sounds. It is this element that gives music much of its character and its individuality and mood. Texture describes how different musical sounds occurring at the same time relate to one another. You have heard various musical textures: monophonic, heterophonic, homophonic, and polyphonic. Texture refers to the density of the sounds—the degree to which they are active or inactive, thick or thin. It can indicate how the melodic element of the music connects with

In music, texture describes how different musical sounds relate to one another.
Can you name an example for each of the four musical textures—monophonic, heterophonic, polyphonic, and homophonic?

Caption answer
Responses will vary but might include: a soloist performing *a cappella* (monophonic); a mariachi piece sung in thirds (heterophonic); a round or canon (polyphonic); a soloist accompanied by instruments or a choir (homophonic).

Monophonic—*a single melodic line with no accompaniment.*

Heterophonic—*the same melodic line repeated in different ways.*

Polyphonic—*the simultaneous combination of different melodies and rhythms.*

Homophonic—*a single melodic line supported by chordal accompaniment.*

the tones that sound simultaneously with it—a series of chords, a rhythmic line, another melody, several other melodies, or even a repetition of the same melody.

Our Western music is highly developed in timbre, harmony, and form. Music from other parts of the world is sometimes more highly developed in other ways. As you have seen and heard, rhythm in the music of India and Africa can be sophisticated and complex. It can go far beyond our steady two- and three-beat patterns. Highly developed rhythm is also characteristic of some of the music from the Arab world, the music of Syria being a good example.

The Culture of Syria

Syria has a long history as an important Middle Eastern province because its trade routes connect Mediterranean countries with those to the east. One of Syria's great river systems, the Euphrates, is interrupted by several hydroelectric dams that drive the industrial development of the major cities, Damascus, Aleppo, and Homs. For centuries these cities have served as inland "ports" to a desert "sea," welcoming caravans to and from Europe, Asia, and Africa.

Syrians view their culture as deriving from ancient civilizations such as Mesopotamia and from the Arabs who conquered the region in the seventh century. Most Syrians are Arabic-speaking Muslims. The way of life in Syria is similar to that in neighboring Lebanon, Jordan, and, to some extent, Turkey. This larger Arab cultural area, which reflects the similarities that exist among the Arab people of the region, is sometimes referred to as Greater Syria. The music throughout this area also has many similarities.

Music & CULTURE

Sabah Fakhri, a Syrian from the city of Aleppo, is pictured here in a performance with his ensemble. Like many contemporary Syrian musicians, Fakhri draws on the rich classical music of the Middle East and Spain during the Arab Empire.

The Bulgarian State Women's Choir regularly tours and performs in the United States, portraying the long Bulgarian history of women's choral groups. They wear their traditional attire during performances, adding visual impact to their remarkable vocal textures and haunting timbres.

The Culture of Bulgaria

The Balkan peninsula includes the countries of Albania, Romania, Bulgaria, Greece, and former Yugoslavia. The position of the Balkans between Europe and Asia has affected its history as well as the ways these people live, work, dress, and make music. At one time or another they have been dominated by their large and aggressive neighbors—the Mongol Empire, the Byzantine Empire, the Ottoman Empire, the Austro-Hungarian Empire, and the Soviet Union. These dominations and many other influences have enriched the Balkan culture.

Bulgaria is slightly larger than the state of Ohio, and although somewhat industrialized, it is a predominantly agricultural country. Until 1918, Bulgaria was part of the Ottoman Empire, so it has absorbed some Middle Eastern customs. The culture is still tied closely to village life.

Balkan Vocal Textures

Much of the musical life of Bulgaria is connected to the daily or seasonal customs and tasks of country village life. The people use their abundant folk songs to celebrate weddings, births, and religious holidays. The same songs, sung and/or played on a variety of instruments, provide music for dancing, which is one of the main forms of entertainment at all festive occasions. The people use songs to help pass the time while working in the fields or to coordinate their movements during certain kinds of tasks such as harvesting crops, sorting vegetables, or weaving and spinning. Even today, when technology has eliminated many of these jobs, the songs are remembered and performed.

There is a long tradition of women singing in Bulgaria. Over the centuries, they have developed remarkable vocal textures and haunting timbres. Singing distracted women from the tedium of their work. As with all folk music, these unusual vocal practices were created communally by the village people doing the singing. One of the most prevalent textures in Bulgarian singing is homophony, two or more different pitches sounding simultaneously, all with the same melodic rhythm.

ACTIVITY ▶ *Examine Bulgarian Singing*

Can you discover the characteristics of Bulgarian singing in "Bajo le Ivane"?

Use these questions to help you in your analysis:
1. Are the singers all singing the same rhythm? Asked another way: Are they singing the words at the same time?
2. Are the singers all singing the same melody throughout the song?
3. How are the singers creating musical variety in their song?
4. What makes this Balkan homophonic sound different from that of a church hymn?
5. What is different about the sound of the singers' voices? What does this tone quality add to the musical expression?

Activity *Examine Bulgarian Singing*
Instructor's Guide, pages 205–206
CD 9 [12] "Bajo le Ivane" (2:44)

The folk song "Bajo le Ivane" (BOTCH-oh lay ee-VAHN-ay) ("Brother Ivan") is a typical example of homophonic texture. Women sang the song as they worked in the fields harvesting crops such as wheat, rye, and barley. In the song, an older sister gives her brother advice about how to choose a hardworking wife. In the field, the hardest workers are at the front of the line!

Texture and Rhythm Combined

Homophonic texture is given additional interest when a more complex meter and a rapid (and challenging) tempo are used. The song "Mome odi" (MO-may oh-DEE) ("A Girl Walks") is from the region known as Macedonia, a cultural area now situated in the three nations of Bulgaria, Greece, and former Yugoslavia. It uses a combined meter of 3+2+2, or seven beats per measure. Like many of the songs from this region, the beats go by quickly (the tempo is fast)! The two parts begin together, separate, and finally merge again at the cadences, alternating between monophonic and homophonic texture. Translated, the text says: "A girl walks through the grassy fields, through the wide sunny fields."

Activity *Test Your Voice and Ears*
Instructor's Guide, page 206
CD 9 [13] "Mome odi" (3:02)

ACTIVITY ▶ *Test Your Voice and Ears*

Listen to the homophonic song "Mome odi" and learn to clap the rhythm and sing the words.

Perform the 7/8 meter by clapping the first beat of each group of three or two beats while you count to seven quietly:

beats:	1	2	3	1	2	1	2
claps:	●			●		●	

Your clapping should produce a long-short-short pattern. When you are comfortable with this rhythmic pattern, try singing the song. Much of the melodic rhythm of this song uses the same long-short-short rhythmic pattern.

*Use section A. in the *Music Theory Handbook* to review beat and meter.*

Technology Option
Use Project 15 in the *MIDI Activities* binder.

MIDI TECHNOLOGY OPTION

■ **Music with MIDI** Use a MIDI program to improvise and compose with 7 beats to a measure.

Mome odi ("A Girl Walks")

First line is in the Bulgarian dialect. Second line indicates the phonetic pronunciation.

Harmonizing

As we have heard in the previous two musical examples, making up a harmony part is an art that can be accomplished in a variety of ways. We can assume that the women who sang these songs knew the tune but made up the second part as they went along. They did not learn the second part from notation but created it "by ear" according to their folk song tradition.

Harmonizing is one of the tools of music making. **Harmonizing** is *the ability to invent on the spot a vocal line that will complement a melody.* "On the spot" means that the harmonization is being created spontaneously, as the melody is sung. Harmonizing is usually done by ear without the benefit of printed notation.

You know from your experience with Mexican music that the singers often prefer to harmonize at an interval of a 3rd, creating a second part that is parallel to the melody. Much of this kind of vocal harmonization is in just two parts. Gospel choirs also create harmony by ear, but in this instance, there may be several parts, each corresponding to the general range of the singers' voices. Altos, tenors, and basses may create individual parts to form chords that support the soprano melody, while a solo voice adds still another **obbligato**, or *subordinate melody above the main melody.* The texture here becomes dense and complex.

Caption answer
Responses will vary.

Harmonizing fills out a melody. Two or more people sing together and invent a complement to a melody. Boyz II Men, shown here, is a popular harmonizing group. **Can you name others?**

ACTIVITY *Harmonize "The Golden Vanity"*

Harmonize by singing (and inventing) a new part that stays within the three chords of the song.

Use the following steps:
1. *Find and Mark the Chord Changes.* Follow the music for "The Golden Vanity" as you listen to the recording of the song. As you listen, put an "X" above each measure where you hear the harmony (or chords) change. The first four are done for you on the music. Your job is to find the remaining five chord changes.

Activity *Harmonize "The Golden Vanity"*
Instructor's Guide, page 207
TRB 15-1, *"The Golden Vanity"*
CD 9 14 "The Golden Vanity" (3:10)

Use section E. in the *Music Theory Handbook* to review harmony.

2. *Write in the Chord Names.* "The Golden Vanity" uses the three basic chords in the key of A major: I or A, IV or D, and V7 or E7. Next to the "X" where you have marked chord changes, write in the proper name and symbol of the chord.

3. *Sing the Chord Roots as a Harmonization.* Use your chord symbols as a guide to select the pitches for your harmonization. Use solfège syllables to sing the chord roots: Sing DO every time you hear the I or A chord; sing FA (up a 4th) every time you hear the IV or D chord; and sing SOL (up a 5th) every time you hear the V7 or E7 chord. Sustain each pitch until the song moves to the next chord. Put the two parts together, maintaining the same rhythm as the melody. This gives you a basic harmonization.

In much of this folk music, instrumentalists also add parts by ear, following the appropriate chord patterns. These parts complement the melody and enrich its overall effect. This is the essence of improvisation in jazz. The instrumentalists know the chord changes, and they invent a part for their own instrument that weaves through that pattern of chords.

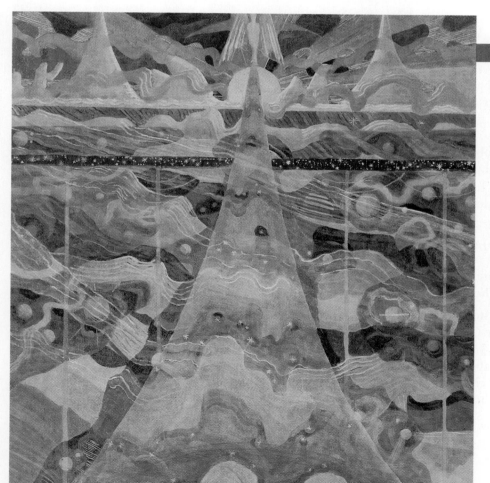

Music & Art

Lithuanian painter and composer Mikolajus Konstantinas Ciurlionis (1875–1910) frequently combined the themes of nature, mountains, clouds, stars, and ocean waves. In Star Sonata, Allegro *he communicates a visual harmony, in much the same way that musicians communicate a harmony of sound.*

Mikolajus Konstantinas Ciurlionis. *Star Sonata, Allegro.* 1908. Ciurlionis Museum, Kaunas, Lithuania.

Modulation

Another device often used for expressive purposes is **modulation**, *the changing from one key to another within a composition.* This effect can be compared to the sun coming out after a rain. A new key can give a feeling of refreshing brightness. It can also create the reverse feeling—a darkening or dampening of the spirit. Then, too, modulation is often used as a device for marking the divisions in a musical form, setting them off in a related tonality.

Modulation is fairly common in longer musical works. One simple way of modulating is to use a chord that is common to both keys. This "pivot chord" is used to go from the old key to a full cadence in the new key:

Use section D. in the *Music Theory Handbook* to review tonality and key signatures.

Activity *Analyze Modulation*
Instructor's Guide, page 208
CD 9 [15] "One More Valley" (3:18)

ACTIVITY ▶ *Analyze Modulation*

How does the composer of "One More Valley" use modulation to reflect the meaning of the words?

Follow the different ways the same melody is presented as you listen to this gospel song, written and performed by Wintley Phipps. Determine how many times the melody is repeated. Does the melody sound higher or lower each time it is repeated?

- What does the text of "One More Valley" describe?

- What musical characteristics help support the words of the text?

- Why do you think the composer chose modulation to illuminate the meaning of the text of this song?

Musical Creation

As you have heard in these examples, music is the result of a combination of various musical elements working together. For anyone who chooses to create music, then, the task is to plan how all the elements can be used to reinforce each other in one cohesive design. It is not much different from a painter who has to consider how line, shape, form, space, color, and texture can be brought together to realize a visual idea or concept. If you were creating a teleplay, you would have to be concerned with such matters as plot (conflict, climax, and resolution), setting, characterization, dialogue, and tempo. The creator has to think in several dimensions simultaneously. This is certainly true of the composer and musical arranger.

The Composer

Composers decide what they want to express and then assemble the combination of sounds that will communicate their intent. A composer, for example, might choose to convey the emotion of real or imagined events and use an array of orchestral timbres as the medium. Such is the case with Hector Berlioz's *Symphonie Fantastique*, originally titled "Episode for the Life of an Artist" (1830). Here, the composer deliberately sets out to express a fantasy based upon an event in his own life.

He composed a **program symphony**, *a pictorial or descriptive orchestral work in several movements.* The composer may or may not supply listeners with a verbal description of the music's content.

Berlioz strongly believed that listeners would benefit by knowing the details of the story. He wrote the following recommendation about knowing the extramusical program before hearing the music: "The distribution of the programme to the audience at concerts where the symphony is to be performed is indispensable for a complete understanding of the dramatic outline of the work."

Symphonie Fantastique

This program symphony is in five movements, and its story sounds much like a contemporary soap opera. It is about a young musician who has a very sensitive personality, a wild imagination, and an uncontrollable romantic interest in a woman who simply does not love him. This is how Berlioz outlined the story in his preface to the work:

> A young, morbid, ardent musician in a state of amorous despair poisons himself with opium. The dose, insufficient to kill him, plunges him into a delirious sleep during which his sensations take the form of musical ideas in his sick brain. His beloved becomes a melody, an *idée fixe* (fixed idea) which he hears everywhere.

The musician's dreams are transformed into musical imagery. The five movements tell the progression of the story: "Dreams and Passions," "A Ball," "Scene in the Country," "March to the Scaffold," and "Dream of Witches' Sabbath." The love theme or **idée fixe** (ee-day FEEKS), *a fixed melodic idea that recurs throughout all movements of a symphony,* is a device Berlioz created to give the composition unity. Here is how Berlioz describes the fourth movement, "The March to the Scaffold":

> [The young musician] dreams he has killed his beloved, that he has been condemned to death and is being led to the scaffold. The procession advances to the sound of a march now somber, now wild, now brilliant, now solemn. Loud outbursts are followed without pause by the plodding sounds of marching feet. The idée fixe appears for a moment like a last thought of love cut short by the fatal blow of the guillotine.

As a Romantic composer, Berlioz had the enriched harmonic resources, the colorful orchestration, and the free creative sense of expression that enabled him to communicate his ideas in graphic detail. This work shows what an imaginative and brilliant composer can do with the resources of a symphony orchestra.

ACTIVITY ▶ *Themes in "March to the Scaffold"*

Activity *Themes in "March to the Scaffold"*
Instructor's Guide, pages 208–209
CD 9 [16] "March to the Scaffold," *Symphonie Fantastique,* fourth movement (4:50)

By comparing the two themes below from "March to the Scaffold," can you determine which is the love theme (idée fixe) and which is the march theme? How do you know?

Study the score as you listen to the final moments in this movement. Try to hear the love theme (idée fixe). The clarinet plays the idée fixe love theme one final time, suggesting that the man's last thought is of his beloved. Hear the blow of the guillotine and the man's head rolling into the basket on the scaffold. Can you detect where these events take place in the score?

Orchestra Score

Fantastic Symphony

Excerpt, Movement IV, "March to the Scaffold"

Hector Berlioz

PROFILE

Hector Berlioz

Hector Berlioz
French Composer
1803–1869

Hector Berlioz was born in France and moved to Paris at the age of 17. His father wished him to follow in his footsteps and study medicine, but Berlioz became inspired by the rich musical life in the city. He abandoned medicine, even though this alienated his parents for years. After studying in Italy, he settled permanently in Paris.

Berlioz was a passionate man, and he poured his emotions into his scores. *Symphonie Fantastique* is a strong example of how he translated his life into music. His obsessive love for the actress Harriet Smithson (whom he later married) is revealed by the recurring love theme in the piece. Literary works also inspired many of his compositions, among them the symphonies *Harold in Italy* (based on Lord Byron's *Childe Harold*) and *Romeo and Juliet* (based on Shakespeare's play). His choral works include *The Damnation of Faust* (based on Goethe's *Faust*), the monumental *Te Deum*, the *Requiem*, and the oratorio *L'enfance du Christ*. He composed a number of works for solo voice and orchestra, as well as works for the stage, including the great opera *Les Troyens*.

The Musical Arranger

In the broadest sense, composers arrange all the elements of music when creating a work. However, the term **arranger** means *someone who reworks preexistent musical material*. It is usually applied in a more limited way. The arranger adapts a composition written for one performing medium to another or recomposes a work to suit different circumstances. The composer and the arranger manipulate sound in all its dimensions, but their roles are different.

The composer often starts with a blank canvas and creates a totally new musical work. Occasionally, the composer will base his or her ideas on an existing theme or work, but what emerges is essentially a new piece of music. In contrast, an arranger takes a composition and adapts it, or otherwise alters it, to make it suitable for a performing medium, occasion, or purpose different from the one for which the composer originally created it. For example, in celebrating the inauguration of a new president, a composer may be commissioned to write a new work, whereas an arranger may be hired to create an updated version of "The Battle Hymn of the Republic" scored for heralding trumpets, brass bands, and mixed chorus.

You may wish to use "Create Your Own Arrangement" at this time. Lesson plans for the activity are found on page 211 in the Instructor's Guide.

The jazz band is common to nearly all high schools, colleges, and universities in the United States. Musical arrangements for these groups are made for saxophones, trombones, trumpets, a rhythm section of piano, bass, drums, and sometimes a guitar. **Can you name the instruments used in your school's jazz band?**

Caption answer
Responses will vary.

Musical arrangements exist from all periods of music history. Arrangers often update a musical work, giving it a contemporary sound and feeling. They will arrange a popular work such as Rimsky-Korsakov's "Flight of the Bumblebee" so that it can be performed by every conceivable combination of instruments—even voices. They might even attempt to popularize this musical masterpiece by jazzing it up for use in a television advertisement! Arrangements of Bach's instrumental music for synthesizer or for voices (for example, the Swingle Singers) have brought his works to the attention and admiration of new and younger audiences.

Like the ingredients that go into a recipe, each of the elements of music—the composer and arranger's tools—have to be figured out. Each ingredient of the musical pie has to work with the other ingredients to create the desired overall result. Change one of these elements and you change the effect. That is what is so fascinating—and challenging! Arranging and composing are exacting arts involving many choices. The person creating the music has to be able to hear all the musical elements and their combinations in order to achieve the intended effect.

ACTIVITY ▶ *Identify Unity in a Medley*

How does the arranger manage to hold a medley of songs together?

Listen to the medley arranged for marching band by William T. (Ted) McDaniel, Jr. Working in small groups, listen to the medley and answer the following questions:

1. Which of the songs can you identify?
2. What musical tools hold the medley together and create a unified work?
3. Since this arrangement was done for the football field, why is it more appropriate than the original songs might have been?

Activity *Identify Unity in a Medley*
Instructor's Guide, page 209
TRB 15-2, *Interview with an Arranger*
CD 9 [17] "Michael Jackson Medley" (2:18)

Transcribing Music

The artistic involvement of the arranger can vary greatly. An arranger can simply take the exact notes of the composer and score them for any combination of instruments or voices. This is largely a mechanical process involving few, if any, musical decisions. Usually, such arrangements are called transcriptions, because they adhere so closely to the original. **Transcriptions** are *arrangements of music transferred from one medium to another.* For example, composers often transcribe vocal music for instruments. This allows a band to play what is essentially a vocal composition.

Transcriptions take many forms. In Europe during the Baroque era (c. 1600–1750), composers borrowed freely from themselves and from one another by transcribing or arranging preexistent compositions, as well as by transcribing music from one medium to another. Today, of course, borrowing the music of another composer is a violation of copyright, unless the arranger acquired permission or the rights to use the material.

ACTIVITY ▶ *Compare an Original and a Transcription*

Which version of "Eternal Father, Strong to Save" do you find more moving—the original or the transcription?

Thousands of vocal works have been arranged for instrumental ensembles. One example is this famous navy hymn. While you follow the score, listen to two different versions of the hymn: first, a choral version; second, the hymn (without words) played by a concert band. After you have listened to both examples, answer the following questions:

1. How does the arrangement for band differ from the choral original?
2. Which do you find more moving? Why?

Activity *Compare an Original and a Transcription*
Instructor's Guide, page 210
CD 9 [18] "Eternal Father, Strong to Save" (3:06)
CD 9 [19] "Eternal Father, Strong to Save" (1:06)

Eternal Father, Strong to Save

William Whiting, 1825-1878   John B. Dykes

1. E - ter - nal Fa - ther, strong to save, Whose arm doth bind the
2. O Sav - ior, whose al - might - y word, The winds and waves sub -
3. O Ho - ly Spir - it, who didst brood Up - on the cha - os
4. O Trin - i - ty of love and power! Our breth - ren shield in

rest - less wave, Who bidd'st the might - y o - cean deep Its
mis - sive heard, Who walk - edst on the foam - ing deep, And
dark and rude, Who bad'st its an - gry tu - mult cease And
dan - ger's hour; From rock and tem - pest, fire and foe, Pro -

own ap - point - ed lim - its keep, O hear us when we
calm a - mid its rage did sleep, O hear us when we
gav - est light, and life, and peace, O hear us when we
tect them where - so - e'er they go; Thus ev - er - more shall

cry to thee, For those in per - il on the sea.
cry to thee, For those in per - il on the sea.
cry to thee, For those in per - il on the sea.
rise to thee, Glad hymns of praise from land and sea. A - men.

Telling the Difference

An arranger can be enormously innovative with an original work, filtering it through his or her imagination to create a work of wholly new merit and expressiveness. Gioacchino Rossini's *William Tell* Overture (1829) has been transcribed and arranged for various performing media. Most transcriptions remain fairly close to the original. They usually do not substantially alter the melody, rhythm, or harmony. Arrangements, on the other hand, are often very different from the original in musical treatment and effect.

ACTIVITY *Compare a Transcription and an Arrangement*

Can you tell the difference between a transcription and an arrangement?

The notes below represent one of the most famous musical themes of all time. You may recognize it as a cartoon theme or as the music from old Western films that featured the Lone Ranger. The music was originally written by the composer Gioacchino Rossini as an overture to his opera *William Tell.* Try to read and tap the rhythm of the melody with your index fingers until you recognize it.

Listen to the original version of the overture so you can familiarize yourself with Rossini's intentions.

Now listen to the other versions of this melody and see if you can tell which are transcriptions and which are arrangements. Mark your answers on a sheet of paper. Identify the performing medium in each of the examples. Then answer these questions:

1. Which excerpt is the closest to Rossini's original overture?
2. Which excerpt is the furthest from Rossini's original?
3. Which one might be most likely to displease Rossini? Why?
4. Which of the examples (original, arrangements, or transcriptions) do you find most creative? Why?

Activity *Compare a Transcription and an Arrangement*
Instructor's Guide, pages 210–211
CD 10 ⃞1 *William Tell* Overture (2:36)
CD 10 ⃞2 *William Tell* Overture (1:55)
CD 10 ⃞3 *William Tell* Overture (2:28)
CD 10 ⃞4 *William Tell* Overture (2:08)

Arrangements may modify the work slightly or radically. The arranger uses his or her creativity to rework the piece, and perhaps even to add to it. In the process of arranging, all the musical elements may be reworked so that a new musical creation results. As musical styles and tastes change, arranging permits music to be updated. This is an important way that music is kept vibrant and alive.

PROFILE

Gioacchino Rossini

Gioacchino Rossini
Italian Composer
1792–1868

Gioacchino Rossini was a great opera composer who was unrivaled in prestige and influence during the first half of the nineteenth century. He began formal music training in Bologna, Italy, at the age of 14. Soon after graduation, he gained a position in the operatic limelight by rapidly composing well-crafted operas, earning a worldwide audience by the time he was 21.

Rossini's music is characterized by rhythmic verve and melodic lyricism. Catering to the popular tastes of opera fans in Italy, Rossini composed in the bel canto style, which emphasized the beauty and range of a singer's voice rather than emotion. His opera orchestrations could be opulent, and his overtures were often masterpieces in their own right. He satisfied audiences by turning out at least one new opera every year. These include the popular *Barber of Seville*, a comic opera, and *William Tell*, a dramatic opera.

Rossini stopped writing operas at the height of his popularity at age 37, partly because he disliked the new styles. He spent his remaining 39 years in Bologna and Paris.

SUMMARY

Composers and arrangers use every possible musical device—rhythm, melody, harmony, dynamics, texture, timbre, and form—to create musical works. Folk, popular, and classical music are created from these same musical elements and processes. So is most of the music of the world. Although we sometimes single out one or more of these elements to listen to individually, it is the coordination of all these elements that gives the music its overall effect. That is why it is important to pay attention to the musical texture—how all the elements are combined.

Composers and arrangers fulfill different roles in the creation of music. Both manipulate and integrate the musical elements to create an original work, but the arranger generally starts with an existing work, whereas the composer most often invents. That is the challenge of the creative process in music—to devise a unified and communicative statement out of a combination of many elements. That is the challenge to the listener as well—to hear the larger overall musical effect that emerges from the details.

Complete answers for the Chapter 15 Review are found in the Instructor's Guide, pages 211–212.

Building Music Vocabulary

On a sheet of paper, write the term from the list that best matches each description below.

(5) arranger   (6) obbligato

(1) harmonizing   (3) program symphony

(7) idée fixe   (4) transcriptions

(2) modulation

1. The ability to invent on the spot a vocal line that will complement a melody.
2. Changing from one key to another within a composition.
3. A pictorial or descriptive orchestral work in several movements.
4. Arrangements of music transferred from one medium to another.
5. Someone who reworks preexisting musical material.
6. A subordinate melody above the main melody.
7. A fixed melodic idea that recurs throughout all movements of a symphony.

Reviewing Music Facts

Answer each question in a complete sentence.

8. Name four kinds of musical texture.
9. What was the original purpose of Bulgarian folk music?
10. What does it mean to play or sing music "by ear"?
11. Why did Berlioz want his audience to know details of the story about his *Symphonie Fantastique*?
12. Write at least three reasons why a piece of music might be arranged.

Thinking It Through

On a sheet of paper, write your responses to the following:

13. **Analyze** Describe the unusual features of the Bulgarian folk song "Mome odi."
14. **Analyze** How can you tell when a person or group is performing music "by ear"?
15. **Explain** In your own words, explain the difference between arranging a piece of music and transcribing it.

Making the Connection

Applied Arts Choose pieces of music from the chapter. Then find and share cloth or other material that reflects the texture of the music.

Theatre Find an example of a Shakespearean play that has been adapted for a modern audience. Explain how your Shakespearean example parallels either a musical arrangement or a transcription.

 Composers Berlioz and Rossini as well as the music of Bulgaria are explored at **www.glencoe.com/sec/music**

Answers to Chapter 15 Review

8. Monophonic, heterophonic, homophonic, and polyphonic.
9. To help pass the time and for village events and celebrations.
10. Creating spontaneously, without the benefit of printed notation.
11. He believed listeners would benefit, and that it would lead to better understanding of the music.
12. To make it easier to perform, to bring it up to date, or to adapt it for a specific purpose or medium.

13. Answers may include homophony, complex meter, very rapid tempo.
14. No written notation, parts will vary from one performance to another, performers will be improvising freely, and so on.
15. An arranger manipulates the notes, harmonies, rhythms, and other musical elements. A transcriber assigns the music to a different set of players or singers, changing the medium of the music but not the arrangement of the material.

Making Musical Decisions

Composers are people who speak their mind primarily through music. Every human being needs to communicate, and we all do so in a variety of ways—through the medium of words (written or spoken), through scientific or mathematical symbols, through gestures and movements (including acting and dancing), through pictures (drawings, photographs, film, paintings, and video), and through sound. Music is one of the major ways humans convey certain kinds of thoughts and feelings.

Creating music is a unique way that both composers and performers comment on their world and their relation to it. As with all creative people, they learn to challenge and refine their creative expressions. **How would you describe your creative process?**

Caption answer
Encourage a variety of responses.

Objectives

By completing the chapter, you will:
- Explore the creative process in music.
- Learn about the organizing device that underlies the 12-bar blues.
- Learn how the Balinese use interlocking rhythms expressively.
- Find out how composers achieve unity and variety in the musical form called "theme and variations."
- Learn about and be able to describe the tone-row system.
- Be introduced to the work of Arnold Schoenberg.
- Acquire some perspective about your own creativity.

Vocabulary

blue notes
blues
interlocking rhythms
Kecak
retrograde
theme and variations
tone row

Musicians to Meet

W. C. Handy
Arnold Schoenberg

Conveying Reality

Some messages are better told through one medium than another. For example, to give someone a general idea of the Grand Canyon, you could use a verbal description: "The Grand Canyon, the world's largest gorge, is a spectacle of multicolored layers of rock." If we want to convey its vastness, we might use mathematics: "The Grand Canyon is more than one mile deep, four to 18 miles wide, and more than 200 miles long." If we want to depict the Grand Canyon in visual terms, we might choose to photograph or paint it. If we want to convey the emotional impact of the Grand Canyon, we might write a poem or depict it in music, as did Ferde Grofé when he wrote the *The Grand Canyon Suite*.

Each of these media conveys a different aspect of reality. When we want to communicate, we select an appropriate medium of expression. If we want to tell people the size of the canyon, we would not choose music as our medium. However, if we want to convey the emotional meaning, music might be a better choice than words or mathematical symbols. Each medium is important because it conveys something unique, something that cannot be communicated as well any other way.

Whatever medium we choose to communicate our insights about, feelings toward, and reactions to the world around us, we have to create our own message. If we choose to communicate in spoken words, we have to know a language and how to speak or write effectively. If we choose to communicate through music, we have to know musical language and how to use it expressively. When we set out to represent aspects of the world through an art form, we must learn how to manipulate the elements of that art so that they communicate what we want to convey. In this chapter we will explore how we can use the medium of music for expressive purposes.

The Creative Process

We know from the appearance of Beethoven's sketchbooks that his tonal ideas went through many revisions, but he discovered many gems. Musical creation did not come to him easily or in finished form. In contrast, music seemed to sing in Chopin's head or flow out of his piano. Only rarely did he have to agonize over a passage in order to make it please him.

Inspiration

Composing can be a struggle or a spontaneous act. The difference is often attributed to inspiration—a mysterious force not easily explained. The original idea for a creative work may seem to be inspired because it appears to come from nowhere and seize the imagination. In spite of the romantic notion of inspiration, creativity is essentially a mental process. Even the excitement and emotion that may accompany the initial idea originate in the mind. Creativity is probably the most demanding of all the thought processes because it appears to produce something where there was previously nothing.

Purpose

As you learned in Chapter 15, composers use melody, rhythm, harmony, dynamics, timbre, form, and texture to create musical expression. One of the mysteries of the art of music is how one composer can use all these devices to little or no effect, while another can use the same devices to achieve electrifying impact. In music, as in any other art, the composer has to have a mission—a need to say something.

Making Decisions

Composing, like painting, sculpting, writing, designing, and choreographing, involves making decisions. The composer has to decide what he or she wants to say and what is the best musical means to express it.

It takes considerable thought and planning to combine the materials of music into a statement that is cohesive and balanced, yet varied enough to be interesting. Musical creators cannot be careless about anything, or the result might sound hasty and slipshod. Many factors have to be brought together in musical expression. All the musical elements must merge together to create a cumulative, unified effect.

In the creative process, composers make decisions about each of the musical elements. The rhythm can be simple or complex, plodding or upbeat, subtle or driven. The melody might be conjunct or disjunct, flowing or angular, narrow or wide-ranging, short or long. The dynamics can remain constant at one level of loudness, contrast several levels, or change gradually or abruptly. The elements can be ordered through repetition and contrast, by the use of motives, imitation, and emotional unity, or by allowing performers to make decisions about order.

Composers give their music texture by using a single line or melody (monophony), or by combining many lines or melodies in a dense blend

Beethoven's sketchbooks reveal his careful and deliberate attention to details. His creative process was one of constant revision and has provided music scholars with a tool to examine his creative process. **How would you describe your creative process?**

Caption answer
Responses will vary. Students might apply the creative process to their artistic endeavors, problem solving, and managing tasks.

You may wish to use "Create a Love Theme." Lesson plans are found on page 217 in the Instructor's Guide.

of sound. They can combine sounds in a number of ways by using polyphony, homophony, or heterophony. Like visual artists, composers select a music palette—one consisting of a particular selection of tone colors or timbres that will best realize their musical idea. The sounds they choose may be produced by conventional instruments, voices, or electronically. They may use a single instrument, a symphony orchestra, a band, a chorus, a synthesizer, or a combination of these. In all these ways, composers shape sound into expressive statements. The number and range of musical decisions the composer makes are astounding.

Getting Started

How does the creative process in music begin? Andrew Lloyd Webber (contemporary composer of the musicals *Jesus Christ Superstar*, *Evita*, *Cats*, and *The Phantom of the Opera*, among others) says he really does not know how he composes. He "doodles" on the piano, and when he finds something he likes, he writes it down. "If I remember it," he says, "it must be all right." Sometimes he starts with the lyrics, at other times, the music.

Music making is a popular pasttime for many Americans. They not only learn how to play instruments and sing, but also to improvise and compose their own music. They learn how music can be used as a means of communication between people.

Sometimes composers start with a musical form. Form in music is like a plot in literature. It is the outline, the skeleton. This structure provides only the format, leaving ample leeway for many different expressions. Form does not control thinking, feeling, or message; it provides a blueprint for releasing these things.

Certain musical devices, such as interlocking rhythms or the twelve-tone technique, can also provide the creative impetus. In this chapter, you will be invited to create by composing a blues song or a theme and variations, or by using interlocking rhythms or twelve-tone technique.

British composer Andrew Lloyd Webber is famous for his popular musicals as well as film scores. Although he states that he begins his works with casual "doodles" on the piano, his finished compositions show that he composes with effort and care.

The 12-Bar Blues

Many of the songs you hear daily are based on the **blues**, *a genre of African-American music often expressing frustration, ordeal, or longing.* Usually blues are based on a 12-bar (sometimes an 8- or 16-bar) harmonic pattern that is repeated over and over. This simple yet elegantly ordered framework gives musicians a means of expression that is limited only by their imagination. To recognize a 12-bar blues tune, you must be able to recognize the pattern of repeated harmonies. The blues form is usually based on just three chords:

I   IV   V   I
DO   FA   SOL   DO

Use section E. in the Music Theory Handbook to review harmony.

The tonic or I chord is built on the first degree of the scale. The dominant or V chord is built on the fifth degree of the scale. The subdominant or IV chord is built on the fourth degree of the scale (that is, on the fifth scale degree *below* the tonic, hence the name *sub*dominant). These chords are often made into dominant-seventh chords by the addition of the seventh above the root tone:

I7   IV7   V7

You may wish to use "Create Your Own 12-Bar Blues." Lesson plans are found on page 218 in the Instructor's Guide.

Activity *Perform the Blues Chord*
Instructor's Guide, page 213

ACTIVITY ▶ *Perform the Blues Chord*

Can you play and sing the roots of the blues chords?

Look at the notation on page 321 and play on a keyboard or mallet percussion instrument the roots of the three chords printed here: C, F, and G. Try to sing these roots using the proper solfège syllables: DO, FA, and SOL.

As an extra challenge, try to play all three chords. One way to do this would be to play each one using the right hand in the following manner:

1. Locate and play each note separately.
2. Arpeggiate the chord by playing each note separately in rhythm.
3. Sound the entire chord by playing all four notes simultaneously.

Muddy Waters (McKinley Morganfield, 1915–1983) became the most important electric blues performer in post-World War II Chicago, along with Buddy Guy. Known all his life by his childhood nickname, Muddy Waters accompanied his amplified blues singing on guitar, backed by harmonica, piano, drums, bass, and rhythm guitar. This combination influenced the development of popular music in the 1950s and 1960s.

By knowing the harmonic pattern and repeating it over and over, musicians can improvise vocally and instrumentally by creating melodies that are compatible with these chords. In the blues, harmony serves as the basis for musical organization. This continuously repeating, sequential pattern of chordal changes provides the foundation upon which each blues tune is built. A repeated harmonic pattern, then, is another fundamental way that music is given order. You, too, can use this pattern to create blues.

ACTIVITY ▶ *Understand the 12-Bar Blues Pattern*

Can you hear and hum the 12-bar blues pattern?

Listen to Buddy Guy's "There Is Something on Your Mind" and try to follow the harmonic movement to detect when you hear the chord changes. Follow these steps:

1. Use the 12-bar grid supplied by your teacher to help keep your place in the music. As you listen to the music, count the measures like a musician and mark an "X" in each blank "measure box" (top row) where you hear a chord change. Listen to the music again and check your changes.

2. As you listen to the music once more, hum the root of each chord. I or DO, IV or FA, V or SOL. See if you can discover which chord (I, IV, or V7) is played on each change. (Hint: The first chord change is in measure 5; after that there are four more changes in the sequence.)

3. Listen again and label each measure (bottom row of boxes) with the syllable (DO, FA, or SOL) of the chord root. (Hint: You will begin in measure 1 on DO and continue this harmony for four measures until it changes in measure 5.) Use your voice and audiation skill to tell you the scale degree (FA or SOL) that is the root of the new chord in measure 5. Continue this labeling through measure 12.

4. Now relabel your syllables with their chord numbers: DO = I; FA = IV; and SOL = V7. Once you have completed this step, you will have written out the complete harmonic sequence for the 12-bar blues!

5. Listen to Buddy Guy one more time to check your chord pattern. Hum the roots of the chords or quietly sing the chord numbers as you listen.

TECHNOLOGY OPTION

■ **Music with MIDI** Use a MIDI program to play along with, improvise within, create variations of, and compose lyrics to a 12-bar blues.

Activity *Understand the 12-Bar Blues Pattern*
Instructor's Guide, pages 214–215
TRB 16-1, *Blues Listening and Performance*
CD 10 [10] "There Is Something on Your Mind" (4:45)

Technology Option
Use Project 16 in the *MIDI Activities* binder.

Bessie Smith (c. 1894–1937) was known as the "Empress of the Blues." She composed blues songs, and she recorded many with such jazz greats as Louis Armstrong, Fletcher Henderson, and Benny Goodman. She had a powerful voice with a talent for improvisation that made her one of the greatest blues singers of her time.

The Words

The lyrics of the blues are simple and direct. They usually express painful experiences that reveal the darker side of life. The poverty-stricken area known as the Mississippi Delta, which lies on the east bank of the Mississippi River south of Memphis, Tennessee, is generally thought to be the birthplace of the blues. In the years following the Civil War, African Americans developed this form of music to express their feelings of misery and desperation. They used the blues to vent their personal anguish.

These very honest, personal expressions dealt with basic concerns that flooded the lives of the poor and downtrodden. Blues lyrics do not just complain, however. They express both the grief and the reason for it. In this way, blues lyrics give hope. They put people in charge of their own problems. In the blues, each 12-bar section represents a verse that consists of three lines. The first states the situation, and the second usually repeats it exactly, assuring clarity and building tension. Then the third, or rhyming, line resolves the situation:

> Gonna lay my head right on the railroad track,
> Gonna lay my head right on the railroad track,
> If the train come 'long, I'm gonna snatch it back.

If you see humor in the third line, you are correct. The third line often dashes the self-pity that was built up in the other two lines.

Blues songs typically have many verses. As you might guess, the problems of love are also a favorite subject. The great blues composer William Christopher (or W. C.) Handy (1873–1958), called the "Father of the Blues," published his "St. Louis Blues" in 1914. Here is the first verse:

> I hate to see de ev'nin sun go down,
> Hate to see de ev'nin' sun go down,
> Cause my baby, (s)he done lef' dis town.

Many blues songs like this one became classics that jazz artists used for their improvisations, a practice that has led to confusion about the blues as a form distinct from jazz and other types of music. Whether it is rendered in a jazz, rock, or pop version, the 12-bar blues chord pattern is a highly individualistic musical form and expression. Even its deliberately plain, everyday street language is part of its down-home attraction.

The blues serve as the basis for much of the rhythm and blues (R & B), jazz, and popular music that we hear today, such as the music of B. B. King. Therefore, the ability to distinguish this form is important.

The themes of human frailty and triumph expressed in the blues probably account for the fact that this original, rural African-American musical form became the most extensively recorded of all folk music. The blues have been the single most important influence on the development of Western popular music.

Blue Notes

The blues vocalist typically "bends" or flattens certain tones of the diatonic major scale, imitating the sliding of the jazz trumpet or clarinet that gives the effect of wailing or sighing. What makes a blues melody really distinctive, however, is the use of the blues scale with its flattened **blue notes**, *the lowered notes on the third and seventh scale degrees.* The flatted fifth degree is a more recent addition.

Use section C. 3 in the *Music Theory Handbook* to review scales.

The Melody

Like most good melodies, the blues melody breathes. It takes up only two-and-a-half bars of each 4-bar phrase. This resting time allows the singer time to make up new verses. During this break, the accompanying instrument(s) improvise(s), or if the vocalist is certain of the lyric, he or she can improvise as well. In W. C. Handy's "Joe Turner Blues," this break is filled in with the improvised "Oh Lawdy." Because few, if any, of the musicians who created the blues could read music, they relied on verbal and musical improvisation.

Each line of the lyrics in a blues song represents a complete thought. The melody reflects this finality. At the end of each line, the melody comes to rest on the tonic (DO) or on one of the tones of the tonic chord (DO, MI, or SOL). This frequent return to the tonic produces an almost hypnotic effect.

You may wish to use "Sing Along" at this time. Lesson plans for the activity are found on page 218 in the Instructor's Guide.

PROFILE

W. C. Handy

W. C. Handy was one of the first artists to popularize Negro folk blues, the secular counterpart of Negro spirituals. Born to former slaves in Florence, Alabama, in 1873, William Christopher Handy grew up listening to folk and country music. In his youth, he played the cornet in a band and sang tenor in a quartet. He tried to keep this secret from his father, a Methodist preacher who did not approve of secular music. However, Handy just had to play music!

After a slow start, Handy became an accomplished professional musician, performing with a minstrel show throughout the country. He began to arrange songs for his own band, which had a total of 67 people. It became so popular he had to split it into three bands. Unable to find a publisher for his music, Handy decided to publish it himself.

In 1912, Handy published the popular "Memphis Blues," providing a break from the prevailing ragtime style and starting a blues craze. His success grew with his many compositions such as "Beale Street Blues," "St. Louis Blues," and "Joe Turner Blues." Handy contributed something new and unique to American and world music.

W. C. Handy
American Blues and
Jazz Composer
1873–1953

Balinese Interlocking Rhythms

Musical creation can take many forms, and the impetus to create can come from many sources. Borrowing ideas from other cultures is one way to initiate the creative process. For example, the music of Bali provides a good illustration of how borrowing can serve as the stimulus to our own creativity.

The Balinese combine different sounds in a highly complex and coordinated way. Music is fundamentally a social art, and the Balinese make the most of it. Balinese music illustrates the expressive possibilities afforded by an ensemble. In Balinese music, rhythmic precision between performers is carried to its ultimate. One particularly interesting example can be heard in the *Kecak* (Keh-CHAK), sometimes called the "Monkey Dance." This theatre spectacle, which was derived from trance rituals, is now performed outdoors for tourists after sunset.

Kecak is *a Balinese musical theatre work based on the Hindu epic the Ramayana* (Rah-MI-yah-nah). After a long struggle, Rama and his friends, Sugriva, the king of the monkeys, and Hanuman, the white monkey general, overcome Rawana and rescue Sita. The story is told by a chorus, narrators, and dancers who portray different characters. The chief narrator sometimes comments upon the action but more often translates the words of the second narrator, who speaks in *Kawi*. Kawi is the formal language of these old sacred texts that is no longer understood by most Balinese. But it is the men's chorus that "steals" the show.

Prince Rama is aided by the monkey king and his monkey army, portrayed by 100 to 150 men seated in five or six tight concentric circles, their backs to the audience. The shirtless men, including many teenagers, wear checkered black and white loincloths symbolizing good and evil in equal measure. (In Hindu epics, good does not necessarily triumph over evil, but the two exist in an eternal struggle.) The leaders of the chorus sit on one side of the inner circle; the narrators sit on the other. In the middle, where much of the action takes place, the army faces a large branching wooden torch with a flickering flame. With their voices and bodies, the men express their reactions to the events. They sway, circle, and bend, thrusting up and stretching out their hands as they chant *chak-a-chak*, with almost threatening energy. They may sway like the trees in the forest or act the role of a serpent, the wind, or other elements

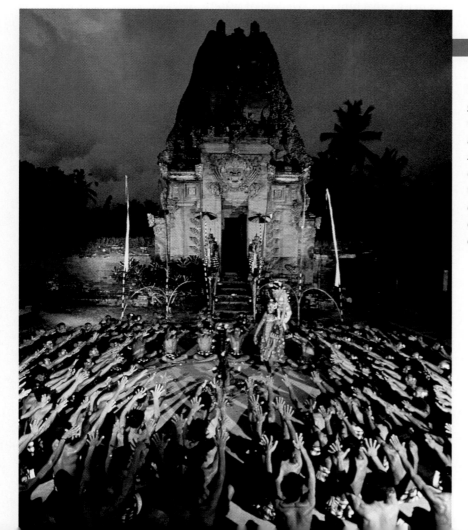

Music & CULTURE

The Balinese music drama Kecak *tells the story of the great hindu epic* Ramayana. *Often more than 150 men sit in concentric circles and rise, sway, fall backwards, and extend their arms, chanting with explosive, precisely executed rhythms. Their music expresses the many emotions of the unfolding drama.*

in the story. Throughout the drama, they imitate the sound of monkeys in intricate, **interlocking rhythms,** *a complex rhythmic line created by several individual rhythms that intermingle with each other.* The Balinese term for interlocking rhythms is *kotekan* (ko-TEH-kahn).

The Literary Drama

In one of the dramatic high points, Prince Rama's wife is abducted by Rawana, the evil king of Langka (Sri Lanka), and is carried off. Rama, Sita's husband, is in trouble, and his brother, Laksmana, has gone off to help him. Before leaving Sita, Laksmana has drawn a protective circle around her on the ground in the forest. As the scene starts, we see Rawana disguised as Pedanda, a priest, reciting a religious passage as a pretext for talking to Sita. The *Chak* chorus, heads bowed, sings and sways slowly. Pedanda addresses Sita using the guttural Low Balinese, as would a high priest in talking to an inferior. He tells her that he has been meditating for seven days and has not eaten or had anything to drink. He asks her to give him one swallow of water.

Sita offers Pedanda her food, but when she leaves her protective circle and gets close to him, he grabs her and changes into Rawana. Now the *Chaks* chant excitedly, bobbing their heads up and down. Sita calls to Laksmana for help, but Rawana asks her not to call out but to go with him to his kingdom. The *Chaks* seem possessed by Rawana's power. At his gesture, they rise to a crouch and wave their arms. As Rawana dances to tell the world he has captured Sita, they clap their hands in celebration. At the end of the scene, the men form a mountain of frenzied energy around Rawana. As they raise their arms and shake them intensely, Rawana vanishes, and they fall backwards.

Activity *Experience* Kecak
Instructor's Guide, page 215
CD 10 [11] "Sita's Abduction,"
Kecak (5:48)

ACTIVITY ▶ *Experience* Kecak

Listen to this excerpt from the Balinese music drama *Kecak* and note the important role the chorus plays in the telling of the story.

Read the story from the *Ramayana,* the great Hindu epic (above).

While you are listening to the scene of Sita's abduction, answer the following questions:

1. Can you distinguish a difference between the narrators, the characters, and the chorus?
2. Are the interlocking kotekan rhythms in the chorus easy or difficult to perform?
3. How does the chorus add to the drama?

The kotekan configuration in the chorus is composed of two rhythmically opposing parts that interlock to create a perpetual flow of sound. The two interlocking parts that form the kotekan are known as the *melos* (may-los, meaning "simple and direct") and the *nygangsi* (yahng-SEE, meaning "differing"), although each part is as rhythmically complex as the other. These negative and positive forces unite to create a continuous current of rhythms that is broken only for phrasing or at the close of an episode. This same principle of kotekan is used in the gamelan orchestra. Balinese performers learn their intricate melodies and rhythms by ear, through repetition and practice. They are not written down.

ACTIVITY ▶ *The Interlocking Rhythms of Kotekan*

Practice the following rhythms until you can perform them together in interlocking style with accuracy and speed.

1. Count and clap each of the rhythms until you can perform them securely.
2. While you tap the two beats, chant the rhythms using the words. Practice breathing at the breath mark ('). Increase the tempo.
3. Transfer the rhythms to wood blocks and claves, observing the higher and lower pitches as indicated. Start slowly with each line separately, then together. Gradually increase the tempo.
4. Now, decide on your tempo and repeat the four-measure phrase according to the following dynamic pattern (or make up one of your own):

5. For a more complex variation on these rhythms, try performing them in four parts.

Activity *The Interlocking Rhythms of Kotekan*
Instructor's Guide, pages 215–216
TRB 16-2, *Master the Principle of Kotekan*
CD 10 [11] "Sita's Abduction," *Kecak* (5:48)

You may wish to use "Create a Dramatic Scene using Interlocking Kotekan Rhythms" at this time. Lesson plans for the activity are found on page 219 in the Instructor's Guide.

Theme and Variations

You may wish to use "Create a Theme and Variations" at this time. Lesson plans for the activity are found on page 220 in the Instructor's Guide.

Composers often base a composition on a theme that is systematically presented in many guises. The theme, or melodic idea, can be borrowed from another composer or be newly created. **Theme and variations** is *a musical form in which a theme is stated then varied in a succession of statements.* The theme can be ornamented, its tempo altered, its harmony changed, its texture transformed, and so forth. There are as many possible variations to a theme as there are different ways to fix a hamburger. Sometimes variations are continuous. At other times they are set off from each other by pauses between them. In both instances, theme and variations achieve unity by basing the whole composition on the same theme, and they achieve variety by presenting the theme in different treatments.

American composer Frederic Rzewski (CHEFF-ski) (b. 1935) wrote a set of 36 variations for piano in 1975 entitled *The People United Will Never Be Defeated!* Rzewski used the theme from the Chilean song, *¡El Pueblo Unido Jamas Sera Vencido!* by Sergio Ortega and Quilapayun.

The variations reflect the meaning of the song. There are moments of struggle and defeat, of confidence and victory. The 36 variations are organized into six sets of six. The sixth variation of these sets is in six parts; the first five parts summarize the previous variations of the set, and the sixth provides new or transitional material. The sixth set of variations summarizes all of the preceding variations, ending with a triumphant and inspirational feeling of unity. What holds the work together is the use of one basic theme throughout, but note the variety and contrast that Rzewski achieves.

Music & ART

Music & Art
Students will notice that the color behind some of the shapes is reversed out with others. Also, the shape in each box evolves into a new shape with each repetition.

Theme and variations may be one of the most common expressive qualities found worldwide. Here, artist Albert Ayme portrays a visual theme and variations with the combination of color, shape and box. **How does each restatement of the visual "theme" vary?**

Albert Ayme. *Sixteen and One Variations.* (3 segments).1963. Collection du Fonds regional d'art contemporain, Languedoc-Roussillon.

ACTIVITY ▶ *Describe Variations of a Theme*

Can you identify a familiar theme even when a composer varies it?

Listen to five variations from *The People United Will Never Be Defeated!* To determine how Rzewski varies the theme, follow these steps:

1. Listen again to the original song as sung by Quilapayun to familiarize yourself with the melody. This is what inspired the composer.
2. Follow the musical score below to see how the composer first presents the theme in the opening of his theme and variations. Describe what he has done to the theme here.
3. Now listen to variations 1, 13, 15, and 18. These variations are described on your worksheet, but not in the correct order. On a piece of paper, match the variation number with its proper description: A, B, C, or D.
4. Listen to the final statement (variation 36) and describe how Rzewski varies the theme to create a dynamic finish.

Activity *Describe Variations of a Theme*
Instructor's Guide, pages 216–217
TRB 16-3, *Variations*
CD 10 |13| "Opening Theme" (1:22)
CD 10 |14| "Variation 1" (0:53)
CD 10 |15| "Variation 13" (1:44)
CD 10 |16| "Variation 15" (1:19)
CD 10 |17| "Variation 18" (1:27)
CD 10 |18| "Variation 36" (4:19)

The People United Will Never Be Defeated!

Thema

Frederic Rzewski

Twelve-Tone Music

Another technique for musical invention and organization is the twelve-tone system. In the early decades of the twentieth century, classical music became less dependent on a specific tonal center, such as DO. The major and minor scales that had served as the main tonal materials for music were increasingly overlaid with additional chromatic tones. To enliven musical expression, Claude Debussy (1862–1918) and other composers used clusters of tones, whole-tone scales, and other devices that incorporated all 12 tones of the chromatic scale, not just the eight in the diatonic scale. Still, there was a semblance of a tonal center.

During the second decade of the century, Arnold Schoenberg (1874–1951), an Austrian-born composer, decided to use all 12 tones in his compositions. This new freedom came at a price. Without a tonal center, the traditional sense of tonality was lost. The twelve-tone approach required a method of organizing tones and harmonies. Schoenberg soon set about devising a system of musical composition based on using a series of the 12 semitones that divide the octave.

Composer Arnold Schoenberg
Austrian-born Composer
1874–1951

PROFILE

Arnold Schoenberg

Arnold Schoenberg was among the most influential composers of the twentieth century. Born into a humble Jewish family in Vienna, he began violin lessons at the age of eight and soon began writing musical arrangements. At age 16, after the death of his father, he left school in order to support his family. Yet he continued his education and even taught himself to play cello. He completed his popular string sextet, Transfigured Night, at the age of 25.

Schoenberg's symphonic tone poems *Pelleas und Melisande* (1903) and *Pierrot Lunaire* (1912) and his other early works established his reputation internationally. However, as his works became increasingly dissonant, the public became hostile to his music. He persevered and invented the method of composition known as serialism in the early 1920s. Among his great accomplishments is the opera *Moses and Aron* (1932).

The rising tide of anti-Semitism in Berlin in 1933 forced Schoenberg and his family to immigrate to America. Settling in Los Angeles, he taught in universities and remained in Los Angeles until his death in 1951. A man of enormous integrity, his innovative spirit took courage and rested on deep religious convictions.

In Schoenberg's system, a **tone row** is *an ordering of the 12 pitches of the chromatic scale in a series that forms the basic material for a musical composition.* The composer can give these tones any order. A note can be repeated immediately, but it cannot be reintroduced until all 12 tones have been used. The tone row can then be used successively to create melody and simultaneously to create harmony.

The serial, or tone-row, technique of composition provides the musical material for an entire musical work. The composer manipulates the original row of 12 semitones by transposing it up or down and by setting it to any rhythm. It can be used in four basic versions:

1. In its original form, designated P (Prime) or O (Original);

2. *Sounded backward,* or in **retrograde**, designated R;

3. Turned upside down, or "inverted," designated I; and

4. Sounded upside down and backward, or in "retrograde inversion," designated RI.

The following example presents the four basic forms of the tone row that Schoenberg used in his *Suite for Piano*, Op. 25, published in 1924:

These four basic forms may be transposed so that, in total, each form can be made to sound at 12 different levels (pitches). (Forty-eight forms are, therefore, at a composer's disposal.) In the minuet from his *Suite for Piano*, Schoenberg uses the four basic forms of the tone row notated above, as well as four transposed forms. Two of the transposed forms that are used at the beginning of the trio section of the minuet movement are presented on page 336. They include the original row

transposed up six semitones (designated O_6) and the inversion of the
tone row transposed up six semitones (designated I_6):

The *Suite for Piano* that Schoenberg created with this tone row is
modeled on dance suites from the time of Bach and Handel. As in a
Baroque suite, Schoenberg's suite contains a number of dance movements: prelude, gavotte, intermezzo, minuet, and gigue. However, the
expressive effect of twelve-tone or serial technique is very different. Here
is the way Schoenberg used the original tone row and its transpositions
at the start of the trio section of the minuet:

ACTIVITY ▶ *Hear the Tone Row*

Listen to the minuet from Arnold Schoenberg's *Suite for Piano* and see if you can detect the tone row.

Study the music (on page 336) to see how the tone row is used. "O" is the original tone row; "I" is the inverted row. O_6 is the original row transposed up six semitones, and I is the inverted row transposed up six semitones. Now listen to the recording. Can you detect when Schoenberg uses the original row, when he transposes it, inverts it, or uses it in retrograde or in inverted retrograde?

Much of the effect of music composed in the twelve-tone or serial technique is psychological. The system does not negate repetition, but it certainly obscures it. Schoenberg and other composers who championed this system believed that the built-in relationship between the sounds and their fixed patterns of succession are recognized subconsciously. The tone row creates a psychological order that our subconscious recognizes, but which our ear may not be able to delineate clearly. It may operate like our "sixth sense"—our ability to sense danger even though it is not readily apparent.

Activity *Hear the Tone Row*
Instructor's Guide, page 217
CD 10 19 Minuet, *Suite for Piano*
(3:52)

You may wish to use "Create a Tone-Row Composition" at this time. Lesson plans for the activity are found on page 220 in the Instructor's Guide.

Music & ART

Artist Vasily Kandinsky (1866–1944) was a contemporary of Arnold Schoenberg. Like the composer, Kandinsky wrote theories about his art. Unlike Schoenberg, he improvised on the canvas rather than hold to strict form.

Vasily Kandinsky. *Accompanied Contrast.* 1935. Solomon R. Guggenheim Museum, New York, New York. (37.338)

How Are You Creative?

Creative people are natural problem solvers. Their answers tend to be unconventional. Instead of thinking convergently, that is, in the customary and expected way, they think divergently, finding different or unusual ways to think and operate. Creative people tend to deviate from the normal or typical in their thinking. They look for new connections, new orders, and new possibilities. They invent.

Artists vary in the degree of their originality. Some prefer to work in the prevailing styles and modes of their day. Others, like Schoenberg, formulate wholly new ways to use sound expressively. That kind of thinking is highly valuable. It has permitted the human race to reach beyond the ordinary and achieve new marvels. Every human being has some sense of creativity. Creative people are often unconventional. They have an ability to go off in new directions, to "diverge" from the customary and the known.

SUMMARY

Composers and performers sometimes rely upon frameworks to help them create musical expressions. For example, there are certain "givens" when one is creating blues: the chord pattern, the number of bars, the structure of the lyrics, the use of blue notes, and so forth. There are strict rules about composing a piece using the tone-row system. There are certain ways one goes about creating a theme and variations, a pop song, a fugue, a march, or any other type of musical composition. These frameworks reduce the number of decisions a composer has to make. They make the composing of music manageable. In a sense, a composer starts by setting boundaries and limitations within which to work, just as a painter starts with a particular size of canvas.

Creating music within these general outlines challenges the mind to its fullest. There is a great deal of figuring out to do. There must be unity and variety, order and emotion, tension and release. The composer chooses the most appropriate musical means, elements, and form in order to tailor the musical sound to his or her expressive idea. The creative process can take place spontaneously, as improvisation, or it can involve hearing the sound in the mind, then producing it or representing it on paper with symbols. The composer speaks directly through sound. Creating music is another way to communicate, another way that human beings comment upon the world and their relation to it.

Building Music Vocabulary

On a sheet of paper, write the term from the list that best matches each description below.

(2) blue notes   (5) retrograde
(7) blues   (3) theme and
(6) interlocking rhythms   variations
(4) *Kecak*   (1) tone row

1. An ordering of the twelve pitches of the chromatic scale in a series that forms the basic material for a musical composition.
2. Lowered notes on the third and seventh scale degrees.
3. A musical form in which a theme is stated, then varied in a succession of statements.
4. A Balinese musical theatre work based on the Hindu epic *Ramayana*.
5. Sounded backward.
6. A complex rhythmic line created by several individual rhythms that intermingle with each other.
7. A genre of African-American music often expressing frustration, ordeal, or longing.

Reviewing Music Facts

Answer each question in a complete sentence.

8. Why might a composer begin a composition with a specific musical form?
9. Which music genre had the most effect on the development of Western popular music?
10. What are four ways a composer might change each statement in a theme and variations?
11. What was the new method of composition developed by Arnold Schoenberg?
12. Name the four basic versions in which a tone row might be used.

Answers to Chapter 16 Review

8. It provides an outline or structure for creating musical expression.
9. The blues.
10. Changing the tempo, the harmony, the rhythm, the texture; or, the theme may be ornamented.
11. The tone row, or twelve-tone method of composition.

Complete answers for the Chapter 16 Review are found in the Instructor's Guide, page 221.

Thinking It Through

On a sheet of paper, write your responses to the following:

13. **Analyze** What are some of the reasons the Balinese *Kecak* is so powerful to an audience?
14. **Explain** In your own words, describe the harmonic structure of a typical 12-bar blues song.
15. **Apply** How did serial composers believe the listener would be able to hear the tonal relationships in their dissonant and atonal music?

Making the Connection

Math Calculate how many different possible sequences, or how many different "rows" of twelve tones, are mathematically possible. Describe how you arrived at your result.

Theatre Choose a myth or legend to serve as the focus of a short musical drama similar to the Balinese drama *Kecak*. Invent characters and write lyrics for their songs. Use a divided chorus to perform the interlocking rhythms.

 Connect to sites where you learn more about blues artists and classical composers at **www.glencoe.com/sec/music**

12. In its original order, in retrograde, inversion, or in retrograde inversion.
13. Responses may include: the intensity and rhythmic excitement of the music, the spectacle and sound of the huge male chorus, the colorful spectacle, the emotions of the drama.
14. The blues song is usually divided into a harmonic pattern, using only the I, IV, and V chords, repeated over and over in the same sequence.
15. They believed the tone row and the tonal relationships would be subconsciously recognized by the listener.

CHAPTER 17

Creating with Technology

Technology is the place where art meets science. Today, music technology is advancing rapidly, expanding the possibilities of musical expression beyond anything ever dreamed of just a decade or two ago. Music technology has opened a new world of sound. It has already made a major impact on the way we hear and on the way we express and interpret our world. It has given musical creativity a new reach, allowing ordinary people to make music in new ways. It allows us to do with ease what was previously impossible.

*Longtime Rolling Stones keyboardist Chuck Leavell, shown here, continues to experiment with musical expression using advances in technology. In this way, he helps open doors to new possibilities. **What developments in music technology can you share with the class?***

Caption answer
Encourage a variety of responses and, if possible, ask volunteers give class demonstrations with synthesizers or MIDI programs.

Objectives

By completing the chapter, you will:
- Find out how technology is changing the role of composers and performers.
- Learn how electronic sounds are generated and how they are used for expressive purposes.
- Be able to distinguish between electronically and conventionally produced sounds.
- Learn the history of electronic music and the meaning of its most important terms.
- Become acquainted with the work of some outstanding living arrangers and composers who use technology to create music.

Vocabulary

drum machine
hyperinstruments
MIDI
musique concrète
sampling
sequencer
synthesizer
telharmonium

Musician to Meet

Tod Machover

Electronic Timbres

Electronically generated sounds are all around us. The invention of new sound technology, particularly the extraordinary developments of the last quarter of the twentieth century, has enabled us to extend the range of musical timbres. The expressive potential of these sounds is infinite and only awaits the imagination of new composers to probe their possibilities. Already there are literally thousands of new musical compositions that owe their existence to this technology.

Activity *Realize the Potential*
Instructor's Guide, pages 222–223
CD 10 [20] *Secrets of Synthesis,*
Track 1 (2:06)
CD 10 [21] *Secrets of Synthesis,*
Track 2 (2:55)
CD 10 [22] *Secrets of Synthesis,*
Track 3 (4:19)

ACTIVITY ▶ *Realize the Potential*

Listen to a demonstration of some samples of sounds and expressive effects that can be created on a synthesizer.

Listen to American composer Wendy Carlos (b. 1939) explain and demonstrate how she made the public conscious of the Moog synthesizer with her recording *Switched-On Bach*, the first classical album to go platinum.

What feats are required to make electronic music expressive and musical in a way similar to music made with acoustic instruments? Discuss such matters as vibrato, the need for overdubbing, touch sensitivity, and the need for taste.

Why is a perfect automated rhythm less exciting than a human's imperfectly performed rhythm?

MIDI TECHNOLOGY OPTION

Technology Option
Use Project 17 in the *MIDI
Activities* binder.

■ **Music with MIDI** Use a MIDI program to create a composition featuring unique and original sounds from your MIDI gear.

Most of us are so accustomed to electronic sounds in television commercials, on pop recordings, and in film scores that we may not be able to distinguish these sounds from the more traditional acoustic sources (musical instruments, voices). Although electronic technology has produced hundreds of new timbres, we do not yet have a common language or vocabulary to describe these new sounds. Quite often, however, sounds that are generated electronically deliberately mimic acoustic instruments or human voices and can be labeled accordingly. Often, instruments are electrified—the organ and guitar are common examples. The trick is to get our ears to distinguish sounds that are produced acoustically from those that are produced electronically.

Throughout the world of popular and commercial music, we hear electronic music every day, but we do not always realize how the sound is generated. Can you recognize synthesized sounds when you hear them? For many composers of popular music, the creative combination of synthesized and acoustic (conventional) sounds has become a standard.

ACTIVITY ▶ *Distinguish the Origin of Sound*

Can you distinguish the electronically produced sounds from those produced by conventional instruments when both are combined in the same piece?

Listen to the "Electronic Montage," which consists of musical excerpts, each of which lasts approximately 40 seconds. As you listen, write down on your worksheet the instrumental sounds in each piece that you believe are acoustic and those that are synthesized.

The Beginnings of Electronic Sound

The roots of electronic music go back to the beginning of the twentieth century, when Edison's phonograph, a mechanical invention, was electrified. Here was an electric machine that could reproduce sound. It could perform! Music would never be the same. Electricity was a natural sound producer. Electric motors and generators hummed with discernible pitch. As early as 1900 in the United States, Thaddeus Cahill invented the **telharmonium** (also known as the Dynamophone), *a machine that used electrical current to produce sound.* It proved impractical. For one thing, it weighed 200 tons! But the telharmonium showed that electricity could be used to make sound.

The earliest sound recordings were made by Thomas Edison on a device he designed in 1877. He used a metal cylinder wrapped in tin foil that rotated on a long metal screw, which was cranked by hand. Eleven years later, in 1888, the first recording by a recognized artist was made when Josef Hofman, at the age of 12, played a brief passage on a piano located in the Edison laboratories.

In 1923 the Russian Leon Theremin introduced the aetherophone (better known as the theremin), an electric instrument that a number of composers incorporated into their music. It had a haunting, vocal-like sound, similar to a musical saw. In France during the same decade, Eduard Coupleux and Joseph Givelet applied the concept of the paper piano roll with its punched holes to control electric oscillators and filters that could create pitch, volume, and timbre. Perhaps the most sophisticated of the early electric instruments was the Hammond organ, which appeared in 1934. There were many other experiments, but most of the electric instruments that were built tried to imitate existing acoustic instruments.

The theremin, named after inventor Leo Theremin, was an early electronic musical instrument that generated only a single tone (pitch). Users controlled pitch and loudness by moving their hands near an antenna and a loop attached to the device. It produced a wavy, eerie sound used in early film scores. **In what kind of movie would you expect to find the theremin's sound?**

Caption answer
Students will mostly likely identify science-fiction movies.

Tape Recorder Music

The real development in electronic music began after the Second World War. By then, the tape recorder was perfected. Magnetic tapes could be cut and spliced together, sped up or slowed down, and played backward, making it possible to manipulate the sound, reprocess it, and rerecord it. The potential of the tape recorder as a machine to create music, not merely to reproduce it, was quickly realized.

In 1948, the first electronic music studio was established in Paris by a group of experimenters. They called their work **musique concrète**, *a system of electronic composition in which natural sounds are taped, edited, and shaped into a composition recorded on magnetic tape.* The music they constructed consisted of natural sounds—birds and other sounds in nature, and man-made sounds such as sirens and car horns—recorded and manipulated on magnetic tape. During the 1950s, electronic music studios were established in major cities around the world. One of the earliest (1951) was the Columbia-Princeton Electronic Music Center in New York. Others in Cologne, Tokyo, Milan, and Warsaw, like the Paris studio, were established at major radio stations. Composers in these centers were dedicated pioneers who explored the new electronic medium and established the tape recorder as both a creative device and a performer. These composers dared to make music without using traditional musical instruments. This was revolutionary!

In the United States, the first public demonstration of tape recorder music was given by Vladimir Ussachevsky (useuh-CHEV-ski) in 1952. No matter what his original sound sources—flute, piano, or any other

Pioneering American electron composer Milton Babbitt (left) and Vladimir Ussachevsky (right) stand with engineer Peter Mauzey in front of the first music synthesizer, the RCA Mark II, at the Columbia-Princeton Electronic Music Center in New York City, c. 1959. Composers composed music on the tape in the center and at the left.

instrument—they were often completely transformed. In the days prior to the existence of the keyboard-controlled, electronic sound-generating devices we now have, the composer had to manipulate the sounds by hand, working with several tape recorders. The composer composed directly on tape, altering sounds and organizing them into expressive compositions.

In 1960, Ussachevsky (1911–1990) was commissioned to compose an electronic work to commemorate the inventions of Lee De Forrest, inventions that had led to the development of radio. As basic sound material in this work, Ussachevsky used some authentic, wireless spark-generated code signals that he recorded in the Wireless Museum in Trenton, New Jersey. He also included a fragment from Richard Wagner's opera *Parsifal,* which he electronically treated to resemble a shortwave transmission. (*Parsifal* had been the first musical work ever to be broadcast.) The orchestral composition gradually emerges from the montage of wireless signals.

Activity *Recognize the Elements of Music*
Instructor's Guide, pages 224–225
CD 10 ⬚31 *Wireless Fantasy* (4:32)

ACTIVITY ▶ *Recognize the Elements of Music*

Is electronic music—music?

Listen to *Wireless Fantasy* (1960) by American composer Vladimir Ussachevsky and determine whether this has elements that define it as music. Does it have melody, rhythm, dynamics, timbre, harmony, mood, texture, and form?

How is this work descriptive of the period of wireless communication (1899–1925)?

Otto Luening (b. 1900) and Ussachevsky worked together on joint compositions, testing the feasibility of combining tape recorder music with a live symphony orchestra. The difficulty was in synchronizing the fixed sounds on tape with musicians performing live. Their *Rhapsodic Variations* (1954) and *A Poem in Cycles and Bells* (1954) left little doubt about the enormous potential of combining the new with the old medium.

At the electronic studios of West German Radio in Cologne, Karlheinz Stockhausen (b. 1928) created musical compositions in the mid-1950s using electronic sounds from oscillators and generators. In those days, producing music by electronic means was highly technical. Stockhausen's mathematical specifications for creating just one minute of music from electronic sources in 1953 filled a one-foot-thick stack of 8½ x 11-inch paper covered on both sides. Every aspect of each particular single sound had to be specified! It was a complex, time-consuming, scientific process.

By the 1950s, many musicians as well as most of the public had not yet subscribed to John Cage's belief that all sounds, including noise, have musical potential, depending upon how they are used. People were accustomed to musical sound coming from acoustic sources—musical instruments and the human voice. The Italian composer Ottorino Respighi (ruh-SPEE-gee) (1879–1936) had incorporated a recording of a nightingale in the third movement of his orchestral work *The Pines of Rome* (1924), but after all, this was a bird singing. It was at least musical. What about, however, using other natural sounds? Can music be made from the clatter of garbage cans, the whirling of machines, and the din of car horns?

ACTIVITY ▶ *Perform Nonacoustic Music*

Create and perform a composition made from nonacoustic sources of sound.

Suggestions for sounds at hand:

Spinning a coin on a desk	Rolling a marble in a cup
Plucking elastic bands	Ticking clock
Tapping a pencil on a desk	Running water
Tapping on a cardboard box	Dripping water
Blowing across bottles of various sizes	Shaking marbles in a closed container

Look around the classroom and find other objects that can be used to create sound. When you have three sources in mind, use the following procedures:

1. Using a portable cassette tape recorder, record about 20 seconds of each of the three sounds to equal one minute of continuous sound.
2. Extend the sound resources of your composition by using three cassette tape recorders as follows:
   - Tape recorder A: Play your original composition and re-record it on the other two tape recorders according to the following plan.
   - Tape recorder B: Start to record when segment 2 begins on tape recorder A, and record segments 2 and 3. Stop. Rewind tape on tape recorder A, then record segment 1 onto tape recorder B. (The order of the segments on tape recorder B will be 2, 3, 1.)
   - Tape recorder C: Start to record when segment 3 begins on tape recorder A. Stop. Rewind tape on recorder A, then record segments 1 and 2. (Order of segments here will be 3, 1, 2.)
3. Now rewind each tape recorder and then play all three tape recorders at the same time. The student operating each tape recorder may use the volume control on his or her recorder to fade in, fade out, turn volume control rhythmically, and turn volume high to create static.
4. Use a fourth tape recorder to record the composition.
5. Perform your composition for the class. See if your classmates can identify the original sound sources for each of the three segments. Decide which composition has the most unique sound sources.

The Synthesizer

You may wish to use "Analyze Musical Commercials" at this time. Lesson plans for the activity are found on page 227 in the Instructor's Guide.

A **synthesizer** is *a machine that produces sound electronically.* The first synthesizer, Mark II, was built in the early 1950s by Radio Corporation of America (RCA). Later it was donated to the Columbia-Princeton Electronic Music Center. It was a huge machine—an early computer— covered with dials and switches and filled with 18,000 vacuum tubes, but it allowed a composer to exercise much control over the sounds that were generated. The composer programmed the machine by punching a paper tape with holes that, according to their position, told the machine what to do. The trouble was, it took a genius to understand how to use it.

Electronic technology developed rapidly during the 1960s. Robert Moog and Donald Buchla in the United States and Paul Ketoff in Italy designed synthesizers that replaced the old vacuum tubes with transistors. Moog's main contribution was the invention of the voltage-controlled oscillator, a device that allowed the operator to vary the current in order to modify the sound. These early synthesizers permitted the creation and control of all the properties of sound—pitch, envelope (the growth and decay of a tune), amplitude (volume or loudness), timbre, reverberation (repetitions of sound like overlapping echoes), and so forth—through an elaborate system of patch cords, similar to those on early telephone switchboards. The Moog synthesizer soon had a keyboard connected to it that immediately simplified the operation. The first commercial synthesizers were made available to the public in 1964, eliminating the need to rely upon an established studio.

Whereas the early synthesizers required the composer to create and record one sound at a time—a tedious process—the new keyboard models permitted the construction of continuous sound sequences. They could therefore be used to create music in live performance (or in "real time"), not just on tape in a studio. Performers began to use synthesizers in performance. These instruments, however, were monophonic—like the human voice. They permitted only one tone to be generated at a time. Many different melodic lines and timbres could be created, but they had to be recorded separately and then mixed through the process of over-dubbing on multitrack taping equipment. The recording *Switched-On Bach* was created this way. The process was time-consuming—like creating thousands of tiny colored tiles in many hues and then assembling them into a mosaic.

Keyboards were attached to synthesizers in the 1960s. They became portable and could be played through a guitar-like amplifier, outside of a studio. Pop groups such as the Beatles and the Who began using them regularly. Soon they were a standard sound in pop music.

Activity *Orchestrated and Synthe-*
sized Arrangements
Instructor's Guide, page 225
TRB 17-3, *Judging Quality*
CD 11 [1] *Moonlight Sonata*, first
movement (5:37)
CD 11 [2] *Moonlight Sonata*, first
movement (5:39)

ACTIVITY ▶ *Orchestrated and Synthesized Arrangements*

Listen to and compare the original orchestration of Beethoven's
***Moonlight Sonata* with a synthesized arrangement.**

For the comparison, write evaluative notes in the "timbre," "expressiveness," and "impact" columns on a Judging Quality worksheet.

First movement (*adagio sostenuto*—slow and sustained) from Beethoven's *Moonlight Sonata*:

    A. Original for piano (Misha Dichter, pianist)

    B. Synthesized transcription (Don Dorsey, synthesist)

After completing the comparison, answer the following questions:

1. How do you suppose the original creator of this composition, Beethoven, would react to the synthesized version?

2. Some people might consider the synthesized version to be a musical distortion of the original. Do you agree? Why or why not?

3. Which version of the composition has the greater musical impact? Why?

4. Which is more creative? Why?

Leo Fender began mass producing electric guitars in the 1940s, making them affordable to musicians. Country and jazz artists were the first to popularize them. The sound of a Fender instrument, along with its amplifier, eventually defined rock and roll.

"Pop" Electrified

During the 1960s, the pop world eagerly assimilated the new electronic technology. These musicians were flexible and creative. The Hawaiian guitar had been electrified by Leo Fender in 1936, about the same time the standard electric guitar appeared. Now the electric guitar became the focal instrument of rock music. New amplification technology allowed rock musicians to perform outdoors and in stadiums for audiences that numbered in the thousands. As synthesizers became smaller and more manageable, pop musicians everywhere began to use them for both performance and composition.

By the late 1970s and early 1980s, keyboard synthesizers had become a regular fixture in popular music, and so had the wide variety of sounds that these new instruments made possible. Patch cords, now a thing of the past, were replaced by sliders and push buttons. Monophonic synthesizers had been replaced by polyphonic (more than one voice) synthesizers that could play several tones simultaneously. The development of touch-sensitive keyboards gave the performer added control. Making

A master showman and virtuoso guitarist, Jimi Hendrix (1942–1970) experimented with a whole new range of amplified sound effects on his Fender Stratocaster. His rendition of "The Star-Spangled Banner" at Woodstock (1969) has been called by music reviewers "the most powerful work of American art to deal with the Vietnam War…One man with one guitar said more in three-and-a-half minutes…than all the novels, memoirs, and movies put together."

and using synthesized (electronic) sounds became easy and relatively inexpensive. In fact, the technology itself has prompted the development of two new musical styles: "New Age" and "Space" music.

From Analog to Digital

The first commercial synthesizers were "analog" machines. They had moving parts like the hands on a watch. Sound was stored on a magnetic tape that also relied upon mechanical movement. By 1983, microprocessors, or chips, transformed synthesizers from analog to digital. The latter is the same technology that allows a watch to display the time in numerals. Microprocessors are commonplace today in home appliances such as microwave ovens and VCRs. In digital technology, sounds can be stored in the computer in the binary "language" of 1s and 0s. A compact disc (CD) stores sound in this way, rather than by cutting grooves into vinyl that represent the actual vibrations.

This new digital technology has further simplified the process of creating music for both the composer and the performer. It gives added flexibility. For example, when sound is stored on tape, increasing the tempo (speeding up the tape) causes the pitch to sound higher. Using digital technology, the tempo can be altered without changing the pitch, and vice versa. This is because the sound is not stored as sound but as information (data). Another advantage is that the sound is clearer. The machines, moreover, are compact. One silicon chip that you can barely see now performs the function of 18,000 vacuum tubes!

You may wish to use "Demonstrate Music Technology" at this time. Lesson plans for the activity are found on page 227 in the Instructor's Guide.

Computers and Music

The new digital technology is now standard. In 1983, Yamaha introduced the first all-digital commercial synthesizer, its DX-7. The same year, Casio introduced its CZ-101 digital synthesizer—for under 500 dollars! Today, the rapidly evolving development of digital synthesizers continues the advancement of this technology. These instruments are computers and synthesizers. The combination has greatly simplified the way in which electronic sounds are generated and used for musical purposes.

MIDI

The computer adds another dimension to electronic music making. It can be programmed to react to cues and translate them into musical sounds. These musical signals in computer form are recorded in **MIDI**, *Musical Instrument Digital Interface.* MIDI uses a standardized "language" of digital bits that the computer can store. These bits can be translated into sound when the computer is connected to a music synthesizer (or "synth"), drum machine, or other instrument designed to read MIDI.

MIDI is simply an interface or link that allows a performer or composer to connect and synchronize a number of machines and tell them what to do. The Biomuse, for example, uses electrical sensors that are wrapped around the musician's head and forearms to amplify brain and muscle waves. The computer is programmed to convert these waves into sound. It controls the music synthesizer. MIDI software even permits the musical information to be printed out in the form of a notated score. The composer or performer plays a melody or a rhythm; the machinery prints it out. Because the music is in digital form, it can be easily altered in pitch, tempo, volume, and timbre.

Live Performance

Just as a TV broadcast signal needs a television set to translate the signal into a visual image, a computer needs a synthesizer to translate its data into sounds that produce music. One of the problems for popular musicians is duplicating their recordings in live performance. In the recording studio, as many as 24 or more tracks are recorded and mixed. In live performance, the same musicians are limited to the number of parts that can be played with two hands and two feet. With MIDI, however, one musician can link different instruments and synthesizers and cue different sound sources so that many sounds can be "played" simultaneously—some live, some prerecorded. Parts of the score are stored in offstage computers that are synchronized with the performance and are cued in by the performer. The MIDI controls permit the onstage performers to appear to do more than is humanly possible, but the computers are actually functioning as additional performers.

Electronic music studios now exist in most colleges and universities and in some high schools. Today, good keyboard synthesizers can be relatively inexpensive. They are rapidly becoming commonplace in the home. Increasingly, the synthesizer is being accepted as a legitimate musical instrument. For many young people, the synthesizer is the first instrument of choice. In the future, no doubt, composers will write for the synthesizer as they have composed in the past for the harpsichord and the piano.

In a recording studio, computers add new dimensions to music making. A traditional sound source such as the human voice can be shaped and manipulated to make new expressions. However, musical performance still remains a living art involving live performers.

Sequencing

The new synthesizers have a built-in memory system so that composers and performers can play back their musical creations. Sequencers have replaced the earlier tape decks. Whereas a tape deck stores the actual music itself, a **sequencer** is *an electronic system that stores data about music.* This is the basic difference between the old analog and the new digital technology. A sequencer greatly simplifies the process of constructing a musical score with many voices (parts) that are synchronized. It allows a single composer-performer to become a whole band or orchestra. The various parts are stored on different tracks that can be altered individually. Then the composer-performer can go back and correct or change individual pitches and rhythms. He or she can reorder the measures, just as sentences or paragraphs might be moved in word processing. Best of all, the revised sound can be retrieved instantaneously and even presented in the form of a printed score. Sequencers facilitate the composing process and make it convenient to retrieve musical information in performance.

Sampled Sounds

The computer permits composers to take small bits of prerecorded sound and manipulate them into musical expression. In the film *Indiana Jones and the Last Crusade*, the adventuresome professor finds himself surrounded by thousands of screeching rats, but the sound actually came from a flock of chickens. The sound of the chickens was sampled and then sped up. **Sampling** is *a recording process that begins with real sounds*, just as the early musique concrète did.

This new technology has many other applications. Composers and performers can now take the sound of a trombone, violin, or any other instrument and create a part for that instrument that can go much higher or lower than the actual instrument. Through sampling, the synthesizer/computer can duplicate real musical timbres with amazing exactness. The reason is very simple—the sound is recorded from the actual instrument. You start with the real sound rather than some electronic simulation of it. Digital recording enhances the process by assuring amazing fidelity. Sampling allows performers to take a real drum stroke and duplicate it, playing any rhythm they choose to tap.

What Technology Allows Us to Do

Electronics are changing the nature and meaning of composing and performing. Through electronics, composers have a new palette of timbres at their command, but this is just the beginning. Computers enable composers to share the process of creation with the performers or with one or more engineers who manipulate the sounds electronically as they are played or sung. Instead of being a solitary act, composing becomes a group endeavor, and performance, becomes a far more creative process.

Expand Technique and Expression

You may wish to use "Debate" at this time. Lesson plans for the activity are found on page 226 in the Instructor's Guide.

Today, the electronic keyboard has been given a degree of intelligence that enables the performer to take the performance to wholly new dimensions. A computer accepts the performance information and stores it in its memory, enabling the performer to alter this information in many ways, then play it back. In a very real sense, electronics gives the performer a powerful and versatile helping hand—or 100 hands. With a computer, as many notes at one time can be played as the piano has keys, and they can be played with incredible speed. The performer can exercise a degree of control over dynamics not humanly possible, so that the range of dynamic gradation is multiplied tenfold. With the help of these new technologies, a single performer can become an entire orchestra. That is quite a feat!

Alter and Add Sounds

For his science-fiction opera *Valis* (1987), Tod Machover (MACK-over), a young American composer, used electronics to create an orchestra out of just two musicians—a keyboard player and a percussionist. In addition to the two instruments, the opera is scored for seven voices, prerecorded tape, and live computer manipulation. Computers analyze the MIDI signals received from the performers and interact with them, altering and adding sounds to create a densely interesting and compelling musical score. His **hyperinstruments** are *instruments that, with the help of computers, respond to live musicians.* They can transform a solo singer into a chorus and an instrumentalist into an ensemble of many timbres and textures. They can prolong live tones or echo them. They can integrate prerecorded rhythms and melodies into the live performance by following the musical score and interacting with it!

Jazz artist Herbie Hancock stands out as an early pioneer in the use of technology in making music. His 1983 album Future Shock, *which features computer-based compositions, won a Grammy for best R&B Instrumental.*

Make Prerecorded Parts Responsive

These hyperinstruments even allow for melodic errors and tempo fluctuations in a live performance and adjust their response accordingly. Machover explains that "special extensions to the instruments let the players delicately control and shape a vast sound world." Prior to this development, musicians had to adjust to the rigidity of any prerecorded parts. Now, Machover says, "These computer programs analyze a musician's gestures and performance [e.g., notes played, loudness, aftertouch, etc.] and react immediately, sending MIDI data out to an array of synthesizers, samplers, and sound transformation modules." Computers react intelligently to a live performance and add to it instantaneously.

PROFILE

Tod Machover

Tod Machover
American Composer
1953–

One of the reasons that composer Tod Machover is so comfortable with technology and music is that his mother was a concert pianist and his father a pioneer in computer graphics. Growing up he learned to play both the classics and rock, and he was encouraged to take technology for granted.

Now, as the director of Massachusetts Institute of Technology's Media Lab, Machover tries to bridge the seemingly polar worlds of technology and art, as well as popular and classical musical styles. The main task of the composer, he says, is "to express and communicate something essential about being human." He believes that "technology has to be used to enhance humanity, not to lead us around."

Called "the wunderkind [wonder-child] of the computer-music world," Machover helped develop computer programs that actually respond to live musicians. He calls the system that produces this interaction hyperinstruments. In 1996 one of his most important works, *The Brain Opera,* premiered in New York. It incorporates contributions made by both live and on-line audiences.

The Opera *Valis*

The story of *Valis* is based on a novel of the same name by the American science-fiction writer Philip K. Dick (1926–1982). Dick wrote about a strange experience he had in March, 1974, when he claims to have been bathed in a pink light that brought mystical revelations. Most of Dick's novels are explorations of everyday life that are melded with dreams and visions. It is Dick's notion that our inner world of fantasy and spirituality is real and that we must look beyond the face value of events if we want to find true reality. In the novel, Dick divided himself into two characters, one being Phil Dick, the science-fiction writer, the other Horselover Fat, the weak, unhappy, and neurotic other side of himself.

As the opera opens, Horselover Fat is experiencing an unnerving revelation. In the midst of video monitors, Fat is pierced through the head by a pink laser beam. Based on this experience, Fat thinks that the human mind is like a computer that is not working properly. His various encounters are odd and disconnected. He has strange dreams. Is he having a nervous breakdown? He asks one of the opera's main questions: "How many worlds do we exist in simultaneously?" He writes a journal (his "Exegesis") in which he attempts to explain the universe. Sounds and images flow from his mind uncontrollably.

Eric and Linda Lampton ("lamp" being a reference to light), two somewhat sinister rock musicians, appear and tell him that the source of his strange experience is Valis, an acronym for Vast Active Living Intelligent System. (Valis proves Dick's belief that there is a single force behind life's seemingly fragmented experiences.) At this point in the opera, the conductor climbs out of the orchestra pit and uses the magic of art and technology—his only language—to sculpt music into the voice of the angel/god/hologram Sophia. It is Sophia who heals Phil/Fat of his duality. Later, she bids him goodbye in a dream—using another's voice.

Valis is the story of painful search and hopeful redemption. It is about synthesis, of bringing strange and seemingly unrelated experiences back together. It is essentially religious. At the end of the opera, Phil/Fat now made whole again and renewed, sits down to await life's next challenge.

To express all the odd and seemingly unrelated events, Machover uses an extraordinary range of music styles—rock, romantic, medieval, serial, rap, new age, and futuristic "sound poetry." This makes the final synthesis even more powerful. "Above all," the composer says, "I have viewed *Valis* as an opportunity to write the most beautiful music that I could, bringing to life a story that I feel strongly about. I have given free reign to my lyrical impulse. . . . I have tried to develop a rich palette of sonic colors to best shade every nuance of emotion. . . ."

You will hear three excerpts from *Valis*:

1. "Lampton Scene" (excerpt). Two rock musicians, Eric and Linda Lampton, are joined onstage by the pianist and percussionist who have been accompanying the opera. They become the two musicians in the Lampton's rock band performing in the atmosphere of a high-tech rock

This scene is taken from the 1987 Paris premiere of the opera Valis *by American composer Tod Machover. At the left, one of the singers stands in front of a video wall. At the right, the two live musicians, a keyboard player and a percussionist, create the musical accompaniment using computers that are connected to "smart" or "hyper" instruments.*

concert. In the presence of Fat, the Lamptons sing about the magic and mystery of Valis, giving Fat his first fascinating, but unclear, description:

VALIS.
Does it come from the stars?
VALIS.
This place where we are is one of the stars.
Is VALIS a man? Is VALIS a god? Is VALIS a satellite?
Or does it destroy?
(Vast Active Living Intelligent System.)

The Empire never ended,
The Buddha is in the park.
He lived a long time ago,
But he's still alive.

VALIS, etc.

The mind is ever active,
In his crafty designs.
It conjures up great plans
But is broken.

VALIS, etc.

2. "Mini's Solo." Mini, a disabled composer of computer music, uses his hands to sculpt sounds on an invisible instrument. The music here is created from bits of the human voice that are deconstructed at first so as to be unrecognizable. Gradually, the sounds are molded into the singing voice of a young girl, Sophia, who appears on a video monitor. (The next excerpt follows immediately.)

3. "Sophia's Scene" (excerpt). Sophia (angel or hologram?) sings a sermon accompanied by sweet, shimmering synthetic sounds over long pedal tones. Tones that she sings are prolonged or echoed electronically on the spot, giving her an otherworldly presence. Phil/Fat is alone facing her image. He is now one person. She has made him whole again.

Sophia: I can see only one person.

Phil/Fat: Where is the other? You destroyed him?

Sophia: Yes.

Phil/Fat: Why?

Sophia: To make you whole.

Phil/Fat: Are you God?

Sophia: I am what I am.

Phil/Fat: Can you help me?

Sophia: I have already helped you. I have helped you since you were born.

Phil/Fat: I am still afraid. . . .

ACTIVITY ▶ *The Potential of Music Technology*

How can technology be used to expand the expressive capability of musicians and musical instruments?

Listen to the three excerpts from the opera *Valis* by Tod Machover that are explained on pages 357–358, then, working in small groups, answer the following questions:

1. What can the performers do that they could not do without technological assistance?
2. Is there variety of timbres? musical styles? tempos? textures? intensities? moods?
3. Are the timbres orchestral imitations?
4. Does this music, much of which is computer generated, have emotional impact?
5. Do you need to know anything about technology to be receptive to this music?

Activity *The Potential of Music Technology*
Instructor's Guide, page 226
CD 11 ③ "Lampton Scene," *Valis* (2:01)
CD 11 ④ "Mini's Solo," *Valis* (1:36)
CD 11 ⑤ "Sophia's Scene," *Valis* (1:17)

Caption answers
Students who have experience with the drum machine might demonstrate both for comparison.

Effects of the New Technology

A great debate is raging throughout the music world. In its early stages, electronic music was the art of creating and assembling unusual synthetic sounds into musical compositions. Increasingly, synthesizers are being used not mainly to create new sounds but to duplicate the familiar acoustic sounds that in the past have been produced exclusively by musical instruments and voices. Sampling and samplers are now making this duplication acutely accurate. The sound is so exact, in fact, that musicians who have spent decades learning to perfect their flute or oboe playing are finding themselves replaced by a sampler, a machine that can play back the actual sampled sounds of their instrument. A **drum machine** is *a machine with the sounds of a whole range of percussion instruments stored in its memory.* These sounds can be applied to any rhythms the operator of the machine might want to perform. Does the drum machine put real drummers out of work?

Sampling has intensified this threat because the sounds of traditional instruments can be reproduced so well. When asked about

*Synthesized drum machines first began to appear in the 1980s. Their popularity may have come from the disco music of the 1970s, which needed a steady beat on the bass drum and cymbal. Both were easily synthesized. **Could you distinguish between a drum machine and a real drummer?***

You may wish to use "Discuss" at this time. Lesson plans for the activity are found on page 228 in the Instructor's Guide.

the use of drum machines in England, drummer Neil Lancaster says that "the community of drummers has totally collapsed. . . . Amateurs are just sitting there in the [recording] studios and hacking away at these things, and in fact half the time the engineers have to do it, because the guys with the machines don't have a clue how to operate them." Mike Comins, a violinist, says, "Even though the synthesizer hasn't replaced a symphony orchestra in public or on record, it will have the capability of doing so, and that's frightening." However, he also acknowledges that "it's really kind of fun to listen to Bach played on a synthesizer—but you know it's a synthesizer. [It's not] meant to displace anything."

Derek Austin, a studio synthesist, does not believe that digital sampling machines will replace orchestral instruments. When a middle C trumpet sample is played up two octaves, he says, "it does not sound like a trumpet hitting a high C." He acknowledges that the problem often boils down to money. Yes, you can create a string wash with a synthesizer, "but if you really want to fool the human ear to think you've got a full orchestra, you put six or eight live violins on top as well."

Seeking a Balance

In England, the Musician's Union has succeeded in banning the use of synthesizers to imitate acoustic or percussive instruments. In the United States, the American Federation of Musicians (AFM) has ruled that contracts should "ensure that electronic devices will not be used to replace or reduce the employment of conventional instrumentalists in circumstances where these members may be reasonably expected to be used. However, the electronic devices may be used to produce sounds that cannot be produced by conventional instruments." Such regulations are not easily enforced. On Broadway, for example, synths rather than traditional instruments are being added to orchestras for a fresher sound. Who can say that conventional musicians are being displaced?

Some Limitations

Does technology make the composer's work easier or more difficult? There appear to be two schools of thought regarding the application of music technology. On the one hand, Dominic Milano, editor of *Keyboard* magazine, says, "Musician dexterity is still important, but no longer a must. The computer can correct a lot of your errors. The result may not be brilliant noise, but it will be useful noise." On the other hand, composer Wendy Carlos says people who pride themselves on not being able to read music or to play even a simple musical passage without computer corrections (e.g., quantizing rhythms) are both arrogant and ignorant.

Robert Silvers. *Vincent van Gogh*. 1997. Photomosaic™.

Music & ART

The introduction of the computer as an art medium generated the same concerns in the art world as did the introduction of the synthesizer in the world of music. However, as art critics became familiar with the tools and qualities of the computer, they saw that computer art could be judged by the same criteria as other art. **Does technology still require artistic choices?**

Caption answer
Encourage a discussion on the pros and cons of using technology versus traditional techniques for both music and art.

Creating great music, she says, is difficult and requires "a profound knowledge of many details."

One of the problems with the new machines is that the product is too mechanical, clinical, and purified. The soul has been wrung out of it. The machine rather than the composer seems to dictate the result. When human imagination and creativity take a backseat and the machine rules, the music that is produced tends to be trite and uninteresting. It is a musical cliché—an expression that has been repeated so often that it is boring. Worse, it lacks warmth and emotion. The potential of the new music technology is not realized.

Unquestionably, the new technology makes it possible for people with very little understanding of music to duplicate or create elaborate compositions. The machine makes it easy for anyone. The drawback is that the end products tend to sound monotonously alike, and they often lack the warmth and emotion that are central to any expression we call musical. Technological breakthroughs in music have caused some problems, as any new way of doing anything normally does. However, the potential is enormous. This technology could produce a generation of musicians, some of whom may turn out to be the Mozart or Ellington of our time.

SUMMARY

Technology is not meant to relieve us from doing the work of imagining, thinking, creating, and learning. It can facilitate these tasks, and it can provide us with tools that shape and amplify. It is an external resource. It permits us to reach for new worlds of understanding and ability. It provides new ways for us to see and hear who and what we are.

Electronics are extensions of ourselves. They are not replacements. We are using technology to make new expressions possible, but people are still in control and central to the process. Musical performance remains a living art involving live performers. Just as electronic tools provide music with new possibilities, they also pose new problems.

Some performers who use conventional instruments believe they are being put out of work by synthesizers. Will the keyboard synthesizer replace the piano, the harpsichord, and all the other instruments it can simulate? Or will the synthesizer/computer assume its own independent musicmaking role, much as it has for composer Tod Machover? Technology opens the door to a vast and previously inaccessible world of musical expression. That is justification enough for whatever adjustments must be made to accommodate it.

Building Music Vocabulary

On a sheet of paper, write the term from the list that best matches each description below.

(2) drum machine   (7) sampling
(6) hyperinstruments   (8) sequencer
(1) MIDI   (4) synthesizer
(5) musique concrète   (3) telharmonium

1. Musical Instrument Digital Interface.
2. A machine with the sounds of a whole range of percussion instruments stored in its memory.
3. An early machine that used electrical current to produce sound.
4. A machine that produces sound electronically.
5. A system of electronic composition in which natural sounds are taped, edited, and shaped into a composition recorded on magnetic tape.
6. Instruments that, with the help of computers, respond to live musicians.
7. A recording process that begins with real sounds.
8. An electronic system that stores data about music.

Reviewing Music Facts

Answer each question in a complete sentence.
9. What is a theremin?
10. What electronic device was used by the composers of musique concrète?
11. When did rock musicians begin to use electric guitars?
12. What is a DX-7?
13. How are computers used as additional performers in live concerts?

Complete answers for the Chapter 17 Review are found in the Instructor's Guide, page 228.

Thinking It Through

On a sheet of paper, write your responses to the following:
14. **Analyze** How can you distinguish between an acoustic instrument and a sampled or synthesized instrument?
15. **Explain** In your own words, explain what MIDI stands for and how it is used.
16. **Apply** What are some of the objections to the use of synthesizers?

Making the Connection

Science Find out more about an early pioneer in the field of electronic music or recording. What was that person's contribution to the development of electronic music?

Theatre Working in groups, use electronic instruments or recording devices to create a "mood piece" for a short dramatic scene. Using a script, improvisation, or simple pantomime, add electronic or manipulated sound to create musical sound effects that reinforce your scene.

 You'll find interactive MIDI sites to explore at **www.glencoe.com/sec/music**

CHAPTER 18

Musical Creators

Composing may appear to be an unusual or exotic career, an occupation for a rare few. How many people can you name who make their living partly or wholly from the music they create? There is no doubt that being a composer is a highly specialized profession, akin to sculpting or painting. You would be wrong, however, if you thought there were very few composers. In truth, there are hundreds of composers at work in the United States, Canada, Mexico, and other countries around the globe.

Objectives

By completing the chapter, you will:
- Become familiar with a representative sampling of music by three twentieth-century composers: Aaron Copland, Duke Ellington, and Libby Larsen.
- Learn what makes these composers effective musical communicators.
- Learn about the characteristics that make their works American.
- Find out about the lives of these composers.
- Learn about what it takes to be a composer.

Vocabulary

bridge
cadenza
chromatic
composition
creative license
glissando
swing
swing era

Making music is a profession for English musician Evelyn Glennie, shown here. She may be the first full-time solo percussionist, performing with world orchestras while writing and producing music for television and films. **What professional music career would you choose?**

Caption answer
Encourage students to explain their responses.

365

The Role of the Composer

You may wish to use "Write a Review" at this time. Lesson plans for the activity are found on page 234 in the Instructor's Guide.

You may wish to use TRB 18-1, Profile—*Aaron Copland,* at this time.

Almost every university and many colleges have one or several composers on their faculty. Some classical composers attach themselves to major symphony orchestras or opera companies. For example, Shalamit Ran, a professor at the University of Chicago who received the 1991 Pulitzer Prize in Music for her *Symphony,* serves as composer-in-residence for the Chicago Symphony Orchestra. Others, particularly composers who work in the popular field, work independently or combine composing with performing. Popular artist Jewel, for example, writes most of the song she performs.

According to American composer Aaron Copland (1900–1990), composing is the mysterious and challenging process of "exteriorizing inner feelings." What the composer does, he says, is to take what is personal and internal and make a statement of it in sound that is so compelling that listeners and performers can experience what the composer was feeling. Composers learn the art of **composition**, *the craft of putting together sounds to create a musical work.* These works are represented symbolically, usually with the language of notation. Composition differs from improvisation by giving an account of the musical statement, permitting it to be repeated with some degree of exactness. Composers often prepare a written musical score, but their account can also take the form of a tape recording or computer program.

Composers are communicators who use music as their language. To be effective communicators, they must affect their audience. They must be able to convey their meaning so that it is understood and felt by those who hear their work. Like a good speech, their message must be convincing, and it must stir their listeners. They have to know how to use sound as a way to express feeling. In this chapter, you will become acquainted with three American composers, and you will discover what makes them effective musical communicators.

Use Artsource® VHS Segment 9 in the Performing Arts Package to show a performance from *Billy the Kid*.

Choreographer Eugene Loring broke with traditional ballet to create an historic ballet with American themes, music, and movement based on the notorious outlaw, Billy the Kid. After he organized the events of Billy's life sequentially, he sent a storyboard of the ballet to composer Aaron Copland in Paris, who wrote the classical score based on old cowboy songs.

The Joffrey Ballet. Tom Mossbrucker dancing *Billy the Kid*, composed by Aaron Copland. Eugene Loring, choreographer. Photo by Herbert Migdoll.

Aaron Copland

Oddly enough, American composer Aaron Copland learned how to write distinctly American music in Mexico! He went to Mexico City in 1932 to work with Carlos Chavez (1899–1978), the distinguished Mexican composer and conductor, and was impressed by his respect for and use of Mexican folk music. Copland tried his own hand at using Mexican melodies in his orchestral work *El Salón México* (1936). Then he set about applying the principles he had learned. During the next decade, he wrote a number of works based on American folk music. He had already experimented with jazz in his *Piano Concerto* (1927). Copland was determined to express his American roots in music, and he succeeded.

The excitement of Mexico City and its people found its way into Aaron Copland's orchestral work El Salón México. *He came back to the United States determined to incorporate American folk music in order to express the spirit of its people.*

El Salón México

Copland's inspiration for *El Salón México* came from a visit to a nightclub named Salón México. "It wasn't the music that I heard there, or the dances, that attracted me so much as the spirit of the place," Copland said. "In some inexplicable way, while milling about in those crowded halls, one really felt a live contact with the Mexican *people*—the electric sense one sometimes gets in far-off places, of suddenly knowing the essence of a people—their humanity, their separate shyness, their dignity and unique charm. . . . At any rate, I soon found myself looking for suitable folk material for *El Salón México*." He began work on this piece in 1933 and completed it the following year. The orchestration followed in 1936.

ACTIVITY *Identify Order in Folk Melodies*

Can you identify the order in which Aaron Copland used the Mexican folk melodies and rhythms as you listen to *El Salón México*?

In preparation for listening, familiarize yourself with the main rhythmic and melodic themes. Perform this melody on a keyboard instrument, xylophone, or other tuned percussion instrument.

Activity *Identify Order in Folk Melodies*
Instructor's Guide, page 229
TRB 18-2, *El Salón México*
CD 11 ⑧ *El Salón México* (5:20)

Perform the rhythm of this melody.

What are the musical characteristics of these two themes that are typical of the style of Mexican folk music?

Each of the lettered "blocks" on the illustration provided by your teacher represents a specific musical event in *El Salón México*. As you listen, determine the order of the blocks in the composition. Write down the letter of each section in the order in which you hear them. Use the musical descriptors and the musical examples you have performed and analyzed to help make your decisions.

Aaron Copland may have been America's most American composer. He composed deliberately and proudly for all people, believing that classical music belonged to everyone.

"Simple Gifts"

After his experiences in Mexico, Copland began to incorporate American folk music into his work. He was always looking for American tunes. One day in a library, he ran across Edward D. Andrews' book of Shaker rituals, songs, and dances entitled *The Gift To Be Simple*. In it he found the melody and words to one of the favorite hymns of this religious sect, "'Tis a Gift to Be Simple." To his credit, he recognized the beauty of this unknown and forgotten song, and he revived it and made it popular around the world. He used the tune in the closing section of his ballet *Appalachian Spring* (1944) and later wrote an arrangement of the song for his first set of *Old American Songs* (1950). He called the song "Simple Gifts"; it might have been a motto for his own life.

Copland was a modest man. He tried to write music that was as ordinary as possible, music that could enchant the listener. He also had a more complex side that led him to compose profound music using the modern idioms of his day, including twelve-tone or serial technique. It is his simpler style, however, that the American public loves.

'Tis a Gift to Be Simple

American Shaker Tune

'Tis the gift to be sim - ple 'tis the gift to be free,

'Tis the gift to come down where we ought to be.

And when we find our - selves in the place just right,

'Twill be in the val - ley of love and de - light.

When true sim - pli - ci - ty is gained,

To bow and to bend we shan't be a - shamed.

To turn, turn will be our de - light,

'Till by turn - ing, turn - ing we come round right.

Activity *Perform "'Tis a Gift to Be
              Simple"*
Instructor's Guide, page 230
CD 11 9 "Simple Gifts" (1:43)

ACTIVITY ▶ *Perform "'Tis a Gift to Be Simple"*

**Sing and perform a simple accompaniment to the Shaker song
"'Tis a Gift to Be Simple" and compare your performance to the
composed arrangement of the same song by Aaron Copland.**

- Identify the number of phrases in the song and decide if the
  phrases are of equal or unequal length.

- Perform this harmonic ostinato as you sing "'Tis a Gift to Be
  Simple":

- Decide what the folklike qualities are in your performance of
  "'Tis a Gift to Be Simple."

- Listen to Aaron Copland's composed arrangement of "'Tis a Gift
  to Be Simple" and decide what is similar about the two
  performances. What is different?

- Perform your arrangement of "'Tis a Gift to Be Simple." Notice
  that the harmonic ostinato sounds on the first beat of each
  measure. Listen to the Copland arrangement to determine on
  what beat the chords change in each measure. Can you figure out
  the pattern of chord changes in Copland's arrangement?

- How does Copland's arrangement reflect the influence of classical
  or "art" music? Does the Copland arrangement of "Simple Gifts"
  destroy or preserve the folklike quality of the song? Justify your
  answer.

Clarinet Concerto

Single-handedly, Copland pieced together an aural American orchestral
quilt that listeners around the world found easily likeable. Some of his
works were unashamedly based on American subjects: the ballets *Billy the
Kid* (1939) and *Rodeo* (1942), and *Lincoln Portrait* (1942) for narration
and orchestra. In some of his works, he combined popular and classical
music styles. This is the case with his *Clarinet Concerto* (1947–1948). This
work, commissioned by Benny Goodman (1909–1986), one of the great
jazz and classical clarinetists, illustrates another of Copland's strengths as
a musical communicator—his direct and honest expression of emotion.
First and foremost, his music relates to human beings and to life. He
believed that one of the great qualities of music was its capacity to
"enlarge the sense of who you are and what life is all about."

Copland's *Clarinet Concerto* is in two parts connected by a **cadenza**, *a section of a piece designed to show the virtuosity of a soloist.* The first movement, like a slow dance, is lyrical and expressive, almost heartbreaking. It is in simple A B A song form. Jazz elements, first introduced in the cadenza, take over in the fast second movement, a free rondo that ends with an elaborate coda. Copland said that some of the musical material he used "represents an unconscious fusion of elements obviously related to North and South American popular music." The contrasts between slow and fast, gentle and jazzy, classic and popular seem natural and right.

ACTIVITY ▶ *Identify the Characteristics of Jazz*

What characteristics of jazz did Copland use in creating his *Clarinet Concerto*?

Listen to the opening measures. Identify the instruments you hear. Which of the instruments you identified are not usually associated with jazz? Perform this bass ostinato on either a keyboard or tuned percussion instrument:

Activity *Identify the Characteristics of Jazz*
Instructor's Guide, pages 230–231
CD 11 ⑩ *Clarinet Concerto* (16:53)

Clap this over-the-bar-line syncopated pattern:

Use section A. in the *Music Theory Handbook* to review beat and meter.

Clap this rhythmic pattern set in dialogue style:

(1) [rhythmic notation]

Count: 1 2 3 4   1 2 3 4   1 2 3 4   1 etc.

(2) [rhythmic notation]

All of these patterns you have just performed are characteristic of jazz.

Listen to the end section of the concerto and decide how many of the three jazz style techniques you just performed are used in this composition. Identify other musical characteristics associated with jazz that are also used in this concerto.

Would you classify this work as classical music or jazz? Justify your answer.

The Later Years

After the Second World War, Copland's style changed. Like many American composers at that time, he became fascinated by Schoenberg's serial system. His *Piano Fantasy* (1957) and *Connotations for Orchestra* (1962), among other pieces, used this method of composition. Perhaps he realized that he had achieved the American style he had searched so long for, and he took up new challenges. Whatever the case, he left a storehouse of works that are known and loved by a vast American public and another set of more complex works that await the public's discovery.

Duke Ellington

Duke Ellington's contribution to American jazz was significant. In addition to many popular dance-tune arrangements and compositions, he wrote extended works for the concert stage such as Black, Brown and Beige: A Tone Parallel to the History of the Negro In America *(1943 debut in Carnegie Hall).*

One of America's most original composers, Edward Kennedy ("Duke") Ellington (1899–1974) took jazz and made it a sophisticated art. Previously, jazz had been an informal, improvised group expression. Ellington did what no one had done before. As the leader of his own extraordinary jazz band, he applied the craft of composition, yet he accommodated the improvised solos of his individual musicians. He gave jazz form and substance and timbres it had not known before. By combining his own creativity as composer, pianist, and bandleader with that of his players, he achieved a new level of distinction in jazz.

Ellington brought intellectual depth and originality to everything he created. That immediately set him apart. He was the thinking person's jazz creator. His songs, for example, had a richness and elegance due to their imaginative and colorful harmonies. The melodies of these songs were often generated by these harmonies, not the other way around. In creating his popular songs, Ellington thought harmonically, while most songwriters think melodically. His approach was instrumental rather than vocal. As a result, his melodies are often **chromatic**, *incorporating notes that lie outside the regular diatonic scale*, and they contain wide leaps and have angular contours that are difficult to sing and demanding to listen to. Because of this, Ellington's songs— "Satin Doll," "Sophisticated Lady," and "Don't Get Around Much Anymore," to name a few—achieve a special richness.

*Music & **History***

Duke Ellington and his band are shown in this photo. An American bandleader, pianist, and composer, Ellington took jazz to new expressive heights. He and his band attained great popularity in the 1940s, and they were the first African-American musicians to perform at New York's Carnegie Hall.

"It Don't Mean a Thing"

One of his songs, "It Don't Mean a Thing If It Ain't Got That Swing" (1932), anticipated the whole **swing era**, *a period of music that extended roughly from 1935 to 1945.* Ellington wrote the theme song long before the era started! This was a period when people danced and listened to "big" jazz bands such as the Duke Ellington Orchestra. With its rhythmic energy and swinging beat, this music was made for dancing. Even though many people primarily associate the term "swing" with Benny Goodman, who was known as "The King of Swing," Ellington was probably the first person to use the word in a song. In many ways, this song says what swing is all about. Irving Mills' lyrics try to define it: "It ain't the melody, it ain't the music, there's something else that makes the tune complete." That something else is what Ellington simply called "its rhythmic vitality."

Swing is *a special rhythmic characteristic that jazz musicians add to the music.* It is notated one way and played another—a perfect example of the old axiom that you can't make music until you go beyond the notes. This is true of all music, but it is well illustrated by swing. Although swing is sometimes improvised by ear, when it is read from a score or "chart," the musicians interpret the notation freely. In classical music, performers refer to this personal touch as "musicality" or "musicianship." In jazz it is called "soul" or "swing."

You may wish to use TRB 18-3, Profile—*Duke Ellington,* at this time.

Activity *Perform Swing Music*
Instructor's Guide, page 231
CD 11 |11| "It Don't Mean a Thing
        If It Ain't Got That
        Swing" (2:13)

ACTIVITY ▶ *Perform Swing Music*

Can you sing with "swing"?

To illustrate, many songs written in "straight" eighth notes are actually "swung" rhythmically in a triplet fashion. For example:
Straight rhythm:

When "swung," sounds like:

Listen to Ella Fitzgerald's rendition of Ellington's song "It Don't Mean a Thing If It Ain't Got That Swing." Note her improvised scat singing. Practice singing along on the highly syncopated "doo wah, doo wah" part of the chorus. It is all on one pitch: B flat.

(doo wah,— doo wah, doo wah, doo wah, doo wah,—

— doo wah, doo wah, doo wah,)

You may be able to perform the syncopation from notation. Is it easier to perform the rhythm by imitation or from the notation? Can you "swing" this rhythmic pattern without looking at the music?

Mood Indigo

Ellington was a ground-breaking musical pioneer. Even early in his career, he was creating jazz compositions for orchestra that were more than merely functional dance pieces. His *Black and Tan Fantasy* (1927), for example, was longer than the usual jazz work. It was meant to be listened to for the feelings it generated. This was one of several compositions dedicated to the dignity and history of African Americans.

At first, Ellington's group sometimes consisted of one or two other musicians. During the early years, from about 1920 to 1927, he used as many or as few musicians as he could round up and afford. Later he was fond of his sextet. In 1927 the group that played at the Cotton Club in New York had ten musicians. This later expanded to 12 musicians in 1930, 14 in 1932, and finally to its biggest size of 19 in 1946. The group varied in size, depending on the situation and the location. One thing remained constant; the orchestra played Ellington's compositions.

The changing instrumentation of the Ellington orchestra:

1927 (10)	1930 (12)	1932 (14)
1 trumpet	3 trumpets	3 trumpets
1 trombone	2 trombones	3 trombones
3 reeds (sax/clarinet)	3 reeds	9 reeds
4 rhythm (bass, drums, banjo, with Duke on piano)	4 rhythm	4 rhythm (1 female singer)
1 violin		

In many ways Ellington was an experimenter. He played with different combinations of instruments and invented new sonorities. He tried using the highest and lowest registers of instruments to draw out sounds that were less familiar than those in the comfortable middle range. His excellent musicians gladly took up the challenges he proposed. The band operated as a team. Ellington thought of the musicians as his family, and they had a deep respect for him. They also grew in their own musical ability because he counted on them to add their own creative skill to the whole.

Because his music spoke with a different sound, Ellington's creations rarely became as popular as those of George Gershwin, Irving Berlin, or Cole Porter. His most popular piece was *Mood Indigo* (1930). It was originally written as an instrumental work called "Dreamy Blues" in which he used the instruments in unexpected ways.

Playing in juxtaposition with a saxophone quartet were vibratoless muted brass and a clarinet in very low register. In 1931, lyrics by Irving Mills and Albany Bigard were added. The song became a major hit. Here again, it is the creative harmonies that generated an unusual, and very memorable, melody.

ACTIVITY ▶ *Analyze* Mood Indigo

Can you play the theme and harmonies from Duke Ellington's famous work?

Look at the first four measures of the famous theme from *Mood Indigo*. How many different pitches does the theme use? Listen to the recording of this popular hit while you follow the 4-bar theme. Keep the harmonies (or supporting harmonic color) in your mind's ear.

Activity *Analyze* Mood Indigo
Instructor's Guide, pages 231–232
CD 11 12 *Mood Indigo* (3:04)

Working in a small group of three to four students, try to play this theme on any instrument that you can play. Have everyone in your group play the theme in unison.

Now ask someone in your group to play the 4-bar theme while the other members play both sets of harmonies below. Which one (No. 1 or No. 2) comes closer to the harmonic color and mood that Ellington had in mind when he composed this tune?

Use section E. in the *Music Theory Handbook* to review harmony.

After playing the melody and underlying harmonies, answer these questions:

1. How would you describe the mood of *Mood Indigo*?
2. Do you hear any blue notes in the 4-bar theme? If so, where?
3. What color is indigo?

Cotton Tail

Ellington reached his creative plateau in the 1940s. His collective approach now included the expert work of Billy Strayhorn, who served as Ellington's arranger and second pianist. Strayhorn joined the band in 1939 and did much of the arranging during the 1940s. One of the great achievements of Ellington and the band was *Cotton Tail* (1940). The piece is a brilliant variation based on the chord changes of George Gershwin's famous song "I Got Rhythm," written ten years earlier (see the chord changes that follow).

Cotton Tail is a trendsetting piece. Prominent American composer and jazz expert Gunther Schuller observes that this work "changed the face of jazz and foretold in many ways where the music's future lay." Both in its conception and performance, it established the big-band style of modern jazz that was to follow. Ellington was clearly ahead of his time.

What made *Cotton Tail* unique? As was usual in jazz, Ellington constructed this piece on an established set of chord changes—in this case, those from "I Got Rhythm"—but he used them in a startlingly new way. He dropped the customary introduction and dived immediately into the melody. Trumpets and saxes announce the theme together in octaves, set against a simple walking bass (see example above). The idea of stating the theme simply and directly at the start became common after this, particularly in the form of jazz known as "bop." Then, too, if you look and listen carefully, Ellington had the courage and imagination to begin the melody on a ninth (C) and not on the usual tonic (B♭).

<table>
<tr><td>DO</td><td>MI</td><td>SOL</td><td>(TI)</td><td>RE</td></tr>
<tr><td>1</td><td>3</td><td>5</td><td>(7)</td><td>9</td></tr>
</table>

Tonic Triad

Use section E. 1 in the Music Theory Handbook to review triads.

Activity *Find the Bridge*
Instructor's Guide, page 232
TRB 18-4, *Cotton Tail*
CD 11 [13] *Cotton Tail* (3:09)

Tenor saxophonist Ben Webster (1909–1973) joined the Duke Ellington Orchestra in 1939. Along with Coleman Hawkins and Lester Young, Webster was one of the premier tenor saxophonists of the swing era.

ACTIVITY ▶ *Find the Bridge*

Can you detect the B section, or the "bridge," in a classic saxophone solo?

As an example of Ellington's creative genius, listen to the way he composed *Cotton Tail* using the chord changes in George Gershwin's classic song "I Got Rhythm." The melody of the A theme for *Cotton Tail* is shown on page 377.

In 32-bar song form, the B section in the A A B A structure is known as the **bridge,** *the connective part of a composition.* You have heard this in Ellington's "I Got It Bad (and That Ain't Good)" and several other songs. Ellington uses this form in the 1940 composition *Cotton Tail.* Your challenge is to detect this bridge in the brilliantly improvised tenor sax solo by Ben Webster. (Hint: After 16 bars, the 8-bar bridge is announced by a strong harmonic shift.)

As you listen, follow the notation of Ben Webster's solo that covers two choruses in this work. You will hear the bridge twice. In what measures does the bridge begin? Where does it end? What makes Ben Webster's improvisation so outstanding?

One of the other remarkable achievements of *Cotton Tail* is the improvised tenor sax solo of Ben Webster (1909–1973). This improvisation builds overwhelmingly to the upper reaches of the instrument. It engages us as listeners and carries us along by its spontaneous and virtuosic invention. Schuller calls *Cotton Tail* "creative on all fronts simultaneously"—in melody, harmony, rhythm, orchestration (timbre), texture, and form. In this work Ellington and his entire band speak as one voice, one force.

Ellington was especially adept at devising accompaniments for his players' improvisations. He knew how to use and combine instruments. When he composed, he took into account the virtuosity of his musicians. No wonder they liked him: He gave them a showcase, and he knew how to make them shine. He invited them to enter into the creative process, to feel the spirit of the work, and to add their own skill to it.

Circumstances changed for Ellington around 1950. At that time, his longer compositions were not accepted. His innovative individuality kept him outside the mainstream of jazz. There was a turnover of musicians in his band that caused his creative forces to become unsettled. Nonetheless, his contributions as a composer were indelible. With Ellington, American jazz became the highly respected musical form it is today.

Libby Larsen

You may wish to use TRB 18-5, Profile—*Libby Larsen*, at this time.

As you read this, a great many living American composers, both male and female, are busy composing music. Among the latter is Libby Larsen, a highly talented composer who has written a large body of works in many different genres. Her music is vivid and picturesque—and very American. She enjoys interpreting poetic images, crystallizing them in musical portraits. Her musical works have all the clarity and sparkle of ice sculptures.

Larsen is a product of her era. She accepts the keyboard synthesizer as a legitimate musical instrument and uses electronic sounds comfortably in her scores. She is visually oriented, often incorporating video images and other media effects in her operas. Her music is dramatic and direct in its communication, evoking picturesque images and a wide range of feelings.

American composer Libby Larsen (b. 1950) strongly believes in the power of sound. A composer, she feels, gives order to sound, enabling us to add meaning to our lives.

"Comin' to Town" from *The Settling Years*

In "Comin' to Town," Larsen connects us with the raw energy of the nineteenth-century pioneers who settled the untamed West. To express their frontier attitude, she began with the poetry of actual pioneers—plainspoken, forthright, and heartfelt. The work consists of three movements. The first, "Comin' to Town," expresses what it must have been like when the cowboys came to town after being out on the range for a time. The second, "Beneath These Alien Stars," describes the great Western expanse:

> The desert wind has waved my hair:
> Desert sands have etched my face,
> And the courage of the mountains
> Has bound me to this place.

The third movement, "A Hoopla," is a celebration describing country fiddling and having a good time. The work is scored for chorus, piano, and woodwind quintet (flute, oboe, B-flat clarinet, horn, and bassoon), and the movements are fast, slow, and fast.

In "Comin' to Town," Larsen created a sentiment that is rowdy and raucous. She says, "I've asked for three members of the chorus to double as a 'whooper,' a 'whistler,' and a 'rowdy,' and I've scored them into the piece. The whistler must have a really piercing whistle, the kind that would have been used on roundup." Larsen adapted the text by Robert V. Carr:

> The boys are comin' to town!
> What does the marshall do?
> He's gone and hid, that's what he did,
> For he knows a thing or two.
>
> The boys are comin' to town!
> What does the dogs all do?
> They hits the trail with a canine wail,
> For they know a thing or two.
>
> The boys are comin' to town!
> What does the old town do?
> She goes to bed while they paint her red,
> For she knows a thing or two.

Activity *Characterize American Music*
Instructor's Guide, pages 232–233
CD 11 [14] "Comin' to Town," *The Settling Years* (2:43)

ACTIVITY ▶ *Characterize American Music*

What makes Libby Larsen's music so American?

Listen to "Comin' to Town" from *The Settling Years* and make a list of the musical elements that give it a distinctive American flavor.

Try speaking the following rhythm:

Ti - yi   yi - yi - yi - yi - yi - yah.

In the text, what word or words does Larsen choose to create word painting? Word painting is the art of portraying the meaning of a word through sound. Signal when you hear the music modulate.

Four on the Floor

In *Four on the Floor*, a short work for violin, cello, bass, and piano, Larsen's theme is again American. The title refers to gunning a car in high (or fourth) gear by putting the gas pedal down to the floorboards.

Larsen says, "Breakneck is the theme of the piece—an America that is speeding up faster and faster, jazzing into eternity." She has marked quarter notes to be played at 138–l44 to the minute!

Four on the Floor, Larsen says, "is inspired by boogie-woogie." After a short three-measure introduction, the boogie beat is set by the piano with its characteristic eight pulses to the measure and the use of triplets (three notes to the beat). Larsen was influenced by the piano styles of Jerry Lee Lewis and Pine Top Smith. The walking bass figure in the left hand continues through most of the piece:

Composers work in all kinds of ways. Some compose at the keyboard, others at the desk away from any musical instrument. In the latter case, they invent the music in their heads (audiate) and then write it down. Here Libby Larsen is shown notating her work.

This walking bass figure is repeated later, giving the piece an A B A structure. Toward the end of the piece, after a **glissando**, *a continuous or sliding movement from one pitch to the other,* from high to low on the white keys of the piano, the string instruments invent "ad lib runs, glissandos" that Larsen has indicated by the following "notation":

*Play any note you land on. Use marcato at the very least.

Here and in some of the following measures, she asks the string players to invent their own parts. The piece comes to a boisterous conclusion.

Activity *Identify Tempo Changes*
Instructor's Guide, page 233
Music! VHS Segment 10, *Four on the Floor*

ACTIVITY ▶ *Identify Tempo Changes*

How does Larsen use tempo to give variety and mark the sections of a piece in A B A form?

Listen to *Four on the Floor* and see if you can detect where the tempo changes.

Clue Listen for a jazzy pizzicato (plucked) section for the three stringed instruments (no piano). When the piano comes in again, there is a new tempo. Is it slower or faster?

Then discuss the following with your classmates: When does the tempo return to what it was at the beginning? Did Larsen take a risk when she asked the performers to invent their own parts? Do you think they realized her intent?

Discuss why Larsen calls this work "a celebration of American music and American musicians."

Opening of the autograph short score of Copland's Inscape," composed in 1967.

Just as each human being has a distinct style of handwriting, each composer has an individual style of writing musical notation. They show their personalities by the way they set their notes on the page. **How might the computer programs used to compose music change the personal style that composers add to their compositions?**

Caption answer
Students may wish to debate the value of personal style over the speed and convenience of computer notation programs.

Frankenstein, a Musical Drama

When she was a child, Larsen was fascinated by the old *Frankenstein* film (1931) with Boris Karloff playing the Monster. Later, during the 1970s, she came across the original book by Mary Shelley, called *Frankenstein, or the Modern Prometheus* (1816–1817). In the book, the Monster talks incessantly. In the film, the Monster does not have any dialogue whatsoever—a good example of **creative license**, *the liberty that artists sometimes take in reinterpreting another artist's work.* Larsen is more faithful to the original story. In the opera, for example, the Monster speaks, yet its voice is electronically created and performed on keyboard samplers and synthesizers. As in the book, Dr. Victor Frankenstein uses electricity to bring the Monster to life.

The main idea of the opera is not about scaring and killing people. The story is about consequences. In Greek legend, Prometheus was a giant who stole fire from heaven and gave it to humankind, raising the human race above the animals. As punishment, Zeus, the king of all the gods, chained Prometheus to a rock where a vulture came each day to eat his liver, which Zeus replaced each night. Larsen says, "The Promethean myth is a myth about consequences." Victor creates the Monster but sees it as an evil creation. Forced to survive alone, the Monster learns to survive and even to speak and read and love. It becomes touchingly human, but the people whom it approaches in search of companionship are repelled. The Monster asks Victor to create a mate, but he refuses. Condemned to a life alone and rejected, the Monster strikes back.

The tragedy is that Victor was not prepared to be responsible for the consequences of his act of creating the Monster. His goal was simply to create the life, not nurture it. When Victor rejects the idea of caring for his Monster by creating a companion for it, he refuses to assume responsibility for the change that he has produced. The Monster then gets even.

This story has reverberations today. "If you set change in motion," Larsen says, "you are also responsible for what happens." She explains: "We face that dilemma in our environmental concerns. If we create roadways and cars, we have to be responsible for the greenhouse effect." The story also points to our inclination to misuse technology in the service of personal ambition and ego. So the story of this opera has applications in our own lives, in our own time.

The story of Frankenstein *is about consequences. Humans need to accept responsibility for their actions. Dr. Frankenstein created the monster but was so repelled by his creation that he chose not to fulfill his responsibility for its care.*

The Music

"One problem with today's opera," Libby Larsen says, "is that there are too many words; they are really plays set to music." Her most radical innovation is in the portrayal of the Monster by a mime and video screens that show what it is seeing, thinking, and feeling. The opera set—designed in black and white except for the videotape of the Monster—extends outward precariously over the audience. It consists of hanging ropes and ladders and various constructed levels hidden mysteriously behind scrims. The orchestra consists of 15 performers, including woodwinds, horn, trumpet, percussion, a string quintet, and keyboards. The story is told in a prologue and 14 scenes.

Throughout the opera, music joins with the visual action to carry the emotional content of the opera. Here is Scene 4: The Act, in which Victor creates the Monster (stage directions have been shortened):

The scene is a dark laboratory, dimly lit. The Monster lies on a table.
A large suspended cable with switches that can be reached by rope ladders
is connected to the Monster. Victor is hunched over the table working furiously.
He checks passages in one of the many books strewn about.
There is a knock on an unseen door.

Elizabeth: Victor, dear, what are you doing?

Victor: Work, Elizabeth, work!

The scene is gruesomely lit. Victor climbs high on the rope ladders and begins to descend.

Elizabeth: Victor, please, at least take some dinner. If you won't come out, let Henry bring you food.

Victor descends the ladder, looks up, and stops in frustration. The cable connection is coming apart. He climbs to reconnect it. When he reaches the top, he is interrupted by a knock on the door. Elizabeth and Henry have returned.

Elizabeth and Clerval: Victor, come on now. You must eat. Victor, let me in. I have food. Victor, Victor!

A tremendous wind rushes through the open roof door. Victor scurries back down the ladder and approaches the table. Another knock.

Clerval: Victor, you can stop now. I believe you. I'm convinced. Now open the door. Victor? Victor!

Victor: (*With great irritation*) Go away, both of you. Now!

He looks up. It is lightning. He is exhilarated. He is just about to connect the cable to the Monster when the cable disengages. He scrambles up the ladder with one end of the cable and finally manages to connect it. He scrambles back down, waits for the right bolt of lightning, and connects the cable into the Monster's chest. Silence. We hear only the storm. Victor remains poised over the Monster. Nothing. Then, suddenly, one of the Monster's arms shoots straight up, then drops back. Victor goes back up the ladder and connects another cable. When he starts back down, the ladder breaks. He barely manages to grab a nearby beam. He manages to connect the cable. Still hanging, he waits for a bolt of lightning to send more electricity into the Monster. Silence.

*More silence. He swings to a nearby pipe and slides down.
The Monster lies quietly.*

*Victor takes an eye out of a small container and puts it in place.
The videotape starts. The image is of a hand backing away from the eye.
The videotape is what the Monster sees. He sees Victor.*

*The Monster rises. Images of Victor are mixed with other images. The
Monster reaches out to touch Victor. Before he makes contact, we see a clear
picture on videotape of Victor, terrified. There is the look of a scream. Victor
backs away. The Monster tries again. Victor pushes past the Monster and
runs from the room, leaving the images on the video a muddle of confusion.*

Activity *Analyze a Scene*
Instructor's Guide, page 234
CD 11 15 *Frankenstein*, Scene 4:
         The Act (6:12)

ACTIVITY ▶ *Analyze a Scene*

**How does Larsen's music in her opera *Frankenstein* help to add
atmosphere and activate our imagination?**

Listen to Scene 4: The Act and follow the stage directions and
dialogue. What does Larsen do with rhythm, melody, dynamics,
timbre, and texture to make the scene and section believable?

TECHNOLOGY OPTION

Technology Options
Use Project 18 in the *MIDI
Activities* binder.

■ **Music with MIDI** Use a MIDI program to score a scene from a
play or movie.

SUMMARY

American composers have had a difficult time finding their
individual styles. Should they copy European models? Should
American composers develop their own compositional style, or should
they strive to establish a distinctly American voice? Charles Ives, George
Gershwin, Aaron Copland, Duke Ellington, Leonard Bernstein, and Libby
Larsen exemplify this latter approach.

American music is often characterized by a driving rhythmic energy
and syncopation, a strong use of percussion and brass, a sense of free
expressiveness and invention, a reveling in contrasting timbres, a sense of
spaciousness and sweep, and a direct and stirring emotional outpouring.
American music blossomed in the hands of composers like Aaron Copland,
Duke Ellington, and Libby Larsen. American music speaks to all of us.

Building Music Vocabulary

On a sheet of paper, write the term from the list that best matches each description below.

(3) bridge
(8) creative license
(5) cadenza
(7) glissando
(1) chromatic
(6) swing
(2) composition
(4) swing era

1. Incorporating notes that lie outside the regular diatonic scale.
2. The craft of putting together sounds to create a musical work.
3. The connective part of a composition.
4. A period of music that extended roughly from 1935 to 1945.
5. A section of a piece designed to show the virtuosity of a soloist.
6. A special rhythmic characteristic that jazz musicians add to the music.
7. A continuous or sliding movement from one pitch to the other.
8. The liberty that artists sometime take in reinterpreting another artist's work.

Reviewing Music Facts

Answer each question in a complete sentence.

9. Where was Aaron Copland living when he became determined to express his American roots in his music?
10. What famous American instrumentalist commissioned Copland's *Clarinet Concerto*?
11. What were some of Duke Ellington's experimental techniques?
12. Name the expert arranger who contributed greatly to Ellington's work in the 1940s.
13. What piano style inspired Libby Larsen's *Four on the Floor*?
14. How does Libby Larsen create the monster's "speech" in her opera *Frankenstein*?

Answers to Chapter 18 Review

9. In Mexico.
10. Benny Goodman.
11. He experimented with different combinations of instruments and new sonorities; he used the highest and lowest

Complete answers for the Chapter 18 Review are found in the Instructor's Guide, page 235.

Thinking It Through

On a sheet of paper, write your responses to the following:

15. **Compare and Contrast** What are some of the similarities and differences between the music of the three composers in this chapter?
16. **Analyze** In what way was Duke Ellington's approach to songwriting different from that of most popular songwriters?
17. **Explain** How did Libby Larsen create a strong American pioneer spirit in her work "Comin' to Town"?

Making the Connection

Social Studies Find out more about what was happening in the world during the "swing era." Discuss whether the upbeat energy of swing music reflected the mood of world events during that time.

Visual Art Find and share an artwork that shows the "American spirit" in a way that parallels the work of one of the composers in the chapter.

 Explore more about the music of Copland, Ellington, and Larsen at **www.glencoe.com/sec/music**

registers of the instruments; he used creative harmonies; and he incorporated improvisation by his band members.
12. Billy Strayhorn.
13. Boogie-woogie.
14. With keyboard samplers and synthesizers.
15. All three use(d) American materials and American subject matter in their music; all three used elements of popular music. Copland worked in traditional classical forms and used traditional instruments; Ellington worked in a jazz/swing style and used traditional instruments in new ways; Larsen works comfortably with both electronic and traditional instruments.
16. It was based largely on the harmonic structure; most songwriters focused on melody.
17. She used American pioneer poetry for "The Settling Years," included fiddling in the instrumental part and incorporated shouts and whistles for a rowdy, raucous frontier spirit.

You may wish to use
Assessment Master 9,
Unit Nine Test, in the TRB.

Chapter 15 Project
Instructor's Guide, page 236
TRB Unit 6 Evaluation: Chapter 15,
Perceptive Listening
CD 11 16 "What's New?" (2:59)
CD 11 17 "What's New?" (4:46)
CD 11 18 "What's New?" (4:14)

Chapter 15 Project

 Understanding Arrangements

What musical tools have been used to create vocal and instrumental arrangements of a stock pop tune?

Use the Perceptive Listening Grid provided by your teacher to compare and contrast three arranged versions of the same classic love song, "What's New?" Work independently and follow the steps below:

1. Listen to the song as it was arranged to be played by Benny Goodman and his band. Make notes about what makes this arrangement distinctive.
2. Listen to the arrangement played by J. J. Johnson on trombone. How is this arrangement different?
3. Listen to the song arrangement performed by Billie Holiday. Again, how is it unique?

Based on your notations on the grid, describe how music arrangers can use their tools of the trade to become just as creative as composers.

Chapter 16 Project
Instructor's Guide, pages 236–237

Chapter 16 Project

▶ *Examining Creativity*

How would you describe the creative process in general and musical creativity in particular?

Discuss the following questions in your small study groups. Take notes on your deliberations. Use your notes and the information in the text to describe the characteristics of musical creativity.

Discussion Questions

1. Is everyone creative? What are creative people like? How are creative people different from noncreative people?
2. How do teachers usually respond to highly creative students? Why?
3. When someone creates a musical composition or arrangement, what kinds of decisions have to be made?
4. Compare the most and least creative composers you know. How are they similar and different? Is their thinking convergent or divergent?
5. What is the role of the composer in today's world? What is the usefulness of musical expression?

Unit Six Evaluation

Chapter 17 Project

 The Language of Music

How well do you know your technological terms?

Based on your reading of the text in this unit and on the class demonstrations of music technology, select five terms that you believe should be in the common language of musically informed young adults. Then, write a brief and clear definition for each term. Hand in your list of five definitions. Your teacher will compile from the class a vocabulary list of the most significant technological terms. Identifying the terms on this list will become your end-of-unit project.

Chapter 18 Project

 The Characteristics of American Music

What characteristics make music American?

Pick one piece in this unit that you feel characterizes American music. Write a one-page essay discussing what makes this music American. Cite specific musical events in your selection to support your viewpoint.

Chapter 17 Project
Instructor's Guide, page 237

Chapter 18 Project
Instructor's Guide, page 237

American painter Thomas Moran (1837–1926) captured the drama and beauty of the Western landscape in this artwork titled The Mirage. *Although the experiences of the early settlers were far from ideal, Moran's offered a vision of America that still lingers today.*

Thomas Moran. *The Mirage*. Stark Museum of Art. Orange, TX.

The History of Recorded Music

Before recorded sound, music was heard primarily through live performances. Whether in a park setting with a band, in groups of people performing music, in a concert hall, or around a piano, music relied on human performance.

Recorded sound is not only one of the many conveniences of modern life, but it also offers you the chance to experience and share music in unique ways. Follow this reverse time line to trace the evolution of recorded sound.

A Montage of Recording History
Instructor's Guide, page 238
CD 19 [3] "Some of These Days"
(4:11)
CD 19 [4] "Back Water Blues"
(3:18)
CD 19 [5] "Mr. Tambourine Man"
(2:17)
CD 19 [6] "Allegro," Concerto in D
Major for Trumpet and
Orchestra (2:54)

▶ *A Montage of Recording History*

Listen to four music selections and match the examples you hear with the four recording mediums described in this lesson.

■ Which example was the easiest to identify? Why?

■ Which examples were the most difficult to identify? Why?

■ In which examples were the differences very subtle?

■ Which of the playback mediums had the smallest listening audience? Which had the greatest listening audience? Explain your answer.

■ Where do you think each of these playback machines might be located in a home? How would that location affect the way listeners shared and enjoyed music?

The Cassette Tape, 1968
The cassette tape was instantly popular when first introduced. It was small enough to fit into a shirt pocket. It held up to 45 minutes of music on each side of the tape and was easy to use—lift the lid; push the play button. It could be played in the car, in any room in the home, or in a battery-operated cassette player. It introduced global recording technology.

The Compact Disc, 1982
The compact disc is perhaps the most common playback machine. It holds up to 75 minutes of sound without surface noise or scratches, without tape hiss or background noises. The CD player offers the random choice of selections and the convenience of remote control. Digital technology has become very user friendly!

The LP Record and High Fidelity, 1950
Before the development of the long-playing record around 1950, records were limited to about ten minutes of music. The LP (long-playing) record, along with "high fidelity" sound, gave listeners the chance to hear up to 30 minutes of uninterrupted music. The development of the 45-rpm (revolutions per minute) disc (shown here) made a large selection of popular recordings available to the public at a modest price.

The Talking Machine, 1880–1920
Thomas Edison is usually given credit for the inventing the first device that could reproduce sound mechanically from a recording. Edison's system placed the recording on a wax cylinder. Sound was amplified by a megaphone-like horn. Other inventors refined Edison's work and created the flat disc known as the "record."

▶ Sound Recordings—Sharing and Influencing Culture

Consider whether modern technology preserves a record of shared culture or influences culture.

English composer David Fanshaw's "African Sanctus" demonstrates a technique of music making that was only possible with modern sound technology. Using a portable tape recorder, he made field recordings of an Ugandan dance called "Bwala." He then returned to England and composed a composition for choir, piano, and percussion, which also included his "on-the-spot" tape recording of "Bwala."

Listen to the piece and answer the following questions.

■ What musical characteristics do you hear that are usually associated with Western music?

■ What musical characteristics do you hear that are usually associated with music from Africa?

■ What part of the "African Sanctus" is a record of shared culture?

■ What part of the "African Sanctus" influenced culture?

Sound Recordings—Sharing and Influencing Culture
Instructor's Guide, page 239
CD 19 [7] "African Sanctus"
(3:09)

391

Mariachi music, uniquely Mexican, originated in the rural Western areas. Born in Jalisco, Mexico, Natividad (Nati) Cano, grew up in a family of jornaleros (day workers). Working hard all day, they considered music a necessity—a means for earning additional money, as well as a personal expression of the love, joy, and community that was at the center of Mexican life. Los Camperos de Nati Cano performs mariachi compositions using violins, guitars, vihuelas, trumpets, harp, and guitarron. What type of music would you choose to describe the story of your life?

Mariachi Los Camperos de Nati Cano.
"Malagueña Salerosa," composed by Elpidio Ramírez. Photo by Craig Schwartz.

392

Music!...
To Tell the Story of Our Lives

You may wish to use Fine Art Transparency 7, *At the Opera*, in the TRB to introduce Unit Seven.

Chapter 19
Musical Theatre

Chapter 20
Opera

Chapter 21
Film

Use Artsource® audio tape segment 2 in the Performing Arts Package to hear a performance of "Malagueña Salerosa" by Mariachi Los Camperos de Nati Cano.

Musical Theatre

Storytelling may be the oldest art. Humans have been telling tales since they could draw and talk, certainly as far back as the caveman, perhaps earlier. Why do we tell stories? We tell them to share our experiences and learn from them, to try to invent explanations for what we do not understand, to remember what is valuable, and to delight and amuse ourselves. These are some of the reasons we still tell stories to each other today.

Objectives

By completing the chapter, you will:
- Be able to relate musical theatre to real-life experience.
- Learn about the differences between a drama and a musical.
- Recognize how music sets the atmosphere and the scene.
- Understand how music develops and reveals character.
- Learn about and be able to describe the dramatic tools of expression (sets, costumes, lighting, makeup, dialogue, and music).
- Discover more about musical theatre on Broadway.

Vocabulary

Broadway musical
dialogue
librettist
libretto
lyrics
soliloquy
vaudeville

Musicians to Meet

Oscar Hammerstein 2nd
Richard Rodgers
Andrew Lloyd Webber

Musical theatre combines the art of drama with music. The result is a story told with greater emotional impact. Shown here performing a duet are the Phantom and Christine, two principal characters in Andrew Lloyd Webber's 1988 Broadway production of The Phantom of the Opera. *The musical is a retelling of the 1911 novel by Gaston Leroux (1868–1927).* **How would you describe the music that would accompany this scene?**

Caption answer
Most students would predict music with a slow tempo about love or, perhaps, sorrow.

395

The Broadway Musical

When music is added to the drama, the storytelling becomes musical theatre. A rock concert with its format of continuous music, singing, costumes, lighting, and movement might be considered musical theatre, except for one thing—the absence of a coherent story line. Musical theatre combines the art of drama with song (and often dance) in order to tell a story with greater emotional impact. Among the many forms of musical theatre are the Broadway musical and opera.

Along with jazz, the Broadway musical is an American invention that tells a story with songs, dancing, costumes, scenery, lighting, and **dialogue**, *the spoken lines of a play or musical show.* It is an outgrowth of the minstrel show operettas and **vaudeville**, *an early staged variety show that included songs, dances, and skits.*

Like opera, the **Broadway musical** is *a dramatic stage form that combines the arts of acting and singing.* However, since opera was considered a bit too stuffy and long-winded for some of the general public, America invented its own type of opera, a form that spoke more simply and directly to the people. The answer was the Broadway musical, or what is now called, simply, "the musical."

You may wish to use "Write About a Musical" at this time. Lesson plans for the activity are found on page 246 in the Instructor's Guide.

Andrew Lloyd Webber
English Composer
1948–

PROFILE

Andrew Lloyd Webber

Sir Andrew Lloyd Webber is the most successful musical-theatre composer of the late twentieth century. Born in London, England, Lloyd Webber was the son of a college music professor and piano teacher. He learned to play piano, violin, and French horn before attending college, where he met lyricist Tim Rice.

Lloyd Webber and Rice worked together on many successful productions, including *Joseph and the Amazing Technicolor Dreamcoat* (1967), which became a hit in Britain. Most of Webber's later shows were also smashes on Broadway. Some of these include *Jesus Christ Superstar* (1971), *Evita* (1978), *Cats* (1981), *The Phantom of the Opera* (1986), and *Sunset Boulevard* (1993). His success continued with a London show in 1998 called *Whistle Down the Wind*. Some of his nontheatre works include *Variations,* composed for cello, and *Requiem,* written for his father.

Influenced by composers such as Paul Hindemith and Krzysztof Penderecki as well as pop and rock music, Lloyd Webber's music has a broad appeal. His contributions to musical theatre earned him a knighthood in England.

The style of the musical was established in the 1920s and 1930s by George Gershwin (*Lady Be Good*), Jerome Kern (*Show Boat*), and Cole Porter (*Anything Goes*), among others. After the Second World War, it was further developed by Frederick Loewe and Alan Jay Lerner (*My Fair Lady*), Jule Styne (*Gypsy*), Leonard Bernstein (*West Side Story*), and Stephen Sondheim (*A Little Night Music*)—Americans all. For the last thirty years, Andrew Lloyd Webber (b. 1947), a Londoner, has made many of the most memorable contributions to the great traditions of the Broadway musical (*Cats, Evita, The Phantom of the Opera*).

Carousel

One of America's greatest Broadway musical writing teams was Richard Rodgers and Oscar Hammerstein 2nd, and one of their greatest achievements was the musical *Carousel*. Like many other Broadway musicals, *Carousel* (1945) was an adaptation of an already existing work, in this case the play *Liliom* by the great European playwright Ferenc Molnár. The story is about a young, shiftless, manly carousel (merry-go-round) barker in Budapest who marries a shy and honest young servant girl. He loses his job, and when he learns that he is about to become a father, he participates in a robbery to get money to support his family. The robbery attempt fails, and in order to avoid capture by the police, he stabs himself and dies.

Liliom is tried in the Court of Heaven but refuses to apologize for his actions. He is too proud to admit that he really loves his wife and regrets what he has done. He is therefore sentenced to a term of 16 years in the purifying fires of the penitential plains, after which time he will be allowed to return to earth for one day to atone for his sins.

Returning to earth dressed as an old beggar, he tries to give his daughter, now 16 years old, a star he has stolen from heaven, but she refuses to take it. Forgetting his situation, he slaps her and is led away. The daughter asks her mother, "Is it possible for someone to hit you—hard like that, real loud and hard—and not hurt you at all?" In the final line of the play, the mother replies, "It is possible, dear—that someone may beat you and beat you and beat you—and not hurt you at all."

From Play to Musical

In adapting the play *Liliom* to a musical, Oscar Hammerstein 2nd wrote the book (the story and dialogue) and the **lyrics**, *the words of a song*. His adaptation reset the action in New England. He was the

librettist, *the person who writes the text for a musical*, also known as the **libretto**, *the dialogue and/or lyrics for a musical work.* His partner, Richard Rodgers, composed the finest musical score of his career, surpassing their previous triumph, *Oklahoma!*

Activity *Describe the Theatrical Setting*
Instructor's Guide, page 243
CD 12 ☐1☐ "The Carousel Waltz," *Carousel* (4:20)

As creators of musicals, the team of Richard Rodgers and Oscar Hammerstein 2nd was innovative. Instead of the usual overture, they opened Carousel *with a dance-pantomime. This prologue of actions and gestures introduces the audience to a carnival setting in the late 1800s. The music of "The Carousel Waltz" sweeps the audience up in the nostalgic sound of a calliope.*

ACTIVITY ▶ *Describe the Theatrical Setting*

How does music help set the scene?

Carousel opens with a "prologue" that introduces the carnival with a ballet-pantomime set to "The Carousel Waltz."

■ Describe the character of this melody.

■ How does music convey the atmosphere of a carnival?

One of the problems the creators of a musical have to solve is the transition between dialogue and singing. Although it is natural for characters to speak to one another, when they suddenly break into song, their singing can appear to be very unnatural, because it is not something people normally do. The transitions into song, therefore, take careful preparation in order to ease the audience into the music. The less noticeable (smoother) these transitions are, the better.

ACTIVITY ▶ *Analyze the Transition*

How does the composer make a smooth transition from speech to singing?

Early in *Carousel,* Julie and her friend Carrie Pipperidge are talking about their boyfriends ("beaux"). Their conversation is quietly underscored with music. Soon they are conversing in song in their duet, "You're a Queer One, Julie Jordan."

- Are you aware when they move from speech to song?
- Is the transition successful?
- What makes this duet a conversation set to music?

MIDI TECHNOLOGY OPTION

- **Music with MIDI** Use a MIDI program to compose a piece of musical theatre that features both spoken and sung text.

Sets, costumes, makeup, and lighting are tools of the stage. The musical adds one more tool: music. Rodgers and Hammerstein use music to convey emotion and drama. The addition of music to the dialogue adds to the emotional power. It influences the reaction of the audience and deepens their level of feeling. The difference between telling a story with dialogue and telling it with dialogue and music can be startling. Music heightens the emotions, making them more obvious, more vivid, and, often, more intense. Some dramatic stories are told more effectively with music; other, subtler tales are better told with dialogue alone.

ACTIVITY ▶ *Play the Part*

Understand the difference between the play and the musical.

In adapting the play to the musical, both Rodgers and Hammerstein tried to maintain the spirit of the original while they conveyed emotion and drama through the music. To understand the difference between the play and the musical, compare the scene in the play *Liliom,* in which Liliom meets Julie for the first time, with the same scene in the musical *Carousel.*

Assume the roles of the characters and read aloud their parts.

Then learn the musical version that appears on pages 402–410. Girls sing Julie's part, boys sing Billy's. Can you act the scene so that you feel the emotion?

What differences are there between the play and the musical setting?

Activity *Analyze the Transition*
Instructor's Guide, page 244
CD 12 [2] "You're a Queer One, Julie Jordan," *Carousel* (1:19)

Technology Option
Use Project 19 in the *MIDI Activities* binder.

Activity *Play the Part*
Instructor's Guide, pages 244–245
CD 12 [3] *Carousel,* Act 1, Scene 2 (9:11)

PROFILE

Richard Rodgers and Oscar Hammerstein 2nd

Richard Rodgers and Oscar Hammerstein 2nd left an indelible mark on the American musical. Their talents complemented each other in such a way that they were both better because of their association. Rodgers' ability to build a melody and make music uplifting meshed perfectly with Hammerstein's sense of drama and lyric purpose.

By the age of six, Richard Rodgers could play the piano by ear and improvise. Later, he wrote popular songs. In 1918 he began collaborating with the lyricist Lorenz Hart. They produced many hit shows, including *Babes in Arms* (1937). It was after Hart's death in 1943 that Rodgers formed his famous partnership with Oscar Hammerstein 2nd.

Hammerstein was already an established wordsmith. For example, he had written the musical *Show Boat* (1927) with Jerome Kern. But his new and lasting association with Rodgers made him the most significant author of musicals during this period. From their first hit, *Oklahoma!* (1943), to their last, *The Sound of Music* (1959), Rodgers and Hammerstein created many of the great masterpieces of American musical theatre.

Richard Rodgers
Composer
1902–1979

Oscar Hammerstein 2nd
American Librettist and Lyricist
1895–1960

Excerpt from Act I of *Liliom*

The scene is a lonely place in the park, half hidden by trees and shrubbery, near the amusement park. Center Stage: Under a flowering acacia (uh-KAY-shuh) tree stands a painted wooden bench. From afar, very faintly, comes the music of a calliope. Blending with it are the sounds of human voices, now loud, now soft. It grows progressively darker until the end of the scene. There is no moonlight. In this excerpt, "that Muskat woman" refers to Mrs. Muskat, the woman who owns the carousel and who has fired Liliom from his job as barker.

In the original play, Liliom and Julie have the following conversation at the end of Scene l.

Liliom: But you wouldn't dare to marry anyone like me, would you?

Julie: I know that—that—if I loved anyone—it wouldn't make any difference to me what he—even if I died for it.

Liliom: But you wouldn't marry a rough guy like me—that is—eh—if you loved me—

Julie: Yes, I would—if I loved you, Mister Liliom. [*There is a pause.*]

Liliom: [*Whispers.*] Well—you just said—didn't you?—that you don't love me. Well, why don't you go home then?

Julie: It's too late now, they'd all be asleep.

Liliom: Locked out?

Julie: Certainly. [*They are silent a while.*]

Liliom: I think—that even a low-down good-for-nothing—can make a man of himself.

Julie: Certainly. [*They are silent again.*]

Liliom: Are you hungry?

Julie: No. [*Another pause. The CALLIOPE stops.*]

Liliom: Suppose—you had some money—and I took it from you?

Julie: Then you could take it, that's all.

Liliom: [*After another brief silence.*] All I have to do—is go back to her—that Muskat woman—she'll be glad to get me back— then I'd be earning my wages again. (She is silent. The twilight folds darker about them.)

Julie: [*After a pause. Very softly.*] Don't go back—to her—[*Pause.*]

Liliom: There are a lot of acacia trees around here. [*Pause.*]

Julie: Don't go back to her—[*Pause.*]

Liliom: She'd take me back the minute I asked her. I know why—she knows, too—[*Pause.*]

Julie: I can smell them, too—acacia blossoms—

[*There is a pause. Some blossoms drift down from the treetop to the bench. Liliom picks one up and smells it.*]

Liliom: White acacias!

Julie: [*After a brief pause.*] The wind brings them down.

[*They are silent. The MERRY-GO-ROUND is heard in the distance. There is a long pause before*]

THE CURTAIN FALLS

Carousel is an adaptation of a play, Liliom, *written by Hungarian playwright Ferenc Molnár (1878–1952). In the Broadway musical, much of the play's dialogue was changed to music.* **What effect does the addition of music add to the characters' dialogue?**

Caption answer
It deepens the emotional impact of a scene and helps convey drama.

In the musical version, the dialogue is similar in the first meeting between Julie (now cast as a factory worker) and Billy Bigalow (the new name for Liliom), but much of it is underscored with music or sung. Julie and Billy develop their sentiments in the song "If I Loved You." Note that the title of this song comes directly from Julie's line in the original play. The music and the lyrics however, probe more deeply into their characters. The lyrics show how awkward Julie would feel if she were to love Billy. Later, Billy expresses similar feelings about Julie.

Julie and Billy never admit they are in love, but the music lets the audience know they are. In this way, the music heightens the drama. It adds a dimension of emotional feeling that reveals what is going on inside the characters. One of the achievements of *Carousel* is the way in which the musical numbers consistently enrich the drama. The story is *in* the music.

Excerpt from *Carousel,* Act I, Scene 2

Oscar Hammerstein 2nd
Richard Rodgers

gaze ab - sent - mind - ed at the roof. _____ and half the time the shut - tle - 'd

tan - gle in the threads, And the warp - 'd get mixed with the woof. _____

BILLY: *(speaks)* JULIE: *(speaks)*
But you don't! No, I don't. *(sings)*

_____ If I loved you   But

Broadly   *rall.*

pp some - how I ken see   jest ex - ack' - ly how I'd be.

Moderato espressivo
a tempo

p If I loved you,   Time _____ and a - gain _____ I would try to say

All I'd want you to know _____

If I loved you,   Words _____ would - n't come _____ in an

eas - y way.   Round   in   cir - cles   I'd   go! _____

Long - in'   to   tell   you,   but   a - fraid   and   shy,

I'd   let   my   gold - en   chan - ces   pass   me   by!

p Soon   you'd   leave   me   Off ___ you would go ___ in the   mist   of   day,

Nev - er,   nev - er   to   know _____

To Coda ⊕, page 410 (second time)

How   I   loved you   If   I   loved   you! _____
mf molto espr.   *mp*

(They sit in silence, he studies her for a moment, then turns away)
L'istesso tempo

pp

sky's   so   big   the sea looks   small. _____   And   two   lit - tle

p

rall.   *a tempo*

peo - ple.   you and   I,   We don't   count   at   all. _____   > *pp*

BILLY: You're a funny kid. Don't ever remember meetin' a girl like you.

Lento

pp   molto legato

BILLY: You! Are you trying   JULIE: No!   BILLY: Then what's
to get me to marry you?   puttin' it into my head?

Piu mosso

sfz   *sempre legato e* **pp**

You're different all right.   Don't know what it is.   You look up at me with that little-kid face like—like you

Most musicals provide the audience with comic relief. In Carousel, *the main story is embellished with a subplot involving Julie's best friend Carrie, who has fallen in love with Mr. Snow, an older fisherman. Their happy relationship contrasts with that of Julie and Billy.* **Speculate about the role of comic relief in a dramatic story.**

Caption answer
It provides a contrast to the serious characters and scenes, and it relieves the tension within the drama. Musically, humorous lyrics, harmonies, and melodies set the comedy apart from the dramatic music.

Using Music to Convey Character

In musical theatre, music is used to convey character and to make us like and relate to the people in the story. Both the words and the music express and communicate meaning. Most people in the audience get the meaning of the text; they may be less aware that the music is also telling them something. Shortly after the duet "You're a Queer One, Julie Jordan," Carrie sings a solo in which she admits to Julie, her best friend, that she has fallen in love with "Mr. Snow," an unlikely older man who happens to be an overbearing and smelly fisherman. She sings: "The first time he kissed me the whiff of his clothes knocked me flat on the floor of the room, but now that I love him, my heart's in my nose, and fish is my favorite perfume!" This song is designed to let the audience get to know and like her.

ACTIVITY ▶ *Analyze the Character*

What kind of a person is Carrie?

As you listen to Carrie sing the song "Mr. Snow," jot down all the characteristics that she reveals about herself in the *lyrics.*

Now consider what the *music* is telling you about Carrie.

Write the adjectives that best describe the character of the melody in the refrain "When I marry Mr. Snow." How does this melody affect our thoughts about Carrie?

Activity *Analyze the Character*
Instructor's Guide, page 245
CD 12 [4] "Mr. Snow," Carousel (3:27)

In the play, Liliom is not a very likeable character. He is shiftless and seemingly satisfied not to work. He gambles and keeps bad company. His marriage with Julie is far from ideal. At one point, when Julie asks him why he won't go back to work on the carousel, he hits her. She even has a difficult time telling him that they are going to have a child.

In spite of the fact that Liliom, or Billy in the musical, has never done anything worthwhile, Rodgers and Hammerstein were determined to treat him empathetically; that is, to help the audience project their own personalities into his personality to share his predicament and thus understand him better. They succeed brilliantly in getting the audience to have some sympathy for him through the "Soliloquy" he sings when he first learns that he is to become a father. A **soliloquy** (suh-LIL-uh-kwee) is *spoken or sung text that reveals the inner thoughts of a character to the audience, but not to the other characters.*

Rodgers and Hammerstein had spent many days talking about this song, what it would be about, who would sing it, and how it would fit into the action. Hammerstein took two full weeks to write the lyrics, but then Rodgers completed the music in less than two hours! "Soliloquy" tells the audience that Billy, in spite of his rough edges, has a decent, caring side.

Activity *Explore Theatrical Character*
Instructor's Guide, page 246
CD 12 ⑤ "Soliloquy," *Carousel*
(7:26)

ACTIVITY ▶ *Explore Theatrical Character*

How does "Soliloquy" show us Billy's good side?

In this soliloquy, Billy is imagining what it will be like to be a father. At first he imagines that his child-to-be is a boy, he is proud of his son "Bill," and he dreams of the fun they will have together.

■ List adjectives that describe the character of this section of music.

Then Billy interrupts himself. Suppose Julie has a girl! What would he do then? He'd have to be a real father to a girl. He describes how delicate she will be and how popular she will be with the boys.

■ List adjectives that describe the character of this section of music.

Again he interrupts himself. His fragile little girl will go hungry if he continues his shiftless ways. He vows he will do anything to get enough money to bring up his daughter the way she deserves: "I'll make it or steal it or take it—or die."

■ List adjectives that describe the character of this section of music.

Working in small groups, compare your list of adjectives. Discuss what the music reveals about Billy and debate these questions:
1. Would he make a good father?
2. Are these fair expectations for boys and girls?
3. In what ways are they stereotypes?

In the same way that "Soliloquy" reveals Billy's character, the song
"What's the Use of Wond'rin?" expresses Julie's. In this song, as in Billy's,
Julie is thinking out loud about Billy. By accepting Billy with all his faults,
Julie reveals herself as sweet and trusting, but also foolish and naive.

>What's the use of wond'rin
>If he's good or if he's bad,
>Or if you like the way he wears his hat?
>Oh, what's the use of wond'rin
>If he's good or if he's bad,
>He's your fella, and you love him
>That's all there is to that.
>Common sense may tell you
>That the endin' will be sad,
>And now's the time to break and run away.
>Oh, what's the use of wond'rin
>If the endin' will be sad
>He's your fella, and you love him
>There's nothing more to say.
>Somethin' made him the way that he is
>Whether he's false or true.
>And somethin' gave him the things that are his
>One of those things is you.

Years after his death, Billy revisits earth to do a good deed. He arrives at the time of his daughter's high school graduation. He urges her to believe in herself and rise above life's setbacks with the song "You'll Never Walk Alone." Through his actions, Billy has redeemed himself.

The Message

Rodgers and Hammerstein made the ending of the musical more fitting to their New England setting and a good deal more hopeful than the ending of the play. Rather than end the musical with the touching but still tragic scene at Julie's front porch as in the play, Hammerstein added a brief finale—a graduation scene at the local high school. In his speech to the graduates, one of whom is Louise, Billy's 16-year-old daughter, the town doctor exhorts them to stand on their own two feet. They will come out all right, he says, if they have faith and courage.

The doctor is reminded of a song he used to sing in school, and soon all the students, except for Billy's daughter Louise, have joined in singing "You'll Never Walk Alone," a song that was first sung to Julie after Billy's death. The lyrics tell us to "walk on, walk on, with hope in your heart, and you'll never walk alone." Rodgers and Hammerstein are saying to the audience that it is hope that will carry us through the dark times.

Coming as it did in 1945, during the last year of the Second World War, *Carousel* raised people's spirits and gave them hope. The moral of the story is that sacrifice is rewarded, that goodness wins out in the end. It was idealistic, perhaps a bit sentimental, but its uplifting musical message is one feature that makes for very effective musical theatre.

Activity *Put Yourself on the Stage*
Instructor's Guide, page 246
CD 12 [6] "You'll Never Walk Alone," *Carousel* (2:37)

ACTIVITY ▶ *Put Yourself on the Stage*

Sing "You'll Never Walk Alone."

Note how the melody climbs gradually higher. Where is the climax in this song?

What is the range of this song (lowest pitch to highest pitch)?

What makes this song right for the ending of *Carousel*?

You'll Never Walk Alone

Oscar Hammerstein 2nd

Richard Rodgers

Since the first Broadway performance of Carousel *in 1945, "You'll Never Walk Alone" became a familiar song at high school graduation ceremonies. Like the moral of the story, the song carries a message of goodness, optimism, and the rewards of sacrifice.* **How is this message appropriate to graduates?**

Caption answer
Students will likely see the hope and encouragement the song reflects to graduates as they prepare to take their places in the world as adults.

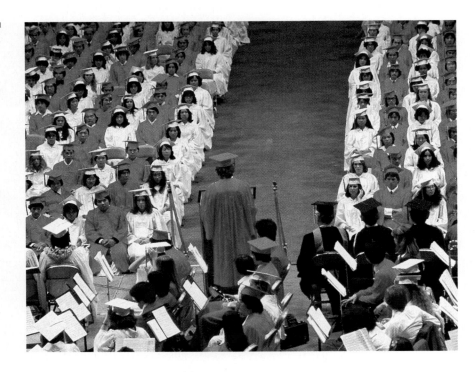

SUMMARY

Good oral storytellers know how to create suspense to hold the attention of the audience, how to build the story to a climax and a satisfactory conclusion, and how to use dramatic words and inflections of the voice to create character and feeling. Writers tell tales in the form of short stories and novels. Dramatists create plays. Theatre and film are two of the more elaborate ways we communicate stories. Probably the most elaborate form of storytelling is musical theatre, a form that encompasses elements of all the others.

Musical theatre is a particularly American way of relating a story through drama and music. The Broadway musical, or the musical comedy, is lighthearted entertainment consisting of a story line or plot, usually with some romantic twist, told through dialogue and a series of catchy songs, dances, and ensembles. People are drawn by the central message of these stories: American optimism—the belief that goodness will triumph over evil.

Building Music Vocabulary

On a sheet of paper, write the term from the list that best matches each description below.

- (4) Broadway musical
- (5) dialogue
- (7) librettist
- (3) libretto
- (2) lyrics
- (1) soliloquy
- (6) vaudeville

1. Spoken or sung text that reveals the inner thoughts of a character.
2. The words of a song.
3. Dialogue and/or lyrics for a musical.
4. A dramatic stage form combining acting and singing.
5. The spoken lines of a play or musical show.
6. An early staged variety show that included songs, dances, and skits.
7. The person who writes the text of a musical.

Reviewing Music Facts

Answer each question in a complete sentence.

8. What is the principal difference between opera and the Broadway musical?
9. Name at least two of the composers in the 1920s and 1930s who helped establish the style of the Broadway musical.
10. Where did Rodgers and Hammerstein find the story for their musical *Carousel*?
11. Why is it necessary to create careful transitions between dialogue and singing in a musical?
12. What feelings are expressed in the song "If I Loved You"?
13. What side of Billy Bigelow's character does the soliloquy reveal to the audience?
14. Why was the year 1945 a good time for the message of a musical like *Carousel*?

Complete answers for the Chapter 19 Review are found in the Instructor's Guide, page 247.

Thinking It Through

On a sheet of paper, answer each of the following:

15. **Explain** Why are some dramatic stories better told with music?
16. **Analyze** How does Billy's "Soliloquy" reveal more to the audience than might be conveyed by regular dialogue between several characters?
17. **Apply** What is the difference between the endings of *Carousel* and the original play? Why did Rodgers and Hammerstein alter the original?

Making the Connection

Language Arts Find a story, play, or television show you think would make a good musical and explain why.

Science Is our response to music something that is inherent or is it something we learn? Find at least one study of animals and their response to music, and describe whether the same observations and conclusions can be applied to humans.

 Discover more about musical theatre at **www.glencoe.com/sec/music**

---

8. The Broadway musical is less stylized and more natural, with more immediate emotional appeal.
9. Possibilities include George Gershwin, Jerome Kern, and Cole Porter.
10. The play *Liliom*.

11. Speaking is more natural than singing, and the transitions between straight dialogue and singing must carefully ease the audience into the music.
12. Billy and Julie express their awkwardness about the idea of being in love with one another.
13. The more decent, caring side of his character.
14. 1945 was the last year of World War II, and a musical like Carousel raised people's spirits and expressed hope.
15. Music adds a dimension of emotional feeling that helps us understand more about the characters and their actions.
16. Billy's "Soliloquy" is more honest because it reveals his thoughts and feelings, not just what he wants others to hear.
17. To make it less dark and depressing, giving it a feeling of hope and triumph that is missing in the play.

CHAPTER 20

Opera

New York's Metropolitan Opera celebrated its one hundredth year in 1983. The celebration saluted a major American cultural institution. Now, in the new millennium, the "Met" and opera are stronger than ever. In the nineteenth century, successive waves of immigrants brought their culture with them—their songs, instruments, and love of music. They wanted America to have symphony orchestras and opera companies, just like their old countries. Even as they moved west during the nineteenth century, the settlers longed for culture. That is why they built opera houses in mining towns like Central City, Colorado.

Concepts to Learn

By completing this chapter, you will:

- Understand how a story is told through the medium of opera.
- Learn to define and use some of the terms associated with opera.
- Become familiar with one opera (*Carmen*) in detail.
- Recognize how the parts of the opera—overture, recitatives, arias, duets, trios, entr'acte music—all contribute to its total effect.
- Learn some of the names of different voice types and timbres used in grand opera.
- Observe how the different timbres of the solo voices add to the interest and overall expression.

Vocabulary

absolute pitch
aria
entr'acte music
grand opera
opéra comique
recitative
seguidilla

Musicians to Meet

Georges Bizet
José Carreras
Placido Domingo
James Levine
Luciano Pavarotti

Opera weaves together dialogue, music, costumes, set design, and lighting to tell a story. In Georges Bizet's opera Carmen, *the main character's strong, but fickle, nature unfolds through the memorable songs that have made the opera one of the most popular ever. Here, mezzo soprano Denyce Graves portrays Carmen.* **What experiences or knowledge of opera can you share?**

Caption answer
Encourage students to find and listen to a live Met broadcast of opera to expand their awareness.

Opera

Today, there are more than 120 opera companies in the United States with yearly budgets of over 100,000 dollars. Together, these companies give well over 7,000 performances of opera each year, reaching a combined audience of 8 million people. As a form of storytelling, opera has been around since the early 1600s, when Italian composers first tried to combine singing with theatre. At first, audiences were excited because they liked the music and stage spectacle. The story dealt with imaginary or symbolic subjects, often gods and goddesses. They were a celebration of the glories of the past and were performed as entertainments in the courts of nobles. The concept of opera, born in Italy, soon spread throughout Europe, becoming less serious, more public, and distinct in national style and character.

Today, a successful opera must achieve dramatic excitement and sustain it throughout the performance. It must have expressive music that reveals and heightens the emotion of the story. The story line or plot must revolve around interesting characters and situations. Costumes, scenery, lighting, and music must combine to dramatize the characters and their predicaments. Achieving this synthesis is a creative process so complex that it is roughly equivalent to making a movie. When an opera is successful, it is therefore a considerable achievement for all involved.

Caption answer

Listeners would rely on imagination to re-create the stage, scenery, lighting, and costumes. Also, they could concentrate on music and words more closely.

The New York Metropolitan Opera Company was first established in 1883. Since 1966 it has been located, along with the New York Philharmonic, in the Lincoln Center for the Performing Arts. Weekly, the Met broadcasts live performances to over 300 radio stations across the nation. **How would the experience of listening to opera differ from watching a performance?**

PROFILE

James Levine

James Levine
American Conductor
1943–

James Levine is one of America's and the world's great conductors. He may be best known for his energetic conducting in his prestigious role as music director of the Metropolitan Opera, but his career has been filled with many musical accomplishments.

Born in Cincinnati, Ohio, Levine made his debut as a piano soloist with the Cincinnati Symphony Orchestra at the age of ten. He went on to study piano, conducting, and other music subjects intensively for many years both privately and at the Juilliard School in New York City. He then became assistant conductor of the Cleveland Orchestra, where he stayed for six years.

Levine made his debut with the Metropolitan Opera in 1971 and was soon appointed music director. He has also conducted the Berlin and Vienna Philharmonic Orchestras as well as the Chicago Symphony. He led "The Three Tenors" concerts and conducted Disney's *Fantasia 2000*. Yet he has not neglected his piano skills. He often performs chamber music and concertos and is considered an outstanding interpreter of Mozart, both as a pianist and as a conductor.

Carmen

One of the most successful operas of all time is *Carmen*. The story is fast-paced and believable. The characters in the story are all people to whom we can relate. Don José (ho-ZAY), a corporal in the regiment, is corrupted by his own passion. His love for the brusque and free-wheeling Carmen turns into a destructive jealousy. To make matters worse, Carmen turns her attention to the pompous and heroic matador, Escamillo (es-cah-MEE-yoh), which further infuriates José. To complicate matters, there is Micaëla (mick-eye-AY-la), José's sweet and innocent girlfriend, the direct opposite of Carmen. Then there is the band of gypsy smugglers and Captain Zuniga (zoo-NEE-guh), José's very proper and law-abiding superior.

The work was composed by Georges Bizet (zjorge bee-ZAY), a brilliant French composer of the nineteenth century who lived in Paris for most of his life. The text of the opera—called the libretto—was adopted from a popular French novel by Prosper Mérimée. The tale takes place in Seville (Spain) in 1820. Bizet's vivid orchestral scoring provides splashes of Spanish color to add atmosphere to the story. His music was unusual for its time because it moved the action along and supported the drama.

Activity *Follow the Themes*
Instructor's Guide, page 248
CD 12 [7] Overture to *Carmen*
           (3:34)

ACTIVITY ▶ *Follow the Themes*

How does Bizet establish the atmosphere for *Carmen*?

As you listen to the Overture to *Carmen,* follow the "map" of the overture to determine how Bizet sets up the atmosphere of the opera. The map uses a different letter for each new melody (musical theme) and the same letter when it is repeated.

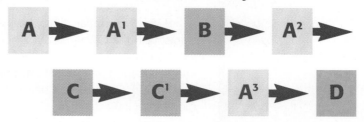

■ Which section of the music represents the toreador? What in the music tells you?

■ Which section represents the excitement of the bullfight? What are its characteristics?

■ Which gives us Carmen's "fate motive" (the recurring melody that predicts her fate)? Study the melody on page 424. What clue to the story does it provide? Why is this clue given at the start?

MUSIC in the WORLD

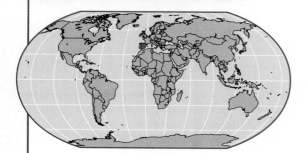

SPAIN is a European country whose music was influenced by both Muslim and Christian styles. In the 1600s Spain developed early musical theatre that was overshadowed by Italian opera in the 1700s. It is from these rich and varied traditions that Bizet shaped the sound of *Carmen.*

Background

Carmen is an *opéra comique* written for and first performed at the Opéra-Comique theatre in Paris. While the name indicates this should be a comic opera, this is not the case. The fact that the opera is a tragedy was a big part of the controversy that surrounded its premiere.

By definition, an opéra comique was supposed to have some comical moments and, certainly, a happy ending. Given the violence in Bizet's new opera, it is not surprising that the management of the Opéra-Comique theatre was horrified. Upon hearing what the composer had created, one of the directors became hysterical. He begged Halévy, one of the librettists, to let Carmen live. "Death has never been seen on this stage, do you hear, never!"

Carmen changed all that. After *Carmen,* opéra comique differed from grand opera only in the amount of spoken dialogue. **Grand opera** is *a type of music drama in which everything is sung.* **Opéra comique** is *a type of opera in which some dialogue is sung, some spoken.* The same thing has happened to the Broadway musical. We no longer maintain that there must be spoken dialogue. Musicals such as *Les Misérables* or *The Phantom of the Opera* are sung throughout. Nor do we call the form "musical comedy," as we used to. Composers simply wanted to be able to use more serious plots, so the label had to be changed. The distinctions have become unimportant. Today there are other versions of *Carmen*. The composer Ernest Guiraud, a friend of Bizet, revised the dialogue and set it in **recitative**, *a speechlike style of singing*, so that the opera could be sung throughout.

ACTIVITY ▶ *Critique Two Performances*

Use a "Judging Quality" form provided by your teacher to compare two different interpretations of Carmen's aria, "Seguidilla."

- Performance No. 1: Carmen is played by Tatiana Troyanos; the conductor is Sir Georg Solti.
- Performance No. 2: Carmen is performed by Maria Callas; the conductor is Georges Prêtre.

After forming your critical evaluations, try to answer the following questions:

1. Which performer do you think has the tone quality that best reflects the character of Carmen? Justify your decision.
2. The "Seguidilla" is based on a Spanish dance rhythm. Which performance do you think captures the spirit of the undanced dance? Why?
3. Describe the differences in tempo between the two performances. Which tempo best captures the mood of the text? Why?

Activity *Critique Two Performances*
Instructor's Guide, page 249
TRB 20-1, *Judging Quality*
CD 12 ⑧ "Seguidilla," *Carmen* (4:42)
CD 12 ⑨ "Seguidilla," *Carmen* (4:31)

Act I of Carmen *is set in a public square in Seville, in southwest Spain. At noontime the girls from the factory enter the square to take a break. It is here that Don José, a corporal, first becomes infatuated with Carmen. This photo is taken from the 1983 San Francisco Opera Company production.*

Act I

When Act I opens, a group of soldiers is lounging in front of the guardhouse watching the people in the square. Soon a relief guard, with Don José and his captain, Zuniga, assumes the watch. At noon, the girls from the cigarette factory pour out into the square. The last to appear is Carmen, the beautiful and brazen gypsy girl, who flirts with Don José and lets him know her thoughts about love. She sings, "If you don't love me, then I love you. If I love you, beware!" She tosses him a flower, and everyone laughs at his embarrassment. The factory bell rings, and the cigarette girls go back to work.

When Micaëla appears, Don José quickly hides the flower. She brings greetings from his mother. She gives him a kiss from her, and he sends one back. Alone, he opens his mother's letter. "Yes," he says, "I'll do what you wish. I'll marry Micaëla."

Suddenly there is a loud noise from the factory. There has been an argument. Captain Zuniga sends Don José and two other guards into the factory. They emerge with Carmen. Don José has caught her with a knife. The women identify her as the culprit. Carmen is insolent. Zuniga tells Don José to tie Carmen's hands while he goes into the guardhouse to make out a warrant for her arrest. Left alone with Don José, Carmen uses her charm to complete her conquest of him. She sings the **aria** *(song)* "Seguidilla" (seh-gee-DEE-yuh).

In the finale to Act I, Zuniga emerges from the guardhouse and commands Don José to take Carmen to prison. She whispers to José to stay in back of her. She will give him a push in order to make her escape. As they walk away, she reminds him, "If I love you, beware!" At the bridge, Carmen pushes José. He falls, and she escapes, laughing loudly. The curtain falls.

Activity *Play Carmen's "Fate Motive"*
Instructor's Guide, page 249
TRB 20-2, *Carmen's "Fate Motive"*

ACTIVITY ▶ *Play Carmen's "Fate Motive"*

Go to a keyboard and try to play the "fate motive" from the notation below.

Perform the first five notes connected as the phrase marking (⌒) indicates, followed by the two Ds performed staccato. Perform the second line, making one long, connected phrase with a crescendo (gradual increase in intensity) and a diminuendo (gradual decrease in intensity) in the last three measures.

ACTIVITY ▶ *Explore the Seguidilla*

Activity *Explore the Seguidilla*
Instructor's Guide, page 250
CD 12 ⑨ "Seguidilla," *Carmen*
(4:31)

A **seguidilla** is *a Spanish dance, or the music for such a dance.* It uses the rhythm below. Before you listen, try to clap this seguidilla rhythm.

Follow the music and text to the "Seguidilla" to see how the story progresses (from below). When Carmen begins the aria, she is Don José's prisoner. When the song ends, how has her situation changed?

After the introduction by the orchestra with a flute solo and oom-pah-pah accompaniment, you will hear the following sections:

(A) Carmen sings the melody to the dance rhythm of the seguidilla. She tells Don José, "Near the ramparts of Seville, at my friend Lillas Pastia's tavern, I'm going to dance the seguidilla (a gypsy dance)."

(B) New melody: Carmen says that she wants company there. She has just showed her lover the door. "All alone, one gets bored. Real pleasures are for two."

(A) Seguidilla melody returns: "Near the rampart of Seville," etc.

(C) Don José sings. The style becomes somewhat less melodic and more recitative. He forbids Carmen to talk. She says she is just thinking out loud about a certain officer who loves her. (You will hear fragments of the seguidilla melody in the flute.) Even though he is only a lowly corporal, she will be happy with him. Don José becomes more impassioned. "If I free you, will you keep your word? If I love you, will you love me?" he asks.

(A) Seguidilla melody returns again: Carmen says yes, and Don José, blinded by his love for her, unties the cord that binds her hands. They will meet later at the tavern.

MIDI TECHNOLOGY OPTION

Technology Option
Use Project 20 in the *MIDI Activities* binder.

■ **Music with MIDI** Use a MIDI program to compose an aria in which the music changes character to reflect the story line.

In Act I, Carmen charms Don José by singing the "Sequidilla," and he is persuaded to help her escape. In this 1995 production by The Washington Opera, the characters are played by Denyce Graves (Carmen) and Neil Rosenshein (Don José).

Act II

Act II opens with Carmen leading the gypsy girls in a wild dance for the officers of the guard. The setting is Lillas Pastia's tavern. Gypsies on guitars and tambourine accompany the dancing. The plucked strings of the orchestra give the effect of guitars. The music gradually grows faster and more intense. The insistent rhythm drives the dancers into a whirlwind. The chorus of "tra la las" adds to the frenzy, and the full orchestra enters to give the dance a feverish finish.

Activity *Compose a Gypsy Rhythm*
Instructor's Guide, page 250
CD 12 ⑩ "Gypsy Dance," *Carmen* (4:16)
Tempos in the Activity are found at the following times on the CD track:
Orchestra—0:00
First tra-la-la— 1:36
Second tra-la-la—2:33
Third tra-la-la—3:30
Final orchestra—3:54

ACTIVITY ▶ *Compose a Gypsy Rhythm*

Use tambourines, finger snaps, or other sounds to mark the three basic beats in the "Gypsy Dance." As the tempo of the music accelerates, speed up the pulse.

Use your accompaniment only when the orchestra plays alone and when the voices sing "tra-la-la." (The dance ceases during the other singing.) Your parts will move through the following tempos:

Orchestra	*Andantino* ($\downarrow$ = 100)
First tra-la-la	*A tempo* ($\downarrow$ = 108)
Second tra-la-la	*A tempo animato* ($\downarrow$ = 126)
Third tra-la-la	*Piu mosso* ($\downarrow$ = 138)
Final orchestra	*Presto*

Challenge

- Test your skill by accompanying on the offbeat. Try half the class accompanying on the beat and half on the offbeat.

- The "tra-la-la" section repeats the note E on every beat in the bass throughout. Play the E on the recurring beats on a keyboard or mallet percussion instrument.

Captain Zuniga is prominent among the observers, even though the tavern is a meeting place for a gang of gypsy smugglers. In the month that has passed since he ordered Carmen's arrest, he too has succumbed to her charms, though she does not hide the fact that she prefers other company. To win a smile from Carmen, Zuniga tells her that her soldier-boyfriend José has been released from prison.

Suddenly, the crowd outside shouts greetings to Escamillo, the popular bullfighter. He enters the tavern and sings the "Toreador Song," an aria that reveals his character.

Escamillo, too, makes a play for Carmen's affection, but she tells him he is wasting his time. As the tavern closes, he leaves with the soldiers. Only Carmen and a few of her gypsy friends linger to plan their next smuggling escapade. The girls are delighted to take part, but Carmen excuses herself. She tells them she has fallen in love again, this time with a man who went to prison for helping her.

Music & Art

As part of the planning for stage productions, an artist might be asked to sketch a scene. This work, showing a street scene in Seville for Bizet's Carmen, *was created by Russian artist Aleksandr Golovin (1863–1930).* **How would this sketch help the stage designers and construction crews?**

Aleksandr Yakovlevich Golovin. *A Street in Seville* (sketch for the stage set for Bizet's *Carmen*). 1906. State Russian Museum, St. Petersburg, Russia.

Music & Art
Encourage a variety of responses, including its usefulness as a model for buildings, to identify and maintain proportion and accuracy of details, and to plan for unity in color.

ACTIVITY ▶ *Describe and Sing*

What does the "Toreador Song" tell us about Escamillo?

The Setting: After the orchestral introduction, Escamillo sings a toast to the soldiers and the gypsy girls. Then he sings of the crowds that await him, their shouts, and the fame he wins for his courage. Then, boastfully, he sings the refrain "Toreador, en garde!" ("Toreador, on guard!"), and the assembled crowd joins in. As he sings of the dark eyes that watch him in the ring, he looks at Carmen.

Describe: What two adjectives best describe both this music and Escamillo?

Sing: Learn to sing the "Toreador Song." Practice singing the grace notes and the triplets separately until you have mastered them. Try to give a marchlike snap and vigor to the dotted rhythms. Can you sing it with the French text?

Activity *Describe and Sing*
Instructor's Guide, page 251
CD 12 [11] "Toreador Song,"
Carmen (4:48)

Toreador Song

Georges Bizet
Translation by Ruth & Thomas Martin

To - ré - a - dor, — en gar - - de! ___ To - ré - a - dor! ___
To - ré - a - dor, — on gaurd! _____ To - ré - a - dor! ___

Georges Bizet
Composer
1838–1875

PROFILE

Georges Bizet

Like many outstanding composers and musicians, Georges Bizet grew up in a musical family. His mother was an excellent pianist and his father coached opera singers. In this environment, his musical gifts emerged early, and by the age of ten his **absolute pitch** (*the ability to recognize and reproduce pitches exactly*), knowledge of harmony, and piano skills won him acceptance as a student at the Paris Conservatory.

By the age of 17, Bizet had composed his first symphony, and two years later he won the coveted Grand Prix de Rome, a scholarship that enabled him to study musical composition in Rome for four years. At 22, he returned to Paris where he spent the rest of his short life supporting himself by teaching and composing.

In 1875 Bizet composed the operatic masterpiece *Carmen*. Although it was not an immediate success, this work would be very influential in creating a more realistic style of opera in the late nineteenth century. It may now be the most popular opera ever written. Bizet died just three months after its premiere.

Hearing Don José's voice offstage, the girls peer out at him approvingly. Can Carmen get him to join their band? To get rid of them, Carmen says she will try. Don José enters and Carmen greets him warmly. She begins to sing and dance for him, as she promised. But as she dances, a trumpet sounds in the distance, a signal that Don José must report for duty. When he informs her that he must leave, Carmen gets angry. "Go," she tells him, "they are waiting for you. So much for your love."

Stung by her taunts, Don José shows Carmen the flower she gave to him before his imprisonment. He tells her in the "Flower Song" how the sweet scent of the dried flower reminded him of her. She took possession of his heart. His one hope was to see her again. To sweet harmonies and harp arpeggios in the orchestra, he tells her that he loves her.

Carmen is not persuaded. "If you loved me, you would come away with me into the mountains," she tells him. "You wouldn't have to obey any officer." Don José wants her love, but not at the price of being a deserter. He begs for her understanding, but she is determined to have her way. "Farewell forever," she tells him.

Don José is about to storm out when someone knocks. It is Zuniga, captain of his regiment. Spotting Don José, he chides Carmen for wasting her affections on a mere corporal when she could have an officer like himself. He orders Don José to get out. Don José refuses. Zuniga commands him again to leave, and again Don José says no. Zuniga strikes him and calls him a scoundrel. Don José seizes his sword. Frenzied music expresses the tension. Carmen, calling Don José a jealous fool, throws herself between them and summons the other gypsies. Rushing to her aid, they seize Zuniga and disarm him.

Carmen informs Zuniga that he must be held captive. The gypsies point their pistols at him and enjoy having the upper hand. They treat Zuniga with mocking politeness. Don José now has no choice. He has disobeyed his commanding officer and has been a party to his entrapment. The gypsies urge him to join with them and enjoy a life that is free. "La liberté!" ("Freedom!") they shout, as the curtain falls on Act II.

Activity *Discover the Romance of the "Flower Song"*
Instructor's Guide, page 251
CD 12 [12] "Flower Song," Carmen
(3:48)

ACTIVITY ▶ *Discover the Romance of the "Flower Song"*

As you listen to the "Flower Song," make a list of the characteristics of the music that help to convey its romantic message.

Divide your list into three categories:
1. **The Orchestra (accompaniment).** How does it convey the mood?
2. **The Melody.** What characteristics make it a love song?
3. **The Singing.** How does the tenor, Nicolai Gedda, who performs the role of Don José, express his love by the way he sings? Discuss your observations.

As the opera unfolds through four acts, Bizet's music foretells the tragic fate that awaits Carmen. In contrast, Carmen fears no one and refuses to heed the warning of death that will be told through the cards in Act III. Here, Carmen is played by Denyce Graves.

Act III

The **entr'acte music**—*light instrumental music that is performed between acts*—suggests the open countryside and the tranquility of nature. This music is in direct contrast to the tense and boisterous music that has just preceded.

ACTIVITY ▶ *Apply Your Conducting Skills*

Can you conduct the entr'acte music to the third act of *Carmen*?

Follow the section map below to conduct these 43 measures of music that precede the third act of Carmen. (Use the pattern for 4/4 meter found on page 139.)

Activity *Apply Your Conducting Skills*
Instructor's Guide, pages 251–252
CD 12 [13] Entr'acte Music, *Carmen* (2:57)

Intro-duction, *pizzicato:* 2 bars	Flute melody: 10 bars	Clarinet melody with Flute *obbligato:* 10 bars	English Horn melody: 4 bars then strings and winds, *crescendo:* 6 bars	Oboe and Strings: 4 bars + Clarinet: 1 bar + Oboe: 1 bar + Flute: 2 bars + Ending: 3 bars
2 Bars	10 Bars	10 Bars	10 Bars	11 Bars

As the curtain rises on a dark, mountainous place, a gypsy smuggler appears on the top of the rocks and gives a signal. Others come down the rocky hillside carrying large bales on their shoulders. Looking down on the village below, Don José recalls his mother. "Then you should go home. The kind of life we lead is not for you," Carmen tells him. At this, Don José's temper flares. Carmen is already growing bored.

Mercedes and Frasquita, Carmen's gypsy girlfriends, spread out cards to tell their fortunes. Lightheartedly, they learn that one finds a passionate lover, while the other marries a rich old man. Carmen, who has been watching, then asks to see what the cards hold for her. She turns up the cards. Diamonds! Spades! We hear the "fate motive." These are signs of death, and Carmen believes them.

Activity *Find the Musical Contrasts*
Instructor's Guide, page 252
CD 12 14 Trio from the Card Scene, *Carmen* (6:50)

ACTIVITY ▶ *Find the Musical Contrasts*

How does Bizet's music contrast the fortunes?

Listen to the Card Scene, a trio sung by Frasquita, Mercedes, and Carmen, to determine how the music contrasts the fortunes of Carmen with her girlfriends.

In the beginning section, sung by Frasquita and Mercedes, how does Bizet tell us that their fortunes are happy?

When Carmen takes the cards, how does Bizet use the orchestra to tell us that her fortune is death ("la mort!")?

Now Frasquita and Mercedes take up their lighthearted fortune-telling, while Carmen sings "Toujours la mort!" ("Always, death!"). Again Mercedes becomes an heiress; again Frasquita finds true love; again Carmen finds death. The trio ends "Encore!"

The band of gypsies depart, leaving Don José to guard their smuggled goods. Micaëla creeps up on the camp to find Don José at the request of his dying mother. She catches sight of Don José, but at that moment he raises his carbine and fires in her direction. Micaëla fearfully hides behind the rocks, but Don José has not fired at her. It is Escamillo who emerges unharmed and introduces himself. Don José's pleasure at their meeting quickly turns to bitter hatred when Escamillo calmly announces his mission—to meet his sweetheart, Carmen. The two engage in a vicious duel fought with knives. Carmen arrives and intercedes once more, saving Escamillo's life. Gallantly, Escamillo thanks Carmen and invites everyone to the next bullfight in Seville. He leaves the scene defiantly.

The smugglers find Micaëla and bring her from her hiding place. She asks Don José to return home, but he is not about to leave Carmen. Then Micaëla reveals that his mother is dying and wants to see him once more. Carmen contemptuously tells him to go. Don José warns Carmen that he will return, and swears that only death will ever separate them.

Act IV

The setting for Act IV is a square in Seville facing the walls of an ancient amphitheatre where bullfights are held. When the curtain rises, we see vendors hawking beverages and souvenirs. The crowd is excited, anticipating the arrival of the matadors.

ACTIVITY ▶ *Read These Rhythms*

Select one of these three rhythms and practice it quietly on a drum or tambourine, so you can accompany the opening of Act IV.

Once you have it, play your rhythm throughout the recording. Can you keep it going all the way through?

Divide the class into three groups and perform your rhythms together.

Challenge Try alternating two or even all three of these rhythms in sequence to accompany the recording.

Activity *Read These Rhythms*
Instructor's Guide, page 252
CD 13 ☐1☐ Act IV Opening Chorus, *Carmen* (1:55)

Music & Art

The sport of bullfighting is a tradition in Spain, Portugal, Mexico, and some other Latin American countries. As the painting here shows, the events were popular and full of pageantry. Bullfighters dressed quite formally and were announced with a musical fanfare. **Why would such a bullfighter as Escamillo appeal to the young Carmen?**

Ramon Casas. *The Bullfight.* 1884. Museo de la Abadia, Montserrat, Catalonia, Spain.

Music & Art
She would be attracted to his fame and the drama associated with the sport of bullfighting.

Directly

Directly following this opening, the orchestra announces the bullfighters with the "A" theme that was heard in the overture. Now the children call, "The Parade! Here they come!" The people in the street salute the brave toreadors. As each one enters proudly with his retinue, they shout cheers and insults. Escamillo, their favorite, enters last with Carmen, radiantly dressed, beside him. The music is a brassy rendition of his Toreador Song, sung by the crowd.

Carmen and Escamillo exchange brief vows of love before he enters the arena. While the crowd moves into the arena, Frasquita and Mercedes approach Carmen and warn her not to stay. Don José is hiding in the crowd. Carmen sees him and tells them she fears no one. They warn her, but she defiantly remains outside the arena alone.

Activity *What Does the Crowd Tell You?*
Instructor's Guide, page 253
TRB 20-3, *Toreador Map*
CD 13 [2] Escamillo's Entrance, *Carmen* (3:49)

ACTIVITY ▶ *What Does the Crowd Tell You?*

How does Bizet make Escamillo's entrance more important than the other toreadors?

At the start of each toreador entrance, we hear the orchestra alone on the bullfight theme ("A"). This is always followed by the reactions of the crowd. Compare those reactions.

Don José appears in a ragged shirt in pitiful contrast to Carmen. Mad with jealousy, guilt, and despair, he makes a last plea to win her. Though he promises not to harm her, horns in the orchestra betray his inner rage. Like a caged animal, the menace in him is about to tear loose.

Activity *Follow the Libretto*
Instructor's Guide, page 253
CD 13 [3] Finale of Act IV, *Carmen* (5:18)

ACTIVITY ▶ *Follow the Libretto*

Here is the final scene as it appears in the libretto with the original French (as heard on the recording) and, next to it, the English translation, line by line. To find out how the story ends, follow the French text with your ears while you read the English translation!

Libretto, Finale of Act IV	English translation
Don José Tu ne m'aimes donc plus?	Then you love me no more?
(Carmen is silent and Don José repeats)	
Tu ne m'aimes donc plus?	Then you love me no more?
Carmen Non, Je ne t'aime plus.	No, I no longer love you.
Don José Mais moi, Carmen,	But I, Carmen,
je t'aime encore;	I still love you.
Carmen hélas!	Carmen, alas,
moi je t'adore.	I adore you!

Carmen	A quoi bon tout cela? Que de mots superflus!	What good is all this? Useless words!
Don José	Carmen, je t'aime, je t'adore! Eh bien, s'il le faut, pour te plaire, Je resterai bandit, tout ce que tu voudras, Tout, tu m'entends, mais ne me quitte pas, ô ma Carmen, Souviens-toi du passé, nous nous aimions naguère.	Carmen, I love you, I adore you. Very well, if I must, to please you, I'll remain a bandit, anything you like. Anything, do you hear me, only don't leave me. Oh, my Carmen! Ah, don't you remember the past when we loved each other?
Carmen	Jamais Carmen ne cédera. Libre elle est née et libre elle mourra!	Never will Carmen give in. She was born free, and free she will die!

Chorus and Fanfares *(In the arena)*

Viva! La course est belle Sur le sable sanglant Voyez! Le taureau qu'on harcèle En bondissant s'élance, voyez! Frappé juste en plein coeur! Voyez! Voyez! Voyez! Victoire!	Viva! What a fight! On the blood-stained sand Look! The angry bull charges! They goad the bull, he leaps forward and charges, look! Now he's pierced to the heart! Look! Look! Look! Victory!

(During this chorus, Carmen and Don José have been silent,
both listening and hearing the cries of "Victory, victory."
Don José does not take his eyes off Carmen. At the end of
the chorus, Carmen takes a step toward the bullring.)

Don José	*(Placing himself before her)* Où vas-tu? . . .	Where are you going?
Carmen	Laisse-moi!	Let me pass!
Don José	Cet homme qu'on acclame. C'est ton nouvel amant!	That man they're cheering is your new lover!
Carmen	Laisse-moi!	Let me pass!
Don José	Sur mon âme. Tu ne passeras pas. Carmen, c'est moi que tu suivras!	On my soul, You will not pass, Carmen, you will follow me.
Carmen	Laisse-moi, Don José! Je ne te suivrai pas.	Leave me, Don José, I will not follow you.
Don José	Tu vas le retrouver, dis . . . tu l'aimes donc?	You will go to him, tell me . . . do you love him?

Carmen	Je l'aime! Je l'aime et devant la mort même, Je répéterai que je l'aime!	I love him! I love him, and in the face of death itself, I will repeat that I love him!

Chorus (In the arena)

	Vivat! Bravo! Victoire! Frappé juste en plein coeur, Le taureau tombe! Gloire au torero vainqueur! Victoire!	Viva! Bravo! Victory! Struck right in the heart, the bull falls! Glory to the victorious torero! Victory!
Don José	Ainsi, le salut de mon âme, Je l'aurai perdu pour que toi, Pour que tu t'en ailles, infâme! Entre ses bras, rire de moi. Non, par le sang, tu n'iras pas, Carmen, c'est moi que tu suivras!	So, I will have lost my soul for you, you wretch, so that you can go to his arms and laugh at me. No, by my blood, you will not go; Carmen, you're coming with me!
Carmen	Non! non! Jamais!	No, no! Never!
Don José	Je suis las de te menacer!	I'm tired of threatening you.
Carmen	Eh bien! Frappe-moi donc, où laisse-moi passer!	Well then, strike me now, or let me go!

Chorus (Inside the arena)

	Victoire!	Victory!
Don José	Pour la derniére fois, démon, Veux-tu me suivre?	For the very last time, devil, will you come with me?
Carmen	Non! non! Cette bague autrefois tu me l'avais donnée, tiens!	No! No! Here, this ring you once gave me, take it!

(She flings it at him.)

Don José (Drawing his dagger) Eh bien, damnée!		All right, you devil!

(Don José rushes toward Carmen. She attempts to escape, but he catches up with her, stabs her, and she falls as fanfares come from the arena.)

Chorus	Toréador, en garde, Et songe bien, oui, songe en combattant Qu'un œil noir te regarde Et que l'amour t'attend.	Toreador, on guard, And remember, yes, remember as you fight That dark eyes are watching you And that love awaits!

(Carmen falls and dies. Don José, distracted, falls on his knees beside her as the crowd comes out of the arena.)

Don José	Vous pouvez m'arrêter . . .	You can arrest me . . .
	C'est moi qui l'ai tuée!	It is I who have killed her!
	O Carmen!	Carmen!
	Ma Carmen adorée!	My beloved Carmen!

The Message

The story of Carmen is a good example of a "love triangle," a basic plot that can take many forms. In this particular example, two men seek the love of one woman. Don José is a man caught in a fierce internal struggle between the forces of good and evil. His love for Carmen compels him to betray his promise to his mother and sacrifice his loyalty to his country. As Don José's status is reduced from lowly corporal to an outlaw member of a band of gypsies, Carmen's status improves as she becomes the sweetheart of the popular bullfight hero Escamillo. Carmen is more interested in the game of conquering her male idols than in keeping them. She casts Don José aside with contempt, caring nothing for his feelings or the honor he has given up for her. The result is tragic for both of them. His uncontrolled passion and her stubborn selfishness lead to her death and his ruin. The message: The jealousy and madness of rejected love can lead to murder and self-destruction.

In Act IV, set in a public square in Seville at the entrance to the bullfight arena, the love triangle between Carmen, Don José, and Escamillo is finally resolved—tragically. In Michigan Opera Theatre's 1981 production, Don José is played by Barry Busse, Carmen by Victoria Vergara.

PROFILE

The Three Tenors— Domingo, Carreras, Pavarotti

The extraordinarily rich and powerful voices of the musicians known as the Three Tenors has done much to revive interest in opera around the world. Each a star in his own right, José Carreras, Plácido Domingo, and Luciano Pavarotti first performed together in Rome in 1990 on the eve of the World Cup Soccer Championship finals. The recording of this event became the best-selling classical concert recording of all time.

Carreras and Domingo were both born in Spain. Carreras made his debut in the early 1970s and soon became well established in the opera world. Domingo sang his first major roles in the early 1960s and went on to become one of the world's leading dramatic tenors. Italian-born Pavarotti made his debut in the early 1960s. His resonant voice has brought him lasting success in opera houses around the world.

Following their highly acclaimed 1990 concert, the Three Tenors did not perform together for four years. Yet after another highly successful concert in 1994 in conjunction with the World Cup Championships, the three went on tour, performing on most of the world's continents. The World Cup final brought them together again in Paris in 1998.

Plácido Domingo
1941–

José Carreras
1946–

Luciano Pavarotti
1935–

SUMMARY

Musical theatre can be a powerfully expressive form. By opening a curtain to see ourselves and our human delights and dilemmas, we feel our own human situation more clearly, and we learn to empathize with other humans about their situations. Musical theatre gives us a way to dream and listen to our feelings. It is a way that we indulge in our own foibles and celebrate our triumphs.

More than anything, musical theatre lets us feel all the emotions of life. It does not appeal to our intellect as much as to our inner, soulful being. Because it can speak so personally, it can move us as only humans can be moved. It can cause us to feel. It can put us in touch with a most important element of our being—our emotions. That is an essential part of why music is important in our lives.

Complete answers for the Chapter 20 Review are found in the Instructor's Guide, page 253.

Building Music Vocabulary

On a sheet of paper, write the term from the list that best matches each description below.

- (6) absolute pitch
- (2) aria
- (7) entr'acte music
- (1) grand opera
- (5) opéra comique
- (4) recitative
- (3) seguidilla

1. A type of music drama in which everything is sung.
2. A song.
3. A type of Spanish dance, or the music for such a dance.
4. A speechlike style of singing.
5. A type of opera that uses some spoken dialogue.
6. The ability to recognize and reproduce pitches exactly.
7. Light, instrumental music performed between acts of an opera.

Reviewing Music Facts

Answer each question in a complete sentence.

8. During what century did the first examples of opera appear?
9. What are the differences between opéra comique and grand opera?
10. How did *Carmen* break tradition with the usual opéra comique?
11. What dance song does Carmen use to escape from Don José?
12. What is the purpose of the "fate motive"?
13. During the parade scene in the last act, what is the music that greets Escamillo's entrance?

Thinking It Through

On a sheet of paper, write your responses to the following:

14. **Identify** Name the creators who work together to make a successful opera production.
15. **Analyze** Why do you think the spoken dialogue of Carmen was later set in musical recitative form?
16. **Apply** Bizet combines the tragic music of Carmen and Don José's last scene with the joyous music of the offstage bullfight crowd. How does this contrast add to the drama of the final moments of the opera?

Making the Connection

Social Studies Find out more about gypsies, their origins and lifestyles. Then use what you have learned to discuss whether Bizet's portrayal of Spanish gypsy life was accurate.

Theatre In groups, create a brief "opera" scene to present to the class. Use recitatives (which may be improvised) instead of spoken lines. Your scene may be funny, sad, or filled with action, but every line must be sung.

 You can learn more about *Carmen* and the Metropolitan Opera at **www.glencoe.com/sec/music**

Answers to Chapter 20 Review

8. During the 1600s.
9. Grand opera was sung throughout; opéra comique had some spoken dialogue. Grand operas were often tragic; opéra comique had comical sections and usually a happy ending.
10. By having a tragic story.
11. The seguidilla.
12. It reminds the audience that Carmen's fate is a tragic one.
13. The theme from the "Toreador Song" that he sang in Act II.

14. Creators include the composer, librettist, performers, and the people who create scenery, costumes, and lighting.
15. So that the opera could be sung throughout, making it a grand opera rather than an opéra comique.
16. The contrast makes onstage drama more intense and frightening. The offstage cheering and singing make the scene more realistic.

440

CHAPTER 21

Film

Music has been an essential part of motion pictures from their earliest days. During the silent era (1896–1927), live music gave the moving images sound and life. Later, when sound became an integral part of the motion picture, music added to the dramatic impact. Like the acting, the sets, and the costumes, it became an expressive force that enhanced the storytelling. Should the moviegoer hear a movie score? Yes—being conscious of the music and responsive to it adds to the total conception of cinema. In the same way that recognizing the technical work of the camera or appreciating effective acting increases our under-standing of film, music completes the picture.

*In Titanic (1997, 20ᵗʰ Century Fox/Paramount), composer James Horner wrote a dramatic score that served as the backdrop to the love story of two young people, Rose and Jack, who fall in love aboard the doomed ocean liner. For this work Horner was awarded an Academy Award for Best Original Dramatic Score. **Can you name any songs from this movie?***

Caption answer Most students will identify "My Heart Will Go On," written by Horner and Will Jennings and awarded Best Song. Other titles include "Southampton," "Rose," Leaving Port," "Hard to Starboard," "The Sinking," and "Death of *Titanic.*"

Objectives

By completing this chapter, you will:
- Understand the development of sound as a part of the storytelling art of motion pictures.
- Understand the role of the film composer and the purposes that music serves in film.
- Become familiar with the work of a number of film composers.
- Be able to explain how appropriate music enhances visual images and gives a film continuity.

Vocabulary

background music
dubbing
incidental music
mag track
scoring
soundtrack
spot

Musicians to Meet

Samuel Barber
Alan Menken
John Williams

The Beginnings

Thomas Edison and his assistant William Dickson invented the Kinetoscope in 1889. The Kinetoscope, which contained 50 feet of film that moved, was a simple device that an individual viewer operated by turning a crank. The "peep show" soon became a popular form of entertainment in the penny arcades of the time. This was the beginning of the motion picture.

In 1896 Edison presented his latest invention, the Vitascope, a machine that projected the Kinetoscope's images on a wall. The Vitascope changed what had been a private experience into a public one. Audiences were soon flocking to storefront "nickelodeons" to enjoy this amazing novelty. For all the preceding thousands of years of human history, people had never been able to record the way they looked and moved in such a realistic way. And what did they see? The brief films showed circus acts, dances, boxing bouts, comic scenes—snippets of this and that. The flickering scenes were usually accompanied by the continuous sound of a piano.

However, the novelty of seeing moving pictures began to wear thin. The medium had to be used in a new way, or the public would lose interest. The creativity of Edwin S. Porter came to the rescue. In 1903 he

EDISON STEREO-PROJECTING KINETOSCOPE

Music & HISTORY

This poster, dating from 1902, shows a later generation of the Kinetoscope (a moving-picture machine, also known as the Vitascope) that Thomas Edison (upper right) invented in 1896. **Can you guess the origins of the word "Kinetoscope"?**

Music & History
Kinetic=movement; scope=to watch.

produced, directed, and wrote *The Great Train Robbery*, an 11-minute film that told a complete and exciting story, the first successful Western. This was the beginning of film as an art form, a medium of human expression.

It is important to remember that the images in a film are two dimensional. Images on the screen are a theatrically contrived "world" that has been edited and spliced together. At first this world was silent. Although the phonograph had been invented by Edison in 1877, there was still no way to coordinate sound and film.

ACTIVITY ▶ *Trace the Influence on an Overture*

Where did the idea of using music in films come from?

Listen to the overture from *A Midsummer Night's Dream* (1826) by Felix Mendelssohn (1809–1847). This was written as incidental music for the Shakespeare play. (The term **incidental music** refers to *music that occurs in connection with, but is less important than, the drama it serves.*) What is the function of this music when it is played prior to the theatrical performance?

Listen to the overture from the musical *Mame* (1966) by Jerry Herman (b. 1933). What is the function of the overture in an opera or musical?

Incidental music and overtures had been in vogue long before the advent of films. Can you conjecture (guess, theorize) what influence they might have had on early filmmakers?

Music for Silent Films

There probably never was such a thing as a "silent" film. Long before films had sound, they were accompanied by music. At first, the music was provided by a pianist or an organist in the theater who improvised a musical score on the spot. These musical performers had to watch the screen intently, size up the mood being portrayed on the screen, then quickly adjust the music accordingly. The trick was to marry the image with appropriate mood music. These performers had to have a large repertoire of music of many different moods at their fingertips.

In film, the visual image is dominant. Film takes advantage of the stronger sense of the eye over the ear. Because the visual image dominates, the music is adjusted to go with it. The character of the music, its

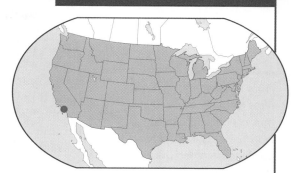

MUSIC in the WORLD

LOS ANGELES is one of the largest metropolitan areas in the United States, and its name is linked with the film and recording industries. It was here that the technology and talent that connects sound and film began. *What song(s) do you identify with a movie? How did that music affect your enjoyment of the film?*

Music in the World
Although responses will vary, encourage students to discuss the quality of the music they identify and its role in telling the story, creating mood, enhancing drama, and contributing to the film's continuity.

Activity *Trace the Influence on an Overture*
Instructor's Guide, pages 255–256
CD 13 4 Overture, *A Midsummer Night's Dream* (4:59)
CD 13 5 Overture, *Mame* (4:01)

form, its length, and its loudness all must fit the image. As early as 1909, the Edison Company introduced cue sheets to help the musicians plan appropriate music to go with the Edison films. The live music added an immediacy and life to the film that audiences found appealing.

In silent films, music served the practical purpose of covering the clatter of the movie projector as well as the chatter of audiences and noise from outside the makeshift theaters. Later, the projectors were housed in soundproof booths so that the audience was not distracted by the mechanical noise. New theaters were soundproofed, and audiences became quieter and better behaved. The expressive function of music, far more than its practical value, assured its continued role in the development of the art of film.

Erno Rapée, a pioneer composer of scores for silent films during the 1920s, compiled a book of *Motion Picture Moods for Pianists and Organists* that was published in 1924. The portion of the page shown on page 445 shows a piece he suggested as appropriate for the firefighting scenes that were so popular in silent films. While playing this music, the performer could scan the column along the side of the music to find music suitable to the next mood on the screen.

From the beginning, silent films were accompanied by music. At first, a pianist watched the film and played appropriate mood music to accompany the images. The music became increasingly important and elaborate until, in the 1920s, the large theaters in New York, Chicago, and Los Angeles accompanied the silent films with a live symphony orchestra of 80 to 100 musicians.

Hurry No. 2

Otto Langey

Copyright © 1915 (Renewed). G. Schirmer, Inc. Used by Permission.
International copyright Secured. All Rights Reserved.

Prior to Rapée's book, musicians had to develop a vast repertoire of music, in many different moods, that they played by ear or had committed to memory. Otherwise they had to leaf frantically through a stack of musical scores with one hand while they improvised a transitional passage with the other. The real talent, of course, was being able to match the moods of the music with the visual images as the film went along. These musicians seldom had the opportunity to preview the film in advance, and films changed every few days. Rapée's book gave the pianist over 200 themes organized in 52 moods.

During the silent movie era, the Keystone Comedy Company produced a series of films featuring policemen known as the Keystone Kops. Their slapstick comedy, crazy antics, and wild chases were accompanied by wild piano music that added to the humor and excitement of the moment.

Activity *Assess the Role of Music in Silent Films*
Instructor's Guide, page 256
CD 13 6 "Hurry No. 2" (1:08)

ACTIVITY ▶ *Assess the Role of Music in Silent Films*

How was music used to accompany silent films?

Listen to "Hurry No. 2," a piano piece used with firefighting scenes in silent films, then discuss the following:
1. What makes this music appropriate for a firefighting scene?
2. What might this music add to the silent visual images?
3. What was the role of music in these early film theaters?

In 1915, the use of a live orchestra that accompanied American producer D. W. Griffith's silent film *The Birth of a Nation* showed the possibilities of the aural-visual partnership. Every sound was carefully matched to the visual image. Themes selected from operas and symphonies were combined with original music by Joseph Breil, including tom-tom beats that evoked Africa and transitions that connected the various themes. Singlehandedly, this film established the symphony orchestra as the ideal sound in the picture palace.

As silent films became more popular during the 1920s, the live musical accompaniment became more elaborate. The two seemed to prosper together. Music became an important part of the art of film presentation, and as the presentation improved, audiences grew. By the mid-1920s, symphony orchestras of 90 to 100 musicians, along with a "Mighty Wurlitzer" organ, were being used in large New York theaters to accompany the otherwise silent films. During this period, **scoring,** *composing music expressly for a film,* became the standard practice. The composer now assumed responsibility for marrying image with music.

Activity *Analyze a Film Score*
Instructor's Guide, page 256
Music! VHS Segment 11, *The Stranger* (excerpt)

ACTIVITY ▶ *Analyze a Film Score*

Watch the video excerpt from *Film Scores: The Music of the Movies,* and answer the following questions:

1. What does Bronislaw Kaper's music add to the scene in the film *The Stranger* (1946) in which Loretta Young climbs the tower?
2. Why was music added to silent films?
3. What makes motion pictures an art of many arts?

The silent motion picture brought a wholly new musical medium into existence. Although film music was new, it was an extension of a very old tradition. Dramatic presentations had often used "incidental" music at the start and during scene changes. This music established the general mood of the play, much as overtures and entr'acte music do in opera.

There is evidence that Greek dramas were presented with musical interludes. Medieval religious dramas that related the biblical stories to audiences who were illiterate and, therefore, unable to read Scriptures, used music as a part of the storytelling. In the seventeenth century, Shakespeare's dramas were often accompanied by incidental music. Film music operates in much the same way. Like program music and music for opera and ballet, it is music in the service of telling, showing, and feeling.

The "Talkies"

Edison and other inventors worked for many years to find a way to synchronize sound with the motion picture. While sound reproduction existed as a separate device, no way had been found to synchronize the sound with moving images. How could motion picture images and the sounds that went with them be recorded and reproduced together? That technological problem was mind-boggling in the 1920s.

The first attempt at synchronizing sound and image was accomplished through a phonographic machine called the Vitaphone. It was used to create the first talking film, *The Jazz Singer* (1927, Warner Bros.). Audiences were stunned to see Al Jolson actually singing, dancing, and speaking. Here for the first time was an image of real life captured and immortalized. In "talking" films, the lifelike presence of sounds and dialogue helped to create a sense of realism. But the Vitaphone process took careful coordination during each showing. It was not a satisfactory solution.

The answer was the film **soundtrack,** *a strip along the film to the side of the visual image that contained visual representations of the sound* (an alternative to the grooves in a record or the electronic signals on a

Caption answer
Dialogue and music added a deeper level of meaning and understanding to the images. Background music helped shape the story and portray emotions.

Al Jolson actually sang to his mother (played by Eugenie Bessemer) in the first talking film, The Jazz Singer, *in 1927. Images and sound were synchronized by the newly developed Vitaphone sound-on-disc system.* **In what way(s) do you think sound changed how people enjoyed film?**

Movie palaces that were built across America during the 1920s gave the art of the motion picture respectability. The Ohio Theater in Columbus, built in 1928 and meticulously restored, shows the Spanish Baroque-style opulence and craftsmanship that made going to the movies a fantasy. Designed by Thomas Lamb, it lives on today as a performing arts center.

compact disc). This "track" could be retranslated into sound by the mechanism in the movie projector.

When the soundtrack was invented in the late 1920s, there was no way to include musical background. At first, only the talking was recorded on the soundtrack—hence the name "talkies." It was several years before the soundtrack for speaking could be overlaid with continuous musical background. Therefore, the early sound films still had live music provided in the theater.

By 1933, improvements in technology permitted the background music to be included on the soundtrack along with the voices and other sounds. Now music did not have to be used throughout the film as a way to fill the vast silence. It could be used when it was needed. This innovation led immediately to the end of live orchestral accompaniments.

The Process

Certain steps must be followed when a composer creates music for a film. First, the composer views the film after it has been edited and is considered to be in its final form or "cut." Then the producer and director help **spot** the music: that is, *to determine which scenes should have music.* This may take several screenings. Good film music is used sparingly.

Since a film is usually near completion at the time it is scored, there is very limited time for a composer to complete the scoring. Composers generally view all the sequences in a film that are to be scored to get a feel for them before they begin sketching musical ideas. Film composers must write rapidly. They must be versatile in expressing a range of moods.

After the film has been scored, the music is recorded while the conductor watches the filmed sequence. Usually, the composer conducts the recording session. This assures that the music will be synchronized with the images as the composer intended. Until the digital age, the music was recorded on magnetic track or **mag track**, *music recorded on film coated with an oxide surface like sound tape.* Mag tracks move at exactly the same rate of speed—24 frames per second.

The final step in the process is **dubbing,** *putting all the elements of sound—dialogue, sound effects, and music—onto one soundtrack.* During this process, the sound level of the music is adjusted to the other sounds. Film music is a carefully crafted element and is integral to the total artistic statement of the picture.

A Film Composer Speaks
by Aaron Copland, American composer

The next time you settle yourself comfortably into a seat at the neighborhood picture house don't forget to take off your ear-muffs. . . . Millions of moviegoers take the musical accompaniment to a dramatic film so much for granted that five minutes after the termination of a picture they couldn't tell you whether they had heard music or not. . . . But it's the spectator, so absorbed in the dramatic action that he fails to take in the background music, who wants to know whether he is missing anything. The answer is bound up with the degree of your general musical perception. It is the degree to which you are aurally minded that will determine how much pleasure you may derive by absorbing the background musical accompaniment as an integral part of the combined impression made by the film.

"Tip to Moviegoers: Take Off Those Ear-Muffs," from *The New York Times Magazine.* Copyright © November 6, 1949. *The New York Times Company.* Reprinted By Permission.

Soundtracks have increasingly become a way for composers and performers to reach a wide audience. Sometimes the popularity of the score or soundtrack might outlast that of the film or stage production. **Are you familiar with the music soundtracks shown here? Can you name others that are memorable to you?**

Caption answer
Encourage students to identify a wide range of songs that became popular because of their connection with a film or theatre show.

Composer John Williams was awarded an Academy Award for his original score for the 1977 movie Star Wars. *This award recognized the contribution that his music made to the film's success. Additionally, the music composed for this soundtrack became popular apart from the movie and was often played in orchestral concerts.*

The Purposes

Film music serves a number of purposes. In a musical film, it is a central part of the storytelling. In *Saturday Night Fever* (1977, Paramount), for example, John Travolta and Karen Gorney dance to music that is an integral part of the visual telling of the story. Similarly, the film *Star Wars* (1977, 20th Century Fox) has a considerable amount of music as part of the plot and dramatic action.

In most films, however, music may be purely **background music,** *music that has no visual or logical source.* It may be a part of the action on the screen, such as the music that is playing on a car radio while a character is driving. In these films music serves three main purposes: to establish mood, to enhance the drama, and to give the film continuity.

Music Establishes the Basic Mood

More, perhaps, than any of the other film elements, music points out clearly the time and place and the feeling of what the story is about. Music accomplishes this by conveying a particular mood or by evoking time and culture.

Music also evokes the spirit of the picture. It shows an audience the essence of what the film is—its heart. It may do this by announcing the film's essential theme. Music reassures the audience that they are in tune with the images, that they are getting the message.

ACTIVITY ▶ *Label the Mood*

Determine how opening music sets the mood and spirit of a film.

Without seeing the visual images, you will hear musical examples that are used in the opening of a motion picture to set the mood of the film. In each case, try to characterize the music with descriptive words selected from the list below or other words of your own.

serious	mid-1700s	out-of-tune piano
urgent	late 1800s	orchestral
majestic	the future	chimes
exciting	lively	harpsichord
lofty	heroic	religious
dramatic	comic	spacious
stately	romantic	

MIDI TECHNOLOGY OPTION

- **Music with MIDI** Use a MIDI program to compose a film score. Explore the ability of music to enhance drama, establish character, and add psychological insight in a film.

Activity *Label the Mood*
Instructor's Guide, page 257
CD 13 [7] Opening Music, *An American in Paris* (1:37)
CD 13 [8] Opening Music, *Star Wars* (2:02)
CD 13 [9] Opening Prelude, *Ben-Hur* (2:00)

Technology Option
Use Project 21 in the *MIDI Activities* binder.

Music Enhances the Drama

If music can establish the general setting and mood of the film, it can also enhance the drama. In a mystery, music can add to the suspense. In a story that tugs at the heartstrings, music can add to the emotional intensity, and in a comedy, music can add a lighthearted touch.

Music also enhances the drama in three quite specific ways. Used well, it helps establish character, it gives psychological insight into a particular character or the meaning of an event, and it intensifies the overall impact. Film composer Ernest Gold believes the music must put a quality in the picture that was not there before. He gives this illustration: A man is refused a job and walks back to his apartment in a New York neighborhood. The music could play to his emotion, conveying the feeling of despair. Far better, Gold says, the composer could play rock and roll on a radio in one of the apartments the man passes. In this way the music comments on the indifference of the neighbors to his plight. That solution is more powerful, more telling, and more imaginative.

PROFILE

*John Williams
American Composer
1932–*

John Williams

John Williams may be the most successful film composer ever. His background could not have been more perfectly tailored to prepare him for his career. Born in New York City, Williams' father was a jazz drummer. Growing up he learned to play piano, trombone, trumpet, and clarinet. At age 16 his family moved to Los Angeles, where his father freelanced for film studio orchestras. Williams studied piano and composition before being drafted into the United States Air Force. Even this experience was musically valuable because he conducted and arranged music for service bands.

Williams began writing film scores in the 1960s but really made it big in the 1970s. He has written spectacular scores for blockbuster hits such as *Jaws, Star Wars, E. T.: The Extra-Terrestrial, Raiders of the Lost Ark, Home Alone,* and *Schindler's List.* Many of his scores have earned Academy Awards. Williams has also conducted the Boston Pops and London Symphony Orchestras.

You may wish to use "Create Music for a Film Segment" at this time. Lesson plans for the activity are found on page 261 in the Instructor's Guide.

Music helps establish character. By adding an aura of feeling around a player, music can reveal the nature of that person. It can suggest the affection of one character for another. It can also convey what is going on in the mind of a character, even though it may not show on the face.

Music helps the viewer attach certain emotions to people and events as they recur throughout a film story. Like the "hook" that organizes a pop tune, or the melodic motive that recurs and gives coherence to most classical music, musical themes in film are repeated to recall important associations. When such themes recur, they help us remember what has happened earlier in the film. By attaching the theme to a character, situation, or object when it is introduced, we tend to set up an association that the theme recalls when it is replayed.

Some films have a central musical theme that is attached to a character and follows that person throughout. In his score for *Superman* (1978, Warner), composer John Williams created a main title theme that we immediately identify with the hero:

Similarly, the "Tara" theme by composer Max Steiner in *Gone with the Wind* establishes Scarlett's love for the land and the strength that she derives from it. Steiner gave this theme many orchestrations and tempos to convey Scarlett's moods. The film is based on Margaret Mitchell's novel about life in the South during the American Civil War.

ACTIVITY ▶ *Compare Themes*

What qualities make the theme music appropriate to represent Superman and Scarlett?

A. Listen to the main theme composer John Williams created for Superman and write down qualities of the (1) melody, (2) rhythm, and (3) orchestration that convey the idea of Superman. Is this melody (below) conjunct (moving from one scale degree to the next) or disjunct (moving by intervals larger than a second)?

While maintaining a steady beat, tap this rhythm.

B. How does Scarlett O'Hara's music in the film *Gone with the Wind* convey her character and mood? ("Tara" Theme 1)

When Scarlett (Vivien Leigh) returns to the plantation to find it in shambles, the "Tara" theme conveys her feelings. What does it tell us and how? ("Tara" Theme 2)

At the end of the film, Scarlett's child has died and her husband Rhett Butler (Clark Gable) has left her. She realizes too late that she loves him. Again the "Tara" theme enters to tell us how she reacts. What does it tell us and how? ("Tara" Theme 3)

C. How does Scarlett's music compare with Superman's? What are the similarities and differences that make each theme work?

Activity   Compare Themes
Instructor's Guide, page 258
CD 13 ⑩ Theme, *Superman* (4:23)
CD 13 ⑪ "Tara" Theme, *Gone with the Wind* (3:16)
CD 13 ⑫ "Tara" Theme (Scarlett returns to Tara), *Gone with the Wind* (2:23)
CD 13 ⑬ "Tara" Theme (Rhett's departure), *Gone with the Wind* (2:09)

Use section A. in the *Music Theory Handbook* to review beat and meter.

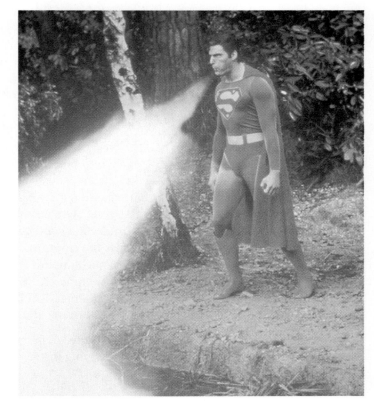

Superman, played by Christopher Reeve, uses his superpowers in the 1978 film about this famed comic-book hero. The music in this film, composed by John Williams, enhances the drama by influencing the audience how to react emotionally to what is on the screen.

Music gives psychological insight. As viewers of a film, we generally accept the unreality of film background music. We seldom ask where the background music is coming from. It is part of the unreality that puts us in the frame of mind to accept the fantasy of what we are viewing. Music adds to the psychological impact, whether it is offscreen (background) or a part of the onscreen action. In either case it functions to complement the action and reinforce its emotional intent.

In *Platoon* (1986, Hemdale), Oliver Stone's film about the Vietnam War, *Adagio for Strings* by American composer Samuel Barber

(1910–1981) is used as background music in a number of scenes. The music is particularly appropriate for the scene in which American soldiers enter a Vietnamese village, interrogate the villagers, and burn their houses. Scored for stringed instruments, the music gives a heart-wrenching feeling of sadness. There is a notable use of tones that conflict and are close, creating a sense of anguish and tension.

Because film music is important to a story, members of the Academy of Motion Pictures Arts and Sciences recognize one original song each year to receive their highest award—the Oscar. Shown here are James Horner, Celine Dion, and Will Jennings receiving this award for "My Heart Will Go On" from Titanic *(1997).*

Activity *Examine Background Music*
Instructor's Guide, pages 258–259
CD 13 ☐14 *Adagio for Strings*
(9:55)

ACTIVITY ▶ *Examine Background Music*

What qualities in background music make it work well with a scene?

Listen to this soundtrack music. The scene is the burning of the village from *Platoon*. The music is American composer Samuel Barber's *Adagio for Strings*, which he composed in 1938.

As you listen, describe on paper the characteristics of this music that make it a good choice as background music for this scene. Discuss the emotional intent.

Learn to sing this melody (right) expressively using the syllable "nah." *Cantando* (kahn-THAN-do) means to sing in a smooth and flowing manner. Is this melody conjunct or disjunct? How does the tempo add to the emotional effect?

Challenge Ask a member of your class to perform this melody on a wind or string instrument to accompany your singing.

PROFILE

Samuel Barber

Samuel Barber
American Composer
1910–1981

American composer Samuel Barber was born in West Chester, Pennsylvania, in 1910. He entered the Curtis Institute of Music in Philadelphia at the age of 14 and graduated in 1932. He received the Prix de Rome in 1935, which allowed him to compose at the American Academy in Rome. He also received the Pulitzer Prize in 1958 for his opera *Vanessa* and again in 1963 for *Piano Concerto*.

While other twentieth-century composers were experimenting with alternatives to the traditional tonal system, Barber found success with a lyric and dramatic style from the late nineteenth century based upon harmony. Like Johannes Brahms, Barber did not create any new style or technique. Instead, he wrote beautiful pieces that bore his own personal style. "I write what I feel," he stated. "It is said that I have no style at all, but that doesn't matter. I just go on doing my thing. I believe this takes a certain courage." Some of his popular works include *Adagio for Strings, Dover Beach, Prayers of Kierkegaard,* and *Knoxville: Summer of 1915.*

Adagio for Strings, Op. 11

Samuel Barber

Music intensifies the drama in a film. Music sets us up for the action and deepens our emotional involvement. It may foreshadow a sinister event by announcing a threatening mood. It may increase our excitement by helping to drive the pace of the action forward. It may give an emotional charge to what is happening. In these ways, music can trigger our anticipation, heighten our sense of suspense, urge our emotional reaction, and strengthen the climactic moments.

In the "chase" that opens the film *Midnight Express* (1978, Columbia), composer Giorgio Moroder uses this ostinato pattern almost throughout:

An offbeat drum gives urgency and added character to this largely electronic score. This is the true story of a 22-year-old American named Billy Hayes who was subjected to the horrors of a Turkish prison during a lengthy imprisonment, beyond the power of the U.S. government or his parents. Hayes not only survived, but he also triumphed.

Activity *Play a "Chase" Ostinato*
Instructor's Guide, page 259

ACTIVITY ▶ *Play a "Chase" Ostinato*

Working in small groups, learn to perform the ostinato pattern (above) that composer Giorgio Moroder wrote for the opening of the film *Midnight Express*.

Discuss why the ostinato pattern is appropriate for a chase. What does it suggest about life in prison?

Music Gives Film Continuity

Music is often used to give film coherence, a sense that it is one continuous, unified flow of action from beginning to end. This quality of connectedness between the beginning, the middle, and the end is conveyed partly by the consistency in the style of music. The return of the opening theme at the end of the film is a commonly used device to tie the film into one statement. The "Tara" theme in *Gone with the Wind* at the beginning and end is an example. A consistency in the style of the music gives the film a feeling that it is cut from one piece of cloth. At the end of a film, music can also give a sense of finality. We know it is over by the event that is pictured and also by the conclusion that the music reaches.

The burning of Atlanta and the flight of Scarlett O'Hara and Rhett Butler is one of many memorable scenes in the American film classic Gone with the Wind *(1939), set during the Civil War. In his musical score, composer Max Steiner used a symphony orchestra to intensify the emotions and give the film a sense of continuity.*

ACTIVITY ▶ *Find the Elements of Suspense*

Listen to the music from these eight scenes from the film *Psycho* (Universal, 1960). While you listen, write brief descriptions about the music that you hear during these scenes:

1. "Prelude"—The opening with the titles.
2. "Temptation"—The money is on the bed, and Marion wonders if she should take it to the bank or not.
3. "Flight"—Marion is driving away and is seen by her boss.
4. "The Rainstorm"—Marion hears voices, then sees the lights of the Bates Motel.
5. "The Madhouse"—Norman says, "You mean a madhouse?"
6. "The Peephole"—Norman watches Marion through the wall.
7. "Finale"—the famous murder scene in the shower. Later, face-to-face with the killer (Norman dressed as his mother).
8. The chord at the end.

   How does the music establish a sense of continuity and coherence?

Activity *Find the Elements of Suspense*
Instructor's Guide, pages 259–260
CD 13 ⒂ "Prelude," *Psycho* (1:59)
CD 13 ⒃ "Temptation," *Psycho* (1:04)
CD 13 ⒄ "Flight," *Psycho* (1:12)
CD 13 ⒅ "The Rainstorm," *Psycho* (1:27)
CD 13 ⒆ "The Madhouse," *Psycho* (2:09)
CD 13 ⒇ "The Peephole," *Psycho* (1:10)
CD 13 ㉑ "Finale," *Psycho* (2:57)
CD 13 ㉒ Chord at the End, *Psycho* (0:17)

PROFILE

Alan Menken

Born in New Rochelle, New York, Alan Menken majored in music at New York University in New York City. Not long after graduation, he was chosen by the already experienced lyricist and playwright Howard Ashman to collaborate on stage musicals. One of their most highly acclaimed theatre productions was the off-Broadway show called *Little Shop of Horrors* (1982).

Yet, Menken and Ashman achieved their greatest successes in film scores and songs. They helped revive the American movie musical with the Disney animated hits *The Little Mermaid* (1989) and *Aladdin* (1992, shown here). After Ashman's death in 1991, Menken continued to compose for theatre, film, and television. Some recent works include the musical version of Charles Dickens's *A Christmas Carol*, the Disney movie *Pocahontas,* and the television miniseries *Lincoln*.

Alan Menken
American Composer
1949–

SUMMARY

In films, music adds to the meaning of the visual image in several important ways. The mood of the music helps to establish the spirit of the film. By touching our feelings, music enhances the dramatic effect of a film by sharpening character, giving us psychological insight, and intensifying our emotional reactions. Music also gives a film continuity, making us feel that the film is one statement from beginning to end.

Music adds to a film's meaning and impact. It is one of the ways that a film conveys its message. Change the music, and we alter that meaning and impact. Music does this in spite of the fact that, alone, it is not as specific as dialogue in what it says. It is one of the expressive forces that make the cinematic image a commanding storytelling medium.

Complete answers for the Chapter 21 Review are found in the Instructor's Guide, page 262.

Building Music Vocabulary

On a sheet of paper, write the term from the list that best matches each description below.

(7) background music   (6) scoring
(4) dubbing   (1) soundtrack
(5) incidental music   (2) spot
(3) mag track

1. A strip along the side of the film containing a visual representation of the sound.
2. To determine what sections of a film need music.
3. Music recorded on film coated with an oxide surface like sound tape.
4. Putting all sound elements together on one soundtrack.
5. Music that occurs in connection with a drama.
6. Composing music expressly for a film.
7. Music that has no visual or logical source.

Reviewing Music Facts

Answer each question in a complete sentence.
8. How was music added to showings of silent films?
9. What is the name of the earliest sound movie with music?
10. Why were early sound movies still accompanied by live music?
11. What is the purpose of attaching a recurring theme to a particular character or emotion?
12. What famous piece of classical music is used in the movie *Platoon* to express sadness and anguish?
13. How can music contribute to the coherence and continuity of a movie?

Thinking It Through

On a sheet of paper, write your responses to the following:
14. **Analyze** How can music establish the time and place in which a movie's action takes place?
15. **Explain** How did dubbing change the way music was used for films?
16. **Apply** How does the "Tara" theme in *Gone with the Wind* tie the film together?

Making the Connection

Science Find out more about how early movie-makers were able to combine voices and music on a soundtrack. Compare what you have learned to what you know or learned in Chapter 17 about current sound recording technology.

Theatre Listen to the soundtrack of a popular film and pay particular attention to the lyrics and mood of each musical selection. Use what you have learned about music in film to explain how the music gives continuity to the film.

 Discover more about silent films and film composer John Williams at **www.glencoe.com/sec/music**

You may wish to use Assessment Master 7, Unit Seven Test, in the TRB

Chapters 19 and 20 Project
Instructor's Guide, page 263

Chapters 19 and 20 Project

▶ *Compare and Contrast the Musical and Opera*

Make a list of the similarities and differences between the Broadway musical and opera.

To discover what is similar and different about these musical forms, compare what you have learned about the Broadway musical *Carousel* with what you have learned about the opera *Carmen*.

For example, one similarity is that both generally include dance. One difference is that the Broadway musical is usually performed in a theater, while an opera generally requires a larger stage, usually an opera house. How many other similarities and differences can you find?

Today, the difference in style between a musical and opera are becoming less distinct. In the musical Sunday in the Park with George, *for example, American composer Stephen Sondheim sets the text to continuous music throughout, as in grand opera. Notice how well the set designer captured the detail and the feeling of the painting by Georges Seurat, shown on the next page.*

Unit Seven *Encore!*

A Divine Diva

Meet Denyce Graves, a young superstar on the stages of the world's leading opera houses. *The Washington Post* proclaims that "she is almost too good to be true—a vital artist, a beautiful woman, a regal presence." Critics in Europe and the United States have called her the best mezzo soprano to sing the role of Carmen—ever!

▶ Describe a Voice

Do you know that no two voices are identical? The human voice—its timbre, inflection, and range in both speech and song—is an aural thumbprint. Your voice makes you unique. Yet, how would you describe someone's voice, even if you know it well?

Critics around the world have used many adjectives to describe the singing voice of Denyce Graves. Some of these, taken from concert reviews, are listed below.

big	clear	full	resonant
burnished	deep	hearty	rich
classic	dusky	lush	soulful
clean	earthy	magnificent	warm

As you listen to Denyce sing a cappella the spiritual "This Little Light of Mine," write down three new adjectives that describe her voice. After hearing Denyce sing, can you tell why some musicians call the human voice an instrument?

▶ *Find the Tessitura*

As you listen to Denyce Graves sing the well-known spiritual "Swing Low, Sweet Chariot," use your ears to find the tessitura—the general range or "lie" of a vocal part or song.

Hint: She begins on A' (above middle C) and goes to F' (a major 3rd lower). How much higher than the A' and how much lower than the F' does she sing? Is this within the typical range of a mezzo soprano? Use the notation of ranges shown below to help you decide.

Vocal Ranges

contralto   mezzo soprano   soprano

Challenge "Swing Low, Sweet Chariot" uses the pentatonic scale, harmonized in the key of F major. If you go up one half step, playing the first two pitches as A sharp and F sharp, you can perform this spiritual entirely on the black keys of any keyboard. Try to pick out the melody, then arrange the spiritual for other instruments and voices in the key of F-sharp major.

Describe a Voice
Instructor's Guide, page 264
CD 19 ⑨ "This Little Light of Mine" (2:34)

Find the Tessitura
Instructor's Guide, pages 264–265
CD 19 ⑩ "Swing Low, Sweet Chariot" (2:24)

Unit Seven *Encore!*

▶ *Apply Your Knowledge*

As Denyce Graves sings "La Pascua," try to identify the following:
1. The language in which the song is written
2. The instruments played
3. The function of this song

   In what country and continent would you conclude this song has its origins? Explain your response.

Apply Your Knowledge
Instructor's Guide, page 265
CD 19 [11] "La Pascua" (2:47)

▶ *From High School to the Opera House*

How does a talented musician such as Denyce Graves achieve this level of success?

   Becoming a star performer requires hard work. Watch the video of Denyce Graves performing in the National Cathedral with students from her alma mater, the Duke Ellington School for the Arts. Imagine what Ms. Graves needed to do in her career to progress from this high school to the stages of the world's leading opera houses. Discuss your answers in class, then read the *Essence* article to learn more about Ms. Graves' remarkable journey from Washington D.C. to the glittering fame of the Metropolitan Opera House in New York City.

From High School to the Opera House
Instructor's Guide, pages 265–256
Music! VHS Segment 12, "Carol of the Drum"
Teacher's Resource Binder
Unit Seven Encore! *Denyce Graves: Diva*

The **Golden Age of radio** lives again with the sounds of the "Vocalworks Radio Hour," which features the swing music of the 1930s and 1940s. The Great Depression and World War II were difficult times, and swing music helped raise the spirits of people. They were times when people gathered around the radio to hear news, music, drama, or comedy programs. Do you listen to the radio? Can you guess how the content of today's radio programs might differ from the period brought to life by Vocalworks?

Vocalworks. Bruce Cooper, Michael Geiger, Tim and Debbie Reeder, and Dave Eastly perform "Vocalworks Radio Hour." Photo: Richard Hines.

Music!...

To

Characterize

the Age

You may wish to use Fine Art Transparency 8, *Improvisation No. 30,* in the Teacher's Resource Binder to introduce Unit Eight.

. . . .

Chapter 22
Music of Our Generation

Chapter 23
Music of
Previous
Generations

Chapter 24
Jazz

 Use Artsource® audio segment 3 in the Performing Arts Package to play "Vocal-works Radio Hour."

Music of Our Generation

Today's music reflects today's people. Our music mirrors our time. Social trends have a direct bearing on the music we create and the music we embrace. Musical creation is not haphazard. It relates to the way we think and the way we live. As our ways of thinking and working have changed, so has our music. The music of our generation directly reflects the trends of contemporary civilization. Like the world we live in, music has become more visual, more urban, and more global. Our music reflects these trends. When viewed from this larger perspective, the music of today is easier to understand.

Objectives

By completing this chapter, you will:
- Learn about the musical characteristics of some of today's popular and classical styles.
- Discover how the increasing visualization, urbanization, and globalization of cultures affect current musical trends.
- Understand how the addition of visual elements can alter your musical perceptions.
- Learn about the styles of New Romanticism and minimalism.
- Understand how music is a reflection of its time and its society.

Vocabulary

globalization
minimalism
New Age
New Romanticism
program music
urbanization
visualization

Musicians to Meet

Philip Glass

*Today's musicians continue to expand their contributions to music. One example is percussionist Sheila E (born Sheila Escovedo), shown here, who became the first female bandleader for a late night show (*The Magic Hour, 1998*).* **Select a music performer or group to represent the music of your generation and explain your choice.**

Caption answer
Encourage a variety of responses to demonstrate the wide range of performers and genres available.

467

Culture as More Visual

Since the advent of motion pictures (1903), broadcast television (1946), and the microcomputer (1979), especially with the Internet (1994), people have become more visually oriented. Without even thinking about it, we take in enormous quantities of information through our eyes (often in combination with our ears). Prior to television, however, radio dramas forced listeners to envision the characters and scenery from clues in the script. In contrast, television dramas create the settings, the costumes, and the characters for the eyes so that the viewer does not have to invent them. It is the difference between reading a novel and seeing a motion picture.

Music Videos

Popular music has become a visual medium. With the first MTV cable broadcast in 1981, music videos became popular in the United States as a way to advertise popular artists and their new releases. These videos are commercials that begin and end with product information, including the name of the artist and album. Music videos soon became art forms in and of themselves and established a market of their own. Today, cable television's MTV, BET, and VH-1 literally define youth culture.

Activity *Analyze Music Videos*
Instructor's Guide, pages 269–270
TRB 22-1, *Analysis of Music Videos*

ACTIVITY ▶ *Analyze Music Videos*

Watch at least three different music videos on either broadcast or commercial video.

Using the music videos worksheet, write down the name of the artist and the title of the song and categorize the video according to its basic type: performance, dance, story, or fantasy. Then jot down all the aspects of each video that show imagination. Finally, try to determine how these visual features affect the musical impact of the song. Report your findings in a class discussion of music videos.

You may wish to use "Imagine" at this time. Lesson plans for the activity are found on page 276 in the Instructor's Guide.

This new world of music **visualization,** *the process of enhancing material that is heard by adding information that is seen,* has altered our perceptions. What we see has a powerful impact on how we think about and respond to a song. The usual music video averages between three and four minutes in length, the standard for a popular song. These videos convey information that we do not get when hearing a recording of the same work. When we listen to music treated visually, we accept someone else's imagination in place of our own. We then associate these visual images with the sound whenever we hear it. Although listening to a recording can stimulate our imagination, watching a music video tends to have the opposite effect.

One of the most widely recognized and influential early music videos was Michael Jackson's *Thriller* from his 1983 record album of the same name. This video helped to set a standard for popular music videos for the remainder of the 1980s. Four main types of music videos were developed in those early days. They are still prominent today:

- Performance videos that present the artist in a concert.
- Dance videos that present the music largely in a dance format.
- Story videos that may or may not relate to the lyrics.
- Fantasy videos that rely heavily on computerized manipulation of visual images that may or may not relate to the music.

Today, concerts of pop music often add a video dimension. On their world tours, rock groups from the Rolling Stones to Mariah Carey create an audiovisual experience for their stadium audiences. Complex technology comprising video walls, mega screens, and random satellite transmissions overlays the live audio elements with images and text. The result is rock theatre, a multimedia extravaganza.

Culture as More Urban

During the twentieth century, increasing numbers of people moved into urban and suburban environments. Because large numbers of people live so close together, a new lifestyle has developed. It is intense, impersonal (anonymous), complex, and varied. Compared to the simple life in rural areas or in small towns, urban living provides more choices. There are more options, not just because of people's different interests, but also because dense populations support a variety of enterprises. These alternatives are necessary in order to serve the wide variety of people and their tastes.

Urbanization is *the development of a culture that is the result of the crowding and intensity of a city lifestyle.* It is a vibrant and exciting culture but also one that is sometimes divisive and unruly. Urbanization has produced its own music. There are about as many different kinds of music as there are distinguishable groups of people. Popular music, especially, comprises a broad mix of different genres. Curiously, the very breadth of this musical variety occasionally polarizes those who favor one style from those who prefer another. Can you cite an example of this phenomenon?

Rhythm and Blues

In the 1950s and 1960s the blues shed some of their rural and country roots to enter the mainstream of musical expression. Rhythm and blues, or R&B, transformed the blues to appeal to a wider audience. This was

The rapid growth in American cities during the past century has brought about new types of music that result from one style influencing another. Popular music often reflects this mutual influence and serves the variety of people found in urban areas.

the popular music of African Americans that evolved into "soul" music in the 1970s. R&B is ensemble music, generally with a raw, sometimes shouted, vocal melody and a strong rhythmic backbeat supplied by a rhythm section consisting of a drum set, bass, keyboard, and/or electric guitar. Other instruments, sometimes including a hard-edged tenor saxophone and backup vocalists, support the harmony and supply riffs and responsive fillers. The lyrics, too, are liberated, sometimes relating to traditional blues subject matter, but more often following the prevailing "pop" style.

B. B. King (b. 1925) is one of the giants of R&B. King, who was born on a cotton plantation in the Mississippi Delta, acquired the initials "B. B." from his billing on a Memphis radio station as the "Blues Boy from Beale Street." King has taken the blues around the world, believing passionately that this music reflects the history of African Americans—not only the pain and misery, but also the love and triumphs. He sings in a natural "bluesy" voice and uses his guitar (named "Lucille") to fill in the breathing spaces in each line of the lyrics, trading back and forth between the emotional vocal statement and the improvised wailing response on guitar. His blues style has commanded a substantial interracial following.

Music & ART

American guitarist, vocalist, and composer B. B. King is a master of the blues. His form of R&B has influenced many other musicians. In this painting, American artist Dane Tilghman depicts the musician wearing his trademark ring. **What does "B. B." stand for?**

Dane Tilghman. *B. B.* 1998. Courtesy of the artist.

Music & Art
"Blues Boy from Beale Street."

ACTIVITY ▶ *Find the Traditional Blues*

Listen to "Go On" performed by B. B. King and determine how the traditional blues have been urbanized.

Discuss such matters as:

■ The instruments and voices that are used.

■ The form of the piece. (Use what you know about traditional 12-bar blues form.)

■ The rhyme scheme. (You will recall that the rhyme scheme in the blues is a simple couplet in which the first line is repeated.)

■ What makes it more sophisticated than a traditional blues song?

■ Why is "Go On" still a blues song?

Activity *Find the Traditional Blues*
Instructor's Guide, page 270
CD 13 23 "Go On" (3:52)

Rock

After the Second World War, the migration of southern African Americans to northern cities brought a new musical influence to the urban culture. The younger generation was no longer entranced by the sweetness of Tin Pan Alley songs or the polished singing of Frank Sinatra and Rosemary Clooney. The younger generation was attracted to rhythm and blues and began to tune in to it on the radio. These lyrics were earthier, and so was the singing. There was more energy in the rhythm, induced by heavy accents on the backbeats (2 and 9). Rock and roll emerged full-blown in 1955 with Bill Haley's recording of "Rock Around the Clock," even though the name "rock and roll" had been coined by Cleveland disc jockey Alan Freed in 1951.

During the 1960s this early style of rock and roll became increasingly electrified and amplified. The electric guitar became the central instrument. Soon many styles were encompassed under the banner "rock," including rockabilly, hard rock, soul rock, punk, heavy metal, new wave, syntho-rock, jazz-rock fusion, grunge rock, and so on.

Rock music has now become so mainstream that some classical composers are weaving elements of it into their symphonic works, and some rock composers have taken to writing symphonically. This kind of musical "crossover" can debase both styles, or it can result in something quite fresh. Now, in the twenty-first century, rock music suffers at times from "copycat" musicians who repeat by formula what others have invented before them.

After the breakup of the Beatles, English composer, singer, and bass player Paul McCartney continued to forge new musical territory, moving away from hard rock, particularly on his solo albums. A versatile musician, he composed the classically styled Liverpool Oratoria *in 1991.*

Rap

Urban African-American youth have invented their own music. One example is rap, an energetic and talky form of accompanied "singing" that often reports on the harsh realities of urban America. Originally, rap music gave voice to disenfranchised youth—those whom society had seemingly left by the wayside. Some rap lyrics have been attacked as obscene, bigoted, and socially irresponsible. In 1990, 2 Live Crew's *As Nasty as They Wanna Be* became the first piece of recorded music to be declared obscene in a U.S. District Court. This led to the arrest of several record retailers and members of the group. It also fueled the controversy over labeling CDs that contain explicit lyrics.

Not all rap lyrics are socially irresponsible. Kris Parker, better known as KRS-One (meaning "Knowledge Reigns Supreme over Nearly Everyone"), has created raps that argue against injustice, racism, drugs, and police brutality and at the same time chide his audience to overcome everyday obstacles and give their attention to education. Similarly, the rap of Will Smith (Big Willie Style), star of the hit movie *Men in Black* (1997), has maintained a positive message in his lyrics for more than a decade.

Rap is the equivalent of a musical newspaper. It can be improvised but often is not. It is aggressive, often rebellious music with confrontational lyrics that address the hard realities of life in urban ghettos. In its lyrics, rap is highly visual, presenting vivid graphic images. The language is the vernacular of ordinary young people.

Rap artist and actor Will Smith, shown here in the movie Men in Black, *helped bring rap music to a mainstream audience. His music has a positive message and a style that appeals to people along with his easygoing personality.* **Do you know under what name he first recorded?**

Caption answer
Fresh Prince.

ACTIVITY ▶ *Arrange and Perform an Original Rap*

See if you can perform an original rap.

To prepare the performance of your own rap, listen to the rap tune "Know How" by Young M. C. and answer these questions:

1. What is the basic purpose of this rap?
2. Who is the intended audience for this rap?
3. Was this rap written or improvised?
4. How often do the words rhyme throughout most of the piece?
5. What is this rap about?

Working in small groups, recite the rap lyrics, written by Kenny Banks, that your teacher will distribute. Figure out how the rhythm of the words might go. Then, using instruments of your choice, create and arrange a rap accompaniment for your performance. An electronic keyboard with its rhythm presets would be an ideal choice.

Activity *Arrange and Perform an Original Rap*
Instructor's Guide, pages 270–271
TRB 22-2, *Perform*
CD 13 24 "Know How" (4:01)

Country music artist LeAnn Rimes (b. 1982) demonstrates the extent to which country and western music has reached an urban audience. In 1997, she became the first country artist to receive a Grammy as Best New Artist. **Can you name other country musicians whose music is popular with urban audiences?**

Caption answer
Possibilities include Garth Brooks, Shania Twain, Trishia Yearwood, and Wynonna Judd.

Country and Western

From its roots in the folk tradition, American country and western music has grown into a well-established style as popular with city dwellers, or more so, as it is with traditional country inhabitants. The music and the lyrics may hold special appeal for the urban population because they are nostalgic reminders of a simpler lifestyle for which many city people yearn. Country and western lyrics often pose basic questions and clear solutions. Some of the best guitar players are in the field of country music, but one instrument that characterizes the style is the pedal steel (or Hawaiian) guitar. Country and western music brings us back to our rural roots and the time when life was not so complex and perplexing.

Many country music traditionalists have lamented the urbanization of their style. Indeed, recording artists such as Shania Twain, Garth Brooks, and Wynonna Judd have gradually introduced a more hard-driving sound that emphasizes searing lead guitar solos and huge trap-sets.

To some, however, the country music of today sounds a lot like the rock of the 1980s. To counter this trend, guitarist and singer/songwriter Vince Gill has "returned to the roots" of country music with a more simple, sparse sound.

Activity *Identify the Stylistic Benchmarks*
Instructor's Guide, page 271
CD 13 [25] "Since I Found You"
(2:46)

ACTIVITY   *Identify the Stylistic Benchmarks*

Listen to "Since I Found You" by Sweethearts of the Rodeo and discuss the characteristics that give country music its appeal.

Try to answer these questions:

1. What tells you that this is a country and western song?
2. Which of the three types of love song is this (lost love, longing for love, or celebration of love)? What is it about?
3. Can you describe the vocal style?
4. What instruments do you hear?
5. How do you think this music is used?
6. Even though the name of this group, Sweethearts of the Rodeo, has a country and western ring to it, why might they appeal to urban audiences?

Salsa

Today's ethnic urban mix of people has embraced a wide variety of musical styles, many of which derive from international sources. Some of these styles are the result of a fusion of different ethnic elements. Reggae, for example, is a Jamaican popular music infused with elements of rock music and calypso. Similarly, salsa is a dance music of Cuban origin that borrows rhythms, harmonies, and improvisatory elements from jazz and from Puerto Rican and South American music. In salsa, the fusion of these components has produced a Latin jazz sound that is distinctive in itself. The form is sectional, and the polyrhythms give the music a particularly "catchy" feeling. The following layered Latin rhythms can be heard in "Descarga—Yema-Ya," an example of this music:

Activity *Identify the Difference*
Instructor's Guide, pages 271–272
TRB 22-3, *Checklist*
CD 14 ☐1 "Descarga—Yema-Ya"
        (6:18)

ACTIVITY ▶ *Identify the Difference*

Can you identify the musical characteristics of "Descarga—Yema-Ya" that are Latin in style and those that derive from jazz?

Read and perform the layered Latin-style rhythmic patterns above. Decide which percussion instruments you think sound best on each rhythmic pattern. Perform all five patterns together while you listen.

Now use the checklist and follow the musical events in "Descarga—Yema-Ya." Decide whether the influence is from Latin music, jazz, or both. Check which of the events exhibit organized form and which exhibit free form.

- Which of the events is the longest?
- Which events could be accompanied by the Latin-style rhythmic patterns you learned?
- Why is this urban music?

MIDI TECHNOLOGY OPTION

Technology Option
Use Project 22 in the *MIDI Activities* binder.

- **Music with MIDI** Use a MIDI program to create Latin jazz compositions as well as those in other popular genres such as rap, hip-hop, rhythm and blues, and country and western.

Music & CULTURE

Like salsa, samba music is a fusion of styles. Samba bands, often called sambateria, are known for their lively performances. **Why did salsa and samba rhythms find an eager dance audience in urban America?**

Music & Culture
The polyrhythms give the music a catchy, infectious feeling.

Culture as More Global

There seem to be as many styles of urban music as there are different people living in our cities. Worldwide communications have created the first human inklings of a global community. **Globalization,** *the process of making information and influence accessible to a worldwide audience,* is expressed more vibrantly in music than in any other art form.

The first music to reach this global audience, accessible within most cultures, is American pop. Prior to electronic reproduction, music was confined to specific locales and societies. During the twentieth century, if there were a common denominator of world taste, American popular music was it. Electronic communication made the commercial reach of this music literally stretch around the world. The range of our pop styles seems to offer something to everybody. Perhaps the international makeup of American culture makes our music speak with a universal voice. However, global communication has also introduced us to many new sounds. Do you suppose these more recent "world music" influences will characterize the new music of the twenty-first century?

The human race appears to be moving in two conflicting directions at the same time. On the one hand, we are seeing ourselves as one gigantic family on a fragile planet, all dependent on each other for survival. On the other hand, we are recognizing and asserting our tribal differences. While we are becoming more interdependent and universally minded on

Music & CULTURE

Music has long been a force for change, and musicians often have combined their talents in an effort to raise the moral consciousness of society. In 1987, American singer/songwriter Paul Simon performed with South African a cappella group Ladysmith Black Mambazo with his Graceland concerts. As a result, people became more aware of the racial prejudice in that country known for apartheid.

some matters, we are proclaiming our independence and singularity on others. These trends are two sides of the same coin. We balance our increasing collectivity with an assertion of individuality. As the world grows ever more democratized, differences are recognized.

Music is also universal and singular. Styles serve the global audience as well as the tastes of individual audiences. The arts are eclectic. They often draw their inspiration from a variety of sources and serve many tastes and interests. There is a definite trend to democratize music so that it has the widest possible appeal and is accessible to all people. Multiple influences are combined to create new styles that speak to new audiences.

One of the recent trends in popular music is a revival of a cappella singing. The groups Take 6 and Boyz II Men, for example, sing complex jazzy arrangements with a passion usually reserved for gospel music. These men vary their sound with intricate rhythms, up-tempo vocal acrobatics, fresh harmonies, a solid bass, and percussive vocal effects. Bobby McFerrin sometimes sings all the parts of his songs himself, overdubbing them to create the sound of an instrumental accompaniment. One of the best-known international a cappella groups is Ladysmith Black Mambazo.

Activity *Discover Common Links*
Instructor's Guide, pages 272–273
CD 14 [2] "Em Lanjeni Yase Bhabhiloni" (0:44)
CD 14 [3] "Pokare Kare Ana" (0:46)
CD 14 [4] "Good Livin'" (0:44)
CD 14 [5] "Eleanor Rigby" (1:05)

ACTIVITY ▶ *Discover Common Links*

Listen to the montage of four different songs excerpts.

Become a "song detective," taking notes on each example. Try to gather enough evidence to answer the following questions:
1. What are three elements all four songs have in common?
2. Which example sounds most unusual in comparison to the others? Why?
3. Which two pairs of examples sound most alike? Why?
4. Which example sounds the oldest? Which sounds newest? Why?
5. This music came from three different continents. Can you name them?
6. What different styles of music are represented in these songs?

New Romanticism

Classical music, too, has been energized with a will to reach new audiences. Whereas much of the classical music of the mid-twentieth century appealed to a small select (some would say "elitist") audience, classical music is now trying to reach out to attract a wider public. Many of today's classical composers set out to write music that is intensely emotional. The self-indulgence that was passed off as self-expression has been replaced by a more urgent drive for communication. Some composers have traded in the tone row and serialism for **New Romanticism,** *a genuine tonal melody composed with exotic textures and timbres.* They like intense drama, splashy effects, virtuoso fireworks, and colossal climaxes. Most of all, they want audiences to react.

To be certain they achieve strong meaning and reaction, New Romantic composers sometimes rely on natural themes as sources of inspiration. For example, while she was composer in residence for the St. Louis Symphony Orchestra, American composer Joan Tower (b. 1938) wrote the riveting tone poem *Silver Ladders* (1986). Tower's genius also produced such exotic compositions as *Sequoia* and *Island Rhythms* for full orchestra and *Show Dreams* for flute and guitar.

Other New Romantics lean on literary subjects. American composer David Del Tredici (b. 1937), for example, has been inspired for more than a decade by the poetry in Lewis Carroll's *Alice in Wonderland* (1865). He has created *Child Alice* (1980), a massive evening-long musical composition that depicts the dramatic contrasts of mood in the poem that is the preface to Carroll's novel *Through the Looking Glass* (1872). Del Tredici's music—a type of program music—was awarded the Pulitzer Prize in 1980.

Although descriptive music has probably existed as long as humans have been creating music, Hungarian composer Franz Liszt (1811–1886) coined the term **program music,** *instrumental compositions that attempt to convey a specific idea without using lyrics.* Such works enable a composer to express something beyond the music itself. These "extramusical" ideas are often provided by the composer in the form of an explanatory note or a program that accompanies the score.

John Corigliano (b. 1938) is another contemporary American composer who is determined to communicate with his audience. His *Symphony No. 1,* an impassioned response to the AIDS crisis, earned him the 1991 Grawemeyer Award, and his score for the film *Altered States* earned him both Grammy and Academy Award nominations. His works capture attention because of his ability to combine many different compositional procedures to attain vivid contrasts and expressive power. His *Pied Piper Fantasy* (1979–1982), a concerto for flute and orchestra, was inspired by Robert Browning's poem *The Pied Piper of Hamelin.* As Corigliano's first work to have a programmatic outline, the concerto is divided into seven sections based on events in the story. In Browning's legend, the town of Hamelin was overrun with rats. The piper played his flute to charm the rats and lead them to destruction.

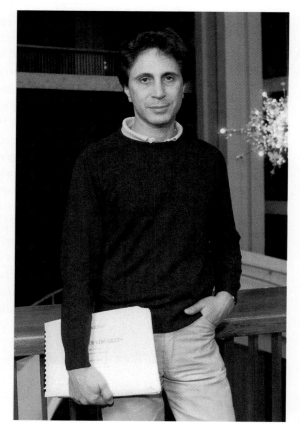

Contemporary composer John Corigliano's opera The Ghosts of Versailles *debuted at the Metropolitan Opera House in New York on December 19, 1992. This was the opera company's first opera premiere in 25 seasons. Corigliano's interest in composing developed in part because his father served as concertmaster of the New York Philharmonic for 23 years.*

Activity *Compare the Generations*
Instructor's Guide, pages 273–274
CD 14 [6] "The Rats," *Pied Piper
Fantasy* (2:00)
CD 14 [7] "The Piper's Victory,"
Pied Piper Fantasy
(3:35)

ACTIVITY ▶ *Compare the Generations*

Can you evaluate how the classical music of our time embodies the expressive dimensions of Romantic music?

Turn back to Chapter 9, pages 161–164, and make a list of the musical characteristics of the Romantic period (c. 1825–1910).

Listen to two short movements from John Corigliano's *Pied Piper Fantasy* and describe this music according to mood, timbre, dynamics, contrasts, and other qualities. How does the mood change? What parts of the story might the composer be expressing?

What characteristics in the music suggest that the rats became hypnotized by the piper's song?

Evaluate How does this music embody musical principles of the Romantic period? How does it embody musical principles of our own time?

Minimalism

During the mid-twentieth century, classical music faced a crisis. The 12-tone or serial music appealed to a very small audience of people who had expert knowledge and highly specialized tastes. Many composers, particularly those who were affiliated with a college or university base, wrote for a small but discerning audience. The public's taste for new classical music was almost nonexistent.

Along came Philip Glass. His studies of music left him dissatisfied. The new music was either too complex or, in the case of John Cage's chance music, too vague and indeterminate. Glass wanted to find a new path for musical expression. His studies in Paris in 1966 with Ravi Shankar, the Indian composer and sitar player, helped him find that expression. He became fascinated by the rhythms in Indian music and began to compose in ways that explored the repetitions of simple rhythms and minimal melodies. Glass's music, which has also been influenced by the insistent and repetitious rhythms of rock music, has been called minimalist. If you have seen the movie *Kundun,* you know how his minimalist score unifies the film. The instrumentation of his touring ensemble resembles that of a rock group, and he has established a sizable, mostly young, audience.

Composers Steve Reich (b. 1936), Terry Riley (b. 1935), and Ellen Toaffe Zwilich (b. 1939) also have used minimalist techniques. **Minimalism,** *tonal music that stresses the element of repetition with changes that are dictated by a rule or system,* is clearly an American invention, attracting audiences in Europe and elsewhere.

One of the ways that contemporary composers have won the interest and following of new and younger audiences is by using real events as their subject matter. The titles of recently composed operas reveal these interests and concerns: *The Death of Klinghoffer, Nixon in China, The Manson Family,* and *X: The Life and Times of Malcolm X.* These works are dramatized portraits inspired by newspaper headlines.

Glass has led the way in making music relevant to today's society. His operas explore global themes—political and social events that have affected humanity. *Satyagraha,* for example, tells the story of Mahatma Gandhi's invention of passive (or nonviolent) resistance. The subject of his orchestral work *Koyaanisqatsi* is respect for nature. The title is a Hopi Indian term meaning "life out of balance," and the subject is nature's desecration. "Islands," one of the movements of *Glassworks* (1977), exhibits the simplicity of musical materials that is typical of minimalism.

PROFILE

Philip Glass

Philip Glass
American Composer
1937–

Philip Glass is one of the most innovative and prolific composers in North America today. He combines Indian, African, classical, and rock elements to create a distinctive style, free of most European tradition. His music, which includes ensemble pieces, dance company collaborations, film scores, and symphonies, is known for its manipulation of repetitive rhythmic units over a static harmony. Glass has also composed several operas, among them *Einstein on the Beach* (1975–1976), *Akhnaten* (1984), and *The Voyage* (1992). Inspired by his intellectual, political, and spiritual heroes, Glass has updated the traditional operatic genre to include modern styles and themes.

Born in Baltimore in 1937, Glass studied at the Peabody Conservatory in Baltimore and then at New York's Juilliard School of Music. There, he was exposed to writers of the beat generation, bop musicians, and alternative theater, in addition to being educated in the conventional forms of music. After earning a master's degree, Glass went to Paris to study with the great French teacher Nadia Boulanger (1887–1979). He also worked with Indian sitar player and composer Ravi Shankar (b. 1920). Glass now lives in Nova Scotia, Canada, with his family.

His score for *Kundun,* the film about the Tibetan Buddhist Dalai Lama, was a nominee for the 1997 Academy Award for Best Original Score (won that year by the score for *Titanic*.)

The tone colors accumulate gradually while the motives are repeated over and over again, but in slightly altered versions. The first ostinato-like motive is introduced by slowly undulating violas:

Glass then adds a static, sustained melody above this ostinato pattern, played first by clarinet, then joined by saxophone:

The combination of these rather simple resources creates an atmosphere that evokes the stark simple beauty of an island.

Activity *Hear and Perform Postmodern Minimalism*
Instructor's Guide, page 274
CD 14 [8] "Islands," *Glassworks*
(7:39)

ACTIVITY ▶ *Hear and Perform Postmodern Minimalism*

Listen to the recording of "Islands" from *Glassworks* by American composer Philip Glass. Try to identify the two basic musical ideas—the ostinato-like pattern and the higher, long-noted melody.

As you listen to the entire composition, you will hear the ostinato rhythms and melody repeat as they modulate to new tonal centers. How else does Glass create variety within all the repetition? What happens to the texture?

Can you point out when these two musical ideas change register, that is, when the ostinato pattern moves to the high register and the long-noted melody shifts to the low register? How does Glass end the composition?

Now, using the keyboard or tuned percussion, perform these fluctuating rhythmic and melodic patterns. Can you play along with the recording?

Music & **ART**

Like minimalism in music, minimal art originated in the 1960s. In this sculpture, artist Dan Flavin uses fluorescent light and geometric shapes in a work that is cool and detached. **How is this artwork similar to the music of Phillip Glass?**

Dan Flavin. *Untitled (In Honor of Harold Joachim)*. 1977. Courtesy, Dia Center of the Arts, New York.

Music & Art
Both seem impersonal; both use technology as a source; both employ repetition with slight alterations in their patterns.

New Age

It has been said that describing the style of New Age music is like trying to nail gelatin to a wall. Yet most record stores have a section for New Age music, and New Age radio stations have sprung up across the country. 50 record companies in the United States, Europe, and Asia now specialize in this music that has commanded its own category at the Grammy Awards since 1987. Today, New Age music generates millions of dollars in sales each year as it continues to increase in popularity. However, is this music a distinct musical genre, or is it, like rock, an amalgam of many styles?

New Age music presents an alternative to the hard-driving, up-tempo, vocal music that usually tops the popular music charts. It appeals to people who want to shut out the abrasive discords of modern life. It is tranquil and pastoral. **New Age** music is *a contemporary type of meditative, mostly instrumental, music.* Musicians combine characteristics of classical and popular music, as well as a wide variety of other cultures, particularly Eastern, to produce a hybrid music that is intimate, peaceful, calming, and meditative. Largely improvised, it often incorporates actual sounds from nature. It borrows its hypnotic repetitions and subtle rhythmic mutations from minimalism. The music often suggests visual images. Guitarist William Ackerman, one of the earliest exponents of the style, calls it "a varied landscape of emotion." New Age is sometimes referred to as the new "easy listening" music.

Styles of music continue to evolve. Old styles give impetus to new ones. Some, like rock and reggae, have become international, appealing to many, but certainly not all, people around the world. Dance music, which avoids the language barrier inherent in vocal music, crosses cultural borders most easily. However, American popular vocal music may help to account for the acceptance of English as the preferred second language around the world.

Activity *Evaluate New Age Music*
Instructor's Guide, page 275
TRB 22-4, *Perceptive Listening*
CD 14 ⑨ "Lullaby from the Great Mother Whale for the Baby Seal Pups" (3:23)

ACTIVITY ▶ *Evaluate New Age Music*

Listen to "Lullaby from the Great Mother Whale for the Baby Seal Pups" by the Paul Winter Consort and try to identify its unique sounds. Take notes about its musical characteristics.

Using your notes, evaluate this piece. What is there about it that is intriguing? Speculate about the uses of this music. Do you know anyone who is a New Age enthusiast? Some people regard this as "elevator music." In what ways might this label be appropriate?

SUMMARY

Our music mirrors us. It emerges from the social fabric of our culture to speak directly to all our different personalities. Taken piecemeal, it can be narrow in scope and limited in how well it reflects us. Taken collectively, it provides a fairly accurate picture of American life today. As our culture has become more visual, so too has our music. As we have become more urbanized, our music has changed to serve the different ethnic groups, classes, and lifestyles in our cities. As our culture has become more global, our music has absorbed and combined musical elements from many cultures. Popular and classical music have both reached out to communicate to a broader public, particularly the younger generation, in all its variety.

In the diversity of its styles, our music tries to accommodate everybody. No group seems to be left out. There is something for everybody, and people generally seek out their own musical common denominator. It is a paradox of today's music that it reflects our narrow and separate individualities and, at the same time, our broad and cosmopolitan oneness.

Building Music Vocabulary

On a sheet of paper, write the term from the list that best matches each description below.

- (2) globalization
- (1) program music
- (4) minimalism
- (6) urbanization
- (5) New Age
- (3) visualization
- (7) New Romanticism

1. Instrumental music that tries to convey a specific idea without using lyrics.
2. The process of making information accessible to a worldwide audience.
3. The process of enhancing material that is heard by adding information that is seen.
4. Tonal music that stresses the element of repetition with changes that are dictated by a rule or system.
5. A contemporary type of meditative, mostly instrumental music.
6. Development of a culture that is the result of the crowding and intensity of a city lifestyle.
7. Tonal melodies combined with exotic textures and timbres.

Reviewing Music Facts

Answer each question in a complete sentence.

8. How does visualization impact our way of hearing music?
9. What kind of music is B. B. King known for?
10. What type of guitar best characterizes country and western music?
11. What literary source inspired much of David Del Tredici's "program music"?
12. Name two musical influences on the minimalist style of Philip Glass.
13. What style of music is sometimes called "easy listening"?

Complete answers for the Chapter 22 Review are found in the Instructor's Guide, pages 276–277.

Thinking It Through

On a sheet of paper, respond to each of the following questions.

14. **Analyze** How has urbanization affected the music created in our society?
15. **Explain** In your own words, describe the development and purpose of rap music.
16. **Analyze** Why does American pop music have such worldwide appeal?

Making the Connection

Visual Arts Create a storyboard for a favorite song that would be a model for a music video. Under each board, write the lyrics that correspond to the visuals. Share your storyboard and explain how the music relates to the visual design.

Language Arts Select an example of modern poetry that appeals to you. Study its form and content. Then consider these four musical styles: New Age, minimalism, New Romanticism, and rock. Tell which of these styles is most like your poetry, and explain why.

 You can explore today's music at www.glencoe.com/sec/music

CHAPTER 23

Music of Previous Generations

Music evokes its time. Each epoch seems to have a particular character— a way of thinking, acting, and living that affects the taste and style of that day. The arts record these attitudes and outlooks. They are indelible imprints of their age. That is why we can live and breathe history through the architecture, drawings, paintings, literature, and music that artists, writers, and musicians create. When we hear the music of a particular historic period, we can begin to experience the feeling and style of that time. Music becomes a very tangible way to touch and be touched by our human heritage. It puts us in contact with those who lived before us.

The development of Western music can be traced through musical styles of the Renaissance, Baroque, and Classical periods. Modern instruments of the band and orchestra also show similarities to those of earlier times.
What familiar Western instrument resembles this Renaissance recorder?

Caption answer
Students will likely identify the clarinet or oboe.

Objectives
By completing this chapter, you will:
- Learn about composers and styles of music in the Renaissance, the Baroque, and the Classical periods.
- Be able to identify and describe the characteristics of these styles.
- Understand the process involved in the evolution of musical styles.
- Understand the relationship and interplay between polyphony and homophony.
- Recognize the connection between the way people think and live and the kind of music they create.

Vocabulary
Baroque period
concerto grosso
concerto style
continuo
madrigals
Renaissance period
terraced dynamics
tutti
word painting

Musicians to Meet
Franz Joseph Haydn
Antonio Vivaldi

487

Renaissance

One of the greatest flowerings of art, literature, and learning occurred in Europe during the fifteenth and sixteenth centuries. The rediscovered classical ideals of the ancient Greeks inspired a rebirth and revival of human creativity. The change in thinking began in Italy and spread gradually northward through Europe, awakening a new spirit that overtook the age. That new spirit marked the transition from the medieval world to the modern. Much of our thinking today is rooted in the remarkable achievements of the Renaissance.

The **Renaissance period,** *a stylistic period between approximately 1400 and 1600*, was a time of brilliant accomplishments in literature, science, and the arts. In Italy, economic expansion brought contact with other cultures and a flourishing urban vibrancy. The de' Medici family in Florence, the doges in Venice, and the popes in Rome, among others, became patrons of the arts. During the Renaissance, secularism asserted itself. Humanism—the emphasis on human values and capabilities—moved society away from the pervasive authority of the Church that had dominated life during medieval times. There was a conscious return to the classical ideals of ancient Greece. Human possibilities were exemplified by Leonardo da Vinci, a universal genius as talented and creative in science as in the arts. This was the age of the artists Michelangelo, Raphael, Titian, and Tintoretto.

Use Artsource® audio segment 4 in the Performing Arts Package to hear Diana Zaslove perform a Renaissance song.

During the Renaissance period, composers began to emphasize the expressiveness of the human voice as a solo instrument. Poetry and music were combined for the purpose of expressing a variety of emotions, especially aspects of love. Contemporary vocalist Diana Zaslove, shown here, has been a featured soloist with many music ensembles specializing in medieval, Renaissance, and Baroque music.

Diana Zaslove, lyric soprano. "It Was a Lover and His Lass," composed by Thomas Morely, with words from William Shakespeare's play *As You Like It*. Photo by Craig Schwartz.

The Rise of Instrumental Music

In music, secular subjects assumed a place alongside the sacred music that had formerly commanded so much attention. Italian composers wrote sacred motets and secular **madrigals,** *nonreligious vocal works in several parts (usually five).* They asserted their sense of harmony in direct competition with the counterpoint that had long dominated music. In Renaissance music, for the first time, the horizontal (polyphonic) and vertical (homophonic) aspects were balanced. Music was no longer primarily vocal. Instrumental music was given greater emphasis and began to flower. It no longer merely supported the voices. Instruments were given their own parts!

The great German composer Michael Praetorius (1571–1621) was a church musician who wrote many sacred hymns, motets, and songs as well as secular madrigals, songs, and dance pieces. His instrumental music shows the new independence that instruments were given in the late Renaissance. In his "La bourrée," from *Terpsichore* (1612), for example, he used the tempo, meter, and character of a traditional French dance in a quick duple meter to create a purely instrumental piece. For contrast, he delighted in using loud oboelike double-reed instruments called shawms, soft flutelike recorders, and reedy and nasal crumhorns.

ACTIVITY ▶ *Accompany a Renaissance Dance*

First, listen to the "La bourrée" from *Terpsichore* (1612), a collection of instrumental French dances, by the German composer Michael Praetorius. Then, try to identify the basics.

- Describe the tempo and metric organization of the music.
- Describe how contrast is achieved in the music.
- In what historical period would you place the instruments you hear?
- Now use the accompaniment score for "La bourrée" to read and perform the melodic (recorder or keyboard) and rhythmic (tambourine and triangle) parts as written. The first melody you hear is six measures long. How many times is it repeated after its first statement?

 TECHNOLOGY OPTION

- **Music with MIDI** Use a MIDI program to compose a Renaissance-style instrumental dance piece. Explore elements of tempo, metric organization, and compositional structure.

Activity *Accompany a Renaissance Dance* Instructor's Guide, pages 278–279 TRB 23-1, *"La bourrée"* CD 14 ⟨10⟩ "La bourrée," *Terpsichore* (2:14)

Technology Option Use Project 23 in the *MIDI Activities* binder.

Word Painting

With the Renaissance came a greater interest in the music's text and its meaning. During the Middle Ages it was common for several texts to be set to music simultaneously, the polyphonic treatment making it difficult to follow any one of them. In the sixteenth century, composers discovered that music could portray human emotions, not just express religious texts. To explore this new phenomenon, composers tied music more closely to poetry. In their madrigals, Renaissance composers expressed the meaning of the text musically by coloring words with new harmonies and chromaticism. They used the device of **word painting,** *music that portrays the literal meaning of the words of the text.*

The English composer Thomas Weelkes (1575–1623) wrote both sacred and secular music, but he is clearly one of the great composers of madrigals. His music is ordered through repetition of sections and by

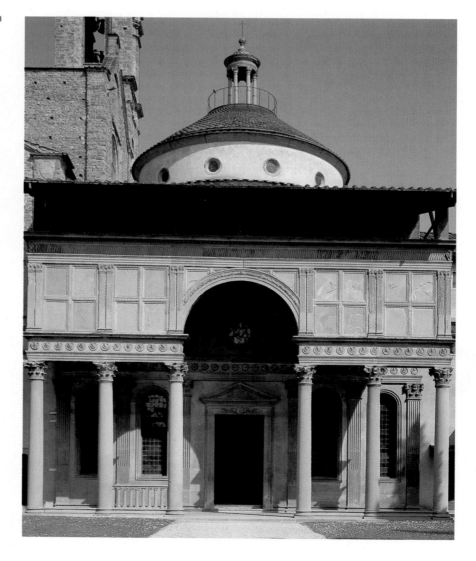

In his Pazzi Chapel (built c. 1429–1433), architect Filippo Brunelleschi demonstrated the new Renaissance style. The curved Roman arch, the mathematically spaced Classical column, and the overall symmetry of the design show a new sense of geometrical clarity, unity, and logic. Renaissance music exhibits similar characteristics.

imitation between the parts. His six-voice madrigal, "As Vesta Was Descending" (1601), demonstrates how he used music to convey shades of meaning in the text. The subject matter is about goddesses; Weelkes tried to portray their human feelings. After all the serious music of the Middle Ages, Renaissance composers were actually having fun.

ACTIVITY ▶ *Follow the Text*

Listen to the madrigal "As Vesta Was Descending" by Thomas Weelkes and follow the text (below) to figure out how Renaissance composers used word painting.

- What is this madrigal about?
- Describe the mood of the music and the text. What musical characteristics helped you make your decision?
- How did Weelkes "paint" the meaning of the text in his music?
- Is the word painting in the madrigal obvious or subtle? Why?

Activity *Follow the Text*
Instructor's Guide, page 279
TRB 23-2, *"As Vesta Was Descending"*
CD 14 |11| "As Vesta Was Descending" (2:53)

As Vesta Was Descending

As Vesta was from Latmos hill descending,
she spied a maiden queen the same ascending,
attended on by all the shepherds swain,
to whom Diana's darlings came running down amain.
First two by two
then three by three together,
leaving their goddess all alone, hasted thither,
and mingling with the shepherds of her train
with mirthful tunes her presence entertain.
Then sang the shepherds and nymphs of Diana
Long live fair Oriana!

Baroque

The **Baroque period** *is the stylistic period between approximately 1600 and 1750.* The term "baroque" derived from a French word for an imperfect or irregular pearl. The term describes a way of thinking that reached beyond the classical Greek ideals of symmetrical organization and highly ordered statements. Why not ovals and curved lines and highly embellished and ornamented melodies? Such Baroque artists as Peter Paul Rubens and Judith Leyster saw beauty and emotion in the imperfect shapes and forms that abound in the real world. They relaxed the "laws" of expression. Baroque composers continued the exploitation of emotions in music, but now they did it with greater drama and freedom.

The Beginning of Opera

The great Italian composer Claudio Monteverdi (1567–1643) was one of the first composers to infuse the meaning of the text with feeling. During the Baroque period, composers found that their music could represent and contrast basic emotional states: sorrow, fear, love, anger, and other "affections," as they were called. The main purpose of Baroque music was to move the affections by sustaining and contrasting them.

The Baroque style was exuberant and emotional. Spanish architect José Benito de Churriguera's ornate altarpiece for the church of San Esteban, Salamanca (1693), shows this extravagant style. **How did Baroque music exhibit a similar exhuberance?**

José Benito de Churriguera. Altarpiece. 1693. San Esteban, Salamanca, Spain.

Caption answer
Melodies were highly embellished and ornamented; terraced dynamics were used to provide contrast.

In their attempt to portray human emotions in sound, Baroque composers established states of feeling that were fixed or that shifted abruptly. Each section of a work maintained a single mood throughout. Rhythms and melodies in the section, based on one or two short motives, retained a consistent character. They used **terraced dynamics,** *layered dynamic levels within a composition.* These contrasts, including dramatic changes in tempo, helped to provide interest and impact.

The Baroque period in music developed around 1600 and ended with the death of Johann Sebastian Bach in 1750. While Bach expended his genius in taking the old contrapuntal style to its final, glorious heights, other composers explored simpler and less regimented schemes of expression. The solo voice was recognized as the best means for communicating the meaning of a text. While polyphony remained important, a new style was emerging that was quite unique. Composers experimented with assigning melody to one voice rather than keeping all the voices equally busy. Instrumental accompaniments were simplified to support the voice with a solid bass line and chords. The **continuo** was *a Baroque accompaniment consisting of a harpsichord sounding the chords and a viola da gamba (a low, bowed string instrument) reinforcing the bass line.* (The delicate sound of the harpsichord could not by itself emphasize the bass line sufficiently.) Composers left it up to the harpsichord (continuo) player to fill out the inner parts by improvising within the chord patterns that were specified. The outer voices were thereby emphasized. The melody in the upper voice was supported by the constantly moving bass line. Harmonies changed rapidly. Composers were now generating music vertically as well as horizontally.

These developments set the stage for opera, which made its first appearance around 1600. In order to dramatize a story through music, the characters had to speak for themselves and convey emotion at the same time. The idea of a solo voice supported by accompaniment was absolutely essential. So was the development of "recitative," a way of speaking musically. Recitative is a combination of singing and speaking. It mimics the inflections of speech but uses melody and rhythm as a way to give the words emotional meaning. The events of the story are told through recitatives. In contrast, the singing of an aria is more sustained. It marks a pause in the storytelling while a character reacts to the events.

One of the earliest operas is Monteverdi's *Orfeo* (1607). The story of this ancient Greek tragedy relates Orpheus's descent into Hell to retrieve his dead bride Eurydice from the powers of the underworld. Monteverdi scored the opera for soloists, chorus, and orchestra. The music succeeds in depicting real human character

One of the earliest operas that is still performed today is Orfeo *(1607) by Italian composer Claudio Monteverdi (1567–1643). Of the many operas he composed, only three survive. His music is inventive and touching. Monteverdi was musical director at St. Mark's in Venice from 1613 until his death.*

and passions. The melodious recitative "Tu se' morte" ("You are dead") conveys grief with a melody and rhythm that follow the natural inflection of the text. There are climaxes on high notes, on the words *rimango* (remain), *stelle* (star), and *sole* (sun), that give the singer opportunities to express emotion. High notes convey excitement and grief, low tones despair and death. As in his madrigals, Monteverdi uses word painting; for example, he sets the word *stelle* (star) on the highest note and *profondi abissi* (profound abysses) and *morte* (death) on the lowest. There are built-in pauses for breathing that remind us of speech.

Activity *Compare the Baroque with the Renaissance*
Instructor's Guide, pages 279–280
CD 14 [11] "As Vesta Was Descending" (2:53)
Cd 14 [12] "Tu se' morte," *Orfeo* (2:42)

ACTIVITY ▶ *Compare the Baroque with the Renaissance*

Follow the English translation (below) of the Italian text as you listen to the recitative "Tu se' morte" ("You are dead") from the opera *Orfeo* by Claudio Monteverdi. Be prepared to describe the feelings about which Orfeo is singing.

Compare "Tu se' morte" with "As Vesta Was Descending" and discuss your observations about the following questions:
1. How many voices are singing in each composition?
2. What instruments can you identify in each one?
3. Which composition is homophonic? polyphonic?
4. Which composer has set the words of the text much like the speech of an actor in a play?
5. Which setting of text makes the meaning clearer? Why?

Tu se' morte

Tu se' morte, se' morte, mia vita,
ed io respiro? Tu se' da me partita,
se' da me part.ita per mai piu,
mai piu non tornare, ed io rimango?
No, no che se i versi alcuna cosa ponno,
N'andro sicuro a' piu profondi abissi,
e intenerito il cor del re dell'ombre,
meco trarotti a riverder le stelle,
o se cio negherammi empio destino,
rimarro teco in compagnia di morte!
Addio terra, addio cielo, e sole, addio.

You are dead

You are dead, dead my darling
And I live; you have left me,
You have left me forever,
Never to return and I remain—
No, no, if verses have any power,
I shall go boldly to the deepest abysses,
And have melted the heart of the queen of shadows,
Will bring you with me to see the stars,
Or if cruel fate will deny me this,
I will remain with you in the company of death,
Farewell earth, farewell sky, and sun, farewell.

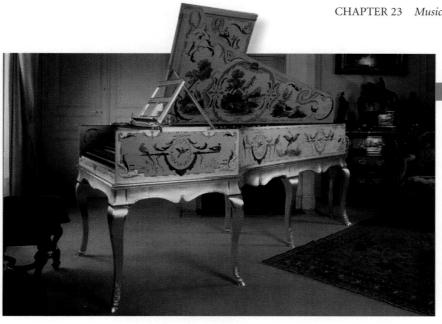

Music & History

The harpsichord is a stringed instrument that dates back to the sixteenth century. Similar to a small modern piano, its strings are plucked, not hammered, with an attachment to the strings. Its soft, vibrant sound is associated with Baroque composers. **The harpsichord was often used with what other instrument as a continuo?**

Music & History
The viola da gamba.

Harmonic Foundations

The French composer and theorist Jean-Philippe Rameau (1683–1764) invented the names of the basic harmonies: tonic, dominant, subdominant, and so forth. Although composers were now using these harmonies, they had not explained their relationships scientifically. The way these harmonies progressed or functioned in homophonic music was now formulized. The principles of chord movement were clarified and codified (explained systematically).

Baroque composers began to think in terms of chords, not just melodies. The harmonic foundation of music became its fundamental expressive force. Like many composers in the Baroque period, Rameau composed instrumental suites comprising stylized dances. During this period, dance rhythms permeated music of all kinds.

Use section E. in the Music Theory Handbook to review harmony.

ACTIVITY ▶ *Describe Baroque Traits*

Why did Baroque composers favor a single melody supported by chords more than the complex contrapuntal music of the past?

Is Jean-Philippe Rameau's composition "Tambourin" for solo harpsichord contrapuntal or homophonic? What musical characteristics give the music its expressive force?

Identify the form of the composition. How is contrast achieved in this composition? How would you describe the melody in the opening and closing sections of the composition?

What percussion instrument is Rameau attempting to suggest in sound?

Activity   Describe Baroque Traits
Instructor's Guide, pages 280–281
CD 14 ⃞13 "Tambourin" (1:09)

The Concerto

In Italy, the Baroque was the age of the great violin makers and of great string music. Baroque composers wrote for strings with the intensity that Renaissance composers wrote for voices. In instrumental music, the suite, the sonata, the concerto, and the "sinfonia" (a forerunner of the Classical symphony) were invented. Composers became increasingly interested in exploiting contrasts of timbre, especially in their instrumental works. In the new **concerto style**, *solo parts alternated with a group of instruments.*

Undoubtedly, the Italian composer Antonio Vivaldi (1678–1741) was the greatest creator of concertos. He wrote more than 500 of them! Vivaldi established the favored three-movement scheme: fast, slow, fast. Most of his concertos are for a solo instrument—chiefly violin—and orchestra. He also composed concertos that contrasted a group of solo instruments with the orchestra. The **concerto grosso** (grand concerto) is *a work in which there is contrast between ripieno (full or tutti) sections for a small string orchestra and concertino (small group of soloists) sections.* The ripieno had the simpler parts and were usually assigned an easily remembered theme or refrain—a *ritornello*—that is repeated. The soloist had the more difficult part. The whole idea of a concerto was the give-and-take between these forces. The "argument" or contest between soloist and orchestra came to a resolution at the end.

PROFILE

Antonio Vivaldi

Antonio Vivaldi was a Venetian composer of the Baroque era. Born in 1678, Vivaldi studied to be a priest, but he also became an accomplished violinist and harpsichordist. When, for reasons not entirely known, Vivaldi left the ministry, he was appointed in 1703 to be the director of music at a girls' orphanage. For nearly 40 years, he composed music suited to the excellent orchestra and chorus at the orphanage. His success and popularity led to commissions and publications of his pieces outside of Italy. One of his most influential publications, *L'estro armonico,* a collection of violin concertos, so impressed J. S. Bach that he transcribed several of them for keyboard.

From 1718 on, Vivaldi traveled widely, composing operas and concertos for various European courts. Unfortunately, much of his prolific output has been lost, but his surviving orchestral works display Vivaldi's skillful and widely copied use of contrasting solo and orchestral sections.

Antonio Vivaldi
Italian Composer
1678–1741

ACTIVITY *Understand the Baroque Concerto*

Activity *Understand the Baroque Concerto*
Instructor's Guide, page 281
TRB 23-3, *"Spring"*
CD 14 ☐14 "Spring," *The Four Seasons* (3:35)

Determine how the Italian Baroque composer Antonio Vivaldi used the concerto as a dramatic and expressive form.

Listen to "Spring" (first movement) from *The Four Seasons* and distinguish the interplay of tutti and solo sections. Using the "Spring" listening puzzle, arrange the blocks in the order in which you hear them. Before you listen again, decide which blocks are similar. Which programmatic descriptions refer to spring?

The most celebrated of Vivaldi's concertos are those that comprise *The Four Seasons* (1725). The descriptive title indicates a programmatic approach. Vivaldi tried to characterize the four seasons and named the concertos accordingly: "Spring," "Summer," "Autumn," and "Winter." In addition, he introduced each work with a sonnet. The music can be quite descriptive. The work is scored for solo violin and a small string orchestra with harpsichord (continuo). It contains the benchmarks of Baroque musical style: virtuoso figuration, elaborate motivic invention, ornamented melody, rhythmic vitality, harmonic clarity, and a clear sense of form. These add up to exuberant expression.

Classical

Even before J. S. Bach died, his sons were exploring ways to express themselves musically that were simpler than the complex, contrapuntal style of their father. They thought that polyphony was too complicated, too cerebral, too unnatural. They resorted to the ideals of classical antiquity—once again. The excavations of Pompeii in 1763 turned attention back to the ancients.

The Beginnings

Like any new generation, Bach's children saw the world differently from their parents. They aspired to a simpler, more natural form of musical expression. They found the affections of Baroque music too artificial. After all, human emotions are in a constant state of transition. Why shouldn't music convey this continuous flux of feeling? Wilhelm Friedemann Bach (1710–1784), Carl Philipp Emanuel (C. P. E.) Bach (1714–1788), and their brother Johann Christian Bach (1735–1782) followed these new instincts and helped establish the new style.

In music, stylistic changes develop gradually. During periods of transition from one major style to another (for example, Renaissance to

Baroque or Baroque to Classical), elements of the old style and new style usually exist side by side. The German composer Michael Praetorius spanned the late Renaissance and early Baroque. His music shows stylistic features of both periods. At the same time that J. S. Bach summed up the contrapuntal style of the Baroque, George Frideric Handel (1685–1759) emphasized melody and harmony.

The mature musical style of the Classical period (c. 1725–1810) can be heard in the works of the greatest composers of the era—Franz Joseph Haydn (1732–1809), Wolfgang Amadeus Mozart (1756–1791), and Ludwig van Beethoven (1770–1827) in his early years. The concertos of Mozart provide a good example of mature Classical style. The overall plan of these works is the same as Vivaldi's concerti: three movements in fast, slow, fast order. The resemblance ends there. Mozart's orchestra is bigger. To Vivaldi's strings he adds woodwinds, trumpets, horns, and timpani. He also uses the orchestra differently, often blending it with the solo parts, rather than alternating tutti with solo sections. **Tutti** indicates *a section of a piece in which all the instruments and/or voices perform together.* Instead of melodies created from short motives, there are fully developed themes. Contrasts of emotions are created within movements by continual changes of instrumental timbres and dynamics. Polyphony is reemployed as an element of the basically homophonic texture.

ACTIVITY ▶ *Tell the Difference*

Compare the first movement of Vivaldi's "Spring" concerto with the second movement of Mozart's Piano Concerto No. 21.

Can you differentiate between Baroque and Classical concertos? Try to answer these questions:
1. How are the two orchestras different?
2. Which concerto has more "songlike" melodies?
3. Which concerto exhibits the most dramatic contrasts of dynamics, texture, and density?
4. How do the roles of soloist and accompaniment differ?
5. Which concerto uses the more subtle dynamic shading?
6. Which concerto would be more difficult to perform? Why?

Activity *Tell the Difference*
Instructor's Guide, pages 281–282
CD 14 ⌷14 "Spring," *The Four Seasons* (3:35)
CD 14 ⌷15 Piano Concerto No. 21 in C Major, second movement (2:57)

A Simpler, Clearer Art

In the eighteenth century, an avid new and influential middle class established a market for music and the other arts. This was the beginning of public concerts. Concertos and sonatas became popular with this new public as vehicles to showcase musical skill. Audiences liked instrumental soloists to display their technique in the same way that singers did in opera. The rise of the middle class was a result of the enormous scientific

Music & ART

American painter Winslow Homer (1836–1910) drew inspiration from European ideals. His artworks were skillfully and carefully constructed, and he often chose regional and local people or events as subjects for his works.

Winslow Homer. *The Studio*. 1867. The Metropolitan Museum of Art, New York, New York. Samuel D. Lee Fund, 1939. (39.14).

and intellectual advances of the preceding century that emphasized natural law and human progress. This Enlightenment or Age of Reason favored common sense, equal rights, and faith in the individual. This was the time of the American Declaration of Independence and the United States Constitution and the Bill of Rights.

In accordance with the scientific thinking of the time, music had to be easily understood and ordered. Classical art was a people's art, dignified and free of complexities. It had to be instantly appealing, natural, universal, and noble. Whereas the Baroque had been grand, intricate, and sometimes pompous, the new music was given a simpler and more direct expression. Instead of the motivic phrases of the Baroque, Classical composers gave balance to their melodies by organizing them in regular two or four-measure antecedent and consequent (or question-and-answer) phrases, sometimes with an extension.

Classical Opera

Mozart's operas have retained their popularity from the time he wrote them in the late 1700s into the twenty-first century. The stories are logical, and characters are delineated musically. Melodies are developed to give the characters greater depth of emotion. Rhythm follows the natural accentuation of the words of the text. Different instrumental timbres in the orchestra produce a variety of moods. The harmonic language is expanded, and dynamics are used expressively. The bass is slowed down, and so are the chord changes.

In the opera *Don Giovanni* (1787), Mozart took musical Classicism to its heights using timeless human themes. This is the story of a scoundrel and his punishment. Don Giovanni is a nobleman whose

Mozart's opera Don Giovanni *combines Classical styles with a timeless theme. In this scene from a 1990 Metropolitan Opera performance, played by Samuel Ramey and Dawn Upshaw, Giovanni tempts Zerlini with a promise of marriage that he does not intend to keep.*

notorious and deceitful pursuits of women finally catch up with him. When he tries to charm Donna Anna, her father, a Commandant, tries to defend her honor. The old man challenges the Don to a fight and is killed. Donna Anna swears to avenge her father's death. In the final act, the statue of the Commandant returns as a ghost, stomping into Don Giovanni's banquet and asking him to mend his ways. The Don refuses. Suddenly, flames engulf the Don, the earth opens, and he is dragged unrepenting to his final persecution.

In Scene 3 of Act 1, the nobleman's decidedly "un-noble" character with women is revealed. Don Giovanni and his friend Leporello happen upon Zerlina and her fiancé, Masetto, two peasants celebrating their engagement. Left alone with Zerlina, Don Giovanni flatters her with a promise of marriage. They sing a duet in which Zerlina is torn by temptation, forced to choose between Masetto and Don Giovanni.

Activity *Sing and Play with*
Classical Balance
Instructor's Guide, page 282
CD 14 16 "La ci darem la mano,"
Don Giovanni (3:11)

ACTIVITY ▶ *Sing and Play with Classical Balance*

**Listen to the duet "La ci darem la mano" between Don Giovanni
and Zerlina, while you follow the music.**

■ Compare the antecedent and consequent phrases sung by Zerlina
to the two phrases sung by Don Giovanni (see notation on page
501). How are they similar, how are they different, and why?
Which phrases end on a strong, tonic cadence?

■ Learn to play these opening phrases on a keyboard instrument.
Try to sing them in Italian. What makes the phrases easy to learn
and remember?

The Development of the Symphony

*Like the symphony, the string
quartet came into existence
during the Classical period
and remains an important
means of expression today.
This ensemble of four instruments usually sounds best in
small places where the
audience is close to the
performers.*

   The symphony came of age as a major instrumental musical form
during the Classical period. Its beginnings can be traced to the Italian
opera overture or sinfonia. As soon as these sinfonias were performed
separately from the opera, they assumed a life of their own. When
composers began to write pieces just for orchestra, they borrowed the
form of the sonata with its several contrasting movements. One of the
early symphonists in Italy was Giovanni Sammartini (1700–1775), who
composed more than 70 symphonies. In Mannheim, a cultural center in
southwest Germany, Johann Stamitz (1717–1757), the director of the
court orchestra, wrote symphonies in four movements with a minuet for
the third. The first movement was in
sonata form.

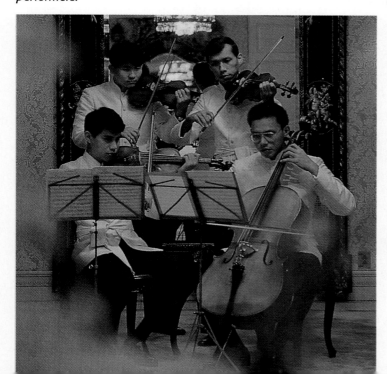

   In addition to Mozart, one of the first
truly great composers of symphonies
was Franz Joseph Haydn, who wrote
more than 100. In his hands the symphony became a powerful new vehicle of
human expression. Haydn's reputation
grew, and he was invited to England
in 1791 and 1794 to conduct performances of his music, including a dozen
new symphonies that he composed for
his visits. In creating the "London"
symphonies, he gave his utmost, not
wanting to disappoint the discerning
English audiences. In these, his final
symphonies, Haydn achieved order,
expressivity, and a noble simplicity.

PROFILE

Franz Joseph Haydn

Franz Joseph Haydn developed many of the basic characteristics of symphonic and string quartet forms and, in the process, established the Classical style. At age eight, Haydn became a chorister in Vienna and remained there studying and performing for 20 years. He met many important people during these years, and he began to compose.

In his late twenties, he was taken into the service of the Hungarian Esterhazy family, one of the wealthiest patrons of the arts. Haydn enjoyed 30 years in their employment. Prince Esterhazy had a theater for opera, a skilled orchestra, and several talented singers. It was Haydn's job to write music, conduct performances, and manage the musicians. The prince became a great champion of Haydn's work.

By the time he was in his forties, Haydn was receiving commissions from all over Europe. During his lifetime, he wrote an astounding number of works, including 104 symphonies, 83 string quartets, scores of other chamber works, 52 piano sonatas, 23 operas, as well as cantatas, masses, and other church music. His oratorios *The Creation* and *The Seasons* retain a place in today's standard repertoire.

Franz Joseph Haydn
Austrian Composer
1732–1809

ACTIVITY *Find the Classical Order*

Listen to the opening section of the second movement of Haydn's Symphony No. 101 in D (*The Clock*). Then answer the following questions to determine how Haydn conveyed an aural sense of classical order:

1. What is the meter? the tempo?
2. How many measures of the "clock" rhythm are present before the main theme enters?
3. What instrument plays the main theme?
4. Listen again and count the number of measures of both presentations of the main theme in the violins. Are both presentations of the theme of equal length?
5. What is the form of this movement?
6. How is a sense of unity achieved?
7. How is contrast accomplished?
8. What in the music suggests that Haydn had a sense of humor?

Activity *Find the Classical Order*
Instructor's Guide, pages 282–283
CD 14 ⟨17⟩ Symphony No. 101 in
    D, (*The Clock*), second
    movement (8:03)

Composers in the eighteenth century almost always wrote their works for specific occasions. As is the case today, composers depended upon a system of patronage for their livelihood. Many eighteenth-century composers were employed in one of the many courts of the nobility where they composed under contract. Some composers held musical posts in churches, while others taught privately or in schools. They wrote on commission, often dedicating a work to the patron who paid for it. Music publishing, which started in the Renaissance, flourished in the Baroque and Classical periods, providing composers with another source of income. During this time, music evolved into a major cultural force. There was a constant demand for new works.

SUMMARY

Much of the history of the human race can be traced from the alternation between periods of Classicism and Romanticism. There appears to be a natural tension between ideal beauty and sensuousness, between the head and the heart, and between thought and emotion that can be traced back to the Greeks and the Romans who also went through periods of stressing one style, then the other. Changes represented by the different musical styles of the Renaissance, Baroque, and Classical periods are a study of these reversals.

Music defines its time, and the times circumscribe the music. How people think and live affects the way they compose and perform. Music characterizes its age. At all points in human history, people react in different ways to the forces of life around them. Some take a conservative view, some a progressive one. Composers choose to write in the old well-worn style or in the new emerging style. A momentum gathers that makes one style dominant. However, there are always alternatives nipping at the edges. These are the prospects that keep cultures moving and changing. That is the excitement of knowing how people were creating and performing in previous generations. Our own twentieth-century music emerges from the same forces.

Building Music Vocabulary

On a sheet of paper, write the term from the list that best matches each description below.

(3) Baroque period
(6) Renaissance period
(5) concerto grosso
(4) terraced dynamics
(9) concerto style
(1) tutti
(7) continuo
(8) word painting
(2) madrigals

1. A section of a piece in which all the instruments and/or voices perform together.
2. Nonreligious Renaissance vocal works in several parts (usually five).
3. The stylistic period between approximately 1600 and 1750.
4. Layered dynamic levels within a composition.
5. An orchestral work which contrasts the tutti, or full orchestra sections, and the concertino sections for a soloist or group of soloists.
6. The stylistic period between approximately 1400 and 1600.
7. A Baroque accompaniment consisting of a harp sounding the chords and a viola da gamba reinforcing the bass line.
8. Music that portrays the literal meaning of the words of the text.
9. Solo parts alternated with a group of instruments.

Reviewing Music Facts

Answer each question in a complete sentence.
10. How did Renaissance composers use the text of their vocal works in a new way?
11. What kind of music is Thomas Weelkes best remembered for?
12. Which Baroque composer created names for the basic harmonies?
13. What is Antonio Vivaldi's most familiar and popular composition?
14. Who wrote the "London" symphonies?

Complete answers for the Chapter 23 Review are found in the Instructor's Guide, page 283.

Thinking It Through

On a sheet of paper, write your responses to the following:
15. **Analyze** Describe how terraced dynamics added feeling and emotion to Baroque music.
16. **Contrast** Describe some of the important differences between the music of the Baroque and Classical periods.
17. **Explain** In your own words, explain why the viola da gamba was added to the harpsichord continuo part.

Making the Connection

Science Find examples of the anatomical sketches of Renaissance artist Leonardo da Vinci. Prepare a display of his work for the class.

Social Studies Find out more about the Age of Reason. Explain how this new way of thinking may have affected the musical styles of the same period.

 Learn more about composers Mozart, Vivaldi, and Haydn at **www.glencoe.com/sec/music**

CHAPTER 24

Jazz

Jazz is America's musical gift to the world. This unique invention, born in New Orleans and bred largely in Memphis, St. Louis, Chicago, and New York, is still alive and kicking and going into its second century of high status. Without a doubt, it is the most original and influential music to emerge from the American continent—so far.

The most original, influential, and American of all our music is jazz, and one significant jazz artist was Miles Davis (1926–1991) shown in this photo. Playing a trumpet from the age of 13, his crisp solos were unforgettable. **What musicians do you associate with jazz?**

Caption answer
Possibilities are: Dizzy Gillespie, Charlie Parker, Benny Goodman, John Coltrane, Ella Fitzgerald, Al Jarreau, Wynton and Branford Marsalis, Herbie Hancock, and Chick Corea.

Objectives

By completing this chapter, you will:
- Learn about the beginnings of jazz.
- Become acquainted with the early contributions of Jelly Roll Morton, Fletcher Henderson, and Louis Armstrong.
- Be able to distinguish between the many styles of jazz, such as Dixieland, small band jazz, swing, bebop, and fusion.
- Learn some examples of classic jazz.
- Find out about the contributions of other jazz performers, such as Charlie Parker and Dizzy Gillespie, and learn what made them so great.

Vocabulary

bop
break
Dorian mode
fusion
scat singing
swing

Musicians to Meet

Benny Goodman
Charlie Parker

The Beginnings

The roots of jazz in and around New Orleans extend back into the second half of the nineteenth century, perhaps earlier. Brass bands, made up of African Americans, played there during the War of 1812. During this period, African Americans participated in a rich, expressive music of their own. In churches they sang spirituals. Outside they sang work songs and the blues and played dance tunes.

While spirituals and blues had some influence on the development of ragtime and jazz, the New Orleans brass bands and the minstrel bands of the period seem to have been their most direct ancestors. These bands used the classical instruments of the day—trumpets, trombones, clarinets, saxophones, and drums. Jazz seems to have evolved slowly from many sources.

Ferdinand "Jelly Roll" Morton (1885–1941) was one of the key figures in the early jazz movement in New Orleans. Morton was a pianist and bandleader who helped bring together many of the varied African-American musical elements that were the building blocks of early jazz. In particular, he helped perfect the New Orleans jazz style that featured a unique blend of polyphonic improvisations. The music had a highly contrapuntal texture in which a melody would be stated by a trumpet (or in the early years, a cornet), and, at the same time, countermelodies would be improvised on the trombone and clarinet. This was group improvisation.

Morton's improvisations at the piano, his use of blue notes, jazz harmonies, and a looser beat established a Dixieland style of music. During the first decade of the century, he broke out of the confines of ragtime, creating a music that expressed a wider range of emotions. Morton claimed to have begun using the term "jazz" in 1902 as a way to distinguish this style from ragtime. As a musician, Morton exhibited unusual versatility and a preference for music that spoke from the heart. He and his group—Jelly Roll Morton and His Red Hot Peppers—introduced a swinging drive. They held back so that they could give their all in a rousing finale. This technique is exemplified in his recording of his "Black Bottom Stomp" (1926).

The Jazz Age

Jazz found its dancing feet in the early decades of the twentieth century. It was an earthy urban music that invited people to celebrate themselves. During the First World War, musicians went north from

---

You may wish to use "Survey the Public About Jazz" at this time. Lesson plans for the activity are found on page 290 in the Instructor's Guide.

Music in the World
Memphis, Tennessee, and St. Louis, Missouri

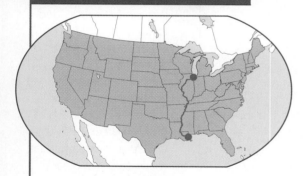

MUSIC in the WORLD

THE MISSISSIPPI RIVER became the route of travel for jazz musicians moving from New Orleans, Louisiana, to northern states where they sought work. As a result, jazz increased in popularity and influenced other music styles. *What two other cities famous for music are located along this route?*

New Orleans up the Mississippi seeking work in Memphis, St. Louis, and Chicago. Their new sound drew a wider audience, including the white cornetist Bix Beiderbecke, one of the most creative jazz musicians of the 1920s. The style of music was New Orleans Dixieland jazz, and the bands were small, with little, if any, duplication of instruments.

During the Roaring Twenties—the Jazz Age—teenage youths shocked their parents by dancing to the Charleston and the Black Bottom. This was also the decade of the passage of the nineteenth amendment, in 1920, giving women the right to vote. Jelly Roll Morton's "Black Bottom Stomp" is typical of this new rhythmic urgency. Jazz is primarily a rhythmic feeling that is induced by combining the steady beat with rhythms that play around and tease it. Soloists improvised melodies rhythmically, shifting accents to the weak beats and emphasizing syncopation and offbeats. The custom of clapping on the offbeats (2 and 4) sets up this competition with the strong beats (1 and 3). The rhythm of jazz is actually polyrhythmic.

Among the many distinguishing features of Dixieland jazz is its march-like feeling and reliance on duple meter. Dixieland features a "front line" of instruments: trumpet, clarinet, and trombone. (These instruments attained their front line position in the New Orleans marching bands.) Chordophones such as banjos and mandolins were often included in these early ensembles. In the interweaving of various lines, the melody or lead line is meant to stand out, and the others are supposed to be less obvious. There is a definite distinction between foreground and background. In polyphonic music with several different parts sounding simultaneously, there is a need to give the music focus.

Use section A. in the *Music Theory Handbook* to review meter.

Music & CULTURE

The Crescent City Joymakers perform their brand of Dixieland jazz at New Orleans Preservation Hall in 1982, preserving a musical tradition that started there early in the twentieth century. **How many instruments can you identify?**

Music & Culture
The clarinet, bass, piano, banjo (left to right).

Activity *Identify the Instruments*
Instructor's Guide, pages 284–285
CD 14 |18| "Black Bottom Stomp"
            (3:09)

ACTIVITY ▶ *Identify the Instruments*

As you listen to "Black Bottom Stomp," an example of early jazz from New Orleans, work with a classmate to identify how many performers make up Jelly Roll Morton's Red Hot Peppers.

The best way to do this is to write down all the instruments you hear being played. (Here are two hints: Morton himself plays piano on "Black Bottom Stomp," and there is only one player per instrument in the remainder of the band.)

Once you have identified the instruments, try to answer the following questions:

1. There are three main improvised solo sections in this piece. Can you name them in order?
2. There are four very short "breaks" in this piece. (A "break" is a measure or two where everyone stops except the soloist.) Can you name the breaks by instrument in the order they are played?
   (Hint: One of these short breaks is played by two instruments; another occurs in the middle of one of the three solo sections.)

When you have figured out the ensemble makeup and the location of the solos and breaks, listen again for Jelly Roll's characteristic New Orleans improvised counterpoint. These are the roots of Dixieland.

Among the distinctive traits of early jazz was the "stride" piano style of Eubie Blake, James P. Johnson, and Earl Hines. It was built on a steady, "oom-pah-pah," timekeeping, left-hand bass, against which the right hand shifted the accents as it embellished the tune. A good stride pianist could imitate the entire band. The early stride pianists were influential in carving out an important place for the piano in jazz. In turn, their work influenced successive generations of pianists. Thomas "Fats" Waller, Art Tatum, and Thelonious Monk followed in their footsteps, taking jazz piano into all the prevailing new styles.

The art of jazz very often involves taking an existing song and embellishing its melody. This was very characteristic of the Dixieland jazz bands. They favored the technique of short improvised "riffs" or "licks" in a call-and-response format, a form which derived from spirituals and work songs. The tune "When the Saints Go Marchin' In" lends itself very well to this type of improvisation. The Preservation Hall Jazz Band epitomizes the New Orleans Dixieland style. This is polyphony with a beat!

ACTIVITY ▶ *Improvise a Dixieland Classic*

Activity *Improvise a Dixieland Classic*
Instructor's Guide, page 285
CD 14 |19| "When the Saints Go Marchin' In" (1:51)

Can you find four appropriate places for a responsive improvisation in "When the Saints Go Marchin' In"?

Before you listen, sing the tune "straight"—just as it is printed. As you sing, see if you can determine where it would be suitable and musically interesting to add an improvised "lick."

Try first to tap out the rhythms of your improvisations in the places where you think they will fit. Then, sing your improvisations. You may use actual words (derived from the lyrics) or scat syllables (nonsense words such as "doo-wah, doo-wee.")

Now listen to the Preservation Hall Jazz Band play this tune. Although they are improvising primarily on instruments, keep an ear out for the similarities between the improvisational ideas in the band and your own improvised musical ideas.

When the Saints Go Marching In

Negro Spiritual

The Emergence of Swing

Fletcher Henderson (1897–1952) was a pioneering bandleader, composer, and arranger. During the 1930s, other bands adopted the basic Henderson style as their model. Toward the end of the Roaring Twenties, a new type of jazz was emerging in his band—swing. Although the music was not fully developed swing, it certainly contained its roots.

Henderson led the field. He enlarged the band and established the instrumentation that became standard. There were three sections: a brass section, a reed section, and a rhythm section. His arrangements used a call-and-response form in which the various sections of the "orchestra" took turns speaking to each other. Solos alternated with the larger ensemble. This "antiphonal" style became the trademark of swing bands. Consequently, jazz music evolved into a sectional form.

Activity *Distinguish the Sections*
Instructor's Guide, pages 285–286
CD 14 [20] "Henderson Stomp"
          (2:50)

ACTIVITY ▶ *Distinguish the Sections*

Can you hear the various sections in a jazz tune?

Listen to the recording of Fletcher Henderson's classic dance tune, the "Henderson Stomp." After an eight-measure introduction, try to figure out the precise length of each thematic section. This means you must concentrate and count measures aurally. You will be successful if you count measures in a meter of two rather than four. The secret to this problem may be found in counting the length of the stride piano solo by band member Fats Waller.

Composer/arranger and pianist Fletcher Henderson (1897–1952) is credited with inventing the structure of the big band with its sectional instrumentation. Shown here is Henderson and his band in 1936 at the Grand Terrace in Chicago. **What jazz style emerged from his band?**

Caption answer
Swing music.

In the mid-1920s, the great jazz trumpeter Louis Armstrong made musical history leading his Hot Five—brothers Johnny and Warren Dodds, Kid Ory, and Lil Hardin Armstrong, his wife. Recordings he made with the Hot Five (1925–1927) and later with the Hot Seven (1927) set new standards for jazz solo virtuosity.

Louis Armstrong, one of the giants of jazz, trumpeted his way out of New Orleans into international stardom. Armstrong's playing was unique and masterful, and he took the trumpet to new heights of musical expression. He gave a different emphasis to the rhythm with well-placed, subtle accents that swung. His way of playing influenced the way every other musician in the band (and many others who heard him) played.

Armstrong is given credit for turning the Henderson band, and those that copied it, into swing bands. The term **swing** refers to *the special rhythmic character that jazz musicians add to the music.* Swing became a label for the style as well as an era (1935–1945) in jazz history.

Single-handedly, Armstrong established the standard for solo jazz artistry. His facility on trumpet was phenomenal. Vocally, he complemented his instrumental improvisations with spontaneous singing on nonsense syllables. This **scat singing**—*a form of vocal improvisation*—became a characteristic that many jazz singers adopted. They would sing a chorus straight, then follow it with an improvised scat chorus. Scat singing became a form of creative expression in jazz, but the singing, too, was different—an African-American creation that was more rhythmic and hard-edged than the mellow crooning of the time.

During the 1920s, jazz evolved into a sectional form with the full ensemble alternating with solo sections. If the jazz composition was built on a blues tune, it might be segmented into 12- or 16-bar sections. Many of the tunes that were created maintained a basic 32-bar length. When an instrument improvised a chorus, it was usually 32 bars long, often with a 2-bar break just before the next 32-bar section began. These short **breaks** were *cadenza-like improvisations by a jazz instrumentalist or singer that were inserted between ensemble passages.* Like the cadenza in a classical concerto, breaks added an interesting textural variety to the composition.

"Hotter Than That" (1927) is a brilliant example of the new style of "hot" jazz. This work was composed by Lil Hardin Armstrong, the pianist in the Hot Seven band and Armstrong's wife. In the A^3 section, the guitarist maintains the steady 4/4 pulse while Armstrong improvises vocally in what is essentially a 3/4 rhythm. The performances throughout are improvisational within the format of a fairly strict sectional structure:

Hotter Than That

Sections	Performers	Length
Intro	Everyone	8 bars
A^1*	Trumpet & rhythm Clarinet Breaks (2)	32 bars
A^2*	Clarinet & rhythm Vocal Break (2)	32 bars
A^3*	Voice & guitar	32 bars
B	Voice/guitar duet **	16 bars
C	Piano interlude	4 bars
A^4*	Trombone & rhythm (14) Trumpet Break (2)	16 bars
B	Everyone (14) Guitar Break (2)	16 bars
Coda	Trumpet (2) Guitar (2)	4 bars

*There are also 2-bar breaks in these sections just ahead of the second 16 bars. **Alternating 2-bar breaks.

From *Early Jazz: Its Roots and Musical Development* by Gunther Schuller.
Copyright © 1968 by Oxford University Press, Inc. Reprinted By Permission. All Rights Reserved.

Activity *Detect the Improvisation*
Instructor's Guide, page 286
CD 14 21 "Hotter Than That"
    (3:00)

Louis Armstrong
American Jazz Trumpeter
1901–1971

ACTIVITY ▶ *Detect the Improvisation*

Can you hear and identify improvisation in Louis Armstrong's performance of "Hotter Than That"?

Follow the sectionalized analysis map (above) as you listen to this 1927 masterpiece. The first time you listen, make a list of all the sections in which you hear improvisation.

During a second listening, make a list of all the sections in which you hear breaks.

Discuss: Why do this group and this piece represent the 1920s concept of "hot" jazz?

The Big Band Era

The Wall Street crash of 1929 led to the Great Depression of the 1930s that began in the United States and spread abroad. Many people lost their fortunes. Jobs were scarce, and unemployment was high. Survival was difficult. It was a time when people turned to motion pictures and music to lift their spirits. These were years when people drew together, and the Second World War united Americans as they had never been united before. At its best, swing reflected this cohesiveness in its ensemble—musicians and dancers caught up totally by the beat. Radio spread the joy across the country.

The big band era began in earnest in the mid-1930s and went on until nearly the end of the 1940s, a period of about 15 years. Swing, we should not forget, was primarily dance music. Teenage youth abandoned the serene fox trots and waltzes of their parents in favor of the frantic gyrations of the jitterbug and the Lindy Hop. The two-beat meter of early jazz gradually gave way to a solid four. The beats were now evenly accented and of equal value. Swing was a technique that could be applied to just about any existing piece of music. Now more than a half century later, swing has become a dance craze again. Do you have friends who enjoy swing dancing?

Bandleader, arranger, and clarinetist Woody Herman (1916–1987) and his Thundering Herd rode the crest of jazz from 1936 well into the 1980s. The popularity of the band was assured in 1939 with the million-selling recording of "Woodchopper's Ball."

PROFILE

Benny Goodman

*Benny Goodman
American Clarinetist and
Swing Band Director
1909–1986*

Clarinetist Benny Goodman was born into a poor Russian-Jewish family in Chicago. A child prodigy, he took lessons at the local synagogue and played in a band. When he was 16, he joined the Ben Pollack band in Los Angeles and three years later went with them to New York, which became his home base.

In 1934, at the age of 25, he formed his own band and hired Fletcher Henderson as his chief arranger. The Goodman Orchestra was featured on the Saturday evening coast-to-coast radio show *Let's Dance*, causing a national craze for jitterbugging. The band is credited with beginning the swing era. In 1936 Goodman formed his trio, one of the first interracial musical groups. He later expanded it to a quartet and then a septet. In 1949 he disbanded his orchestra, marking the end of the swing era.

Goodman is also noted as the first jazz artist to establish an equally successful parallel career as a concert artist. He commissioned clarinet concertos from composers Aaron Copland and Paul Hindemith, and he appeared as a soloist with all the major American symphony orchestras.

The bands of the 1930s were first and foremost dance orchestras, not jazz bands. The tunes that were best for dancing often became the popular, commercial successes. Compared with the best of the jazz that was produced by these bands, much of this music was mediocre. The need to make a living caused many jazz artists to compromise their art for the sake of commercial success.

The best of the swing bands—those of Jimmy Lunceford, Fletcher Henderson, Count Basie, and Duke Ellington—were African American, but there were many excellent white bands as well, among them, those of Tommy Dorsey, Benny Goodman, Woody Herman, Harry James, Stan Kenton, and Glenn Miller. The genre is defined by the artistic excellence of many fine performers and creators who contributed to its development.

By the beginning of the swing era, around 1935, the saxophone had replaced the clarinet as the reed instrument of choice for solo jazz work. The one clarinetist who stayed very much in the forefront of jazz, however, was Benny Goodman. He was known as a virtuoso clarinet performer. Like Wynton Marsalis today, he played the classical literature as well as jazz. His big band was highly successful. In fact, he became known as the "King of Swing"—an unfortunate label because it suggested that other great bandleaders were somehow less competent. As an artist, Goodman could take almost any tune and polish it into a miniature gem; he was among the best.

As the saxophone began to define the swing era, many exceptional sax soloists began to set new standards for tonal beauty, technical wizardry, and improvisational creativity. According to jazz critic Grover Sales, "The saxophones became dominant jazz instruments because musicians sensed they were akin to the human voice and that you could make these instruments sing." The saxophone gradually established itself as a jazz instrument largely in the hands of Coleman Hawkins (1904–1969). He demonstrated how his tenor sax could negotiate solos, and his influence helped to establish the sax section in swing bands.

Count Basie's nine-piece band honed its style in Kansas City, where jazz and dance melded artfully. These musicians knew how to swing, and the band had a rhythm section—guitar, bass, and drums—that urged the musicians on. Basie's piano filled in and kept the rhythm swinging. The lead tenor saxophonist with the Count Basie Orchestra during the 1930s was one of the all-time great tenor players—Lester Young. While Coleman Hawkins had established the tenor saxophone as a gutsy robust instrument, Young showed its lyrical and subtle richness. His playing became the model for other jazz musicians, including the incomparable alto saxophonist Charlie Parker. Young inspired most of the artists who dominated jazz in the early 1950s, showing them a new sensitivity and artistry.

ACTIVITY ▶ *Debate Your Preference*

Activity *Debate Your Preference*
Instructor's Guide, pages 286–287
CD 14 [22] "China Boy" (2:33)
CD 14 [23] "Cherokee" (2:14)

While the clarinet enjoyed a prominent role during the early history of jazz, the saxophone became the favored reed instrument during the later swing era.

Which of these two reed instruments would you argue is better for improvised jazz solos? In groups of three or four students, choose an instrument (clarinet or sax) and prepare to debate this issue. All of your information must be gathered by listening carefully to two different swing hits: "China Boy" featuring Benny Goodman (clarinet) and his trio, and "Cherokee" featuring Lester Young (tenor sax) and the Count Basie Orchestra.

Before you begin, it is important to note that both soloists are considered by jazz critics and historians to be among the finest musicians ever to have played these reed instruments. They are virtuosos. Also, the tunes were recorded within a year of one another (1938 and 1937 respectively), and both are composed in the standard A A B A song form. Finally, each features extensive improvisation on familiar melodies.

Start your clarinet-versus-sax debates after listening and taking notes. When you have concluded, answer this question: Why are these versions of "China Boy" and "Cherokee" classified as swing?

Music & ART
Romare Bearden (1914–1988) grew up in Harlem, New York, and drew inspiration from the rhythms and textures of African-American music, especially jazz. Jazz musicians used the term "woodshed" to mean "practicing," although it also might refer to a jazz club where these musicians are performing.

Romare Bearden. *The Woodshed.* 1969. The Metropolitan Museum of Art, New York. George A. Hearn Fund, 1970. (1970.19)

The 1940s and Bebop

Right after the Second World War, interest in jazz intensified. While big band jazz had become a formula, another style was emerging. Some of the younger jazz musicians wanted the freedom to create outside the confines of swing. This new style—called "bop" or "bebop"—was invented in Harlem jam sessions that took jazz back to a small combo. **Bop,** *a complex and sophisticated type of improvised jazz,* was an art for listening rather than dancing to. It was a reaction against the rigid conventions of swing. The jazz world was suddenly split into two camps: swing versus bop.

Trumpeter John Birks "Dizzy" Gillespie (1917–1996) and alto saxophonist Charlie "Yardbird" Parker (1920–1955) led this new movement and changed the face of jazz in the 1940s. They introduced melodic and harmonic innovations that established the style of contemporary jazz. These pioneers gave bop the sophistication of classical chamber music. Melodies became more chromatic. Harmonies and rhythms became far more complex. Beats were often doubled from four to eight, and constantly shifting accents created intricate polyrhythms. There were rapid tempos and dazzling technical displays but, at the same time, a seething soulfulness. Improvisations on the lips of these masterful musicians became more complex, dissonant, and daring. Parker's brilliance as an improviser was not measured just by the notes he could spin, but with the blues he could wrap them in. His bop could be melancholic. Through his improvisation a tune was transformed into a higher state—a reincarnation through invention.

Bebop or "modern jazz" was a more intimate art than the big band jazz. Jazz artists realized that what they were doing and saying went deeper than just easy entertainment or music for dancing. They could be profound and virtuosic, subtle and sophisticated, sensitive and expressive. With bebop, jazz declared itself an art, and the performers, artists. One of the goals of these beboppers was to see how far they could stretch a musical composition while still maintaining its basic formal structure. Fast and creatively complex improvisation became the highest form of art. Together Parker and Gillespie expanded the language of jazz, and other musicians studied their innovations and learned from them.

Charlie Parker
American Saxophonist
1920–1955

PROFILE

Charlie Parker

Saxophonist Charlie Parker, nicknamed "Bird," was one of the most creative and brilliant musicians in jazz history. His smooth technique, harmonically daring ideas, and inspired solos are still widely imitated, and many of his compositions, such as *Confirmation* and *Ornithology,* are now jazz standards.

Growing up in Kansas City, Missouri, Parker hung out in night clubs, where he heard "blowing matches," or competitions between local and visiting sax players. He began playing baritone saxophone in high school. Later his mother gave him an alto saxophone, and he soon dropped out of school to devote himself to the instrument.

After gaining experience in the Kansas City clubs, Parker joined the Jay McShann swing band in 1938. It was during this period that he met Dizzy Gillespie, and they, along with a handful of other musicians, went on to invent a new kind of jazz called bebop during the mid-1940s. Bebop was more complicated rhythmically and harmonically than earlier jazz styles. In the late 1940s and early 1950s Parker made many great recordings and memorable performances. However, a heroin addiction and other health problems began to take a physical and emotional toll and brought about his tragically early death.

Activity *Sing a Jazz Classic*
Instructor's Guide, page 288
CD 14 |24| *Cotton Tail* (3:09)
CD 14 |25| "Shaw 'Nuff" (2:57)

ACTIVITY ▶ *Sing a Jazz Classic*

Can you sing the melody of "I Got Rhythm" while you listen to two different jazz tunes?

You already know this hallmark tune in the world of jazz. Review it by reading and singing the sheet-music version below.

To compare the complex and intricate improvisational style of bebop with the more dancelike feeling of swing, listen to two recordings based on George Gershwin's "I Got Rhythm." First, listen to Duke Ellington's *Cotton Tail* (1940) swing with its tenor sax solo performed by Ben Webster. (You studied this tune and Webster's brilliant improvisation in Chapter 18.) Then listen to "Shaw 'Nuff" (1945), bebop by alto saxophonist Charlie Parker and trumpeter Dizzy Gillespie. While you listen to each tune, try to sing Gershwin's famous melody.

- In which composition does the improvisation seem more "far out"?

- In which is it more difficult to stay true to the original melody?

Based on these performing and listening experiences, how would you describe the difference between bebop and swing?

MIDI TECHNOLOGY OPTION

Technology Option
Use Project 24 in the *MIDI
Activities* binder.

- **Music with MIDI** Use a MIDI program to create a bebop solo over an emulation of a jazz band accompaniment. Explore different approaches to jazz improvisation.

I Got Rhythm

Words by Ira Gershwin

Music by George Gershwin

Although jazz is largely an instrumental expression, there have been a number of outstanding jazz singers, beginning with Louis Armstrong and Billie Holiday and continuing with such greats as Sarah Vaughan and Ella Fitzgerald. Jazz singers developed many of the techniques of the jazz instrumentalist—a natural brassy tone, a rhythmic delivery, and the ability to improvise. Jazz is not a simple art. It takes considerable practice and an excellent ear.

The term "jazz" gradually became the umbrella label for a number of styles—"swing" in the 1930s, "bebop" in the 1940s, "cool," "progressive," or "hard bop" in the 1950s, and "fusion" in the 1960s and 1970s. From ragtime, blues, and early jazz to the swing era and the bebop period, the jazz scene absorbed many dramatic and creative new directions. The new styles generally emerged even when the old style was still popular. Inevitably, there was a time when the old and new styles existed side by side. That is why the dating of these styles can appear to be confusing, and there is disagreement among the experts as to when these styles began and ended. Often, there was a transition period during which the old style was waning while the new style was establishing itself.

You probably can easily distinguish ragtime from Dixieland or tell the difference between swing and bebop. Through all these stylistic changes, however, many of the basic musical forms and performance values (e.g., 12-bar blues and 32-bar A A B A song form, improvisation, syncopation, and the instrumentation of brass, saxophone, and rhythm) remained constant into the twenty-first century. It is the consistency of these "basics" that solidifies the musical linkage between all the evolving styles within the broad history of jazz.

With her rich contralto voice, singer Ella Fitzgerald (1918–1966) became well known for her scat singing—vocal inventions that are the counterpart of instrumental jazz improvisations. Her finest work can be heard in "Lady Be Good" and "How High the Moon." **Can you name two other female jazz singers?**

Caption answer
Billie Holiday and Sarah Vaughan.

Two visual trademarks for which Dizzy Gillespie was noted were his "chipmunk-pouch" facial appearance and the bent bell on his trumpet. He was featured in medical journals because his cheeks were so unusual.

The 1950s and Cool Jazz

Change often stems from dissatisfaction. That was the case again in the 1950s when there was a reaction against the complexity of bebop. The white reaction to bebop was a revival of older forms of jazz— Dixieland, ragtime, and the jazz style of King Oliver. The African-American reaction was a return to blues dressed up with a danceable beat, a style called "rhythm and blues." Still another reaction was the invention of a simpler style through the use of different modes—musical scales other than the major and minor. One of the leading players of this "modal jazz" was trumpeter Miles Davis (1926–1991). Another innovator during this time period was the great jazz pianist Thelonious Monk (1917–1982). Davis and Monk are legends to millions of "hip" jazz fans.

Jazz now took a turn at being cerebral. The emotional intensity of bop was cast aside. Stan Getz, Miles Davis, Stan Kenton, Bill Evans, Dave Brubeck, Woody Herman, George Shearing, and Gerry Mulligan expanded the language of jazz technically. In the 1950s "progressive" or "cool" jazz, which incorporated a simpler melody and rhythm than bop, flourished chiefly on the West Coast. Sonny Rollins and John Coltrane led a wave of "hard bop." The 1950s was a time of diverse styles and rapid changes. Jazz was transforming itself once more.

The Miles Davis Sextet in the late 1950s included alto saxist Cannonball Adderley, pianist Bill Evans, and alto (later soprano) saxophonist John Coltrane. The Sextet was the principle jazz group of that time, producing influential albums such as *Miles Davis + 19* (1958) and

Kind of Blue (1959). Davis' style of playing was restrained and moody, and it was copied endlessly. These albums brought a new public to jazz. The tune "All Blues" on the latter album is a 12-bar blues set in the **Dorian mode,** *a scale with the pattern of whole step, half, whole, whole, whole, half, and whole.*

Activity *Test Your Knowledge*
Instructor's Guide, page 288
CD 15 ☐1 "Smoke Gets in Your
        Eyes" (4:29)
CD 15 ☐2 "All Blues" (3:34)

ACTIVITY ▶ *Test Your Knowledge*

How accurately can you identify traditional forms used in the "new" jazz of the 1950s?

You will hear a composition performed by two greats. Pianist Thelonious Monk plays his 1954 version of the classic song "Smoke Gets in Your Eyes," and trumpeter Miles Davis plays his almost entirely improvised tune "All Blues." The test here is simple. Listen carefully to the musical repetition and contrast in both examples and write down the form of each.

Challenge The influential "All Blues" with Davis and John Coltrane uses the Dorian mode beginning on G. Musicians call this "G Dorian," and it is an easy scale to play. The notes in the scale are G A B♭ C D E F G. You may want to play the following patterns along with the recording, then improvise some new ideas by using either set of just three notes.

Jazz took a back seat during the rock explosion of the 1960s and 1970s. This was a time of experimentation and of looking for new beginnings. There were attempts at collective improvisation. The "free jazz" of Ornette Coleman stretched expression to its ultimate limits, making music that was atonal and intellectualized. New structures were tried that broke away from reliance on repetition of a given harmonic pattern. There were experiments with different tempos and mixed meters, with new textures and densities, and with the use of timbres from other cultures. One of the briefer experiments in jazz was the concept that Gunther Schuller called "third-stream" music—a fusion of jazz with the techniques of Western art music. Jazz presented itself in many guises.

Tenor (and soprano) saxo-
phonist John Coltrane
(1926–1967) crafted his art
while performing with Dizzy
Gillespie, Miles Davis, and
Thelonious Monk. His recordings from 1959 to 1965
demonstrate his majestic tone
and emotional power. He
continued to experiment,
spending his final years
exploring the free jazz of
Ornette Coleman.

In the 1960s, Miles Davis and others managed to merge rock with jazz. This *combination of jazz and rock*, called **fusion**, introduced electronic keyboards to jazz. The synthesizer was invited to become a jazz instrument. Musicians such as Herbie Hancock, Chick Corea, and Quincy Jones continue in this fusion vein today, relying heavily on technology. For purists, the problem is that fusion rather handily obscures two fundamental pillars of jazz: basic forms and improvisation. However, jazz is still reinventing itself.

ACTIVITY ▶ *Distinguish Between Rock and Jazz*

What makes "Birdland" a fusion of jazz and rock?

Listen to the fusion hit "Birdland" (1977), performed by Joe Zawinul and his five-member group, Weather Report. Do you hear a guitar—or is it a synthesizer?

Make a list of the qualities of this music that derive from rock and those that reflect jazz. Is "Birdland" more rock, or more jazz?

Activity *Distinguish Between Rock and Jazz*
Instructor's Guide, page 288
CD 15 ⒊ "Birdland" (3:34)

In jazz today, there is a simultaneous diversity of styles, all legitimate and acceptable. One style no longer dominates. In fact, almost all the jazz styles of the past remain current today. In the 1990s there was a trend of going back to acoustic jazz with a bebop flavor. This jazz reflects a deep reverence for the creative and technical genius of Armstrong and Parker. In the new century, the emphasis is on brilliant, moving, improvisation such as we hear in performances by Wynton and Branford Marsalis, Joshua Redman, Marcus Roberts, and Christian McBride. As was true from the 1940s on, this music demonstrates that jazz is a vehicle for some of the most inspired and artistic creation ever heard. It also proves that exercising one's musical imagination through improvisation is an intellectual and creative process of the highest level.

SUMMARY

The most original, influential, and American of all our music is jazz. It is one of the great contributions of African Americans to Western civilization. When Africans were uprooted and brought to the New World as slaves, their musical culture met head on with the European-based culture already here. Soon Southern African Americans were playing all the new instruments—cornets (trumpets), clarinets, trombones, saxophones, banjos, and guitars—and doing so with the spontaneity, pizzazz, and rhythmic sense that reflected their African heritage. They made the most of these new musical resources, and the result was a wholly original expression—jazz.

Taken as a whole, jazz is largely an "up" music, but its expressive range is as broad as its many styles. Tracing the evolution of this new musical species is difficult. It appears to have made its first recognizable appearance in New Orleans in the early years of the twentieth century. It spread quickly to other urban centers and spawned generations of musicians, both black and white, and a whole series of styles—Dixieland, small band jazz, swing, bebop, free jazz, and fusion, among others. Today, jazz is an important part of every American's musical heritage, a unique and splendid art that reveals the vitality and the variety of our collective being.

Complete answers for the Chapter 24 Review are found in the Instructor's Guide, pages 289–290.

Building Music Vocabulary

On a sheet of paper, write the term from the list that best matches each description below.

(5) bop
(3) fusion
(2) break
(1) scat singing
(4) Dorian mode
(6) swing

1. An improvised singing style that imitates the sound of an instrument.
2. Cadenza-like improvisations by a jazz instrumentalist or singer that were inserted between ensemble passages.
3. A combination of styles, for example, jazz/rock.
4. A scale with the pattern of whole step, half, whole, whole, whole, half, whole.
5. An complex and sophisticated type of improvised jazz.
6. The special rhythmic character that jazz musicians add to the music.

Reviewing Music Facts

Answer each question in a complete sentence.

7. Which early twentieth-century musician has been called the first great jazz composer?
8. What characteristic is common to Dixieland jazz music?
9. What was Fletcher Henderson's contribution to the development of swing?
10. In the 1930s, what instrument became the favorite instrument of solo jazz works?
11. Which two musicians are associated with jazz development in the 1940s?
12. Name at least two jazz singers.
13. What musical style became more popular in the 1960s and 1970s?

Thinking It Through

On a sheet of paper, write your responses to the following.

14. **Explain** Describe how jazz had roots in African-American brass bands as early as 1812.
15. **Compare and Contrast** Describe the similarities and differences between bop and swing.
16. **Apply** What do jazz breaks have in common with the cadenzas of the classical concerto?

Making the Connection

Science Learn more about the way sound is produced on the trumpet. Then investigate possible reasons for Dizzy Gillespie's "chipmunk" cheeks when he played the trumpet.

Visual Art Many artists have created paintings with jazz and jazz musicians as the subject or inspiration. Find at least one example of such a painting, and tell which kind of jazz it most illustrates: bop, big band, cool jazz, and so on.

 You'll discover more about American jazz history and musicians at **www.glencoe.com/sec/music**

Answers to Chapter 24 Review

7. Jelly Roll Morton.
8. An embellished melody.
9. He enlarged the jazz band and initiated innovative instrumental styles.
10. The saxophone.
11. John Birks "Dizzy" Gillespie and Charlie "Yardbird" Parker.
12. Louis Armstrong, Billie Holiday, Sarah Vaughan, and Ella Fitzgerald.
13. Rock music.
14. The players in brass bands used rhythms of the traditional band music; they also brought their styles of gospel music, work songs, and the blues to their music making.
15. Both styles had their roots in jazz. Bebop was art for listening, while swing was for dancing to.
16. Both showcase the skill and artistry of the soloist.

You may wish to use
Assessment Master 8, Unit
Eight Test, in the TRB.

Chapter 22 Project
Instructor's Guide, page 291

Chapter 22 Project

 Write Your Own Editorial

Read the August 27, 1990, editorial from *The Washington Post* **(below) and write an essay that addresses the following questions:**

How can certain types of music be used to attract and repel people? Focusing on one of the musical styles referred to in the editorial, mention specific characteristics that would appeal to some people and offend others.

Easy Listening

Music continues to be the psychic battleground on which the fiercest campaigns of intergenerational culture wars are waged. Forget the Beatles, forget the Stones, forget 2 Live Crew: This time, the aggression is going the other way—and classical and country and western are the chosen weapons. The Associated Press reports a widening circle of 7-Elevens and other convenience stores in the Pacific Northwest have begun to deal with the problem of disorderly young customers "hanging out" by filling the parking lots with music these customers can't stand: for instance, recordings of Mantovani and of Perry Como. The mastermind of the policy, a "loss prevention manager" for the Southland Corporation that owns the 7-Eleven chain, explains that he got the idea when he noticed his teenaged son fleeing the house whenever he played the '60s songs that are now referred to as "classic rock."

If this is the direct-mail philosophy played out in a weird new dimension, it nonetheless seems to work quite nicely. In Tillicum, near Seattle, a convenience store called Hoagy's Corner is blaring a country-and-western radio station in its parking lot to keep young GIs from two nearby military bases from sitting around too long in the parking lot with their own car radios on loud. (The country and western isn't so audible from inside the store, so the GIs still make their purchases, and the neighboring stores have nothing but praise for the selections.) Some 7-Elevens across the border in western Canada have cut down on loitering by playing Petula Clark or even Mozart.

A bemused representative of Muzak Inc., the corporation with perhaps the best handle on how to tailor one's piped-in music to attract a specific audience, calls this the perfect reverse of normal music-customer relations: "Usually you choose your music with an eye to the sort of customers you want to attract; why not for the sort of customers you want to repel?" Muzak is based in Seattle, but its representatives hasten to note that their own product, which they refer to as "environmental music," is not being utilized in this undertaking. We don't know if they should consider it a compliment, however. Going to piped-out Muzak in this particular war of nerves would probably be considered an unfair escalation, the moral equivalent of going nuclear.

Chapter 23 Project
Instructor's Guide, page 291
CD 15 [4] *Brandenburg Concerto No. 5*, first movement (3:00)
CD 15 [5] *Eine kleine Nachtmusik* (2:03)
CD 15 [6] "Sing We and Chant It" (1:13)

Chapter 23 Project

 Classify Musical Compositions

Can you classify musical compositions according to their stylistic periods?

Listen to three selections representing the Renaissance, Baroque, and Classical styles. Write down the period each work represents and justify your choice of classification by relating what you know about the characteristics of each style.

Chapter 24 Project

Chapter 24 Project
Instructor's Guide, page 292
CD 15 [7] "Cherokee" (3:34)
CD 15 [8] "Cherokee" (2:34)

▶ *Classify Musical Compositions*

Which of the following great jazz recordings would you recommend to a friend who asked your advice about contemporary jazz?

Listen to two performances of Ray Noble's song "Cherokee": one by the great jazz trumpeter Clifford Brown (1930–1956), the other by the young jazz trumpet phenomenon Marlon Jordan. Then write a letter to a close friend recommending only one of these two recordings. Pick the one you like better and give good reasons why it is your preference. Follow these steps:

1. As you listen to the performances, follow the sheet music of "Cherokee," the tune (in A A B A song form) that both Brown and Jordan use as the basis for their improvisational interpretations.
2. Notice how each man moves away rhythmically and melodically from the basic theme. As you listen, jot down notes that will help you evaluate the performances and decide on your preference.
3. Although both recordings feature virtuosos, pick the one you would recommend and describe your own level of understanding.

Cherokee

Women in Jazz

Picture yourself at a jazz club. You watch fingers flying over piano keys and arms crashing the cymbals and toms of a drum set. Who do you visualize when you imagine jazz musicians playing an electronic organ, a piano, or trap-set?

Like many careers, the jazz world has traditionally been dominated by men, but there are many women whose creativity stands out. In the following activities, you will learn about four women who have distinguished themselves as jazz vocalists and instrumentalists.

Find and Play the Pattern
Instructor's Guide, page 293
CD 19 [12] "Gemini" (2:08)
TRB, Unit Eight Encore!,
Performance Guide to "Gemini"

Name This Musical Form
Instructor's Guide, page 294
CD 19 [13] "Birthday Blues" (3:26)

▶ Find and Play the Patterns

Listen to "Gemini" by Mary Lou Williams (1911–1968). See if you can find three distinct patterns as you listen.

These patterns can be described in order as follows:
1) Bass arpeggios [BA]
2) Rhythmic scales [RS]
3) Piano boogie [PB]

Listen again, and use these questions to describe each pattern:
1. [BA] Do the pitches in the bass arpeggios move downward then up, or upward then down?
2. [RS] By counting groups of eight in a quick tempo, how is the pattern organized?
3. [PB] Beginning on C, how many notes of the scale does the boogie pattern go upward before it does back down?

Go to a keyboard and figure out each of the patterns by ear so you can play them along with Mary Lou Williams. Here are some hints:

- [BA] The bass arpeggios begin on middle C (C') and go downward on the notes C', A, F, D. This pattern is played twice before playing the C major arpeggio upward.
- [RS] The rhythmic scales begin on E' (above middle C) and use every white note for an octave. For adventure, try playing the scale in parallel thirds: C' + E'/D' + F' and so on.
- [PB] Start on low C and play octaves up a 4th until you turn around.

Jazz pianist and composer Mary Lou Williams strongly influenced modern jazz musicians. She also wrote arrangements for many popular swing bands of the 1930s, including Benny Goodman's.

▶ Name This Musical Form

Barbara Dennerlien (b. 1963) is a native of Munich, Germany. You will hear her play a tune in which she is featured on her main instrument—the Hammond B3 organ.

Listen to her performance and answer these questions:
- How quickly can you name the form of the piece?
- In what chorus does Barbara improvise as a soloist on the organ?
- What other instrument often accompanies her in a melodic duet?
- Can you improvise a scat-singing solo to the chorus immediately following the one that includes a drum solo?

▶ *What Makes This Music Bebop?*

Toshiko Akiyoshi is a Japanese musician born in Manchuria who studied music at the Berklee School of Music in Boston.

Listen to the tune she composed and arranged entitled "Be-Bop."

■ Why is the title appropriate to the piece?

■ Can you tell which parts of the piece are arranged (actually written down on staff paper) and which are improvised by the band?

■ There are two extended solos in "Be-Bop." Identifying the solo instruments should be easy. Using your watch, can you tell how long each solo lasts?

What Makes This Music Bebop?
Instructor's Guide, pages 294–296
TRB, Unit Eight Encore!, *Video Observation Report*
Music! VHS Segment 13, *Jazz Is My Native Language*
CD 19 ⟨14⟩ "Bebop" (6:37)

International jazz musician Toshiko Akiyoshi composes and arranges most of her material. "Be-Bop" was inspired by a Dizzy Gillespie piece. Her accomplishments include 18 big band albums and 14 Grammy Award nominations.

▶ *Conduct the Changing Tempos*

As a trap-set drummer, Cindy Blackman (b. 1966) has the coordination of an Olympic athlete. Her sophisticated jazz playing has impressed the critics.

Listen to "A Strawberry for Cindy" and try to keep up with her tempo changes. She begins with an extended "press" roll on the snare drum, then moves to her toms and cymbals.

■ As you listen, first find the beat, then try to keep the beat as it speeds up and slows down by conducting a basic duple (2-beat) pattern.

■ To make things interesting, assign one-third of the class to the snare part, a second third to the tom-toms, and the final third to the cymbals. Conduct your assigned part when it is featured predominantly.

Challenge Use a high-hat cymbal to improvise a solo to accompany Cindy Blackman. Remember to use both hands and one foot!

Conduct the Changing Tempos
Instructor's Guide, page 296
CD 19 ⟨15⟩ "A Strawberry for Cindy" (4:30)

The African American Dance Ensemble
presents "African Roots in American Soil."
Based on extensive research, their performances are a blend
of traditional African and African-American styles. In African
cultures, dance is not seen simply as an artform, but as an
integral part of the economic, political, social, and religious
aspects of life. Chuck Davis and his company use dance and
music to bring the message of "peace, love, and respect for
everybody." In what ways can the arts help to bridge cultural
differences?

The African American Dance Ensemble. "African Roots in American Soil."
Chuck Davis, artistic director. Photo: Courtesy of African American Dance Ensemble.

Music!...
To
Share Our
Humanity

You may wish to use Fine Art Transparency 9, *Blessing Rain Chant,* in the TRB to introduce Unit Nine.

A R T
S O U
R C
ARTSOURCE

Use Artsource® VHS Segment 10 in the Performing Arts Package to show a performance of "African Roots in American Soil."

CHAPTER 25

Folk, Popular, and Classical

Like all the arts, music serves as a window to the world, presenting us with insights that reinforce, clarify, or challenge our perceptions. Each of us, as a listener or a performer, engages with music to derive some kind of satisfaction. The knowledge we bring to music—our own familiarity with this communication system—helps us to understand it. We must know the "language" of music in order to be able to enjoy its revelations. One way we learn this language is to grow up with it. We hear the music around us, become accustomed to it, and gradually come to understand it. The society we live in conditions us to its musical traditions.

Objectives

By completing the chapter, you will:
- Review how you can get the most out of new music you listen to.
- Realize that you can value many kinds of music for many different reasons.
- Recognize the basic differences between folk, popular, and classical music.
- Understand that the music of other cultures is not all folk music.
- Learn that we all have a responsibility to respect differences in musical tastes.

Vocabulary

country music
folk music
genre
popular music
rock music

All music in the world can be classified into one of three categories: folk, popular, and classical. Moreover, all three types are available to you in various ways. One way is to attend a live concert, such as the one pictured here with singer/songwriter Elton John. **Have you attended a live concert? How did the setting help you enjoy the music you heard?**

Caption answer
Encourage various responses.

Unlocking Musical Meaning

In this section, you will be asked to put the knowledge you have acquired to work and to come to terms with a broader vision of musical styles. The music of the world can generally be classified as folk, popular, or classical. All of the many different styles of music that you have studied fall into these broad categories. All of these styles have something to say, but their messages are received with different degrees of familiarity and understanding. Some give us their meaning with relative ease. Popular music is generally presented in a simple and direct form that speaks to us immediately. That is what makes it popular. Our familiarity with a particular tradition enhances our understanding of folk music. Other music may require serious effort in order for the meanings to be unlocked. New music, or music that is different from any we have heard, poses the greatest challenge. If we are willing to listen several times and make some effort, we may be treated to some new revelation. We have to communicate with the music before it can communicate with us.

Activity *Refine Your Approach*
TRB 25-1, *Perceptive Listening*
Instructor's Guide, pages 299–301
CD 15 ⑨ "The Pines of the Appian
Way," *The Pines of Rome*
(6:31)

ACTIVITY ▶ *Refine Your Approach*

Can you determine what affects your perception and reaction to a new musical composition?

You will be listening to "The Pines of the Appian Way" from *The Pines of Rome* by Ottorino Respighi (1879–1936). Before listening, ask yourself the following questions:

1. What image comes to mind when you read the title?
2. Have you ever heard of the composer? Speculate about his nationality.

Now listen, using these questions to guide your perception:

1. Was your reaction to the work different from the image that came to your mind when you read the title?
2. In listening, did you put to work some of the new musical perceptions that you have acquired?
3. What other knowledge might help you understand this work? Would knowing more about the composer help?

Enhance your perceptions of "The Pines of the Appian Way" by going to the library and investigating the composer. Use these questions as a guide for your research: (a) Where did Respighi live? (b) Did he study with other composers? (c) What other works did he compose? (d) What is the style of his music? (e) What other works that you have studied are similar in style?

Listen to the work again, putting your musical perceptions to work as well as the knowledge you have acquired. How does this technique affect your reaction?

Discuss what makes one musical work so readily understandable and others more difficult to grasp. What should you do to make a musical work more understandable?

Why We Value Music

Throughout this text, you have listened to and studied many different kinds of music at the same time. This approach was deliberate, so that you could see how various kinds of music address many of the same general social themes and purposes, achieve unity and variety, and touch us emotionally. We can treasure music for its simple emotional direct-ness, its mysteriousness, its spirituality, its compelling fascination, or many other reasons. We can savor a work because of its particular musical qualities or because of the way it serves a special purpose or function.

Each **genre**, or *style of music,* does something different. Each is necessary because no one style of music can say everything or serve all the functions required of music. These stylistic differences are important and comple-mentary. They permit music to speak across entire populations and to serve broad, comprehensive purposes.

Caption answer
Although students will have various responses, encourage them to examine how varied the experi-ences are and how frequently they hear music.

The Boston Pops Orchestra, started in 1885, has become the world's most recorded orchestra. Through Evening at the Pops, *its public television program, and world tours, it is probably the most watched orchestra.* **What live musical experience has most influenced you?**

Activity *Show Your Wisdom*
TRB 25-1, *Perceptive Listening*
Instructor's Guide, page 301
CD 15 [10] "Gloria in excelsis
Deo," *Missa Solemnis*
(5:04)
CD 15 [11] "Ay te dejo en San
Antonio" (2:48)
CD 15 [12] Piano Concerto No. 2,
first movement (3:05)
CD 15 [13] *Liberty Fanfare* (4:12)
CD 15 [14] "Hush, Hush, Some-
body's Callin' Mah
Name" (3:56)

ACTIVITY ▶ *Show Your Wisdom*

Why do people value a wide variety of musical styles and genres?

Listen to the following examples. Decide why each musical example is regarded as significant and important for the society in which it functions as a mode of expression. Focus on musical descriptors to validate your responses. Draw upon the musical knowledge and understanding you have acquired.

Title	Source/Composer
"Gloria in excelsis Deo"	Ludwig van Beethoven
"Ay te dejo en San Antonio"	Flaco Jimenez
Piano Concerto No. 2	Sergei Rachmaninoff
Liberty Fanfare	John Williams
"Hush, Hush, Somebody's Callin' Mah Name"	(traditional) Spiritual

Can one person value all these different types of music?

Distinguishing Styles

Categorizing music is a tricky business. There are no easy definitions or answers. There are many styles of folk, popular, and classical music throughout the world. This is a major reason for inventing names to distinguish specific styles within the large categories: hard rock, heavy metal, folk rock, country rock, and so forth.

Yet these labels are sometimes used negatively. The term "classical" is sometimes used to mean "stuffy"; the label "folk," to imply "simplistic"; and the term "popular," to suggest "trivial" and "unimportant." The terms are used to pit one kind of music against another: popular versus classical, or vice versa. We shall look at these broad genres of music one more time. The object is to make certain that their real meaning is clear.

Popular Music

In the nineteenth century, popular music in America originated in minstrel shows and other popular entertainments and even included some folk music and "light" classical music. It was music that met the tastes and interests of the broader public. Popular music served to raise the morale of the growing industrial population who had little access to the more formal music of concert halls.

During the first half of the twentieth century, popular music came from operettas, vaudeville, and Broadway revues and musicals. It was the ever-present dance music of the day. When sound was introduced to motion pictures in the 1930s, film became a rich source of popular music. Today in the United States, popular music is everywhere—in dance halls, on radio and television, in theaters and concert halls, in stadium concerts, in films, and on recordings. It is the mainstream musical culture of American democracy. It can be entertaining, and it can be serious. The intent is almost always pleasurable. Fortunately, a number of highly inventive composers have brought particular distinction to American popular culture.

The Style

Popular music generally refers to *relatively short works with a prominent melody and a simple chordal accompaniment.* Often the work is sung. What appealed to the masses about popular music is that they could readily understand music that was relatively simple in construction and easy to perform. This new popular music was made widely available through published sheet music and, later on, through recordings and broadcasting. In the 1960s, inexpensive portable radios and record players permitted young people to make this music a passionate avocation.

Rock Music

Rock music is *a popular music style that began in the 1950s with a blending of gospel, rhythm and blues, and country music.* It emerged in response to social and political events of the times, in which young people rebelled against the social mores and rigidity of the 1950s. They sought a new openness and personal liberation. Music became one of the centerpieces of this largely youthful rebellion.

Music & CULTURE

Although music can be identified by different styles, it is sometimes difficult to categorize an individual performer. Garth Brooks, shown here, began his career as a country and western musician. Eventually, his music had a strong appeal to a popular audience as well. **Can you name others like Brooks?**

Music & Culture Encourage students to consider musicians who represent many styles: folk, rap, classical, country, new age, world music, and so on.

Like every major musical genre, rock consists of many individual styles. The music of the Jefferson Airplane, the Beatles, the Rolling Stones, the Who, Led Zeppelin, and other groups was not alike, even though there was a common spirit.

The first artist to bring rock and roll to a broad public was Elvis Presley (1935–1977). Born in Mississippi, Presley was influenced by gospel music, rhythm and blues, and country music. He blended these African-American and white musical influences to help create the style known as rock and roll in the mid-1950s. His first major hit was "Heartbreak Hotel" (1956). From then on, he had a succession of hits, and he commanded a large audience of faithful fans. He constituted a major threat to the establishment singers such as Bing Crosby and Frank Sinatra, who could not and would not sing this new style of music. Presley is the only singer whose popularity rivaled that of the Beatles, who admired his work and were greatly influenced by him. He is the most important performer of the rock and roll era.

Rock music itself took advantage of the new possibilities afforded by electronic amplification and distortion. The electric guitar became the main musical instrument.

Musicians burst out of the confines and constraints of the prevailing popular forms. There were distinctive soloists: Janis Joplin, Bob Dylan, Jimi Hendrix, and Jim Morrison, among others. They experimented with freer forms, new harmonies, driving rhythms that emphasized syncopation, and different timbres. The lyrics were sometimes political, sometimes very personal and poetic.

During the 1960s, the Beatles became pacesetters. Their music was highly original, artful, and expressive. Their four-piece ensemble consisted of the standard lead (or solo) guitar, rhythm guitar, bass guitar, and drums. Later they supplemented their sound with other instruments, including sitar and violins. They took advantage of the creative possibilities afforded by the development of multiple-track tape recording. They recorded different tracks and then overlaid the sounds to create textures of considerable sophistication and complexity in recordings—effects they could not reproduce in live performance.

Cleveland's Rock and Roll Hall of Fame is full of well-known personalities, from Elvis Presley to Jimi Hendrix and from the Doors to Booker T. and the MG's. Candidates for this honor must have been affiliated with rock music for at least 25 years to become eligible for induction. The question arises, however, is all rock the same?

Singer/songwriter Bob Dylan was an early contributor to the growing popularity of rock music. His lyrics were often political, and his music often showed the influence of the folk tradition.

ACTIVITY ▶ *Describe the Characteristics of Rock*

How do the musical characteristics of rock vary?

Compare an early rock piece with Scandal's "The Warrior," a rock ballad that made its way into the Top 10 in the mid-1980s, featuring Patty Smythe. Working in small groups, listen to these two very different rock hits and make a list of the differences and the similarities, paying particular attention to all the musical and stylistic characteristics of each.

Can you and your group list other identifying characteristics of rock that these two pieces do *not* illustrate?

Country Music

Soon after radio broadcasting was started in the United States in 1920, **country music**, *a popular musical style that began in rural areas of the South and West*, was being sent over the airwaves. This was the music of isolated rural populations; urban populations had little taste or liking for it. They thought of it as "hillbilly" music. Country music then was a mixture of narrative ballads; lively instrumental dance music played on the fiddle, guitar, and banjo; and religious music in the form of hymns and gospel tunes that were highly emotional and personal. Much of this music reflected the Scottish traditions that immigrants had brought to this country. The music was homespun and largely amateur. It was the antithesis of European art music.

Today country and western music is a popular style of American music. How did it happen? In the 1920s, the new southern and western radio stations began to showcase their local country performers. Public interest was aroused. Barn-dance programs soon became the rage. Americans everywhere took to square dancing, and country music was "in." A recording industry arose in Nashville and elsewhere to exploit this new public interest. By the mid-1930s, cowboy singers such as Gene Autry became folk heroes through their films and recordings. Nashville's Grand Ole Opry became an American musical institution, and broadcasts from there helped to establish country music as a major and respectable form of American musical entertainment. Country and western music continues to evoke the simplicity of rural life. Although it is now broader in style and message, and somewhat more sophisticated than in earlier days, styles such as bluegrass maintain the folk tradition.

Folk Music

Folk music is *uncomplicated music that speaks directly of everyday matters.* It was the first popular music. The indigenous music of the world evokes the culture and the lifestyle of the people from which it comes. It evokes the human qualities of those people. It speaks directly to us of the simple pleasures of life and of life's foibles and difficulties.

Use the Artsource® VHS Segment 11 to show a performance by AMAN International Folk Ensemble.

The AMAN International Folk Ensemble is dedicated to preserving the traditional dance and music of many ethnic groups. The "Suite of Appalachian Music and Dance" gives a perspective on different dance forms found in the Appalachian Mountains around the turn of the nineteenth century. The clogging doll used in the dance shown here serves as a musical instrument; its movements provide the rhythmic patterns of the dance.

AMAN International Folk Ensemble. "Suite of Appalachian Music and Dance." Jerry Duke, choreographer. Photo by Craig Schwartz.

We distinguish folk music as music that has been handed down by the aural/oral tradition. The original composer is not usually known. Indeed, there are many composers, because successive performers created their own versions. They altered the melody, rhythm, harmony, dynamics, and/or lyrics—the character—to suit their own musical technique, taste, message, and purpose. Folk music is music that people feel they can make their own.

Folk songs often do more than tell stories; they promote a cause. Music can give a cause more immediacy, vitality, and impact. Some folk songs have a "message" and are specifically created to publicize or criticize a controversial political or social issue.

You may wish to use the Unit Four Encore!, "Music and the Civil Rights Movement," at this time.

American Music of Protest

The struggle of working men and women to gain fairer wages and working conditions is one of the oldest civil rights campaigns in our country. Miners have a long history of protest and struggle to improve their working conditions. In 1931, Florence Reece, the wife of a Kentucky coal miner, wrote the words to the song "Which Side Are You On?" to bring the miners together to join the union. The melody was originally an old hymn tune, but the lyrics have an almost militant edge.

Music & HISTORY

In 1931, some 10,000 miners went on strike in West Virginia, demanding better working conditions. Striking miners and sympathizers march along the road near their homes from which they have been evicted. **What song was inspired by the cause of these union workers?**

Music & History "Which Side Are You On?"

Which Side Are You On?

Words by Florence Reece

Music: Old hymn tune
Arranged by Waldemar Hille

ACTIVITY ▶ *Discuss Social Issues in Folk Music*

How does "Which Side Are You On?" reflect a sense of struggle?

Listen to the Weavers sing "Which Side Are You On?" Discuss and debate the following questions:

1. How would you answer this question yourself?
2. How might this question divide a community?
3. Which verses could be sung about any union?
4. Without changing the chorus, for what other social issues could this song be adapted?
5. What qualities make this a folk song?

Activity *Discuss Social Issues in Folk Music*
Instructor's Guide, page 303
CD 15 [15] "Which Side Are You On?" (2:33)

The issues embodied in folk music are important to the people singing and listening to them. Such music is socially conscious. It may make a case for caring about people in need, our environment, or an endangered species of animal. It may issue some form of political statement of protest. The feature that these songs share is the expression of a longed-for ideal (such as civil rights) on the part of the creators, singers, and listeners. These are songs of struggle that help us to react to the world around us.

ACTIVITY ▶ *Compare Popular and Folk Music*

Can you define the differences between popular music and folk music?

Listen to one example in each of these musical genres (popular and folk) as the basis for writing two short paragraphs about each category. Listen carefully and apply what you have learned about analyzing musical genres. The challenge is to write accurate descriptive definitions of both popular and folk music—*without* comparing the two examples in your definitions. Cite as many characteristics as you can. After writing your paragraphs, be prepared to answer the following questions:

1. What are the greatest similarities between folk and popular music?
2. What are the greatest differences between these two categories?
3. Would you classify either one of these two pieces as rock music? Why or why not?

Activity *Compare Popular and Folk Music*
Instructor's Guide, pages 303–304
CD 15 [15] "Which Side Are You On?" (2:33)
CD 15 [16] "Mr. Bojangles" (Phantom Track)

Ethnic Folk Music

You may wish to use "Find Your Musical Roots" at this time. Lesson plans for the activity are found on page 308 in the Instructor's Guide.

People who share a common culture, ancestry, and language also generally share a common music. Ethnic folk music reflects this ethnicity. Americans of Puerto Rican extraction, for example, share a musical tradition called *musica jibara* (MOO-see-kah HEE-bah-rah), the *jibaros* being the farmers, fishermen, and laborers who developed their own unique culture. This is music of the people.

This music requires the skills of both the musician and poet. The typical *jibara* musical ensemble, called *conjunto jibaro* (kohn-HOON-toh), centers upon a *cuatro* (KWAH-troh), a uniquely shaped guitar with ten metal strings, that plays the melody, accompanied by a guitar, *guiro* (WEE-roh—a gourd rasp), and often bongos. The songs consist of a series of ten-line poetic stanzas called *décimas* (DEH-see-mahs). Each line of the décima must be eight syllables long and fit into a fixed rhyme scheme: A B B A A C C D D C.

Caption answer
Musica jibara.

Ethnic folk music, like ancestry and language, is a reflection of the culture that shares it. Here, Puerto Rican singer Olga Tanon is shown in a 1995 performance in Central Park, New York. **What musical tradition might you expect to hear at her performance?**

In some cases décimas are improvised on the spot. The text may discuss current events or report on everyday situations. A poet/singer might be hired to perform at a birthday party to sing improvised décimas about the person celebrating, the guests, or other topics.

The singer Enrique Galarza composed the décimas of "Mi triste lamento" ("My sad lament") to express his feelings of sadness about his loss of skill at improvising décimas. All he has left is his "amor a la cancion" (love of song). In this song, he mentions the *pie forzado* (pee-EH for-SAH-doh), literally the "forced foot of poetry," a reference to the fixed last line of each décima (or stanza) that adds to the challenge of improvisation.

Activity *Analyze the Décimas*
Instructor's Guide, pages 304–305
CD 15 ⟦17⟧ "Mi triste lamento"
(3:13)

ACTIVITY ▶ *Analyze the Décimas*

Do all four décimas of "Mi triste lamento" ("My sad lament") adhere to the typical décima rhyme scheme of A B B A A C C D D C?

Listen to this traditional Puerto Rican song-story and check the rhyme scheme of each décima, or stanza, to see if it complies with the pattern.

■ Does each décima (stanza) have the same melody?

■ Why is improvising décimas so challenging?

■ How does the instrumental part of the music allow the meaning of the text to be heard?

■ How does this ethnic music define Puerto Ricans and their culture? What does it tell us about them?

Classical Music

Not all classical music is great. Not all classical or so-called art music is profound. Length and complexity do not automatically make music better. At its best, however, there are moments of extraordinary revelation in classical music that enlighten our humanity. The mystery and meaning of life is probed. The human spirit is revealed, rejuvenated, and replenished. The classical music of the ages can put us in touch with the accumulated wisdom and insight that preceded us. That is why we call some music and art "classic." It continues to relate to the here and now. The reason we call Shakespeare's plays "classics" is that they continue to speak to our concerns today. This is true of classical music as well. It reaches out across the ages to say something important to us now.

Like the genres of popular and folk music, the genre of classical music consists of not one style but of many. In spite of the individual styles it encompasses—Renaissance, Baroque, Classical, Romantic, and Modern—its broad characteristics clearly distinguish it from other major musical genres such as folk and popular.

Music & ART

At the age of ten years, Mozart is captured in this painting by French artist Ollivier Michel Barthelemy (1712–1784), as he plays for the aristocracy. While Mozart's music is of the Classical period or style, many of his compositions are regarded as classic *pieces.* **Do you know why?**

Ollivier Michel Barthelemy. *Le thé à l'Anglaise au Temple Chez le Prince de Conti.* 1766. Louvre, Paris, France.

Music & Art
Because they reach across the centuries to touch us deeply and speak to our concerns of today.

Child prodigy David Helfgott faced many emotional challenges in his life. However, his training in classical music helped him overcome these difficulties. His life was the basis for the 1996 movie Shine. *The photo shown here is his performance at the Academy Awards ceremony in March, 1997.*

Activity *Compare Classical and Popular Music*
Instructor's Guide, pages 305–306
CD 16 ☐1 "My Funny Valentine" (3:52)
CD 16 ☐2 *Ninth Symphony*, fourth movement (26:17)

ACTIVITY ▶ *Compare Classical and Popular Music*

What are the basic differences between classical and popular music?

Compare the following compositions: "My Funny Valentine" by Richard Rodgers, and the fourth movement of the *Ninth Symphony* by Ludwig van Beethoven. Use the following criteria to make your comparison.

- Text/message
- Vocal style
- Timbre/instrumentation
- Degree of complexity
- Intended audience

Write a short paragraph focusing on the following:

1. What are the most obvious differences between these compositions?
2. What are the similarities?
3. What are the differences in the technical demands on the composer and performers?
4. Is one of the compositions "better" music than the other one?

Classical Traditions Elsewhere

Just as American musical culture spans folk, popular, and classical styles, other cultures embrace a variety of styles. Mexico, for example, has a strong folk tradition that includes mariachi, but it also has a classical tradition with composers as world-famous as Carlos Chavez (1899–1978). In the twentieth century, many nations around the world have been influenced by our Western system—politically, economically, and culturally.

We may never be able to hear or understand the music of another culture in the same way as a person from that culture does; however, we can derive pleasure from it and have some sense of its emotional impact. To do so, we must spend time with the music and try to understand the tradition behind it. We have to avoid dismissing this music by assigning it a label that stereotypes it as unworthy of our interest. Even the term "folk" can be a put-down, depending on how we use it.

Music & CULTURE

When you spend time listening to and learning about music, you begin to understand the people and culture who make the music. For example, this performing group from the Celebes Islands draws upon a musical tradition as rich as that of other cultures.

ACTIVITY ▶ *Classify Balinese Music Drama*

Is the traditional music of other countries simple folk music?

Listen to the excerpt from the Balinese music drama *Kecak* (keh-CHAK). This is the scene of "Sita's Abduction" (see page 328).

1. Is this music simple or complex? How do you know?
2. Can this music be learned quickly or does it take considerable time and effort to learn? How do you know?
3. Is this music easy or difficult to perform? Why?
4. Is the subject matter simple or profound?
5. How would you label this type of traditional music—popular, folk, or classical? Why?

MIDI TECHNOLOGY OPTION

- **Music with MIDI** Use a MIDI program to compose with elements of different folk musics and to explore different degrees of musical complexity within your composition.

Activity *Classify Balinese Music Drama*
Instructor's Guide, pages 306–307
CD 16 ③ "Sita's Abduction," *Kecak* (5:48)

Technology Option
Use Project 25 in the *MIDI Activities* binder.

All the Music for All the People

Democracy begs the question: Can we have quantity and quality at the same time? The French observer Alexis de Tocqueville thought not. In 1835, after a year of travel in the United States, he wrote in his book *Democracy in America:* "Is it your object to refine the habits, embellish the manners, and cultivate the arts, to promote the love of poetry, beauty, and glory? . . . If you believe such to be the principal object of society, avoid the government of a democracy, for it would not lead you with certainty to the goal." In the production of goods, America has shown that quality and quantity need not conflict. The fact that a product is made widely available does not mean that it is necessarily shoddy. We have made the visual arts and music accessible to all through inexpensive reproductions, including recordings. The commercial mass market manages to produce for a variety of tastes and does not cater just to the lowest common denominator, although the latter often commands the most attention.

America is a pluralistic society that is held together by a belief in freedom, the opportunity to work and acquire, and a culture born of commerce and industry. Music expresses our similarities and differences as a nation comprising many ethnic groups. It represents and interprets the many worlds of our composite nature. Through music, we acknowledge that as human beings we are not just cold brains and logic but also emotional, caring persons who dream, hope, fear, and suffer.

Technology has made all music accessible to all people. One no longer has to be rich to be able to have access to opera and symphonic music. We live in a pluralistic society. We can enjoy it all.

The music you prefer tells something about who you are. It reveals something about you. **Describe what your musical preferences say about you.**

Music: Where and When?

Music can be used indiscriminately and inappropriately. It can be made so pervasive in our lives that it becomes tiresome. We shut it out. When music is constant over long periods, it can become annoying. We may end up treating it with indifference or even hostility. Music requires its counterpart—silence—in order to be special. The right kind of music in the right circumstances will speak to us with full intent and impact.

Music making (and listening) depends upon certain conditions. Primitive peoples do not make music when they are hungry. According to ethnomusicologist John Blacking, the forces of self-preservation tend to separate people from each other. Only after self-preservation is assured do people restore their sense of community. Then they rebalance their lives by placing the self back into its social context. They make music together. They have the time and the energy to tend to their spirit.

In our busy, high-tech world, the conditions for using and enjoying music are sometimes haphazard. We cannot always control them. Electronics have advantages and disadvantages. They permit us to have music any time, whether we want it or not, whether it is appropriate or inappropriate. They also allow music—often the wrong kind of music—to invade our privacy in food stores, elevators, on the telephone, and at other times and other places.

Ann Landers

Dear Ann Landers:

I love and appreciate good music but spare me the stuff that is piped into every bank, doctor's and dentist's office, store, restaurant, beauty parlor, mall, etc. There is no escaping the merciless din. It's even in the elevators. We have no choice and are forced to listen to what somebody else enjoys. I hope the store managers will take note because I have walked out of several shops in which I could no longer stand the racket. Where are my rights to a little peace and quiet? Companies pay good money for this so-called entertainment. What a waste.

What is wrong with our culture that we cannot go anywhere—and I mean anywhere—without being entertained? What does this say about us? Please respond in print. It's time someone spoke up.

—*Anybody, Anywhere, U.S.A.*

Activity *Offer Your Advice*
Instructor's Guide, pages 307–308

Above is a photo of a sign in the parking lot of Porky's Bar-B-Que in Pine Mountain, Georgia. **Who do you think the owners had in mind?**

Caption answer Possibly the sign is a warning to people using portable music players or car sound systems. It might also suggest that street musicians congregated at the business.

ACTIVITY ▶ *Offer Your Advice*

When does music become "noise pollution"?

Read the letter Ann Landers published in her advice column in August of 1991. Do you agree or disagree with the writer?

1. Working on your own, jot down notes that support your viewpoint. Take a definite stand (agree or disagree) and outline the arguments you would make in response.
2. Working in a small group of three or four classmates, compare your viewpoints and discuss the different arguments each person made. Answer the following questions as a group:

   ■ Can you think of a time when you were genuinely bothered by music over which you had no control? Why? Did the style of the music have anything to do with your reaction?

   ■ Can you think of a time when you actually liked the music you heard in some public place? Why? What was the music?

   ■ When is piped-in music or forced listening appropriate? Where or when is it inappropriate?

   ■ Is it one's civic responsibility to respect the privacy and musical tastes of others?

3. After concluding your discussion, return to individual work and write your advice in response to this letter, summarizing your opinion. Write clearly and persuasively.

SUMMARY

Thanks to recorded sound, all styles of music are available to us. No one in the United States has to be stuck in a musical ghetto—even if that narrowly focused style is hard rock, rap, folk, or classical music. We can like various kinds of music for different reasons. This is not to say that all dance music is equally good, or that dance music is as good as classical music, or that classical music is better than popular music. We can still discriminate within the types. We can still have our likes and dislikes. We can choose music for entertainment, and we can choose it for its profound emotional insight. We do not have to limit ourselves to one or the other. We can have it all. The wider our choice, the more that music will reflect our mental and emotional life in all of its vast diversity.

Building Music Vocabulary

On a sheet of paper, write the term from the list that best matches each description below.

- (4) country music
- (5) folk music
- (3) genre
- (1) popular music
- (2) rock music

1. Relatively short works with a prominent melody and a simple chordal accompaniment.
2. A popular music style that began in the 1950s with a blending of gospel, rhythm and blues, and country music.
3. A style of music.
4. A popular musical style that began in rural areas of the South and West.
5. Uncomplicated music that speaks directly of everyday matters.

Reviewing Music Facts

Answer each question in a complete sentence.

6. What is the best way to learn a musical "language"?
7. What are the three broad general classifications of music?
8. What were some of the early origins of popular music in Europe and America?
9. Why was Elvis Presley a threat to singers such as Frank Sinatra and Bing Crosby?
10. What musical mixture produced early country music?
11. What style was the first popular music?
12. Why is *musica jibara* considered to be music of the people?

Complete answers to the Chapter 25 Review are found in the Instructor's Guide, page 308.

Thinking It Through

On a sheet of paper, write your responses to the following:

13. **Compare and Contrast** Describe some of the similarities and differences between popular music and folk music.
14. **Analyze** Using what you have learned, tell why you think rock music gained such sudden and widespread popularity in the 1950s.
15. **Explain** Describe how décimas are structured and tell why these Puerto Rican songs are so difficult to perform.

Making the Connection

Social Studies Find a protest song and investigate the political or social situation that generated it.

Language Arts Discover more about the poetic form of the sonnet, ballad, haiku, or limerick. Bring examples to class to share what you have learned. Draw comparisons between poetic language and musical language.

 Classical, popular, and folk music are further explored at **www.glencoe.com/sec/music**

Answers to Chapter 25 Review

6. To grow up with it.
7. Folk music, popular music, and classical music.
8. Operettas, vaudeville, and Broadway revues and musicals.
9. He was extremely popular, and singers like Frank Sinatra and Bing Crosby were unfamiliar and uncomfortable with his style.
10. Narrative ballads; dance music on fiddles, guitars, and banjos; and gospel tunes.
11. Folk music.
12. It is music of Puerto Rican farmers, fishermen, and laborers.

13. Similarities include simplicity, simple melodic and harmonic structure, often brief, often sung; texts are about familiar subjects of love, home, adventure. Differences include pop music as a composed style and folk music as an evolving style that is passed through generations.
14. Mention should be made of the response to the social events of the time: strict social mores being challenged, personal liberation, and so on.
15. Décimas are stanzas of ten lines each, with eight syllables in a fixed rhyme scheme: A B B A A C C D D C. The performer must be able to "freely" improvise within a rigid structure, becoming poet and singer at the same time.

CHAPTER 26

Styles Influencing Styles

Music has a good deal of influence on itself; this works in a number of different ways. Sometimes, for example, the music of one culture will affect the music of another. An American classical piece, for example, might incorporate Latin rhythms. One example you are familiar with is Aaron Copland's *El Salón México.* Cross-cultural influences can be even more sweeping as, for example, when the Japanese adopted Western symphonic music. Most Japanese cities have a symphony orchestra that performs a largely Western repertoire—Mozart, Beethoven, Brahms, and so on. This is cultural adoption and absorption on a grand scale. The Japanese have become so Westernized that they now export classical artists who perform around the world.

Objectives

By completing the chapter, you will:
- Discover how different styles of music can affect each other.
- Learn how music in one culture is influenced by the music of another.
- Learn how some classical music has been used to create popular songs.
- Become familiar with music of American composers Louis Moreau Gottschalk, George Gershwin, and John Lewis.
- Become acquainted with and able to discuss "crossover" music by Antonín Dvořák, Claude Debussy, Igor Stravinsky, Modest Mussorgsky, and Heitor Villa-Lobos.

Vocabulary

acculturation
clave
crossover
pentatonic scale
time line

Musicians to Meet

Claude Debussy
George Gershwin
Louis Moreau Gottschalk

*Musical styles are not fixed. They often evolve through a blending of different styles, as is the case with American music. Musicians Odetta and Kathleen Battic, shown here, represent the significant contribution of the African-American musical tradition. **Through what means do American music styles influence those of other countries?***

Caption answer Through sales of records, videos, and CDs; through worldwide concert venues, movies distribution, and television programming.

Influences from One Musical Style to Another

Not all influences of music upon itself are of this magnitude, but they are always of consequence. The blending of styles, however modest, is significant. As traditions are adapted and transformed, the resulting music exhibits a different character.

Folk to Classical

Folk songs have served as a major source of inspiration for classical composers. During the nineteenth century, many composers expressed their nationalism by incorporating their country's folk music into their compositions. Some accomplished this by imitating folk music; others actually incorporated the tunes. In Norway, for example, Edvard Grieg (1843–1907) was one of the first composers to cultivate the rhythmic and melodic flavor of native (Norwegian) folk songs in his works. In the same way, the Finnish composer Jean Sibelius (1865–1957) created

Louis Moreau Gottschalk
American Pianist and
Composer
1829–1869

PROFILE

Louis Moreau Gottschalk

Louis Gottschalk was the first solo musician from America to become world renowned. His many trips abroad spread goodwill, particularly to the Latin American people. This virtuoso pianist was also a highly gifted composer whose great works for the piano include *The Banjo, Louisiana Trilogy,* and the popular piece *The Last Hope.*

Born in New Orleans, Gottschalk could pick out tunes on the piano when he was only four. When he was 11, he went to Paris where he studied privately and made his debut there at the age of l6. Both Frédéric Chopin and Hector Berlioz, highly regarded composers of the day, praised his playing.

In his many piano and orchestral compositions, Gottschalk was a pioneer in incorporating native folk song materials, especially Caribbean and Creole rhythms and melodies. As a result, his music is uniquely American, and he deserves to be recognized as our first nationalistic composer.

Ben Shahn. *Four-Piece Orchestra.* 1944. © Estate of Ben Shahn/ Licensed by VAGA, New York, NY.

Music & Art

*In this artwork, American painter Ben Shahn (1898–1969) visualizes an unlikely musical ensemble. He is expressing the social themes of equality and integration. The house painter (left), the worker (center), and the classical musician join together to create a harmonious mix of styles. **Why is the artwork titled** **Four-Piece** **Orchestra when it depicts a trio of performers?***

Music & Art
The center musician plays two instruments at one time—the guitar and the harmonica.

melodic patterns that were characteristic of Finnish folk music. In Hungary, both Béla Bartók (1881–1945) and Zoltán Kodály (1882–1967) collected Slavic folk songs and were influenced by them. Bartók often evoked this Slavic feeling in his music, while Kodály quoted these folk songs directly. All these composers were considered "nationalistic" because their music deliberately reflected and asserted their culture.

One of the earliest composers to incorporate native folk themes in his work was an American. Louis Moreau Gottschalk (1829–1869), a composer and pianist, composed *The Banjo*, Op. 15, around 1854–1855. This piano work has been called "one of Gottschalk's most virile compositions." It uses themes common to the spiritual "Roll, Jordan, Roll" and Stephen Foster's "Camptown Races." The piece was written by Gottschalk for his New Orleans concerts of 1855. It is a clever imitation of the banjo that was popular in the minstrel shows of the period.

To add to its folklike flavor, Gottschalk used a five-note, or pentatonic, scale in *The Banjo*. The **pentatonic scale** is *any scale that is made up of five tones within the octave.* It therefore has many forms because there are many choices. Although much of the music we hear is based on the diatonic (or major) scale, the pentatonic scale is very common, particularly in folk music.

You may wish to use "Challenge" at this time. Lesson plans for the activity are found on page 317 in the Instructor's Guide.

Activity *Perform American Folk
Music*
Instructor's Guide, pages 310–311
CD 16 ☐4 *The Banjo,* Op. 15
(3:53)

ACTIVITY ▶ *Perform American Folk Music*

Hear how the American composer and pianist Louis Moreau Gottschalk incorporated the flavor of American folk music in *The Banjo*.

Sing, play, or hum the melody of Stephen Foster's song "Camptown Races," a folklike tune that was very popular at the time Gottschalk composed *The Banjo*.

Camptown Races

Stephen Foster, 1850

The Camp-town la-dies sing this song, doo-dah doo-dah. The

etc.

Camp-town race-track five miles long, oh doo-dah day.

Listen to *The Banjo* to determine how Gottschalk imitated this folk instrument on the piano and how he evoked the melody of "Camptown Races," particularly the "doo-dahs."

Why does Gottschalk's music sound so American?

What other American composers incorporated folk music in their works?

Jazz to Classical

Classical music has also been influenced by jazz, particularly during the first part of the twentieth century. At that time jazz was making its way around the world as a new form of musical expression. The French composer Claude Debussy (1862–1918) heard American ragtime music at the turn of the century, perhaps at the Paris Exposition in 1900. It gradually became popular in the bistros of Paris, where people danced to its lively beat. France has had a long love affair with American jazz, one that was revived in the 1990s. In 1991 the French government bestowed on American jazz trumpeter Miles Davis its highest distinction—the French Legion of Honor. Debussy, too, was taken in by this new rhythmic wildness, and he mimicked ragtime in some of his works. One example is his "Golliwogg's Cake-Walk" from the *Children's Corner Suite* for piano (1908). This was not ragtime as Scott Joplin had created it, but it was definitely influenced by his use of syncopation.

PROFILE

Claude Debussy

French composer Claude Debussy was one of the most important musical figures at the turn of the twentieth century. His compositions were the musical counterpart of the French poetry and Impressionistic painting of that time—fluid, colorful, and atmospheric. His most well-known piano work is "Moonlight" ("Clair de lune"). His works for orchestra include *Prelude to "The Afternoon of a Faun," Clouds, Festivals, Nocturnes,* and *The Sea (La Mer),* among many others.

Debussy is credited today for being the creator of the musical style known as Impressionism. His compositions were free from standard musical forms, and he explored new avenues of harmony, delicate timbres and textures, subtle moods, and rhythms that evolve almost improvisationally. Debussy prepared the world for the modern expression of the twentieth century.

Claude Debussy
French Composer
1862–1918

ACTIVITY ▶ *Trace the Influence*

Activity *Trace the Influence*
Instructor's Guide, page 311
CD 16 ⑥ "Maple Leaf Rag" (3:02)
CD 16 ⑦ "Golliwogg's Cake-
        Walk," *Children's
        Corner Suite* (3:05)

How did American ragtime music influence Claude Debussy?

Listen to the "Maple Leaf Rag" and review the musical characteristics of ragtime. Half the class should tap the steady duple beat, while the other half taps the following melodic rhythm of "Golliwogg's Cake-Walk" from Debussy's *Children's Corner Suite* (1908):

Now tap along with the recording while you decide which characteristics of ragtime Debussy used here.

What is the main difference in the way Joplin and Debussy treat the steady beat?

As part of the fun, Debussy mocks the dramatic, Romantic style of Richard Wagner by introducing a melodic motive from his opera *Tristan und Isolde:*

How does Debussy let you know he is not being dramatic and serious himself?

American popular music, in particular the music of African Americans, has made a strong impression on composers around the world. Many, like the Russian Igor Stravinsky (1882–1971), incorporated some element of it in their work. Stravinsky lived in Paris from 1911 until the First World War broke out in 1914, when he moved to Switzerland for the duration of the war. As a result of the shortages and poverty that many people suffered during the war, he developed the idea of economy in the use of musical resources. This idea was in direct opposition to the post-Romantic inclination toward the end of the nineteenth and beginning of the twentieth century to inflate the length of musical forms, the number of performers, and the bigness of the sound.

To show this new approach, he wrote a musical stage play, *L' Histoire du Soldat* (1918), for seven instruments and narrator. Following this same reasoning, on Armistice Day (November 11) that same year, he composed a work for just 11 instruments that he called *Ragtime*, a piece inspired by the popular American style. As you might imagine, it is joyous, celebratory music to mark the end of the First World War. With this work, Stravinsky, whose compositions are full of dance rhythms, followed a tradition of bringing a popular dance form into the concert hall, just as composers had used the minuet, gavotte, waltz, and other dances before him.

Activity *The Fusion of Classical and Popular Music*
Instructor's Guide, page 312
CD 16 [8] *Ragtime* (4:20)

ACTIVITY ▶ *The Fusion of Classical and Popular Music*

How did Igor Stravinsky introduce a form of popular music into the concert hall?

Listen to Stravinsky's *Ragtime* for 11 instruments and write a paragraph or two describing the fusion of the two styles of music—classical and popular. You may wish to use the following questions as points of discussion.

1. Name some of the instruments you hear in this composition. Are they usually associated with popular or classical music?
2. What characteristics of the popular style does Stravinsky borrow?
3. What characteristics of classical music does Stravinsky use?
4. Where might Stravinsky have heard ragtime? Why do you think he chose to base his composition on this style of American music?

Classical to Pop

Sometimes classical music influences popular music. For example, classical melodies are often popularized. The pop composer takes the main theme of Tchaikovsky's Piano Concerto No. 1, sets words to it, gives it a popular treatment, and it becomes "Tonight We Love."

Whole Broadway shows have been created by these means. The musical *Song of Norway* was based on the music of Norwegian composer Edvard Grieg. *Kismet* (1953) used popularized versions of the melodies of the Russian composer Alexander Borodin (1833–1887) for its score.

Jazz musicians frequently base their improvisations on the themes of other composers. One of the masters of this type of improvisation is John Lewis (b. 1920), who for nearly 30 years has been the pianist for the Modern Jazz Quartet. He has recorded an entire album based on the music of Johann Sebastian Bach. One of these tunes, entitled "One Diamond," starts with the beginning of Bach's Prelude No. 16 in G Minor from Book 1 of *The Well-Tempered Clavier*. Very gradually, he moves into a jazz improvisation based on Bach's contrapuntal piece.

ACTIVITY ▶ *Pinpoint the Change in Style*

Can you identify the moment when John Lewis changes styles?

Listen to the first few minutes of John Lewis' "One Diamond." At some point in this piece he gradually changes styles, going from Bach's contrapuntal, Baroque sound to a more contemporary style. Pinpoint the exact place (the minute and second) where the change occurs.

Work with a friend and write down the exact time at which you hear a stylistic change. Can you identify the two different styles? How did you know that a change in styles had occurred? You may need to listen to the work more than once.

Activity *Pinpoint the Change in Style*
Instructor's Guide, page 312
CD 16 ⑨ "One Diamond" (4:11)

*The Modern Jazz Quartet, shown here in 1961, presents jazz as a serious art form worthy of tuxedos and concert halls. As leader and pianist, John Lewis is as adept at classical music as he is at jazz, and he mixes the two styles freely. **Why do tuxedos signal a "serious art form"?***

Caption answer
They are formal wear, calling attention to the music and the group as a whole, not the performers as individuals; jazz is usually an informal musical form that emphasizes individuality.

Musicians are inspired by each other, and musical styles are influenced by others. For example, contemporary artists might draw on classical pieces for their compositions. In his recording of "C U When U Get There," singer Coolio drew on Pachelbel's Canon, *a classical piece.*

You may wish to use "Create a Composition" at this time. Lesson plans for the activity are found on page 317 in the Instructor's Guide.

Musical styles have been influencing one another for centuries. One example is the transformation of Hans Leo Hassler's seventeenth-century secular song, "My peace of mind is shattered (by a tender maiden's charms)," into J. S. Bach's eighteenth-century sacred chorale, "0 Sacred Head, Now Wounded." In 1973, Paul Simon continued the tradition by using this same melody in his composition "American Tune" as a setting for the words, "Many is the time I've been mistaken, and many times confused," making it secular again.

This trading back and forth between styles is common practice for a very good reason. These "parodies" of songs are adaptations that keep the creative fountain flowing. Musicians, like architects and actors, get inspiration from each other. One of the serious problems that afflicts commercial music is the tendency to imitate the popular fad of the moment. Sometimes there is little real innovation or originality. Groups tend to sound a great deal like each other. For the popular artist who wants to create an individual sound, classical music can sometimes provide a fresh approach. On the record jacket for his 1985 hit album, *The Dream of the Blue Turtles,* the rock star Sting acknowledges that he borrowed the theme for his song "Russians" from the classical Russian composer Sergei Prokofiev (1891–1953). Prokofiev created this theme in 1934 for his orchestral work, *The Lieutenant Kije Suite,* Op. 60. In the Evaluation for Chapter 9 on page 188, you learned that the singer/pianist Eric Carmen borrowed the theme from the first movement of Sergei Rachmaninoff's Piano Concerto No. 2 as the basis for his popular hit, "All by Myself." In the late 1990s, the rap star Coolio made use of the popular *Canon* by Pachelbel in his performances.

It is not unusual for classical music to be popularized—made more appealing through an arrangement, orchestration, or adaptation. Consider, for example, the way that Modest Mussorgsky's "The Great Gate of Kiev" from *Pictures at an Exhibition* (1873) has been popularized during the past 100 years. This work has become a favorite of many musicians, including pop groups. It was written in memory of one of Mussorgsky's friends, Victor Hartmann, an artist whose paintings inspired the composer. Like many other programmatic works, *Pictures* is in several sections. In this case, Mussorgsky walks the listener through an art gallery where a number of Hartmann's paintings are displayed. The composer uses a "Promenade" theme to depict himself walking between pictures:

(The original is in B♭)

With its shifting rhythm, the theme is a bit awkward, suggesting, perhaps, Mussorgsky's own uneven gait. Although the theme is presented in a different color and character each time it appears, it serves as a connecting and unifying element between the sections and is heard in the finale, "The Great Gate of Kiev." The sections of this program suite portray ten different paintings in the gallery, and Mussorgsky took his inspiration directly from them, often in surprising ways.

Mussorgsky originally wrote this program suite for piano. His own musical training, like that of many of today's rock musicians, was limited. He simply did not have sufficient skill to score the work for an orchestra. Consequently, other composers have arranged the work for orchestra. The most memorable and familiar orchestral version is by Maurice Ravel (1875–1937).

Popular artists of our own time have found Mussorgsky's work so appealing that they have arranged it for their own performances. For example, the rock group Emerson, Lake, and Palmer arranged several movements from *Pictures* in the early 1970s. Later in that decade, Tomita, a Japanese musician well known for his electronic transcriptions, arranged the work for synthesizers.

ACTIVITY ▶ *Analyze "The Great Gate of Kiev"*

Compare four versions of Mussorgsky's work.

Listen to four different versions of "The Great Gate of Kiev" from *Pictures at an Exhibition:* (1) piano, (2) orchestral, (3) electronic, and (4) brass ensemble.

As you listen, write down terms that describe and characterize the musical impact of each version. What do two of these versions have in common?

Knowing that the original composition was written for piano, how do the other three arrangements help to popularize this work?

Activity *Analyze "The Great Gate of Kiev"*
Instructor's Guide, page 313
CD 16 ⑩ *Pictures at an Exhibition,* "The Great Gate of Kiev" (4:30)
CD 16 ⑪ *Pictures at an Exhibition,* "The Great Gate of Kiev" (5:09)
CD 16 ⑫ *Pictures at an Exhibition,* "The Great Gate of Kiev" (6:21)
CD 16 ⑬ *Pictures at an Exhibition,* "The Great Gate of Kiev" (1:19)

Influences from One Culture to Another

Although many societies existed in almost total isolation at the beginning of the twentieth century, very few do today. This awareness of others has made people conscious of different ways of living. Lifestyles are imported and exported. For better or worse, American popular music provides an excellent example of how a particular form of contemporary expression can encircle the world.

When two or more cultures exist in proximity, there is apt to be some exchange between them. Some traits of one will be adopted by the other, and vice versa. In anthropology, the study of cultures, this process is known as **acculturation,** *the mutual influence of different cultures in close contact.* Examples are common, particularly in music.

Antonín Dvořák (1841–1904), a Czech composer, traveled to the United States for the first time in 1892. He had accepted a two-year appointment as director of the National Conservatory of Music in New York City. Dvořák was already well known for establishing a distinct Czech national music by embracing elements of Czech folk-song style in his works, particularly in his Slavonic dances and rhapsodies. During his stay in the United States (1892–1895), he produced his most frequently performed composition, the Symphony No. 9 in E Minor, Op. 95 *(From the New World)* (1893). In it he incorporated references to the Negro spirituals that he heard here. Dvořák was as interested in the music of African Americans as he was in his own Czech folk music.

Dvořák's use of American folk music in a classical composition started a controversy that lasted for years. Suddenly, American composers became aware that it was possible to create their own nationalistic music based on African American, Native American, and other folk sources.

However, they learned their lesson from a foreigner rather than from the American composer Louis Moreau Gottschalk, who had used the same techniques! Dvořák encouraged this development as a way for American composers to free themselves from European models and establish their own style of American music. Some composers embraced the idea; others objected, believing it would corrupt and destroy both styles of music. The American public had no difficulty with the idea as it was seen in this work; they claimed Dvořák's symphony as their own.

Dvořák did not lose his Czech identity by incorporating the feeling of the American spiritual into his symphony. It is still essentially a Czech work. By reaching outside his own familiar territory, he enriched his musical expression.

Activity *Apply Your Skill and
        Knowledge*
TRB 26-1, *Perceptive Listening*
Instructor's Guide, pages 313–314
CD 17 ⃞1 Symphony No. 9 in E
        Minor, *From the New
        World,* second
        movement, (12:08)

ACTIVITY ▶ *Apply Your Skill and Knowledge*

How was Antonín Dvořák's compositional style in the largo theme from the second movement of his Symphony No. 9 in E Minor *(From the New World)* influenced by the character and pathos of the Negro spiritual?

Perform the spiritual "Nobody Knows the Trouble I've Seen." Be sure to focus on the tempo, dynamics, and relationship between the words and the music.

What are the musical characteristics of this spiritual that are usually associated with folk music?

Crossover

Fortunately, in music, acculturation is not usually total or exclusive. Usually some characteristics rub off; others do not. There are influences that alter the music in certain ways, but not in every way. The alterations that are induced by the other culture can be very exciting. They can add new life and vitality to a staid tradition.

The sharing of musical ideas across cultures happens in many ways. In music, ideas are borrowed quite freely. Generally this is a harmless, invigorating indulgence. As humans, we tend to copy what we like and what moves us. New styles often overturn previous styles. Sometimes, however, there is a **crossover**, *a merging of styles*. This is how new styles such as "country rock," "blue-bop," (an amalgam of bebop and bluegrass), and "fusion," to name a few, were developed.

From Europe to Africa

The centuries-old contact of Africans with Europeans and with Christian culture is reflected in African music. By the early 1900s, choirs of mixed voices and the use of the Tonic Sol-fa system were established traditions in some African churches, schools, and communities. The dense (thick) musical texture that results from this multipart organization is now a dominant characteristic of South African Nguni vocal music. African composers do not view these elements as "weeds" that will kill or endanger their own traditions. The music of South Africa retains a number of characteristics that are typically African. The European elements are viewed as additional resources that provide an expanded range of musical choices.

The Protest Song in South Africa

Perhaps no other country in the world has used music so effectively as a means to communicate dissent than South Africa, where music serves as a powerful vehicle of protest against racial injustice. In 1886, when the largest gold strike ever recorded happened there, mine workers came into the country from many places in Africa and throughout the world. The population of South Africa is one of the world's most complex mixes of ethnic and racial types. Four racial categories are recognized in the population of more than 30 million: *whites* of European descent, *coloreds* of mixed origin, *Asians* mostly of Indian ancestry, and *blacks* of African descent. Blacks are subdivided into six major groups—Nguni (which includes the Zulu); Xhosa; Ndbele; North Sotho, South Sotho, Tswana; Tsonga or Shangaan; and Venda.

Music & HISTORY

During the period of apartheid in South Africa, music was a medium through which protest was broadcast. Ladysmith Black Mambazo, a South African a cappella group founded in 1960, often criticized apartheid through coded lyrics. Here they are shown in a 1996 performance with leader Jack Shabala.

For many decades, the official policy of the social system was *apartheid* (a-PAR-tite), an Afrikaans term for separateness or racial segregation. When the Afrikaner Nationalist Party won electoral victory in 1948, apartheid was soon enshrined in hundreds of laws. These laws restricted ownership of land according to race, provided for segregation of public facilities by race, assured lower quality education for nonwhites, and made nonwhites permanent residents of "independent" homelands, whether or not they had ever been there. Thanks to the resistance of the South African people and the sanctions of the international community, apartheid laws have been repealed. Nelson Mandela is the foremost leader of the struggle for liberation in South Africa.

The Music

Blacks have demonstrated their resistance to apartheid with protests and civil disobedience and through artistic expression. Songs, dances, plays, and other art works are proving to be an effective means of exposing cruelty. In South Africa today, culture and politics can no longer be separated. Of all these artistic expressions, music has played the most pivotal role. South African musicians have become the most outspoken critics of the system, chroniclers of the people's suffering, and uncompromising fighters for a new, democratic, and nonracial nation.

South African music has established a worldwide reputation because of its powerful message, its vast array of styles, and its excellent creators and performers. Its effectiveness has caused the Pretoria government to force musical artists into exile and to make it illegal for their music to be aired on radio or even to be listened to privately. Miriam Makeba, Abdullah Ibrahim (Dollar Brand), Hugh Masekela, Jonas Gwangwa, and Julian Bahula are just a few of the many superb, internationally acclaimed artists who were exiled. Their efforts have succeeded in reducing censorship. Most of these artists are now free to return home. Artists around the world have repeatedly voiced their sympathy and support for the plight of the South African people.

"Sobashiya" (soh-bah-SHE-ya) is a freedom or protest song that means "we will leave" in Zulu. It is performed by Amandla (a-MAN-dlha), the cultural group of the African National Congress. "Amandla" is the Zulu term for power. The meaning is "power to the people," the basic demand of the oppressed majority. This musical ensemble, founded in 1978, comprises exiles from virtually all ethnic groups. It performs the best music, dance, poetry, and theater of the South African peoples. The group is directed by John M. Gwangwa, probably best known in the United States for his musical score for the film *Cry Freedom*.

The song expresses the determination of people who have no choice but to leave the country and join the liberation movements abroad.

Sobashiya   **We Will Leave**
  (**S** = soloist; **C** = chorus)
Zulu text: English translation by
                                                 Thami Makwakwa:

1. (Verse)
  S: Sobahizy abazali ekhaya   We will leave our parents
  C: Saphuma, sangena   We will leave for other countries
     kwamanye amazwe

(Refrain)
  S: Kwamanye amazwe   For other countries
  C: Lapho kungazi khona   Where our parents don't even
     uBaba noMama   know
     Silandeli nkululeko.   In Search of Freedom

2. (Verse)
  S: Sithi salani, salani, salani ekhaya   Stay well at home
  C: Sesi ngena kwamanye amazwe   We're now entering other countries

(Refrain, as above)

3. (Verse)
  S: Sobashiya aBafowetu   We left our brother
  C: Saphuma sangena kwamanye   We left for other countries
     amazwe

(Refrain, as above)

Sequence of the repetitions is 1, 2, 3, 2, 1, 2

Sobashiya

Amandla, South Africa

Transcribed from Amandla, African National Congress Cultural Group, by Salomoa Julio Manhica.
Zulu translation by Thami Makwakwa. Used by Permission. International Copyright Secured. All
Rights Reserved.

The tune of this song is traditional, but the arrangement is modern. The most obvious outside influence is the arrangement of the voices in soprano, alto, tenor, and bass parts, no doubt an adoption of the format of the Christian hymn or chorale with its chords and cadences.

ACTIVITY ▶ *Discover South African Music*

Identify the African and non-African characteristics.

Listen to the South African protest song "Sobashiya" ("We Will Leave") as sung by Amandla. Note the following musical characteristics:

1. The multipart organization of the chorus into soprano, alto, tenor, and bass parts (like a hymn).
2. The use of call-and-response or antiphonal (alternating) style, marked by the independence of the solo and choral parts.
3. The use of polyrhythm or polymeter:

Melody (triple)

Foot stamping (duple)

4. The extensive use of repetition (with slight variations in the solo part dictated in part by the text).

Which of the above characteristics were adopted, and which are African in their origins?

Aside from the text, what makes this music work as a protest song?

Activity *Discover South African Music*
Instructor's Guide, page 314
CD 17 [2] "Sobashiya" (2:39)

From Africa to the Americas

West African music has had enormous influence on our popular musical styles. Between the fifteenth and nineteenth centuries, some 10 million Africans were uprooted from their culture and brought to the new world as slaves. Their descendants in North America, the Caribbean, and South America forged new traditions with double roots. One side drew upon the cultures of Europe (English, French, Spanish, and Portuguese), and the other side fed upon a rich variety of African traditions. Because these Africans had come largely from central and western Africa, the musical traits of these regions were evident in African-American music. The threads of continuity include leader-and-chorus (also called call-and-response) singing, the use of repetition as a unifying principle, the combination of relatively simple rhythms to create complex polyrhythms, an emphasis on percussive sounds and dense textures, and highly developed forms of improvisation.

The Time Line

In much West African drumming there is a **time line**, or *a basic rhythmic pattern that provides the foundation for the complex rhythms played by multiple drums.* This pattern or time line is asymmetrical; it is made up of two different halves. Frequently, the pattern is played on an iron bell, struck wooden sticks, or some other instrument that makes a loud enough sound to penetrate the thick, sonic texture that is created when multiple drummers play interlocking patterns.

Activity *Play a Time Line Pattern*
Instructor's Guide, page 315
CD 17 ③ Gome drumming (1:20)

ACTIVITY ▶ *Play a Time Line Pattern*

Learn to play the time line pattern and recognize it by ear.

Perform the time line by counting evenly and clapping on the dots:

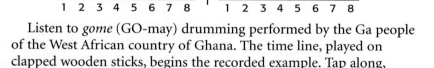

Listen to *gome* (GO-may) drumming performed by the Ga people of the West African country of Ghana. The time line, played on clapped wooden sticks, begins the recorded example. Tap along, keeping the time line steady as the master drummer improvises.

The time line is important as an organizing ostinato. It helps all the musicians stay together. In African drumming, the musicians have to be able to perform their own rhythms while they hear all the others. Their attention must be divided among the various parts without losing their focus. This is why the time line is so important. Even very experienced drummers use it to reorient themselves if they lose their place during a particularly tricky improvisation. Because the time line is asymmetrical, it is easy to hear which half of the 16-beat pattern is being played and to reenter the flow of the music.

This time line pattern in West African music has influenced the rhythms in the Cuban cha-cha, in Latin jazz, and in rhythm and blues, among other African-American musical styles. **Clave** (KLAH-vay) is *the time line in Afro-Cuban music.* The word also refers to two round wooden sticks that are struck together to produce the pattern. It is an excellent example of how different musical cultures have borrowed from each other. Yet in each case, the pattern appears in its own very different musical and cultural context. It provides a link back to its origins.

ACTIVITY *Perform a Clave Pattern*

Try to hear the clave pattern in each of the two musical examples and tap along with them.

1. In this Afro-Cuban cha-cha, the clave pattern is the reverse:

First half | Second half
1 2 3 4 5 6 7 8 | 1 2 3 4 5 6 7 8

This pattern is called the *reverso* ("reverse") or 2–3 clave, in contrast to the *primero* ("first") or 3–2 clave you learned in the previous activity. Try to maintain the pattern as other percussion instruments enter and add layers of rhythmic complexity.

2. In this early rock and roll piece, recorded in 1955 by Ellas McDaniel (Bo Diddley), you will hear a rhythmic pattern called "hambone" that is closely related to the West African time line and the Cuban clave. The pattern, which is elaborated by the drummer on the tom-tom and by Bo Diddley on the guitar, is common in the music of the Mississippi Delta where Diddley was born. Can you hear it and tap along?

Activity *Perform a Clave Pattern*
Instructor's Guide, page 315
CD 17 4 Cha-cha (1:28)
CD 17 5 "Bo Diddley" (1:05)

The African dance group Teye Sa Thiosanne Ban toured the United States in 1992, bringing their culture to audiences here. They help cultural influences to flow both ways, and they help people to develop respect for cultures different from their own. **Why is dance an effective form of cultural communication?**

Caption answer The physical nature of dance literally "embodies" culture and makes it easier for people to grasp and understand it.

The Blending of Styles

Today, classical music also continues to be enriched by cultural exchange. As composers absorb ideas from other cultures, they tend to establish new communicative musical "languages." Often, classical composers are inspired by the work of other classical composers. This is the case with the Brazilian composer Heitor Villa-Lobos (1887–1959), who, as a young man, fell in love with the music of J. S. Bach. It was Bach's music that led him to compose a series of nine works he called *Bachianas Brasileiras*, a series of dialogues between Bach and Brazil. Each of the works sets up a contrast between elements of Baroque and Brazilian musical styles.

The *Bachianas Brasileiras No. 5*, scored for soprano and eight violoncellos, is the most celebrated work in the series. Here the contrasting pairs are Aria (Cantilena) and Dance (Martelo). In the first section, Villa-Lobos combines the formality of a Bach aria with the Brazilian *modinha* (mo-DEEN-huh), a lyrical and sentimental song. The first part of the composition is a vocalise for soprano—an aria without a text!

Activity *Evaluate a Blend of Musical Styles*
TRB 26-1, *Perceptive Listening*
Instructor's Guide, pages 315–316
CD 17 ⑥ "Aria," *Bachianas Brasileiras No. 5* (7:51)

ACTIVITY ▶ *Evaluate a Blend of Musical Styles*

Can you distinguish the different musical styles that the Brazilian composer Heitor Villa-Lobos brought together in the "Aria" from his *Bachianas Brasileiras No. 5*?

- What elements of Baroque musical style—the style of J. S. Bach—did he copy?

- What elements of Brazilian musical style does his music evoke?

- Does this type of interplay between two cultures help or hinder the music?

MIDI TECHNOLOGY OPTION

Technology Option
Use Project 26 in the *MIDI Activities* binder.

- **Music with MIDI** Use a MIDI program to compose a piece featuring elements from different styles of music and explore different approaches to combining styles.

Like their European counterparts, American classical composers were impressed by the new music called jazz, impressed enough to integrate some of its basic characteristics into their music. George Gershwin (1898–1937) went to Harlem nightclubs and was so impressed by the vitality of this new music that he incorporated some of its features into many of his works. Gershwin extended the borders of musical style. He created a hybrid form of musical communication that combines and

PROFILE

George Gershwin

George Gershwin
American Composer
1898–1937

In spite of his short life—not quite 39 years—George Gershwin left an indelible mark on American music. Born and raised in Brooklyn of Russian immigrant parents, Gershwin learned to play and improvise on the piano. While working in Tin Pan Alley, he wrote his first hit, the song "Swanee," at the age of 19. It sold more than one million copies and brought him early recognition. He was soon writing a string of Broadway musicals—*Lady Be Good* (1924), *Oh Kay!* (1926), *Strike Up the Band!* (1927), *Funny Face* (1927), *Girl Crazy* (1930), *Of Thee I Sing* (1931), which won him a Pulitzer Prize, and many others. In most of his songs, he teamed up with his brother Ira, who wrote the lyrics.

His music possesses an infectious rhythm derived largely from the popular jazz of the day, which he applied to his songs with great originality. Yet Gershwin's musical ambitions stretched well beyond songwriting. He composed *Rhapsody in Blue* for piano and jazz band in 1924. *An American in Paris,* a work for orchestra, followed in 1928, and *Porgy and Bess,* undoubtedly the most American of all operas, was premiered in 1935.

merges elements of both classical and popular music. His *Rhapsody in Blue,* an extended work for piano and orchestra, premiered in New York in 1924 with Paul Whiteman's jazz orchestra and the composer at the piano. In this work the worlds of classical and popular music met on congenial terms. Gershwin's aim was to show people that jazz could be just as respectable as classical music.

ACTIVITY ▶ *Test Your Knowledge*

How did George Gershwin (1898–1937) merge popular musical expression with traditional forms of art music?

Listen to the opening of Gershwin's *Rhapsody in Blue* and make two lists—one of the musical characteristics that are classical, the other of the characteristics that are related to jazz or popular music.

Clues Consider the following; instrumentation (timbre); size of the orchestra; rhythm; melody; harmony; use of dynamics; and overall feeling.

How would you classify this composition? Jazz? Classical music? How did you arrive at your answer?

Activity *Test Your Knowledge*
Instructor's Guide, pages 316–317
CD 17 ⟨7⟩ *Rhapsody in Blue*
    (15:43)

Today composers and performers continue to mix and merge different stylistic influences. Why? The combining of styles gives new vitality to musical communication. Musical styles influence each other because musicians are fascinated by the new sounds that they hear. They are continually borrowing and absorbing these new sounds and blending them with, or discarding, the old sounds in order to create new expressions that are fresh and vibrant. Stylistic blending is one of the ways musical creators reach out to embrace the world around them.

SUMMARY

In our global society, music absorbs and reflects unique sounds from many different cultures. As cassette players, CDs, and broadcasting have made all kinds of music accessible to people everywhere, musical styles have tended to blur. Culture may be America's biggest export. American popular music has traversed the globe, influencing music in many other cultures. You can hear Janet Jackson and the Oak Ridge Boys in Bangkok, Berlin, Buenos Aires, Baghdad, Bogota, and Bombay. The music of these seemingly faraway places can also be heard here. These sonic influences are persuasive, altering musical tastes, and changing our musical preferences.

Musical styles are continually being modified. One of the ways music evolves is through a blending of different styles. This occurs when the musician or composer views different musical styles as opportunities rather than as barriers. When musicians become explorers, they combine styles to create their own individual sound. This is one of the fundamental ways that music evolves. In a very real sense, this is the way music breaks down boundaries, an important concept in a world prone to conflict.

Building Music Vocabulary

On a sheet of paper, write the term from the list that best matches each description below.

(3) acculturation   (4) pentatonic scale
(1) clave   (5) time line
(2) crossover

1. The time line in Afro-Cuban music.
2. A merging of styles.
3. The mutual influence of different cultures in close contact.
4. A scale made up of five notes within the octave.
5. A basic rhythm pattern that serves as a foundation for more complex patterns in other parts.

Reviewing Music Facts

Answer each question in a complete sentence.
6. Name at least four classical composers of the nineteenth and twentieth centuries whose music was often inspired by folk songs.
7. What scale did Gottshalk use in *The Banjo*?
8. What piano piece by French composer Claude Debussy was inspired by the syncopated rhythms of ragtime?
9. What Russian composer also used ragtime as inspiration for one of his pieces?
10. Which Baroque composer inspired a jazz album by John Lewis and the Modern Jazz Quartet?
11. Why did Ravel create an orchestration for Mussorgsky's *Pictures at an Exhibition* instead of the composer himself?
12. Why were many South African musicians exiled during the struggle against apartheid?
13. What is the purpose of the time line in West African drumming?
14. Who composed *Bachianas Brasileiras*, and what composer's music inspired it?

Answers to Chapter 26 Review
6. Edvard Grieg, Jean Sibelius, Béla Bartók, Zoltán Kodály, Louis Moreau Gottschalk, and Antonín Dvořák.
7. The pentatonic scale.
8. "Golliwogg's Cake-Walk."

Complete answers to the Chapter 26 Review are found in the Instructor's Guide, page 318.

Thinking It Through

On a sheet of paper, write your responses to the following:
15. **Analyze** How does music benefit from the crossover and mixing of musical styles?
16. **Analyze** Why is following a trend in popular music considered harmful?
17. **Apply** How can music benefit from acculturation?
18. **Explain** How did the assimilation of European elements into South African choral music enrich the South African musical style?

Making the Connection

Science Find out more about a genetic phenomenon called hybrid vigor. Then relate it to music and the positive effects of crossover and assimilation.

Math Create a new and different rhythmic time line pattern. Then invent another rhythm to be played against your basic time line pattern.

 You'll discover more about composers Gershwin, Gottschalk, Stravinsky, and Debussy as well as information on African music and dance at **www.glencoe.com/sec/music**

---

9. Igor Stravinsky.
10. J. S. Bach.
11. Mussorgsky did not have the skill or training to orchestrate the work.
12. Their music was used to protest apartheid.
13. To organize the complex drumming patterns and help the musicians stay together.
14. Villa-Lobos; J. S. Bach.
15. It creates new expression and promotes greater understanding between cultures.
16. It leads to a lack of innovation and originality.
17. It can lead to an enrichment of both cultures with the sharing of different styles and techniques
18. It expanded the range of musical choices.

CHAPTER 27

A Unique Record of Humankind

None of us can escape the mystery of human life. What is the purpose of our existence? Music commands our attention because it is one of the expressions of civilization through which we connect with other human beings—those around us, those who came before us, and those who will come after us. In many ways, music serves as humanity's memory, stirring our feelings today as it stirred others' yesterday, decades ago, or even in centuries past. Feelings are at the core of our existence. They radiate the life within us.

Objectives

By completing the chapter, you will:
- See how your tastes have changed over the term of this course.
- Understand how music establishes a sense of time and place.
- Understand how music expresses our humanity.
- View music as a fundamental means of human communication.
- Realize how much you have learned about musical styles and how well you are able to recognize them.

*Music brings us back to our basic humanness. It permits us to express who we are and what we feel about the world we live in. It also serves as an important means of communication within and between all humans. **How does music help identify who you are?***

Caption answer
Encourage a variety of responses.

Music Is Human Communication

Music turns the beat of the human heart into a drum and the feelings of human experience into a melody. Just as a drawing captures the rhythm of the hand, music captures the pulse and the passion of its creator. It represents the essence of the person who created it and, because of our human sameness, the essence of all people. This human essence is given representation in sound so that it can be relived and shared. Music permits us to express and communicate our emotional reality. It is both an extension of our being and a representation of it.

Musical communication may be more important to us than we have yet recognized. In America, our sense of community depends on our establishing linkages across our many ethnic and racial differences. Music is one of the splendid connectors between different peoples and cultures. It is a way for America to speak to itself in all its different guises. It is a way for Americans to attain a feeling of unity and of oneness.

ACTIVITY ▶ *Radio Scan*

How have your musical tastes changed?

Early in this course, you listened to ten brief musical selections as if you were scanning a variety of radio stations. The idea was to indicate your reactions to each musical example by writing down how long you would want to listen to the music playing on those stations.

■ Listen to these same selections again and indicate how many minutes or seconds you would want to stay tuned in to each musical example.

■ Compare these results with your first reactions. Have your musical tastes and interests changed?

■ Has learning more about music helped you to be open to a broader range of music?

Establishing Connections

Through the arts we can make connections with other people and with our own inner being. To be willing to listen to music that is different from what we know is to begin to open ourselves to human differences as well. The idea is not just to tolerate what is alien to our comfort sphere, but also to accept. Acceptance calls for a deeper understanding and commitment. Tolerance does not reach out and embrace, acceptance does.

Activity *Radio Scan*
Instructor's Guide, pages 320–321
TRB 27-1, *Radio Scan*
CD 1 [1] Symphony No. 3 in F Major, Op. 90, first movement (0:40)
CD 1 [2] "I Fall to Pieces" (0:44)
CD 1 [3] "Kogetsu Cho" (0:42)
CD 1 [4] "Your Smiling Face" (0:46)
CD 1 [5] "Menuetto/Vivace" (0:45)
CD 1 [6] "Changing Opinion" (0:43)
CD 1 [7] "Kyrie eleison," *Missa Papae Marcelli* (0:40)
CD 1 [8] "Pick Up the Pace" (0:49)
CD 1 [9] "Dovúnque al mundo lo Yankee," *Madama Butterfly* (0:44)
CD 1 [10] "A Foggy Day" (0:45)

*Music can bring people of all kinds together. It is one of the main ways that we make connections with other human beings. **Why would music serve as an important link between humans and extraterrestrial beings?***

Caption answer
Because it reaches inside us to express our being and our humanness.

As social animals, it is our nature to seek alliances. We want to establish contact with other creatures. If there are other forms of consciousness in the universe, we want to make connections with them. Will we, however, be able to communicate? Words may not suffice. Some sort of sign language may prove more effective. So might pictures or music. Sharing our music is like baring our souls, our feelings, our spirit. Music offers another form of basic communication that reaches our humanness.

ACTIVITY ▶ *Analyze How Music Connects People*

How can music connect people who do not otherwise relate?

Watch the short film *Caesura* by Frank Kerr, then write an essay on how music was able to bridge the hostility between these two men. Use these questions as the basis of your discussion:

Were any words spoken? Did they need to be? Could words have accomplished the same thing? Why can music work this way?

Activity *Analyze How Music Connects People*
Instructor's Guide, page 322
Music! VHS Segment 14, *Caesura*

If other creatures out there in the vastness of the universe have their own forms of music, then we cannot be so far apart. Sharing the soundscapes we have invented breaks through some of the barriers of fear and distrust. Music could provide a possible basis for the beginning of an

Music & CULTURE

Music puts us in touch with our own humanness and with the humanness of people in other cultures. That is its mission and its power. The musicians in the Ecuadorian ensemble shown here communicate who they are through their music. **What music would you share with them to communicate who you are?**

Music & Culture
Encourage a variety of responses.

alliance based on one form of intellectual and emotional understanding. It provides a way for us to see something of ourselves in other creatures and they in us. It is not by chance that our discovery of the songs of the whales, and our ability to record and hear them, coincides with worldwide efforts to "Save the Whales." Their songs helped to give us empathy for these magnificent creatures.

When we deal with the minds of others—human or animal—we are necessarily dealing with degrees of consciousness. One of the most impressive features of the human mind is its capacity and determination to understand itself and the farthest reaches of the universe. There may be life forms somewhere out in the universe that have intelligence far superior to our own. These beings might possess a far greater understanding of the meaning of their own lives and the nature of the universe and their place in it. It is conceivable that their physics and mathematics might be so astonishing and fantastic that they would be unintelligible to us. Their insight may so eclipse ours that our greatest attainments would appear primitive by comparison. If so, they would have enormous advantages over us.

If the social, emotional, and intuitive insights of aliens are as remarkable as their scientific knowledge, then we could hope to establish bonds based on mutual trust, respect, cooperation, even true admiration and affection. Empathy for other creatures depends upon being in tune with our own feelings so that we can understand the feelings of others. This scenario provides a good reason why we might be wise to develop the capacities of our senses as well as our minds. In the long run, our sensibilities may play as large a part in our survival as our intellect.

Voyager and Its Music

Launched by the United States in 1977, the Voyager 1 and Voyager 2 robot spacecrafts completed the first human reconnaissance of the planets in our solar system. They explored Jupiter and Saturn, then went on to visit Uranus and Neptune. Both spacecrafts are now continuing on their long journey to the stars, and both are still transmitting data back to Earth. The Voyager spacecrafts are now traveling at the rate of 1 million miles a day! Even at this rate, it will take them 20,000 years to break entirely free of the gravitational shackles of the sun. Then they embark on phase two: possible contact with an extraterrestrial civilization.

Affixed to the outside of each spacecraft is a gold-coated copper phonograph record encased in a mirrored aluminum jacket containing selected examples of the Earth's music. Carl Sagan of Cornell University, who served as Distinguished Visiting Scientist at the National Aeronautics and Space Administration's Jet Propulsion Laboratory in California, wanted to include music because "there is much more to human beings than perceiving and thinking. We are feeling creatures." He included music as "a creditable attempt to convey human emotions."

What music should be included? Two criteria for choosing the music were established: (1) The selections should represent a wide range of cultures, not just music familiar to the society that launched the spacecraft; and (2) every selection should touch both the mind and the heart. The result was 90 minutes of the Earth's greatest musical hits—Eastern and Western, classical and folk, including a Navajo night chant, a Pygmy girls' initiation song, a Peruvian wedding song, a Japanese piece for

One of the two Voyager spacecrafts that were launched in 1977, shown as it would appear to an alien spacecraft approaching it a billion years from now in interstellar space. The recording of Earth's music is centered on the side panel. ***What noted scientist wanted to include music as part of the mission?***

Caption answer
Carl Sagan.

*The Voyager recording, enclosed in this golden, mirrored jacket, is mounted on the outside of the spacecraft along with a stylus and cartridge. Among its contents are almost 90 minutes of Earth's greatest music. **Why was music included?***

Caption answer
It was a way to communicate human emotions.

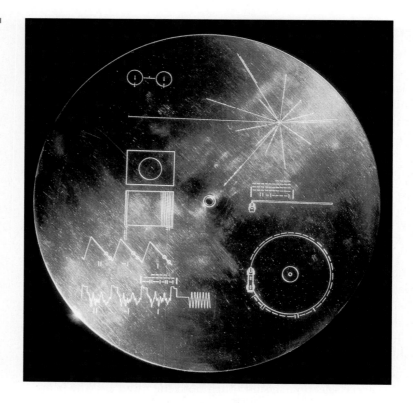

shakuhachi, Bach, Beethoven, Mozart, Stravinsky, Louis Armstrong, and Chuck Berry. Also included on the recording are greetings in 55 human languages and one whale language; a 12-minute essay of the sounds of Planet Earth, including a baby's cry and a kiss; and 118 pictures, digitally encoded, that reveal our science, our civilization, and ourselves.

Activity *Evaluate the Music on Voyager*
Instructor's Guide, page 322

ACTIVITY ▶ *Evaluate the Music on Voyager*

How well does the music included on the Voyager recording represent the variety and the depth of the world's music?

Look on page 585 at the list of 27 musical works that were included on the recording attached to the Voyager spacecraft. To analyze the list, answer the following questions:

1. What balance was achieved between classical, popular, and folk music?
2. What balance is there between the old and the new?
3. Is the entire world represented, or only a small part of it?
4. What is the balance between works that are relatively simple and works that are complex?
5. How much music of Americans is included?

The Music on Voyager

1. Bach, Brandenburg Concerto No. 2 in F, First Movement, Munich Back Orchestra, Karl Richter, conductor.
2. Java, court gamelan, "Kinds of Flowers," recorded by Robert Brown.
3. Senegal, percussion, recorded by Charlcs Duvelle.
4. Zaire, Pygmy girls' initiation song, recorded by Colin Turnbull.
5. Australia, aborigine songs, "Morning Star" and "Devil Bird," recorded by Sandra LeBrun Holmes.
6. Mexico, "El Cascabel," performed by Lorenzo Barcelata and the Mariachi Mexico.
7. "Johnny B. Goode," written and performed by Chuck Berry.
8. New Guinea, men's house song, recorded by Robert MacLennan.
9. Japan, *shakuhachi*, "Cranes in Their Nest," performed by Coro Yamaguchi.
10. Bach, "Gavotte en rondeau" from the Partita No. 3 in E Major for Violin, performed by Arthur Grumiaux.
11. Mozart, *The Magic Flute*, "Queen of the night" aria, No. 14, Edda Moset, soprano. Bavarian State Opera, Munich, Wolfgang Sawallisch, conductor.
12. Georgian S.S.R., chorus, "Tchakrulo," collected by Radio Moscow.
13. Peru, panpipes and drum, collected by Casa de la Cultura, Lima.
14. "Melancholy Blues," performed by Louis Armstrong and His Hot Seven.
15. Azerbaijan S.S.R., bagpipes, recorded by Radio Moscow.
16. Stravinsky, *Rite of Spring*, "Sacrificial Dance," Columbia Symphony Orchestra, Igor Stravinsky, conductor.
17. Bach, *The Well-Tempered Clavier*, Book 2, Prelude and Fugue in C, No. 1, Glenn Gould, piano.
18. Beethoven, *Fifth Symphony*, First Movement, the Philharmonia Orchestra, Otto Klemperer, conductor.
19. Bulgaria, "Izlel je Delyo Hagdutin," sung by Valya Balkanska.
20. Navajo Indians, "Night Chant," recorded by Willard Rhodes.
21. Holborne, *Paeans, Galliards, Almains and Other Short Aires*, "The Fairie Round," performed by David Munrow and the Early Music Consort of London.
22. Solomon Islands, panpipes, collected by the Solomon Islands Broadcasting Service.
23. Peru, wedding song, recorded by John Cohen.
24. China, ch'in, "Flowing Streams," performed by Kuan P'ing-hu.
25. India, raga, "Jaat Kahan Ho," sung by Surshri Kesar Bai Kerkar.
26. "Dark was the night, Cold was the Ground," written and performed by Blind Willie Johnson.
27. Beethoven, String Quartet No. 13 in B-flat Major, Opus 130, Cavatina, performed by the Budapest String Quartet.

At right is a view of the moon and Earth as they might appear from the Voyager spacecraft as it sped outward into the universe to explore the planets and interstellar space.

The hope is that somewhere out there in the vastness of space, a sufficiently advanced civilization will intercept the spacecraft and be able to decipher the messages on the recording. Voyager will provide these beings with news of our existence. Visual instructions for playing the record are included.

Activity *Select Music for the Next Voyager Mission*
Instructor's Guide, page 323

ACTIVITY ▶ *Select Music for the Next Voyager Mission*

Create your own list of the world's music to be included on the next interstellar spacecraft mission to the cosmos.

Write down your set of criteria for deciding what you will include. Limit yourself to 15 works. Select your music primarily from the music you have studied in this course, but pick out at least one work from your own collection that reflects the best example of a new style that has emerged since the original 1977 spacecraft launch. Justify every piece you include, based on what it might tell some extraterrestrial being about us as humans.

When you are finished, share your lists with each other and determine how much your lists differ and agree. Listen to the five selections that appear most often on all the lists. Discuss the various reasons behind the choices of these five examples. Is there a consensus in the class on the selection criteria?

Music Expresses Our Humanity

Music permits us to relate to other people and their lifestyles in a highly personal, emotional way. Through music, we can feel the way they feel. There is a near miracle here, because as soon as we have a glimpse of other people's humanity, we have crossed the cultural chasm that separates us. We must remember that intellect alone seldom connects us to other people; feelings do. Once we achieve empathy for others, we have

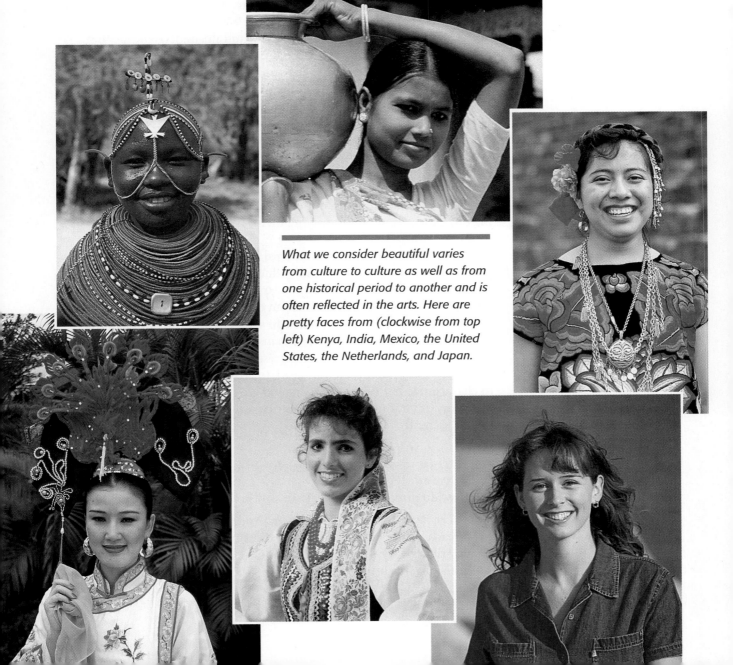

What we consider beautiful varies from culture to culture as well as from one historical period to another and is often reflected in the arts. Here are pretty faces from (clockwise from top left) Kenya, India, Mexico, the United States, the Netherlands, and Japan.

acquired the basis of respect. It is respect for other people that provides the basis for any worthwhile relationship across cultures. You do not have to like the music of other people; you should, however, strive to respect it. If we respect what people have been able to create, then we can appreciate people.

Because the music of a people gives such a clear representation of their essence, it provides a powerful means for understanding them. Music can help to lift the veil of ignorance that sometimes stands between people who differ in race, ethnicity, religion, economic well-being, and lifestyle. If we accept their music and have some understanding of it, we have established a way to relate. As their music moves us and ours moves them, we share our humanity. We cross the boundaries and obliterate the walls of prejudice, hostility, and misunderstanding that so often persist among peoples.

America is a microcosm of the world. Our population is the world in miniature—a cross-section of all the world's people. But the challenge is to embrace our differences and to find ways to link arms in spite of, and because of, them. Music is a bridge. It is a fundamental human connector. Its power is that it can join us not just intellectually but also empathetically and emotionally. Feelings are the basis of any real attachment we have for others. Music presents us with a stream of sounds that we can equate with our lives. By putting us in touch with our emotional fiber, it communicates with our essence, drawing us into its fold, arousing our expectations and satisfying them. We do not just perceive music, we live it.

The arts represent the way we reveal our humanity, the way we express our being, the way we see our individuality and our commonality. Music gives shape to the feeling of human experience. It is one way in which we express our insight and wisdom about our emotional and spiritual being. In studying how humans use music to serve their human needs, we see how similar those needs are. As humans, we have a need to define who we are, to move and perform, to express ourselves, to communicate, to celebrate, to commemorate our dead, to create, to tell stories of our lives, to characterize our time, to understand life's meaning, and to share our humanity. All humans use music to express these needs, but they express them differently.

ACTIVITY ▶ *Determine the Place*

How do musical characteristics and style convey a sense of "place"?

Listen to examples of music that you have studied. On the basis of each work's musical character, determine its geographic "home" or origin. If it helps, refer to a world map. Be ready to justify your decisions musically.

Activity *Determine the Place*
Instructor's Guide, pages 323–324
CD 17 [8] *The Blue Danube* (0:40)
CD 17 [9] "La Negra" (0:40)
CD 17 [10] "Baishe Zhuan" (0:40)
CD 17 [11] "West End Blues" (0:40)
CD 17 [12] "Bajo le Ivane" (0:40)
CD 17 [13] "Sobashiya" (0:40)
CD 17 [14] "El Sapo" (0:40)
CD 17 [15] Overture to the Balinese Barong Dance (0:40)
CD 17 [16] "Ana fi intizarak" (0:40)
CD 17 [17] "Offerings for General Protectors" (0:40)

Music Expresses Our Differences— and Similarities

The means of musical communication are infinite. Music is valued by people everywhere—but not the same music. Nor are cultures as unified in tastes as we might like to believe. While there are common threads in all cultures—values, lifestyles, and music are representative—there are also tastes that are uncommon. These differences keep cultures vibrant and moving. They excite and stimulate. They cause us to rethink, to reevaluate, and to change. This is the great strength of America. Yet as America becomes increasingly diverse, there are people who choose retrenchment in racial and ethnic enclaves and resistance to intracultural exchange. They honor just their own music.

Bringing People Together

Still, as humans, we are not all that different. What we think and feel is not vastly unlike what most other people think and feel. Our problems, our inner doubts, our hurts and hopes, our feelings of defeat and inferiority, our successes and failures, our pleasures and pain are similar to what all people experience. Music lets us know that we are not alone in our feelings.

If music can bring all kinds of people together by uniting them in spirit and feeling, it surely has a role to play in world peace. Any force that can bring people together and cross cultural boundaries should be valued highly in today's world. Technological advancements continue to

Music & ART

This woodblock print by Hokusai captures a moment in time for us to enjoy and reflect upon. Although the setting and style of the print is Japanese, the event is familiar to people of all cultures. **How do art and music communicate what humans have in common?**

Katsushika Hokusai. *A Gust of Wind at Ejiri.* 1831–33. The Metropolitan Museum of Art. New York, New York. Rogers Fund, 1936.

Music & Art They unite people in spirit and feeling.

bring the people of the world together. Yet contact alone does not assure understanding. We need to rely upon the arts to improve the human communication process. For many years, cultural exchanges between different countries have been recognized by governments as a way to open the doors to human understanding. Such exchanges acknowledge that the arts are one of the great treasures of the human race through which we define ourselves, our world, and our era.

Activity *Determine the Time*
Instructor's Guide, pages 324–325
TRB 27-2, *Time Line*
CD 17 [18] Minuetto, Symphony No. 40, third movement (0:40)
CD 17 [19] "Maple Leaf Rag" (0:40)
CD 17 [20] "Alleluia, *Vidimus stellam*" (0:40)
CD 17 [21] "Siegfried's Funeral Music".(0:40)
CD 17 [22] "As Vesta Was Descending" (0:40)
CD 17 [23] "China Boy" (0:40)
CD 17 [24] "Mini's Solo" (0:40)
CD 17 [25] Toccata and Fugue in D Minor (0:40)

ACTIVITY ▶ *Determine the Time*

Can you place a musical composition or style in its proper era?

Listen again to the following musical examples that you have studied. Evaluate the musical characteristics and designate where the composition would best be placed on a time line. Be ready to justify your decision musically and to explain how music conveys its era.

1. The Third Movement—Minuetto from Symphony No. 40 by W. A. Mozart
2. "Maple Leaf Rag" by Scott Joplin
3. "Alleluia, *Vidimus stellam*" (Chant)
4. "Siegfried's Funeral Music" from *The Twilight of the Gods* by Richard Wagner
5. "As Vesta Was Descending" by Thomas Weelkes
6. "China Boy" performed by the Benny Goodman Trio
7. "Mini's Solo" from *Valis* by Tod Machover
8. Toccata and Fugue in D Minor by J. S. Bach

MIDI TECHNOLOGY OPTION

Technology Option
Use Project 27 in the *MIDI Activities* binder.

■ **Music with MIDI** Use a MIDI program to compose futuristic music and to explore what new approaches music making of the future might include.

SUMMARY

In a world of technology, facts, and information, music brings us back to our basic humanness. It is one of the fundamental methods we have invented to search for life's meaning and to express our human essence in this world. Through music we can find our roots as global human beings—members of the human race. We can stretch ourselves to be bigger, to be more, to realize our fullest human possibilities. In these ways, music gives balance to our existence. The real wonder of it all is that these rewards can be ours for a lifetime.

Reviewing Music Facts

Answer each question in a complete sentence.

1. What discovery led to greater awareness of the plight of whales?
2. Why was music one of the cultural elements sent to outer space on the Voyager spacecrafts?
3. How are alien beings expected to be able to hear the music on the Voyager recordings?
4. Identify at least five human needs that are expressed in music.

Thinking It Through

On a sheet of paper, write your responses to the following:

5. **Analyze** Why is musical communication particularly important in America?
6. **Explain** Based on what you have learned, explain in your own words why the Voyager's selections represent the variety and depth of the world's music.
7. **Compare and Contrast** Describe the benefits of listening to and making an effort to understand unfamiliar music.
8. **Explain** In your own words, explain how a listener might identify the time and place to which a piece of music belongs.
9. **Apply** What are the implications for world peace in the sharing of music of diverse cultures?

Complete answers to the Chapter 27 Review are found in the Instructor's Guide, page 325.

Making the Connection

Science Find out more about the physical changes that occur to people when they listen to music. Use what you have learned in class discussions about how music can bridge cultural differences.

Language Arts Choose three of your favorite pieces of music from the course, selecting those you consider to come from your own culture. Pick one from each of the categories: popular, folk, and classical. Then write three short paragraphs presenting and describing each piece to a person from another culture.

 Music sites from around the world and a NASA discovery site are explored at **www.glencoe.com/sec/music**

Chapter 25 Project
Instructor's Guide, pages 326–327
TRB Unit Nine Evaluation: Chapter
25, *Name the Musical Genre*
CD 17 26 "The Trolley Song"
(0:55)
CD 17 27 "Vigilante Man" (0:49)
CD 17 28 "Roll Over Beethoven"
(0:52)
CD 17 29 "Semarandana" (0:41)
CD 17 30 "Shaw 'Nuff" (0:44)

You may also wish to use
Assessment Master 9,
Unit Nine Test, in the TRB.

Chapter 25 Project

▶ *Identify Music Genres*

How would you categorize these five musical compositions?

Listen carefully to each example and place it in the category you believe is most fitting: (a) Folk; (b) Popular; (c) Jazz; (d) Classical; or (e) Rock.

After you have completed your worksheet, reflect on how you would answer the following questions and prepare to take part in a lively class discussion:

1. What is the arguably correct answer for each example?

2. Why might someone who knows very little about music confuse these different styles?

3. Do you see any problem with generalizing about stylistic categorizations of music? If so, what are some of the issues that arise?

Artists sometimes try to capture the essence of another culture. For example, American artist John Singer Sargent (1856–1925) painted El Jaleo *(1882), a large artwork depicting a Spanish dancer and the musicians accompanying her. In 1879 he visited Spain and saw the famous dance* jaleo de jerez. *He captured the impassioned performance with the energy and spontaneity of his brush work.*

John Singer Sargent. *El Jaleo.* 1882.
Isabella Stewart Gardener Museum.
Boston, Massachusetts.

Chapter 26 Project

▶ *Examine Cultural Influences*

Artists of all kinds are inspired by cultures other than their own. Shortly after the French composer Georges Bizet captured the sound of Spanish music in his opera *Carmen* (1874), American painter John Singer Sargent, also living in Paris at that time, painted *El Jaleo* (1882) featuring a Spanish gypsy dancer (see page 592). Sargent was inspired by his visit to Spain and perhaps by the wave of interest in Bizet's opera. Similarly, the American composer Aaron Copland was inspired to compose *El Salón México* based on his experience of and admiration for Mexican culture.

Choose one of the following subjects and write a research paper. Your task is to discover the cultural influences that inspired the composer by reading and by listening to appropriate musical examples:

A. The influence of Slavic folk songs on the music of Hungarian classical composer Zoltán Kodály (1882–1967). (Possible work to study: *Hary Janos Suite*, 1927)

B. The influence of the music of other cultures on the music of American popular musician Paul Simon. (Possible albums to study: *Graceland*, 1986, or *Rhythm of the Saints*, 1990)

C. The influence of jazz and Negro folk idioms on the music of African-American composer William Grant Still (1895–1978). (Possible work to study: *Afro-American Symphony*, 1930)

Chapter 27 Project

▶ *Assessing Your Growth*

How broad has your aural knowledge of musical styles become?

In the activity called Musical Style Check on page 9, you were asked: "How familiar are you with the many styles of music heard daily in the United States?" Listen again to all 20 of the original musical examples and try to identify them with 100 percent accuracy.

If you completed all the chapters in the text, then you have studied each of these musical pieces. Your greater awareness of musical style and the vocabulary you have learned should enable you to earn a high score this time around. You may be surprised at how well you do!

Chapter 26 Project
Instructor's Guide, page 328

Chapter 27 Project
Instructor's Guide, pages 328–329
TRB Unit Nine Evaluation: Chapter 26, *Musical Style Check*
CD 1 [11] "How I Got Over" (0:32)
CD 1 [12] "A Mighty Fortress Is Our God" (0:35)
CD 1 [13] *Choral Symphony*, fourth movement (0:30)
CD 1 [14] "Sweet Home Chicago" (0:39)
CD 1 [15] Concerto No. 21 in C Major, second movement (0:35)
CD 1 [16] "The Entertainer" (0:34)
CD 1 [17] "Ice Nine" (0:30)
CD 1 [18] "Northern Plains" (0:34)
CD 1 [19] "Islands," *Glassworks* (0:34)
CD 1 [20] "La Negra" (0:30)
CD 1 [21] "Know How" (0:34)
CD 1 [22] "As Vesta Was Descending" (0:30)
CD 1 [23] "Which Side Are You On?" (0:37)
CD 1 [24] "Stone Coal" (0:38)
CD 1 [25] Toccata and Fugue in D Minor (0:34)
CD 1 [26] "When the Saints Go Marchin' In" (0:38)
CD 1 [27] "Mr. Snow," *Carousel* (0:37)
CD 1 [28] "Cherokee" (0:37)
CD 1 [29] "The Washington Post March" (0:30)
CD 1 [30] "Since I Found You" (0:40)

Memphis: Birthplace of an American Music Style

Memphis, Tennessee, is best known as the home of Elvis and Graceland. However, this city on the Mississippi River is also the setting for an American success story—of how musicians of all races crossed cultural barriers to create rock and soul.

The Memphis story is one of musicians influencing musicians, and styles influencing styles. The result was a unique record of humankind that now has universal acceptance.

Describe the Early Memphis Styles
Instructor's Guide, page 330
CD 19 [16] "Dark was the Night, Cold was the Ground" (3:15)
CD 19 [17] "Joe Turner Blues" (2:00)
CD 19 [18] "Just as Long as I Have You" (3:00)

▶ *Describe the Early Memphis Styles*

Can you define the difference between music styles heard in Memphis during the 1930s–1940s?

Blues, country, and gospel were part of the musical tapestry in Memphis during the early decades of the twentieth century. Blind Willie Johnson, W. C. Handy, Thomas Andrew Dorsey, and Ernest Tubbs were popular performers, playing to audiences of all races. Although Memphis was a socially segregated city, music bridged the races and cultures.

Listen to these three musical examples of blues and country music and answer the following questions:

1. What are the greatest similarities between these three styles?
2. What are the greatest differences between these three styles?
3. Describe the instrumental accompaniment in all three selections.
4. What is the message depicted in each style?

In 1949, a Memphis radio disc jockey named Dewey Phillips created a popular radio show called the *Red Hot & Blue* program. It was the beginning of the rock revolution in Memphis. He broke the segregated city's musical color line, playing black rhythm and blues records for an audience mostly made up of white teenagers.

Phillips played the first recordings of Elvis Presley, Carl Perkins, Jerry Lee Lewis, Johnny Cash, Roy Orbison, and B. B. King. By the end of the 1960s, rock and roll had an international audience. This new generation of "rockabilly" musicians (a word Dewey coined) became internationally known through their recordings on Sun Records.

1930

BLIND WILLIE JOHNSON

THOMAS ANDREW DORSEY

W. C. HANDY

ERNEST TUBBS

1950

B. B. KING

CARL PERKINS

Unit Nine *Encore!*

▶ *Define the Memphis Sound*

Listen to and compare a later blues song with the earlier blues style of
W. C. Handy and Blind Willie Johnson.

- Describe the treatment of the blues harmonic progression in the three selections.
- Identify and compare the instrumental accompaniments.
- What musical characteristics of the country music style are found in this selection?
- What message is conveyed in each selection?
- List the musical characteristics that define the "Memphis Rockabilly" sound.

Define the Memphis Sound
Instructor's Guide, page 331
CD 19 [16] "Dark was the Night, Cold was the Ground" (3:15)
CD 19 [17] "Joe Turner Blues" (2:00)
CD 19 [19] "All Your Love" (3:14)

▶ *The Beginning of the Memphis Soul Sound*

The 1960 Memphis style originated at Stax Records, where multiracial studio bands and songwriting teams joined forces. The Stax artists mixed a Memphis "stew" of rhythm and blues, country, rock and roll, and the raw emotion of gospel that resulted in the "Memphis Soul Sound."

This generation of Stax Stars included Booker T. & the MGs, Rufus Thomas, William Bell, and Otis Redding, the superstar in the Stax stable.

Listen to an example of the Memphis style and identify reasons why the public responded so powerfully. Was it the

- message of the text?
- tone color of the accompaniment?
- invitation to dance?

Can you name contemporary styles of popular music whose roots are planted in Memphis style "soul" music?

The Beginning of the Memphis Soul Sound
Instructor's Guide, page 331
CD 19 [20] "I'm Your Puppet" (2:57)

ROY ORBISON

ELVIS PRESLEY

JOHNNY CASH

1960

RUFUS THOMAS

BOOKER T. AND THE MGS

WILLIAM BELL

OTIS REDDING

1970

595

Music Theory Handbook

Table of Contents

A. Beat and Meter

Music occurs within a span of time. Time elements in music include the underlying pulse or beat of the music and the organization of the beats into a grouping of meter. These elements are similar to the beat and meter in poetry.

1. Beat

Beat is a steady recurring pattern of time that is "felt" in music. Beats are organized into recurring patterns that define meter.

2. Meter

Meter is a pattern of strong and weak beats. All meters can be simplified to duple or triple meter. Other meter types are called combined or mixed, compound, asymmetrical or irregular, and nonmetric.

Use *Feeling Meter* lesson plans.
Instructor's Guide, page 333

Duple and Triple Meter

There are two basic meter patterns: duple and triple.

Duple meter is a group of two beats in a strong-weak pattern. It can be shown in two ways:

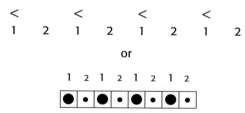

Triple meter is a group of three beats in a strong-weak-weak pattern. Like duple meter, it can be shown in two ways:

Use *Hearing Duple and Triple Meter* lesson plans.
Instructor's Guide, pages 333-334

Recurring beat patterns or the meter are divided into measures. A measure is shown by a vertical bar line separating the staff into parts.

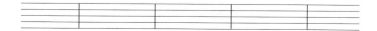

Meter signatures, also called time signatures, are sets of numbers used at the beginning of a piece of music to
    a) indicate the number of beats in each measure, and
    b) define the note that represents the basic beat.
Notating a meter signature is similar to writing a fraction, with the number of beats in the top number, and the unit of measure or note value that represents the beat, directly below it.

$$\frac{2}{4} \quad \frac{4}{4} \quad \frac{2}{2} \quad \frac{6}{8} \quad \frac{3}{4} \quad \frac{9}{8}$$

For instance, in the first example there are two beats per measure with a quarter note receiving one beat. In the last example, there are nine beats per measure with an eighth note receiving one beat.

If the upper number of the meter signature is divisible by two, but not divisible by three, the meter is duple meter. The first three meters shown above are examples of duple meter.

If the upper number of the meter signature is divisible by three, then the meter is triple meter. The last three meters above are examples of triple meter.

Combined and Compound Meters

Combined or mixed meter is the mixture of duple and triple meters. The beat continues as a steady pulse, with alternating accented beats according to the meters. Combined meter signatures are shown in the measure of meter change.

```
<           <                 <           <                 <
1    2      1    2    3      1    2      1    2    3      1    2
```

Compound meters have two or more groups of triple meter.

$$\frac{6}{8} \quad \frac{9}{8} \quad \frac{12}{8}$$

Asymmetrical Meters and Nonmetric Music

Asymmetrical or irregular meter is the unequal pairings of beats in a meter. These meters can be

$$\frac{5}{4} \quad \frac{5}{8} \quad \frac{7}{8} \quad \frac{11}{8}$$

and may be designated in the music as follows:

$$\frac{3+2}{4} \quad \frac{2+3+2}{8} \quad \frac{3+2+2}{8}$$

Nonmetric refers to music with no fixed grouping of beats, no time signature, and no measure bars. Plainsong or chant is nonmetric. It is also used in twentieth-century music.

Use *Musical Instruments and Sound* lesson plans. Instructor's Guide, page 334

Use *Combined Meter* lesson plans. Instructor's Guide, page 334

Use *Paired Meter* lesson plans. Instructor's Guide, page 335

Use *Unpaired Meter* lesson plans. Instructor's Guide, pages 335-336

Use TRB Music Theory Transparency 1, *Time Signatures*

B. Notation and Rhythm

Music notation is a system of symbols designed to represent the elements of time and sound. Musicians read, write, and "hear" the symbols of music.

1. Notes

Notes are musical symbols. Each note represents the duration of a musical sound or pitch—the length of time value in beats. The note names indicate the relationship of each note to the longest commonly used note value, the whole note. The length of a half note is half as long as the whole note; the quarter note is one-quarter as long as the whole note; and so on.

The value of the notes is indicated by the meter signature, designating the type of note that receives the basic beat. In the following example, the quarter note represents the basic beat:

Use *Rhythmic Durations* lesson plans.
Instructor's Guide, page 336

2. Rests

Silence, or the absence of sound, is indicated by a symbol called a rest. There is a rest that corresponds with each note. The names and durations for the rests are the same as the notes. The rests are shown with their corresponding notes below.

Use TRB Music Theory Transparency 2, *Notes and Rests and Their Values.*

name	note	rest
whole	𝅝	▬
half	𝅗𝅥	▬
quarter	♩	𝄽
eigthth	♪	𝄾
sixteenth	♬	𝄿

3. Dotted Notes and Rests

Dotted notes and rests have augmentation dots added to lengthen their durations. The dot is added to the right of the note or rest and it adds half of the original note or rest value.

For example, a half note receives two beats; a "dotted" half note receives three beats. The following two equations show how the dotted half note relates to combinations of half and quarter notes.

Use *Duple and Triple Meter* lesson plans.
Instructor's Guide, page 337

4. Rhythm

Use *Rhythm and Meter Quiz*
TRB Theory Master R-7.

Rhythm is a pattern of sounds and silence. Sounds are defined by a variety of characteristics such as loudness, pitch, and timbre. They are also defined by the intensity of the sound and the length or duration of the sound. Rhythm in a song or vocal piece is determined by the text. In an instrumental piece, rhythm is determined by the specific notation durations chosen by the composer.

C. Pitch

Sounds are vibrations that travel through the air. Vibrations are heard as sound when they reach our ears. The speed of the vibrations affects the sound or the pitch of the sound. Pitch is based on how high or how low a sound is heard. The faster the vibration, the higher the pitch. A pitch vibrating 440 times per second is heard as the absolute pitch A, the A above middle C on a keyboard instrument. It is called A-440 and is used as a baseline note for tuning instruments.

1. Notating and Measuring Pitch

Use *Sound Vibrations and Pitch* lesson plans.
Instructor's Guide, pages 337-338

In Western musical culture, absolute pitches are labeled with seven alphabetical letters: A-B-C-D-E-F-G. The musical alphabet repeats as the pitch ascends, or gets higher. When the pitch descends, the letters are reversed. Relative pitches using solfège, DO-RE-MI-FA-SOL-LA-TI-DO, correspond to the musical alphabet.

An octave is the distance between two pitches that share the same letter name and are eight notes apart. Octaves are pitches that have special relationships. When two pitches are one octave apart, the higher pitch vibrates twice as fast as the lower pitch.

The staff is a system of five horizontal lines and four spaces between the lines.

The staff is used to show how high and low the pitches are. Notes may be written on the lines or in the spaces between the lines. Notes written on the lower lines and spaces of the staff are lower in pitch than notes written higher on the staff. Each line and space represents a different pitch letter. Notes on neighboring lines and spaces are neighboring pitches in the musical alphabet.

Clef signs on a staff assign absolute pitch names to specific lines and spaces on the staff. The following three clefs are commonly used: G clef, or treble clef; F clef, or bass clef; C clef.

Each clef is named for the pitch it indicates on the staff. The G clef marks the pitch G on the second line of a staff. When the F clef is used, it designates the fourth line of a staff as the pitch F. The center of the C clef indicates the pitch C below A-440, called middle C. When the C clef marks the third staff line as C, it is called an alto clef. When the C clef marks the fourth staff line as C, it is called the tenor clef. Clefs are used to keep a range of notes on the staff.

treble clef   bass clef   alto clef   tenor clef

2. Organizing Pitches

The octave is divided into twelve equal parts or pitches. A specific pitch name identifies each of the twelve parts. A half step, or semitone, is the distance between neighboring pitches. Half steps are adjacent keys on a musical keyboard. The distance of two half steps is a whole step, or wholetone.

Use *Notating Highness and Lowness of Pitch* lesson plans. Instructor's Guide, page 338

Use TRB Music Theory Transparency 3, *Clef Signs* and Transparency 4, *Grand Staff.*

Use *Semitones and Wholetones on the Keyboard* lesson plans. Instructor's Guide, page 338

The seven pitches of the musical alphabet include two half steps and five whole steps as illustrated by the keyboard pitches. Look at the example and find the half steps (⋀) and whole steps (⎍).

Use *Notating and Hearing Semitones and Wholetones* lesson plans.
Instructor's Guide, page 338

Altered pitches, or accidentals, are changes to the musical alphabet to name notes that do not have their own letter names. On the musical keyboard, any pitch can be raised one half step by using a sharp (♯) sign. When the pitch F is raised, the new pitch is called F-sharp. Flats (♭) are signs used to lower pitches one half step. Pitches that do not have a letter name are named as sharps or flats. Locate these pitches on the music keyboard. Notice that the black keys on the keyboard may be named as either sharp or flat. For example, F♯ is also called G♭. F♭ is also called E. Pitches that sound the same but have different names are called enharmonic pitches.

3. Scales

A scale is a group of pitches organized in an ascending pitch order. Each scale uses a certain number of pitches, which are organized in specific patterns. The patterns create the same type of scale when started on any pitch. The scale patterns are frequently described as ascending orders of half steps and whole steps.

Solfège syllables are frequently used to represent the scale patterns. Each syllable represents a pitch in the scale. Singing musical patterns and melodies with solfège is a useful tool for musicians. It helps to improve a musician's sense of relationships between tones in musical patterns.

The Major Scale

Use *Major Scales* lesson plans.
Instructor's Guide, page 339 and TRB Music Theory Transparency 5, *Intervals*

The major scale is the most familiar scale in Western music culture. A major scale contains seven different pitches that can be repeated in the continuation of the scale beyond one octave. The ascending pattern is shown in the following example using a musical keyboard, letter names, and solfège. In the ascending scale pattern, five of the scale steps are whole steps, and two of the steps are half steps. The major scale pattern is whole-whole-half-whole-whole-whole-half, beginning from any starting pitch. The half steps occur between scale steps 3 and 4, or MI and FA, and between scale steps 7 and 8, or TI and DO.

Each pitch of the scale is spelled with different letter names. For example, there cannot be an A and an A♯ in the same major scale. Instead of A♯, the scale step is spelled as B♭.

DO RE MI FA SOL LA TI

The Minor Scale

The minor scale is also a familiar scale in Western music. There are three patterns, or forms, of minor scales. They are natural minor, harmonic minor, and melodic minor. All three scales share similar patterns for the first five scale tones. The differences in the scale patterns are the sixth and seventh scale tones. The example below shows the different sequence of whole steps and half steps for each minor scale. Half steps in the natural minor scale occur between scale steps 2 and 3 and between 5 and 6. The harmonic minor is unique. It has three half steps and one scale step that is 1½ steps. The melodic minor scale is the only scale that uses two different patterns, one for going up the scale, and another for coming down the scale. The ascending pattern has half steps between scale steps 2 and 3 and between 7 and 1. The descending pattern is just like the natural minor pattern.

Use *Minor Scales* lesson plans. Instructor's Guide, page 339

natural minor (aeolian)

harmonic minor

melodic minor (ascending)

More About Scales

There are many varieties of scales. While many have seven pitches just like the major and minor scales, some have more or less pitches. Each scale has a unique pattern.

Modal scales originated with early Greek civilization. They are called Ionian, Dorian, Phrygian, Lydian, Mixolydian, Aeolian, and Locrian. The

Ionian scale later became the major scale and the Aeolian became the minor scale. Early European folk music, chant, and jazz use modal scales, including the major and minor forms.

Pentatonic scales have five pitches. They are common in folk music of cultures around the world, including Eastern Europe, Asia, North and South America, and Africa. Commonly used jazz scales are the whole-tone, blues, bebop-dominant, and the Lydian-dominant scales. Many scales used around the world cannot be labeled with the Western twelve-pitch name system.

4. Intervals

Use *Introduction to Intervals* lesson plans. Instructor's Guide, page 339

The distance between two pitches is called an interval. Musical intervals are primes (unisons), 2nds, 3rds, and so on. To count an interval between two pitches, include each letter name of the two pitches and all letter names between them. For example, the distance between B up to the next higher E is a 4th. The pitches B-C-D-E are counted as four consecutive pitches, or a 4th. Sharps and flats do not affect this general measurement. Therefore, measuring from B♭ to E is still some type of 4th. The difference between these two types of 4ths is discussed later.

Use TRB Music Theory Transparency 5, *Intervals*.

Counting intervals between two notes on the staff is similar to counting them with letter names. On the staff we count each line or space that the two notes are on, and we count all lines and spaces between them. A clef sign is not needed to count intervals in this general way. Count the line and spaces for each of the intervals shown below.

Prime   2nd   3rd   4th   5th   6th   7th   8ve

Use *The Smaller Intervals* lesson plans. Instructor's Guide, page 340

More About Intervals

As shown above, intervals measure the general distance between two pitches. They also measure quality. When you measured the intervals between B and E, and between B♭ and E, you found that both were 4ths. However, they are not the same exact size. They are not the same "quality" 4ths.

Intervals in a scale have a quality for each interval. Primes (unisons), 4th, 5ths, and octaves are called perfect. The intervals of a 2nd, 3rd, 6th, and 7th can be major or minor quality depending upon the scale. Intervals are made larger or smaller by raising or lowering one of the pitches one semitone. Sharps and flats are used. Major intervals made smaller are called minor. Minor and perfect intervals made smaller are called diminished. Major and perfect intervals made larger are called augmented.

Use *Intervals of the 4th, 5th, and Octave* lesson plans.
Instructor's Guide, page 340

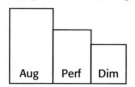

Use *Interval Review* lesson plans.
Instructor's Guide, page 341

Now return to the two different sized 4ths and use semitones to measure the difference between them. From pitches B to E is five semitones, while B♭ to E is six semitones. The distance from B to E is called a perfect 4th (P4). The distance between B♭ to E is called an augmented 4th (A4).

Use *Intervals of the 6th and 7th* lesson plans.
Instructor's Guide, page 341

The quality of intervals can also be analyzed by comparing the intervals in the major scale. If pitches are contained within the major scale, the intervals are all major or perfect intervals. If there are altered pitches, the quality of the interval is named based on this comparison.

Use *Interval Review* lesson plans.
Instructor's Guide, page 342

Intervals from middle C to high C are shown in the example below. Count the number of whole steps and half steps in each interval.

Use *Pitch Quiz*
TRB Theory Master P-21.

MI2   MA2   MI3   MA3   P4   A4   D5   P5   MI6   MA6   MI7   MA7   P8

D. Tonality and Key Signature

Musicians organize melody or sound elements into groupings or patterns, just as time elements are organized into beat, meter, and rhythm. Patterns of sound can be defined and have a relationship that connects one pattern or element to the next.

Use *Notating Scale Degrees and Key Signatures* lesson plans. Instructor's Guide, page 342

1. Scales and Tonal Centers

A scale is a group of pitches organized in an ascending and descending order. The order of pitches always follows the order of letter names: A-B-C-D-E-F-G. The pitches of a scale are called degrees; that is, the first pitch of a scale is called the first degree, and so on. Each type of scale uses a particular order of semitones and wholetones.

The first degree of a scale is called tonic. Tonic is the goal tone of melody and harmony. It is "home base." A melody and harmony can go away from tonic and visit the other notes in the scale, but eventually they will come back to tonic. Sometimes this return is temporary, but in the end the melody and harmony will return to the tonic.

Each pitch in a scale has a name. The names come from their relationship to tonic. Tonic is the tonal center of a piece of music. In the following example we put tonic in the center of the scale rather than at the beginning. This lets us see how the other notes relate to tonic. The fifth note of the scale is the dominant because it is a P5 interval above tonic. The fourth note of the scale is the subdominant (below the dominant) because it is a P5 below the tonic. The other note names also show their relationships to tonic.

2. Keys and Key Signatures

Key is a general term used to describe the pitches used in a piece of music. A key, or a scale, is groups of pitches that create melodies and harmonies. As you have seen, a scale is a specific order of the pitches. The key of C major implies the same pattern as the C major scale.

The groups of sharps or flats shown at the beginning of each staff is called a key signature. A key signature is the symbol for a key or a scale, and it is a collection of all the sharps or flats in the scale. A key signature can have as many as seven sharps or seven flats.

The sharps and flats are organized in particular orders. The order of the sharps is as follows: F♯ C♯ G♯ D♯ A♯ E♯ B♯. The order of flats is as follows: B♭ E♭ A♭ D♭ G♭ C♭ F♭.

Notice that the two orders are reversed from each other. We increase the number of sharps or flats in key signatures using these orders. For example, a key signature with one sharp is F♯. A key signature with two sharps is F♯ plus C♯. This pattern continues up through seven sharps. The pattern is similar for the key signatures that use flats.

Major keys are associated with major scales. The keys form an interesting pattern of relationships. As the number of sharps or flats increases in the key signature, the names of the keys form a series of P5 intervals. The pattern is called the circle of 5ths. The circle of 5ths is a convenient way to see, learn, and think about keys and key signatures.

Use *Major Key Signatures* lesson plans.
Instructor's Guide, pages 342-343 and
TRB Music Theory Transparency 6, *Circle of Fifths*

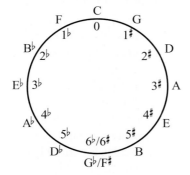

Even though there are three types of minor scales, there is only one minor key signature for each tonic pitch. The key signature is taken from the natural minor scale. The key signature for C minor is 3 flats. Minor keys form a series of circle of 5th relationships similar to the major keys.

Use *Minor Key Signatures* lesson plans.
Instructor's Guide, page 343

Major and minor keys are the most common keys used. Other tonalities also form keys and have key signatures. Examples of these are the modal scales, C Dorian, and C Mixolydian. The key signature for C Dorian is two flats and for C Mixolydian is one flat. Although these keys are used in contemporary music, most commercial publishers do not use the key signatures. They often prefer the familiarity of major and minor key signatures and indicate the changed or altered pitches in the music.

Use *Tonality Listening Activity* lesson plans.
Instructor's Guide, page 343

3. Key and Scale Relationships

Different keys that share the same key signature are called relative keys. The keys of F major and D minor share the same key signature of one flat. F major is called the relative major of D minor, and D minor is called the relative minor of F major. Because these keys share the same key signature, they also share the same pitches. The scales of relative keys overlap. The first note of the minor scale is the sixth note, or LA, of the major scale. The first note of the major scale is the third note of the minor scale. See the following example on page 608.

Use *Relative and Parallel Key Relationships* lesson plans. Instructor's Guide, page 344

Use Key *Signature Quiz TRB* Theory Master K-11.

Although relative keys share the same group of pitches, they do not share the same scale. This means that they do not share the same tonic. It also means that patterns in the melody and harmony are different. Because the tonic is always the goal tone or "home base" of melody and harmony, the role of each pitch is different in different scales. The role of the pitch F in F major is tonic and is the goal tone of melody. In D minor F is the mediant of the scale and is not the goal tone of melody.

It is the scale—the organization of pitches—that determines the tonic rather than the particular group of pitches. Many keys can share the same key signature and the same group of pitches. It is the scale and tonic pitch that defines the way the pitches interact. Other relative keys to F major are G Dorian and C Mixolydian.

Parallel keys are keys that share the same tonic pitch. Their key signatures are different. For example, G major (one sharp) and G minor (two flats) are parallel keys. The scales for these keys are different, but they both begin on the same pitch, G. Other keys with a G tonic— G Dorian and G pentatonic—are parallel to G major.

E. Harmony

Musicians add more dimension to time and sound elements with a vertical sound relationship called harmony. Harmonic relationships developed in later music history and were not found in all world music.

1. Triads

Use *Basic Triad Spelling* lesson plans. Instructor's Guide, page 344 and *TRB* Music Theory Transparency 7, *Major and Minor Triads*

Use *Triads I* lesson plans. Instructor's Guide, page 345

The simultaneous sound of tones is called harmony. Groups of two or more pitches that sound together are called chords. In traditional harmony, chords are built on intervals of 3rds. Chords made of three pitches are called triads.

When a triad is written as two consecutive 3rds, the triad is in root position. The lowest pitch in a triad in root position is called the root. The middle pitch is called the 3rd because it is an interval of a 3rd above the root. Likewise, the top tone is called a 5th because it is a 5th above the root. Chords or triads are often found as inversions. Inversions are the chord or triad pitches used in a pattern other than root position. The triad must be repositioned in root position in order to name the triad by its root.

a) root position   b) first inversion   c) second inversion

fifth
third
root

root
fifth
third

third
root
fifth

Use *Triads II* lesson plans.
Instructor's Guide, page 345

Qualities of Triads

There are four types or qualities of triads. These are major, minor, diminished, and augmented. When the quality of the 3rd is major and the 5th is perfect, the quality of the triad is major. Major triads are built on any pitch by putting together these intervals above a given root. A minor triad contains a minor 3rd and perfect 5th above the root. A diminished triad also has a minor 3rd above the root, but the quality of the 5th is diminished. An augmented triad is built with a major 3rd and an augmented 5th.

Use *Primary Chords in Major* lesson plans.
Instructor's Guide, page 346

F+   F   Fᴍɪ   F°

Triads can be built on any scale pitch. The pitches in the triad are all pitches contained in the scale. We label triads with Roman numerals below the staff to show the position of the triad in the scale. The tonic triad is built on the first note of the scale and labeled with the Roman numeral I. Uppercase numerals indicate major triads. Lowercase numerals indicate minor triads. Diminished triads are marked with lowercase numerals and a degree sign (vii°). This indicates that the diminished chord contains a minor 3rd and diminished 5th. Augmented triads are marked with uppercase numerals and a plus sign (V+).

Use *Secondary Chords in Major* lesson plans.
Instructor's Guide, page 346

Chords are also labeled with chord symbols above the staff. Chord symbols indicate the root of the chord by pitch name and the quality of the chord. All symbols use uppercase letters. Other symbols are added to show the quality of the chord.

In major keys there are three major triads, three minor triads, and one diminished triad.

Use *Primary Chords in Minor* lesson plans.
Instructor's Guide, pages 346-348

C   Dᴍɪ   Eᴍɪ   F   G   Aᴍɪ   B°

I   ii   iii   IV   V   vi   vii°

Minor keys have several possible chord qualities, as there are three forms of minor scales. Frequently used chord qualities are shown below.

Use *Secondary Chords in Minor* lesson plans.
Instructor's Guide, page 347

Cᴍɪ   D°   E♭   Fᴍɪ   G   A♭   B°

i   ii°   III   iv   V   VI   vii°

Use *Major 7th and Minor 7th Chords I* lesson plans. Instructor's Guide, page 347

2. Seventh Chords

A seventh (7th) chord is a four-note chord that combines a triad with an interval of a 7th above the root. There are five commonly used 7th chords in major and minor tonalities. These are the major 7th, dominant 7th, minor 7th, half-diminished 7th, and the diminished 7th chords.

- A major 7th chord combines a major triad and a major 7th.
- A dominant 7th chord combines a major triad with a minor 7th.
- A minor 7th chord combines a minor triad with a minor 7th.
- A half-diminished chord, minor 7♭5, combines a diminished triad with a minor 7th.
- A diminished chord combines a diminished triad with a diminished 7th.

Use *Diminished 7th Chords I* lesson plans. Instructor's Guide, page 348

Just like triads, 7th chords can be built on every note in a scale. The qualities of 7th chords in a major key are shown below. Notice that the dominant 7th chord is unique to the dominant tone of the scale.

Use *Major 7th and Minor 7th Chords II* lesson plans. Instructor's Guide, page 348

The 7th chords commonly used in minor keys are shown below. Notice that the dominant 7th chord is used on the dominant note in a minor key just as it is in the major key.

Use *Diminished 7th Chords II* lesson plans. Instructor's Guide, page 349

The most commonly used qualities of 7th chords are the dominant 7th and minor 7th. Some styles of music use very few 7th chords. Folk music is typically limited to triads, the dominant 7th, and occasionally, minor 7th chords. Other styles, such as jazz, regularly use all types of 7th chords.

3. Primary Chords

Primary chords are the principle harmonies in a tonality. The primary chords in major keys are tonic, subdominant, and dominant.

Use *Melody and Harmony* lesson plans.
Instructor's Guide, page 349

These chords collectively contain all the notes in the major scale. Every pitch in a simple melody can be harmonized with one of these chords.

4. Secondary Chords

The other chords in a major key are secondary chords. Secondary chords substitute for primary chords to add interesting contrast to the music.

Use *Chord Progressions* lesson plans.
Instructor's Guide, page 349

Primary chord:	I	IV	V7
Secondary chord:	iii or vi	ii or vi	vii°

Secondary chords are typically found in the middle of musical phrases. Primary chords are typically used to harmonize the beginnings and ends of phrases.

The primary chords in minor are also tonic, subdominant, and dominant, but the quality of the tonic and subdominant chords is minor. This makes the minor tonality distinctive from the major tonality.

Use *CD Listening* lesson plans.
Instructor's Guide, page 349

Use *Harmony Quiz*
TRB Theory Master H-18.

Glossary

A

absolute music music without extra-musical associations, as opposed to program music

absolute pitch the ability to recognize and reproduce pitches exactly

a cappella without musical accompaniment

accelerando (aht-cheh-leh-RAHN-doh) a gradual increase in tempo; gradually growing faster

accent the emphasis placed on a beat

accidentals sharp, flat, or naturals occurring outside of the given key signature within a composition

acculturation the mutual influence of different cultures in close contact

adagio (ah-DAHJ-ee-oh) slow tempo, but not as slow as largo

aerophones instruments that produce sound by a vibrating column of air, including wind instruments such as woodwinds and brass and reed instruments such as the accordion and the organ

aleatory music music with sections that are left undetermined, or left to chance; see also chance music

allegretto a little slower than allegro

allegro fast and lively tempo

alto the low female register; see also contralto

andante moderately slow

andantino a little faster than andante

animato with spirit; antecedent term for the question half of a melodic phrase

anthropologist a scientist who studies the characteristics and customs of a group of people

antiphonal describing musical groups that perform alternately in a call-and-response manner

aria a song for a solo singer and orchestra, usually in an opera, oratorio, or cantata

arpeggio (ahr-PEJ-ee-oh) a broken chord whose pitches are heard successively

arrangement an adaptation of a composition from one medium to another

arranger someone who reworks preexisting musical material

articulation clarity and distinct rendition in musical performance

a tempo in normal time, or a return to the preceding tempo

atonal without tonality or a tonal center

audiation the ability to hear, think, or imagine music in your head

authenticity performing music as closely as possible to the way it was performed at the time it was created

B

backbeat in popular music, accents on beats 2 and 4 that answer the normal accents on 1 and 3

background music music that has no visual or logical source

ballet a physically strenuous style of classical dance that originated in France in the sixteenth century

band a large instrumental ensemble consisting primarily or solely of wind and percussion instruments

baritone the intermediate male voice

bar line vertical dividing line between measures on the musical staff

Baroque period the stylistic period between approximately 1600 and 1750

bass a lower male voice, with a rich, robust, resonant, full quality; the lowest instrument in the violin family, also called contrabass

bass clef (𝄢) F clef that indicates the placement of F below Middle C

basso continuo bass line and accompanying chords for keyboard instruments, used extensively in the Baroque period

basso profundo the lowest male voice, with a dark, rich, powerful quality

beat steady recurring pulse; a unit of time

bebop see bop

bel canto a style of singing characterized by flowing phrases and beauty of vocal color

binary form a two-part form

bluegrass a type of American country music using acoustic instruments

blue notes lowered notes on the third and seventh scale degrees

blues a genre of African-American music often expressing frustration, ordeal, and longing

book the story and the dialogue of a musical

bop a complex and sophisticated type of improvised jazz

bourrée (BU-ray) A French dance usually in quick duple meter with a single upbeat

brass wind instruments that derive their sound from vibrations transmitted through cup-shaped mouthpieces (trumpet, French horn, trombone, and tuba)

break a cadenza-like improvisation by a jazz instrumentalist or singer

bridge the connective part of a composition; a support to raise the strings from the soundboard

Broadway musical a dramatic stage form combining acting and singing

bugaku danced portions of Japanese gagaku; see also gagaku

C

cadence a breathing break; punctuation or termination of a musical phrase

cadenza a section of a piece designed to show the virtuosity of a soloist

cakewalk a dance with syncopated rhythms, perhaps an early form of jazz

call and response a question-and-answer pattern, with a group responding to a leader

cancion (cahn-see-OHN) **ranchera** a popular type of Mexican song, usually in AAB form

canon a musical form that using imitation; melody performed similarly to a round

cantata an accompanied vocal work in a number of movements with a sacred or secular text

chamber music music played by small groups

chance music music in which aspects such as melody, rhythm, dynamics, timbre, and form are left wholly or partly to the discretion and creativity of the performer; see also aleatory

child prodigy someone who excels at a very early age

chorale a hymn tune; a hymn melody of the German Protestant church

chorale prelude a composition serving as an introduction to congregational singing

chord simultaneous combination of at least three different pitches

chordophones instruments that produce sound when a string or chord is struck, rubbed, or plucked

chromatic incorporating notes that lie outside the regular diatonic scale; indicated by a sharp (♯), flat (♭), natural (♮), double sharp (✕), or double flat (♭♭)

classical music a style of "art" music, as distinguished from popular music; European music of the Classical period, composed from about 1750 to 1825

clave the time line in Afro-Cuban music; also, the two round wooden sticks struck together to produce the pattern

clef symbol indicating pitches for the lines and spaces of the staff

coda a short concluding section of a piece of music

coloratura the highest female voice that is light and flexible enough to perform scales and trills

composer a person who creates musical works

composition the craft of putting together sounds to create a musical work; a musical work

concert band an expanded version of the wind and percussion sections of the orchestra

concertino the section of a Baroque concerto played by a small group of soloists

concerto a composition usually written in three lengthy sections or movements featuring interplay between one or more soloists and an orchestra

concerto grosso a work that contrasts the tutti, or full orchestra sections, and the concertino sections for a soloist or group of soloists

concerto style solo parts alternated with a group of instruments

conductor the director of a performing group

conjunct a melody employing successive pitches of the scale; stepwise movement

conjunto a dance music created by Texas Americans

consequent the answer of a melodic phrase

consonance absence of tension or discord in music

continuo a Baroque musical accompaniment consisting of a harp sounding the chords and a viola da gamba reinforcing the bass line

contour the shape of a melody or its rise and fall

contralto a low female voice with a full, dark, rich, and powerful quality; see also alto

contrapuntal in the style of counterpoint; the combining of melodic lines

counterpoint music that counters one note against another

countersubject a secondary melodic pattern used at the same time as the principal subject

countertenor the highest adult male voice, with a register in the female alto range

country music a popular musical style that began in rural areas of the South and West

creative license the liberty that artists take in reinterpreting another artist's work

crescendo (kreh-SHEN-doh) a gradual increase in the loudness of a sound

crossover a merging of styles

culture the customs, ideas, tastes, and beliefs acquired from a person's background

D

decibel unit for measuring volume of sound

decrescendo (day-kreh-SHEN-doh) a gradual decrease in the loudness of a sound

development the section of the sonata form in which thematic reworkings and modifications occur

dialogue the spoken lines of a play or musical show

diatonic the tones of a major or minor scale

diminuendo a gradual decrease in the loudness of a sound; decrescendo

disjunct a melody formed by intervals larger than a 2nd

dissonance discord in music, suggesting a state of tension

dominant the fifth pitch of a diatonic scale; the chord built on the fifth degree of the diatonic scale

Dorian mode a scale with the pattern of whole step, half, whole, whole, whole, half, and whole

double bass the largest instrument in the bowed, stringed family

downbeat the accented first beat in a measure

drone a long sustained note, usually in the lower part

drum machine a machine with the stored sounds of a whole range of percussion instruments

dubbing putting all the elements together on one soundtrack

duet composition for two performers

duple beats grouped into sets of two (strong-weak)

dynamics the volume of sound, the loudness or softness of a passage

E

electrophones instruments that generate sound from electricity

empathy the ability to look at the world from another person's perspective

ensemble a group of musicians performing together; the quality of togetherness

entr'acte music light instrumental music between acts of an opera

ethnomusicologist a professional who studies the music of different cultural groups

exposition the opening section of a sonata form, in which the main thematic material is given its first complete statement

extramusical the idea that inspires a programmatic piece of music

F

"felt" time the space that music appears to carve out for itself; one's subjective sense of time, in contrast to time measured by real time

fermata a hold

finale concluding movement or passage in a musical work

flat (♭) symbol that lowers a pitch by one half step

folk music uncomplicated music that speaks directly of everyday matters; the first popular music

form musical design, incorporating repetition and contrast, unity, and variety

forte loud

fortissimo very loud

fugue a polyphonic composition consisting of a series of successive melody imitations

fundamental the main pitch from which the harmonics of the overtone series are generated

fusion a combination of styles, for example, jazz/rock

G

gagaku Japanese orchestral music (sometimes with singing) that is used at imperial court, ceremonies and shrines; see also bugaku

gambamg a Balinese sacred instrumental ensemble

gamelan a Balinese instrumental ensemble; an ensemble of 25 performers or more who play on metallophones of several sizes and pitches, gongs of different sizes, cymbals, drums, a flute, and a simple string instrument

genre a style of music

gig an engagement to perform music, especially jazz

glissando a continuous movement from one pitch to the other

globalization the process of making information accessible to a worldwide audience

gospel a type of religious folk or popular music sung largely in African-American churches

grand opera a type of music drama in which everything is sung

Grand Staff the combined treble and bass staffs

H

half cadence see incomplete cadence

half step the closest pitch above or below any given pitch on the keyboard, such as C to C♯ or F to E

harmonics series barely audible tones generated by the vibration of a fundamental sound; see partial

harmonizing the ability to invent on the spot a vocal line that will complement a melody

harmony vertical blocks of different tones that sound simultaneously; a progression of chords

heterophony a musical style where all performers sing or play the same melody in a manner appropriate to each voice or instrument

homophonic texture musical texture in which a single melodic line is supported by chordal accompaniment

homophony a single melody with chordal accompaniment

hook the motive or "grabber" phrase in a song that often accompanies the words of the song's title

hymn a strophic song sung within a religious service

hyperinstruments instruments that, with the help of computers, respond to live musicians

I

idée fixe (EE-day FEEKS) a fixed melodic idea that recurs in all movements of a symphony

idiophones simple, solid instruments that produce sound by being struck, scraped, or shaken

imitation exact repetition or resemblance between parts

Impressionism a French style of atmospheric music created by Claude Debussy in the late nineteenth century as a reaction to the emotion of Romantic music

improvisation spontaneous musical invention, commonly in jazz

incidental music music that occurs in connection with a drama

intensity degree of loudness; dynamics

interlocking rhythms a complex rhythmic line created by several individual rhythms that intermingle with each other; see also kotekan

interval the distance in pitch between two tones

inversion arranging the tones of a chord in an order different from the way they are derived; performing a melody by turning the contour upside down

J

jazz a popular style of music characterized by strong, prominent meter, improvisation, and dotted or syncopated patterns

K

Kecak (keh-CHAK) a Balinese musical theatre work based on the Hindu epic *Ramayana*

key the basic scale and tonality of a composition

keynote the tonic pitch; number one of the scale

key signature designation of sharps or flats at the beginning of a composition to indicate its basic scale and tonality

kotekan (ko-TEH-kahn) the Balinese term for interlocking rhythms; see also interlocking rhythms

kritis (KRI-tees) Hindu religious songs sung in praise of a particular god or gods

L

Lali a warrior dance

largo very slow

legato a smooth articulation of a series of tones, each connected to the next

lento slow

librettist the person who writes the text of a musical

libretto the text of an opera; dialogue and/or lyrics for a musical

lieder German art songs

lyricist the writer of lyrics, particularly for popular songs

lyrics the words of a song

M

madrigals nonreligious Renaissance vocal works in several parts (usually five)

mag track music recorded on film coated with an oxide surface like sound tape

major scale a scale built on the pattern of two whole steps, one half step, three whole steps, and one half step

major triad three tones that form a major third (bottom) and a minor third (top), such as C E G

mambo an African-Cuban dance in syncopated 4/4 time with heavy accents on 2 and 4

march music with a steady beat in 2/4, 4/4, or 6/8 time, suitable for a parade or procession

mariachi a Mexican instrumental ensemble consisting of violins, trumpets, and guitars

marimba a wooden xylophone that can be played by as many as eight musicians

mass the principle form of the Catholic liturgical service

measure the division of beats into set groups; a measure is denoted by a bar line

melismatic a melody in which each syllable of text is set to several pitches

melody a logical succession of musical tones

membranophones instruments that produce sound when a membrane or skin is struck or rubbed

mestizo a Spanish term for "mixed culture"

meter a rhythmic measure of a certain number of beats

mezzo medium

mezzo forte (*mf*) medium loud

mezzo piano (*mp*) medium soft

mezzo soprano the intermediate female voice; one who sings in the lower part of the soprano range

MIDI Musical Instrument Digital Interface; a "language" of digital bits that the computer can store

minimalism tonal music that stresses the element of repetition with changes that are dictated by a rule or system

minor scale a scale built on the pattern of one whole step, one half step, two whole steps, one half step, and two whole steps

minor triad three tones that form a minor third (bottom) and a major third (top), such as C E♭ G

minuet an old French dance, rather slow and stately, in triple meter

mixed meter changing meter

moderato moderate tempo

modulation changing from one key to another within a composition

monophonic a musical texture having a single melodic line with no accompaniment; monophony

monophony a single melodic line with no accompaniment

motive a short, distinctive musical pattern or figure, often used by composers as a building block

movement one part of a larger composition that is relatively complete and independent

musical expression the feeling a performer brings to music

musical style the distinct manner or character of musical expression

music critic a person who judges the quality of a musical performance

music dramas Wagner's term for his operas of the Romantic period

musique concrete a system of electronic composition in which natural sounds are taped, edited, and shaped into a composition recorded on magnetic tape

N

national anthem a song of praise or devotion to one's country

natural (♮) a mark that cancels out a sharp or a flat

neumes marks written over the words of a song

New Age a contemporary type of meditative music

New Romanticism tonal melodies combined with exotic textures and timbres

O

obbligato a subordinate melody above the main melody

octave an interval of eight pitch names, such as C to the next C above or below; a distance of twelve half steps

offbeat emphasis of the weak beats in a measure

opera a staged drama that is predominantly sung, most often with orchestral accompaniment

opéra comique a type of opera that uses some spoken dialogue

opus a musical work or set of work; a number indicating the order in which works were composed

oratorio a sectional form for soloists, chorus, and orchestra

orchestration the process of scoring for an orchestra

ostinato a repeated musical figure

overtones faint tones that are generated when any one tone is sounded

overture an extended orchestral introduction to an opera, ballet, or similar type of musical presentation

P

parallel organum an early type of polyphonic music (ninth and tenth century) in which the voices move together note-for-note at the interval of a fourth, but begin and end on the same pitch

partial a harmonic generated by a fundamental tone; see overtone

passing tone nonharmonic tone that moves between two chordal tones

Peking opera a Chinese musical art form that combines instruments, speaking, singing, acrobatics, martial arts, and pantomime

pentatonic scale a scale made up of five notes within the octave

perceptive listening the ability to discern musical characteristics and describe them

percussion instruments that derive their sound from being shook or struck, including drums, cymbals, triangles, xylophones, gongs, chimes, and rattles

phrase a musical thought—a series of pitches that makes sense

pianissimo (*pp*) very soft

piano (*p*) soft

pitch the highness or lowness of sound determined by its frequency of vibration

pivot chord chord that is common to two tonalities or keys and is used as the basis of modulating from one to the other

pizzicato playing string instruments by plucking with the fingers rather than bowing

plainsong a religious melody of early Christianity; Gregorian chant

polka a rapid dance in duple meter

polychoral music music for several groups performing in answer to each other

polyphonic music a texture in which several melodies sound at one time

polyphony the simultaneous combination of different melodies and rhythms

polyrhythms a combination of two or more contrasting rhythmic patterns played at the same time

popular music relatively short works with a prominent melody and a simple chordal accompaniment

presto very fast; faster than allegro

prima donna the principal female singer in an opera

primary chords the chords built on the first, fourth, and fifth degrees of the scale

program music instrumental music that tries to convey a specific idea without using lyrics

program symphony a pictorial or descriptive orchestral work in several movements

Q

qawwali (kha-WAA-lee) a popular form of religious music in Pakistan and parts of India

quartet a combination of four voices or instruments; also music written for such an ensemble

quintet a combination of five voices or instruments, for example a woodwind quintet; also music for such an ensemble

R

raga Indian melodic material; a traditional melodic pattern or mode, or the improvisation based on it

ragtime a style of American popular music, often for piano, in which the syncopated melody conflicts with the steady 2/4 or 4/4 rhythm

range distance between the highest and lowest pitches used in a melody, that is, its outer limits

rap a highly rhythmic, talky form of contemporary popular music

recapitulation the section of a sonata form that is a repetition of the exposition (main thematic material)

recitative a speechlike style of singing

refrain a chorus (melody and text) that is repeated at intervals in a song, especially following each verse

reggae Jamaican dance music, mixing African and Caribbean rhythms

register the high, middle, or low section of the vocal or instrumental range

Renaissance the stylistic period between approximately 1400 and 1600

repertoire an inventory of compositions mastered and performed by a musician; also the historical listing of similar pieces in any one period

Requiem Mass part of the Catholic ritual for the dead

resolution in harmonic analysis, the succession of a dissonant sound to a consonant sound

retrograde sounded backwards

rhumba a ballroom dance that imitates the African-Cuban rumba; see also rumba

rhythm the way music paces itself and moves through time

rhythm combinations of long and short sounds that convey a sense of movement

rhythm and blues (R & B) a style of American music that combines blues harmonies and rhythm with gospel-like vocals in up tempo

rhythm cycle a fixed number of beats in a series that repeats itself over and over

riff jazz ostinato

ripieno the orchestral sections of a Baroque concerto

ritardando the gradual slowing of tempo; gradually growing slower; abbreviated as rit; also called ritard

ritornello a refrain-like repeated section in a Baroque concerto

rock music a popular music style that began with a blending of gospel, rhythm and blues, and country music; also called rock and roll

Romantic music music of the nineteenth century that stressed the expression of feeling

Romantic period a period during the nineteenth and early twentieth century marked by music that emphasized emotion

rondeau a fixed poetic form of the thirteenth century

rondo a composition consisting of a recurring theme alternating with contrasting sections

root the pitch that is the foundation or building block of a chord

round a composition in which the same melody is started at different times and sounded together; also called canon

rubato "robbed time"; the free treatment of meter in performance

rumba an African-Cuban popular dance; see also rhumba

S

sacred of or dealing with religious music; see secular

salsa a type of Latin American dance music of African-Cuban and Puerto Rican origins

samba (SAHM-bah) an African-Brazilian dance that is fast and jazzy

sampled sounds prerecorded bits of sound that are reprocessed

sampling a recording process that begins with real sounds

sarabande a dance in stately triple meter with an accent on beat two

scale a sequence of tones arranged in rising pitches

scat singing an improvised singing style that imitates the sound of an instrument

scherzo a vigorous and lighthearted movement usually in triple meter

score a notation showing all the parts of a musical composition, aligned vertically on staves

scoring composing music for film

secular music without religious associations; see sacred

seguidilla a type of Spanish dance, or the music for such a dance

sequence repetition of a melodic idea or phrase at a higher or lower pitch level

sequencer an electronic system that stores data about music

sharp (♯) a symbol that raises a pitch by one half step

solfege (sohl-FEZH) a method of sight reading, using the syllables DO, RE, MI, FA, SOL, LA, TI, DO

soliloquy spoken or sung text revealing the inner thoughts of a character

solmization a method of sight-singing by syllables

solo composition for one performer

sonata a work in several movements for one or more instruments

sonata-allegro form a large ABA form consisting of three sections: exposition, development, and recapitulation

son jarocho (SOHN hah-ROH-choh) a traditional Mexican song

song form ternary form in ABA

soprano a high female register

soul music a form of rhythm and blues

soundtrack a strip along the side of the film containing a visual representation of the sound

spiritual a religious song of the American Negro (Negro spiritual)

spot to determine which scenes of a film need music

staccato played in a detached manner, as opposed to legato

staff a set of five lines and four spaces on which music is notated

stanza the verse of a text

stretto a polyphonic texture in which the imitating voices overlap, creating a heightened sense of drama

string quartet an ensemble of four stringed instruments including two violins, a viola, and a cello; also music performed by the ensemble

strophic the repetition of music for each new verse in a song

style the particular character of a musical work, a performance, or a historical period

subdominant fourth pitch of a diatonic scale as well as the triad built upon that pitch

subject the principal musical idea, synonymous with the theme but usually applied only to the main melody of a fugue

suite a set of instrumental pieces, each in the character of a dance

swing the special rhythmic character that jazz musicians add to the music

swing era a period of music roughly from 1935 to 1945

symphony an extended work for orchestra, with several movements; also an orchestra configured to perform symphonic music

syncopation deliberate shifts of accent so that it conflicts with the steady pulse and tries to upset it

synthesizer a machine that produces sound electronically

T

tango a Latin-American dance performed at a moderately slow, walk-like tempo

technique the ability to perform an instrument or sing music in tune and in proper rhythm

telharmonium a machine that used electrical current to produce sound

tempo the pace with which music moves

tenor a high male voice, with a powerful, ringing quality

ternary a three-part form, such as ABA

terraced dynamics layered dynamic levels within a composition

tessitura the general range of a voice part, considering the commonly used pitches not the lowest and highest extremes

texture the way sounds are woven together

theme a melody that assumes importance in a composition because of its central and continued use

theme and variations a musical form in which a theme is stated then varied in a succession of statements

through-composed a setting of text in which different music is provided for each stanza of the poem

timbre the quality of a sound

time line a basic rhythm pattern that serves as a foundation for more complex patterns in other parts

tintal a popular 16-beat rhythmic cycle in the music of India

toccata keyboard piece (usually) that displays the performer's manual dexterity

tonality the major or minor system of pitches

tone row an ordering of the twelve pitches of the chromatic scale in a series that forms the basic material of a musical composition; see also twelve-tone music

tonic first pitch of a diatonic scale or the triad built on such a pitch

transcriptions arrangements of music transferred from one medium to another

transpose to move a whole piece, or a section of a piece, or a twelve-tone series, from one pitch level to another

treble clef (𝄞) a sign on a staff showing the tone G above middle C

tremolo an effect found in string or keyboard music that involves the quick repetition of one or two pitches; in singing it refers to excessive use of vibrato

triads a chord consisting of three tones: a root, a third, and a fifth

trio a work or movement for three voices or instruments

triplet three notes performed in the time of two

tutti a section of a piece in which all the instruments and/or voices perform together

twelve-bar blues jazz form based on three phrases of four measures each in 4/4 time, using a set of progression of I, IV, and V chords, often with added 7ths

twelve-tone music twentieth-century system of writing music in which the twelve tones of the chromatic scale are arranged into a series (number 1 to 12) and subsequently used as the basis of melodic and harmonic variation

U

upbeat a weak beat preceding the downbeat

urbanization development of a culture that is the result of the city lifestyle

V

vaudeville an early staged variety show

verse a line of metrical writing or a stanza

vibrato a slight wavering or pulsating of a tone

visualization the process of enhancing material that is heard by adding information that is seen

virtuoso a performer with brilliant, flawless technique

vocal range the span from the highest to the lowest pitch you can sing

vocal register how high or low someone speaks

W

waltz a dance in triple meter, made famous in Vienna in the late 1800s

whole step distance of two half steps in the same direction, such as between C and D or E and F sharp

whole-tone scale scale in which all intervals are whole steps, such as C, D, E, F♯, G♯, A♯, and C

word painting music that portrays the literal meaning of the words of the text

Z

zydeco the music of black Creoles that originated in south Louisiana

Artists and Their Works

Composers, Musicians, and Their Works

Index

Acknowledgments

PHOTOGRAPHY CREDITS Cover: *From left to right; top to bottom:* Robert Frerck/Odyssey Productions/Chicago; Bill Aron/Tony Stone Images; ©John Elk/Bruce Coleman Inc.; Andy Sacks/Tony Stone Images; ©David Madison/Bruce Coleman Inc.; Bob Thomason/Tony Stone Images.

William Anderson 283; AP/Wide World Photos 111 114 120 184 215 249 278 321 438 479 562; Archive Photos: 94TL Fotos International, 97B 140 159 247 RKO Radio Pictures, 319 344B 351 Joe Sia, 512 594C Frank Driggs Collection, 548 Reuters/Gary Hershorn, 595R; Armadillo Enterprises 359; Art Resource, NY: 117B 503 Giraudon, 225R John Bigelow Taylor, 271 280 Erich Lessing, 490 Nicolas Sapieha, 492 Scala, 559 Lauros-Giraudon; Artists Rights Society, NY: 483 © 2000 Estate of Dan Flavin; Artsource vi; Associated Press Pool/Paul Hackett 293; Ray Avery Photo 322, 372, 530 531; Warren Berman Photography 106M; Boston Symphony Orchestra/Miro Vintoniv 537; Dan Bryant 258; Syndey Byrd 12 32L 269 509; Campanas de America iv, 26; K. W. Cobb 463; Bruce Coleman, Inc.: 56 Lois Greenfield, 107L Bob Burch, 106T J. C. Carton, 148 David Madison, 1 155 IFA, 486 C. Bradley Simmons; Columbia University Computer Music Center 345; Corbis 75, 97TC UPI/John Keating, 266 Robert Maass, 303 Lynn Goldsmith, 316 Gunter Marx, 324 391R Bettmann, 343 Henry Diltz, 347 Ted Streshinski, 353 Neal Preston, 367 Charles & Josette Lenars; Corbis (NY) 94, 522 Hans Fahrmeyer; Corbis-Bettmann 42 68 158 163T 176 205 213 236 246 263 277 334 368 428 442 444 493 496 513 514 515, 78 81CL 96TC 191B 519 543 561 UPI, 320 Agence France Presse; Corbis-Westlight: iv Bob Waterman, 60 C. Goldin, 81L R. W. Jones, 161L Jim Zuckerman, 161R 225L 240 470 Michael Yamashita, 171 D & J. Heaton, 296 Prisma, 420 Bill Ross, 502 R. Ian Lloyd; Culver Pictures 447; Dia Center for the Arts/Cathy Carver 483; Dominic Photography 96R; Thomas A. Dorsey 238; Drum Workshop, Inc. 466; Everett Collection, Inc. v 1 16 52 58 67 83 86 94BC 112 142 152 157 168 182 194 196 199 237 288 314 394 398 400 440 445 450 452 453 472 473 474 481 525 539 540 541 554 594R 595L 595CL, 117T 191T 286 309 326 373 455 516 556 575 594L CSU Archives, 121 Kraig Geiger, 396 454 Robert Hepler, 458 Walt Disney Co.; Clem Fiori 498; Charles Fowler 272 552; FPG International/Jack Zehrt 586; Gamma Liason International: 104 Frederick Charles, 253 Bassignac-Simon, 356 Dominique Nabokov, 458 Craig Filipacchi; Glencoe Stock 457; Globe Photos/Arvind Garg 523; The Granger Collection 344T 391L 592; Houston Grand Opera/Jim Caldwell 217; Houston Grand Opera/Jim Caldwell 411 413; Korg USA 340; Frac Languedoc-Roussillon 330; Libby Larsen 379 381 383B 384; Library of Congress 136, 207; Metropolitan Opera Association/Winnie Klotz 96TL 97TL; Michigan Opera Theatre 437; MIT Media Laboratory/Carl Machover 357; NASA Media Services 583; National Endowment for the Arts/Dan Sheehy 24; National Geographic Society Image Collection/Gilbert Grosvenor 327; Odyssey Productions/Chicago: 4 92 124 231 578 582 Robert Frerck; 133 210 Daniel Aubry; Ohio State University Marching Band/Ed & Karen Crockett 181; The Ohio Theater 448; Kingsavanh Patthamavong 127; David Perry v, 462; Photo Reserve/Paul Natkin 355 469 506; PhotoDisc iv vi 48 50 80 151; PhotoEdit: 7 Michael Newman, 9 Spencer Grant, 47 Gary A. Conner, 62B 109 390L 573 David Young-Wolff, 81TR Michelle Bridwell, 102 Jeff Greenberg, 126 Gary A. Conner, 132 390R Tony Freeman, 220 Bill Aron, 229 Mark Richards, 257 Spencer Grant, 449 Amy C. Etra, 581 Myrleen Ferguson; 587TL 587TR Anna E. Zuckerman, 587TC Alan Oddie, 587LR Myrleen Cate, 587LC Bonnie Kamin, 587LL Bachmann; Red Willow Songs/John Rainer 128; Ebet Roberts 65 349 477; Kevin Roznowski vi; Runaway Technologies, Inc. 170, 361; San Francisco Women's Philharmonic 138; Tom Stack & Associates/TSADO/NASA/JPL 584; StageImage: 33TL 48l 49 96BL 97TR 107R 163B 241 244 299 364 378 416 418 423 426 431 495 Ron Sherl, 421 Steve Sherman; Tony Stone Images: 6 David Young-Wolff, 88 550 Robert E. Daemmrich; SuperStock, Inc.10 14 28 29 32R 33R 33BL 62T 70 81CR 94BL 106B 116 144 166 350 354 549, 233 Stock Montage; SuperStock International 175 337, 290 Gary Neil Corbett; Time Life/Martha Swope 69 90 460; University of New Mexico Archives 401.Jack Vartoogian 35 38 61 71 172 214 227 300 310 476 500 546 568 595CR.

REPRINT CREDITS The following material has been reprinted by permission. International Copyrights Secured. All Rights Reserved. P. **34**, "Kye Kye Kule," from the repertoire of Abraham Kobena Adzenyah, as sung in *Let Your Voice Be Heard: Songs from Ghana and Zimbabwe.* © 1997 World Music Press; P. **190**, "We Shall Overcome," Musical and Lyrical adaptation by Zilphia Horton, Frank Hamilton, Guy Carawan and Pete Seeger. Inspired by African American Gospel Singing, members of the Food & Tobacco Workers Union, Charleston, SC, and the southern Civil rights Movement. Royalties derived from this composition are being contributed to the We Shall Overcome Fund and The Freedom Movement under Trusteeship of the writers; P. **198**, "You are the Sunshine of My Life," by Stevie Wonder. Copyright © 1972 Jobete Music, Co. Inc. and Black Bull Music, Inc. Used by permission of CPP/Belwin, Inc., Miami, FL. International Copyright Secured. Made in U.S.A. All Rights Reserved; P. **211**, lyric for "Prendes i Garde" from *The European Musical Heritage.* Copyright © 1987 McGraw-Hill; P. **216-217**, lyric for "Bess, You Is My Woman," from *Porgy and Bess,* George Gershwin, Ira Gershwin, and DuBose Heyward. Copyright © 1935 Chappell & Co. (Renewed); P. **263**, Gerald Abraham, 1812 Criticism, from *The Music of Tchaikovsky.* Copyright © 1946 W.W. Norton & Company, Inc.; P. **273**, excerpt from *A House in Bali,* by Colin McPhee. Copyright © 1987 Oxford University Press; P. **292**, "Do Not Go Gentle into That Good Night" by Dylan Thomas, from *The Poems of Dylan Thomas.* © 1952 by Dylan Thomas. Reprinted by permission of New Directions Publishing Corp.; P. **306-307**, Berlioz quotes from *The New Oxford Companion to Music, Volume 2.* Copyright © 1983 Oxford University Press; P. **336**, Five Measures of the Trio Section from *Suite for Piano,* by Arnold Schoenberg. Copyright © Belmont Music Publishers; P. **355-358**, *Valis* excerpts and Tod Machover quotes, printed by permission, Bridge Records, Inc., from the CD recording of *Valis,* BCD 9007; P. **360**, excerpts from "The Great Synthesizer Debate," by Bob Doerschuk, *Keyboard,* December, 1983. Copyright © 1983 Miller Freeman, Inc.; P. **367-372**, Copland quotes from *Aaron Copland; 1900-1942,* by Aaron Copland. Copyright © 1984 Aaron Copland and Vivian Perlis. Reprinted by permission of St. Martin's Press Inc.; P. **377**, "Cottontail," from *The Swing Era,* by Gunther Schuller. Copyright © 1946. Renewed 1968. Robbins Music Corporation. Rights Assigned to EMI Catalogue Partnership. All Rights Administered by EMI Robbins Catalog Inc.; P. **379-386**, Libby Larsen material copyright by Libby Larsen; P. **550**, *Democracy in America, Volume 1,* by Alexis de Tocqueville. Copyright © 1965 Arlington House.